ONCE UPON A LIFETIME

The Epic True Story of Corporal William Wesley Bennett, U.S.M.C.

by Brent A. Peterson

*To Kristi —
Enjoy the book!
Brent A. Peterson*

Copyright © Brent Peterson 2019

Registration Number TXu 2-071-993

Edited by Belle M. Peterson

Design and Art Direction: Stephen Hawk / Hawk Design

All rights reserved. No part of this book may be used or reproduced in any manner whatsoever without the written permission of the Author. Printed in the United States of America.

For information:

info@bpetersonbooks.com

Facebook: bpetersonbooks

Website: bpetersonbooks.com

ISBN: 978-1-7328051-0-1

Printed by Versa Press, Inc., Spring Bay, Illinois

FIRST EDITION

10 9 8 7 6 5 4 3 2 1

Dedicated to the memory of
William Wesley Bennett, Sr.

An uncommon combination of
grace and courage.

A man after God's own heart.

Semper Fidelis.

Table of Contents

1. A Guy Named Bill 1
2. True Pioneers 2
3. A Change In Direction 4
4. A New Bennett Family 5
5. Arrival 8
6. The Early Years 10
7. A New Kid In Town. 14
8. A Change of Address. 17
9. A New School 20
10. Close To Home 25
11. Becoming Bill 27
12. Champs! 29
13. A Tale of Red and Black 33
14. The 1937 Tomcats 43
15. From Denver, With Love 48

Begin "Quick Read" Feature. 51

16. The End Of An Era. 51
17. Wedding Bells. 54
18. The Clippers. 57
19. The Unexpected 59
20. A Bitter Pill 63
21. Moving On 65
22. Different Directions 73
23. A New Flame 79
24. Looking Ahead 87
25. The Winds of War 91
26. Commitment 93
27. The Wonder City. 95
28. The Corps. 102
29. Semper Fidelis 108
30. The 2nd Pioneers 114
31. Company A 120
32. 746 Automatic Rifleman . . .127
33. Shipping Out 131
34. At Sea 138
35. Final Preparations 141
36. Into The Fray 145
37. Orphans 154
38. Stranded 157
39. The Reunion 168
40. Letters From Home 171
41. Naval Nightmares 174
42. Relief. 179
43. A Land Down Under 187
44. Company D 190
45. Liberty 195
46. The Stoner Weekly News. . .205
47. 533 A New Specialty 207
48. Camp Life. 213
49. Sentimental Ties 215

50.	Broken Hearts. 221
51.	A Combat Flier 231
52.	The Sable and The Wolverine 232
53.	This Is It! 236
54.	Tarawa 237
55.	Getting Ready. 246
56.	The Gauntlet 253
57.	The Whisper. 262
58.	Hell On Earth 269
59.	A Bitter Farewell. 275
60.	Tarawa: The Aftermath 282
61.	Blue Hawaii 285
62.	Disillusion. 291
63.	The Meeting. 294
64.	Replacements. 298
65.	USS Nehenta Bay 301
66.	"Island X". 302
67.	The Marianas 308
68.	Counterattack. 317
69.	Collateral Damage. 319
70.	The Long Haul. 321
71.	The Silver Star 334
72.	The Combat Zone 336
73.	Banzai! 342
74.	Recuperation 348
75.	Tinian. 350

76.	Bulls Eye! 356
77.	The Unthinkable. 361
78.	The Homecoming 373
79.	Swamp Lejuene 384
80.	Home At Last 389
81.	A New Beginning 393
82.	Like No Other 398
83.	Challenges 401
84.	Terry Allen 404
85.	The Good Life 407
86.	Full Circle 421
87.	Getting To Know Bill Bennett 427
88.	To Japan 433
89.	The Enemy Has A Face. . . . 434
90.	Losing His Girl. 436
91.	Reliving Saipan 439
92.	Marine Corps Monument. . . 443
93.	A Historic Record 445
94.	A Historic Flight 446
95.	The Arms of God 450
96.	Memorial Day 453
	Epilogue 458
	The Gospel According to Bill . 462
	Research, Interviews, Bibliography and Sources . . 464

A Word of Thanks from the Author

Without the exemplary life lived by Bill Bennett, there would have been nothing for me to write and nothing for you to read. Bill would want you to know that without the constant work of The True and Living God and the cross of Christ, there would have been nothing remarkable about him. Bill's mother, Jessie Jean Phrangle-Bennett was highly influential in molding Bill into the man that he was and her records contributed greatly to the success of this book. Though I never met Jessie, I have come to know her through Bill.

My wife, Belle M. Sands-Peterson contributed countless hours assisting me on this project during a very challenging time in her own life. She refined my writing again and again until it was ready for others to read. Without her support and assistance, this book would not have been finished, and that is a fact.

Stephen Hawk from Hawk Design, for his valuable assistance with the final edit, page layout and design work, and bringing our cover concept to life.

Pete and Kathy (Bennett) Andrews opened their Bennett family archives and allowed me to research 100 years of photos, letters and memorabilia. Without their willingness to answer my questions and assist me with family history, the book could not have been written.

My dad, Arlen D. Peterson, served in the United States Army (1954-56) and contributed to my interest in military history and specifically World War II. His keen interest in Bill's story resulted in countless "updates" from me as the story came together.

My late mother, Patricia Carter-Peterson, never knew about this book, but she prepared me to write it. She instilled a love for reading in me from my earliest memories and demonstrated a love for others at every turn.

The Marines of Company D, 2nd Battalion, 18th Marine Regiment served our country when defeat was not an option. All of these Marines gave a part of their lives to secure our current freedom and many of them lost their lives in the process. This book is, in part, dedicated to this fine group of men. Emanuel "Manny" Bud shared his soul as he recounted the horrors and hardships of the Pacific with me. Sam and Margaret Stoner poured their hearts into their little newspaper, *The Stoner Weekly News*, between 1942 and 1946. These surviving editions, along with Bill's letters home from the Pacific, were instrumental in rebuilding these events. The family members who contributed photos and family history through interviews and email were vital toward filling in accurate details within this story. You will find a complete list of those who contributed in Research, Interviews, Bibliography and Sources at the back of this book. I want to thank each and every one of them.

How to Use the "Quick Read" Feature of this Book

The beginning of "Once Upon A Lifetime" contains a detailed account of William Wesley Bennett Sr.'s early life and social involvements. If your interest in this book is primarily the account of Bill's experiences during WW II, you may choose to follow the "Quick Read" Feature. Simply read the Prologue and Chapter 1, then skip to the short summary between Chapters 15 and 16 on page 51.

Forward

"December 7th, 1941 ... a date which will live in infamy." These were the historic first words, in an address to Congress, by our 32nd president, Franklin Delano Roosevelt, committing this country into the Second World War. The surprise attack on Pearl Harbor, by 353 Japanese aircraft, was the impetus for the speech. It was also an attack that would affect the lives of every American. War has a way of doing that.

In this book, author Brent Peterson describes, in vivid detail, the tragedy of war and how that violence changes everyone it touches. And in this reading, you will also come to understand how trusting in God can work to balance such human calamity. In the pages that follow, you will meet Bill Bennett, a man whose life is turned upside down by global events, over which he has no control. What is under his authority is how he responds to them. *Once Upon a Lifetime* is a true story of personal and global tragedy and how faith in God works in Bill's life to strengthen him. You will also experience the ordinary and the extraordinary of the American spirit. It's a story all Americans should read.

Historically, we have been a people who value loyalty, fellowship, family, and God. We are a people who have cherished personal freedom ... resisting tyrants similar to those who have ruled over other people and cultures. Our personal freedoms have produced, in the American people, a fierce independence and self-reliance not found in most cultures. Our liberties have also produced a connection with fellow countrymen who share in these values even if we don't always share common origins. Historically, we as a people have bonded together and understood that we all have a responsibility to protect and defend our way of life. It is, after all, up to the people of this country to defend America from enemies, foreign and domestic. It is this freedom and this way of life that our servicemen and women have lived, fought, and died to defend throughout our history.

I now invite you to meet Bill Bennett ... a member of a generation we commonly refer to as the "Greatest Generation." Bill was a man of honor, integrity, and great faith. He was a man who personified the red, white and blue of the American spirit.

Bela "Bill" Suhayda
Educator, Coach and Author of *From Tyranny To Liberty*

Prologue

I have heard it said that we all have connections to the past, whether we think about them or not. I am certain that this is true. No matter who we are or what we do in life, we stand on the shoulders of those who came before us. I have known people who were much older than I, who told wondrous stories of long ago when they were young and the world was in turmoil. Most of them are gone now, and they have taken libraries of information with them. Gone too, are countless stories of brave men and women who stood in the gap for us long before we were born. These were heroes who lived life and gave us examples, standards, goals and ideals. Some were role models who loved God and lived for their fellow man and did not shrink away from responsibility when duty called. Many were ordinary people who had no choice but to do extraordinary things. These Americans, who lived through the Great Depression and World War II, became known as "The Greatest Generation." I learned that it was not only their accomplishments that made them great, but also who they were on the inside. I fear that mankind is quickly forgetting what honor, integrity and loyalty look like. I hope that I am wrong. If I am not, here is a true story that I want to make sure is not lost to the ages. This is the true story of one man who successfully set a standard for what it means to be an American and what it means to be a man.

I was born in Aurora, Illinois, in 1962, 17 years after the Germans and the Japanese surrendered, marking the end of World War II. Our neighborhood on the city's east side was very close knit, with many older neighbors, including my grandparents and great grandparents. From my earliest memories, I loved to listen to the stories of how things had been long ago. My brother, sister and I shared a newspaper route which brought me into contact with many older neighbors within several city blocks. On some Saturday mornings I spent more time talking to my customers than I did collecting the *Beacon News* fees. There was talk of the Great Depression, when everyone struggled for normal things that I had taken for granted. Many of these older people would use the phrase, "back during the war," as they began to relate some of their memories, whether they had been veterans or not. World War II had left an indelible stain on the culture into which I was born.

My family had lived in the same neighborhood for four generations, and I went to the same elementary school as my mother and my grandfather, who lived next door to us. There was a path through our backyard that led to my great grandparent's house, so if I wanted to know anything about history, there were plenty of people to ask. My dad grew up in the small town of Plano, where he spent his early years with "the war" affecting just about every aspect of his life. Dad had spent a few years in the Army in the early 1950s and he and mom lived in Germany for 18 months where my older brother, Eric, was born. My dad and I developed a common passion for military history, and especially World War II history. I loved to read and began reading history books at a very early age. When I was in third grade, the Aurora Public Library made me bring a note from my mom and dad before they would let me check out *The Rise and Fall of the Third Reich.* Looking back on all of this now, I can see where my somewhat unusual early life had prepared me for the most incredible story that I would ever encounter. As with just about everything in life, you must have an interest and pay attention. Otherwise, some of the most beautiful parts of life will just slip away without notice.

About These Maps

The following maps were developed by the author during the research phase of this book. They are included so that the reader may better understand the geography described in the story. The maps are ordered to correspond with the progression of the story.

Author's maps digitally edited by Mike Lesus.

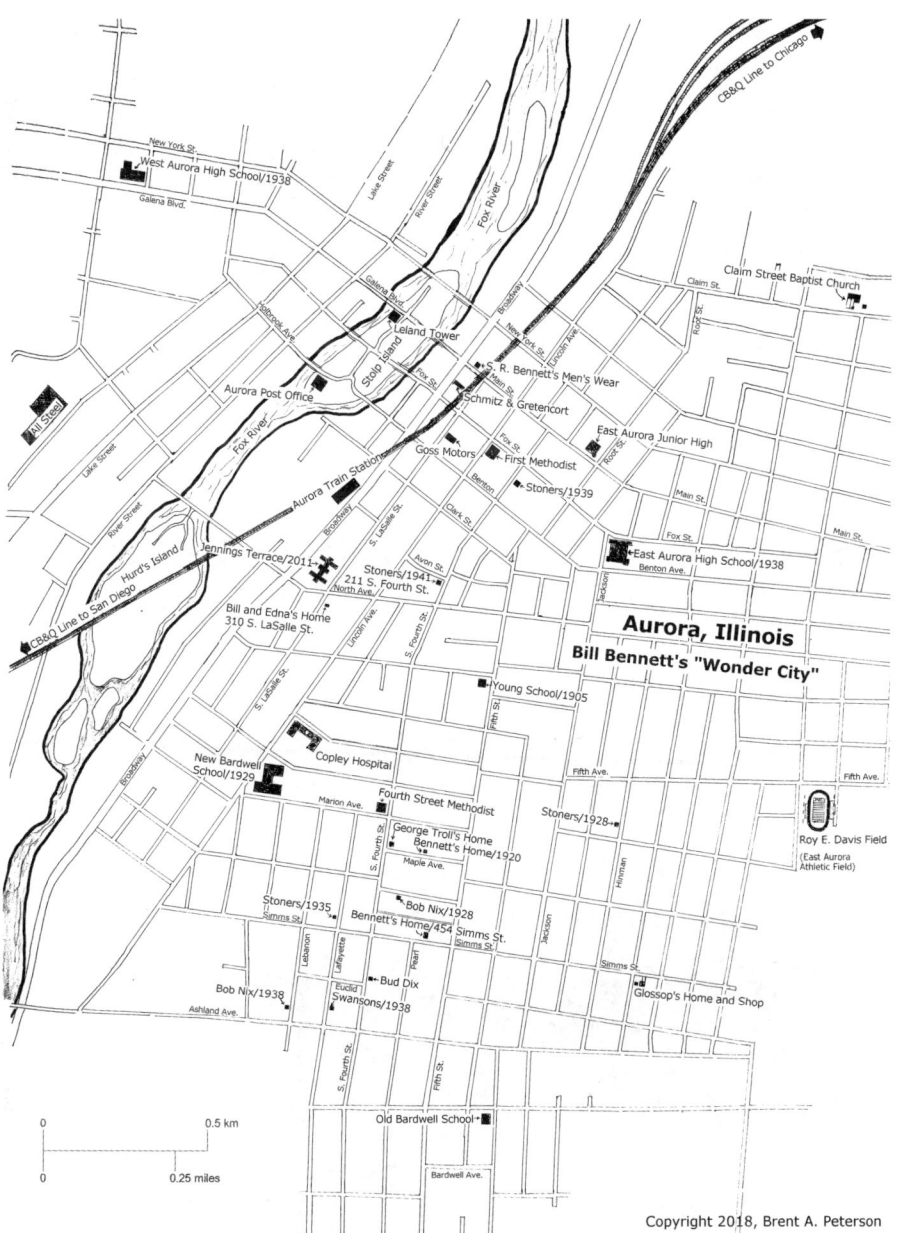

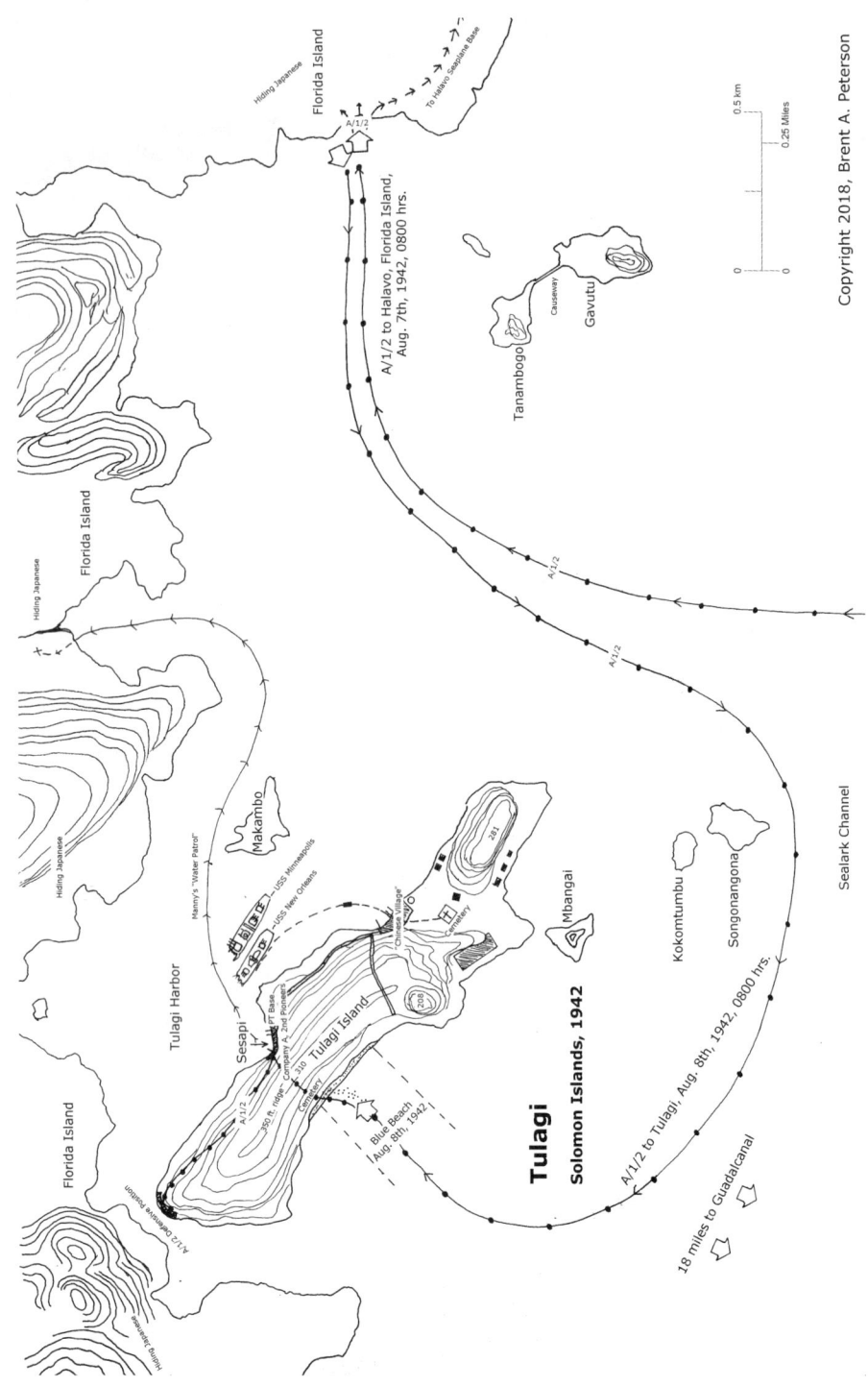

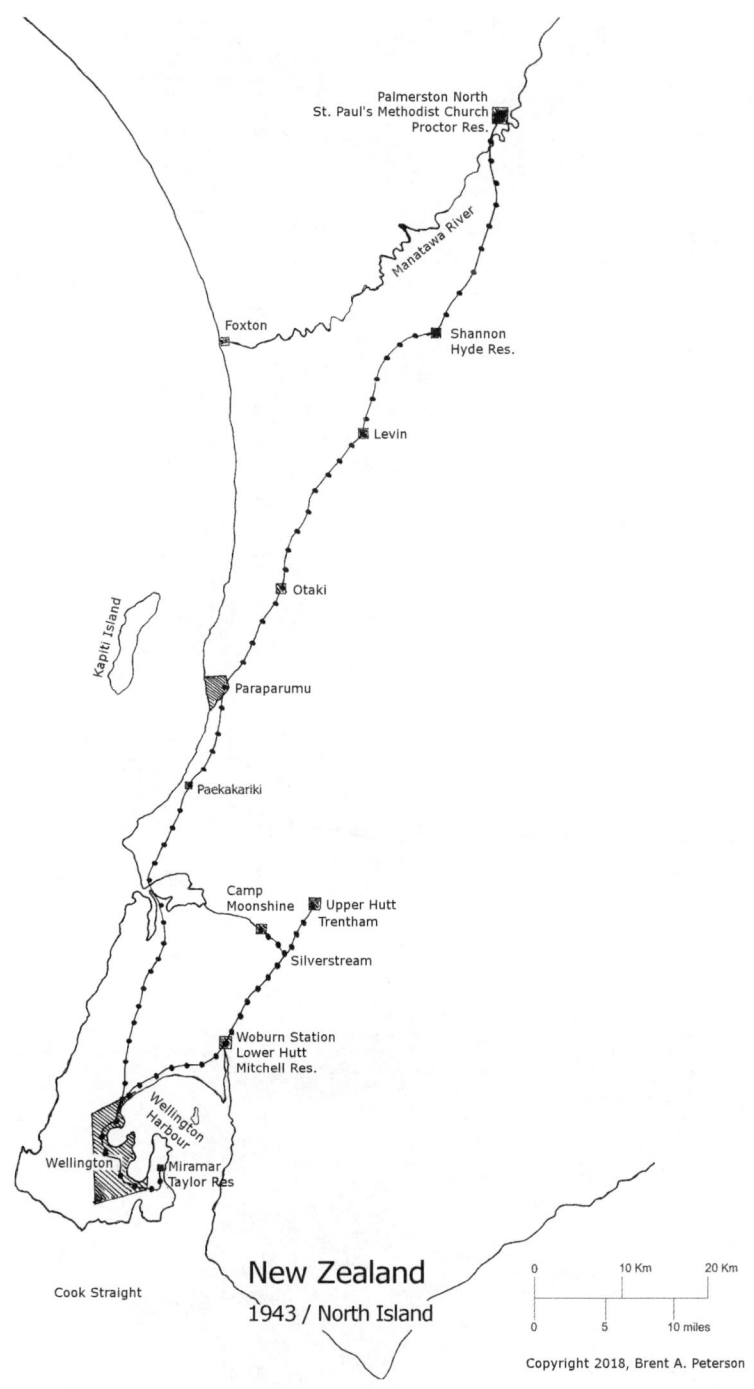

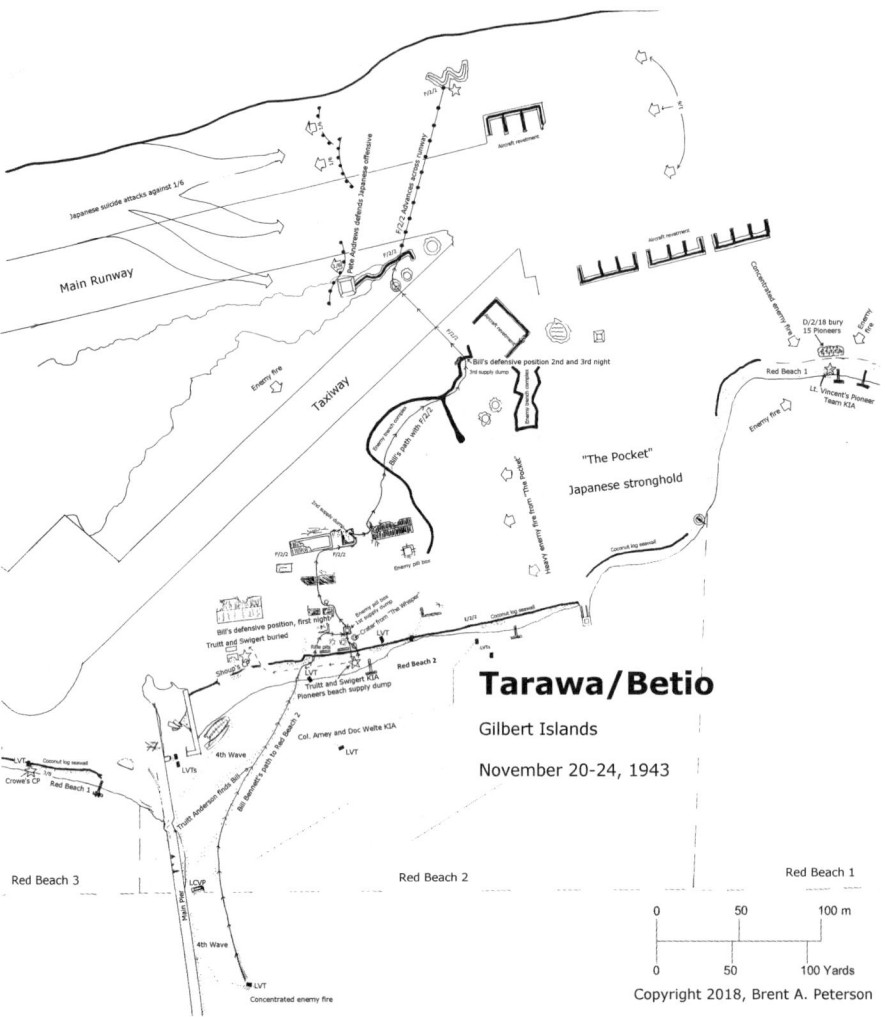

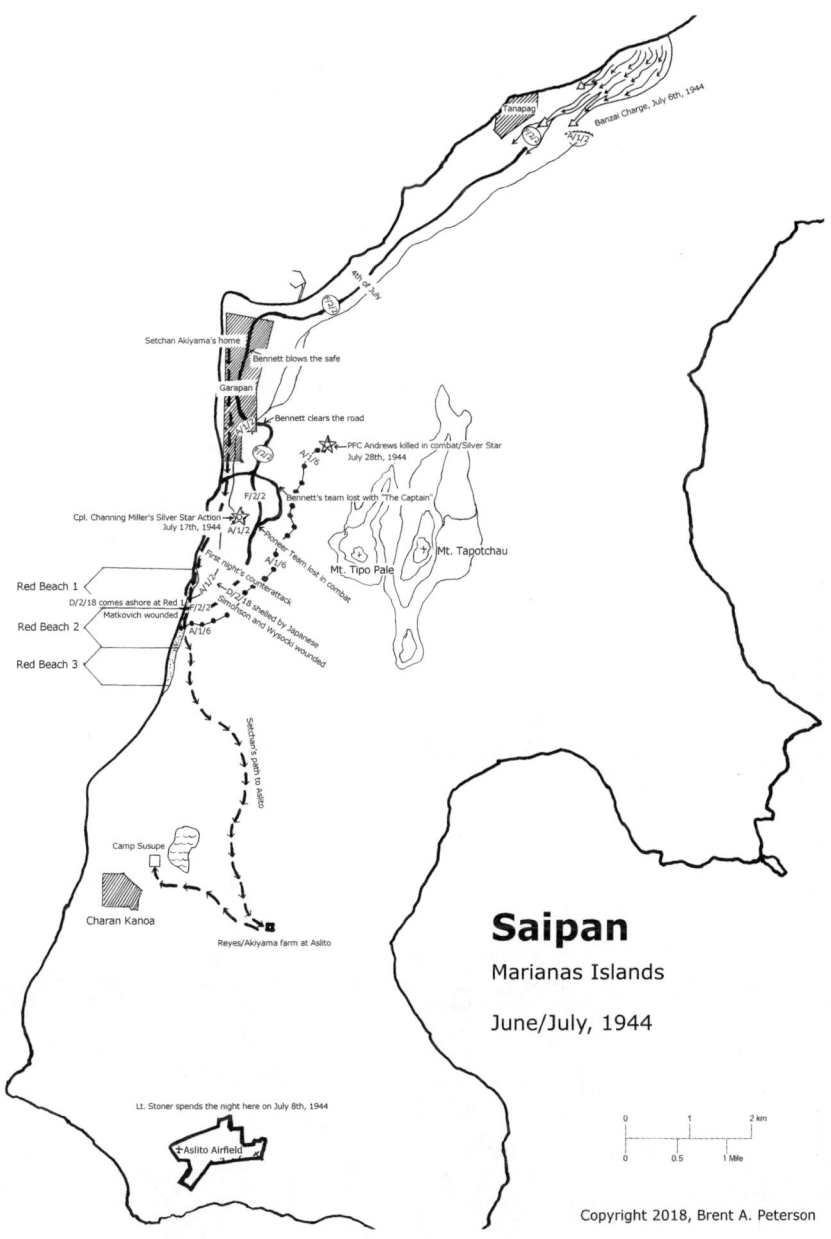

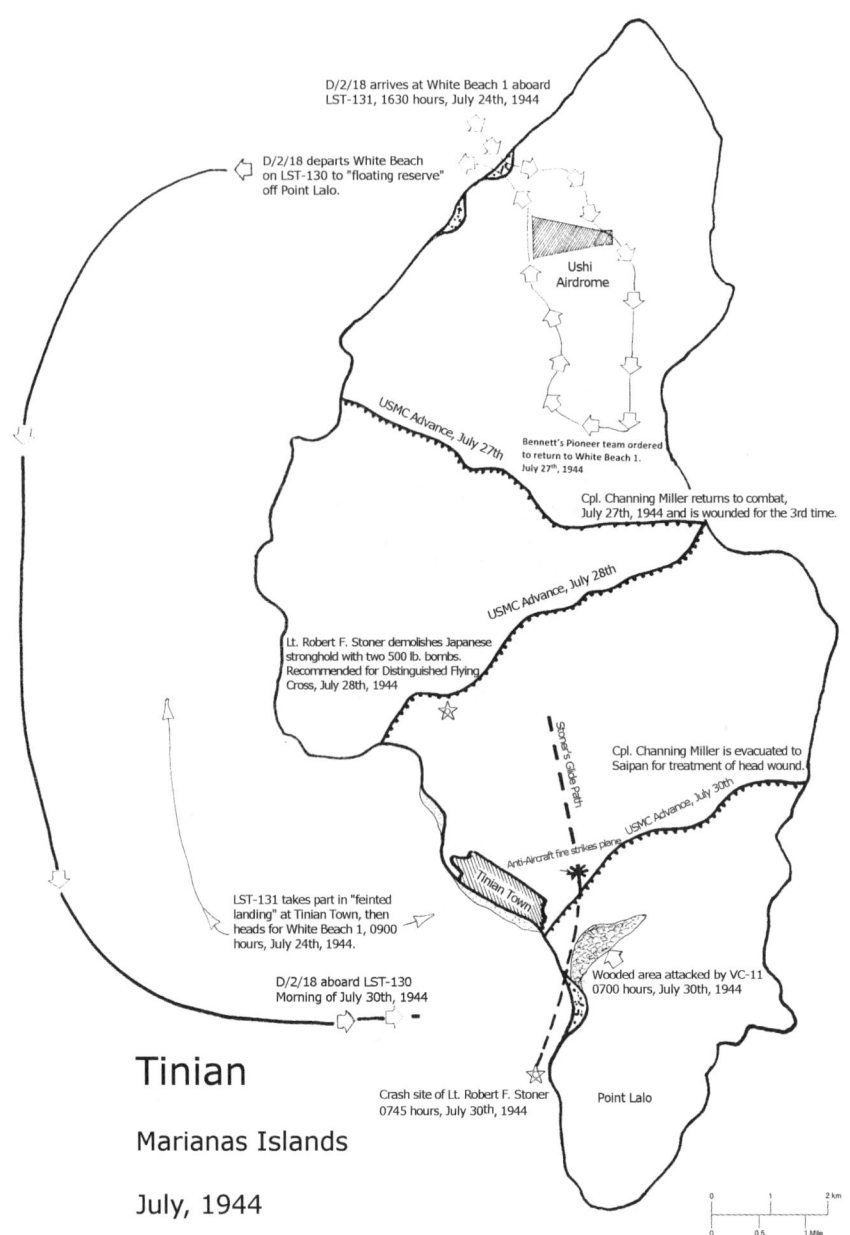

1. A Guy Named Bill

May 25th, 1975 brought a beautiful, sunny Sunday morning to my home town of Aurora, Illinois. I was nearing the completion of 7th grade and I enjoyed being able to get to church on my own, occasionally by walking about a mile to Claim Street Baptist Church. On this particular day, I remember going into the church auditorium and finding a seat on the east side of the main floor. Those already present were involved in conversations as the organist played through the prelude. As the volume of the organ music crescendoed into the last powerful chords, people flooded into the church to find their seats. The auditorium had a high A-frame ceiling with arching wooden beams and the music filled the building with the sense that something big was about to happen. The church was filled to a capacity of 400 to 500 people, and the voices of the congregation joined in powerful refrains of familiar hymns. Pastor Adamson eventually came to the pulpit and announced that in observance of Memorial Day, the church wished to remember the fallen and recognize those in attendance who had served our country in the various branches of the service. He asked those who were serving, or had served, to stand when their respective branch was called so they could be recognized.

Private William Wesley Bennett, U.S.M.C., 1942

(Cochran-Larson Family Photo)

He called out "Army!" and quite a few veterans stood up. "Navy!" and about a half dozen stood. "Air Force!" and three or four stood. When he called out, "Marines!" a very loud bellow of "YO!" rang out across the auditorium. Heads turned toward the lone figure of a man who had sprung to his feet. There was a slight burble of laughter that washed across the room, a reflex from the exuberance that this man had just shown for the United States Marine Corps. From my seat, I could clearly see him. He was in his late 50s with graying sideburns, glasses and a strong-looking physique for his age. He had a stern look on his face as he looked straight ahead. No one else in the room could see what he saw within his gaze. No one else could hear the echo of distant battlefields or smell the stench of war. We were comfortable in our pews and probably concerned about the lunch menu. Although I would not fully understand it for many years to come, I recognized that there was something special about this man. From what I had read about the United States Marines, he fit the picture. The first thing I ever knew about Bill Bennett was that he was without question, a proud Marine. (For "Quick Read" Feature, go directly to Chapter 16.)

2. True Pioneers

Stephen Bennett was born in 1811, in Dutchess County, New York. A rural upbringing during those early years of America allowed very little time for activities that were not directly related to survival or food production. He learned how to grow crops and build buildings. Stephen's dream was to one day own his own farm, and he grew up hearing the stories of hearty and adventurous pioneers moving westward across Pennsylvania, Ohio and the Indiana Territory. As a young man, Stephen courted the attention of Betsy Knickerbocker, who shared his deep Christian faith and his excitement for venturing out into the frontier. The two were married in 1836 and they carefully made plans to head west to the Illinois Territory which had recently become the 21st state. The Pottawattamie Indians had recently made a deal relinquishing their possession of the wilderness just to the west of Lake Michigan, and explorers had reported some of the most fertile ground known to mankind. This opportunity, although dangerous and uncertain, provided the best chance for the newlyweds to own a sizable homestead on which to raise a family and prosper. Within a few months, Betsy announced that the Bennett family would be expanding, and the couple made the decision to move west before travel would become impossible for Betsy and the baby.

Stephen and Betsy said goodbye to friends and family and set out overland for Buffalo, New York. At Buffalo, they bought passage aboard a Great Lakes steamship and sailed west on Lake Erie for Detroit. Upon arrival at Detroit, they changed ships for the second half of the trip to Chicago. The Bennett's ship took them north through Lake St. Claire, then onto the St. Claire river which opened up onto Lake Huron. The vastness of the Great Lakes was beyond belief for the pair who had spent their entire lives near the banks of the Hudson River. There was so much territory to be had, and they prayed they would soon own a piece of it. Passing Mackinac Island, Huron gave way to Lake Michigan and soon the western shores of Lake Michigan came into view. The crew pointed out areas of the Wisconsin Territory as the ship headed south, including a small settlement north of Chicago called Kilbourntown, which would one day become Milwaukee.

The arrival at the Port of Chicago was filled with excitement as ships were loading and unloading supplies. There were raw materials moving back to the East Coast for sale and farming supplies moving out into the frontier. The population of Chicago was about 8,000, with 400 being Pottawattamie working with traders, suppliers and shippers. New construction was visible in every direction and the now empty Fort Dearborn told the story of wars fought here just a few short years before. The Bennetts bought a wagon and a pair of oxen to carry their belongings and new supplies in search of their future. Stephen gathered all the information he could regarding the immediate opportunities and heard about a man named George Ela who was settling an area just a few days travel to the northwest. A new publication by S. Augustus Mitchell entitled *Illinois in 1837* provided ample information about every type of challenge the pair might encounter in the new territory. Within a few short days, Stephen and Betsy headed north away from Chicago to find George Ela.

The Bennetts located George Ela twelve miles west of the western shore of Lake Michigan, just east of modern day Lake Zurich, Illinois. The word that had been brought back to New York did not exaggerate the beauty and fertility of the land. A homestead of 160 acres was claimed and a house was built. Frances "Betsy" Bennett was born on October 20th, 1837. The family prospered, and by 1850, the Bennett family boasted seven children: Frances, Louisa, Samuel, Sylvia, George, Robert and baby Owen. On April 2nd, 1850, Ela Township had the first official meeting at the new town hall and Stephen Bennett was elected the first Township Supervisor. Stephen and Betsy had built a beautiful farm, owned a General Store and had become prominent citizens of Ela Township. On October 17th, 1853, their youngest son, Owen, died tragically at the age of four. The entire community was devastated by little Owen's death as they gathered to bury him at the new Diamond Lake Cemetery. Not long after Owen's death, Stephen and Betsy decided to sell their land and move the family farther west. The Bennetts loaded everything they owned into two wagons and left Ela Township. This time they set their sights on Osage, Iowa, and the current frontier.

As Stephen was leading his family very near to their destination in Iowa, he died suddenly. Betsy and the children buried Stephen very near what is now Floyd, Iowa. Stephen Bennett was 42. The area was unsettled and still considered dangerous. Many settlers were warned that this area of Iowa remained dangerous due to Indian raiding parties and wilderness conditions. Betsy believed the Lord would take care of her and her family and she wanted to honor Stephen's desire to move the family to this area. After burying Stephen, Betsy loaded the children, took the reins of the ox team and moved ahead. William Howard was the first settler in this area and he marveled at the sight of this small woman with six children in tow driving the huge covered wagon into the Floyd County area. William and his brother Sanders, held land rights to a vast area of prairie and Betsy looked it over with her children. Within hours, she came to a stretch of prairie that she recognized as a terrific spot for a farm. Betsy dug into the soil and recognized a similar texture of fertile soil to that which she and Stephen had found in Illinois. She told the children that this was their new home, and then she led them in prayer as they asked for God's blessing upon this new place. She arranged to purchase 216 acres from the Howard Brothers. Betsy and her oldest children picked out a prime location for a cabin, barn and shed. Betsy and 18-year-old Frances, 16-year-old Louisa, 15-year-old Samuel, 13-year-old Sylvia, 11-year-old George, and nine-year-old Robert, worked tirelessly to build their new homestead. The Howard, Bennett, Neville, Newton, Walling, Harris, Schermerhorn, and Wright families all worked together to build up their homes and farms, and the closely-knit community of Howardville, Iowa, was established. It would be a long hard road for the Bennett family, but they would stick together and take care of each other.

Betsy became known in their part of Iowa as "Mother Bennett" and she earned a reputation for being a tireless follower of Christ. She read the family Bible and taught her children the teachings of Jesus. She lived out her faith in plain view for all to see on a daily basis. She not only took care of her own family, but she also tended to the sick in the area, including many who were dying. She fed the hungry and aided the frontier pastors as they arrived in the area. The Bennetts and the other families were friendly to the Sioux Indians that migrated annually through their homesteads on the way to and from the Mississippi River. The families traded with these Indians and even built shelters that the Sioux could use as they passed through. At times of Indian attacks on the frontier to the west, settlers would flee their homes and many found refuge with the Howardville families. Betsy was instrumental in organizing and building the first United Weslyan Methodist Church in this region of Iowa, the Howardville Methodist Church.

George Bennett served with the 6th Iowa Cavalry from 1862 to 1865, fighting in the Sioux War in the Dakotas. Betsy organized the Howardville women to hand sew a large American flag in 1864, along with church banners that became part of the area's historic treasures.

3. A Change of Direction

Betsy's youngest son Robert eventually built a store in Osage, Iowa and Samuel took over the farm as she moved to town with Robert. Robert married Margaret Neville in 1872 and their first son, Charles, was born in 1875. Their first daughter, Missy, was born two years later. On October 16th, 1879, Robert and Margaret's second son, Stephen Robert Bennett, was born into their house on Pleasant Street. Two years later, Maggie was born. The family grew as Grandmother Betsy watched the frontier fade away into civilization.

Robert and Margaret Bennett made a very difficult decision to sell the family store and relocate in 1891. Betsy decided that she wanted to stay in Iowa and moved in with her daughter Louisa and eventually went back to the farm to live with Samuel and his wife Sarah. Robert and Margaret were attracted to the growing city of Aurora, located in Northern Illinois along the Fox River. Aurora had been one of the first cities in America to use electric streetlights, warranting the nickname, "The City of Lights," and it had one of the best public education programs in the state. The city of nearly 20,000 had a bustling downtown district that was split right down the middle by the river. The city's east and west sides were expanding across flat plains that were perfect for developing residential neighborhoods. The elevation dropped down into the river valley by 60 feet, creating clear views of the downtown area from the streets above. In the heart of the downtown area, the river forked around Stolp Island, which was the centerpiece of the city. The main east and west streets dropped down the hill to the river, across two bridges, over the island, and then back up the hill to the neighborhood on the other side of the city. Across the river, and up into the neighborhood of the east side, Robert and his family found a new church family at First Methodist Church.

The Bennetts bought the house at 185 Spruce Street, on Aurora's near west side, and Stephen Robert Bennett enrolled into the West Aurora schools. On March 18th, 1892 Margaret gave birth to George Oswald Bennett and their family was complete. Steve adapted quickly to the new city life, so very different than what he was used to back on the prairie at Osage. Steve grew into an impressive young man of 5' 10," with a lean frame, black hair and steel gray eyes. Aurora had everything a young man could want in a city and the most important was opportunity. Steve was drawn to another new aspect of city life, that being stylish men's wear. The clothing stores in Aurora featured the latest fashions that one would expect to find in Chicago or New York. Steve was fascinated by the immaculate tailors that could measure a man in a few minutes and produce a custom-made suit in a matter of hours.

Betsy Knickerbocker-Bennett, 1870
(Osage County, Iowa, Historical Society)

After graduating from West Aurora High School in June of 1898, Steve set about the task of building a career in the men's clothing industry. He was hired by Fernberg's Clothing Company as a clerk and went to work full time right in the heart of the city's business district at 8-10 S. Broadway. His years of hard work in the family store had taught him a work ethic that was easily spotted by Mr. Fernberg as Steve was given increasing responsibilities. His favorite part of the business became tailoring itself and he applied himself towards learning every detail of the craft. Steve used some of his first paychecks to buy himself a "proper suit." Looking good in public was now a must as his appearance was one of the best forms of advertisement. His 5' 10" frame in a tailored suit with shined shoes and straw hat would become a daily sight in downtown Aurora for many years to come.

A telegram arrived at the Bennett home in Aurora on October 15th, 1902, informing the family that Grandmother Betsy had passed away in Floyd, Iowa. She was a true pioneer woman who lived to be 90 years old.

4. A New Bennett Family

In 1903, Steve began the courtship of Miss Jessie Jean Pfrangle, a 1901 graduate of East Aurora High School. Jessie was now an elementary school teacher at the east side's D. W. Young School on the corner of Fifth Street and Center Avenue. Steve had known Jessie for many years through church activities and was impressed by her sense of direction and kind personality. Jessie was the grand-daughter of German immigrants and she lived with her parents, William and Sarah, on Aurora's near east side at 279 S. LaSalle Street. William was a postal clerk at the sizable Aurora post office and Sarah maintained an immaculate home. Steve went to call on Jessie at the Pfrangle home and the two began to get to know each other beyond their previous casual conversations. Jessie expressed a closeness to the Lord that was at the very core of all she aspired to in life. Prayer, for Jessie, was a part of her everyday life, not just something she saved for Sundays. She brought decisions and plans to the Lord in prayer and believed that He answered prayer and guided lives according to His will. She was the most loving person that Steve had ever met and this spilled over into her work as a teacher as well. Jessie loved her students at Young Elementary and they loved her back. Perhaps Jessie reminded Steve a little of his Grandmother Betsy. Steve took it all in and came to believe that Jessie had the ingredients to be a very, very good mother one day.

The city offered an almost unlimited opportunity for activities for Steve and Jessie during their courtship, with church, social and family gatherings. The two fell in love and Steve proposed marriage. They were married at the Fourth Street Methodist Church on August 30th, 1905 and a new Bennett family was formed. They rented a spacious two-story home at 228 Avon Street on Aurora's east side, close enough to D. W. Young School for Jessie to walk to work. Steve was already in the habit of catching the electric trolley for his ride downtown to Fernberg's. The new couple had their work cut out for them with the Bennett and Pfrangle families to interact with, and each family was excited about their new addition. When Christmas time arrived, Jessie shared the wonderful news that another Bennett would soon be living in Aurora, as she was expecting their first child. Jessie taught the remainder of the school year of 1906, but when she closed up her classroom in June, that would be her last day as a school teacher. Stephen Robert Bennett, Jr. was born on August 16th, 1906 at Aurora's City Hospital on the east side. Steve and Jessie decided to call the new arrival "Bobby" to avoid any confusion with Steve. The families were so excited about the new baby, and Grandpa Robert Bennett was honored by the name choice. Knowing that he and his father Stephen's name would live on into the future meant a lot to Robert. The honor proved a timely choice as Robert passed away nine months later on June 4th, 1907.

Jessie Jean Phrangle-Bennett on her Wedding Day, August 30th, 1905.

(Bennett Family Photo)

With Jessie staying home to care for Bobby, the Bennetts decided to rent out the extra two bedrooms to occasional boarders. As kindergarten was approaching for little Bobby, Jessie, again, had happy news for Steve and the family as they were expecting their second baby. Albert Eugene Bennett was born on January 11th, 1912 and there would be no more room for boarders at the Bennett house. Steve worked long hours at Fernberg's and he had been promoted to management, so his income had been able to increase along with their bills. Jean Pfrangle Bennett was born on February 11th, 1914 and Steve and Jessie began to look for a bigger house. They found a large two-story, four bedroom house for rent nearby at 430 Maple Avenue, and the Bennetts moved from Avon Street, right up Fourth Street about seven blocks to the new neighborhood. Jessie was thrilled with the bigger house and the fact that they would only be a short walk from church. Marian Virginia Bennett was born on January 2nd, 1917. Three-year-old Jean was over the moon with excitement upon the arrival of her little sister. Al had already proven to be a very dependable young lad at the age of four, and ten-year-old Bob was busy getting used to the new neighborhood. The new house on Maple Avenue brought new friends to the children and a better area for playing. Bob and Al changed elementary schools as they started at the Marion Avenue School just a few blocks away. Another huge change in the Bennett's lives arrived when Steve bought a used Ford Model T and Jessie and he learned to drive it.

Steve and Jessie's lives were extremely busy with the children and all that went along with having a large family. Besides the children and housework, Jessie was active with the Parent-Teacher Association as she had experience on both sides of the equation. She was also very active with the Sunday school organization at Fourth Street Methodist Church. In spite of the busy schedule that came with motherhood, Jessie continued to find time for prayer and devotional reading of her Bible on a daily basis. She prayed for each one of the Bennett children and her husband daily. She wanted her children to come to know and love God more than anything else.

A very well-dressed Stephen Robert Bennett, circa 1910.

Over the following months, the United States would learn that Germany had been trying to convince Mexico to attack the U.S. on Germany's behalf. On April 2nd, 1917, Congress declared war on Germany and on June 5th, the military draft was begun. By the middle of August, 1918, Jessie told Steve that there would soon be a boy's bedroom, a girl's bedroom and a nursery at the Bennett home as the doctor had confirmed that child number five was on the way. Steve's age bracket was called to register for the draft and he went and filled out his card as was his duty as an American. No one knew how long this war would last or if family men like Steve would actually be called to serve. For Jessie, the thought of having a loved one in harm's way would be more than she could bear, but on November 11th, 1918, Germany surrendered, ending the "War to End All Wars."

5. Arrival

A lot of people say that they "wouldn't want to bring a child into a world like this." The truth is, there has never been a time in recorded history when it seemed like a good time to bring a child into the world. The world seems to find a way to provide all kinds of evil and danger, so someone has to watch out for the vulnerable. The year 1919 had more than its share of turmoil, both in the U.S. and around the world. Americans were trying to put the war in Europe behind them while race tensions came to a boiling point. Communism was raising its ugly head all around the world, and anarchists were bombing innocent Americans. In the middle of all of this, life with the Bennetts kept moving forward. Mr. Fernberg had promoted Steve to Vice President of the company, which meant he could fairly well run the business by himself, if necessary.

Jessie's friends were especially excited about this new baby as there had been other new arrivals in the neighborhood. Two friends from church had new babies that had actually been born on the same day last June 18th. Gertie Meyers had little Rodney and Florence Morey had Jack. John and Gertie Myers lived directly across the street from the Bennett's, so Jessie saw her and the baby often when the weather was nice. It had been mentioned, more than once, how nice it would be if the next Bennett baby just happened to be a boy so that Rodney would have a playmate. Wilbur and Florence Morey lived just a few blocks away on Jackson Street. Jessie's next-door neighbor, Margaret Keck, was a high spirited Scottish gal that had no children of her own, so she paid great attention to Jean and little Marian and could lend a hand if Jessie needed one. The Bennett children were a great help to their mother and they looked forward to the baby's arrival.

Jessie Bennett and Billy during the spring of 1920.
(Bennett Family Photo)

Another friend of Jessie's from church, Maude Troll, lived a half block west on the corner of Fourth Street and Maple Avenue. Maude had been born into the Riley family in Aurora in 1877 and had married Ernest Troll, an immigrant from Germany. Their son Robert was about the same age as Bob Bennett and the two were buddies. Two months after Jessie had told Maude about the new baby on the way, Maude had walked down for a morning visit after the kids were off to school. The great news was that Maude was pregnant and her due date would be sometime in June. Another nice thing about the neighborhood was that the hospital was only a few blocks away, close enough to walk if one went into labor.

As March gives way to April, the new life of spring is an exciting time for Midwesterners who have just been through a tough winter. Looking forward to having the baby made the spring all the more welcome. With Easter Sunday just a few weeks away, Jessie was planning out what needed to be done for Sunday school and what she and the girls would wear for Easter. When it came to the boy's suits, she had to consult Steve, of course. Perhaps the baby would wait until after Easter when all these decisions had been taken care of and Jessie's schedule had been cleared. On Monday, April 14th, 1919, Jessie Bennett gave birth to William Wesley Bennett and the word traveled quickly through the city. Jessie held this baby in her arms and thanked the Lord for His blessing. Flowers were delivered from friends and family and Steve was congratulated at Fernberg's. The Bennetts had quite a family.

The Bennett home at 430 Maple Avenue, where they lived in 1919 when Baby William was born.

(Bennett Family Photo)

6. The Early Years

Siblings Bob, Al, Jean and Marian welcomed baby Billy into the family routine and the neighborhood was excited with the news of the latest Bennett arrival. Jean was old enough to be a real help to Jessie, and Marian couldn't wait until Billy was old enough to play. Jessie and Steve tried to make sure that the other Bennett children didn't feel overlooked as Billy required most of the attention for a while. Bob and Al knew the ropes by now. Of course, Gertie Myers was elated about Billy's arrival, and within a few months Wilbur and Florence Morey moved into the house right next door to the Myers.

On June 11th, Maude Troll went into labor. Ernest called Jessie that evening to tell her that the Troll's had a new baby boy named George. The Maple Avenue neighborhood was going to be a busy place for Jack, Rodney, Billy and now George. These four boys were together playing on the floor long before any of them could walk. Jessie enjoyed having the ladies over for tea and coffee during the day, and she was often over at the other's homes with Billy and Marian during the school days. Getting together over tea and baked goods became a standard way to break up the day. The east-side neighborhoods had concrete sidewalks and curbs at the streets, so walking with a stroller or a baby carriage was quite nice. The streets were fairly quiet with an occasional motor car or truck. Most of the commercial vehicles were still horse and wagon. On some of the main streets, the electric trolleys ran on their tracks delivering Aurorans back and forth across the city. When the weather was nice, a walk with the other ladies and their babies was very enjoyable. Occasionally, Jessie and the kids would walk to the trolley stop to meet Steve on his way home from work.

Fourth Street Methodist Church
(Bennett Family Photo)

Fourth Street Methodist Church was expanding its membership at a record pace. Within a year, Elsie Dix gave birth to Earl, Jr., who became known as "Bud," and Louise McElroy gave birth to Harley. The following year, Helen Nix delivered baby Robert and the nursery was a busy place on Sundays. As these seven little boys grew, they became a close group of playmates both at home and at church. Billy had Jack and Rodney just across the street and George just a few houses down on the corner. The younger boys lived a few blocks away, and as they became old enough to play, Jessie would set up visits both to and from for Billy. Billy also had built-in playmates with his sisters Jean and Marian. Jean was more of an overseer for most of the young years, but Marian loved to be involved with any kind of play that included little Billy. She had gotten her wish for a little brother to play with, and then some. For some reason, early on, Billy decided that Marian should be called "Pete," and that's the way it was. As extended families grew, the Bennett kids had regular visits and lots of fun with their cousins. George and Nellie Bennett and their little girls were regular visitors and Billy and his family called them "The West Side Bennetts" as their house was across the Fox River.

Preschool years were made up of long days with Jack, Rodney and George. Favorite play consisted of steel trucks and cars that could be used in the yard, various ball games, tag, hide and seek and "kick the can." The older kids in the neighborhood passed along the games and supervised the instructions for each one. When it came to boy's issues, older brother Al watched over Billy and his friends most of the time. Billy knew that Al would help him with almost anything and the two became close to each other in spite of the age difference. Bob was so much older that he had other things to do and didn't seem to pay much attention to Billy. Learning to be a part of this extended play group became a very important learning experience for little Billy, and he learned very early in life that you must learn how things work, then work within those boundaries. Jessie taught Billy that prayer was an important part of life and Billy had a wonderful example of love and kindness from his mother.

Rodney Myers, George Troll, Billy Bennett and Jack Morey at play at 430 Maple Ave. 1922.

(Bennett Family Photo)

Steve had become dissatisfied with his position at Fernberg's and had been kicking around the idea of opening his own shop for a few years. With his extensive interaction with Aurora's business elite, he was sure that he could make his own business work. He convinced Jessie that the family would be better off and the decision was made. Steve found a suitable store front that was available right around the corner from Broadway at 104 Main Street and located the best stock and supplies to focus the marketing towards the fashion needs of "the younger man." Bob and Al helped Steve with the set up at the shop and Jessie pitched in as she could while taking care of the home front. Finally, in 1923, S.R. Bennett's Men's Shop opened to the public. Many of Steve's customers from Fernberg's transferred their loyalty to his new shop, and the advertising he aimed at the younger men's market worked well. He placed advertising in all the right places, including inside both the East High and West High school yearbooks. His location also made it necessary for many of his competitor's customers to walk past Bennett's window display on their way to the other shops, and a popular cigar store was located right next door. Steve was now an Aurora merchant, not just an employee. His increasing interaction with Aurora business led him to become the Treasurer of the Kiwanis Club as well as the President of the Advertising Club of Aurora.

In the spring of 1924, Jessie and Steve's oldest son Bob graduated from East High and set about starting his own career. He worked with his dad down at

Bennett's as needed and Al helped at the shop occasionally. September of 1925 brought a huge change to Billy's life as he enrolled in kindergarten at the Bardwell Elementary school on Bardwell Avenue between Fifth Street and Jackson Street. Jessie took Billy by the hand and walked him to the classroom door and into the care of his new teacher, Miss Kathryn Mitchell. With Billy being off to school now, it was the end of an era for Jessie, and she cried as she walked home alone. Jean and Marian were Billy's escorts to and from school and Jessie could drive them during bad weather as Steve always rode the trolley to work downtown. Jessie's new freedom during the daytime allowed her to become more involved with work at the church as well as the freedom to get together with her family and neighborhood friends. She could also focus more time on her involvement with the PTA at Bardwell School and she became President. Jessie and Steve became fond of having dinner parties at their home and the usual guests would be other families from church, school or Steve's business associates. Jessie loved to cook meals and bake cookies and cakes. Having the fresh scent of baked cookies in the kitchen when the children came home from school became a regular occurrence. Billy developed a love for cookies and cold milk that would last throughout his life.

Billy's Sunday school classes and his lessons from Jessie, in particular, were exposing him to the detailed teachings of Jesus Christ. His mother taught him that going to church was something that grew out of a love for Christ and that Christ Himself had paved the way for this relationship by dying on the cross as payment for our sin. Going to church itself held no "magic power" to change Billy's heart,

Billy Bennett as an energetic five-year-old beginning Kindergarten at Bardwell School.

(Bennett Family Photo)

it would be the result of Billy asking for and receiving forgiveness from Christ Himself. On their own, people have no power or ability to be cleansed from their sinful nature. As a believer admits sinfulness and accepts the forgiveness offered by Christ, the believer is not only forgiven, but transformed by the indwelling of the presence of Christ, the Holy Spirit who brings along the promise of eternal life. As Jesus taught, "I am the resurrection and the life. He who believes in me will live, even though he dies; and whoever lives and believes in me will never die." As Jessie began to make things clear to Billy, she also told him that any decision he would make regarding his acceptance of Christ's offer for forgiveness would be up to him.

Left: Even as a young lad, Billy Bennett's jovial personality was plain to see.

(Bennett Family Photo)

Below: Billy Bennett and his beloved fire truck on his 6th birthday, April 14th, 1925.

(Bennett Family Photo)

Eventually the day came when young Billy decided he wanted to follow Jesus as he prayed with his mom and asked Jesus to forgive his sin, cleanse his heart and live with him eternally. As Jessie tucked Billy into bed and turned off the light, she knew that this had been one of the most important days in her life; certainly, a day that she had prayed about for many years. It would certainly be the most important day in Billy's life as well. As Jessie prayed, her thankfulness to the Lord was overflowing as He had allowed her to play such a vital role in bringing her child to the knowledge of who He is. Although this was only the beginning, Billy was on the road to an abundant life.

7. A New Kid in Town

During the summer of 1927, Sam and Margaret Stoner moved their family from Oak Park (Chicago's first suburb on the western edge of the city) some

45 miles west to Aurora. Sam had been offered a new sales position at the Wentzel-Foster Dodge Brothers dealership on Lake Street in Aurora and they decided that the schools on Aurora's east side would be a good change for their five children. They bought a house on Talma Street and the Stoner kids had some time to get familiar with the neighborhood. The Stoner's were members of a Methodist church in Oak Park, so they naturally looked into finding another Methodist church after the move to Aurora. They visited the Fourth Street Methodist Church a few Sundays after the move and friendships began almost immediately. Sam Stoner and Steve Bennett had so much in common that it would take the pair years to uncover it all. Jessie and Margaret both had five children that were roughly the same ages, with the oldest and youngest being offset a few years. With Sam and Margaret's oldest son, Dexter at 13, Harley at 11, Eleanor at 10, Robert at nine and Helen at four, the families had a lot in common. Billy's brother Al was nearly the same age as Dexter and Harley. Jean and Marian fit right in with Eleanor while Billy and Robert were only a year apart. As the children were introduced after church, Margaret Stoner noted that her Bobby and Jessie's Billy were almost the same age, with Bobby starting third grade at Bardwell and Billy starting the second grade. Bobby and Billy shook hands and Billy welcomed him to Aurora. Bobby's bright blue eyes and big smile sent out a sense of excitement at the prospect of making a new friend, and he had a firm handshake just like Billy had been taught by Steve.

Jessie asked Billy to take Bobby and introduce him to some of the other Fourth Street gang and the two boys were thrilled to be released from the adults. Jean Bennett took Eleanor to introduce her to some of the teenage girls while Dexter and Harley were busy talking to Al and some of his friends. As Billy was leading the way, looking for George and the other boys, Bobby was explaining to him about the move and how he missed some of his friends from Oak Park. He asked Billy about school and wondered if the teachers were nice or mean. Billy told him that they were pretty nice if you did what they told you, but could be mean if you didn't. Pretty much like all teachers. Bobby was very well spoken and seemed like a pretty smart kid. Even though he was older than Billy, he was a bit smaller. Billy found George and Bob Nix running around behind the church with Jack Morey and "Bud" Dix. When Billy approached them with the new kid in tow, they naturally stopped what they were doing out of curiosity. Having another boy to join in the play was great as far as they all were concerned. The more the merrier. Billy and Bobby joined in the brisk game of tag which had to be somewhat low key so that no one ruined their Sunday clothes.

When it was time to go, the Stoner's walked down Marion Avenue to their parked car and the Bennetts walked up Fourth Street toward home. Jessie and Steve were planning to have the Stoner family over for one of their dinner parties so that they could all get to know each other better. Billy and the girls already knew that having the Stoner kids over to the house would be a lot of fun.

When the day came for the Stoner family to come over to the Bennett's for dinner, there was a lot of excitement around the house. Jessie began cooking some of the dishes just after lunch and the kids pitched in to make sure that the house and yard were presentable. By late afternoon the whole house smelled of pot roast and baking from the oven. Billy ended up out in the front yard with Jean and Marian as they waited for their guests to arrive. The girls were looking forward to playing with Eleanor and Billy was eager to show Bobby around his neighborhood. A Packard sedan turned the corner at Fifth Street and Maple and rolled toward the Bennett place. As the car came closer, the familiar faces of Margaret and Sam could be seen smiling through the windshield. Sam pulled the Packard over to the curb right in front of the Mitchler's house next door and the back doors exploded with the five Stoner kids. Margaret stepped out onto the grass and Helen waited near her while eying the Bennetts as they welcomed their guests. Sam came around from the street side and took Helen's hand while Margaret produced a huge bowl covered with a cloth. Billy greeted Bobby excitedly and told him of his plans for after dinner. By the time he turned towards the house, Jessie and Steve were already down the front steps and welcoming Sam and Margaret. The dishes clanged and the silverware clinked away as dinner was devoured. Aside from the dining room table, some folding tables accommodated Billy, Bobby and the girls. After dinner, everyone helped to clear the table and get things put away. Billy and Bobby slipped out the front door and down to the corner to see what George was up to. George was still eating dinner, so Billy showed Bobby the alley short cut to the Bennett's backyard.

Sam and Margaret Stoner family in 1927. Bobby is top center with Harley just below. A well-dressed Dexter is kneeling on the far right, little Helen is looking down in the front next to her big sister Eleanor with the golden curls. Cousin Marjorie MacGibbon is at the top right.

(Stoner Family Photo)

The house was loud that evening as all of the Bennetts and Stoners were getting acquainted. Dexter and Harley had just landed a newspaper route and they spent a lot of time with Al. All three of these fellows were very serious about school and had hopes of going to college after high school. Dexter and Harley both loved to write and thought that being a reporter or writing books would be great jobs. Harley was especially gifted as an athlete and loved sports. Billy and Bobby stopped by the three older boys several times to see what they were up to. Eleanor's bubbly personality made her a lot of fun to be around and there was a lot of giggling from the girl's room when Billy and Bobby came down the hall. Eleanor shared her older brothers interest in writing and she was also a very good student; "smart as a whip," one might say. Her wavy blonde hair and bright blue eyes made it easy to see that she and Bobby were related. The boys knocked on the door and Jean opened the door just wide enough to tell the boys to go away; girls only. Of course, little Helen got a pass to attend the girls get together.

Downstairs, laughter roared occasionally as Sam and Steve talked at the dining room table while Jessie and Margaret were out in the kitchen. Sam Stoner had piercing blue eyes and a thin mustache that he wiggled from side to side. With a wink of the eyes and a wiggle of that mustache, it was easy to believe that Sam Stoner could sell anything. He and Steve talked of business and how things were situated in Aurora. Before the night was over, they forged an alliance that would have Steve sending customers to Wentzel-Foster Dodge and Sam sending customers to Bennett's Men's Store. As the young boys made their way into the kitchen, Margaret was helping Jessie with dessert plates. They were preparing to bring out the cake that Jessie had baked earlier that afternoon. Jessie had been answering a lot of questions that Margaret had about the east side schools and the start of the coming year. Spending the evening with the President of the PTA was just what she needed. As the new school year began in 1927, one of Jessie's responsibilities as the President of the Bardwell Parent Teacher Association was to make sure that new families moving into the Bardwell district were welcomed. This usually meant a phone call, meeting at the school or dropping off some information at the new family's homes. She would make sure that Margaret Stoner had everything she needed.

The boys ended up in Billy's room and they pulled out all the great toys that Billy wanted to show his new friend. One of Billy's favorites was his huge metal fire truck that had been his birthday present when he turned six. The two boys exchanged ideas about what they wanted to be when they grew up. They shared stories about their friends and the things that they liked to play. They both had a love for sports, bicycles and adventure. Bobby had a great interest in the Navy and had a favorite sailor hat that he wore frequently. Having lived near Chicago, he was familiar with Lake Michigan and loved to watch the ships when he went near the lake. They both thought that airplanes were awesome and they thought it would be great to be a pilot like Lindbergh or Doolittle. Billy told Bobby about some of the friends that he would meet at Bardwell and the play groups around the Maple Street neighborhood. He wanted Bobby to come back and play with George, Jack, Bobby Nix and the others. Bobby was a quick wit and the two boys laughed and had a great time. By the end of the night, as the Stoners gathered on the Bennett's front porch, it was obvious to all that there would be many more gatherings of the two families.

8. A Change of Address

Billy loved to stop in and see his dad down at Bennett's Men's Store, and Jessie would sometimes pull up to the curb and have Billy run in a sandwich, chocolate milkshake or something else that Steve needed at the shop. The shop itself afforded all kinds of adventures as there were many places to hide: in the dressing rooms, under the racks, shelves or counter. The mannequins were very interesting and Billy liked it when his dad was setting them up with different clothes in the window display. Steve liked having the kids around the shop as long as there was no "horseplay," especially if there were customers present. Billy was fascinated by the shop in the back where the sewing machines and tailoring tools were all set up. If it had to do with tools, he liked it. It was amazing to him how his dad's hands worked so fast with exacting skill. Many years of experience had given Steve abilities that were hard for a young boy to understand. Steve's business had been running well for over five years now and the venture had been good for the family. Jessie and Steve had been discussing the possibility of buying a house instead of renting the place on Maple Avenue. They both agreed that they wanted to stay in the same general area as the family was involved with the neighborhood in so many ways.

One morning in 1928, as Jessie was returning from dropping the kids off at Bardwell School, she turned down Pearl Street to head home. As she came to the T-section where Pearl Street ends at Simms Street, she looked left and then right. Something caught her eye to the right and as she looked back, she noticed a "House for Sale" sign in the front yard two doors to the east. She turned the wheel and took a long slow look at the two-story frame house with a large wrap-around front porch at 454 Simms Street. This could be exactly what she and Steve had been talking about. Arriving at home, she made a few phone calls to arrange for her and Steve to take a look at the house. The house belonged to an older woman named Ruhama Nicholson who had moved to Aurora some years earlier from Plano, Illinois. She had been using the extra bedrooms to take in boarders for several years, but now she had found a larger house that was more suitable for boarders.

The front steps were made of concrete with knee-walls made from heavy block on both sides. The porch gave the front of the house a picturesque look and offered a great place to sit on pleasant days, welcome guests or play when it was rainy. The siding on the front of the porch was a "fish scale" design of cedar shingles whereas the rest of the house was clad by four-inch wood siding. Just inside the front door, a beautiful wooden staircase ascended on the right hand side. The landing near the bottom of the stair had a stained-glass window just above it. The newel post was made from white oak and had Grecian wreaths carved at the top with cascading ribbons carved below them. The foyer led straight ahead and opened up into the dining room and kitchen on the right, with the family room and parlor to the left. The floors were made from heart pine and the lighter color gave a contrast to the darker stained woodwork above. There were built-in cabinets to the right of the door leading from the dining room to the kitchen at the back of the house with a double window looking out from the dining room. Just through the door into the kitchen there was another door to the right which revealed a small pantry. The kitchen had a back door that led out onto a large roof-covered back porch. Just to the left of the back door was a utility stair leading down to the basement and up to the second floor. The second floor had four bedrooms, two large, one medium and one small, as well as one huge bathroom with a stand-alone bathtub. Overall, this house was considerably larger than their house on Maple Avenue, and it had a lot more charm.

Steve and Jessie went back for a second look and this time the whole Bennett family came along. It was an easy decision as everyone was both excited about the idea of the Bennetts owning their own house as well as the obvious upgrades. Billy looked the house over and wanted to know how the bedrooms would get divided up. More than likely, the small room would be his, but it was a nice room at the back of the house and it would do nicely. The back staircase was like a secret passage down to the kitchen or up to the spacious attic. The back yard was quite large and led back to an alley that split up the block just like on Maple Avenue. There would still be a shortcut to George's house and Bob Nix lived right across the alley less than 100 yards away. Another great thing about the prospect of moving to 454 Simms Street was the fact that it was only two blocks south of the Maple Avenue neighborhood. The Bennetts would be two blocks closer to Bardwell, two blocks farther away from Fourth Street Methodist and they could all keep their current friends. Steve and Jessie worked out the details with their bank and a move-in date was set.

Everything that the Bennetts owned had to get ready for the move north, albeit two blocks. However, moving into a new house is always a big deal for a nine-year-old boy and it was quite the same for the girls. When moving day came, the moving truck came to load all of the big items, but Jessie had set aside quite a few things that she wanted to move in the car. It was a busy day for all of them, but they had plenty of help from friends and family. As they were making their first trips to the new house, Billy was curious about the new neighbors. The most notable upgrade to the move was the fact that Bobby Nix lived at 421 Linden Avenue, just one street north and the Nix's back yard and the Bennett's yard almost lined up across the alley in the middle of the block. Billy could run from his new back porch to Bobby Nix's back porch in about 17 seconds. As far as the play group went, there would be no major changes that came along with the new address. One thing that did change was the walk to school. For years Billy and Marian had stopped by to join up with George down on the corner. With the Bennett's move toward school, George now stopped by their house in the morning to join up with them. They would continue on to the corner of Simms and Fifth Street, then four blocks up Fifth Street to the school.

Billy's play with the other boys at school and in the neighborhood changed in many ways during these early school years as the boys became increasingly interested in sports versus the old standby neighborhood games. Al was eager and available as a teenager to help Billy with learning the basics of football, baseball and basketball, although he was not much of an athlete himself. Al recognized that Billy had very good eye-hand coordination and he learned the basics of sports quickly and with eagerness. Billy began to realize, and Al could see as well, that Billy was becoming strong. The other boys he played with were realizing it too as they were regularly involved in the games. Any boys involved in running a football soon learned that being tackled by Billy Bennett was going to hurt. As Billy grew stronger, it was not something he would use to get his own way or push people around, but quite the opposite. Jessie and Steve were very strict parents, and they would not allow one of their children to behave badly in any sense of the word without assured punishment. Billy decided at a very young age that disappointing his parents or his family in general was not something he wanted to do. He also took to heart the teaching of Jesus to "treat others the way you want to be treated," known as the golden rule. However, knocking people down was, at times, just part of the game.

Bobby Stoner became a regular part of the play group in the Maple Avenue neighborhood and Billy was frequently over at the Stoner's house. Both Bobby and Billy benefited from the input and example of Dexter and Harley when it came to several areas. Dexter and Harley had their paper route which made the younger boys think about what they could do to earn some spending money. Mowing lawns, carrying junk, pulling weeds, small painting jobs and shoveling snow in the winter all became possibilities.

As Billy grew into the middle grade school years, the casual backyard and school yard sports took a more serious turn as he began to take part in activities at the Aurora YMCA. One of the best things the YMCA had to offer was a gymnasium with a real basketball court. The neighborhood gang would regularly meet for open gym at the YMCA. Billy, George, Bobby Stoner and Bobby Nix developed a love for basketball. George and Bobby both began to play the clarinet with the Bardwell band, but Billy had no interest in playing an instrument. After many of his friends had decided to join band, he felt a bit off to the side. Billy's bicycle changed his world as much as that Ford changed Jessie's. He could get over to his friend's house or over to school in a few minutes. The neighborhood kids would regularly play at the nearby Catholic Church parking lot, or walk up to the school playground with a group to play football or baseball. Billy's favorite activity during these years would be to invite a few of the gang over for the night at the Bennett house. They would be able to have some special treats in the evening while they listened to the radio and imagined being a hero in one of the stories, or laughed at the crazy comedians doing their routines. Jean and Marian had their turns at this and it was always fun for Billy when the house was filled with giggling girls too. Sometimes he would get to spend the night at George's house if the girls would be taking over the Bennett place. Being at George's house became like a second home for Billy as Maude Troll became known as "Ma Troll" to Billy and the gang. All over the east side neighborhood, Billy became familiar with dozens of families through church, school and playing at each other's homes. These were truly wonderful years for Billy and his friends as their world was very friendly and very safe.

9. A New School

During 1928, it was announced that the school district planned to tear down the Marion Avenue School and build a new Bardwell Elementary School on the corner of Lincoln Avenue and Marion Avenue. This new school building was to be a huge building with all the modern construction features available, and large enough to combine the students of Marion Avenue School and Bardwell School. The new Bardwell Elementary would be one of the nicest schools in America and something that Aurora could be proud of for decades to come. As construction began and progressed, Billy would ride his bike over to the site with a few of the gang or the girls. The framework was so large that it was hard to imagine being in a school that big. In fact, the new school building dwarfed Copley Hospital, which was right across the street. Hundreds of workmen crowded the site with trucks, loaders, scaffolding and piles of construction material. The talk all over town was that the students who would be attending the new Bardwell School would indeed be fortunate. Jessie would occasionally take a drive past the new building to keep up on things first hand. As President of the Bardwell PTA, she would get regular updates from the school, but it was fascinating to see the beautiful building going up. This new building would feature a large auditorium as well as gymnasium, so the boys were eager to shoot some baskets when it was ready. The huge two-story, orange brick school featured a steep gabled roof with dark red tile shingles. Some of the attic space created by this steep roof would be utilized as a third-floor play area where the 700 students could play at recess or lunch break when the weather was foul outside.

The day finally came in 1929 for the students from the old Bardwell and Marion Avenue Schools to move into the new Bardwell School. The school had been opened for tours about two weeks before and word had traveled quickly about the amazing, if not unbelievable, new school building. Billy began the fourth grade in this brand-new building with his sister Marian, George, Bobby Nix, Bobby Stoner, Bud Dix, Rodney, Jack and hundreds of other students. The newspaper reporters and photographers were a regular sight for the first week or so as the building received statewide and national attention for being the ultimate elementary school building. The huge gymnasium was everything that Billy had hoped it would be and more. He was able to enjoy the games during gym time at school and "open gym" was held almost every Saturday morning for the Bardwell students. This open gym time, combined with regular visits to the gym at the YMCA, gave Billy and his friend's ample time to develop their basketball skills. The boys began to learn offensive and defensive strategy and they began to have thoughts of becoming real players one day. For the next several years, Fourth Street Methodist, Bardwell Elementary and playing sports together became central to these boys lives.

Billy had regular help with his studies at home from Al, Jean, Marian and Jessie. His favorite tutor was Al. Al was a senior at East High, and he seemed to know just about everything from Billy's view. The Bennetts attended the home football and basketball games at East High and the excitement was, at times, epic. At the same time that Bardwell School had been putting on the finishing touches, Billy and his friends had also been keeping an eye on the raising of giant light poles around the East High football field. East Aurora High School became one of the first high schools in America to install lights on their football field. The use of the lights resulted in the ability to schedule games on Friday nights instead of Saturdays, and the increased attendance eventually paid for the cost of the lights. The school's Athletic Director, Roy E. Davis and his wife Mary, purchased the land for the field and donated it to the school district. Davis personally supervised the construction of the stadium. The beautiful field, complete with metal stands, a cinder track and scoreboard, was named the East Aurora Athletic Field. On Friday night, September 21st, 1929, the Bennetts attended one of the very first night football games in Illinois. East High pounded Downers Grove 43-0. Attending these games on Friday nights with the lights, the band and thousands of cheering fans became a highlight of Billy's young years in Aurora, and filled him with hopes of one day playing on that field. The East Aurora team was led by a fiery young head coach named Glen Thompson. Coach Thompson had moved to Aurora from Michigan and his strict discipline and personal leadership style had overhauled East Aurora's football culture and the team had become a formidable powerhouse.

On October 29th of 1929, the American Stock Market crashed sending the country into economic uncertainty. Billy heard explanations from Jessie, his teachers and quite a bit from Steve and Sam Stoner when the families got together for one of their regular dinners. There was a chance that these economic problems would begin to be felt by stores like Bennett's Men's Store, but for the time being, things seemed to go along fairly normally. The Bennett and Stoner families had become very close over the past two years and it started at the top. Steve Bennett and Sam Stoner had so much in common that they could literally talk all night if the wives didn't remind them of how late it was. Sam had taken a sales job with Goss Motors, located on LaSalle Street, in a block referred to as "Automobile Row" due to the large amount of car and truck dealers there. Goss Motors was the area's Packard dealer and Sam became a true believer in the Packard automobile. The Stoner's drove one to prove it. Goss Motors was only two and half blocks from Steve's shop on Main Street and the pair could arrange for lunch on a regular basis. Sam had his suits made by Steve and recommended the shop to his contacts whenever possible. Steve had a steady stream of customers at his shop that were interested in automobiles, so Sam received many referrals in return. They both knew they were sending folks to the right guy. Sam joined Steve as a member of the Aurora Kiwanis Club that met every Wednesday night at 7 p.m. at the Aurora Hotel on Stolp Island. The club's core beliefs were based on following "the golden rule" and contributing in a meaningful way to society.

Jessie and Margaret had become close over the past two years as their mothering tasks of five children each left them with so much in common. They both kept impeccable homes, in spite of the heavy traffic, loved to entertain and were very active at church. Margaret did not have a driver's license and Jessie did almost all of the driving for the Bennett family. Jessie was always willing to help out in any way she could and frequently picked up Margaret for shopping while the kids were at school. The two made a habit of attending school functions together and they shared the latest news regarding each one of the kids regularly. The dinner parties became a regular event and went back and forth between the two homes. Sam, Margaret, Jessie and Steve formed a habit of playing bridge after dinner with either the "boys against the girls" or the "Stoners vs. the Bennetts." When time would allow, they would opt for an occasional game of the more complicated cribbage, which was Sam's favorite. Margaret's flair for the social graces caused Jessie to grow in this direction, and Jessie's focus on trusting the Lord in her daily life was a good influence on Margaret.

While the friendships and bridge competition grew among the adults, the Stoner-Bennett relations flourished at other levels as well. Eleanor Stoner and Jean Bennett had become close friends during the junior-high years and the two were frequently together with other girls at either house. Marian was included in the activities at home, but being two years younger, she was not a regular part of what the older girls were doing with school. Billy's friend Bobby Nix's older sister, Margaret, was one of Eleanor and Jean's close friends, which always gave Billy, Bobby Stoner and Bobby Nix plenty to talk about. Eleanor's outgoing personality and sense of humor made her a natural leader within the group of girlfriends and Billy liked how Eleanor always joked with him. The girls were a lot of fun at this age for Margaret and Jessie, as school, clothes, music and boys became frequent topics of their conversations. Jessie and Margaret led the girls on frequent shopping sprees into downtown Aurora and occasionally made trips to Chicago.

Dexter and Harley became standouts at school both socially and academically, and Al Bennett enjoyed talking with them on an intellectual level. Although Al was a little older, Dexter and Harley had very similar interests. Al was a very committed Christian, volunteered for activities at church and was a good example to the younger Stoner's. The Stoner boys had been developing a serious game of golf at the Aurora Country Club, funded primarily with money they made from various jobs they landed. They were good looking, industrious and hard-working, which made the girls in Eleanor's circle take notice. Dexter became a leading member of the high school Forensic Debate Team and a member of the High Honor Roll. "Dex," as he was called, was a member of the Drama Club, Delphi and a top reporter for the school newspaper, *The Auroran*. Harley was 19 months younger than Dex, but only a year behind in school. Harley was not only a great student, but a star athlete as well. His 6 ft., 165 lb. frame was recognized on both the basketball court and the gridiron at East High, and he was the top golfer on the golf team. Harley was in the Aurora *Beacon News* regularly for his sports achievements. The middle name of "Hamilton" won Harley the nickname of "Ham" from some of the Stoners. Both Dexter and Harley were inspirational to their younger brother Bobby and his friend Billy. The fact that Steve's shop catered to "the sharp dressed young man" made visits from the Stoner's a regular occurrence. Of course, the Bennett men were known to also dress well.

Bobby Stoner and Billy had become very close friends as Bobby had been accepted into the old Maple Avenue and Bardwell play groups without a hitch. Between school, church and family functions, the two boys were together in some capacity almost daily. Like his sister Eleanor, Bobby was smart, funny and well spoken. When the gang got together for games, Bobby became a leader because he always seemed to have good ideas. What Bobby lacked in size, he more than made up for with brains and speed. In basketball, for example, Bobby understood the game and he helped the others learn how to play it. He could bring the ball down and set up plays. He knew how to shoot and could give some tips to help the others sink more shots. In football, he was fast and could come up with a good play when they needed one. Another area where Bobby was a good influence was his school work. Bobby liked school and liked to read. Since he was a year ahead of Billy in school, he was very knowledgeable whenever Billy needed help. Even though George Troll remained Billy's best old pal, Bobby Stoner had become a great friend.

Christmas time around the Bennett house was a festive occasion to say the least. The whole family worked on decorations and the house seemed to have been built for Christmas. The front porch was a grand location for lights and greens and the inside staircase was decorated with a garland and bows. Jessie's kitchen produced such smells that the other Bennetts couldn't keep from checking in to see when eating some of it would be possible. Steve would always have the latest on where to get a good deal on a tree and Billy looked forward to going with him to pick it out. Jessie and Steve loved to get the decorations up and planned to have an annual Christmas open house so that the house could be filled with guests. Sam and Margaret Stoner formed their own open house tradition by having theirs on Christmas Day from noon to 4 p.m. Billy loved working with Jessie on his ideas for gifts for Jean, Marian, Al and Bob. He also liked to work with the siblings on ideas for Jessie and Steve. Of all holidays, the celebration of our Creator coming to Earth in the form of a vulnerable infant became Billy's favorite.

Christmas morning bore life-long memories for the entire family, and the Christmas of 1930 was especially memorable for Billy. A rather large, heavy present was found under the tree this year with Billy's name on it. All of the Bennetts paused and watched Billy as he tore back the wrapping. "Lionel Electric Trains" was emblazoned across the top of the box and Billy's heart raced. Inside the box were three stacks of train track, a power supply and six brown rectangular boxes. As he eagerly removed the contents of the box, Steve, Jessie and Al were giving him some background on how they decided exactly which Lionel set would be the best one. They had planned this present for many months after deciding it would be the perfect gift. As soon as everyone had finished with opening presents, Billy and Al went to work setting up the track and the power supply in the family room. Billy removed the engine and the passenger cars from the brown boxes and they had a fresh smell of paint and metal. Once the track was connected, they set the "Mojave" colored cars in line and connected them on the track. The engine had a small hole in the top where you could drop mineral oil that would puff smoke out as the train rolled along. Al told Billy to give it a try and he moved the red lever to the "forward" position and the train rolled forward. The yelling of excitement from the Bennett men was cause for the girls to come to see the train's maiden voyage.

The Bennett family had a happy addition in June of 1932 when Billy's oldest brother Bob married Elizabeth "Bess" Parnham. Steve and Jessie invited the couple to live at the Bennett home so they could save money to buy a house of their own. Bob and Bess were married with a small private ceremony, but Steve and Jessie threw a classic "Bennett Open House" for them and the house was packed with well-wishers. Although Billy had never felt particularly close to Bob, he relished the part about "gaining a sister" with his new sister-in-law, Bess. She was very kind to Billy, who was impressed by her intelligence with math and calculations. Bess worked as a statistician for an insurance company in nearby Winfield, so there were times that she came in plenty handy with math homework questions. 454 Simms Street was a busy place.

10. Close to Home

Billy had developed a treasure of friends and he cared deeply for this group that he referred to as "the gang." Although the number of close friends had grown over the years, Billy and George had remained the closest of friends. Billy had spent so much time at the Troll's and George at the Bennett's that the two boys had grown up like brothers. Billy admired George's mastery of the clarinet and he could see how respected he was within the band society. George was also a walking encyclopedia when it came to school work and he had always been willing to help Billy with some of the hard subjects. Maude Troll and Jessie pitched in with rides to and from school as the junior high was quite a walk compared to Bardwell nearby. The two boys had spent countless nights at each other's homes and it was rare to see one without the other around the neighborhood. They were the kind of friends that all parents would hope their sons would have. Billy always called Maude "Ma Troll" and George referred to Jessie as "Ma Bennett."

As Christmas of 1932 was approaching, the entire community was caught up in all the usual festivities and busy schedules. Billy had become almost as comfortable with the Troll family traditions as he was with those at home. Ernest Troll would sing any Christmas song you wanted in German, so Billy was exposed to the international side of the holidays right there in the neighborhood. The Trolls and the Bennetts shared a special evening together every year as Christmas approached. On Friday, December 23rd, the kids had all been released for Christmas vacation a few days earlier and families were scrambling with last minute gifts and shopping. As the Bennetts were cleaning up after dinner that evening, the telephone rang and Steve answered it, as Jessie was busy in the kitchen. Billy could hear the seriousness in his dad's voice as he took the abbreviated information. Steve hung up the phone and went straight to Jessie. Maude Troll had an apparent heart attack at home and had been taken to Copley Hospital, only two blocks away. Ernest and George had followed the ambulance over to the hospital. Steve and Jessie were now grabbing coats and heading out the kitchen door for the car. Jessie reminded the other Bennetts to pray for Maude as she went out the door.

Billy's thoughts immediately were of George and he imagined how he would feel if it were Jessie being taken away in an ambulance. The sudden shock of being faced with a life or death situation brought the excitement of the approaching holiday to a sudden stop. Billy helped Al and the girls clean up the rest of the dishes and then they all listened to the radio while waiting to hear from mom and dad. Jessie and Steve had been gone for well over an hour when the sound of the car pulling in the back alleyway alerted the Bennett household and the girls ran to the kitchen door. Jessie was in tears as she came up the back stairs and everyone knew that the news was not to be good. Jessie explained that attempts to resuscitate Maude had failed and that she had passed away shortly before they had arrived at the hospital. Billy was in shock as the words hit his ears. It did not seem possible that this kind and gentle woman that he had literally grown up with could be gone. He thought of George's pain and he burst into tears. Jessie hugged Billy to her chest and the two cried together for quite some time. Jessie then told Billy that George was going to need him as a friend now more than ever and it would take quite some time for George to get beyond losing his mother. Billy had a great hole in his heart for Maude and how much more so must George? Jessie phoned Ernest later and offered to have George spend the night with the Bennetts, if he thought it might help. Ernest thought it best for George to be home with his brother Robert tonight, but thought it would be good if George could stay with Billy the next day while Ernest attended to arrangements for Maude's funeral.

The next morning Billy looked out the family room window and across the front porch as he expected George's arrival. Jessie was in the foyer looking through the curtains on the front door window when Mr. Troll pulled up along the curb. As George got out of the car, Billy noticed a look on his face that he had never seen before on his friend. Whenever the two were getting together, there had always been an air of excitement and an expectation of sharing good times as friends. Being in mourning was new to both boys. As Ernest and George came through the front door, Billy could see that both of them were stunned by the sudden loss. Billy threw his arms around George as he told him how sorry he was about his mom. Both of them started to cry. After Ernest left, Jessie immediately went to work by explaining to George that he was part of the Bennett family too. She told George he had so many people that loved him and they were all suffering the loss of Maude together. Things were awkward under the circumstances, but as time went by, Billy and George played games and talked and Billy even made George laugh a few times. But Billy knew things could never be quite the same. Jessie and Billy dropped George off at home later that afternoon and George waved good bye from his front porch. Jessie commented to Billy that she felt sorry for George having to spend such a Christmas Eve.

Attending Maude's funeral was the first such experience of Billy's young life. All of "the gang" attended with their families and the Fourth Street Methodist families were extremely supportive of Ernest, Robert and George. The funeral was held at the church and Reverend Schuerman gave an inspiring eulogy about living one's life for others, sacrificially and unselfishly, just as Jesus Himself had demonstrated for us. He also spoke of how our separation from a loved one is only temporary as we will all face death one day and be rejoined with Christ in Heaven. Billy had accepted the fact that everyone must die, and he had known some older folks from church and the neighborhood who had died, but Maude was close to him and he had not experienced this sort of pain before. He was aware of how fragile George's state of mind was now and he did his best not to say anything that would cause George to get upset. Seeing Bobby Stoner, Bobby Nix, Bud Dix and other friends from school gather around George eased the concern that Billy had because he could see how much support George was going to have. As time moved forward, George was going to have a half dozen mothers looking after him.

Jessie made the most of this tragic time in young Billy's life by emphasizing the importance of prayer in a Christian's life. She made sure that he understood

Billy Bennett (L) with close friend, George Troll in 1932.

(Bennett Family Photo)

that painful things were going to happen in the lives of believers and unbelievers alike; the difference would be in how that pain would be handled by the believer. Billy read his Bible almost every day whether in preparation for Sunday school lessons or conversations with the family. Jessie reminded him of how Jesus Himself suffered greatly during His time on Earth and He warned his followers that they too, would suffer. Billy learned that prayer was not only about his wellbeing, but that he was able to "intercede" and pray for his friends and family. Understanding that he could actually engage in prayer that would help the lives of others around him was exciting. His friend George would be included in his prayers for many years to come. Jessie also made sure that Billy understood that Biblical prayer was not only the way we communicate with God, but also the way He communicates with us; a most overlooked detail in the lives of many Christians. Billy's faith and understanding grew during this time and he began to experience a closeness to the Lord which became the core of his life and affected all his decisions. He became determined to live his life in a way that would honor God and in turn, honor his family.

11. Becoming Bill

The move from the glorious Bardwell School building to the junior high was the most disappointing event in Billy's school experience. The junior high on Root Street had been built in the 1880s as the original East Aurora High School. When the new high school was built at Jackson and Benton, the old building was relinquished to serve as the junior high. The Victorian architecture of dark red brick and the round tower on the corner gave the building the look of a haunted castle. The huge open staircase in the middle of the building and the creaking wooden floors added to the horror. This was not the place you would want to spend the night alone. The classmates were mostly familiar to Billy, with the addition of kids that had come from other schools like Beaupre and Oak Park. The school work was harder, the teachers were not as nice, but the sports were a lot more competitive.

Since many of Billy's buddies played in the school band, they encouraged him to join the band's "color guard" so that he could march and carry a flag. It turned out that being a part of a marching band was more complicated than one might think, but it was also quite enjoyable. Billy wore the uniform proudly and was assigned to carry the East Aurora flag, an assignment that he greatly enjoyed. He was extremely proud to lead the band on the field or in a downtown parade carrying the "colors" of East Aurora next to the "stars and stripes."

No one knows for sure why it happens, but there comes a time in every boy's life when decisions are made to become young men. With Billy and his friends, one such decision swept through the ranks during that first year of junior high school. Billy decided that it was time to be known as Bill, not Billy. He discussed this with his mom first, as accepting this change would probably be hardest for her. The rest of the family was informed of the request and the attempt was made to comply. Bill had his own challenges along these lines as both Bobby Stoner and Bobby Nix made the change to "Bob" about

Billy Bennett with his East Aurora flag in the front driveway of 454 Simms Street in 1933.

(Bennett Family Photo)

the same time. The boys had to make many reminders over the next year or so, and an occasional "Billy" or "Bobby" slipped out of a mother's mouth for many years to come.

Sam and Margaret Stoner bought the house at 827 Lafayette Street, just two blocks from the Bennett place, and Bill and the girls could make plans with Bob and Eleanor with ease. The social connection with the Stoner family continued to flourish. Excitement around the Bennett house hit an all-time high when Bob and Bess announced that they were expecting a baby. Of course, this would not be just any baby, but the first Bennett grandchild. Jessie, Jean, Marian and of course, Bess, were consumed with the arrival of this baby so it was a steady topic of conversation around the house. Bill was excited about it too since he was the only one in the family that had not experienced bringing a new baby into the family. Space in the Bennett house was holding up quite well as Jean and Marian shared a room as did Bill and Al. The room arrangement worked well for Bill as he and Al frequently talked at night regarding just about everything, including the family, friends, church, school, and things in the newspaper or on the radio. Al had developed a relationship with God, similar to Jessie's, and he helped Bill out with some of his questions. Al was a full time working man now and taught Sunday school classes at church, so his positive influence on young Bill remained important. Al read the Bible regularly and liked to quiz Bill on what he knew about specific passages. Bill would discuss his thoughts about his friends and his sports and Al was always a good listener. Al knew all of Bill's friends very well since most of them had been around the house for years. As the Great Depression began to eat at the profitability of S. R Bennett's Men's Furnishings, Al's income began to make up the difference, and without complaint from Al. Al's own friendships with the Stoners had steadily developed over the past five years, just as Bill's had with Bob Stoner. Dexter and Harley had both graduated from East High, but with depression-era finances being tight, they both had to put off college to find jobs for the time being.

On November 15th, 1933, Bess gave birth to Robert William Bennett and the whole family welcomed little Bobby home to 454 Simms Street. Bill was elated that he shared at least the middle name with little Bobby and all of the Bennetts struggled with the idea of keeping things quiet around the house while the baby and Bess caught up on sleep. With the usual busy atmosphere of the Bennett place, this was like trying to keep a bus station quiet. Bill was no longer the youngest Bennett, and he was eager to fill the role of being "Uncle Bill" to Bobby. Learning to hold a new born and all that went with it was quite an adventure for a 14-year-old.

12. Champs!

The love of basketball grew into a passion during these years as Bill became a member of the junior high team and the Junior League team at Fourth Street Methodist. The junior high team played from Thanksgiving through to the first of February and the Junior League played through February and March. During the off season, the regular gang played pick-up games whenever possible and often met at the YMCA during open gym times. Bill learned to play the position of forward with George while Bob Nix and Bob Stoner played guard. Bud Schultz, Stan Andrews and Bill Cousland were added to the basketball regulars during these years and this group formed several teams in one configuration or another. Bud was very tall for his age and he became a great center for these teams. Stoner and Nix were good ball handlers who could set up the plays, and Bill and George worked on their jump shots from the outside. The 1933 Junior League team had made quite a run of the season but had come up short on the championship. As Bob Stoner was moving on to high school, this would be the last time Bill and he would play on the same team.

The 1934 Fourth Street Methodist team had a new coach in a college aged fellow named Wayne Mortimer. Wayne and his brother Wilbur were both great athletes, and he had played a lot of basketball in recent years. His manner of coaching the boys was well accepted and he told them they had what it would take to win. Coach Mortimer wanted the boys to put an emphasis on their conditioning and insisted that they run wind sprints at practice until they were ready to quit. He told them that in order to win, they had to outlast their opponents and that games were decided in the final minutes and seconds. This would be their last year in the Junior League and Bill, George and Bob Nix would probably never all be on the same team again. The Junior League played most of their games at the junior high gym with a few at East High or West High. The first game of the year was a disappointing loss to First Evangelical, who always seemed to be the toughest team in the league. The boys tried to come from behind but ended up losing by two points. The next eight games all went to Fourth Street as they posted an 8-1 record before meeting First Evangelical for the second time. This second game was a hard-fought battle that found Fourth Street pulling ahead and holding onto a 12-11 win. The Fourth Street boys were headed into the year-end tournament with a 9-1 record.

Fourth Street won the first two games of the tournament handily, which put them into the League Championship game against none other than First Evangelical. The game would be played at the East High gym on March 24th, 1934. What a season this had already been, with First Evangelical taking the first game by two points, then Fourth Street taking the season closer from First Evangelical by one point. Now for the final showdown, Coach Mortimer told the boys they had already played a great season and they should be proud. They needed just one great effort here today to win the championship and seal up a memorable season. Bill really wanted to win, but he also wanted to win for George and his other teammates. He looked around the locker room at George, Bob Nix, Bud Schultz, Stan Andrews, Emory Dillon and Bill Cousland. With only seven on the team, they all needed to contribute. As the boys took the court for warm ups, they were already surprised by the number of people in the stands and more were still arriving. It was not a big crowd for the size of the gym, but far more people than usually attended a Junior League game. Jessie and the family were there sitting with Al, Dexter and Harley. Knowing the older guys were watching would definitely make Bill a little nervous. Bob Nix's sister, Margaret, was there with Marian and Eleanor Stoner and several other gals from church. Bob Stoner was there as well, cheering his teammates from last year on to the title. There were quite a few East High students there that must have had nothing else to do on a Saturday afternoon.

At the bench, Coach Mortimer said a prayer for the boys and their safety. Then they all put their hands into the middle and yelled, "Fourth Street!" before taking the court. Coach kept a damp towel on the floor along the bench area and Bill wiped his shoes to make sure they would get a good grip on the gym floor. The teams took their positions with nearly-six-foot-tall Bud Schultz at the center position. Bud won the jump and the ball went to George and then over to Bob Nix to set up the play. Bill ran down the court to take his position and moved back and forth to get open. Bill Cousland fired a pass to Bill and he sized up the shot, then noticed George open across the court and threw a sharp pass to George who threw up a shot that hit backboard, rim, then air, as an Evangelical player scooped up the rebound. Evangelical came down the court with precision and one of their forwards put up a jump shot that caught only net. This would be a long game.

By halftime, Evangelical led Fourth Street 13-8 and Coach Mortimer tried to fire up the boys to put more pressure on defense. The third quarter was worse than the first two and at the end of three, Evangelical led 20-13 and it seemed impossible. Coach Mortimer reminded the team that they had been running more than anyone in the league, and it was time to show everyone what they had left in the tank. This was it, no games tomorrow or next week, or even next year for most of them. He told them that Evangelical looked used up, tired and probably thought they could coast through the next 12 minutes. His advice was to get out there and surprise them, and surprise the whole gym while they were at it. Bill took his position and Bud tipped the ball into his hands. Driving down the court, he hit Bill Cousland, who, in turn, hit Emory Dillon, who put up a shot that glanced off the rim and into the hands of Evangelical. As Evangelical brought the ball down, Bill pressed hard on his man and as the opponent tried to pass, the ball caught Bill's outstretched fingers and bounced for open court. Bill gained on the ball and took control as George sped past him. Bill lofted the ball with a two-hand pass out in front of George, who brought it in, then laid the ball up about eight feet in front of the nearest defender. The crowd on the Fourth Street side of the gym went nuts with excitement at the sign of life from their team. Now they were only down by five and they just needed to keep up the pressure. As the Evangelical players brought the ball down again, Bill could see, or maybe just imagine, that they were finished and didn't have the will to finish the game. This time, the Evangelical shot deflected off the rim and Bud went up and took the rebound. He fired the ball over to Bob Nix who brought the ball down court with skill and set up the play. He found George open again and George put up a back board shot that brought the score within three points.

With less than two minutes now left, Bud drew a shooting foul and went to the line for two free throws. Almost miraculously, Bud hit both free throws and the game was now 20-19. A time-out was called by the Evangelical coach and Bill and the guys gathered around Coach Mortimer one last time. "Keep up the pressure, go after the loose balls and hit the open man with a good pass. One basket is all we need, but keep up the pressure!" Evangelical brought down the ball and both sides of the gym were screaming for their team. The Bennett section was standing and jumping up and down as Bill pressed on defense. The ball moved inside toward the basket, then back outside where Bob Nix got his hands on the ball and stripped it cleanly. Bill saw the steal coming and was already in full stride for the Fourth Street bucket when Bob lobbed a pass directly in front of him. Bill took the ball at full speed and drove directly for a right hand lay-in that went nicely up into the orange square and back through the net. For the first time in the game, Fourth Street now held the lead 21-20 with only 40 seconds left on the clock. The Bennett section screamed and yelled and Jessie was a nervous wreck. Bill noticed Al and the guys yelling with their fists pumped into the air and he was excited by their support.

Once again, Evangelical inbounded the ball and came down the court. All they needed was to run the clock down and hit a shot and it would be yet another one-point affair between the two teams. They drove with desperation and the Fourth Street boys held the pressure on defense. With 20 seconds left on the clock, the First Evangelical forward with the best shot on the team let go a jump shot over the hands of George Troll. No breath was drawn in that gym until the ball clanged off the rim and into the hands of Bud Schultz. Bud passed to Bob Nix who brought the ball down the court quickly. Bill moved to the left and then faked right and his man just fell away and Bill was open. The sharp-eyed Bob Nix saw Bill in the clear and fired a baseball-pass right at his head. Bill caught the pass, then turned to the basket and let go a 15-foot jump shot that found nothing but the net. Only one side of the gym was screaming now. Evangelical inbounded the ball and made one last attempt to sink something at the buzzer, without success. As the buzzer sounded, the Fourth Street team all found each other in a huge team hug as Coach Mortimer ran out to congratulate them. George and Bill hugged and jumped up and down and hooted and hollered. The season was over. They had finally won the Junior League Championship!

Bill made his way over to Al and the guys along the court and the Stoner boys patted Bill so hard that they almost knocked him over. Bob Stoner congratulated his old team and Bill said he was sorry they couldn't have done it last year. Bob was already playing lightweight ball at East High as a freshman, so the Junior League was not heavy on his mind anymore. Next season, Bill would be up there too, but this was the finest farewell to the Junior League that Bill could imagine. Then Bill found Jessie and the girls and they were so happy for him that they hugged and kissed him on the cheek. Margaret Nix, Eleanor Stoner and Marian Bennett all told Bill that he was a great player and then Eleanor told him not to get conceited over it, in a joking manner.

Word of the close, hard-fought game traveled fast around town and everywhere Bill and his teammates went, people congratulated them on their win. This was special for Bill because he had played and practiced with these guys for many years. It was especially good, even perfect, for him to be able to win the championship with George, since they had been friends since George was born. Bill could not help but think of how proud Maude would have been to see them win that game. This would be the last basketball game that Bill and George would ever play together as George decided to focus on academics and music in the coming years. In just five short months, Bill would have to report for football training at East Aurora High School. This was something he had been looking forward to for years.

13. A Tale of Red and Black

Bill's favorite sport was definitely football. He had dreamed of being old enough to play for East High for as long as he could remember. Moving on to East High had been a focus of Bill's for many years and the excitement was huge as he graduated from 8th grade and said goodbye to the musty old junior high school. Summer zoomed by as he took on quite a few odd jobs and mowed several neighbor's lawns. Over the past two years, Bill had grown substantially; now standing 5' 8" and weighing about 150 pounds. High school athletic rules divided teams by weight for football and basketball. Anyone 135 pounds and under would be assigned to the "lightweight" team and those over 135 assigned to the "heavyweight" team. The heavyweight teams held the spotlight that would be associated with the "varsity" squads of later years. Bill signed up for football and reported on equipment day at the end of August, a week before school would begin. The players all weighed in and were divided into the two teams. Bill was assigned to the heavyweight squad while Bob Stoner was assigned to the lightweight squad. This was a huge disappointment for both of them, but with Bob only weighing about 125 pounds, there was no other option. This meant that all of their practices and games would be separate, almost like attending different schools. Bob longed to follow in his brother Harley's footsteps, but all he could hope for was a growth spurt between now and next year.

Bill assembled in the gym with the heavyweights as Athletic Director Roy Davis welcomed them to East Aurora Football. Assistant Coach Coleman "Gundie" Gunderson was introduced and he mentioned the tough schedule the team had ahead of them, and the great amount of work that lay ahead. Then, Head Coach Glen "Tommy" Thompson took over and emphasized the work ethic he was expecting from each and every player. They would have three weeks to put a top-notch team together and it would be tough. Coach Thompson told the team to be prepared for hard work, and if they didn't feel up to it, there may still be some cheer-leading spots open. The team roared with laughter with some of the coach's jokes and he had a way of using humor to cut through some of the tension. Coach Thompson had come to East High in 1925, after the football team had been through some lean years. Within two years, he turned the East team into a powerhouse that other teams feared. Eventually, the school newspaper reported that Coach Thompson's team controlled the field like "Big Cats." Because of this article, the team was then referred to as "Tommy's Cats," which was adopted about 1930 as the "Tomcats." Bill was officially welcomed to Tomcat football. After the talks, the team lined up for locker assignments and equipment. Bill was issued pads, helmet and a practice uniform. He couldn't wait to get on the field.

On the first day of practice, it was immediately apparent there would be a common theme to playing football at East High, that being physical conditioning. The team lined up to run wind sprints with Coach Thompson blowing his whistle to signify the start for each line. After the wind sprints, there were push-ups, sit-ups, jumping jacks and a drill where players had to run in place and then hit the dirt with their stomachs when the whistle sounded. After the "warm welcome," several drills were set up on the practice field to assess each player's skills. There was a tackling drill where one player tried to run the ball through markers and another player had to tackle him. Bill lined up as the potential tackler and the whistle blew. The ball runner came toward Bill and tried to juke him to the left but Bill was not fooled. He drove his shoulder right into the runner's waist, lifting him somewhat and driving him backward into the ground. The on-looking players gasped at the sound of the impact and the runner did not get up for about five seconds. He had just learned what George, Bobby and the gang knew about playing football with Bill: either be on his team or get ready to feel pain. The coaches noticed that Bill Bennett was hard to elude and that he seemed to enjoy hitting hard. They quickly decided he would be groomed as a defensive player, whether line or backfield.

On September 14th, 1934, the Saint Charles team came to East Aurora Field for the season opener. It was hard to focus on anything but the game during school that day. The lightweight team would face off at 5:30 p.m. with the heavyweight game scheduled for 7:30 p.m. The team was to be in the locker room no later than 5:30 p.m. to dress and be ready to go by 6:30 p.m. The locker room was strangely quiet as Bill put on his pads and uniform. The coaches did not like a lot of noise in the locker room before games and wanted the players to think about what they needed to do in the game ahead. Bill pulled his number 28 jersey over his shoulder pads and one of his buddies helped pull it down from behind. Pulling the belt through the loops and pulling it tight finished off the job and Bill pulled on his cleats. The metal studs that rounded out on the bottom of the cleats not only made a sound like Fred Astaire on the concrete floor, but they also made the shoes extremely slippery until you stepped onto turf. Once the team was collectively ready to go, Coach Thompson gathered them together. He told them that each of them had been training for a specific job. If everyone did their job the way they had practiced, the team would win the game. He wanted each player to focus on doing his job. Bill envisioned stopping the opposing running back and putting pressure on the backfield if they tried to pass.

The Coach led the team outside to the grassy area at the back of the school where the band, cheerleaders, students and other fans cheered at their appearance. The band played "Wave the Flag of East Aurora" as the cheerleaders screamed, "Go, Aurora, Go, Aurora!" and the fans clapped and cheered for the team. Coach Thompson and Coach Gunderson then led the whole procession of about 300 people south on Jackson Street toward the field about a mile away. As the team walked on the paved street, their steel cleats hitting the pavement created quite a clatter. Cars pulled over to let the huge entourage by and many honked their horns in encouragement to the team. The cheerleaders followed the team with Jimmy Clausen and Ray Orland calling out the chants, followed by the band. This traditional march was conducted prior to each home game and it was quite a sight to behold.

Bill was filled with exuberance when he ran out onto the field to warm up before the game. It was probably the same kind of feeling that one gets when arriving at a vacation spot that you have dreamed about for a lifetime. The Saint Charles Saints warmed up on the north end of the field while the Tomcats warmed up on the south end. The turf was a perfect emerald green as the groundskeepers had been fertilizing and watering it all summer. Finally, the long-awaited kick-off, and the game was underway. The Tomcat offense moved the ball steadily and the defense held Saint Charles back. By the third quarter, East led 13-0 and Coach Thompson told Bill to get ready to go in on defense. Bill tightened the chin strap on his helmet and waited for the Saints to return a punt. The defensive squad waited near Thompson and then it was time to go! The punt team ran toward the bench as the defense ran onto the field. The PA announcer boomed the information that "Number 28, Bill Bennett is now in the game at defensive tackle for the Tomcats." Bill tried to focus on his job, just as Coach Thompson had preached over and over, but it was very difficult as he had never been this nervous before. The ball was snapped and he lunged forward into the wet jersey of the Saints offensive tackle. The running back tried running an end-around to the right side, but the Tomcats pulled him down with a gain of two yards. The next play the Saints tried to run to the left side and the Tomcats ran the running back out of bounds with a gain of three yards. The Saints, faced with a third down and five yards, decided to run straight at the new kid. Bill found himself being forced to the left by the smelly tackle as he saw the running back coming right through the hole. Bill twisted and shoved and got his arms around the running back's waist, then slid down to lock his arms around his calves as other Tomcat defenders swarmed and took him over sideways. Another gain of two yards and the Saints would have to punt. As some other players helped Bill up and smacked him on the back, Bill heard, "Number 28, Bill Bennett on the tackle for East Aurora." The feeling of being out on the field under the lights instead of in the stands was surreal for Bill. He knew that his family members were up in the stands and he felt so proud to be a Tomcat. The Bennett clan was just as exuberant.

Overall, the team ended up 5-5 during Bill's freshman year. Bill did not get to play anywhere near as much as he would have liked, but this was common for a freshman. One of the five wins was the season-closing Thanksgiving Day win over West Aurora 7-0. It felt so good to beat West Aurora, and the turkey had never tasted better. As soon as football season was over, Bill began to practice with the heavyweight basketball team and was surprised to not only make the team, but to become a regular player in his first year. Bob Stoner was on the lightweight team, but they were able to interact more than they did in football and even scrimmaged against each other a few times. Bill thought it was a shame that Bob could not play with the larger guys because his ball handling, speed and knowledge of the game would have made a difference. Basketball coach Stunkel was a southern gentleman with a great sense of humor and Bill really liked him. Everyone knew that the team was up against a tough year and Coach Stunkel wanted steady improvement to be emphasized. Bill played forward again, a position that he was used to, and he played much more than he thought he would as a freshman. Coach Stunkel told Bill that he saw a lot of potential in him and thought he could be a standout player his junior and senior year. The team ended up with a 7-11 record which included a 27-20 loss to West Aurora at their gym.

Socially, East High was wonderful. Bill knew so many other students from various connections over the years that there seemed to be a familiar face everywhere he looked. His brothers and sisters had left a favorable legacy with the teachers and staff at the school. Marian was very well liked and had graduated only months before with Eleanor Stoner and Margaret Nix. The teachers were very strict, but very professional and the entire school seemed to be a class act. Bill became a student council representative his freshman year and enjoyed planning activities and meeting a lot of new faces. It was a great introduction to parliamentary procedure and he enjoyed the fact that everything was conducted in an orderly fashion.

On March 28th, 1935, Bill's oldest sister Jean married Lincoln Charles Schell at Fourth Street Methodist Church. "Linc" was the son of Charles and Pearl Schell and he was raised on their farm on Jericho Road on the far western side of Aurora. Linc and Jean moved in at the Schell farm and had plans to continue farming for a living. Linc was no stranger to hard work and the Bennett family thought highly of him. Just as when Bess married Bob, the family felt they were blessed to have a new member. Bill was very interested in everything at the farm and he went out to help Linc whenever he could. Linc appreciated Bill's eagerness to work and took extra time to show him the right way to do things. Linc was also an accomplished horseman and learning to ride intrigued young Bill. Linc had worked at the cattle pens west of Aurora where the stock was brought to rest for three or four days before being delivered to Chicago. Linc showed Bill how to handle a horse and how to ride like a man without holding onto the saddle. It was all in the legs and the positioning of the rider. Within a short time, Bill had things figured out and he could handle any of the horses at the farm.

Little Bobby had become a very excited two-year-old and Bill loved playing with him and babysitting whenever he could. Things had not been going well for Bob and Bess' relationship and Bill hoped they would be able to work it out. Bob and Bill were so different when it came to personality that it was hard for them to really understand each other. Bob wasn't very social and seemed to resent that Bill was always the center of attention with the family. Bill kept himself very busy being a "people person" and wanted everyone to be happy. He would learn that everyone could not, or would not, be happy.

The first year of high school came and went in a blur as Bill found himself preparing for another summer of odd jobs and getting in shape for another football season. He and Bob Stoner went to the YMCA to lift weights and play basketball. Bob was already thinking that he might be able to go to college and had a few ideas. He encouraged Bill to think about college, but Bill knew that he would be happy to get through high school and find a decent job in one of Aurora's many manufacturing plants. Bob had always been fond of the Navy, as Bill recalled the sailor hat that he used to play in when they first met. Whatever the future held, there were options for a sharp guy like Bob.

Bob had just passed another of life's milestones; that of gaining his driver's license. On a typical Friday that summer, Bob asked Bill and George to go downtown to check out some shops and get something to eat. Bob first stopped by the Nix's house to gather Bob Nix and then he came around to the Bennett's place driving Sam Stoner's sharp blue 1933 Packard. The three of them drove over to George's house on the way downtown, and George was waiting on the porch. George jumped into the back with Bill and the foursome headed toward town on Fourth Street. Bob hung a left at Clark Street, crossed Lincoln Avenue, then right onto LaSalle Street. Crossing over Benton Street, he pulled the huge Packard into a spot just a few doors down from Goss Motors. Bob wanted to stop in and see Sam at work and the other three jumped at the chance to see what Sam Stoner was up to at the dealership. Sam was on the phone at his desk on the side of the showroom and he smiled when he saw his son Bob and the entourage come through the front door. Sam motioned with a single finger that it would be just a minute and he would be with them. Bill and George eyed the '35 Coupe 120 Convertible with huge running boards and a spare tire cover painted the same dark red as the rest of the car. They would be the talk of the town if they could be seen tooling around in such a machine. Sam yelled over to the pair and asked Bill if he wanted to drive it home tonight. Bill laughed at the thought of having a car that was worth more than all the money he had ever seen, combined! The dealership always had the best smell and the thought of someday owning their own cars was exciting for the boys. Sam told the boys to be careful as he said goodbye and they headed back to the blue Packard parked on the street.

Bob waited at Main Street for traffic to clear, then turned right and found another parking spot on the hill just above Bennett's Men's Wear. This would be a good spot as they could walk anywhere downtown from here. They piled out of the Packard and made for Steve's shop door. Bill pushed open the door to the chime of the two little bells attached to the top of the door. Steve was just straightening up a stack of shirts when the bells caught his attention and he saw the smiling young men invading the shop. Bill told Steve that he had brought him some business and Steve smiled and said that he could use it. The guys all laughed. All four of them were actually looking for some things, so they took some time with the shirts, ties and suspenders. All of Bills friends were welcome to a substantial discount at Bennett's and Steve always hated seeing them buy from anyone else. But a shop the size of Bennett's couldn't have everything, and it was inevitable that the guys would have to go to other shops from time to time. Bob Stoner picked out a shirt and some suspenders and he asked Steve if he could hold the box for him and then he would stop by again after they looked around and found something to eat. The bells rang on the door as they headed out to the right and around the corner onto Broadway. Bob told Bill that he wanted to look at some of the jackets at Schmitz & Gretencort Men's Shop a half block down. Bill said that his dad would hate to hear that Bill had been seen in the competitor's store and they all had a good laugh again.

As the guys made their way down Broadway, they ran into a few other groups from East High and stopped to see how some of the other guys were doing. They also stopped to chat with a group of girls they spotted coming out of Sencenbaugh's Department Store across the street. George was complaining that it was time to find some food, and that his 6' 2" beanpole of a body needed some sustenance. They decided the counter at the Carl's Lunch Room next to Bennett's Men's Shop would probably offer the most food for the little money they had on them. Carl's pretty good burgers, plus a Coke and a slice of pie would really make a good dinner. The four of them talked about jobs they were interested in and their future plans. Everyone was consumed with high school at the moment, but they knew it wouldn't be long until it would be time for college or a full-time job. The chatter was interrupted as the waitress started sliding plates in front of them. The guys handed plates back and forth until they all had what they ordered. Bill was blessed with some very good buddies, and on days like these, life was good.

As the start of school approached again, Bill attended his second "equipment day" for football and this time he knew what to expect. Coach Thompson and Coach Gunderson seemed pleased to see Bill again after the summer and Thompson automatically asked Bill what he was weighing. Bill answered 163 pounds and Coach smiled. Once practice began, the coaches could see that Jessie had been feeding Bill quite well. Bill was far more aggressive on defense than he had been the year before and it was plain to see that his experience as a freshman had given him confidence. Although Bill was far from the biggest defensive player, his speed and ability to get to the ball was remarkable. He seemed to have a natural sense as a defender, and the years of Tag, Last Man Over and backyard sports had undoubtedly contributed to his development.

Football consumed Bill's time and he had to make a huge effort to keep schoolwork and social agendas going at the same time. Bill was elected to student council again, and he enjoyed working with Bob Stoner on council issues and planning events. He also joined the Boys Club, which was a social club that stressed good manners; older classmates helping the younger; and planning dances after the home basketball games. Bill and the whole "gang" were members of the East Aurora High School "Hi-Y Chapter." Hi-Y was sponsored by the YMCA, "to create, maintain and extend throughout the school and community, high standards of Christian character." Hi-Y members pledged to live their lives following the four "C's": Clean Speech, Clean Scholarship, Clean Sports and Clean Living. Every other Monday night, Bill, George, Bob Stoner, Bob Nix and Bud Dix, all from Fourth Street Methodist, would attend the Hi-Y meeting at school. They promised to support each other, as well as other students, in their commitment to live their lives consistent with their desire to follow Jesus Christ. Hi-Y also brought members together through city-wide meetings and even regional conferences and activities. Combined with the strong examples Bill received at home, the Sunday school group at Fourth Street and the sermons and friendship of Reverend Schuerman, Bill's faith and commitment to Christ strengthened as he was becoming a man.

On the football field, Bill became friends with Jimmie Smith, an African-American who played tight-end on the offense and could seemingly catch anything they threw at him. Jimmie seemed to always be having fun, wore a huge smile and gave 110% effort in everything he did. Jimmie also shared Bill's commitment to Christ as he attended Main Street Baptist Church, Aurora's largest black church on the east side. Jimmie was a Hi-Y member and also played on the heavyweight basketball team with Bill. The Aurora schools had always been integrated racially, and Bill held respect for Jimmie and other black students based on who they were and what they did. He could not tolerate any nonsense based on a person's skin color. Bill also worked closely with Wayne Warren, Elmer Renner and Bob and Ralph Zilly. Wayne was a smart player and showed great leadership skills on the team. He played quarterback and halfback and had a good passing arm. Elmer Renner played defensive end with Bill and could punt the ball farther than any high school kickers that East faced. Bob Zilly had been a standout player and his little brother Ralph, became an offensive starter as a freshman, with a promising future ahead.

The team looked to be extremely tough this year. Throughout the first four games, the Tomcats outscored their opponents 74-13 while racking up a 4-0 record. The *Beacon News* sports staff described the Tomcats as a powerhouse with possibly the best defense in the conference. Scanning through the newspaper reports of Tomcat games became routine for Jessie. She would lay the paper out on the dining room table, along with the scissors, on the day after games. It seemed as though there was something printed about someone the family knew almost every day. Jessie made sure the clipped articles found their way to mothers or friends who may have missed them.

East Aurora High School's 1935 Heavyweight Football Team. Coach Thompson, top row, far left. Bill Bennett, 2nd row, sixth from right, number 28. (East Aurora High School 1935 Yearbook)

As football season was coming to a close, the Tomcats had a 5-3 record going into the Thanksgiving game against West Aurora. They had narrowly missed winning another Conference Championship, so the big game would only be for yearly bragging rights. The season had been long and hard fought and the thought of getting it over with was welcomed, in a way. Wednesday evening, Jessie served her pot roast for dinner as she always wanted Bill to have a good meal before game days. The family talked about dozens of things as they ate together, and then cleaned everything up to get the kitchen ready for another big food day tomorrow. Bill got ready for bed earlier than usual as he knew he would need the sleep. Saying goodnight, he went up the back stairs from the kitchen, then across the hall into the room he shared with Al. Bill was awake for quite some time thinking about what tomorrow would be like over at the field. He knew that no matter what the team records showed coming into an East-West game, the game would probably be a "knock-down, drag out" brawl. Al came into the room and was trying to be quiet when Bill told him that he was still awake. The two of them talked for half an hour or so before Bill finally fell off to sleep.

The Bennetts at home in 1935. Left to right are Al, Marian ("Pete"), Jessie, and Steve. Bill and Jean are seated.

(Bennett Family Photo)

November 28th, 1935. Bill's alarm jolted awake him from a dream at 7 a.m. and the smell of food was already rising up the stairs from the kitchen. Jessie had been busy with eggs, bacon and pancakes, and the place smelled wonderful. Bill came down the stairs into the kitchen and Jessie plated the kind of breakfast that a defensive tackle should have on game day. He carried the steaming plate into the dining room where Steve sat with the *Chicago Tribune* that he had just brought in from the front porch. The huge headline, "SEIZE RAIL LINES IN CHINA," told the story of the Japanese Imperial Army invading part of China. Steve wondered what these Japanese were up to as the world seemed to be growing increasingly dangerous. At any rate, it didn't seem likely that what the Japanese were doing on the other side of the world could ever have an effect on what was happening right here on Simms Street.

Al dropped Bill off at the back of the school just before 9 a.m. and Bill made his way down into the locker room. The game was scheduled for noon and they needed to be ready for the walk over by 10:30. Coach Thompson gave an unusually rousing talk before they left the locker room. He wanted everyone to focus on doing their job as usual, but he wanted an all-out effort for the seniors, many of whom would be playing the last game of their lives. Once outside, the band, cheerleaders and cheering fans created a circus atmosphere as the Tomcats proudly marched up Jackson Street to Fifth Avenue. The wind was blowing briskly as it chased leaves down the street ahead of the team. The high temperature was supposed to be around 50 degrees, but right now it felt like the sprinkle of rain could turn into snow. Cars were already parked bumper to bumper for blocks around the stadium as nearly 5,000 attended the game. Pre-game warm ups were very welcome as getting warm was on most of the player's minds. The band began "Wave the Flag" and the huge home crowd nearly drowned out the band as they sang and shouted the words. A few minutes later, the teams lined the sidelines with helmets in hand as the band led all in attendance in the singing of the National Anthem. As Bill sang the familiar words, he faced north and watched the flag standing straight out in the brisk wind. The sound of so many singing our wonderful anthem was memorable and inspiring.

East kicked off to West and Bill was right to work trying to stop West's attempts to advance. West was running a new offense this year behind the new head coach "Migs" Apsit. Apsit had been a stand out player at West back in the mid 1920s, then played three years at the University of Southern California, where he played in the Rose Bowl in 1930. He then played three years in the NFL with the Green Bay Packers and the Boston Redskins. Now he was back at West in the head coach's role. Coach Thompson was hoping that the Tomcats would make Apsit's first trip to East Aurora a miserable one. The Tomcats jumped in front with a touchdown in the middle of the first quarter and Bill thought that the offense looked like they were in top form. The Tomcat defense stopped just about everything West tried and the final horn sounded with East beating West 20-0. Welcome back to Aurora, Coach Apsit!

After the game, most of the players were headed home to their Thanksgiving feasts and celebrating their fourth consecutive victory over West Aurora. Knowing that there would not be any football practices for the next nine months was also a cause for celebration. After dinner at the Bennetts, the Stoners were coming over for pumpkin pie and coffee. The house sounded like a bus station with all the conversations, as the families caught up and discussed everything imaginable. Dexter had recently been named "Aurora's Most Eligible Bachelor" in a *Beacon News* contest. There was a photo in the paper of a crowd of his friends carrying "ole Dex" on their shoulders. Of course, this was an item that Jessie would not have missed with her scissors. Dexter had landed a job with Western United Gas and Electric Company and was doing very well. Harley was working for a bond house as a broker's clerk and had been playing in amateur golf tournaments quite competitively. Eleanor was working as a secretary at the Pictorial Paper Packaging Company in Aurora and all the Stoners were encouraging Bob to go to college. With the three older siblings holding down full-time jobs and living at home, they could certainly find a way to make sure Bob could go to college. Bob had been posting outstanding grades and everyone knew that he had potential to do just about anything he wanted to in life.

Bill reported to Coach Stunkel for the start of another year of heavyweight basketball and the team worked extremely hard on conditioning as they knew they may have to overcome a lack of talent, again, this year. Compared to the grueling football season he had just wrapped up, basketball seemed like a piece of cake to Bill. On the court, there weren't any one-inch cleats stepping on your hands or helmets plowing into your ribs. Basketball was pretty neat and clean, all things considered. Nonetheless, it was another long, long winter of riding the bus to distant cities, losing games in front of huge crowds and newspaper clippings about the "struggling" Tomcat basketball team.

June, 1937. At the Bennett house, there was both a cause for celebration and for despair. Ernest Troll remarried a very lovely woman named Edith; everyone was happy for the Trolls, and especially for George. Although it was not possible to ever replace Maude, it would be good for George to have Edith in his life. The despair came when Bob and Bess decided to split up and divorce. This sickened Bill as he thought the world of Bess and did not want to see Bobby lose the presence of both parents. Bess moved her and Bobby in with her sister nearby, and Bob moved to Chicago to distance himself from the situation. The family tried to make it clear to Bob that he needed to be nearer to Bobby, but the decision was made. Bess felt the love of her Bennett family and made sure that Bobby was at Steve and Jessie's as often as possible. With Bess working full time, Jessie was able to watch Bobby on a regular basis. Bill spent a lot of time with little Bobby and taught him everything he knew about anything. He felt as though this was his chance to repay some of what Al had invested in him and he truly wanted to be a stable presence for Bobby. Bill loved Bobby, and Bobby loved him back.

The next two years of Bill's life would follow the patterns now set by athletics, church and social clubs, and it was a fine pattern to follow. Bill became known as a great athlete and a young man of integrity.

"Uncle Bill" with Little Bobby Bennett in front of 454 Simms Street, 1936.

(Bennett Family Photo)

Bill picked up work during the summer scraping and painting trim as well as the usual yard work. Looking ahead to his senior year, he knew this would be the last summer of his life that would allow him any leisure time. George had graduated early, along with Bob Stoner, and they both were headed for college in September. Bob and Bill had discussed the possibility of attending seminary and becoming ministers. Bob decided to attend North Central College to get a "Commerce" degree. There could always be time for seminary later. George was accepted to Illinois State University with a scholarship in academics and band. Playing the b-flat clarinet had really paid off. The gang frequently got together and enjoyed their trips downtown. Bill knew that it would be very different for him next year without some of his old buddies around. Bob would still be living at home as North Central College was in nearby Naperville. George would be two hours away at ISU, so they would not see each other often. As summer came to a close, Bill and Jessie went to the train station with the Trolls to see George off to college and Bill reported to "equipment day" one last time. Bill weighed in at 180 pounds and stood 6-feet tall.

14. The 1937 Tomcats

Bill had learned that all high school coaches preached optimism at the beginning of each season, as they had to encourage the players even if there was no apparent chance for success. However, as the 1937 Tomcats began practice, it appeared to Bill that there was an outstanding team on the field and Coach Thompson told them, in no uncertain terms, he wanted the conference title. Thompson was no foul mouth, but he was known to "let one fly" from time to time. One thing was certain; the players loved and respected him as a coach. Thompson was so exuberant about making his points that several times a year he would show up on the practice field in full gear and actually "bang heads" with the team. He had been a football, basketball and track star at Kalamazoo College and he knew his business. Just as Bill had grown and matured over the last three years, a lot of his fellow players were poised for their best season ever. Harold Urak, at 5' 9" and 166 pounds, was the fastest guy on the team and was hard to stop around the ends. The team nicknamed him "Speed." The Tomcats elected "Tri-Captains" for the first and only time in their history with Wayne Warren, Rich Kalstedt and Merill "Buss" Heagy gaining the honors. Heagy was 6-feet tall and weighed 195 pounds. He was thought by many to be the best player in East's history. Wayne Warren was set to play fullback after being the quarterback the previous year. Bob Ziegler was set to take over the quarterback role. The other captain, Rich Kalstedt, was the smallest guy on the squad at 140 pounds, but he was extremely fast, had a good passing arm and even took the punting job from Elmer Renner. Earl "Rusty" Rottsolk, the 6'3" Center from basketball, was at right end and Willie Vaughn was at left end. Ralph Zilly had grown into a 205-pound monster. Bill was "working in" on the offense, just in case he was needed to cover that role, but he was central to the defensive squad again this year.

The season revealed that the Tomcats were indeed a defensive powerhouse as they outscored their opponents 168-72 throughout the first nine games. Their 7-2 record left them in contention for the Conference Championship with only the 6-2 West Aurora Blackhawks left to play. Like most of the recent East-West games, it was bound to be a nail-biter.

Coach Apsit and Coach Thompson had three long weeks to prepare for the Thanksgiving game. Coach Stunkel approached Bill and wanted him to attend some basketball practices during these three weeks so that Bill could jump right in after football was over. Bill brought up the idea to the family that he may not play basketball this year. His reasoning was that the past three basketball seasons had created nothing but drudgery as practices and games absorbed all of his time. With Jimmie Smith and Don Cooper gone from the team, there was little chance for any big changes this year. In the end, Bill decided not to play basketball his senior year. Coach Stunkel tried to encourage him to play, but he then thanked him for the three years Bill had put in and said he would miss him on the team.

Following the usual routine on Thanksgiving Day, Bill sat in front of his locker knowing that this would be the last time he would wear the Red and Black, and it would probably be the last football game of his life. The seniors were very

Back Row — G. LIMBRUNNER, R. BAUMANN, S. BARTLETT, R. WOLGAST, D. BLAKE, J. PETRAITIS, J. RAAB, R. FOSTER, F. PATTERSON, R. CARLSON, C. KOBELENZ, Q. KYES, W. MUTH, D. HAWKING, A. MUSCHLER, J. HEITKOTTER. *Fourth Row* — A. POLLOCK, R. KRANTZ, H. SWANSON, E. HOLLIS, R. SECORD, H. FELDOTT, G. SPRIGGS, E. PIELET, W. SCHMIDT, W. CONNER, G. SCHOLZ, F. PFEIFFER, H. HEIDELBERG, L. SPEARS. *Third Row* — MR. C. G. GUNDERSON, E. WEINGARTNER, A. BAUM, C. BUMBAR, A. JURGELONIS, G. WASHBURN, S. SPENCE, G. PRESBREY, D. BUHRMANN, R. ROKOP, D. KREITZ, D. ILIFF, L. BARNETT, MR. G. THOMPSON. *Second Row* — E. RENNER, H. URAK, J. PAWLOWSKI, E. ROTTSOLK, B. BENNETT, W. WARREN, R. KALSTEDT, M. HEAGY, D. FAUTH, W. BAILEY, R. ZILLY, W. VAUGHN, F. BIESCHKE, MGR. *Front Row* — W. BJORSETH, MGR., J. HOLLON, R. JONES, R. PAYNE, H. STEIFBOLT, J. DOBBINS, R. ZIEGLER, H. MCKINNEY, R. HOLLE, W. DIRST, R. HILLS, F. HOUGHTBY, W. BOLES.

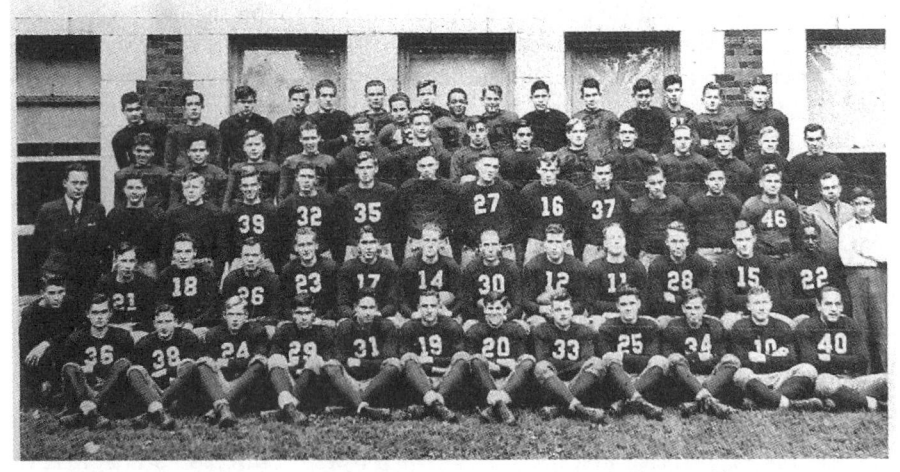

Bill Bennett (17) with the very successful 1937 East Aurora Tomcat Heavyweight Football Team. (East Aurora High School 1938 Yearbook)

quiet as everyone was thinking about the need to win this game. Some of them were thinking about the finality of this last game and leaving behind a way of life. Bill pulled the elastic red knee socks out of his gym bag and rolled them up his calves. Next were the girdle pads and pants, his practice jersey and the shoulder pads. Then he pulled on the white sweat socks before stepping into his cleats. Once the cleats were tied and double tied, he carefully rolled the white sweat socks down to the tops of the cleats, leaving them in a neat three-inch-wide roll. He unfolded his number 17 jersey and pulled it over his head. Rusty Rottsolk pulled Bill's jersey over the pads and Bill returned the favor, silently pulling Rusty's number 23 over his pads for the last time. The sound of the steel cleats clicking on the floor began to grow steadily louder as the team dressed and began to move toward the open area where Coach Thompson would talk to them. Bill sat on the bench in front of his locker and bowed his head. Silently, he thanked the Lord for the years that he was given with this team and these friends. He asked for the safety of all the players in the coming game, on both teams, "Amen." Bill shoved a towel into his helmet, shut his locker and headed toward the team. Coach Thompson told them they were the hardest working team he ever had at East. They were also the most talented over all. He wanted them to remember the tough loss to West from last year and realize that they had the chance to reverse that today. They all knew exactly what they needed to do and they could only play the game one play at a time; one tackle at a time. Coach had the team come in close and put their hands together, the count of three, and, "GO TOMCATS!"

The sun was bright and Bill had to squint hard as he came out of the dark hallway into the parking lot at the back of the school. The air had warmed quite a bit since Jessie had dropped him off earlier. The high temperature would be about 42 today, so that practice jersey under the shoulder pads would come in handy. The band was playing "Wave the Flag" as two hundred people were singing with all their might. Today the Tomcats had the chance to win the title and the crowd was certainly going to be huge. Although Bill had made this walk to the Athletic Field many times before, he was keenly aware that this would be the last time he would be a part of this. It had truly been something special in his life, even before he was a part of the team. The huge throng of fans, students, cheerleaders and footballers made their way into the street at Benton and Jackson and the procession moved toward Fifth Avenue. There were a lot of people who had come out of their houses to wave and cheer as the Tomcats walked by to the sound of 66 pairs of steel cleats clacking on the pavement. As soon as they made the turn at Fifth Avenue, cars were parked bumper to bumper; a sure sign of a big turnout for the game.

Bill Bennett and Little Bobby Bennett in front of 454 Simms Street prior to one of Bill's many big games at East High. Bobby wears Bill's football helmet and warm-up jacket while Bill is in high style. Probably before the East-West game, Thanksgiving, 1937.

(Bennett Family Photo)

The Tomcats gathered outside the gate and Coach Thompson yelled encouragement to them before he turned to lead the team onto the field. The crowd of nearly 8,000 people roared as the teams took the field, with most of the noise coming from the large home stands on the east side of the field. The loudspeakers roared something about the Tomcats, but Bill could not make it out entirely. The defense ran across the field to the far side to set up warm-up drills while the offense stayed on the near side, closer to the bench area. Hundreds of people lined the back of the end zone on either end of the field and the fences were lined with fans all the way around. As Bill warmed up, he glanced over to the Blackhawks' end and spotted number 33, Bob Peterson and number 18, Frank Burgess, warming up together. Burgess was throwing bullet passes to Peterson, as well as to number 25, John Duke, and number 11,

Chuck Wilbur. These were the backs that Bill was going to have to stop if East were to win this game. Either way, he was determined to give his all to keep the Blackhawks scoreless. Bill saw that the Coach was motioning the team to the sidelines and Coach Gunderson and Ossie Federspiel were both busy with some last-minute information. The loudspeaker invited everyone to stand, remove their hats and join in the singing of the National Anthem. Bill removed his helmet and turned to the north end of the field where the flag gently ruffled in the light breeze. As the band played the intro to the Anthem, Bill twisted to look into the stands behind him and found the Bennetts smiling back at him. They all knew that this would be Bill's last game as a Tomcat, either in football or basketball, in light of Bill's decision.

The crowd roared as the Tomcat's kickoff lofted into the air and John Duke ran the return for the Blackhawks. Bill and the defense raced onto the field as the Blackhawks gathered into their huddle. Bill dug his cleats into the turf on the left side of the ball as West's tackle, George Zajicek faced him from the other side. Zajicek nodded with respect across to Bill and Bill nodded in return. Burgess moved in behind the center and looked left and right, sizing up the Tomcat defense. Bill looked into the backfield and decided that he would push through the gap between Zajicek and number 26, Bill Murphy. In a split second, the ball was snapped to Burgess, and Zajicek and Murphy slammed into Bill from both sides. Bill saw number 33 take the ball into his chest and head for the slot that Murphy had made with his block. He reached past Murphy but all he could do was lay a heavy hand on Bob Peterson as he slid past. Wayne Warren and Earl Rottsolk brought Peterson to the ground after a six-yard gain. The teams lined up and Zajicek and Murphy took their positions on the Blackhawks' line. Instead of another double team, the West line pulled to Bill's right as he spotted number 25, John Duke, headed toward East's sideline. Tomcats pursuers rambled to cut Duke off as he rounded the corner for another six yards and a first down. This was not a good start for the Tomcat defense.

On the next play, Bill shoved Zajicek aside as number 31, Frank Scarpino, took the hand-off from Burgess and tried running straight at Bill. Bill's arms went all the way around Scarpino and locked on his side as Bill lifted him off his feet and brought him down on the line of scrimmage. No gain. The defense tightened on the next two plays and the Blackhawks were forced to punt. Bill turned and ran toward the East bench and noticed a smile on Coach Thompson's face as he heard the Coach's voice yelling, "Good job! Way to hold 'em!" Bill made his way to the end of the bench and found a paper cup filled with water. He gulped the water, unsnapped his helmet and wiped the sweat from his head with a towel. Warren and Rottsolk smacked Bill on the back as they knew he had stood tough on the inside.

On the field, the Tomcats were having a hard time getting their offense going. A holding penalty pushed them back 10 yards and then quarterback Bob Ziegler was dropped for a loss in the backfield, forcing East to punt from their own 20-yard line. Rich Kalstedt dropped back to punt for East. On the snap, West's Frank Scarpino split the gap in the East line, tore straight for Kalstedt and slapped the ball immediately after it left Rich's foot. The blocked punt made a sound like a cannon as the ball bounced into the Tomcat end zone. Kalstedt sprinted to the blocked ball and scooped it up just as three Blackhawks smothered him to the ground. The West bleachers went wild as the East stands gasped with horror. The referee held his hands to a point over his head signifying a Safety, and two points for West.

As West took possession of the ball, Bill and the defense again held fast and forced them to punt. The Tomcat offense failed to get a first down and the tiring defense returned to the field. The Blackhawks drove the ball to mid-field and Bill and the guys shouted encouragement to each other as they knew they needed to stop West right there. On the next play, Burgess moved to the outside and Bob Peterson took the snap and headed to Bill's left, looking like he meant to try an end-around play. Peterson stopped on a dime and heaved the ball to a wide-open Frank Burgess, 20 yards down the field. Burgess absorbed the pass without missing a step and proceeded into the end zone with a touchdown. On the extra point attempt, Frank Scarpino kicked the ball through the uprights for the Blackhawks. Bill ran back to the bench with only seconds to go in the first quarter and West was leading East 9-0.

The two rival teams pounded each other through the half and well into the third quarter with no change in the score. In the third quarter, East's Bob Ziegler called time out and ran to the sidelines to talk to Coach Thompson. He ran back to the huddle and the Tomcats lined up for the snap. Ziegler took the snap and he dropped back to pass as Kalstedt and Warren ran down the sidelines. As Ziegler faked the pass, he handed off the ball behind his back to "Speed" Urak, who took the ball in full stride and ran the end-around in front of the East Aurora stands as he broke a tackle into the open field. The crowd roared as they pounded the steel stands with their feet. Just past midfield, Wayne Warren hit Frank Scarpino with a block and Urak was clear for the end zone. Warren got the call on the extra point and was stopped by six Blackhawks before he could dive over the line. The score was 9-6 in favor of West Aurora.

For the next four possessions, Bill pounded his pads against Murphy and Zajicek and man-handled Scarpino, Duke and Burgess. Peterson put together a great game on his way to being named an All State Running Back. As Bill came off the field late in the fourth quarter, his hands were bleeding, his nose was bleeding and his legs felt like jelly; he had left it all on the field. The Tomcats now had the ball on their own 38-yard line and needed to score to win the title. Burgess hit Willie Vaughn with a 15-yard pass and the East stands went wild, again, pounding their feet on the steel stands which made a sound like rolling thunder. Warren, Ziegler, Kalstedt, and Urak all took their turns advancing the ball, but the clock in the south end zone was winding down fast. With 20 seconds left on the clock, East used their last time out and Ziegler again ran to the sidelines. Bill listened in behind Coach Thompson as he ordered Ziegler to send Urak to sweep the left side. "Speed" was left handed and he always ran the left side with power. It was East's best play. Ziegler went back to the huddle and the Tomcats went to the line. Coach Apsit yelled to his defense to watch the pass as East crouched for the snap. The crowd roared with anticipation of a crucial play. In the stands, Jessie was beside herself as she hoped her son would have the chance to experience winning the title. Ziegler took the snap and Urak crossed behind him taking the ball at full stride. The Tomcat line pulled and 22 men headed toward the West sideline. Urak broke the first tackle and gained about eight yards before at least four Blackhawks brought him down hard. Urak fought to get clear of the mass of bodies, but the defenders were in no hurry. The Tomcats raced to the middle of the field to try and reset, as 3 ... 2 ... 1 ... ran down on the clock and the final gun declared the game over. The visitor's stands went wild as several Tomcats dropped to their knees on the field. The sound of the gun sent a sense of disappointment through Bill like he had rarely experienced. He had suffered many losses over the years, but this loss also brought the end of a dream that he had lived with for over 10 years. The Tomcats and the Blackhawks mingled at mid field as they shook hands and the Blackhawks congratulated East on a great season. Bill made his way to Peterson and Burgess and they told Bill they would see him on the court soon. Bill told them that he was not playing basketball this year and they were surprised. They had seen a lot of Bill over the past four years. Many of the West players were members of the West Aurora Hi-Y Chapter and seeing them reminded Bill of things in life that were more important than titles.

After the game, there would be no procession back to the school. The band walked in small groups, the cheerleaders got rides and everyone seemed to want to get to their turkey dinners. Bill made the walk back with about half of the team as he wanted to finish the season with the group. The sound of lockers reverberated through the lower level as frustrations were taken out on inanimate objects. Bill sat on the bench and untied the double knots he had carefully pulled tight four hours earlier. The air was welcome as he pulled the wet jerseys over his head and stepped out of the grass stained pants. Bill shoved it all into his bag as it needed to go home for a washing before being turned in next week. Coach Thompson, Coach Gunderson and Ossie Federspiel made their way around the locker room shaking each player's hand and congratulating them on a great season. It really had been a great season; almost a phenomenal one. Bill looked around the room and yelled goodbye to eight or 10 guys as he shouldered his bag and headed up the stairs for the parking lot. Coming through the door, he scanned the parked cars and spotted Al in the family Ford parked on Benton Street. Bill jogged as best he could with the huge bag over his shoulder and Al jumped out to throw open the back door. Al told Bill that they played a tough game. Not tough enough, Bill thought to himself. Al turned right off Fifth Street into the alley and then pulled into the gravel parking place in the back yard. The sky was darkening by now and Bill could see that the lights were on in the kitchen. Al carried the bag for Bill as they climbed the back stairs and opened the kitchen door. A wave of wonderful food smells hit Bill's nostrils like a soothing hug. Jessie wiped her hands on her apron and slid over to Bill with a hug and a kiss on the cheek. She was proud of her son. Bill had done his job and given 100%. She knew it, because she knew Bill.

15. From Denver, With Love

Going back to school after Thanksgiving, Bill felt a huge relief without the pressure of the basketball schedule. Bill was able to focus on his studies and some of the other activities that were somewhat neglected during football season. Senior Delphi was a group that studied and practiced parliamentary procedure and Bill had been elected President of the club. Every Thursday, Bill made his way down to Clark Allen's room 123, during 7th period, for the Delphi meeting. The group was set up like the U.S. Senate, with students acting as representatives of all 48 states, as well as a few foreign countries. As President, Bill was in charge of the entire proceeding and could direct, deflect or deflate motions with the pounding of his gavel. The club would annually stage a mock trial with all the drama of a Hollywood movie. These exercises gave students the chance to apply their professional and communication skills in a way that would simulate what they were headed for in life. Dotty Gast was a very smart and ambitious student, the Secretary of Senior Delphi and a very pretty blonde to boot. Bill admired Dot as she was a member of the High Honor Roll, numerous clubs and even worked on cars as a member of the Automotive Club with Mr. Burgett. It would be safe to say that nearly everyone at East High knew Bill as an athlete, and many knew him from Student Council, Hi-Y, Delphi, and Boy's Clubs. Since Bill loved interacting with people, the student club societies were a perfect environment for him. He loved to keep the atmosphere light and his frequent smiles and jokes were well known to his peers.

One of Bill's fellow students just happened to be a very spunky and intelligent transfer student from Denver, Colorado, named Mary Anne Swanson. Mary Anne's father, Carl, and mother, Irene, had lived in Aurora years earlier before Carl was transferred by the Chicago, Burlington and Quincy Rail Road to Lincoln, Nebraska. Mary Anne was born in Nebraska in 1922 and grew up in Denver before moving to Aurora to enroll at East High in the fall of 1937. She knew very well who Bill Bennett was from all the football "hoopla" around school that fall, and Bill had particularly caught her eye. The Swanson's rented a house at 940 Lafayette Street and then bought the house at 924 Lafayette, less than two blocks from the Bennett place. Mary Anne was very well spoken and socially outgoing. She made sure that she ran into Bill whenever she could and her tall "fashion-model" looks and bubbly personality were hard to ignore. Bill was soon wondering about this very attractive freshman when word came to Bud Dix and Dick Sheble that Mary Anne had let it be known that she would like to be more than friends with the young Mr. Bennett. Bill decided he would like to get to know Mary Anne, and set about making more frequent conversation with her as was possible at school. One of the first things she let Bill know was that she preferred to be called "Annie" by her friends. She wore her hair pulled back over the top with curls cascading down to her shoulders. Her appearance was always immaculate, her make-up flawless and her manners polished and proper. She was the kind of girl that you wanted to take home to meet your mother.

Bill asked Annie if she could go with him to get some ice cream one night and she informed him that he would have to ask her father, so Bill made arrangements to meet her parents. He made the quick walk over to her house, climbed the wood steps to the porch door and knocked with a firm four taps on the screen door. Inside the house, a torrent of terror broke loose as Annie's

Pekingese guard dog, Teddy, announced to the neighborhood that someone was at the door. Annie came through the door with Teddy in her arms and politely introduced Bill to her guardian. Once inside, Mr. and Mrs. Swanson greeted Bill warmly and said they were very glad to meet him. Conversation turned to football, East High, Steve Bennett's men's store, which was highly recommended, and the neighborhood. Bill explained that he had lived in this part of town his entire life and he knew most of the families that lived near the Swansons. John Dobbins lived right on the corner and the Stoners lived a half block north on the other side of the street. Bob Nix lived right through the block on Lebanon Street and Bill had to walk past Bill Rees' and Bud Dix's house to get over to the Swanson's. It was clear to Annie's parents that Bill knew just about everyone in that neighborhood. Bill was approved, and he and Annie formed a habit of seeing each other outside of school.

Bill Bennett with high school sweetheart Mary Anne "Annie" Swanson, 1938.

(Bennett Family Photos)

    Of course, Bill wasted no time inviting Annie and her parents to Fourth Street Methodist Church and the Swansons became frequent attenders. Annie was very artistic and she loved painting, sketching and sewing. She told Bill about her previous school in Denver and how she had been enrolled in an interior decorating class that she loved. She was very disappointed when she found out that East Aurora had no such class. Bill was very impressed when Annie let him read a letter she had penned to Mr. K.D. Waldo, Superintendent of the East Aurora Schools, introducing herself and admonishing him to adopt an Interior Decorating class into the curriculum. Annie was definitely not afraid to reach out for what she wanted, and Bill admired her assertiveness. Annie attended dinner at the Bennett house and all of the Bennetts were equally impressed. Bill invited Annie when the Stoner family was over and she fit into the group like part of the family. Jessie and Steve invited Annie's parents over for dinner and the Swansons were soon like old friends with the Bennetts.

Begin "Quick Read" Feature

William Wesley Bennett was born in Aurora, Illinois, on April 14th, 1919 to Steve and Jessie Bennett. The youngest of five children, Bill began life within a close-knit family that thrived on relationships within the community and Fourth Street Methodist Church on Aurora's east side. The Bennett's life was centered around their home at 454 Simms Street where they enjoyed entertaining and welcoming their friends and family. In 1927, the Bennetts met Sam and Margaret Stoner and their five children. The two families began an enduring friendship. Bill's brother Al and sisters Jean and Marian became close friends of Eleanor Stoner and her two older brothers, Dexter and Harley, while Bill became a close friend of Bob Stoner. Bill and his friends developed a love for basketball and football as they grew into young men and had seemingly endless adventures. Encouraged primarily by his mother, Jessie, Bill developed a deep commitment to God and the people in his life. When his oldest brother, Bob, divorced and moved away, Bill attempted to fill the void in his young nephew's life.

During high school, Bill developed remarkable skill as a defensive tackle in football and was part of the East Aurora "Tomcats" successful heavyweight squads from 1934 to 1937. Having earned a reputation as an honest, hard-working young man, Bill finished his senior year of football with a disappointing loss to cross-town rival West Aurora and decided to give up basketball to focus on his studies. He met a beautiful transfer student named "Annie" Swanson and the two became regular dates. Aurora had been a great place to live and Bill looked forward to graduation with the hopes of developing a career in one of the trades and having a family of his own one day.

16. The End of an Era

1937 - 1938. The remainder of the school year went by in a blur as there were dinners, dances and meetings on the calendar. Church activities added to the busyness as Bill helped Al and Reverend Schuerman in any way he could. He also pitched in to help Jessie and the girls with some of their activities. As Bill matured into a man, his commitment to Christ and his love of helping others strengthened and became a strong core that kept him centered. Without sports that winter and spring, Bill spent more time with his old friends; they all knew that life would soon be changing for all of them. The Bennetts were guests of Sam and Margaret Stoner, as usual, that Christmas. Sam had landed a new job with International Harvester in sales with the Truck Division. Sam and Margaret had sold the house on Lafayette Street and bought a large, beautiful home at 68 S. Fourth Street, across the street from First Presbyterian Church and very near to downtown. The house was a stunning brick and stucco exterior with a huge flat-roofed porch, big enough to set up tables and chairs for 20 people, if one so desired. The huge living room, dining room and parlor were perfect for entertaining and the dinner parties that Margaret loved to host. The four large bedrooms offered plenty of room for the Stoner kids who all still lived at home.

The news from the Stoners was that Bob had become very successful at North Central, not only academically, as was expected, but also athletically as there were no size distinctions with college sports. Bob not only made the team on football and basketball, but he was on the field and on the court as a major contributor in both sports. This came as no surprise to Bill as he had always known that Bob was a ferocious athlete, in spite of his size. Dexter Stoner had become good friends with a fellow at the Western United Gas Company named Dick Turner. Dick was a Lineman for the company and stood 6' 5." He was from Cedar Rapids, Iowa, and had transferred to the Aurora facility without knowing anyone in the area. He had a great sense of humor and made fast friends with Dexter, and certainly found a wellspring of social connections in doing so. When Dexter invited Dick over to the Stoner's for dinner, Dick was smitten with Eleanor and asked her out on a date. Evidently, Eleanor was quite smitten with Dick as well, and the two had been together regularly ever since. Dick even came with the Stoners to the Bennett's for dinner and he had become friends with Bill's brother Al. Harley Stoner's golf game had become more than a pastime as he was now competing in and winning amateur tournaments in the Fox Valley area. Sam's new job of selling trucks for International Harvester had him frequently on the road throughout the Midwest, leaving plenty of time for Margaret to plan social activities, which was her labor of love. Helen Stoner was now in junior high and was headed for East High next year. It was hard to believe, but the Bennett and Stoner families had been close friends for over 10 years already.

The Bennetts hosted the annual Stoner-Bennett New Year's Eve party and everyone welcomed 1938. The families were growing up and out as time marched on and Margaret and Jessie quietly reveled at the thought of grandchildren in the future. The big news for both families was that Dick Turner had proposed to Eleanor, who had accepted, and a wedding was being planned for October 15th. There was no doubt that this would be quite an event.

At 454 Simms Street, Jean and Linc had become settled in with their jobs, although Linc was keeping his eye on any possibility to get back to farming, his real focus as a vocation. Al had found a good job working for the Pillsbury Flour Mill and was working on a side business of catering dinners. Steve was a great source of contacts, of course, with his connections with the Kiwanis and Elks clubs. Kiwanis was still meeting on Wednesday nights and bowling with the Elks Club was on Thursdays, so Steve kept a sharp edge on the Aurora social scene. Little Bobby continued his regular visits at the Bennett place and Bess was so comfortable with Jessie that she frequently allowed Bobby to stay for several days at a time while she worked at the insurance company. Bill's oldest brother, Bob, stayed in Chicago most of the time and had only been out a few times a year. Bill spent time with Bobby on a daily basis. Bobby thought the world of his Uncle Bill and wanted to play football when he was old enough. Bill took time to help Bobby learn to roller skate and ride his bike; things that Bill knew Bob should be doing with Bobby. The Bennetts knew what Bobby needed in his life and they all contributed to give him a family and an anchor of love. Bill's heart went out to Bobby and he prayed that somehow Bob and Bess would get back together, if only for Bobby's sake. No matter what happened, Bill resolved to spend time with Bobby and try and fill the void of a missing dad. One of Bobby's favorite places was the Phillip's Park Zoo, only a half mile from the house. Bill could take Bobby there after school and spend an hour to look at the bears, elk, and other creatures and then get home to lend a hand with dinner.

As spring arrived, Bill and the EAHS class of 1938 were fitted for caps and gowns with graduation fast approaching. Bill spent a lot of time with Dick Sheble and Bud Dix as the school days wound down to an end. Bud was planning on college, but Dick and Bill were already planning on finding full time jobs as soon as they graduated. Dick and Bud were extremely funny guys who kept Bill laughing most of the time, and they were around the Bennett place frequently. Just as Bill referred to his friend's mothers as "Ma," Jessie became "Ma Bennett" to numerous friends of Bill. Ever since Bill was a toddler, Jessie loved having Bill and his friends around the house. She was so proud of Bill and his buddies as they had grown to be courteous and polite young men. Bill had built the reputation of being extremely nice to his mother; a reputation of which he was proud.

Dick Sheble, Earl "Bud" Dix and Bill Bennett in front of East Aurora High School. Spring of 1938.

(Bennett Family Photo)

On Saturday, June 4th, 1938, Bill walked onto the East Aurora Athletic Field for the last time as a student. Bill crossed the platform and shook the hand of K. D. Waldo, Principal Walters and then Judge Allen, as he placed the diploma into Bill's left hand. As Bill crossed the platform toward the stairs leading down, he glanced toward the stands and let go his biggest smile. He knew that Jessie, Steve and the whole Bennett clan were smiling back. When he returned to his seat, he flipped open the heavy leather diploma cover just to make sure that the page wasn't blank; but there it was, officially finished and approved by the school board!

Bill lay in bed later that night talking to Al about the future and what the logical next steps would be for him. They both agreed that Bill was a "hands on" guy and there would be plenty of opportunities for him amongst the dozens of Aurora manufacturing companies. He would just need to start filling out applications in the coming week. The next morning, Bill was again recognized at church along with other 1938 graduates. After church, Steve and Jessie held a fantastic "Bennett Open House" for Bill and 454 Simms Street was a busy place all afternoon. It seemed as though half of the church stopped by at one point or another, as well as dozens of classmates from school and all of the old "gang" from younger years. Annie helped Jessie, Jean and Marian with the refreshments and Bill introduced her to old friends and family endlessly. Everyone thought that Annie was much older but she was still only 16. The "West Side Bennetts" were there along with the Pfrangle and Cross families. Bill explained to his many inquisitors that he was happy to be finished with school and planned on becoming a working man as soon as possible. The open house worked very well in letting the word out that Bill was looking for work and he would undoubtedly hear back on many leads in the coming weeks. At one point, Bill gathered with a group of his buddies in the back yard so that Al could take a few photos. Bill and George, Bob Stoner, Bob Nix, Dick Sheble, Bud Dix, and even Jack Morey and Rodney Meyers from the early years on Maple Street, were all together for possibly the last time. All these young men were now either working or going off to college somewhere, and they would certainly be spreading out in the coming years.

Within two weeks, Bill landed a full time job at E. W. Eade and Company and then was hired at All-Steel as an "operator" in the shop. Welding, drilling and running the punch press was hard work, but the pay and benefits were good enough to support a family and Bill fell into a "workaday" life.

17. Wedding Bells

As Bill came bounding down the sidewalk after work that August, he could see Bobby's head over the porch rail. Bobby spotted him and jumped over the side rail and ran toward Bill. Bobby giggled with excitement as Bill lifted him and wildly spun him around several times. Bill carried Bobby through the front door, past the front stairs and into the dining room where Jessie was watering her African Violets in the east windows. Jessie noted to Bill that he had mail waiting on the dining room table where she regularly sorted arrivals at the Bennett house. He had the usual YMCA letter, a note from Annie who was in Wisconsin, and a small letter from "Stoner, 68 South Fourth, St." This was addressed to "Mr. William Bennett and Guest." Samuel and Margaret Stoner were requesting his presence at the marriage of their daughter Eleanor to Mr. Richard Turner on October 15th, 1938, at 2 o'clock p.m., at the First Methodist Episcopal Church in Aurora, Illinois; Reception to follow at the Stoner residence, 68 S., Fourth Street, Aurora, Illinois. Eleanor and Richard had decided to have the ceremony at the First Methodist Church with a seating capacity of nearly 1,000, compared to the much smaller Fourth Street Methodist that held about 250. Since the Stoners had moved to the new house at 68 S. Fourth Street, they had attended First Methodist occasionally. The church was two blocks away and the 100-foot-tall spire was visible out their front windows. The huge stone church was built in 1872 and was the highlight of Aurora's architecture. With all the people the Stoner family knew, it made sense to use the bigger building.

As East High began the 1938-39 school year, Bill was getting used to his new life as a working man and returning to the Athletic Field on Friday nights as a spectator. The Tomcats started the season on September 16th by smashing Bloomington 26-0 as their defense played a nearly perfect game. The juniors that had played last year with Bill on defense had taken over the leadership roles with passion and the season looked promising. Ralph Zilly, Floyd Houghtby, George Presbrey, Tony Jurgelonis and Roy Holle were leading the defense and dominating their opponent's linemen. From week to week, Bill was amazed at what he was seeing. Sitting in the stands with the Bennetts, he couldn't help but to tense up with each play. When he saw the opposing halfbacks trying to run through the East Aurora line, he wanted to lower his shoulders and make the tackle. The Tomcats took down Elgin 14-0 on October 14th, with yet another display of defensive mastery. East was now posting a 5-0 record with a defense that had not allowed a single point so far. Everyone in Aurora was talking about the amazing Tomcats and the *Beacon News* would undoubtedly have a great write-up about the game in Saturday's paper. Bill walked Annie home after the game and Teddy caused the usual commotion as they came onto the front porch. They talked about another big day tomorrow as they would be attending Richard and Eleanor's wedding. They discussed the time that Bill would pick her up, and they agreed on 1 p.m. They would walk over to the Bennett's and ride with Al from there. This promised to be a wonderful weekend.

The day of the grand wedding had finally arrived. The huge stone church on the corner of Lincoln Avenue and Fox Street was a hub of activity. The parking lot quickly filled to capacity and the First Presbyterian Church lot next door was used, as were the streets for blocks around. As Bill and Annie walked nearer the church, the sound of the huge organ could be heard through the walls. Guests were lining up on the sidewalk as they waited for the line to move into the church. Inside the doors, signs directed the guests of the bride to use the staircase to the left and the groom, the staircase to the right. The stairs led to the sanctuary on the second floor and as Bill and Annie approached the double doors, Bill could see busy ushers as they whisked guests into the auditorium. Over the heads of the guests in front of them, Bill could see Dexter, Harley, Bob and Dexter's friend Bud Reynolds all dressed in tuxedos and escorting guests to their seats on either the bride's or the groom's side of the church. The boys looked fantastic. Bob returned from delivering a couple to Richard's side of the church and spun himself around to take Annie's right arm. The two stepped forward and Bill fell in behind them. Bob walked Annie to the fourth row on the bride's side where the Bennett clan had mostly been seated by now. Annie slid into the pew next to Marian and Bill sat next to Annie. The organist was busy playing the preludes and Bill spun his head to gather in the sight. The ceiling reached up over three stories supported by seven round columns on either side of the sanctuary. Dark beams reached for the ceiling from each column as they crossed from left to right. The entire room was highlighted by some of the most fantastic woodwork Bill had ever seen. In front of them, the wall behind the altar was almost completely covered by the huge organ pipes that rose up within five wooden frames with gables and spires on the tops. The choir loft was set just below the pipes with the huge organ itself in the center of the loft. The balcony was faced with wooden panels that ran toward the back of the sanctuary, curved around behind and then back to the front on the other side. Bill turned his head to the rear of the sanctuary and looked at the huge stained-glass window that faced Fox Street. A likeness of Christ was in the middle with a shepherd's staff. Smaller symbols arched over the Lord's likeness on the upper part of the window. It was no wonder to Bill why Margaret and Sam liked to attend church here. Today the entire church was decorated with white chrysanthemums and the fragrance was wonderful. Bill had never seen this many people at a wedding before, although he should have expected it to be so, knowing how socially connected the Stoner family was. The *Beacon News* reporter for the Society Page was also a guest, and every detail would be printed in Sunday's paper.

As the two o'clock hour was struck, the flow of guests ceased and Bob and Harley appeared at the front of the sanctuary and took a huge white roll of linen in tow towards the back of the church.

Eleanor appeared on Sam's arm. She had never looked lovelier and Sam had never been prouder. Eleanor was wearing a beautiful egg shell wedding gown that had been worn by her grandmother, Mrs. Harley Stoner, many years before. The matching egg shell veil was held in place by magnolia blossoms and she carried a sheaf of white chrysanthemums, matching the theme of the church decorations. As she drew near to the front of the church, Bill could see Eleanor's smile through the lacy veil and he could also sense her nervousness, which was to be expected. Sam looked dashing with his 5' 10" frame immaculately dressed in the black tuxedo that Steve had fit for him. Sam's graying blond hair and piercing blue eyes, along with the thin mustache and the tux, gave him the look of a movie star. The guests smiled as the storybook bride moved past toward the front of the church and her waiting groom.

Eleanor Stoner on her wedding day, October 15th, 1938.

(Stoner Family Photo)

Reverend Israel asked, "Who gives this woman to be married?" At which Sam replied, "Her mother and I." The veil was lifted and Sam kissed Eleanor on the cheek, and then joined a teary-eyed Margaret in the front row. Eleanor joined Richard in the center of the altar and their height differential was astounding. Even with heels, Eleanor's 5'5" barely came to the shoulders of the 6'5" Richard. Reverend Israel read Scripture from the 13th chapter of 1st Corinthians and explained the Biblical model for marriage. Vows and rings were exchanged and the vocalist performed "At Dawning," during the candle ceremony. Eleanor and Richard turned and joined Reverend Israel as he instructed Richard to "Kiss the bride," then presented "Mr. and Mrs. Richard Turner" to the guests, who applauded loudly. The organ strains filled the room as Richard and Eleanor made their way out of the church, followed by the wedding party and then the guests, row by row. Being in the fourth row was a relief for Bill as it would undoubtedly take quite a while to empty the church through a receiving line. Bill and Annie exchanged handshakes and hugs with the Stoner and Turner families, then with Richard and Eleanor before heading outside.

The bride and groom eventually exited the church through the huge red doors that let out onto Fox Street. They ran down the steps through a blizzard of rice to the waiting Packard limousine decorated with white and yellow streamers. Ken Turner drove the couple away from the church as trailing cans clanged and the guests read the "Just Married" sign on the back of the car. Bill and Annie walked with the Bennetts over to the Stoner home, about 250 yards away as Jessie, Jean and Marian all had plans to help with the reception as needed. Margaret and Sam had catered the food and drinks, but there was still going to be a lot of work with the amount of people that were expected. Within an hour, the house was filled, the porch was filled, the yard was filled and folks mingled along the sidewalk and even in the parking lot across the street. There were family members from near and far, classmates from East High, church members from Fourth Street, fellow employees from Richard's Western United Gas and Electric and Eleanor's Pictorial Paper Packaging. If there had ever been a wedding this big in Aurora, Bill had never heard of it. The huge Packard pulled up in front of the house and all the guests cheered as Richard and Eleanor arrived for the reception. Margaret and Sam loved to entertain, but of all the parties and dinners they organized, nothing ever came close to the party they threw for their oldest daughter Eleanor. Richard and Eleanor had just bought the house at 414 Grant Place on Aurora's east side, so they would remain very near the family.

18. The Clippers

Bill found time to help out at church with the youth meetings and activities and found it very satisfying being able to take part in these events. The direction that he had found in church youth activities and Hi-Y had been formative in his life and the chance to give back to these organizations was valuable. Bill also had the occasion to talk to Reverend Schuerman about direction in his life and again, considered the possibility of attending seminary. Bill was able to help pay some of the bills at the Bennett place and also put some money in the bank. Life was good for Bill in his first year out of school and the future was looking bright. Bill's oldest brother Bob had recently been remarried to Sunshine Dale Shay, who he had met while living in Chicago. "Sunny" had grown up in Tucson, Arizona, and had been living in the same apartment building as Bob. When Bob brought Sunny to the Bennett's for an introduction, it was very awkward for all of them. Jessie reminded everyone that Sunny had absolutely nothing to do with the break-up of Bob and Bess, so she needed to be treated with respect and welcomed into the family with love. Jessie was right, but Bill could not help but realize that Bob's marriage to Sunny also marked the end of his hope that Bob and Bess would somehow reconcile for little Bobby's sake.

The holidays were spent with the usual family gatherings of the Bennett and the Stoner families, and Bill was excited about having money to buy gifts for the family. He took such pleasure in being able to give gifts of any size to family and friends; selecting the gifts was as fun as giving them. Having some spending money also meant occasional flowers for his girls, and Smely's Greenhouse on the corner of Fourth Street and Seminary became a stop for Bill. The spring of 1939 brought Harley Stoner the Aurora *Beacon News* Golf Championship and then the Aurora City Championship. The Beacon sports writers had frequent articles about Harley's amateur golf prowess and some wondered if he had it in him to become a pro. Golf was not Bill's game, but he had to admire the skill that Harley had acquired since he had moved to Aurora and picked up the clubs. Bill thought the world of Harley and seeing him succeed was terrific. Bill and Bob Stoner occasionally got on the golf course with Harley, who enjoyed beating them soundly.

One afternoon that spring, just after getting home from All-Steel, Bill answered the door and was surprised to see his old friend Oscar "Ossie" Federspiel on the front porch. Ossie was now a delivery man for the Aurora Dairy and he was wearing his white uniform and had the white truck parked at the curb. Bill joked that the Bennetts already had plenty of milk, but guessed that Ossie had something else in mind. Ossie explained that he had been working to organize a professional football team in Aurora and hoped to be ready for the 1939 season. He had placed Bill on his list of desired players and wanted to know if Bill would be willing to participate in try-outs this summer. The team was to have about 25 players, a very small team for football, and Ossie would have to take the best players available in order to compete at this level. Bill told Ossie that he was working at All-Steel and Ossie said that practices and games would be scheduled for working men. The team would officially be "semi-pro," as they would be just like a pro team without any pay. Bill said that it sounded exciting and would definitely consider trying out.

After all things were considered, and the fact that Bill did not have a wife and child to support, he decided to try out for the first Aurora Clippers football team. Tryouts started at the end of July on Aurora's Hurd's Island. The island was on the south end of the city and the North Avenue Bridge joined it from east to west. This was a great place to practice, as Bill could get to the island in minutes by bicycle or get dropped off by Jessie or Al in even less time. Hurd's Island was a neutral municipal sports venue that had lights for night time play. When Bill arrived on day one, Ossie had a pile of football gear that the guys were going through to see what they could find and fit. The deal was that if you were cut from the team, you gave back the gear. Ossie had worked hard with both East and West high schools, as well as several area colleges, to forage for the gear. Of course, if any of the guys wanted to buy their own gear, they were more than welcome. Bill was encouraged to see his former

Tomcat team mates Bob Ziegler and Harold "Speed" Urak suiting up near the pile. They were encouraged to see Bill. Bill also found two of his former rivals from the West Aurora team, Bob Lage and Frank Larrabee. There were also football standouts from recent years from both of the schools, as well as some college drop outs and a few older guys. All in all, there were about 50 guys there that wanted one of 22 spots on the new Clippers team.

Bill Bennett (34) with the inaugural Aurora Clippers in the Fall of 1939. (Fox Valley Sports Journal)

Bill was situated with enough of a uniform to get the job done, but there would have to be some improvements before the season. It felt good to be back on the field and it all came back fast once the hitting started. By the third practice, the guys seemed ready to go all out in scrimmages, and Ossie was assembling squads to find out what worked and what didn't. Since Ossie had helped Glen Thompson coach the Tomcats for a few years and he had ex-Tomcat quarterback Bob Ziegler, it was natural to run a similar offense. The guys from West had some input on adjustments, but Ossie seemed to know what he wanted to do. Since this was a tryout situation, Bill had to show Ossie what he had without trying to hurt anyone. The rub on the deal was that anyone breaking an ankle or arm would probably lose their job and it could cause great hardship since the Great Depression was still a harsh reality. Ossie soon had Bill lined up as a defensive tackle, although with a small roster he would have to sub-in on offense as well. The plan was to announce the roster at the beginning of September and the first game would be against Woodstock on October 8th.

19. The Unexpected

Bill and Bob Stoner decided to get together with "the gang" and go downtown on a Saturday night. Bill went over to Bob's and they could either walk or drive from there. Harley Stoner and his friend Chuck Manning hatched a plan to drive out to California to play some golf. As it happened, Richard and Eleanor had been planning to take a vacation and visit Richard's family at Cedar

Rapids, Iowa, and then to St. Paul, to visit Richard's grandmother. The four of them came up with a plan where Harley and Chuck would drive the Turners to Cedar Rapids on Monday, August 14th and drop them off. Harley and Chuck would then press on to California and Richard and Eleanor could use one of the Turner's cars to head up to Minnesota. Harley and Chuck would then pick them up on the return trip. It all made sense and the trip would cost the newlyweds a lot less. That weekend was exciting around the Stoner place as Harley was preparing for the long road trip.

Monday morning came and Bill was off to All-Steel as usual via the bus, while over at the Stoner's house, Harley and Chuck Manning made their way over to Grant Place to pick up Richard and Eleanor. The four of them headed west on Route 30 for Iowa as they had planned. They had great weather and they laughed and had a great time on their way west. Harley pulled into the drive in Cedar Rapids about noon and the elder Mrs. Turner made lunch for the travelers. Harley and Chuck headed west again as Richard and Eleanor settled in for the night, staying up late talking to Richard's parents and his brother Ken. The Turner's loved Eleanor and found her lively personality and sense of humor a pleasure to be around. She was a blond-haired and blue-eyed angel that had come into their lives and they couldn't help but welcome her into the family.

Dick Turner, Harley Stoner and Eleanor Stoner-Turner in front of the Turner home on Grant Place, 1939.

(Stoner Family Photo)

The next morning was clear and bright in Cedar Rapids and Richard and Eleanor enjoyed breakfast with the elder Turners before Ken and Richard's dad went off to work. The plan was to drive up to Minneapolis for about three days and then come back to spend more time in Cedar Rapids. About 9:45 a.m., Richard and Eleanor hugged Mrs. Turner and waved goodbye as they pulled away in the Turner's 1936 Plymouth sedan. They drove a few blocks and headed north on Highway 11 toward Center Point, Iowa. Half an hour earlier, Iowa State Senator Paul Stewart and his wife Lena, left their 320-acre dairy farm at Maynard, Iowa. They headed south for the opening day of the Iowa State Fair at Cedar Rapids. Paul was the President of the Iowa State Holstein Association and the scheduled speaker for the start of the fair. As Richard and Eleanor were nearing Center Point about 10:15 a.m., they came upon a slow-moving vehicle and Richard was looking for an opportunity to pass. As the Stewarts were headed south out of Center Point, Paul came upon a slow-moving truck, and using the unusual center lane of the three-lane highway, swung his Ford sedan over for a look ahead. At the same instant, Richard had the same thought as he headed the Plymouth in the opposite direction.

As he swung the car into the center lane to pass, he was horrified to see Paul Stewart's Ford already taking the lane. The two drivers swerved to avoid one another and tires screeched as the cars slid on the paved road. The Stewart's Ford slammed head-on into the passenger side of the Turner's Plymouth, and both cars seemed to explode into a hail of glass and steel. The impact redirected each car across the opposite lane of traffic, and the Turners slid sideways down into the southbound ditch. The Stewarts car slid sideways as well, and ended up facing north on the southbound shoulder. A huge cloud of smoke, dust and radiator vapor hung over the road as motorists going in both directions came to a stop to lend assistance. The Stewarts were slumped forward in their car with their faces covered in blood. They were conscious, but dazed. Their car was missing most of the front end with huge gashes in the passenger side running the length of the car. The first motorists to the Turner's car were horrified to see that most of the passenger side of the Plymouth had been torn off, including the doors. Richard was dazed and barely conscious as he lay against the driver's door with Eleanor lying against him. Eleanor was bleeding profusely from a large wound on the right side of her head and she had suffered a compound fracture of her right arm. People who lived along the road had heard the wreck and immediately called an ambulance from Center Point. Among those who stopped to help was a doctor from Cedar Rapids who applied pressure to Eleanor's head wound and bandaged the deep lacerations on Richard's right arm. The doctor could feel Eleanor's pulse and he assured Richard that she was still alive.

Within minutes, police and ambulance teams from Center Point arrived and the first ambulance took Eleanor south to St. Joseph's Hospital in Cedar Rapids. The doctor at the scene used the two-way radio to let the emergency doctors know what to expect. Richard was able to tell State Patrolmen Hallgren and Cloud to contact his mother in Cedar Rapids and tell her to meet them at the hospital. They radioed the information ahead and the Cedar Rapids Police sent a car over to the Turner home. Paul and Lena Stewart were transported to the smaller Center Point hospital where they were treated and released. Family members arrived in Center Point to drive the Stewarts back to their home in Maynard.

Once at the hospital, Richard asked the police to notify Dexter at Western United Gas and Electric Company, so that he could go notify Margaret in person. Sam Stoner was out of town on business and Richard knew that Margaret would go to pieces when she heard that Eleanor had been injured. About 11 a.m., as Dexter was starting to think about lunch at the office, his phone rang and a stranger told him that Richard and Eleanor had been in an auto accident. Dexter asked if they were both still alive and the voice told him that they were, but they were seriously injured. Dexter made his way directly home and hurried in through the kitchen door. Margaret thought momentarily that Dexter was coming home for lunch until she saw the look on his face. He told her about the phone call and Margaret quickly called Jessie to tell her where she was going and asked her to pray. Dexter and Margaret were both in the car within minutes and headed for Route 30, westbound. The doctors at St. Joseph's were busy trying to assess the injuries to Richard and Eleanor. Richard's right leg was badly broken above the knee and would need surgery to repair it. He too, had received quite a few stitches to cuts on his right arm caused by flying glass and steel. Eleanor was the doctors' main concern as she had suffered a fractured skull and had not regained consciousness. Her badly broken arm was stabilized, but the head wound was the issue. As Dexter and Margaret sped toward her, Eleanor's life was hanging in the balance. When Bill came home from work about 3:40 p.m., he saw Jessie's face and knew that something was horribly wrong. They both prayed for Richard and Eleanor. They were not entirely sure if Harley and Chuck Manning were in the car, but Bill said that the plans were for the golfers to be heading west that day.

Dexter pulled up to the emergency room door at Saint Joseph's just before 6 p.m., and let Margaret out so that she could go ahead and locate Eleanor. When Dexter found Margaret at Eleanor's side, there was nothing that could have prepared him for what he saw. Eleanor's head was wrapped in gauze and she had a breathing tube in her mouth. It was difficult to believe that the person on the bed was Eleanor. The doctor explained that with a skull fracture of this sort, the brain had started to swell and they would just have to wait to see if she made it through the night. The doctor said that he had to be honest with Mrs. Stoner, and things did not look good for Eleanor. Margaret and Dexter then went to Richard to tell him the news, and though he was heavily sedated, he cried and moaned and wanted to see his Eleanor. Richard had immediately assumed the crash had been his fault, although the police told him it was not. Dexter went back and forth between their rooms for the next five hours, and Margaret held Eleanor's left hand and would not let go.

Shortly before midnight on August 15th, 1939, Eleanor Stoner-Turner went into cardiac arrest and could not be revived. Margaret's agony went beyond measure as her beautiful daughter slipped away into the arms of Almighty God. She was 22 years old. Dexter composed himself to call home and tell Sam the horrific news. Even though it was after midnight, Sam phoned Steve and Jessie and family members. The Wyoming State Police located Harley and Chuck, who were still heading west. They turned around to head back to Cedar Rapids. Harley stopped occasionally to call Dexter at the hospital and this is when Harley got the bad news. While Harley was standing in a phone booth in Nebraska, Dexter told him that their sister, one of their best friends, had passed away. Harley now cursed the idea of the trip in the first place, but there was no way anyone could have foreseen two confused drivers on a strange three-lane highway in central Iowa.

20. A Bitter Pill

The doctors allowed Richard to be wheeled into Eleanor's room to say goodbye. His spirit was crushed with the loss of this wonderful girl that had literally changed his life two years ago. The center of his life and the center of his future lay lifeless before him. Margaret and Dexter consoled Richard knowing that he could not blame himself and also realizing his great loss. Mr. and Mrs. Turner had also been there for hours, along with Ken, and they consoled Richard as best they could. A nightmare would just not suffice to describe the ordeal. In the early hours of the morning, the Turners convinced Margaret to come back to their house to get some sleep and they reluctantly retired there as Ken Turner stayed with his brother.

When morning arrived, phones were ringing across the cities of Aurora and Cedar Falls with the news of Eleanor's death. Friends, family, church members, classmates, co-workers, business associates, newspaper reporters and even radio news staff were all shocked to hear the tragic news of Eleanor's loss. The Bennetts were devastated as Eleanor was dearly loved by the entire family. She was the daughter of Steve and Jessie's best friends. She was a friend and classmate of Marian and Jean for the past twelve years. She was the sister of one of Bill's best friends and a very close friend to Al. Bill and Al rode with Steve and Jessie over to the Stoners later in the morning. Seeing Sam quiet and distraught was unnerving for Bill, as Sam was usually a very pleasant live wire. Bob came downstairs and Bill and Al gave him smothering hugs as they all cried tears of pain. Helen was upstairs in her room and did not want to come down just yet. Jessie wanted to make sure that Sam, Bob and Helen all had whatever they needed in Margaret's absence, and Sam assured her they would be fine. He knew Jessie was, after all, grieving too.

Dexter phoned Sam to let him know what was happening at Cedar Rapids. Harley and Chuck should be back anytime as they were taking turns driving to get back. Sam told Dexter to have Harley take it easy as there was no hurry now. He said that he didn't need anyone else dying at this point. Sam had already been talking to Healey Chapel in Aurora and a funeral director in Iowa to arrange for Eleanor to be brought back home. Even the sounds of the words created a surreal atmosphere, as 24 hours ago no one could have imagined being in this situation. Sam decided that he needed to strike out for Cedar Rapids to be with Margaret and Dexter and take care of the situation. Dexter told him that they were anticipating being able to leave there by noon, which was sooner than Sam could possibly make the drive. The best thing to do would be for Sam to remain home. Sam was not used to waiting. Steve and Jessie made sure every Stoner knew that the Bennetts would be available and on call until further notice. Bill knew that all things work together for good for those who love the Lord, but Eleanor's untimely death made absolutely no sense, and he brought that to the Lord in prayer. Although he knew that God was in control and would be at work within the situation, the sting of death, especially of one so young and lovely, brought pain that Bill had not really felt before.

In one of life's strange ironies, Sam and Margaret had almost no choice as to the location of Eleanor's funeral. The sheer number of mourners that would attend eliminated smaller buildings, so Sam called Reverend Israel and arranged to hold the service at First Methodist Church; where Richard and Eleanor had been married ten months earlier. The service was set for Friday, August 18th, 1939 at 2 p.m., the same hour the wedding had been. When Friday came, the Bennetts were at the church with the Stoners, just after noon. Flowers poured in from all over the city as florist trucks made numerous deliveries. Al had been asked to be a pall bearer along with Bud Reynolds, Chuck Manning, Frank Hawley, Don Barr and Russell Hansop. Bill stood on the Fox Street sidewalk in almost the same spot where he and Annie had watched Richard and Eleanor drive away in the limousine. He watched the black hearse from Healey Chapel come to a gentle stop in front of the huge red doors. Al and the pall bearers lifted the white casket, adorned with white chrysanthemums, out of the hearse and then up the stone steps to the rollers the funeral home had in place. Inside the church, there were staircases to the left and right that rose up to the sanctuary on the second level. The six bearers rose one step at a time as the funeral directors watched carefully from the top and the bottom. Some friends and family cried out loud as the casket was brought into the church. Reverend Israel cried with huge sobs as he privately wondered how he would be able to bring the eulogy to these mourners without breaking down himself. In all his years in the clergy, he had not witnessed so sad a funeral. Richard Turner arrived by ambulance and he was wheeled to the front of the church where he placed his hands on the casket and wept. For anyone who had maintained composure until then, this sight would surely have broken them.

    Annie arrived and she quietly took her place next to Bill and the Bennett family. As two o'clock approached, the huge church filled to capacity. Mourners were still coming in and they stood and lined the back wall. Church members set out as many folding chairs as they could to accommodate as many as possible, but there were nearly 1,000 people in attendance. The huge organ played soft and slow as Reverend Israel took to the pulpit. He reminded the mourners of the joy they had all shared in this very sanctuary just ten months previously. He reminded them that God is both a God of joy and a God of sorrow. That no matter what life brings and no matter what the season, our focus is to trust God, even when we don't understand why things like this happen. He affirmed to all that Eleanor lived a life that was devoted to Christ her Savior, and recounted conversations he had with Eleanor prior to her wedding, when they discussed their faith. Reverend Israel went on to recount how while we were yet sinners, Christ died for us on the Cross of Calvary, paying the price for our sin that none of us could ever pay ourselves. Holding out to us forgiveness of our sin and eternal life, He beckons us now to accept His sacrifice, lay down our lives and live for Him, to the reward and promise of eternal life. If nothing else, this tragedy should drive home the fact that none of us left living has the total assurance of another day. Christ's sacrifice is something that must be accepted today or rejected today. He asked those attending to go forward to live lives for Christ in place of this life that was tragically cut short. Reverend Israel then went on to paint a beautiful picture of Eleanor, now alive with Christ forever, and awaiting the day when all of those who follow Christ will join them in heaven. He wanted the family to understand that Eleanor was truly with Jesus, just as they were with each other in the room. We, the living, are the ones enduring pain and loss at this moment, but Eleanor was safe, secure and joyous with Christ Himself. The real tragedy would be for anyone to ignore the sacrifice of Christ and die not knowing Him.

The church emptied onto Fox Street as police blocked off traffic. The huge crowd of mourners, dressed almost completely in black, surrounded the hearse as the pall bearers brought the white casket down the stone steps and returned it gently to the rollers of the hearse. Automobiles were lined up behind the hearse and the limousines that would carry the family. The Stoners had requested that only family and close friends attend the burial at Lincoln Highway Cemetery on the outskirts of Aurora. The Bennetts followed the procession east on Fox Street then over to Main Street. The curve south onto Hill Avenue then led them out of town to the cemetery. The pall bearers carried the white casket to the frame over the grave and slowly set it down. The Stoner family and their friends gathered under the tent as Reverend Israel read scripture and recounted the resurrection of Christ and His promise of the resurrection of all those who have believed in Him. He declared that one day in the future, Eleanor's grave would become a resurrection site just as Christ's tomb had almost 2,000 years ago. Flowers were laid on the casket and some family members took a white chrysanthemum before they turned away. Slowly, painfully, mourners withdrew until only Richard, Sam, Margaret, Dexter, Harley, Bob and Helen remained. After some time there alone, the Stoners withdrew and returned home. The sobering loss of Eleanor Stoner revealed that although time does heal wounds, those who were close to Eleanor would be scarred for life.

21. Moving On

As Bill and Al were talking in the dark before sleeping that night, Al told Bill that being a pall bearer was the hardest thing he had ever done. They agreed that they didn't see how any of them would ever get over the loss of Eleanor and they were especially concerned about the Stoners. Somehow, sleep came to the Bennetts that night. If there ever were a vivid reminder to the Bennetts that life goes on, it came about 8 a.m. the next morning. As everyone in the house was involved with breakfast, the phone rang and Marian answered it. Her sudden jolt of excitement startled everyone when she yelled out, "it's Bob and it's a boy!" Jessie and Jean hurried from the kitchen and they all gathered around the phone. Everything was fine, the baby and Sunny were both doing well. The baby would be named Stephen Robert Bennett III. Steve could not have been more proud. Although Bill could not have been happier for Bob and Sunny, he privately dealt with the finality of Bess and Bob's divorce and remained very concerned about little Bobby. It was highly unlikely that with a new wife and baby in Chicago Bob was going to be able to spend more time with Bobby. Any way that Bill could slice it, Bobby lost out. Bobby was now six years old and Bill enjoyed doing things with him more and more as he grew.

After a few days, Bill stopped by the Stoner's to visit Bob. The two sat out on the huge porch and watched cars going up and down Fourth Street. Bob told Bill he was very concerned about Sam and Margaret. He was afraid that no one in the family would ever be the same. Bob had already started football practice with the North Central team and Bill had hopes of making the Clippers. Bob was certain Bill would be on the team. He knew that Ossie wanted a strong defense and Bill had proven he could be the backbone of a good defensive line. Even the thought of football brought them back to Eleanor as she had been a huge fan of both of them over the years. Richard and Eleanor had attended every North Central home game last season and Eleanor had hardly ever missed a home game at East Aurora Athletic Field. Bob said he just didn't have the desire for football right now, but he couldn't just sit around and cry all the time. He knew that his big sister wouldn't want that. School would be starting again in a few days and due to Bob's academic "nose to the grindstone," he would be able to graduate early, spending just three and half years to get his degree. Just ten days after Eleanor's funeral, classes started at North Central for Bob. On the very first day of class, Bob met a very attractive freshman from Wheaton, Illinois, named Marijane Mole. Marijane and her twin sister, Marjorie, were the daughters of a successful home builder and they were enrolled in the Commerce program, just as was Bob. He had also found a spot on the college newspaper as a sports reporter. This allowed him to pursue his love of writing that he had honed on *The Auroran* at old East High.

Ossie Federspiel announced the very first Aurora Clippers team in the *Beacon News*. The paper came out in the afternoon and some of the guys at All-Steel had gotten the copy from the office and brought it out to Bill. There were the 22 Clippers players listed and Bob Stoner was right, Bill was on the team. Football would once again be a part of Bill's life and he was eager to play. Bill looked over the list and thought that Ossie had done a good job with his selections. Former West Aurora rivals, Frank Larabee and Bob Lage, would be at the ends, along with Jim Spiers and Leo Smith on defense. Bill would be at tackle along with Bob Dumont, Elmer Shutz, Bill Mosher and Carl Ullom. Floyd Houghtby from East would be at guard along with Dick Payne, Elmer McIntire and Al Theis, while Joe Nelson was the only center. Former Tomcat quarterback Bob Ziegler would share the leadership with Ken Pfeiffer while feeding the ball to halfbacks Charley Critser, Jim Miller, "Speed" Urak and Ed Wagner. Fullbacks Tony Paul and Wayne Foster would be plowing up the middle. Thanks to Ossie Federspiel and the merchant sponsors, the Aurora Clippers were officially a football team.

Bill started regular nighttime practices at Hurd's Island field, under the lights, which was a welcome break from the heat they had been enduring throughout tryouts. The team had so much talent that things happened at a much faster pace than high school games. Having Ziegler and Urak in the backfield was just like old times, and Bill felt a bit exuberant about being able to lay into running backs once again. Although they worked hard at practice, the guys all had an agreement that they would make an extra effort to avoid injuries. Ossie handed out the new uniforms a few weeks before the first game, and Bill received number 34 on a beautiful dark brown jersey with orange shoulders, arm stripes and large white letters. The pants were brown with brown stockings bearing orange stripes. The guys all ponied up the cash for new spikes, since wearing used footwear was a good way to get bad feet. The Clippers were getting good press coverage in the papers and on the local radio stations. People asked Bill how the team was looking just about everywhere he went. The Bennett house was excited to get the Clippers season going, and of course, Annie was the only girl at East High who had a professional football player for a boyfriend.

On Sunday, September 3rd, Bill came downstairs for breakfast prior to Sunday school and church and Steve slid the *Chicago Tribune* across the table as he sat down with his pancakes. "BRITAIN GOES TO WAR," was emblazoned across the top of the paper and the entire front page held stories of Europe becoming unraveled as Germany attacked Poland. Bill asked his dad if he thought the U.S. would get into it and Steve said that he certainly hoped not. Now with Japan invading China and Germany at war with Britain, it seemed like the whole world was in danger of being swept into hostilities in one form or another. Bill noticed an article down on the page that said the U.S. had already sent reinforcement troops to the Panama Canal. American's lives were already starting to change because of what leaders on the other side of the world were doing.

The Clipper's inaugural game would be played on the road at Woodstock, Illinois, on Sunday, October 8th, 1939. Ossie's biggest worry was for the defense. Woodstock had somehow acquired Reino Nori as a running back and Nori had played for the Chicago Bears the previous season. Nori had been one of the best college running backs in history and was considered the best football player to ever play at Northern Illinois University. Nori was known for lightning speed in the open field and his tenacious energy. Ossie emphasized how important it would be for the Clippers to contain him and not let him outside into the open field. The stage was set for a great game and an exciting challenge.

The Woodstock club played their home games at St. Mary's high school and the crowd of 500 spectators was much smaller than either team had hoped for. In the back of Bill's mind, he thought it may be a good thing to have a small crowd until the Clippers knew what they had to offer. For the players from East and West, who had played in front of crowds of over 8,000 fans, the Woodstock game seemed fairly quiet. On Woodstock's first possession, Bill and the defense braced for the onslaught of Reino Nori, known as the "Phantom Finn." On the first play, their QB handed off to Nori who worked down the line on Bill's left side looking for an opening. Bill moved left, eying Nori like a hungry cat while fighting off the opposing blockers. Nori cut into the line and Bill wrapped him up around the shoulders and took him down with a two-yard gain. That seemed pretty normal to Bill and he looked forward to getting his hands on the Finn again. With the score tied 0-0 in the second quarter, Bob Ziegler pitched the ball to halfback Charley Critser, who, in turn, hit Speed Urak with a 20-yard pass that landed him in the end zone with six points. It was the first touchdown in Clippers' history. Woodstock came back with a drive that went into Clipper's territory when Nori ran wide to the left while Bill tried to head him off near the sideline. Bill plowed into Nori's knees just as Ed Wagner hit him high and about six bodies crashed into the Woodstock benches. Nori had racked up six yards on that play, and it would be his best for the day. In fact, Woodstock would not score until late in the fourth quarter, and the Clippers had disarmed Reino Nori with a 19-6 score.

Since the Clippers played their games on Sunday afternoons, it left Saturdays open for other things. Bill was able to borrow the family Ford with some advanced scheduling and he took Annie over to North Central College to watch a few of Bob Stoner's home games. Bob had regained his competitive spirit and was having a good year at running back. His small size and great speed worked well together as he was able to stay low and hit openings in the line quite well. Bill enjoyed the college atmosphere with cheerleaders and a band. He had always hoped that he could play with Bob, but it was just not meant to be.

An unforeseen change for Bob was the announcement that North Central would be offering a Civil Aviation course for the first time. The successful result of the course would be receiving a pilot's license. Bob had been an avid admirer of aviation since Lindbergh crossed the Atlantic. Bob was the kind of guy who appreciated opportunity and he knew that it seldom knocked twice. Sam and Margaret were quietly apprehensive about their offspring leaving the ground, but Dexter, Harley and Richard thought it was perfect for Bob.

Bob worked through the classroom portion of flight training on the campus of North Central while he became familiar with the planes at Lewis Holy Name School of Aviation, just a few miles away. One of North Central's Engineering Professors, Carl J. Cardin, taught the class and was the flight instructor at the field. Carl introduced Bob to a bright yellow Piper J-3 model high-wing tail dragger, a popular light student plane. The J-3 had two seats that were "tandem," with one in front of the other. The instructor would fly from the back seat initially, and then switch with the student as they progressed. From the classroom study and his ever-present aviation book, Bob had already memorized the location and purpose of each feature of the cockpit. Carl's main concern for Bob was keeping him paced with the rest of the class. He could tell Bob was eager to plow through the course and get flying. Bob listened intently as Carl went through his preflight checklist and Bob took diligent notes in the notebook he had already half filled. Carl opened the fuel lines, turned on the magnetos and motioned to the attendant who threw the prop. The little plane jolted as the engine sputtered to life and then revved into a smooth vibration. Carl released the brakes and pushed the throttle forward and the J-3 slowly bounced across the grass as Carl guided it to the strip. The tail swung around to face the prop into the breeze and Carl looked at Bob with a smile. "You ready?" he yelled. Bob smiled and nodded his head affirmatively. He was born ready. The throttle opened and the little plane roared forward as it built speed. Sooner than Bob was expecting it, Carl pulled back on the control stick and Bob sank into the seat. Looking out the right window, the grass strip quickly dropped away as he could feel the wind working on the wings with a few dips and shifts. For the first time in Bob's life, he was airborne, and it was exhilarating.

With a full-time job, football practices and games on Sundays, Bill was staying busier than he wanted to be, but life was very enjoyable for him. The

Clippers lost their second game in a 0-6 upset against the Elmhurst Elms at the "Elmhurst Grounds" on October 15th. Three days later, the offense was tired from running wild as they stuffed Wheaton 32-0 on their own field. On October 22nd, the Clippers edged out Glen Ellyn 6-0 and the Clippers' defense was beginning to gain a reputation as being hard to score against. The 29th of October rolled around and the Clippers had their first home game on the newly marked-out field they had been assigned at Garfield Park. The problem with this field was that there were no fences, so they could not charge spectators. Ossie told the guys that they needed to "pass the helmets" before the game and at half time to raise money for the team. Bill was thrilled to see so many familiar faces in the crowd as he passed his helmet and worked his charm the best he could. There were a lot of East High friends there, as well as Fourth Street families, and the Bennetts and Stoners were well represented. The Villa Park team had their cars backed up on the far side of the field and the cars and their trunks were basically their locker room.

Tony Paul trotted toward the ball on Frank Larrabee's toe and booted the ball down the field as the first home game got underway. Harold Matthews announced the game to the 1200 fans situated on chairs, benches and car bumpers, as well as blankets and just plain grass. Bill dug his fingers into the turf at left tackle and watched the halfback's eyes. The ball snapped and bodies crunched as he took a hard forearm to the neck. The quarterback handed the ball off to the halfback on the right side and he cut into the line at Bill's left tackle position. Bill saw the running back trying the line just behind the Villa Park guard, who was trying to help Bill out of his shoulder pads and Bill got a hand full of the back's jersey. This slowed him down just enough so that Floyd Houghtby could get an arm load of the running back's head and shoulders and toss him to the ground. The referees pushed players aside as they quickly recovered the ball and placed it back in the center of the field. Bill was feeling at home with this defense and they were working together to make sure every offense they played against had to earn their yardage. The Clipper offense had another field day as they wore a path to the end zone. At the end of the game, the Clippers' had done it again, this time 35-0.

Bob Stoner looked out the left window of the little yellow J-3 Cub and noticed cars below rolling down the two-lane asphalt highway. Running with the wind, he was parallel with the strip and dropping in altitude as he prepared to turn into the final approach. He looked up at Carl Cardin in the front seat and Carl nodded his approval, letting Bob know he wanted him to take them down. The engine noise and the rush of air coming in the open windows made sign language the best way to communicate. Bob pushed the stick to the left and pushed the left rudder pedal slightly forward while barely nudging the stick forward at the same time. The plane banked nicely to the left and he held the bank until he could see the strip lining up with the nose. Bob leaned left and then right to size up his position, as it was impossible to see the ground directly in front of the J-3. The altimeter showed 350 feet and dropping; just where he wanted it. His airspeed indicator was showing 55 mph, a healthy amount above the 38 mph stall speed. Looking out the left side window, Bob saw the now familiar dairy farm and the black and white occupants grazing in the pasture. Watching the air speed, Bob brought the throttle back just a bit to aid in their decent. At 50 feet they crossed the end of the grass strip. Bob held the stick tightly in his right hand while he gripped the throttle and readied to push it to "idle" just before the wheels hit the earth. Bob eased the stick back and pulled the throttle back just a bit and the wheels touched down and bounced the plane a bit with a nearly perfect three-point landing. Bob reached back to the throttle and pushed it forward enough to push the plane down the runway towards the hangers and office building.

As Bob turned the plane left toward the hangers, he broke into a huge smile as he saw the blue Packard parked nearby. He recognized his mom and dad, along with Dexter, Harley and his girl, Marijane. Before they got near the hangers, Carl yelled to Bob that this spot was fine. Bob wheeled the J-3 around and came to a stop.

Carl threw his right arm over the front seat and looked back at Bob. Carl wanted everything done exactly as they had rehearsed, over and over, during Bob's training hours. Once in the air, Bob was to climb to 800 feet, descend to landing approach and make a "touch and go," immediately taking the plane back into the air. Bob would repeat this "pattern" three times and bring the plane back to the hanger when completed. Only this time, Carl would be staying on the ground. Bob nodded his head and told Carl that he fully understood. Carl swung his legs out onto the grass. He gave Bob one last look, then gave him a "thumbs up." Bob held up his affirmative thumb as Carl closed the door and jogged back in the direction of the tail. Bob looked over and saw his guests waving in his direction. He gave them a quick wave and then pushed the throttle forward. The little 40 horsepower engine revved and the wheels moved forward as Bob bounced along back to the runway. He rolled the J-3 back toward the dairy farm and then wheeled it around 180 degrees into the wind. Checking over his limited instruments, the oil pressure was good and he had plenty of fuel. Bob paused momentarily as he asked the Lord to watch over him and calm his nerves, then he shoved the throttle forward to full. The plane bounced, then rolled, then sped down the grass strip as Bob eyed the airspeed indicator. As the needle hit 50 mph, Bob eased the stick forward until he felt the tail raise and level out the J-3. Nearing 60 mph, he eased the stick back and he felt the ground vibration stop as he lifted into the air. He glanced out the right-side window as the grass dropped away and he rose above the treetops. The wind blasted his curly blond hair and roared into his ears and he thought this moment was one of the greatest of his life. As Bob banked left at the end of the runway, he let out a shout of joy with the realization that he was finally alone in the sky.

As it turned out for the Aurora Clippers, playing on the "ad hoc" field at Garfield Park was not all they had hoped. Ossie Federspiel worked his magic with his connections and secured the West Aurora Athletic Field as the home field for the Clippers. Most of the players on the Clippers had experience playing on this field in their high school days, and Larrabee and Lage naturally felt right at home there. On Sunday, November 12th, 1939, the East Chicago Avalanche came to Aurora to take on the Clippers on their new home field. Over 1500 spectators paid to get into the game and Bill was scanning the stands for the Bennett clan. Annie was sitting with Marian and Bob, along with Harley and Dexter. The weather and location made this game reminiscent of the past Thanksgiving battles against West Aurora. This time Larrabee and Lage would be friends and not foes. As the game started, the Clippers players noticed right off that the East Chicago team was taking "cheap shots" with every chance they could get. Faces were bloodied, eyes gouged and spikes stepped on ankles after the whistle. The Clippers were not going to tolerate being taken advantage of so they let the Avalanche know it could go both ways. It was an unusually tough game.

Charley Critser had been brought down hard and left the game after being nearly knocked out and Floyd Houghtby had an ankle rolled on before half time. The Clippers offense continued their intricate plays and had run the score to 21-0 at the half. The Clippers gathered at the back of their end zone during half time and the players were complaining to Ossie about the dirty play from the other side. Ossie told everyone to just settle down and not to do anything stupid to get a penalty. Just focus on the game and the job that they each had to do. It sounded a lot like Coach Thompson talking. Part of the frustration of the Avalanche was that the Clippers defense had shut down everything they had tried. Perhaps their only hope was to inflict some illegal pain on the Clippers in return. Before play continued, Bill and the defense had a little talk and decided to double down on the Avalanche and not let them have anything to feel good about. When play continued, the defensive Clippers put the pressure on the East Chicago line and stopped every drive in their own territory. Bill saw the right-side halfback look towards the Quarterback as the ball was snapped and then the pitch-out followed. Bill shoved off the offensive tackle, trying to take him out of the play and pursued the back toward the sideline. As the back made his cut, Larrabee wrapped up his legs, just as Bill slammed into his upper body and plowed him into the turf. Bill heard the air come out of the back's lungs when they hit the ground and he knew that he had doled out some pay back for the earlier cheap shots. The Avalanche punt team ran onto the field and the Clippers lined up for their return. At the snap, Elmer McIntire, the Clippers' right Defensive Guard, split the gap between their tackle and guard, dove straight at the punter and blocked the punt. Bill heard the "ba boom" of the punt block just as he broke through the line and saw the ball spinning back to the left. With his momentum already leading him in the right direction, he cut to the left and followed the erratically bouncing football. With his peripheral vision, Bill saw two East Chicago players converging on the ball from his sides, so he dove full-out and smothered the ball on the seven-yard line. Other players piled on top of Bill and he could feel them trying to strip the ball while the referee's whistles were blowing repeatedly. Bill finally got to his feet with the ball still in his hands and he handed it to the referee. Two plays later, Frank Larabee grabbed a pass in the end zone and the Clippers finished the game with a 33-0 win.

The Bennett and Stoner families were always very supportive of Bill's football play, and wherever he went that fall, it seemed that someone would ask Bill how the team was looking or who they were playing next. Bill always encouraged those he knew to come out and support the Clippers as that was the name of the game. The team needed income to survive and the more tickets they sold, the better. The Monday morning after the win over East Chicago, Burt Olson stopped Bill at the guard house at All-Steel. Burt had taken his family to the game as they lived very near the Athletic Field. He told Bill that he greatly enjoyed the game and he thought it was just like watching the Bears. Bill thanked him for coming and told Burt there would be another home game this coming Sunday. Some of the guys in the shop had been at the game and they congratulated Bill on the win. It was very satisfying to be a part of something that people noticed and respected.

Bob Stoner pulled back on the stick of the J-3 Cub and he felt the plane lift from the grass strip below. His airspeed was at 55 mph and he adjusted his rudder for a slight crosswind. He leaned forward and tapped on the shoulder of his first official passenger, Dexter, who did not look very comfortable. He was holding onto the seat with white knuckles and looking down at the treetops below the right side. Dex glanced back at Bob and showed a huge grin, but Bob could sense that riding in a plane with his little brother at the controls was understandably unnerving for him. Bob banked to the south and then east as he steadily climbed and leveled out at about 800 feet. The fields below stretched out into a sea of golden brown corn and beans, and several plumes of dust arose as farmers were harvesting their crops. Tree lines and clumps of wooded areas were highlighted by the fall colors in the peak of their season. Bob crossed the train tracks and banked down and over the Des Plaines River. The river wound to the south with the straight-edged Chicago Sanitary and Ship Canal cut right next to it. All across the area, there were ponds formed by the gouging of gravel pits and it made for interesting viewing. They followed the river until they came over Lockport, then Bob banked east and overflew the small town. Dexter was fixated on watching the tiny people below as they went about their everyday business. Most of them didn't even look up when they flew over. Plumes of smoke rose from backyards as residents burned their leaves. Bob kicked the rudder and pushed the stick to pull the little J-3 around and head back to the strip. He made a 300-foot pass over the edge of the strip and dipped the wing to get a good view of the young man beside the blue Packard who waved up at them enthusiastically. It was Harley, and he would be Bob's second passenger.

Jessie and Steve invited the Stoners over for the late Thanksgiving feast as they continued their habit of attending the East-West game earlier in the day. After East Aurora's phenomenal season of 1938, they posted a dismal losing season in '39 and West took the big game 20-7. Apparently, Glen Thompson had lost so many good players over the last two years that there just wasn't enough left to live up to the expectations. Bill invited Annie over for her second Thanksgiving with the Bennetts and Bob Stoner brought Marijane for her first official meeting of the Bennett family. Bob only had a few more football games left in his college career and he would be able to get his degree in Commerce in February, only three months away. Bob seemed very serious about Marijane when he talked to Bill, and why would he not? Bob was 22 and almost out of college, and with the hopes of landing a good job in a few months, he felt like a family could be out there on the horizon. Bill knew that Annie still had more than a year of high school left and then she planned on college, so there was no need to even think about such things in his life at the time. Privately, Bill thought that nothing would suit him better than to settle down with a wife and kids.

Almost all conversations eventually turned to the events unfolding in Europe as Hitler's Germany had invaded Poland and naval battles had been raging across the North Atlantic for almost two months now. More countries were being pulled into the war every week. Bob's opinion was that the U.S. would end up being sucked into the war at some point, and the country certainly wasn't ready for it. Bob had confided in Bill that he had thought about the possibility of joining the Navy, and with his love for flying might try for Naval Aviation. Bill had no idea what he would do if the U.S. went to war; he supposed he would join the Army.

The Clippers finished their first season with an impressive record of seven wins and one loss, so Bill felt that the defense had put up a good showing. The holidays came and went in the usual way and life was enjoyable if not somewhat predictable. Bill found he enjoyed teaching his Sunday school class for grade-school boys, and he felt that he was giving back to the influence that others had been for him. He liked to keep up with what was going on in the lives of the boys in his class and most of the boys thought having Bill Bennett for a teacher was particularly interesting. Bill hoped that all of the boys would grow up to be strong believers and serve God.

Bill had developed a habit of letter and note writing which he used to cheer people up and let them know he was thinking about them. He even had some rubber stamps and an ink pad he bought at Sencenbaugh's and kept them in the glove compartment of the car. If he stopped by a friend's house, he was well prepared to leave a note that included some funny comments from one of the rubber stamps. Bill had grown up within a tightly-knit community surrounded by wonderful people. He thrived within these relationships and everyone knew he was truly a "people person." Bill's propensity to look outside of himself and see the needs of others had become one of his finest attributes.

22. Different Directions

The spring of 1940 was a great time for Bill as there was no football and the weather was getting warm again. There was a knock on the door and Bill heard Jessie welcoming someone inside. Then Jessie yelled for Bill. As Bill flew down the front stairs, he saw Bob just inside the front door. Happy to see him as always, Bill presumed that Bob had a trip downtown in mind, or maybe playing some basketball at the YMCA. Instead of the usual, Bob asked Bill to talk out on the porch, so the two closed the door behind them and assumed seats on the block walls along the steps. Bob's blue eyes had a serious look and Bill became both curious and alarmed that there might be some bad news at hand. Bob was direct. "I joined the Navy this morning," he said. Bill was not totally surprised, as Bob had mentioned the possibility several times before. Bill asked him when he would have to leave and Bob told him it would probably be the middle of May. Bill wanted to know what Marijane and his family thought about the decision, but only Sam, Dexter and Harley knew what he was planning. He was going to tell Margaret and Marijane tonight. Bill told Bob they would either be very proud of him or very mad; maybe both. Bob reasoned, again, that the U.S. was headed toward war and we were going to need pilots. He loved to fly and decided that was what he wanted to do with his life. Tomorrow he would have to notify his supervisors at General Electric, in Chicago, that he would be leaving in four weeks. The G.E. job was a wonderful opportunity for Bob, but he just could not stand the thought of business when the country may need pilots soon. If he was wrong about the coming war, having Naval Aviation experience under his belt would certainly not hurt his chances of finding another suitable job in a few years. One could not argue with Bob's reasoning. He was very intelligent and he had thought this all through.

Bob had been thinking about making a trip downtown, so Bill found his shoes and grabbed a jacket. Bob told Bill that he had to stop by the house to grab some money and he was welcome to come in for a minute if he wanted to, but don't let on about the Navy. Sam and Margaret had surprisingly sold their grand home at 68 S. Fourth Street and moved to a lovely American Four Square brick home at 211 S. Fourth Street, just two blocks south on the corner of South Fourth Street and Avon. The memories of Eleanor were hard to take at the old house and the steeple of First Methodist could be seen out the front window. Margaret's enthusiasm for the huge church was gone since Eleanor's funeral, so she and Sam were going to Fourth Street Methodist every Sunday with the Bennetts again. Bob swung the Packard into the driveway and told Bill they could only stay a few minutes as they shared the drive with neighbors to the left. The two came through the front door to find Sam sitting in his chair with a newspaper and Margaret reading a book on the sofa. They both looked up and were surprised, but excited, to see Bill. Bob said he needed to grab some cash and shot up the stairs. Sam and Margaret asked Bill how he was doing and they enjoyed a minute or so of conversation before they heard clunking at the top of the stairs. Bob reappeared with Harley in tow and Harley was carrying his shoes. Bob said that Harley had been working too hard and needed to get out for a while. Bill laughed at Bob's assertion as the Stoner boys always made him laugh. Bill told Sam and Margaret it had been nice chatting as the boys emptied out onto the front porch and to the car.

Bob got behind the wheel and Harley graciously jumped into the back seat. Heading down the hill on Clark Street, Bob turned right onto Broadway. He then turned right again onto Main and found a parking spot just across the street from S. R. Bennett's shop and in front of the pool hall. Bob decided that he could use a quick visit to Bennett's. Bill noticed George and Pete Andrews taking a break in front of Main Hatters, the hat and shoeshine shop next to the pool hall. Their dad, Nikolas Andrews, had moved the family to Aurora from Greece when the boys were both pretty young, and they had been working in the shop for about as long as Bill could remember. Bill asked them how things were going and they said pretty good and asked Bill the same. Bob and Harley came up on the sidewalk and they talked for a few minutes. Bill had known

George casually for quite a few years and knew that he had quit school to work for his dad. Pete was a few years younger than Bill and would be graduating from East High in six weeks. Bob and Harley's little sister Helen went to East High with Pete. The Andrews family lived about a block away from the high school on Second Avenue, just across the street from St. Paul's Church. George and Pete were very hard-working guys and they had frequently sent customers over to Steve's shop, as he did in return. Crossing Main Street, two older gentlemen stood on the sidewalk in front of the Smoke Shop next to Bennett's. The smoke from their apparently brand-new cigars floated up the sidewalk as they reached the door of Bennett's. The usual visit to Steve's shop resulted in Bob running across the street to throw the bag with his new shirt into the back seat. Bill wasn't sure if Bob really needed a new shirt or if the Stoners had a secret agreement to keep Steve in business. After the usual trip up and down Broadway, they ended up at Carl's snack counter with some chocolate shakes. With just the three of them together, they were safe to talk about the Navy. Harley's main concern was for their mother, who he was sure would cry when she found out. There was no doubt that Sam would be proud of Bob for his decision.

The middle of May arrived and Sam and Margaret threw an open house to celebrate Bob's college graduation and to send him off to Naval Training. One great thing about the training would be the location; Great Lakes Naval Training Center in Glenview, Illinois; a little over an hour's drive from home. Marijane seemed happy with Bob's choice and she and Bob planned to get together at every opportunity over the coming months. When the day came for Bob to turn his life over to the Navy, Sam and Margaret drove him to Great Lakes and said their goodbyes. Bill knew Bob's absence would mark the end of an era for him, and he hoped Bob would be proven wrong about the inevitability of war.

Bob finished basic training at Great Lakes and went to Naval Aviation Training at Pensacola, Florida at the end of June. When August came around, Bill was once again working hard trying to make the Aurora Clippers' 1940 squad. When Bill arrived at All-Steel on Tuesday, August 13th, some of the guys had the morning *Tribune* showing the huge headline, "British Cry, Air Blitz Here!" Germany had attacked Britain with thousands of planes and it looked like England would fall as had Poland and France. It sure seemed as though Bob Stoner had foreseen the future. Regardless of the headlines, things in Aurora seemed to just go on as usual. Bill made the Clippers again and resumed his busy autumn schedule. George Troll was back in town after finishing college and had landed a job with Miller-Bryant-Pierce down on South River Street. The company was one of the world's largest manufacturers of typewriter ribbons and carbon-copy paper. George was hired into the sales department and was trying to get used to his new "workaday" life. Having him back around was great for Bill, especially since Bob Stoner was away. Bob, George and Bill had always kept in contact by letter when necessary, so Bill and George were now keeping up with the United States Navy through correspondence with Bob.

At the Bennett house, there were some important changes. Jean and Linc had found a farm to rent and work, outside of Naperville, so there was a little more room around 454 Simms Street. Marian was dating a fine young man named Perry Edwin McIntosh, who was attending Millikin University in downstate Decatur, Illinois. Perry was a "stand-up guy" according to Bill and a fellow football player to boot. He was very polite and had a good head on his shoulders. He fit into the Bennett clan very well and Bill was very happy for Marian. Since Bill had called Marian "Pete" his entire life, the phrase "Pete and Perry" just came naturally.

Bennett's Men's store had not been doing as well as it had in previous years as there was stiff competition downtown. Steve and Jessie had discussed the options of closing the shop and Steve taking a position with one of the competitors. Wheeler's Men's Wear offered Steve the manager's job at their shop and agreed to buy out his inventory. The offer was exactly what he was looking for and he took it. Bennett's had a "going out of business" sale and the whole family pitched in with the task of closing up the shop. Steve started the new job at Wheeler's and also set up for tailoring jobs at the house. Some of his loyal customers would still want Steve to fine tune their suits. The changes for Steve eliminated a lot of stress for him, and although he always missed having his own shop, he did what was best for his health and his family.

Annie was in her senior year now at East High and she was getting ready to attend Illinois State University the following year. It became evident to both Bill and Annie that the two of them were heading in different directions and they parted ways romantically, although they considered themselves friends and talked from time to time. Bill's buddies encouraged him to get out and find another girl, but after two years of dating Annie, there was a void in his life and he was not in a hurry to find a girl just for the sake of having a girl. It would all work out in due time. That was his belief. Bill also knew deep down any woman that he would consider spending his life with would have to live a life that put God first and other things second. He didn't have that feeling with Annie and he knew that she would meet a lot of guys at college.

Al was doing well working in sales for Pillsbury and had started catering dinners on weekends for extra money. Both Bill and Al developed a love for cooking by helping Jessie over the years at home, and she had taught them both a lot about kitchen work. Steve helped Al make connections and he was getting some fairly large dinners of 200 to 300 people. The halls that he would cater in had their own kitchens and service equipment, so it was a matter of buying the food, cooking, serving and cleaning up. Bill helped Al by having members of "the gang" jump in to help as needed, and Bill mentioned Al's services in all of his social circles as well.

Reverend Schuerman left Fourth Street Methodist and Reverend Paul G. Dibble was called to fill the position. Paul had moved to the parsonage at 440 Marion with his wife Marie and two teenage children, Elsie and Jimmy. Jessie wasted no time at all before inviting the Dibbles over for a Bennett dinner to get to know them. Marie had been born in Denmark and spoke with a thick but smooth accent. Elsie was a very reserved teenage girl and Jimmy was thrilled to know that Bill played semi-pro football. Al developed a quick admiration for Reverend Dibble and worked as a teacher and "lay minister" in support of the Reverend. Bill followed Al's example and continued the teaching role of an elementary boys Sunday school class and helped Al and Reverend Dibble with the planning of services and youth activities. As Bill got to know Reverend Dibble, he noticed that he had an emphasis, in his speaking and in his life, on the very personal relationship that believers must pursue with Christ. Of course, Bill had heard this before and read these passages in the Bible, but it caused Bill to think about where his heart really was with the Lord. It was very easy to go to church and even be deeply involved in church and still not have a heart and mind that had been surrendered to Christ, Himself. Bill read Jesus' words about picking up your cross and following Him, and about offering up one's self as a living sacrifice in Christ's service. Bill had long ago decided that he wanted to know the Lord and to serve Him with his life, but he had to reflect on where he was in his life.

The Reverend Paul Dibble in front of Fourth Street Methodist Church, 1940.

(Bennett Family Photo)

Bill was well aware of the pitfalls of being a young man and had seen many of his peers get involved in booze and carousing. Some of the guys he knew not only talked about girls with loose morals regularly, but they treated women without respect altogether. Bill wanted for his future wife to be treated with respect just as he wanted Jean and Marian to be respected and would want to flatten anyone who acted otherwise. He had been raised with the utmost respect for Jessie and would never want to do anything that might make his family ashamed of him. In fact, one day, Bill was being introduced to the friend of a friend and the new guy said, "Oh yeah! You're the guy that is so good to his mother!" which Bill took as a badge of honor. Bill was even known as one of the only guys around school and the sports teams that you would never hear using foul language; although he did let a few slip by from time to time. All of these attributes were great to have and well respected, but not necessarily proof that Bill was living his life in a close relationship with the Living Christ. Bill decided to try and focus on this relationship through regular and heartfelt prayer and study. He began to regularly read the *Upper Room* devotional books that Jessie always had around the house and even took them to All-Steel in his lunch bucket. Keeping his devotion to God in mind throughout the day helped him to focus on his true direction in life.

As 1941 rolled around, George Troll was transferred by Miller-Bryant-Pierce to their sales office in Memphis. George was pretty upset about having to move to Memphis where he didn't know a soul and thought about quitting the job. The guys reminded him how hard it was to get such a job and George reluctantly went. Now Bill was keeping up with Bob Stoner and George via the U.S. Post Office. Bob Stoner's letters to Bill described his short training in the NS-1 Grasshopper, the Navy's version of a Piper Cub, and then Bob's exuberance of training in the 220-horsepower Stearman N2S-2 bi-plane. It seemed as though Bob was made for the Navy and Bill would chuckle to himself when he remembered Bob playing with the sailor hat when they were kids. The Navy had asked Bob if he would be interested in becoming a Flight Instructor upon graduation and he jumped at the chance. Although he would lose out on being assigned to an active combat-ready squadron, he would be able to log far more flight hours than any other position as well as have the respect that the instructor position held. Bob Stoner loved to fly, and his intelligence and communication skills had set him up to be a very competent pilot. After mastering the Stearman, Bob was introduced to the Navy's new single wing trainer, the 450-horsepower SNJ. The SNJ would be a pilot's last plane before getting assigned to a combat aircraft. Bob learned all known aerial combat tactics and participated in mock air-to-air dogfights, bombing, strafing and reconnaissance flying. He learned to be an expert navigator and studied every aspect of the plane's mechanics. Upon graduating at the top of his class, Bob was given the rank of Ensign and given leave to visit his family.

When Bob got back to Aurora, he borrowed Harley's car and went to pick up Bill to visit some of their old buddies. Bob's Florida tan, along with his blonde hair and blue eyes, were highlighted by the pure white Navy dress uniform and Bill could immediately sense the changes in his old friend. Bob looked to be in great shape and he presented himself with a heightened sense of politeness, although he had always been quite polite. Jessie and Marian sounded like school girls when they saw Bob in his dress whites and had to be careful not to smudge him with makeup. Bob answered some questions about flying and life in the navy, and then he and Bill hit the road to do some visiting. Bob had been writing to George, so he knew about his loneliness and his disdain of the south, but Bill filled him in on what had been going on in Aurora. Bob said he was sorry to hear that Bill and Annie had gone separate ways, but Bill told him he was okay with it now. Bill asked how things with Marijane were going and Bob said that it was fantastic. In fact, after he got himself established as a Flight Instructor, he was planning on asking her to marry him. Bill was surprised to hear this, but it made sense. The subject turned to Eleanor, now a year and a half since her death. Bob said he thought the family was doing okay, but that Margaret frequently went for walks when she was becoming overwhelmed. Moving to the new house had helped, but some of these things would never go away. Bob said he frequently thought of Eleanor in heaven with Jesus and wondered what, if anything, she knows about what we are doing down here. When he was flying through cumulus clouds he somehow felt closer to God and he just seemed closer to heaven. Bob held a strong assurance that because of what Jesus had done for both of them, he would be reunited with Eleanor in heaven when he left the Earth.

The conversation turned to war and Bill asked Bob what he was hearing about the Battle of Britain, now raging over the U.K. and the English Channel. Bob said that he thought the Brits had pretty much repelled the Germans by now and that the real threat, as far as the Navy was concerned, would be from Japan. As far as Bill knew, the Japanese had no reason to fight the U.S. They seemed only interested in China and the South Pacific. But Bill led a busy life and he did not spend a lot of time reading about world events. Bob was able to stop by a few more times over the next week and he and Bill went to the YMCA to play a little basketball the following Saturday. His leave came to an end and Bob headed back to Pensacola.

23. A New Flame

May, 1941. After two and a half years at All-Steel, Bill was wondering if running the punch press and the spot welder would be all he had to look forward to for the rest of his young life. He had received two raises since he started and was making $30 per week. Not bad pay, but he wasn't ready to settle for it. Just to see what else was out there, he regularly kept an eye on the jobs section of the Aurora *Beacon News*. One late afternoon before supper, he was sitting at the dining-room table doing just that when he saw an ad placed by Donald L. Glossop Heating and Cooling/Sheet Metal over at 806 S. Spencer in Aurora. They were looking for an individual with sheet metal experience that would train as an air conditioning technician. An air conditioning technician sounded like several levels up from a punch press operator. The next day after work, Bill rode the bus over to Glossop's shop and filled out an application. The shop wasn't very big, but there were ten or twelve guys working there and it seemed quite busy. Besides the heating and cooling business, there was also a truck that had "Glossop Trucking and Roofing" painted on the side. It seemed like there was a lot of work going on around there at any rate. The next day when Bill got home from All-Steel, Jessie handed him a note with Don Glossop's phone number and a message to call him back. Bill called and talked to Don, then changed clothes and drove Steve and Jessie's Ford over to the shop. Bill walked into the shop and Don motioned for him to come into the small office. Bill had a seat and Don pulled out his application from the previous day. Compared to the original interview at All-Steel, this was all very low key, which wasn't all bad. Don asked him about his work at All-Steel and asked him what his plans were for the future. Bill told him that he would like to have a trade that would support a wife and kids someday, although he didn't even have a girlfriend at the time. Don said that he and his wife Helen had three kids and that Bill should take his time. Don told Bill that he knew who he was since he was a football fan. He had been to a lot of the East Aurora games over the years and read the sports pages with the Clippers' game summaries. Bill told Don he was no stranger to working hard and he would do a good job. Don said he was sure Bill would do fine, but he had a few other guys to talk to. Bill asked about the pay situation and Don told him the position would pay $35 per week. That sounded good to Bill. Don said he would call him by tomorrow night. As Bill shook hands and headed out of the shop, he had a good feeling about Don. He hoped that it was mutual.

When Bill came through the kitchen door the next day, there had been no phone calls for him. Jessie said that she had gone shopping earlier, so no one had been home. Bill headed upstairs to clean up and change clothes, but before he could even get fully dressed, the phone rang. Jessie called for Bill to get the phone and Bill came down the stairs like a rock-slide. Don said he had waited to call until now because he knew Bill did not get in until about four. He said Bill could have the job if he wanted it. Bill said he absolutely wanted it, but he needed to give All-Steel a fair notice. While they both looked at their calendars, Bill agreed to start working for Don on May 19th. This was cause for celebration as Bill now had the chance to learn a trade that could carry him through his working years and earn considerably more than an operator at All-Steel. When Bill gave his supervisors at All-Steel his two-week's notice the next morning, they were pretty upset. Bill was called to the foreman's office and they asked him if he would consider staying if they gave him a nominal pay raise. Bill said that he really was after the chance to develop a trade and that heating and cooling sounded like the right path for him. He told all the people he knew at All-Steel he had enjoyed working with them and wished them the best.

On May 19th, Bill rode the Simms Street bus six blocks east to the corner of Simms and Spencer. Don Glossop's shop was just past Spencer Street with the driveway entrance on Simms Street. The bus ride took two minutes and on most nice days, this commute would be a pleasure to walk. Don introduced Bill to his brother, Charles, as soon as he arrived. Charles shared the office but he had a separate business that involved the trucks, gutters and roofing. Don introduced Bill to Wiley Holt who was 26, married and had two small sons, ages three and one. It turned out that Bill had been working with Wiley's brother, Tom, over at All-Steel for the past two years. Bill was also introduced to Marvin Settles, a 19-year-old trainee who had worked at a gas station the previous year. Marvin was a smooth talking southern boy with a great sense of humor. Don's wife, Helen, helped out in the office with the bookwork and she was very pleasant to be around. After a few weeks, work started to feel like a second family and the environment was a lot better than the All-Steel plant. Don and Helen had eight-year-old twins named Donald Jr. and Ronald and a four-year-old daughter named Carol June. The guys called them Donnie and Ronnie, and, due to little Carol's bright blonde hair, she was sometimes called "Butter Head." The children were often around the shop as they lived next door, and Bill enjoyed joking with them. The twins just happened to be about the same age as little Bobby and Bill had a lot of experience relating to that age. The twins were excellent older brothers and they took little Carol just about everywhere they went. There was a large concrete area in front of the shop and Carol would be out on her roller skates almost every day, weather permitting. Bill would tell Carol how good she was on those skates and she would ask him all kinds of questions befitting a four or five-year-old. One day, Carol asked Bill if he had a girlfriend and he had to say no. She told Bill that it was okay because he could be her boyfriend since he seemed so nice. Bill had hardly ever seen anyone so cute.

Bill started going out on house calls with Don to get a feel for interaction with the customers, usually a homeowner or business manager that needed repairs or upgrades. When Bill was sent out with Marvin, he began to notice that Marvin would naturally get involved in conversations with the ladies as they seemed to be enthralled with his genteel southern accent. After a few days of this, Bill had to ask Marvin to try and shut up so that they could get their work done. Marvin said he would try, but it wasn't his fault the good Lord made him so attractive to the ladies.

One of the things that Bill and Al worked on at Fourth Street Methodist was planning youth meetings and activities. They tried to have one activity per month and there was a meeting every Sunday night. Back in 1940, Tommy Fairclough and his wife, Anne, set up a skating floor with a tent over it in nearby Sandwich, Illinois. The makeshift rink was so popular that by late 1940 they were constructing a building across Route 34 from the tent. The rink became popular with kids from Aurora, even though it was a 35-minute drive out of town. Part of the attraction was that Sandwich was a small town with a lot of kids, and visiting the rink and the downtown was a change from the usual nights out around Aurora. The Fourth Street Methodist Youth Group got together to make a trip out to Sandwich for some skating on a Saturday night in early June of 1941. Al, Bill, Bob Nix and Bud Dix were going along as chaperons and they all headed out with five cars. Bob joked with Al as he wondered who would keep an eye on the chaperons. The convoy headed down Route 31 to Oswego, where they picked up Route 34 out through Yorkville, then through Plano and into Sandwich. The new Fairway Skating Palace was the first building coming into town on the big curve, and the parking lot was busy with incoming cars. The group all got in line to pay, then to get their rental skates at the skate counter. Tommy Fairclough sat behind a bright white Hammond organ on a small stage in a corner of the rink and he was playing a lively foxtrot with amazing skill.

Skaters went around and around on the outside of the rink while experienced skaters whirled and twirled in the center. Several young men wore yellow jerseys with "Floor Guard" printed on their backs as they skated around with whistles making sure that skaters followed the rules. There was a snack bar selling popcorn, sodas and candy. Several colored light beams reached up to the mirrored ball that slowly spun in the center of the room, hanging from the huge, curved, wooden roof trusses. Bill got his skates on and took to the floor trying to look smooth enough so that no one would notice how awkward he felt. It had been a while since he had skated so it took a few laps before he started to feel comfortable. With George in Memphis and Stoner in the Navy, it was good to have "Nix 'n' Dix" back in town. The Fairway Skating Palace was packed tonight and it had a festive feel. Bob and Bud were both pretty funny guys and they were frequently hilarious when they were together. Having been at college for the last several years, they had become experts in locating good-looking girls and they were laughing about finding Bill a girlfriend. As it was bound to happen in a crowd this large, the guys located four young ladies skating together without any male companions visible, and Bob made sure that he said hello to them as he skated past. As Bill went by, the girls in turn said hello to him and he replied. Bob told Bill that he should have seen the smile on the cute one with the brown hair when he went by and Bill told him to stop lying. Whether Bob was making it up or not, the idea was enough for Bill to at least keep an eye on her for a while.

Tommy Fairclough behind his Hammond Organ at the Fairway Skating Palace.

(Sandwich Historical Society Photo)

Tommy Fairclough cleared the floor for some specialty skating and most of the skaters headed for the benches, tables, restrooms or just the outside of the half wall. The group of young ladies that said "hello" to Bill were seated at one of the crowded tables and Bob went over for a chat. He introduced himself and was already getting their names when Bill and Bud caught up. Bill reminded Bob that they were supposed to be keeping an eye on the kids that they had brought from Aurora, not the girls from Sandwich. At that, Bob asked the girls if they were from Sandwich. Without a pause, Bob broke into introductions of Bill and Bud and then pointed to Ada, Helen, Shirley and Betty. Helen was the petite, brown haired girl that had reportedly smiled as Bill skated past. She certainly had a beautiful smile and it was very evident as she told Bill that it was nice to meet him. Bill told the girls that it was a pleasure to meet them, as well. Then Bill excused himself as he told the ladies that he was helping to chaperon 18 church kids they had brought out from Aurora.

Bill had seen the smile for himself, and he couldn't help but wonder about Helen. Was she in high school? She seemed more mature than that. She probably had a boyfriend and he was working tonight or something. The questions kept coming. Of course, Bob and Bud fed the flame as they made comments about how sure they were that Helen really seemed to like Bill. Bill was not shy about talking to girls, but he didn't want to seem too aggressive with a girl he had just met a few minutes ago. Before long, Tommy Fairclough called for the "Couples Skate" and told the guys that if they didn't have a girl they had better find one. The organ began the strains of Bing Crosby's recent number one hit, "Only Forever," and the fellas were on the move to pair up for the song. Bill saw Helen and Ada near the opening in the guard wall and skated up for the question. He asked Helen if he might have this skate. She smiled up at him and said certainly. As they rolled into the stream of counter-clockwise traffic, Bill took her hand and they merged in behind the other couples.

Miss Helen Cochran, 1941, Ripon College.
(Cochran Family Photo)

Bill asked Helen if she was in school and she told him she had just graduated from college last week. Bill felt relief on that one. Bill asked about her college and she told him she had just earned a two-year Commerce degree from Ripon College up in Wisconsin. He asked her if she had lived in Sandwich her whole life and she said yes. She supposed that Bill was from Aurora from what she had heard earlier, but asked, "East or West?" Bill proudly proclaimed his loyalty as a Tomcat. He told her that he had worked at All-Steel for the past two and a half years, but just took a new job a month ago. The "couples skate" came to an end and Bill thanked Helen for the skate and told her it had been nice talking to her. She said likewise and smiled as she skated toward her friends.

Bob and Bud just had to ask Bill how it went and what he thought about Helen. Bill said that she seemed very nice. But what did they expect? Bill thought about what his next step might be and he did want to know more about Helen. A short while later, when Helen and her friends took a rest, Bill bought some popcorn and rolled over to their table to share. He just wanted to talk to Helen again, and that was probably obvious to her by now. Bill politely asked Helen if she would mind if he called her on the phone sometime. She said that would be fine and scrounged for a piece of paper. She neatly wrote her number and handed it to Bill, then reminded him that it would be a long-distance call. Bill said he would keep it in mind. He asked Helen for her last name and she told him that it was Cochran. Helen Cochran.

Bill thought about the call all day on Sunday and thought that it might be best to wait a few days. If he waited, he reasoned, she might think that he had forgotten about her or that the call wasn't important to him. He recounted the whole story to Jessie as he was drying dishes and the wisdom that came to the surface was it "never hurt to ask." After supper was cleaned up, he dialed out to Sandwich. A woman answered the phone and he asked if he might speak to Helen. When Helen answered, Bill asked her if she remembered him from last night. She laughed and said, "Bill who?" Bill said he was wondering if she would be busy on Friday night as he would like to come out to skate again. Then he asked her if she might have time to show him the sights of Sandwich. Helen said she would love to see him and that she was uniquely qualified to give him a tour of the city. Helen reminded Bill that it might be helpful if he knew where he should go once he got to Sandwich again. Bill grabbed his note pad and wrote the directions as she gave them.

"Go past the skating rink on Route 34 to Latham, there is a giant root beer barrel on the corner there, and turn right, over the tracks. Three streets to 4th Street, I know that doesn't make sense, but there is no 2nd Street there … anyway, turn left onto 4th Street, and we are on the third corner on the right side. It's 503 East 4th Street, on the corner of 4th and DeKalb. It's a big gray house with a round front porch and a roof that looks like a church steeple. You can't miss it." It was a date. Bill hung up the phone and felt a little strange. His experience with such things had been very limited as he had met Annie at school about three years earlier and they just met in the hall. This was the first time he had actually asked a young lady for an official date so soon after meeting her. Bill told "Nix 'n' Dix" that they could count him out next Friday night because he was going out to Sandwich to see the city and skate with a certain young lady.

When Friday rolled around, Bill hurried home from work so that he could stay ahead of the clock. He wanted to leave for Sandwich by 5:45 so that he could be at Helen's by 6:30. She would show him around town for an hour or so, and then they could go over to the Fairway Skating Palace for another skate. Bill had made arrangements to use the family Ford again and made sure there was more than enough gasoline for the trip. He dressed in a fresh white shirt with his best suspenders, tan cardigan pants with the two-inch cuff and his favorite white dress shoes. No time for the bank today, so he borrowed 10 dollars from Jessie, gave her a kiss and flew out the kitchen door. She yelled out for him to be careful just as she had done since time immemorial.

As Bill drove out Route 34, he thought about how unexpected this had been. When he went to Sandwich last Saturday, he had absolutely no idea he would meet a girl there and be heading back out so soon. Maybe he was nuts, but the whole thing was pretty exciting. Bill drove past the Plano water tower and had to obey the slow speed limit through town, and then he hit the highway on the other side of town. The highway ran right next to the train tracks for a few miles and a freight train rumbled past on the way in to Chicago. Down into a valley there was a bridge over a good-sized creek and then up the hill and Sandwich was dead ahead. Bill passed The Fairway Skating Palace and the parking lot was already half full at 6:25 p.m. He came to the corner of Railroad Street and Latham and there it was: the giant root beer barrel! Somebody had actually made a root beer, barbecue and ice cream shop in the shape of a giant root beer barrel. Bill decided that he and Helen would have to come back here for a root beer later. He made the right, then 1st Street, 3rd Street and 4th street ... indeed, there was no 2nd Street! He made the left and counted the corners. There was the beautiful two-story Victorian house with a huge curved front porch and the round room with what looked like a church steeple. As Bill looked back to the road, he pulled the car onto the gravel in front of the house and Helen came bounding down the front steps toward the car. She welcomed him back to Sandwich and asked if he had any trouble following her directions, he said none at all. She asked Bill if he would like to meet her parents and Bill was thrilled about it.

Yes, there really was a giant root beer barrel in Sandwich, Illinois.

(Sandwich Historical Society Photo)

As Helen led Bill through the front door, the smell of supper was still in the air, and it smelled good. Mrs. Cochran stepped out of the kitchen while drying her hands and Helen introduced her as her mother, Carrie. Helen said that she only had one sister, Phyllis, but she graduated college last year and was living in Chicago now, working as a secretary. Helen asked Bill if he still wanted the tour of Sandwich and he said that he absolutely did. Helen told Bill to follow her as she headed out the kitchen door to the side yard. Helen told Bill that his tour should probably start by meeting the Mayor of Sandwich, as she turned right around the back of the house where a middle-aged man sat reading the paper. "Dad," she said, "this is my friend Bill Bennett from Aurora." "Bill," she continued, "this is my dad, the Mayor of Sandwich!" Bill was somewhat shocked as he reached out to shake Mr. Cochran's hand. "Wally. Wally Cochran," he said. Bill said that it was nice to meet him and asked if he was truly the mayor. Wally admitted that he was truly the mayor and Bill turned and smiled at Helen. She smiled and said, "I told you that I was uniquely qualified, didn't I?" Bill had been played like a fiddle, but it was very funny.

The Pullman train car converted to a diner in Sandwich, IL. (Sandwich Historical Society Photo)

As Helen slid into the car, Bill chuckled about her being the mayor's daughter and asked if there were any more surprises. Helen told him that she could be full of surprises and he should be on his guard. Helen directed Bill to make a series of turns that led them back over to Railroad Street and toward the business district. There was a large building on the left that she identified as the Opera House. She said they didn't really have any opera's there, but they did have a lot of music acts and plays. Just past the Opera House, the downtown area unfolded with a wide-open center where the train tracks ran through. On the left was the State Theater with its well-lit marquis hanging over the sidewalk with Sandwich Motors in the building next door. There was every kind of shop you could think of and it reminded Bill of a small downtown Aurora. Helen directed Bill left and over the tracks. There was a construction site on the northeast corner and a very nice brick building, with four pillars, was having windows installed. Helen identified this as the new Sandwich Library and quite the rage around town, but she admitted that everyone was far more excited about the Fairway Skating Palace. Bill drove down 1st Street until the houses ended and then farther out until he came to the fairgrounds. Helen said that this was the biggest deal in Sandwich. The Sandwich Fair was always the week after Labor Day and literally everyone in town went; everyone.

Bill turned back onto Route 34 and headed to the roller rink. At the stop sign at Route 34 and Main Street there was another unexpected sight. There was a full-sized Pullman train car on the side of the road with "Diner" painted on the front end. Neon signs reading, "Chicken," "Steak," "Open" and "Wright's Diner" were already lit up for the night. Helen told Bill the rumor was the old dining car had actually been Teddy Roosevelt's when he was President. She thought that there was truth to it. She had Bill turn right and they drove a few blocks over to the Sandwich High School. Helen said that this was her old hang out. Bill asked Helen what sort of things she did in high school and she described being the class vice president one year, the editor of the newspaper another year, editor of the year book her senior year, etc. Bill was impressed. Helen had Bill drive back toward the center of town and she pointed out the "Sanitary Cleaners" sign on the end of the block where the State Theater was. She told Bill that the cleaning business was owned by her mom and dad. The mayor's job was only part time and didn't pay very much. As he turned back toward the rink, Bill said that there was something he wanted to do before they went skating, and then he pulled the car in next to the giant root beer barrel. He asked Helen if she would care for a root beer.

24. Looking Ahead

Bill was very impressed by Helen and she soon came to Aurora for a Bennett dinner to meet the family. Bill introduced Helen to Aurora and she continued to introduce Bill to Sandwich. Bill learned that Helen was highly intelligent and very capable in many areas. In high school, she had been very active in several chorus activities, drama productions, Latin Club, Commerce Club, the Girl's Athletic Association, as well as several journalistic activities. At college, she played intramural sports, was Sergeant at Arms in the Kappa Sigma Chi sorority and was a member of the championship women's rifle team. The 1941 team had been undefeated in their matches all over the country, and then they beat the Ripon College men's ROTC team in an unofficial duel at the year's end. Within a few weeks, Bill's outlook changed quite a bit as he now planned most of his free time around activities with Helen. The Bennetts, as usual, opened their hearts to Helen and made her feel very welcome.

Bill learned that Wally Cochran was already in his second term as mayor and he literally knew everybody in Sandwich, and of course, everybody knew him. Wally had business and political connections in abundance and he was very familiar with the Sandwich bars. Carrie Cochran was very impressed by Bill and she thought Helen had been very fortunate to meet him. Bill was invited regularly to the Cochran's for dinner, and Carrie and Helen were surprised by Bill's helpfulness with kitchen work; they were not used to men being involved in that sort of thing. Bill was used to seeing a job and doing it. He thought that often a man could spend more time worrying about doing something than it would actually take to get it done. Being a "people person," he also did not like the idea of one person having an unfair amount of work to do. Al had been a good example for Bill and they had grown up helping Jessie and the girls in the kitchen, so helping at the Cochran house was natural for Bill. Carrie worked at Hornsby's department store on the corner of Railroad and Main in Sandwich, and Bill liked to take Helen there when Carrie was working, just to say hello. Hornsby's was a nice two-story department store that had just about everything you could need around the house and quite a bit of home hardware.

Bill was invited to the Cochran's for dinner on a Saturday evening when Helen's sister, Phyllis, and her fiancé Ken Stroker were out visiting from Chicago. Phyllis had graduated the previous year from college and had landed a secretarial job at The Market Report, Inc., in Chicago. *The Market Report* published several different market guides and, most noteworthy, reports for the auto industry. Ken was from Michigan and he met Phyllis at college. Bill picked up on the fact that Phyllis was a little more of a "daddy's girl," while Helen was closer to her mother. The world that Phyllis and Ken lived in seemed like life on another planet to Bill. Phyllis told Bill about her busy commutes every work day from her apartment on North Kedvale, to the high-rise where she worked, at 20 North Wacker Drive. Bill had always marveled at the huge buildings in Chicago, the busy streets, buses and trains, but the thought of living there didn't appeal to him. Wally Cochran was very proud of his two daughters and their college educations. Phyllis was well on her way with her career now and they were very hopeful that Helen would find her career path soon. Bill was not sure what Helen had in mind for a career, but he knew that new jobs sometimes meant new locations. He learned that first hand from George Troll and Bob Stoner.

Bill loved to have Helen in to Aurora on Sunday mornings and she frequently attended Fourth Street with the Bennetts. Bill, in turn, attended the Sandwich Congregational Church with the Cochrans. Bill was happy to learn that Helen was in the habit of going to church, because he wanted that to be a large part of his future. Should he ever be blessed with a family, he wanted them to be brought up in church, just as he had been.

The summer seemed to be flying by as Bill worked during the days, assisted at church and occasionally worked with Al on his dinners. In spite of the hectic schedule, he tried to see Helen whenever possible. At work, Don Glossop made it a point to ask Bill, "How's your Helen doing?" to avoid any confusion with Don's Helen. Bob Nix and Bud Dix dubbed Helen as Bill's "Sweetie of Sandwich," and of course, they felt personally responsible for getting the two together. Bill found it refreshing to date a person that had college behind her, was very well spoken and knowledgeable about business, government and religion. This was a positive contrast to the past years he had spent surrounded by high school girls. Meeting Helen had made Bill really think about moving forward with his life and focusing on responsibilities even more than he had. He was very focused on becoming a licensed heating, ventilation and air conditioning technician, and Helen's college degree was a good influence on him.

Friday, August 1st, 1941. Bill had several pieces of mail on the table when he got home from Glossop's. One stood out from the rest, as it was a yellow envelope with a red marking that read, "Special Delivery." It was from The Market Report, Inc., 20 N. Wacker Drive, Chicago; obviously from Phyllis Cochran, but how unusual. The letter was addressed to "Bill Bennett, Simms St., Aurora, IL" but it had found its way, nonetheless. Bill sliced open the end of the envelope and pulled out the letter. A very nicely typewritten letter on company letterhead appeared from the envelope. Phyllis wrote that Ken was supposed to stop by the Bennetts to talk to Bill last week, but had failed to do so. Phyllis and Ken were getting married at the Sandwich Congregational

Church on Saturday, August 9th, and they wanted Bill to be one of the ushers. He would need to wear a black tux and there would be a rehearsal on Friday night, the 8th of August, at the church. She told Bill that she was sorry for the short notice and his agreement to the request would be appreciated. Since Bill was on his way out to Sandwich in a few hours, he would take the letter with him and let Helen know that he was more than willing to usher. As always, Steve lined up just the right tux for Bill, at just the right price and Bill was quite the sight as he made the drive out to Sandwich that Saturday. The wedding was not only enjoyable for Bill, but it gave him a chance to meet a lot of Helen's friends and extended family. He met Ada from the roller rink again and she told him how the town had been buzzing about Helen's new beau from Aurora. Helen either didn't know this, or she didn't think Bill needed to. Helen looked beautiful in her bridesmaid's dress, and Bill was proud to be a part of something so special to the Cochran family.

The following week, Bill received a phone call from Ossie Federspiel regarding the upcoming practices and try-outs for the Clippers 1941 team. Bill told Ossie that he had been thinking about whether or not to play again this year, as he was training to be an HVAC technician and wasn't sure if he should invest his time in football. For the first time in his life, there was at least a possibility that he might be thinking about settling down someday, and he had seen quite a few guys carried off the field with serious injuries. Bill decided to think about it for another week, and when the Clippers arrived at Hurd's Island for practice, Bill Bennett wasn't there. He had decided to retire from football. Bill was able to focus more of his time and attention toward other parts of his life. Work and Helen were his priorities.

Bill learned something that any man who has ever dated a woman from Sandwich, Illinois, knows; when the Sandwich Fair opens the week after Labor Day, everyone goes. The Sandwich Fair, or DeKalb County Fair, is the biggest event in or around Sandwich every year and had been for as long as anyone could remember. Beginning the Wednesday after Labor Day, farmers, merchants, politicians, musicians, daredevils, thrill seekers, bakers and the curious of all ages head for the year's most significant social event. Helen had been looking forward to taking Bill to the fair since this was a great way to meet just about everyone she knew, all in the same place. Wally and Carrie Cochran were both heavily involved in the fair and Wally had official responsibilities as the mayor. Bill pulled up to the Cochran place and parked near the kitchen door along DeKalb Street and Helen met him on the porch, as she was expecting him. Carrie told them that she would be at the Arts and Crafts building later if they wanted to find her. The key, on a Saturday, was to get there early since by 5 p.m. the parking line would get pretty long.

The fairgrounds were beautifully kept and the sound of music, machinery, tractor engines, and excited fairgoers combined to create a festive atmosphere. The various smells of the foods cooking were the best advertisement that any vendor could ask for. Every kind of grilled and fried meat you could imagine, combined with doughnuts, elephant ears, cotton candy and corn on the cob gave most of the fairgrounds the smell of a restaurant. Bill noticed that the appetizing smells dissipated quickly as they approached the livestock areas. As exciting as the Midway was with the games, rides, crowds, and food, the agricultural displays and 4H projects were far more interesting and Bill and Helen spent several hours looking at the farm animals. Helen introduced Bill to quite a few farm families that she had known most of her life. Bill had picked up a little bit of farm knowledge from his brother-in-law, Linc, as he had been out to their place quite a few times to lend a hand when it was needed. Life in the country and life in a small town held a lot of attraction for Bill, as he had always been drawn to people who were honest, hardworking and found satisfaction in the simple things in life. As Bill thought about the possibilities for his future, he could see himself living in the city or the country, as both had their benefits. The cool evening spent at the fair was about as enjoyable an evening as one could ask for, and Bill learned a lot about what growing up in Sandwich had been like for Helen and her sister Phyllis. Since he had met Helen, the two had made an occasional trip to skate at the Fairway Skating Palace, so Bill was quite surprised when he received a phone call from Helen a few weeks later to inform him that the skating rink had burned. Being nearly destroyed, it would probably be next summer before it could be rebuilt and reopened. Bill wondered what all those young people from Sandwich would do with their spare time.

Bob Nix had been impressed with Bob Stoner's progress in the Navy and was convinced, himself, that war was inevitable. He stopped by the Bennett's to see Bill one evening after supper and then they both rode over to Bud's house for a visit. Bob told them both that he had joined the Navy and was due to report to Great Lakes on November 12th. The gang was down to just Bill and Bud now and Bill asked Bud when he was joining the Navy, as a joke. Of course, Bud had a wife now and joining anything but a good company was not on his agenda. Bob Nix had no intention of flying in the Navy; he just wanted a desk job.

Margaret Stoner called Jessie to tell her that her son, Bob, would be home on leave again in a few weeks. A lot of things had changed in Bill's life in the last six months, just as they had for Bob. Bob had now become a United States Naval Aviation Flight Instructor and was promoted to the rank of Lieutenant, Junior Grade. Bob had described in his letters to Bill, George and the guys, that his office was now a 450-horsepower Navy SNJ aircraft. Pensacola was the perfect place for naval aviation training as most of their flight time was over the ocean interacting with ships in both offensive and defensive roles. Bob's favorite aspect of flight instruction was air-to-air combat and the mock dogfights that were staged. Bob was now interacting with high-ranking officers and there were plenty of perks that went with the job. Bob's favorite perk was the assignment of his very own SNJ and the ability to fly it when he needed to travel on Navy business. Bill was looking forward to introducing Helen to Bob and Marijane, if they all had the chance to get together when he came home on leave.

When Bob did get home, Sam and Margaret threw a little party at 211 S. Fourth Street and Bill invited Helen to come along. Meeting all of the Stoners was the only way she would understand why Bill thought so highly of them.

Bill privately shared the tragic story of Eleanor's death with Helen, beforehand, just so she would understand and possibly avoid asking any awkward questions. Even though two years had passed and Helen had not known Eleanor, hearing the story was saddening, and her heart went out to Margaret. She also needed to know who Richard Turner was, since he had sold the house on Grant Place and moved in with the Stoners after Eleanor's death. As far as the Stoner family was concerned, Richard was as much a part of the family as any other Stoner sibling. Harley, Dex and Richard seemed inseparable. Since Bill didn't have the option of a county fair, Helen would meet most of his friends at dinner parties, football games and church services. The evening was wonderful as Helen got to meet Bob and Marijane. They had quite a bit in common since all three studied Commerce in college. Helen was very impressed with Bob's enthusiasm for his flying and the Navy. She later told Bill that he had not exaggerated on his assessment of Bob's intelligence. They both figured that Bob Stoner would end up being an Admiral. Both families were excited about the upcoming holidays and the prospects of the family gatherings at Christmas and the annual Stoner/Bennett New Year's celebration. Bob would do everything he could to get home for Christmas, and Marijane would make sure that he tried. Helen was very impressed by the Stoner family. Bill and Bob shook hands and exchanged a bear hug on the front porch as Bill told Bob to be careful up there. Bob said he would see Bill again at Christmas.

25. The Winds of War

The weather was holding out as temperatures were in the upper 40s daily. Not bad for the first week of December, 1941. There had been snow on the ground by this time in many recent years. Bill made a routine of reading the newspapers after work and then helping Jessie with whatever she needed done. Jessie, in turn, tried to get everything handled so that she could tell Bill to go ahead and relax after work instead of getting involved with kitchen work. The papers were filled with stories about the hostilities in Europe and it seemed inevitable that the United States would get involved against Hitler's Germany at some point. Bill noticed in the Thursday, December 4th *Chicago Tribune* that President Roosevelt had plans drawn up to draft as many as 15 million men in the event that America had to take up arms against Germany. The size of the possible mobilization was inconceivable. There were still many experts who were very concerned about the Empire of Japan, although Japan seemed very interested in avoiding war with the United States and was sending envoys to meet Secretary of State Cordell Hull in Washington. There was also an interesting article about scientists deciding it was best to shorten the standard clothespin by a half inch. The world would never be the same on many levels. There was also a nice article about a blind terrier that walked off the open end of the Halsted Street North River Bridge in Chicago. The poor dog couldn't get out of the river because of the walls along the bank. The bridge operator asked another fellow to hold onto his legs and lower him down the wall to pull the little pooch to safety. Now, there was a story that would leave you feeling good about the world in which you live. Bill's attention was drawn to a box at the bottom of the page that said, "Only 18 Shopping Days 'til Christmas!" Just above that was a small story, "Engineers Award Medal to Garand Rifle Inventor." NY Dec. 3rd (AP) "For inventing the Garand Semiautomatic Rifle, John C. Garand of Springfield, Massachusetts, tonight received the Holley Medal of the American Society of Mechanical Engineers." That must be some wonderful rifle. At any rate, Bill knew that he had better get going with his Christmas shopping.

December 7th, 1941. Bill taught his Sunday school class, as usual, and enjoyed Reverend Dibble's sermon during the worship service. Jessie made sandwiches after church and the Bennetts were relaxing and reading while Steve was listening to the radio. At 1:15 p.m., Steve stood next to the radio and yelled for everyone to listen. There was a "special news bulletin" interrupting the regular programming. Bill and Al had been in the kitchen and walked out to the family room. "Washington has announced that Naval and Air Forces from the Empire of Japan have attacked the U.S. Navy fleet at the port of Pearl Harbor in the Hawaiian Islands. There are reports of U.S. ships ablaze and the loss of many American lives." The announcer stated that they would stay with the story and would report more as details emerged. The reports explained that the U.S. Fleet had not been alarmed or ready for the attack when it came at about 8 a.m., Hawaiian time. Many sailors and airmen had just been waking up on Sunday morning. The first thing Bill thought of was that Bob Stoner had been right about the Navy being more concerned about Japan than Germany. Apparently, there had been good reason for that. Reports said that hundreds of Japanese planes had participated in the air raid and they had probably been launched from several aircraft carriers at sea. There were already reports of half-sunken U.S. battleships burning at Pearl Harbor and hundreds of U.S. aircraft had been destroyed. The irony of the attack was that the Japanese had requested "peace talks" with the United States. Bill had just read in the paper that Japanese Admiral Nomura and Envoy Saburo Kurusu were actually in Washington D.C. discussing peace with Cordell Hull. The entire visit by the Japanese now seemed to be part of the surprise attack. The phone rang and Marian announced that it was Sam Stoner wanting to talk to Steve. Steve took the phone in the front hall and Bill could hear him talking about the Japanese and what this meant for America, and closer to home, what it meant for Lieutenant Bob Stoner.

The Bennett phone was ringing off the hook all afternoon. Everybody in America was in shock and calling friends and family. As more information came in about the attack, it was estimated that the number of dead would end up being in the thousands. The thought of servicemen being killed in their beds, or while on deck attending a church service, began to make Americans' blood boil. By the time evening rolled around, the Bennetts all agreed that this would mean the U.S. would be going to war with at least Japan, and probably Germany as well. Bill phoned Helen and she said that her dad had been cussing at the Japanese all afternoon. She said the attack was shocking to her and she felt terrible for the thousands of families that would be getting the word they had just lost a loved one. That night, as Bill and Al turned out the light, their discussion was brief and somber. They both knew that the world had changed today, and it would probably never be the same.

26. Commitment

Monday, December 8th, 1941. As Bill came out of the bathroom drying his hair the next morning, he could smell bacon and coffee and hear the radio down in the family room. The reports of the Pearl Harbor attack had been updated and corrected overnight and Steve and Jessie were already hearing some reports for the second time. As the Bennetts tried to go through their normal morning routines, they were all unusually silent as the radio held their attention. It seemed now that about 2,000 Americans had been killed and quite a few of them were civilians. One report focused on the Japanese envoys, Kurusu and Nomura, who apparently were part of the whole surprise attack plan. Steve blurted out that these Japanese were dirty, filthy subhumans for what they did and he hoped that the U.S. would show them a thing or two. President Roosevelt was scheduled to address the nation later in the day, and it was hard to imagine anyone not making plans to listen. There was a lot of talk of the need for Americans to pull together and do their part. Bill pulled his lunch bucket from the pantry and set it on the kitchen counter top. He made a ham sandwich, wrapped a few chocolate chip cookies in wax paper and dropped in a banana and an apple. He gave Jessie a hug and a kiss and said goodbye to his dad and Marian. Bill didn't say so much, but he had always hated it when people took advantage of others. He fumed inside when he thought about what these Japanese had done to the sleeping and unsuspecting sailors at Pearl Harbor.

Bill jumped off the bus at Simms and Spencer and made his way over to the shop. On most days, there were a couple of guys that had come in early and machines would already be running. As Bill came in the door, he saw Don Glossop talking with three employees in front of his office door. Bill couldn't hear exactly what was being said, but he could tell by the sound of Don's voice that he was not happy. At first, Bill thought that Don was cross about something they may have screwed up, but Don seemed to be trying to reason with them. Bill went about his business and set his lunch bucket under his work bench, where he had been testing AC compressors last Friday. Bill signed in on the time sheet and pulled some tools out of the bench drawer. Don waved his hand over his head and turned and went into the office. The guys went to their benches and picked up some things, then turned and walked out of the shop. Bill heard from Marvin Settles that these three co-workers had gone downtown to join the Army. That's why Don was so upset. He had work scheduled with no one to do it. About eight o'clock, two more employees were talking to Don by the office and a very similar exchange was taking place. Bill could not hear anything this time, as machines were running and there was some sheet metal work in progress. As the other guys walked out the door, Bill knew that he could not just work on air conditioners while the Japanese were killing Americans, and apparently, trying to take over the world with Adolf Hitler. During the break about 9:30 the whole conversation was about Pearl Harbor, the Japanese, and how it seemed that everyone in America was in line to join the service. Bill finished his banana and set the lunch bucket back beneath his bench. As he worked, he silently prayed and asked the Lord to guide him in his thinking and direct him in the right way. The thought that Bill needed to "do his part" remained heavy on his mind and he just couldn't shake it. At 10:15, Bill shut off the testing equipment he was using, turned off the light above his bench, picked up his lunch bucket and headed for Don's door. Before he reached the door, Don came out to the shop with his clipboard in hand and stopped dead in his tracks. "Oh, no! Bennett! Not you too!" he lamented. Bill told Don that he was sorry to do this to him and he thanked him for everything he had done. "I just want to do my part in this," Bill explained. Don replied, "If I thought I could talk you out of this, I would." Bill told Don that he would let him know how things went. Bill crossed Simms Street and headed for home on foot. He didn't want to head downtown with his lunch box, so he set it by the side of the front porch on the way past the house and hoped that Jessie didn't see him. He caught the Fourth Street bus for downtown, the same bus that Steve took to work every day, and thought that he would at least see what the deal was for joining the Army.

As the bus came down the hill toward Broadway, Bill noticed that it was unusually crowded downtown for a Monday morning. When he arrived at the Army Office in the Federal Building, he was surprised that there were only a few people milling around in the hallway. When he got to the office door he saw the reason. A sign in the window said that recruiting activities had been moved to the Aurora YMCA building on Lasalle Street. No problem there, just about four blocks away. As Bill turned the corner on Lasalle Street, he couldn't believe his eyes, as the recruiting line went down the street and around the corner. As he walked past the line, Bill noticed dozens of guys that he knew over the years and many of them said, "Hey Bill"" as he walked past. Finding the end of the line, he wondered how long this could possibly take and how the Army was going to get to everyone in line before dark. As he waited for about an hour, he realized how cold 38 degrees could get when you were just standing there. Some of the guys would get out of line and make a "coffee run," returning with as many cups as they could carry. Dick Sheble came from the direction of the YMCA and saw Bill in line. He came over to Bill and they exchanged pleasantries. Dick got close to Bill, as if he had a secret, and told him that he overheard two guys talking, and apparently there was no line over at the Marine Corps Recruiting Office, so guys could get right in and right out. Dick was headed over there and wanted to know if Bill wanted to check into it.

Bill decided that anything was more promising than this two-block-long line, and headed down to the Post Office/Federal Building on Holbrook Street with Dick. The rumor was right as there were about six guys in line at the U.S.M.C. office. About 15 minutes later, Bill was handed a clipboard and a government fountain pen and told to fill out the form. All the usual things: date of birth, school history, address, physical condition, etc. Next, Bill was called into a very small office and a Corporal "Something or Other," went over the options. If the Marines decided that they would take Bill, there were two possibilities: One, the regular U.S.M.C.; he would have to join for four years straight up. If the war only lasted six months, too bad; you were in for four years. Two, the U.S.M.C. Reserves; he would have to join for the duration of the war plus six months. If the war lasted six months, then you went home within a year; if the war lasted 10 years, too bad. Bill was sure that the war would be short and sweet, so he went for the duration, plus six months. He figured that the U.S. would work the Japanese over quickly and everyone would get back to life as usual. Bill read over the agreement, signed and dated it. The corporal told him that he had made a good decision joining the Marine Corps. He also told Bill that should he get into a "hot spot," there were no better fighting men than the Marines. Bill was hoping that he would find some support role that would keep him away from any "hot spots." As Bill walked with Dick Sheble over to River Street for the North Avenue bus, he realized that he really knew very little about what the Marines actually do.

27. The Wonder City

As Bill rode the bus back to the corner of Simms and Fourth Street, he started to think about what he had just done. Sure, he was going to do his part, whatever that might entail, but he was now faced with telling his family and also telling Helen. He feared that telling Jessie would be the worst of it. Helen was young and strong and had a great head on her shoulders. She would be reasonable. Jessie, on the other hand, was Bill's mother and he was her youngest, her baby. There is no possible way that a mother could not get upset when she finds out that her baby is leaving home, and of all places, headed for war.

Bill didn't have to wait very long to find out what their reactions would be. At dinner time, the Bennetts were bantering about the news from Pearl Harbor, the Philippines, and places no one had ever heard of, like Guam and Wake Island. Bill asked to have everyone's attention for a minute and all eyes went to him, as though there could only be one reason for the request. Bill told them that he had taken off from work early and joined the Marine Corps. He looked at Jessie and knew that his words were tearing her heart out. He hugged her with his best heart-felt hug and he could feel her starting to tremble. Questions started coming. "What? When do you have to report?" And Al's topper of all questions: "Are you nuts?" Al seemed to be the only Bennett that actually had some idea about what United States Marines did. Right now, there were quite a few Marines on Guam and Wake Island who wished that they were somewhere else. Bill explained that he didn't care about being drafted or not, he felt it was his duty to defend his country. In his soul, Bill knew that he had to pull his weight and do his part. It was the way he was raised and it was, in effect, Bill Bennett. Steve read a small editorial at the top of the front page of today's *Tribune*: "We All Have Only One Task. War has been forced on America by a clique of insane Japanese militarists who apparently see the desperate conflict into which they have led their country as the only thing that prolongs their power. Thus, the thing that we all feared, the thing that so many of us have worked with all of our hearts to avert, has happened. That is all that counts. It has happened. America faces war through no volition of any American. Recriminations are useless and we doubt that they will be indulged in; certainly not by us. All that matters today is that we are in the war and our nation must face this simple fact. All of us, from this day forth, have only one task. That is to strike with all of our might to preserve and protect the American freedom that we all hold dear." Bill could not have described his feelings over the matter as well as this editor had done.

As Bill drove the car towards Sandwich, he went over and over how he was going to tell Helen that he had joined the Marine Corps today. The truth was there was no good way to tell her. Bill passed the boarded-up hulk of the Fairway Skating Palace and turned right at the giant root beer barrel, now closed for the season. The car bounced over the railroad tracks and he became nervous as he pulled onto the gravel in front of the Cochran's kitchen door. Helen was very happy to see Bill and he said hello to Wally and Carrie. The news of the Japanese attacks and the declaration of war had changed everyone within a few hours, and the atmosphere in the Cochran house was no exception. Bill asked Helen if he could take her for a walk and she retrieved her coat with a knowing look. What could be so important that Bill would want to take a walk in the dark with it being so cold outside? Once outside, they walked a few feet towards the driveway and Bill stopped and warned Helen that there was no good way to say this. With her prepared, he explained that he had joined the Marines earlier in the day. He explained that he had to do his part and that he had no will to be separated from her or the rest of his family and friends. Helen understood. There had been dozens of young men from Sandwich and Plano signing up today as well, and Wally had been involved with handling the logistics of the process. Bill told Helen that he had opted for the "duration" over the four years and that he hoped it would all be over soon, so that he could get back. At the time, he had no idea when he would have to leave for training, but it wouldn't be long. Bill made it clear that he wanted to come home to Helen and he asked her if she would wait for him. She told Bill that he didn't even have to ask that question as the two embraced in the cold night air. As Helen turned back toward the house, Bill saw her wiping tears from her eyes by the light from the porch. The Japanese had already impacted millions of lives across the world in the past 48 hours, and the heartaches were only beginning.

Tuesday morning, Bill got up and went to work as normal and Don was glad to see him. Bill explained that he had joined the Marines but did not know when he would have to leave. They agreed that Bill would work until that day arrived. This would keep money coming in for Bill and allow Don to get the work out that he had already contracted. Don had just lost half of his crew to enlistment and was scrambling to try and hire more workers to keep up on his work load. Unknown to most of his men, Don had been trying to enlist in the Air Corps, as he was an experienced pilot with single and twin-engine planes. He was also a talented aviation mechanic. Don was frustrated by the fact that at 36, he was one lousy year too old to join. In the meantime, word traveled fast about Bill's enlistment. Bill's main concern was for his girls, Jessie and Helen. His absence would probably affect these two the most. Bill also called Reverend Paul Dibble and asked if he could stop by his office and talk to him. Paul was pleased to have some time with Bill. Bill went over his decision with Paul and explained his feelings, as well as his remorse for hurting his family with the news. Paul explained that there was going to be "dirty work" with this war, that had to be done, and everyone was going to sacrifice. Bill would be sacrificing his former life-style and placing his life in possible danger. The folks at home that could not serve in the military would be sacrificing by missing their loved ones who served. He framed for Bill that his decision to enlist was part of a higher call in his life and that it was undoubtedly the Lord's will that men defend their country at this time. Bill told Paul that he did not want to kill people and that he hated what the Japanese had done, but didn't hate the Japanese. Paul told Bill that the Japanese were loved by God, and that the Japanese soldiers were doing as they were ordered. Seeing it this way helped reassure Bill that he was doing the right thing. Paul prayed with Bill and asked the Lord to watch over him on his mission with the Marines and to keep him safe in the coming days. He asked that Bill be allowed to return home safely after his service was no longer needed. Paul told Bill that he was proud of him for what he was doing.

Bill was notified by mail that he was required to return to the U.S.M.C. office for a physical that would determine his acceptance into the Corps. When he arrived at the office, several guys were coming out the door and there were several more waiting inside. Bill reported to the corporal at the desk and he was handed another clipboard with a form to fill out and a pen. Bill was then assigned to three other fellows and told they would be called in order. The group was summoned to a private area and told to completely undress. There were three doctors all working together to get the physical exams done as quickly as possible. The first requirement was the eye test. Covering one eye and then the other, Bill read the chart quickly and accurately. He felt a little strange having an eye exam while being naked, but he realized that the U.S.M.C. would most certainly be the end of any privacy that he once had. The doctor checked Bill over like he was scrutinizing the purchase of a horse. Height: 6 feet; weight: 187 pounds; eyes: blue; hair: dark brown; vision: 20/20. There was nothing to check that went unchecked that morning and Bill's file was stamped "PASSED" and the process was continued.

Bill was given paperwork notifying him to report to "Central Procurement Division, Lieutenant Colonel Chester L. Pordney, Room 753, U.S. Courthouse Building, Chicago, Illinois, at 10 a.m. on January 7th, 1942." He was to bring a change of socks, underwear and a toothbrush. He had three weeks to wrap up his life in Aurora. Bill kept the outlook positive for his friends and family and used phrases like "when I get back" or "until I get back." Some people thought that Bill would get to come home after basic training, but no one knew for certain. Bill made sure that little Bobby had access to anything he would like to play with while he was away. Christmas was especially meaningful for all this year, as no one knew when Bill would be back for another Christmas. Don Glossop had a party at the shop for all of the employees, their wives and children. Everyone wished Bill well with his future in the Marines.

Bill enjoyed selecting presents more than ever and he wanted to get each Bennett the perfect gift. Privately, this was the first time in Bill's life where he had thoughts that this could be the last Christmas or the last time he saw some of the people he loved. He determined to keep up a positive front no matter what. He didn't want to cause any more emotional distress.

Christmas came and it was wonderful. The services at Fourth Street Methodist were spot on for families that now had loved ones leaving for the service. Bill absorbed family time at the Bennett's and he made sure that he asked each Bennett, individually, to please take care of Helen in any way possible while he was away. The Cochrans all visited the Bennett's house for Christmas dinner. Helen came back to the Bennett's for the traditional Stoner-Bennett News Year's Eve celebration and they all had a great time, despite the absence of Bob Stoner. His leave had been canceled due to the need to train pilots.

As the final week came, Bill found himself driving past numerous places in town just to see them one last time before he left. He went past East High and the snow-covered Athletic Field. He drove down Maple Avenue and recalled the old days and the play group that had accepted Bob Stoner when he moved to Aurora. He remembered George and Maude Troll and those early years when he referred to her as "Ma Troll." Everywhere he looked in Aurora, there were fond memories, and he thanked God for every one of them. Bill prayed more than ever, as he was faced with uncertainty and the possible danger that awaited him. He felt peace from the Lord, that even if his life ended soon, he had lived a remarkable life. He knew from the promises of Jesus that should he die, he would be present with the Lord in eternity. These were the promises and the truths that would have to get him through whatever lay ahead.

January 4th, 1942. Steve and Jessie held an "open house" for Bill on Sunday, January 4th. This would be Bill's last Sunday in Aurora for quite some time. Reverend Dibble made an announcement at the 4th Street service and invited the entire church. Although there were many of Bill's friends that could not attend, many did. The Bennett house was filled for the entire afternoon. Helen was there, alongside Bill, as they welcomed car loads of friends and neighbors, and many who walked to the Bennett's. The church family was well represented, as well as football and basketball team mates. The Pfrangle family attended, as well as the "West Side" Bennetts, the Dix family, the McElroys, Mr. and Mrs. Nix and Reverend Dibble with his wife and children. All of the Stoners, minus Bob, stopped by and Dexter and Harley were teasing Bill about getting his hair "buzzed off," and were generally hilarious as usual. Harley and his new wife, Betty, along with Dick Turner, had driven over with Dexter and Helen Stoner. George Troll came by and brought his girlfriend, Betty Gates. Bill teased Betty and asked her when they were going to get married, mostly to put George on the spot. As food was set out for the occasion, Reverend Dibble asked all to join in prayer and he led them in asking for protection over Bill and for the Bennetts while Bill was away.

Don Glossop and his wife Helen visited and they brought their daughter Carol June along. She had grown quite fond of Bill during the months that he worked for Don and she was a bit upset that he was going away. She was not fully able to understand why Bill had to go away to war, but she had already been impacted by the war in her own small way. Her birthday was December 8th and her parents had planned her fifth birthday party for December 7th. Due to the Pearl Harbor attack and the turmoil that impacted everyone, they had to cancel the party. Carol didn't know who the Japanese were, but she was pretty upset with them. Helen Glossop told Bill that Carol June had something for him and Carol shyly stepped forward and held out a small white envelope. Carol was as bright a five-year-old as any of them had seen, as her brothers already had taught her to read and write. She looked up at Bill with her dark green eyes and said that she had made something for him. The envelope had been handmade by Carol with great care. She had taken a sheet of her dad's letterhead from the office, folded it into an envelope and hand stitched it together with white thread from her mother's sewing kit. On the outside it said, "To Bill," in pencil. Bill got down on one knee and thanked Carol for the card. He carefully opened it and pulled two little pieces of lined paper from inside. The first piece said, "Bill, I don't want you to go away, you are my boyfriend. You are always nice to me." The second one said, "Here is my address so that you can write me a letter, 806 S. Spencer, Aurora." As Bill read the notes, Carol started to cry and said that she didn't want Bill to go away. Bill gave her a hug as he could hardly hold back the tears himself. He told Carol June that he would write to her and that he would come back as soon as he could. Most of those who saw what Carol had made for Bill were touched.

Jessie handed Bill a Western Union telegram that had been delivered from Grandma Phrangle in Los Angeles. The telegram read, "BILL, SORRY TO SEE YOU GO. HAVE FUN, SALUTE, RELAX. WILL BE PRAYING FOR YOU. AL, GIVE BILL FIVE BUCKS." Bill was very grateful that he had so many well-wishers. Throughout the afternoon, about 100 people stopped to visit. Aside from the ladies being present, many of the men encouraged Bill to give the Japanese some grief. Bob Nix's dad asked Bill to, "Get a few Japanese for me." Bill replied politely that he would do his best. Bob Bennett's ex-wife, Bess, stopped by with Bobby and Bill took Bobby upstairs and told him that he was moving some things around so that Bobby could sleep in Uncle Bill's bed while he was away. Bill told Bobby that he could use his football to play with Wayne and Dale Lipke, next door, when the weather got warmer and he told Bobby that he had some favors to ask. He asked Bobby if he would take care of Grandma while he was away, and that would mean giving her extra kisses. Bobby said he could do that. Next Bill asked if Bobby could make sure to write some letters to his Uncle Bill because he would sure be missing him while he was away. Bobby agreed again. Bill knew that he had been filling a gap in Bobby's life, and that was going to be one of the most painful parts of leaving for the Marines. Bill wanted Bobby to shake hands on the deal and he didn't want any old limp fish handshake either. The two shook hands and Bill acted as though Bobby was crushing his hand, to make Bobby laugh. They went back downstairs where the Bennett house sounded like an auction barn with all the talking and the card games that had developed at the dining room table. Steve Bennett stood in the living room and talked with Wally Cochran who had driven in from Sandwich. Wally had developed a fondness for Bill and he was proud of him for joining up to go give the Japanese what they deserved. The "open house" was a huge success and Bill felt blessed to have had such an outpouring of sentiment from so many loved ones.

Bill had dinner with the Cochrans in Sandwich on Tuesday, January 6th. It was there, on the side of the house along DeKalb Street, that he said his goodbye to Helen. Wally and Carrie had been so nice in voicing their concern for Bill and he had felt as though they were saying goodbye to their own son. Bill went out to start the car and came back inside. The temperature had dropped to near zero and would be -10 by morning. Helen put on her coat to come outside with Bill. Neither of them wanted to say goodbye, as it would be left open ended with no reunion in sight. Finally, the inevitable came as the cold wind stung their faces and hands. So, with promises to write and sweet things said, their arms extended until their fingertips separated and Bill turned for the car door. As he pulled forward, his last view of Helen would be of her waving from the light of the side porch. As Bill's tail lights turned the corner and went out of sight, Helen went inside and made her way straight upstairs for her room as to hide the tears from Wally and Carrie. In Bill's mind, he formed a determination to return to that porch, and he would think of it often.

Bill turned down the alley off Fourth Street and then pulled into the crunching gravel behind 454 Simms. The whole family was together as Jean and Linc had come over to say goodbye. There seemed to be an air of unbelief that this would be the last time this close-knit family would be together for quite some time; possibly, for the last time. As Bill and Al talked in the darkness of their room, Bill went over all the things he wanted Al to take care of, mostly regarding mom and Helen. Al reassured Bill that everything here was going to be fine and he wanted Bill to focus on being a good Marine and finding a good "non-combat" position that would keep him out of the front lines. Al prayed with Bill in the darkness and Bill had a sense that he would indeed be watched over while he was gone.

January 7th, 1942. All too soon, the alarm clock jolted Bill and Al from their dreams and Bill was now on a schedule that would last indefinitely. Bill would be catching the 7:30 train to Chicago from the Aurora Station. Al had taken the day off from Pillsbury so that he and Marian could come with Steve and Jessie to say goodbye. Bill shaved in front of the bathroom mirror and then made sure that all of his things were out of the way and out of the bathroom. He dressed in the clothes he had set out before he went to sleep and put his tooth brush, socks and underwear into a bag that he would carry in his pants pocket. Bill stepped back into his room and gave it a quick look to make sure he had everything ready for his long absence. Bobby could sleep in here now while he was away. Bill had a copy of the January edition of *The Upper Room* devotional booklet and a small New Testament lying on the nightstand. He picked them up and dropped them into his pants pocket. Jessie had scrambled eggs, bacon, coffee and toast underway when Bill came down the front stairs. The smell alone would have been enough to get Bill out of bed. Bill paused near the bottom of the stairs and looked at the stained-glass window just above the stair landing. He remembered how beautiful it had been the first time he saw it when they moved there. The morning sun lit the stained glass with heavenly colors through the yellow and blue eye-shaped glass. Bill sat on the landing and tied his shoes, then headed into the dining room.

Steve's chair slid back on the heart-pine floor as Bill walked into the room. The *Tribune* lay on the table with the headline, "We'll Do War Job; Industry." Bill thought that it was heartening knowing that Americans were at least determined to get the military the supplies they would need. Jessie insisted that he sit at the table and she brought out breakfast and set it in front of him. With the temperatures being -10 degrees, Bill recommended that Al just drop him at the station. Steve said that was nonsense, as they would all come out to the platform with him. Bill enjoyed the breakfast and carried his plate into the kitchen. He rinsed the plate and set it in the sink for later. He paused to give Jessie a very strong hug as if to apologize for the pain he was causing her by leaving. Jessie just wanted to savor the hug there in her kitchen, as she knew she would soon be longing to hug her baby without the possibility of doing so. Marian was putting some things away in the kitchen and she came over for the next hug. She told Bill that she would miss her baby brother. Bill smiled and said that he was sure going miss his "Pete." Al came in from warming the car and said that it barely started. He thought they might have had to catch the bus. Bill would have to wear a fall jacket even though it was brutally cold outside. There was no need for a winter coat where he was going and he had to travel light. Steve came into the kitchen and Jessie wanted to pause for a minute for prayer. She praised the Lord for His goodness to the Bennetts over the years and proclaimed His great love and forgiveness that He had supplied. She asked Him to watch over Bill wherever he would go and asked that He would provide peace in their hearts. She asked the Lord to protect our men and women, who would now be in harm's way. Jessie paused in her prayer and Steve continued; then Al, Marian and Bill. Bill echoed the things that had already been said, but asked the Lord to watch over and protect his loved ones that he was leaving behind, and ended with "Amen." He zipped the jacket and stashed the bag with his minimal supplies into the pocket. Together, the five Bennetts loaded into the old Ford and the tires crunched their way down the alley to Fourth Street.

Al drove, with Marian in the front, as Bill sat between Steve and Jessie in the back seat. Al drove past Fourth Street Methodist and Bill turned his head to get one last look. Al turned onto North Avenue and then right onto Broadway and parked in the station lot. Once inside, Bill went to the ticket window and showed the clerk the U.S.M.C. paperwork that would be his train ticket. They stamped his form and told him to go down the stairs and out to platform 2 for the 7:30 to Union Station in Chicago. The Bennetts sat on the waiting benches for about 10 minutes, as waiting outside would not be the least bit enjoyable. Bill sat with his arm around Jessie's shoulder as she told him to be careful for at least the tenth time this morning. They made their way onto platform 2 and the train came in from the west and squealed to a stop. The doors opened and passengers unloaded onto the platform. Bill hugged Al, Marian, Steve and finally Jessie, one last time. Jessie tried not to cry, but it was just more than she could bear. Bill told her not to cry because her face would freeze. He promised that he would write while on the train on the way to San Diego, and he promised that he would visit Grandma Pfrangle in Los Angeles, as soon as it was possible. Bill climbed the stairs and leaned out for one last wave before finding a window seat on the platform side. He waved through the window and the Bennetts wildly waved back. The train jolted forward and started to roll and the Bennetts started to walk along with the train on their way back to the underground stairs. Bill waved until they fell out of sight and he turned to look forward. The train crossed the bridges over Fox Street and Main Street and Bill saw the downtown with plumes of steam coming from every building in the arctic air. As the train passed the roundhouse and then through the Burlington Yards, the tracks curved beneath the Ohio Street Bridge and the Eola Yards lay ahead. Bill looked back to what little he could see of Aurora, and he wondered if he would ever see it again. The word "wonder" stood out in his mind for some reason and he decided to refer to Aurora as "The Wonder City," while he was away.

The Number 2 Platform at the old Aurora Train Station from which Bill Bennett departed for the Marine Corps on January 7th, 1942. It was 10 degrees below zero.

(Aurora Historical Society Photo)

28. The Corps

Bill stepped off the train at Union Station in Chicago and he made his way through the river of people in front of him. Inside the huge terminal, iron supports rose to the arched ceiling that was 60 or 70 feet above the floor. Bill needed to find the sign that read "U.S.M.C. Arrivals," and he located it near a waiting area in one of the corners. There was a Marine officer with a clipboard in hand and Bill announced himself to the officer. The Marine looked at his list and said, "From Aurora?" Bill was affirmative and the officer told him that they would be waiting here until the trains from Milwaukee, St. Paul and St. Louis arrived. Bill could either have a seat or look around for a while. If he chose to walk around, he should not leave the terminal building. Bill walked the length of the room in amazement at the size of the structure and the number of people moving through it. Then he headed back for the meeting area and found a seat in between two other recruits on a bench. Bill introduced himself and the fellow on the right said he was Bob Weir from Libertyville and the fellow on the left said he was Al Swanson from Chicago. They had both enlisted on December 8th for the same reason that Bill had. As they waited for the other recruits to assemble, they got to know each other on all of the basics. Bob's dad worked for the railroad and was the Freight Coordinator at Crystal Lake, Illinois. Al's whole first name was Alfred and he grew up with his mom at 2654 N. Burling in Chicago. He was a genuine city kid. Bill met Joe Sobolewski, also from Chicago, and Al Slowinski from Steven's Point, Wisconsin. Slowinski had just spent the night in Milwaukee with a bunch of recruits, so he had been in the Corps almost 24 hours.

Several trains rolled into the station within 30 minutes of each other and hundreds of out of state Marines began to crowd the meeting area. The Marine officers began grouping the guys in preparation for loading buses to drive them about six blocks east to the U.S. Courthouse Building. There were now about 200 recruits and they moved outside to load onto the buses. Bill stayed with Al Swanson and Bob Weir and they ended up on the same bus. It had only taken Bill 10 minutes to locate some new buddies. The Chicago city streets were ridiculously busy as the bus pushed its way over to the courthouse. They probably could have walked the six blocks faster than the bus ride, but it was still -1° outside and the wind was whipping. The buses pulled up in front of a fantastic building that looked like the state capitol, complete with a huge dome in the center. The recruits marched inside and began to form lines for roll call. Once they all checked in, they assembled in a huge hall and were addressed and welcomed by Lieutenant Colonel Chester L. Pordney, who was the commander of the Central Procurement Division. Colonel Pordney led the recruits in the Oath of Enlistment. *"I, William Bennett, do solemnly swear that I will support and defend the Constitution of the United States against all enemies, foreign and domestic; that I will bear true faith and allegiance to the same; and that I will obey the orders of the President of the United States and the orders of the officers appointed over me, according to regulations and the Uniform Code of Military Justice. So help me God."* They were now officially in the Marine Corps and it was stressed that they act accordingly. The recruits would be assigned groups with group leaders. They would be bused to a hotel for dinner and then back to Union Station, as their train would head out at 10:30 p.m. for the Marine Recruit Depot at San Diego.

A sergeant walked up and down the lines looking the recruits over. He approached Bill and Al and told them they would be leaders of their group. They were to make sure there was no horseplay or trouble within the group and make sure they stayed together. For the trip to the hotel, they were assigned 15 other recruits. The Marine Corps had reserved dining rooms at the Hilton Hotel on South Michigan Avenue, where they would have their dinner. There was a very nice dinner set up in one of the ballrooms with roast beef and chicken. The guys joked about the wonderful amenities and thought that it was the Marine Corps strategy to make sure that most of them didn't run away on their first night in the Corps. Without any issues to speak of, the group that Bill and Al were assigned behaved themselves and everyone had a great meal. One of the Marine sergeants pulled Bill aside and handed him a list with 26 names on it. Bill would be responsible for taking roll call, making sure that no one was out of line and bring issues to the sergeant's attention during the trip out to San Diego. Bob Weir had been assigned as the leader of the entire group, so Bill would be able to report any problems to him. This was a good system as it allowed the recruits to police themselves and relieve the sergeants. The buses had them all back at Union Station by 2100 hours and the train was scheduled to leave at 2230 hours. Moving through Union

Station was very different than it had been this morning. They had all come into Chicago as individuals looking for a connection, but now they were Marines, moving as a group for the first time. Even though they were as of yet untrained, they were moving toward their mission to destroy the enemy. As the group moved through the station, civilians smiled and waved. Calls of "Give 'em hell" and "Good luck, boys" were heard.

Bill was amazed as he boarded the train. The train cars were luxurious with nicely upholstered seats and finely made woodwork and fixtures. He and Al Swanson were assigned to the same state room, which had a nice seating area that folded into a bed and a bunk bed that folded down from the wall. This was much nicer than either of them had imagined. The lounge car had tables where the guys could gather to play cards or talk together and they would be allowed to drink from the bar, but were warned that drunkenness would never be tolerated in the Corps. Some of the guys were still scurrying about when the "All aboard!" calls could be heard. The train doors were pulled shut and shortly after, the jolt signified the beginning of the journey. There was a counter in the lounge car where you could buy all kinds of things that one might need on such a trip, so Bill made his first purchase of 10 penny post cards, so that he could keep his many promises to write home.

As Bill had thought it might, the train used the same tracks that had brought him to Chicago to head back west. As the train rolled through Aurora, Bill excitedly pointed out the landmarks. Bill could see that everything was getting along without him. Steve would be to work downtown in the morning and Jessie would be watering her violets in the dining room. He pointed out the #2 platform where he said goodbye to the Bennetts earlier that morning, and then up the hill to where his neighborhood was located. On the other side of the train was the Fox River and Hurd's Island, where Bill had practiced with the Clippers. Bill felt like it was a gift to be able to come through Aurora one last time; the Wonder City. As the train picked up speed and headed west, Bill realized that there would be one more gift on this trip, as the train would be going through Sandwich before long. Bill went over to the right side of the car and Bob and Al were ready for the sights. There was the Fairway Skating Palace on the left side with construction equipment all around it. A quick glimpse of the giant root beer barrel, then the Latham Street crossing that Bill had bumped over so many times. As the train zoomed past that crossing, he wondered what Helen was doing at that moment. The quick tour of the city and the small town that meant so much to Bill really drove home what he was leaving behind. No young man could have had a better life than Bill had; with his loving family and numerous friends, as well as the church family, school and sports teams. He had truly been blessed. Rolling out into the prairie, Bill and Al retired to their bunks and fell asleep.

Heading southwest, the train went through Kewanee, Galesburg and Stronghurst before crossing the Mississippi from Niota, Illinois, into Fort Madison, Iowa. In the morning, Bill and Al dressed and headed out to the dining car to find breakfast. Then they went back to their stateroom to read for a while. Bob Weir stopped in and he seemed to know just about everything about the railroad, as he pointed out types of cars and engines, and explained the traffic and switching as they rolled along. Joe Sobolewski and Al Slowinski stopped by and chatted away a few hours with Bill and Al. Within 24 hours, Bill had crossed paths with quite a few stand-up guys that he probably would have been buddies with had they grown up in the same town. Bill asked one of the porters how to get a post card in the mail and he was told that they would be taking mail off the train at Kansas City. All Bill had to do was give the mail to the attendant in the lounge car before Kansas City and it would be mailed straight away. The recruits milled about all over the train. Magazines were hot property as some guys even read the same articles side by side. The bar sold small bottles of alcohol for 50 cents and the hot seller was Four Hearts Whiskey. However, the bar would be closed at 10 p.m. on the last night and should anyone try to bring any bottles with them, they would be punished. The sergeant stressed the point that no one would want to begin basic training with a punishment of that type. Drink your Four Hearts, then say goodbye. The train was already past Kansas City by supper time and then card games developed all over the train. Penny poker was the big game and the Four Hearts sold out at the bar. The conductor said that they would pick more up at Wichita. Bill went back to the state room and worked on a few post cards. He wrote a separate card to his mom, dad and Helen, explaining the highlights of the trip so far. He said that he was with a swell group of guys that had been no trouble at all. He let them all know about his surprise at the amenities and the food, but he knew that this would soon change for the worse. Bill posted the cards, but the next post drop for the train would be at Wichita, Kansas.

    As Bill and Al were getting off to sleep, Bill pulled out his New Testament and *The Upper Room* booklet. Al saw what Bill was up to and asked if he could read aloud so that Al could follow along. Bill was pleased that Al was interested and a lengthy conversation ensued. Al said he thought that there was something different about Bill because he hadn't heard him using any foul language. Bill said he tried his best to honor God with his speech, but he wasn't perfect. They read *The Upper Room* and then talked about it for a while. Bill prayed and Al followed up with a short prayer. They both realized they needed to stay close to the Lord in ordinary circumstances and even more so now. Bill enjoyed having that time with Al and thought how nice it was that he had an "Al" to talk to at bedtime just like he did at home.

    The next morning dawned a beautiful day as the train was into heavy snow and vast pine forests near Flagstaff, Arizona. The meals on the train were "all you can eat" affairs and the group leaders made sure that all the guys had eaten before they did. Bill sat with Al Swanson and Bob Weir in the dining car, and after a long conversation, they went to work on their penny postcards. The train tracks were a bit rough in this area, which made writing a bit difficult and the results a bit of a mess, but it was legible. Bill reminded Jessie to have Helen over for dinner, as if she would have forgotten that in three days.

    Another night on the train and the noise from the poker games was growing a bit old. Bill and Al read together again as they had the night before, and they knew that tomorrow morning the train was due at San Diego and the Recruit Depot at 0800 hours. They wanted a good night's sleep as tomorrow was bound to be tiring.

January 10, 1942. The new Marines were rousted out of bed at 0500 while the train was still in the desert east of their destination. Everyone had time to shave and get one more "all you can eat" breakfast down before they arrived at the Recruit Depot. Bill sat with Al and Bob and they agreed that they would do everything possible to stay together once training started. As the sun came up and the train headed down the grade into San Diego, Bill and the guys could see the Pacific Ocean out in front of them. For most of the new Marines, this was their first look at the Pacific, just as it was for Bill. Southern California seemed very brown and dry to the Midwesterners, although there was no snow on the ground, and that had to be good. As the train slowly rolled into the station, there were five olive drab buses in the lot that would finish the job of getting them to the U.S.M.C. Recruit Depot. Bill remained in charge of his 26 recruits until they loaded the buses. He shouted out the names as he went down the list and everyone was there.

As Bill came down the steps from the bus, a very angry sergeant was pointing to the right and telling the recruits to line up with their toes on the line. Recruits scurried to get a place on the line. The sergeant told them to line up and shut up. Once in line, other officers with flat-brimmed hats walked up and down the lines, looking at the recruits and loudly commenting about this being the sorriest looking bunch of losers that the Corps had ever sent them. They said that with a war on they supposed the Marines would take anything that was breathing and they doubted if they could ever make United States Marines of out this sorry lot. Bill learned later that if the Chicago Bears would have gotten off the buses at the Recruit Depot, they would have heard the same degrading welcome. The remarks were meant to be intimidating. The recruits were marched into an area where they had to undress and put everything they had, including the toothbrush, into a cardboard box and put the address where they wanted it mailed on the top. The next step was a roll call where each recruit was issued their "dog tags" and told that these could not be removed under any circumstances while they were in the Marines. Bill signed a form saying that he was William Wesley Bennett and that he had received the dog tags. His new serial number was 352573 and he was officially "U.S. government property." Dozens of Marines were behind counters stacked with uniforms as the recruits shuffled past and two sets of everything was handed out. A sergeant demonstrated how the uniforms were to be worn down to every detail. The next room smelled strongly of leather and the process was similar to renting skates at the roller rink. You told the Marine what size you wanted and he gave you the closest size possible. The boots were not at all what Bill was expecting. They were a shorter split leather boot with white stitching and black rubber and rope soles. Overall, the boots looked similar to the boot part of a roller skate. The size of each pair was stamped in yellow on the instep of the sole. At this point the recruits were given grease pencils and told to put their name, rank and serial number on every item they were issued. They would be responsible for everything issued and would be punished if anything were lost.

The next building would prove to be one of the most memorable as the recruits went in one door with hair and came out the other side without hair.

Bill had watched the sheep being sheared at the fair, and the Marine "barbers" could have taken a lesson from the farmers regarding customer care. The shears were set as low as they could go and Bill rubbed his hands over the stubble on his way outside. Seeing that everyone had the same cut took some of the shock out of the make-over. At this point, it was lunch time and the recruits were treated to their first Marine Corps meal, which was in another category from the food they had been eating since Chicago. Bill took it easy on the lunch chow as he was uncertain about what they would have to do in the afternoon and didn't want to get caught having to run on a full stomach; some discipline that he had learned from the athletic years back in Aurora. After lunch, the recruits were given fiber helmets that looked something like a hunter in Africa might wear, and field gear. Each recruit was then issued a Springfield Model M1903 bolt-action .30-06 (thirty ought six) rifle. It would be some time before any of them would see any ammunition, but they were shown the proper way to carry and present the weapon. These rifles would be with them most of the time from now on and the sergeant told them that they would know this rifle better than any of their body parts within a few weeks. The recruits were now assigned Training Platoons and Bill was assigned to Platoon 55. For the time being, the recruits were housed in four-man tents that were staked over wooden floors that were built similarly to shipping pallets. Each platoon had about 65 recruits and hopefully as many bunks in the tents. After the tent assignments were situated, the first dose of reality set in as the recruits assembled on the parade grounds for physical training. Group calisthenics, consisting of jumping jacks, push-ups, sit-ups, and knee bends were completed prior to a three-mile run. As Bill had expected, there were quite a few lunches lost along the way that afternoon. After dinner, the recruits had a crash course in marching and the sergeants screamed insults as the new Marines turned into each other and presented sloppy lines. Bill watched closely as the sergeants picked people out to use as bad examples. He noticed that listening was the key to avoiding problems and blending in as much as possible would be to your advantage. Keeping your mouth shut was a must. When the Drill Instructors were instructing, any conversation noticed would result in trouble.

    The recruits were told they would be at the Recruit Depot for four days and then assigned to Camp San Louis Obispo, 14 miles away. While at the depot, there would be no lights allowed in the tents and no time for writing letters home. They would be able to write when they got to the new camp. It had been a long day and being able to shower and crawl into the new cot was welcomed enough after all the excitement of the past few hours. Bill pulled the wool blanket around his shoulders and thought about home. He missed everyone terribly and at that moment he thought about what his brother Al might be saying to him if he were at home. As he lay in the dark, there was no one to talk to, as he was accustomed. His New Testament and *The Upper Room* booklet were now in the box being shipped back to 454 Simms Street. This was a new feeling for Bill; completely unfamiliar surroundings, mostly strangers with the same clothes, the same haircuts and nothing to say about anything. The following morning, the recruits were in formation on the exercise grounds and the sergeant told them that there would be religious services available. He told all of the Catholics to step forward, turn right, and march off to mass. All the others should face left and march off to the Protestant services. Any recruit that did not select a service to attend could spend the morning cleaning the latrines. After church, each recruit was allowed to send one post card home and Bill wrote his to Jessie with a brief description of camp life and his new haircut. 96 hours ago, he was Bill Bennett from Aurora, Illinois. Now he was Private Bennett, 352573, Training Platoon 55, Marine Recruit Depot, San Diego, CA. Bill was a Marine; one of many.

29. Semper Fidelis

Platoon 55 moved 14 miles north to Camp San Luis Obispo (SLO) and the sergeants wanted everything done to perfection. The camp was an Army camp that the Marines were borrowing and the sergeants did not want any reason for the Army to disrespect the Corps. In fact, the sergeants wanted the Marines to be so impressive that the Army soldiers would wish that they had joined the Corps. The new quarters consisted of three-man tents with rough wooden floors. Bill managed to bunk up with Bob Weir again, but Al Swanson was assigned to another tent. A cowboy from Wyoming named Al Schlager was assigned the other cot and Bill started to learn a lot about life in the west. Al Schlager said that just about everybody in Wyoming is a cowboy. The daily schedule was set up with a 0430 wake up, then dress for breakfast and organize the tent; in line for breakfast by 0500. After breakfast, 15 minutes to shave, then scrub the tent floor with a bucket and a scrub brush, leaving it perfect or you will scrub it again. Next came the morning exercises and three hours of marching drills before dinner (lunch) at noon. After noon there would be one hour for hand-washing clothes for the next day and then marches and runs of increasing mileage. Supper would be at 1700, followed by three hours of study, rifle cleaning and reassembly. At 2100 there were 30 minutes for showering and getting ready for bed, followed by 30 minutes to write letters or postcards. Lights were turned off at precisely 2200. Sleep became a commodity of survival with only six and a half hours available each night. Anyone goofing off or making noise after 2200 would not be tolerated by the recruits or the sergeants, who liked their sleep as well.

There was absolutely no talk of war or the Japanese enemy during this time. The focus was almost entirely on Marine Corps discipline, protocol and procedure. Unlike the other platoons, 55 was led by a corporal. He was tough and stern, but he needed to make Marines out of this cornucopia of civilians. Not long after arrival at SLO, the corporal had gotten close to Bill's face while yelling criticism of his marching ability and Bill thought that he could smell alcohol on the corporal's breath. Probably just something left over from last night, but more than likely forbidden for recruit or officer.

At long last, Bill was able to get some real letters going home. Bill wrote a post card to little Bobby and told him that he was lucky he was still so young, as he would miss the war. He also asked Bobby to eat some extra candy for his Uncle Bill as the recruits could not have any for 30 days. He also asked

Bobby to give Grandma Jessie an extra kiss goodnight for Uncle Bill while he was away. He wrote to Jessie and filled her in on the daily schedule and told her that Al was right about Bill being nuts to join the Marines. He also told Al to tell the guys in Aurora not to join the Marines because it was hell. After 10 or 12 days, letters from home began to arrive. Little Bobby was sick with the flu, but all else was going well. Al had driven out to Sandwich to bring Helen over for supper a couple of times already. Bill wrote back to Jessie to tell her that he wanted Bobby to have his Lionel train set and that he hoped he was feeling better. He had not heard from Al yet and he wanted Jessie to tell him to get with it. Although the recruits could not have any candy during basic training, they could have cookies from home. Bill loved cookies and he made it abundantly clear that he could use some in San Diego, right away.

The following Monday morning, it was time for U.S.M.C. inoculations, which was a nice way to say that they were about to receive five or six shots at the same time. The shirtless Marines were herded through the medical building with doctors on the left and the right, with several assistants standing behind them readying syringes as fast as they could. The doctors jabbed the needles into the recruit's arms faster than anyone imagined possible. After the second shot, Bill lost count, but there were at least four, maybe six injections. There were a lot of unhappy campers at this point. Over the next few days there were a number of recruits in sick bay for a variety of reasons. On the second day after the injections, Bill felt as though he were coming down with something and a trip to sick bay showed that he had a fever of 101. Possibly a reaction to one of the inoculations, but Bill would be spending the night in the infirmary. Once back to the barracks, the drills, physical training and studies continued. Recruits were taught how to salute, who to salute and when to salute. In a nutshell, anyone that wasn't a private needed a salute and "Sir" when being addressed. The proper salute was a 45-degree slant with the index finger contacting the forehead halfway to the eye. A Marine's head should be covered unless told by an officer to remove the cover.

The pistol range was 3.5 miles from SLO and Platoon 55 would walk over with their Springfield M1903s on their shoulder. At the range, the 1903s were racked and each recruit issued a 1911 .45 caliber pistol. The range instructors and the platoon corporal went over safety issues and procedures and the general operation of the .45. Next, there was a demonstration of the various shooting positions from which they would eventually have to qualify with the 1911. The basic standing position would have the Marine's shoulders pointing a line to the target while firing the 1911 with the right hand. The left hand would be placed on the left hip to stabilize the shoulders. Bill loaded three .45 rounds into the magazine and held it in his left hand. When his group stepped to the firing line, they were ordered to unholster the weapon while keeping the muzzle down range toward the target. Anyone seen pointing a muzzle in the direction of another Marine would be removed from the range for punishment, whether it was intentional or inadvertent. The order came to load the weapon and Bill jammed the magazine into the pistol grip and it clicked into position. In order to "charge" the weapon, the left hand gripped the slide and pulled it abruptly backwards and let it snap forward. "READY!" Bill held the

.45 toward the target. "Aim!" he lined the front sight into the gap on the rear sight. "Fire!" he pulled the trigger and the .45 jolted in his hand. He pulled the trigger again and again and the slide stayed open after the third shot, showing that the .45 was empty. The target showed that Bill needed work. Firing the .45 accurately was harder than it looked.

Pvt. William W. Bennett
(U.S.M.C. Photo)

On the way back from the range, Platoon 55 ran the 3.5 miles with the M1903 rifles in their hands. All of the running a person could do would not prepare them for running with an 8.5 pound rifle at the ready. The "boondockers" were not too bad for running. Bill had worn several pairs of football cleats that were worse over the years. The M1 helmet was a bit heavy but fit well. It consisted of a fiber liner that fit inside the steel pot and a strap that buckled under the chin. Bill set up the helmet strap like he had his football helmet and wore the strap over his chin, just below his lower lip. Bill found that this kept the M1 helmet from tipping forward under normal use. If he suddenly needed to run or secure the helmet, he just pushed he strap under his chin and he was good to go. The liner was a web construction that supported a leather head band that mixed with sweat and gave off the familiar smell of the old football helmets. The weight was a bit hard on the neck at first, but Bill was soon comfortable with his ever-present companion. He had no idea at the time, but his helmet would be a very useful tool for a variety of reasons, including bathing, cooking, bailing, a rain awning and the only privacy that he would have at times. The pack and belt were similar to football pads and getting them adjusted was the key. Carrying the rifle was unlike anything Bill had done previously. Holding the rifle while running began blisters in the grips of his hands. It would be a process of toughening up. The range experiences began to break up the endless drills and marches and the recruits started to get a sense that their job would be at least, in part, to shoot at things. The next trip to the range resulted in the issuance of bolt action, .22 caliber rifles. Bill was shown four positions for the rifle: standing, prone, sitting and kneeling. Standing would be the most difficult, prone the easiest. The rifle was comfortable to Bill and he was on target from the start. Bill told Bob and Al, in the tent, about Helen's championship rifle team from Ripon College and they asked Bill if she had taught him anything about shooting; unfortunately not, as no one had foreseen the need. A week of working with the .22 rifles would be preparation for the Marines finally getting to load and fire the Springfield M1903 rifles that they had been carrying around for weeks. About this time, the platoon was assigned a new sergeant as the corporal had been found drunk the previous night and had been relieved of duty. The sergeant told the platoon what had happened, as it was a strong lesson about U.S.M.C. discipline and the seriousness of breaking the rules. Sergeant Frank Drasil took over the platoon and turned out to be a fine leader who was well respected.

The .30 caliber rifle range was about three miles farther away than the pistol range and there was a train that would carry them back and forth. This train ride afforded the recruits a bit more time for letter writing. The Springfield M1903 .30-06 rifle is a five shot, bolt action, high power rifle, capable of hitting a target up to 1,000 yards away. Bill had carried this rifle for almost a month, studied and cleaned it every day. Now it was time to fire it. When the first recruits went to the firing line, the rest were a bit in awe of the dirt flying up behind the targets and cannon-like sound of the .30-06. Bill's group was called to the line. Five .30-06 rounds were loaded into a steel "stripper clip" and these clips would be carried in the pockets of the ammunition belt. With the rifle bolt pulled back as far as it would go, the five-round clip was pushed down into the receiver. Bill then had to force the rounds down into the magazine with his thumb and remove the steel clip. The bolt was then shoved forward placing the top .30-06 round into the chamber. The first target was at 100 yards and the sergeant stood to the side of Bill with binoculars. When told to fire, Bill shouldered his rifle, brought the front sight into the center of the hole in the rear site, flipped the safety to "fire," slowly exhaled and pulled the trigger. The recoil of the M1903 surprised Bill as it felt as though he had fired a dozen .22s at the same time. The first shot was a little low to the right, but it was on the paper. Bill worked the bolt and the spent casing flung backwards and he brought the next round into the chamber. He sighted the rifle and fired off another round, then another, then another. The fourth shot trimmed the black edge of the bull's eye and the sergeant was pleased with what he saw.

As the M1903 rifle training progressed, a new and sobering subject was introduced to the recruits; the use of the bayonet. Bill was issued an M1905 bayonet with a 17" blade and scabbard. He was taught to carry the bayonet in his pack on the left side with the handle pointing to the sky. The sergeant showed them how the bayonet could be grasped and drawn by reaching back over the left shoulder and then snapped into position on the muzzle of the rifle. Drawing the bayonet and "fixing" it onto the rifle barrel was repeated until the recruits thought that they might lose their sanity. The next step in this training was a demonstration by the drill sergeants showing the proper way to "thrust and parry" the rifle and bayonet as though using a spear. The rifle butt could be alternated as a bludgeon, as could the bolt side of the rifle be thrust into the enemy's face. A dummy was set up and the recruits were taught to select the center of the ribcage to locate the heart, the neck or even the mouth, if possible. This drill brought Bill to a reality that he had not considered before: the face-to-face stabbing of another human being. The platoon was shown that once the bayonet had been plunged into the enemy, it needed to be rotated and twisted to inflict more damage and to loosen it for removal. It was best to have a round in the chamber during battle that could be fired if the bayonet would not come out of the body. Bill took his turn with the dummy and received encouraging remarks from his sergeant. His size, strength and agility allowed him to make some decisive jabs into the sponge stuffed enemy. The sobering part of this training was that each recruit came to the point of realization that there were Japanese soldiers somewhere over the Pacific that were practicing to plunge and twist a bayonet into their hearts too.

The Company was led to an obstacle course that was 100-yards long and had multiple lanes with what appeared to be crudely formed "scarecrows" placed at regular intervals. This course would give the recruits the chance to develop bayonet skills while running full speed, jumping over ditches and facing two and three enemies at the same time. The sergeants demonstrated the course and had several recruits run the course to be criticized, and then lined up the Company for a full speed run through. The recruits were taught to scream like crazy men as they ran through the course, as this was thought to intimidate the enemy. The first group of eight recruits tore out from the line at the chirp of the whistle and this reminded Bill of the sprints from football practice back at East High. At the next chirp of the whistle, Bill sprinted full-speed toward the awaiting scarecrow and plunged the bayonet into its midsection, twisted the blade to the left and pulled it free. He moved on, jumping a pit filled with brown water and jabbed two more mannequins with slanted eyes drawn on with a grease pencil. As Bill's heart rate soared, he was aware of the loss of some dexterity, as it was more difficult to land the bayonet where he was aiming. He completely missed one lunge and the sergeant screamed that Bill would be "a dead Marine" if that happened in real combat. As Platoon 55 chattered about their training in the showers and in the chow lines, no one seemed to be too anxious to use their bayonets in battle; it seemed that using the rifle from a distance would be much preferred.

As Bill regularly sent letters home, many letters began to arrive at the camp. He received letters from his parents, Al and Marian and even Marian's boyfriend, Perry McIntosh. He received cards from Bobby, Helen, Bob Nix and Bob Stoner in the Navy, and Grandma Pfrangle let him know that she would be expecting a visit in L.A. as soon as they would let him out of camp. His sister Jean sent him a tin of her unbeatable chocolate chip cookies that she baked at the farm and his tent mates shared the joy. One of Bill's friends from Fourth Street Methodist, Fran McElroy, sent a letter asking Bill to visit her brother in Los Angeles if he could find the time. She had told her brother all about Bill and she said that they would be happy to show him the sights of L.A. Bill found some very nice U.S.M.C. lapel pins at a little shop on base and sent one home to Helen for Valentine's Day. A few days later, he bought a similar one and sent it to Jessie. He told Jessie that she was still his girl too, and didn't want her to feel bad. He told Jessie that if prayer worked, nothing bad would ever happen to her as he had been praying for her so much.

There had been many tough nights when Bill longed for his family and was truly homesick. He knew that everyone around him was feeling the same things and it helped that they were able to talk about it. Most of the guys had a girl back home and quite a few of them were married. Some of the guys told Bill that leaving a girl back home without a wedding ring on her finger was a mistake. This caused Bill to wonder if he had done the right thing by not asking Helen to get married before he left. He had talked to his dad about this after he enlisted, but Steve and Al both thought that it would be better to wait until the war was over, although no one had any idea how long it would last. Bill knew that his only choice would be to trust the Lord to lead him in the right direction and he prayed each morning when he woke up and before he fell asleep at night. He tried to pray as he went through the day as well, which didn't always work due to all of the excitement around the camp. Bill was confident that God knew that he wanted a family someday, and if Helen were the right girl, then she would be there whenever he returned. Being away from home and away from his comfort zone was a huge trial for him. There was a lot of foul language and crude talk where he was and Bill knew that things that deteriorate morals are very contagious. He had to make a conscious decision to pursue a closer relationship with the Lord and he prayed for strength and protection daily. One bright spot for Bill was the Protestant Service every Sunday morning. These services, although simple, helped to remind the Marines of the importance of maintaining their relationship with Christ. The Chaplain emphasized that no matter where these Marines went and no matter the circumstances, the Lord would be faithful to them as He had promised.

One morning the platoon was scheduled to be at the range at 0530 hours. When Bill woke up at 0430, the rain was pouring down. He figured that they would have to do something else for the day's training, but Sergeant Drasil told them they were going to the range, rain or shine. He told them that they would not be able to put off a fight with the Japanese until the sun was shining. The platoon was at the range all day until dark and rain ponchos or not, everyone and everything was soaked. The range had its own Mess Hall, but the food there was far worse than their regular food, which wasn't very good either. Cleaning the rifles was all the worse that night and Sergeant Drasil inspected every M1903 to make sure that it was cleaned and oiled. The rain and mud they experienced reminded the recruits that there is always a worse form of misery. Bill had become proficient with the M1903 and could load and fire the weapon rapidly. They practiced holding a fresh five-round clip in their left hand while firing so that it could quickly be loaded to continue firing. The range went from the original 100-yards, out to 1000-yards and then to 300-yards for qualification. Bill qualified with his rifle and received his Marksman medal with a score that was somewhere in the middle of the platoon. He qualified with the .45 but by his own estimation, he was no Wild Bill Hickok. The recruits' marching had grown from a disorganized mess the first week into an impressive display of teamwork. Bill became so accustomed to Sergeant Drasil's bellowing of the marching orders that it had actually become soothing. Every recruit in Platoon 55 seemed to know that they needed to acquire skills that would help them get through the war alive. They encouraged each other and wanted the entire platoon to do well. In the final days of basic training, the platoon marched with full packs up to 20 miles. They learned how to dress blisters and take care of their feet. Sergeant Drasil told them that the Navy gets to ride on boats, but Marines have to walk. That's the way it would work.

30. The 2nd Pioneers

February 20th, 1942. After almost five weeks in the Marine Corps, Platoon 55 graduated from Basic Training and everyone received orders for assignment to other units for Advanced Infantry Training. Bill was handed orders that placed him with an experimental new unit called the 2nd Pioneer Battalion. The Pioneers would specialize in "Shore Party" responsibilities, but no one knew exactly what a Shore Party did. The 2nd Pioneer Battalion was part of the larger 2nd Marine Division, so Bill's training would remain at San Diego, for now. Bill was very sad to learn that Bob Weir and Al Schlager had been assigned elsewhere, and they may not be able to see each other again. Bill packed up his "sea bag" and moved into a pretty nice two-story barracks back at the Marine Corps Base. The other guys were all nuts to get into town on a pass, but Bill decided to stay at the new barracks and write a few letters. He wasn't looking to get drunk and he certainly wasn't looking for a girl. His mind was occupied with the life that he left behind in Illinois. It seemed that just about every night, Bill was asked to go into town carousing with a group of Marines. Going out on the town was a temptation, of course, but Bill didn't want to get caught up in living that type of life. He wrote home to Jessie and Steve and told them that they didn't have to worry about their boy. He told them that they raised him right and he was determined to make them proud and never do anything to embarrass them. He had developed a daily sense that the Lord was with him at all times, and he privately didn't want to do anything to shame Him either.

Bill was assigned to the "2nd Pioneer Holding Battalion," with a group of 33 other Marines; they would all start their careers with a 30-day trip to the kitchen. 2nd Lieutenant Clarence B. Allen was in charge of KP duty and he seemed to be a pretty good guy. Three meals per day, seven days per week; that was the work schedule. Bill was assigned as a dishwasher and he worked 0600-0930, 1100-1530, and then 1600 until 2000 hours. As much as Bill liked to work in the kitchen, he grew to hate the dish job quickly. He knew that things could be a lot worse so he decided to smile all day, act as if he loved the job and whistle a lot. His forced demeanor paid off as some of the other guys developed better attitudes and the work environment improved. One good thing about this KP assignment was the abundance of food. There were lots of leftovers. Bill found the empty Mess Hall a great place to write letters in between the meal services and Helen sent him a very nice pad of U.S.M.C. stationery. He sat at a table with a cup of coffee and two leftover doughnuts from breakfast and started to write home. He apologized for not having the Marine photo taken and explained that he did not even have one hour to himself on a weekly basis, for the time being, but he would have a photo taken as soon as he could. The Marine Corps did not take the photos for the Marines, so they would have to find a photographer to get the job done. As Bill described how much he missed the family back home, two tears dropped onto the letter he was writing. It was impossible to hide his emotions, but he did not want anyone at home to know that he was homesick.

The good side of the new assignment was that the second-story balcony of the barracks overlooked the fenced-in area where movies and U.S.O. shows took place. Anytime that there was a show or movie, Bill could sit on the balcony and watch it for free. As Bill got to know the other guys at the barracks and KP duty, they joked around and tried to make the best of things. At times when Lieutenant Allen wasn't around the mess hall, they engaged in some hellacious water fights with sprayers, pans and even buckets. Of course, the trick was to get it all cleaned up before they were discovered. On Bill's first Sunday at MCB (Marine Corps Base), San Diego, he went to the Protestant Service on the base and met Reverend Allen and Mrs. Allen. The Allen's quickly became fond of Bill and they invited him to visit their house which was only a few blocks away from the MCB gate. The Allen's regularly attended First Presbyterian Church of San Diego. Bill put in a request for an evening off and visited with the Allens. They were about the same age as his parents and Mrs. Allen reminded him of his mother. Since they lived so close, Bill had it in mind to get over there as often as he could without being a bother. On any Sunday that Bill could get off base, he would take a Marine buddy, Herb Dale along, and visit First Presbyterian Church with the Allens and listen to the sermons of the Rev. Thomas Law Coyle.

Bill wrote his brother Al and told him that he appreciated the letters that he had sent and would take his advice to try and get into a non-combat job, if such a thing existed in the Marine Corps. Bill reminded Al what a swell bunch of friends they had back home and told Al that he wouldn't really understand until he had to leave them. He also told Al that he had been praying for him every night. Included in letters coming in for Bill was a very nice letter from Reverend Paul Dibble, who congratulated Bill on getting through basic training as well as his firearms qualifications. Reverend Dibble also quizzed Bill on what he thought about the Chaplain's role in the Marines, as he seemed tempted with the thought of volunteering. Herman Dimond, the Fourth Street Methodist Sunday School Superintendent sent Bill a very nice letter thanking him for his service along with blessings of a safe return. These letters helped Bill feel as though he was still a part of what was going on at the church.

After ten days of dish washing, the officers in charge told Bill that he would be their new "bread and butter man." Bill was in charge of getting all of the bread, butter, salads, olives, pickles and canned milk ready for the meals. Bill was thrilled to get the new assignment as his hands had been shriveled for the past ten days. Bill took the time to write Reverend Dibble a letter to let him know that he was doing well and appreciated his advice and insight before he left home. While he was in the middle of writing Jessie and Al, a few fellows from the 2nd Pioneers came through the mess hall and Bill engaged in a conversation with one of them. Bill asked the fellow if he had any idea what the Battalion's job would be. This fellow looked at Bill with a bit of disbelief that he had no idea about the Pioneers. The new Pioneer Battalion would follow the first waves of Marines ashore during an amphibious assault. As the front lines moved forward, the Pioneers would keep them supplied with whatever they needed. The Shore Party would be organizing the ammunition and supplies on the beach as the Pioneers moved it into combat. The Battalion would have to know how to use every weapon there was, including tanks and bulldozers. The 2nd Pioneer Battalion would conduct what some believed to be some of the hardest work of the war. The Marine told Bill that the 2nd Pioneers would begin an intensive 15-week training course as soon as Bill finished up his KP duties. Bill was shocked to hear that he had been assigned to such a unit and it seemed that Al's idea of finding a safe, out of the way job would not pan out.

Pvt. William Bennett in front of First Presbyterian Church, San Diego, 1942.

(Bennett Family Photo)

Bill received news that he would be stuck in the mess hall job until the first of April as the 2nd Pioneer Battalion training had been delayed. Bill had been in line to be the lead man in the mess hall, but was passed over for that job since he would be leaving in a month. At least now that Bill was working in the mess hall, he would be easy to find. As Bill was writing one afternoon, Lieutenant Bill Flentye, from Aurora, found him sitting alone at his table. Flentye said that he heard from his folks in Aurora that Bill was trying to find him, so he thought he would stop by and say hello. They talked about the "Wonder City" and how their folks were doing. The Flentye's were an affluent family that lived in a huge home on the city's west side. Bill Flentye, Sr. was a successful stock and bond trader and he had been a customer at Bennett's Men's Store for years. On another day, Al Bennett's old friend from Aurora,

Bill's close friend, Pvt. Herb Dale of Ryegate, Montana. First Presbyterian Church, San Diego, 1942.

(Bennett Family Photo)

Bob Robinson stopped by for a chat. Bob was in basic training at the MCB, so he could actually stop by the mess hall on occasion. Bob told Bill that he really liked the Marines so far. Since Bill could not get home, or even a few miles up to Los Angeles to visit Grandma Pfrangle, meeting these guys from Aurora was the next best thing. Bill pulled out his stationary and wrote to Al. He had not had a letter from Al in a while and wondered why. As he wrote Al, the base radio station played on the overhead speakers in the mess hall. About halfway through the letter, the strains of "Miss You" by Dinah Shore began. Emotion came over Bill and he set the pencil on the table.

> I miss you, since you went away dear.
> I miss you more than I can say dear.
> Daytime and night time, nothing I do can make me forget that I still love you.
> Kiss you, in my dreams I kissed you.
> Whispering, 'Darling, how I miss you.'
> Tell me, do you ever miss me as I miss you?
> Tell me, do you ever miss me as I miss you?

Bill wiped tears from his eyes again as he picked up the pencil to continue his letter to Al. The song had made Bill think of home more than any other. It made him think of Helen, of Jessie and of his family in general. It was just too tough to get through the song without a tear or two.

On Sunday, April 12th, Bill was able to leave the MCB to attend church at the First Methodist Church on the corner of Ninth and C Streets in San Diego. Bill loved the service as it was nice to see happy people that were not wearing green. Reverend George A. Warner's sermon was about people with endless "lists" of things that they want from God. People need to be content with what they have and have the patience to allow God to give us what He wants us to have. This really made Bill think about the life that he had left behind. He had thus far considered the war and his leaving home to be somewhat of a tragedy, but the thought occurred to him that God was working in his life without it being obvious. The church hosted "The Fellowship Lounge" for servicemen and Bill was handed a card on the way out. He looked forward to attending the lounge as well as the youth meetings on Sunday night.

Back at home, Helen had just been hired by TWA as a ticketing agent and started her training at the Midway facility in Chicago. This meant a long commute for her on the train each day and Bill became concerned about her working so hard. This was the type of career that Helen had wanted and she was not afraid of hard work or even hardship for that matter. Bill thought that it would make sense for Helen to move in with the Bennetts so that her commute would be shortened. He wrote both Helen and Jessie about this and they discussed it. Helen assured everyone that the train time was not a bother and she used the time for letter writing and reading books. After she tried the commute for a couple of weeks, she decided that if she spent two or three nights a week at the Bennett's it would help quite a bit. She brought some things to keep at the Bennett's and used Marian's room since she was away at Millikin College. Helen missed Bill terribly, but being a practical thinker, she knew that there was nothing she could do but get busy, be industrious and wait out the war. Steve and Jessie invited Carrie and Wally Cochran over for Sunday dinner and they got to know each other quite well. Steve was very interested in Wally's role as mayor as well as his business experience with Sanitary Cleaners. Wally enjoyed hearing of Steve's experiences with the Aurora area business associations as well as his vast knowledge of the men's clothing business. The Fairway Skating Palace had been reopened and Al had taken Helen skating a few times. Al was dating a girl named Eunice, who he had met at a Jack Benny show in Winnetka, Illinois. Eunice was there in support of her friend, who was selling cigarettes and cigars. Al had the good fortune of striking up a conversation and Eunice ended up volunteering to drive Al home after the show in her 1938 coupe. Eunice ended up making occasional trips to Aurora to visit Al and the two of them made sure that Helen felt welcome to go out with them whenever she wanted to.

Bill thought that it might be a good idea to propose to Helen on his upcoming birthday of April 14th. He went over the plan with Steve, Jessie and Al by mail and he wanted Al to convey the message personally to Helen. He imagined the Cochrans coming over to the Bennetts for supper and then he would place a call and talk to them all, ending up with the proposal for Helen. But, Bill decided to go ahead and ask Helen about it by letter instead of surprising her and he was on pins and needles to hear back from her.

Bob Robinson finished boot camp and one of Bill's buddies and football team mates, Ray Jones, stopped by the mess hall and told Bill that he would be finishing up boot camp in a week. Ray had grown up at 320 Seminary Avenue, just a few blocks from the Bennetts, and he had played on the Tomcat football team those last two years of high school. It was great to see Ray, and it really brought a feeling of home. Bill decided that it was time to go into San Diego with Bob Robinson and they went to see a floor show at a small club for servicemen and went bowling at the largest bowling alley in the city. Bill went to buy a Hershey Bar at the candy counter and the young lady working the counter asked him where he was from. They talked a bit and Bill told her about his girl back home and the letter he had just written. The counter girl told Bill that her name was Georgia Cobb and she and her husband Al lived a few miles away in Oceanside, California. She wished him luck with the letter and said that he should stop by later and let her know how it all came out. She told Bill that she would introduce him to her husband if he happened to be there the next time Bill and Bob came to bowl. She was the friendliest person that Bill had talked to in months and Bill made a point to talk to her on subsequent trips to the bowling alley. A few days later, Bill received the letter from Helen that he had been waiting for and eagerly tore open the envelope. Helen said that she was honored by Bill's offer, but she would feel much better about it if he waited until he received a furlough so that it would be in person. Bill had a strong feeling that he would not get a furlough until the war was over and that could be years from now. He was very disappointed, but Helen had not turned him down. Helen told Bill that she would look into the possibilities of making a short trip to San Diego to see Bill. She was still in training at TWA but she would eventually receive some time off and a discount on the flights.

Bill, Bob Robinson and several other Marines went to bowl again and Bill was able to meet Georgia Cobb's husband Al, who ran a gas station up in Oceanside and liked football. He figured that he would end up getting drafted within a year, but with a wife and two small children, he didn't want to go to war if he could avoid it. Georgia and Al invited Bill to go to church and have lunch with them the following morning, and gave him directions to their house in La Jolla. The only way that Bill could make the trip was to leave the MCB at 0430 hours and walk the 10 miles or so to La Jolla. Bill left the front gate about 0445 and headed north around Mission Bay. As the darkness started to lift, Bill could see hundreds of sail boats moored on the docks of the bay. The water from the bay had somewhat of a stale smell, but the slight breeze coming in from the Pacific made the air fresh enough to enjoy. Seagulls shrieked as Bill disturbed their morning routines of foraging for dead fish or a snack that someone had dropped.

Bill followed the street north of the bay and came to La Jolla Boulevard which ran next to the sand and rocks of the coastline. There was plenty of light now to see the ocean as the waves broke below on the rocks and expanses of beach. The ocean was so beautiful and peaceful that Bill stopped several times just to take it all in. Being about 0700 in San Diego, Bill figured that it was about 9 a.m. in Aurora. The Bennetts would be heading for church about now. As Bill looked out at the endless Pacific, he knew full well that out there, somewhere, Americans were fighting the Japanese. He knew that before long he would be facing the enemy along with the 2nd Pioneer Battalion. Bill decided to pray with his eyes open as he began to thank the Lord for his goodness and mercy. He asked the Lord to help him to remain faithful to Him in everything he would encounter and to be an example to his comrades in the Corps. Bill liked the Corps' motto of Semper Fidelis, Latin for "Always Faithful." He not only wanted to be faithful in his duty as a United States Marine, but as a follower of Christ. Bill asked the Lord to be with his family and friends and he listed many of them by name. Bill said, "Amen," as he turned and continued on his way. Partly filled with awe at God's creation and partly filled with the sadness of longing for home, he watched the waves roll in one after another. The solitude of this morning and the closeness that he felt to God would be something Bill would long remember. As Bill walked north, he came into the residential area and made a few turns until he located the Cobb's address. His visit with the Cobbs was very enjoyable and they introduced Bill to dozens of people at church and quite a few neighbors when they got back home after church. Bill had to be back at the MCB no later than 1600 so the Cobbs gave him a ride back to the front gate.

Bill received a letter from Jessie telling him that Steve had made another career decision that would come as quite a surprise. After closing Bennett's Men's Wear, Steve had taken the manager's position with one of his former competitors, Wheeler's Men's Wear. This had been an acceptable position for the past year or so, however the pay was somewhat less than Steve thought he was worth. One evening after supper, William Gretencort, President of Schmitz & Gretencort Co. on Broadway rang Steve at home. They had known each other for over 30 years as they both worked in men's wear in Aurora, but Steve was surprised to hear Bill Gretencort on the line. Bill and his partner Ed Schmitz had been talking about Steve in regard to the head sales position at Schmitz & Gretencort. They wanted to offer him substantially more pay, long term job security and a chance to work with the best store in Aurora, according to them, of course. Schmitz & Gretencort knew that Steve had a fine reputation as one of the best men's-wear professionals in the area and employing him would even bring more business in the door. Steve and Jessie had talked about it for a few days and discussed the move with Al. It seemed like a solid opportunity, so Steve took the new job. When Bill heard this, it was almost unbelievable. As Bill was growing up, Schmitz & Gretencort had always been the bad guys and his father would have been upset had he purchased anything from them even though many of his friends shopped there. Having Steve Bennett go to work for Schmitz & Gretencort was similar to when Babe Ruth was traded from the Red Sox to the Yankees. Bill immediately sat down and wrote Steve a letter congratulating him on the new job and encouraging him to be the best "suit guy" in the business. Bill also reflected on how he had not been as respectful to his dad as he could have been at times, and he had not thought as much of Steve's expertise as he probably should have. Bill had always gone a little overboard with treating his mom with respect, but thought that he could have done more for his dad. In his heart, Bill thought that if he ended up dying in the war, he would have left some things unsaid with his father.

31. Company A

Bill was transferred out of the Mess Hall and into Company A, 2nd Pioneer Battalion. Company A was based at the MCB San Diego in a tent area, so Bill moved back into a tent with a wooden floor. Oddly enough, a package came from Jessie on Bill's first day back with the Pioneers and Bill pulled out his

New Testament and the new *Upper Room*. Bill received a letter from his Aunt Emma saying that they would pick him up at the main gate on Sunday morning. But no one ever showed up, so Bill took the train to Los Angeles to find Emma's house. It was the hardest address to find that Bill had ever seen. He stopped to ask a dozen people and no one even knew where the street was. He finally found the house and Emma was already back home. They had their "wires crossed" on the meeting time. Emma was married to Bill's uncle Sammy, Jessie's little brother. Emma drove Bill over to visit his Aunt Ruby, but they didn't have enough time to drive to Grandma's house. Bill arranged to meet Grandma Pfrangle near the bus station the following week and they were able to eat lunch and visit for about four hours. Bill absolutely loved his Grandma Pfrangle and would do anything possible to come back and visit her again. Bill hatched several plans to get back to visit Grandma, but it would take some finagling to make the plans work.

Big news on the base was that Jack Benny was coming to do a U.S.O. show and Bill, Bob and Ray managed to get tickets. Jack Benny brought Joan Bennett along and they were both hilarious. It was a great diversion from the past four months for Bill. Bill made arrangements to meet Grandma and Aunt Emma one Sunday evening but he was fairly late when he finally got to the gate. Bill's surprise for them was that he had managed to make arrangements to bring them both to the Bob Hope U.S.O. show on the base. They not only got into the show, but Bill managed to get them both into the front rows. Bob Hope had Frances Langford, John Hall, and Jerry Colonna, and Clyde "Skinnay" Ennis had his fantastic band along for the show. There were about 10,000 troops there and it was an unforgettable night. Grandma and Emma were quite impressed. The three of them were able to go downtown for a soda together after the show, and then Bill headed back to camp while Grandma and Emma went to a hotel. The plan was to meet again the next day and Bill had the pass all lined up, but all passes were canceled and Bill couldn't get free to see them. About noon, one of the sergeants came up to Bill in the Mess Hall and handed him a pass to the front gate and said that he had a visitor. It was Grandma. Bill was allowed to see her off to the train and all ended very well.

Bill finally went downtown and had a portrait taken and sent two 8" by 10" photos home. He had another pose taken and paid to have it colorized. This portrait was sent to Helen's house in Sandwich. At long last, everyone at home could see what this Marine looked like. Since working in the Mess Hall for two months, Bill managed to get himself up to a healthy 190 pounds; heavier than he had ever been, and a good football weight. Earl Carroll's Vanities Show 1942 came to camp and all of the troops made plans to be there. Those girls could not only sing and dance up a storm, but they were probably the most beautiful group of girls that Bill had ever seen. Bill had found a few weeks of entertainment and a little fun quite refreshing.

The 2nd Battalion training was finally about to begin. As Bill joined Company A, he was sent to the rifle range to catch up on his marksmanship. There was a unit of Marines assigned to running the range and they did maintenance and supply work there. As Bill was preparing himself to take his place on the firing line, Earl Rottsolk from the East Aurora High School days was

Pvt. William Bennett with his beloved grandmother Pfrangle, in front of her home in Los Angeles, Calif. during the Spring of 1942.

(Bennett Family Photo)

carrying ammunition out to the range. Earl was Bill's defensive team mate on the Tomcats and they had lockers next to each other their senior year. Earl enlisted in the Marines back in November of 1941 and had finished basic training before he was assigned to the rifle range at the Marine Corps Base. Bill made plans to visit Earl's barracks over the weekend and stayed overnight so that they could catch up and trade Marine stories. The other guys in Earl's barracks enjoyed hearing the Tomcat football stories and being with Earl made Bill feel like he was back in Aurora for a few hours.

One night when Bill was in downtown San Diego, he stopped in at "The Federal" Uniform Shop at 220 Broadway. In the store window was a mannequin wearing a full set of Marine "Dress Blues." Looking in the front windows reminded him of being back-home on Broadway and he thought of his dad working in his new environment in the Schmitz & Gretencort shop. Having always been a sharp dresser, Bill was imagining himself wearing this classy uniform instead of the olive drab uniform that was standard issue. He asked a few questions in the shop and they told him that any Marine could wear dress blues regardless of rank. The problem was that the blues cost $10 and Bill was pretty much broke. He wrote home to Steve and asked him to check into finding a deal on a set of dress blues and let him know what kind of a deal he could get. As it turned out, wearing dress blues required other accessories such as the hat, shoes and belt, which would drive the whole package out of range. That was probably why there weren't many Marines wearing them. The point became moot as Bill was launched into intensive training again and would not have much time for wearing the blues anyway. Bill wrote back to Steve and told him to forget about the dress blues and apologized. He said that he needed to take care of his own money and should not have bothered anyone else with it.

asked Steve to send him his driver's license and some photos of his friends that he had left in the glove compartment of the old Buick. He also wanted the rubber stamps that he had used for letter and note writing while at home. Bill had just received over twenty birthday cards during the week of his birthday and he asked Steve and Jessie to put a small thank you in the *Beacon News* as he could not possibly write twenty letters to thank all of his friends personally.

By the end of April, Al Bennett's number looked like it might be coming up at the draft board. When Bill heard about this, he was nearly frantic. He knew Al and he knew the military, he could not see the two of them working very well together. Al did not have an aggressive bone in his body and Bill was afraid of what might happen to him in the service. He wrote to Steve and asked for an update and told Steve that he would stay in the Marines for the rest of his life if he knew it would keep Al out. Al had begun to investigate what kind of deal he might get if he enlisted into one of the branches prior to being drafted. Al was still dating Eunice and was serious about her, so Bill did not want him to have to leave his girl behind. Bill told Al that he thought he would make a good officer; with his business experience at Pillsbury, they might even put him in a supply role. So, both brothers had tried to think of a way to keep the other out of harm's way.

Colorized portrait that Bill had specially ordered for Helen Cochran prior to shipping out from San Diego.

(Photo courtesy of Mark Larson and Susan Johnson)

The 2nd Pioneer Battalion began a crash course in Amphibious Warfare and every aspect of the science would be new to most of the new Marines. The first principle would be that of selecting the shoreline of the target most suitable for access by the Marine Corps. Beaches or other similar shorelines were the most likely types of terrain for such assaults. Areas with high-rising coastlines would be the most unlikely assault points. The next thing to consider would be the capabilities and weaponry that would be defending the assault point. Good terrain that was heavily defended could still prove to be a disastrous attack. The logistics of the actual attack were far more complicated than Bill had imagined. A pre-assault bombardment would be conducted by the Navy by both sea and air. In some cases, the Army Air Corps would participate in aerial bombardments coordinated with the Navy. The Marine Corps was, in fact, a part of the Navy, so the Navy was technically in charge of planning the invasions with advice from the Marine Generals. During the time of pre-assault bombardment, specially-trained Advance Units could be used to take out certain targets prior to the main invasion. The attacking Marines would be divided into groups referred to as "waves."

The first Marines onto the beach would be the first wave, followed by the second, etc. In principle, the first wave would take the brunt of the casualties as they faced whatever remained of the enemy defenses after the bombardment ceased. The second wave would hit the beaches within minutes of the first to reinforce that punch and then the third wave would give the attack the boost to move inland. That third wave would include the Command Section and Reconnaissance Sections from the 2nd Pioneer Battalion. These Marines would locate and mark the "Dump Marker" sections of the beach with Battalion markers notifying supply boats where to land ammunition, weapons, food and water. The Pioneer Sections would accompany the fourth wave and move those supplies up to the front lines to make sure they did not run out of anything. The Shore Party would arrive with the fifth wave and set up a "shipping and receiving" scenario on the beach. Once the beach was secured and the enemy pushed back, trucks and trailers would be brought in to carry supplies forward. The 2nd Pioneers would need to be able to drive tractors and build bridges, demolish enemy fortifications with TNT and flamethrowers, and build new structures when needed. The entire 2nd Pioneer Battalion would therefore be trained in the same combat roles that combat units would be, as well as their Engineering roles. The 2nd Pioneers would need to have twice the skills of ordinary Marines. If the front line Marines ran out of ammunition or weapons, they would die and the enemy would advance on the beachhead and push the Shore Parties and incoming Marines into the sea.

Bill remembered what the officer in the Mess Hall had told him about the Pioneers having the hardest job in the Marine Corps. It sounded as though he knew what he had been talking about. The 2nd Pioneer Battalion would be divided into three Companies of about 200 men each and one Headquarters Company of about 200 Marines, leaving the full-strength battalion at about 1,000 men. Bill had been assigned to Company A and the 1st Platoon which had about 65 Marines. Each platoon would need a full variety of specialists that were under the command of a captain, his 1st lieutenants, 2nd lieutenants, various sergeants and corporals. The Private First Class and Private would be the lowest level of Marine Corps existence. The Platoons would be divided into work groups called "squads," "sections" or "work parties" depending on what was needed to be done. The first order of business would be for the individual company commanders to assign a "specialty" to each Marine for in-depth training in that area. Bill was interviewed by Captain Joseph Clerou and they discussed what Bill wanted to do and what the Marine Corps needed him to do. One of the specialties the captain was trying to fill was that of Tractor Driver. As it turned out, all of the Pioneers had to learn to drive the tractors just in case it was needed. Bill thought about how funny it would be to his brother-in-law, Linc, when he found out that Bill joined the Marines and went all the way to California to learn to drive a tractor! The following day Bill was given a card with his name on it ordering him to begin training that afternoon for "Spec. 746, Automatic Rifleman."

1st Platoon. As the entire Company A was pulled together, Bill began to become acquainted with a whole new batch of Marines. He was assigned to 1st Platoon, led by Lieutenant Henderson who was supported by Corporal George P. Gabel from Chicago and Gunnery Sergeant Emory Haaby. Lieutenant Henderson was a good leader who marched, ran and ate with his men. Gabel had been on gunnery duty aboard the USS Maryland at the time of the Pearl Harbor attack and was shaving when the Japanese arrived. Clad only in his skivvies and a T-shirt, Gabel had the key to the munitions locker on a shoe lace around his neck and had to run to unlock the ammunition. He manned a twin .50 caliber machine gun on the super-structure, and fired it into the Japanese planes until the barrels overheated and the guns stopped firing. He then made his way down to the deck where he manned a single .50 caliber gun until its barrel began to melt as well. When Bill had the chance to talk to Gabel privately, and off duty, he learned what a nice guy he was. Gabel had a girl named Verona, who he called "Ronnie," back in Chicago. He had been trying for months to go home on leave and get married, but the Japanese attack on Pearl Harbor put a stop to that. Now he had been assigned to a combat unit getting ready to go in the wrong direction! There was no telling when, or if, he would ever get back to Ronnie now. The sad truth was that there were thousands of young couples in the exact same set of circumstances.

Bill re-connected with Al Slowinski, who he had met the first day at the train station in Chicago, and Al had chosen the specialty of "050 Carpenter" as this had been his job back home. Truitt Anderson was one of the youngest Marines in Company A and also one of the smallest physically, at 5' 6" and 130 pounds. Truitt was a very smart and confident kid. He was a fast runner, tough and wiry, in spite of his size. He had enlisted right after Pearl Harbor and then left his home in Akron, Ohio, on January 14th. He was born in West Virginia and had lived in the south for many of his younger years, which had left strong traces of a southern accent. His small size, blonde hair and deep blue eyes reminded Bill of Bob Stoner, and Truitt had found a friend in "Bennett." Truitt came from a strong Baptist upbringing and his strong faith in the Living Christ became an almost instant bond between him and Bill. They both read their Bibles daily and prayed often. They became buddies as they attended the weekly Protestant Service together. Truitt's buddies nicknamed him "Andy," short for Anderson, and that was how he was known from then on.

Bill noticed a Marine with a sketch pad at the Mess Hall one day and his work was very professional. Bill introduced himself and the Marine's name was John C. Jones from Oklahoma City; his friends called him Johnnie. Johnnie was a Machine Gunner who said that he would much rather sketch people than kill them. It turned out that Jones was also assigned to 1st Platoon and Bill would have plenty of time to get to know him. Jones stood about 6' 2" and had movie actor looks to go with his athleticism. He was a good opponent in football or basketball pick-up games, so Bill and Johnnie had something in common from the start. Bill soon befriended Charles LaPoint, Bill Walzer, Carmen Yonke, Duane Strinden and Leo Renault. 1st Platoon was Bill's new home and he believed that he was with a fine bunch of Marines. Time would prove that Bill was right.

2nd Platoon. 2nd Platoon was led by Lieutenant Saylor with Sergeant John C. Bass, 2nd Lieutenant Barney Boos and Corporal Mike Matkovich. Bill had not seen Joe Sobolewski since they had split up after the train ride to San Diego from Chicago, but now Joe was in 2nd Platoon along with Herb Dale. Herb was from a cluster of buildings called Ryegate, Montana. The town was so small that Herb wasn't sure if he should call it a town or not. Herb's mother had died when he was in high school and his brother and dad didn't write letters. Herb couldn't believe all the mail that Bill had coming in and Bill felt bad for him not having anything to read. Bill began sharing his letters with Herb and he even asked Steve to start addressing his letters to "Bill and Herb," so that Herb would feel included. Herb loved cars and trucks and loved to work on them. No matter what was wrong, Herb could figure it out pretty fast. He was sent to specialize as a truck driver. Bob Swigert, a friendly fellow from Oelrichs, South Dakota, had been a full-time ranch hand and farmer before joining the Marine Corps. Swigert was very polite and mild mannered and Bill enjoyed being around him. Gerald Coate was a cowboy type from Butte, Montana, and Bill noticed how friendly and sensible most of these cowboys and farmers were; much more relaxed than the city boys. Bill Poterola was a plumber from Salt Lake City, and he was training as a truck driver along with Herb. Poterola liked to go downtown and drink, so he and Bill didn't have much of a bond. Harry Cabler was older than Bill and a master carpenter before the Marines. Naturally, Harry was specializing in carpentry with the Corps. George Cothran was a tough little Irish guy from Oklahoma, and he had the makings of a good bull rider. George wasn't a mean fellow by any stretch, but he had grown up as the oldest of four brothers and he was not about to take any guff from anybody. He was a good guy to have as a friend. George's specialty was a 745 Rifleman.

Charles Montague and Gene Seng were life-long buddies from Texas. They worked on cars together, hunted together, played sports together and had been just about inseparable. They both were specializing in the .30 caliber light machine gun, a belt-fed weapon that fired from a tripod base and required two Marines to operate properly. Bill met two Marines from Chicago as well. Corporal Mike Matkovich had been in the Marines for a few years and spent some time on the USS Tennessee. He had experience with all sorts of heavy weapons from the ship and was trained as a .30 caliber machine gunner just like Johnnie Jones. Matkovich had grown up street fighting on the south side of Chicago, and he had that familiar "I don't take any crap" attitude that a lot of the city Marines had. Bill hoped that Mike and George Cothran would become friends or else there might be trouble. Mike was a talented artist and turned out to be a good guy. The tough exterior was more of an outer shell for protection than an attitude problem. He was a good Marine and was very helpful to the new guys.

Another interesting Marine that Bill befriended was Manny Bud from Chicago. Manny was the son of two Russian immigrants who had Americanized their last name. He graduated from Crane Technical High School and was a top student there. Manny had really wanted to be a doctor. Manny's dad worked in retail menswear, something he had in common with Steve Bennett. Manny had been working in shipping and receiving before Pearl Harbor and joined the Marines on December 8th at the huge post office in Chicago. Ironically, Manny had tried to join the Army Air Corps as he wanted to be a fighter pilot, but they took one look at his glasses and told him to find another branch. Since he only had an hour for lunch, he went downstairs to the Army office and found the line was four hours long. He tried to go to the Navy office but the elevator was broken, so he settled for the Marines. After he enlisted, he walked back to work wondering what Marines do. Bill and Manny had a good laugh over this. For most of his time in the Corps, Manny had been the only Jewish Marine in his unit. The fact that Manny was Jewish didn't bother Bill. After all, Jesus was Jewish. Fred R. Ellis was a few years older than Bill and he was a carpenter along with Harry Cabler. Fred told Bill that he was from Basin, Montana, and had grown up on a farm there. In Basin, you had to be a carpenter just to survive. The depression had been particularly hard on the Ellis family and Fred had been working full time since he was about 14. Fred had a gentle air about him and he seemed to have sensible knowledge of just about everything. Bill could sense a genuine spirit in most of these guys and he felt blessed to be around them. Bill referred to Coate, Dale and Ellis as the "Montana Men."

3rd Platoon. Lieutenant Harold A. Hayes, Jr. and PFC Emory Ashurst were leading 3rd Platoon as it gathered the Battalion experts in 533 Demolitions. 3rd Platoon was not as closely associated with the 1st and 2nd initially, so Bill did not get to know many of them the way he had with the others. The 3rd Platoon adopted the nickname, "The Go to Hell Men" due to their job description of blowing up enemy fortifications. The 2nd Pioneers were made primarily out of Midwesterners with Texas, Oklahoma, Montana, and North and South Dakota Marines sprinkled in. 2nd Lieutenant Joseph Clerou was placed as the Battalion Commanding Officer.

32. 746 Automatic Rifleman

Bill reported to the thirty-caliber rifle range with a group of 60 other Marines from mixed units. They were all there to begin their training with the Browning Automatic Rifle, Caliber .30, M1918A2. In the center of the range, a set of bleachers was placed so that the class could overlook the range for a demonstration. As the Marines stacked themselves onto the bleachers, a gunnery sergeant walked to the center and they gave him their full attention. He made sure that everyone was in the right class and explained the overview of what they would be learning during this training. Their mission was to learn and master the operation and care of the Browning Automatic Rifle, or BAR. They would learn the operation, care and maintenance first, just as they had their standard M1903 Springfield Rifles, before firing their weapons. After some technical descriptions of the BAR, four Marines who were instructors on the weapon came to the left and right of the sergeant. As the sergeant again referenced components of the rifle, the instructors held out the rifle for the class to view. The instructors were in full combat gear with large ammunition belts. One of the instructors took his place on the firing line with a row of seven large steel cans arrayed on the range at 100 yards.

A distant Marine yelled out "Clear on the range!" and the instructor clicked a magazine into his BAR, snapped the bolt back and loaded the weapon. The sergeant yelled out the order to "Fire!" and the instructor fired a three-round burst into the first can. It exploded into the air amid a cloud of dust and debris. The next five cans met the same fate in rapid succession and the last two rounds sent the seventh can tumbling down the embankment. The firing lasted ten seconds. The Marines applauded the mastery of the instructor and they loudly commented to each other about the awesome fire power they had witnessed. The sergeant quieted them as another instructor joined the first. At 300 yards out on the range, more cans were arrayed, and the two instructors now fired their BARs with alternating three-round bursts. This provided a constant pounding of 40 rounds that resulted in a huge cloud of dust and tumbling targets. All 40 rounds were expended in about 15 seconds this time. The two instructors on the line snapped the empty magazines from beneath the rifles and put them back into their belts while producing full magazines and rapidly snapping them into the openings. The two other instructors stepped to the line and readied their BARs. The sergeant again yelled, "Fire!" and all four instructors fired on a simulated enemy bunker that was at about 400 yards out on the range. With alternating bursts, the instructors fired 80 .30-06 rounds in under 15 seconds. The entire bunker area flew with dust and debris. The Marines had never witnessed that much concentrated fire before and it was awe inspiring.

The class was divided into groups of 12 and assigned to one BAR instructor. Bill was given a notepad, pencil and small manila-colored book with *FM 23-15, WAR DEPARTMENT, BASIC FIELD MANUAL, BROWNING AUTOMATIC RIFLE, CALIBER .30, M1918A2 WITH BIPOD* printed on the cover. Bill was instructed to read and re-read this manual over the coming week. Everything that he would need to know was covered in this book, so there would be no reason for him not to know everything about his BAR. The M1918A2 weighed 21 pounds with the sling attached and was 47" overall. Each magazine held 20 .30-06 rounds and the magazines weighed 1.7 pounds fully loaded. The rifle would only fire as an automatic weapon, but it had two rates of fire controlled by the "rate of fire change lever." The standard rate of fire was set to 550 rounds per minute while the slow rate would be set at 350 rounds per minute. If the desire was to fire single shots, the slow rate would be selected and the trigger quickly released to only allow one round to be fired. The standard "burst" to be fired would be three rounds, and two rounds would be the short burst and five rounds would be the maximum. The maximum rate of fire on the BAR was more than the rifle could reliably sustain if pushed to the limit. If the rifle was fired with continual bursts of 20 rounds in rapid succession, it would over heat within 120 rounds, with probable damage to the weapon. Keeping any weapon as cool as possible was always the key.

The following day the classes were given a preliminary quiz with the instructor and a BAR. The instructor questioned Bill on the basics of the rifle as described in the manual, and he could tell that Bill had done his homework. After the quiz, the class lined up to receive their rifles. The serial numbers were recorded and Bill signed the card saying that he received the weapon. Bill's BAR was covered with heavy grease called "Cosmoline" which was applied at the factory to keep it from rusting. The first chore for each Marine would be to disassemble, clean off the Cosmoline, reassemble and oil the weapon. Stripping the BAR for cleaning would render the rifle into dozens of individual parts and assemblies, and Marines were not allowed to disassemble some assemblies without the assistance of an Ordnance Specialist. Bill disassembled and cleaned his BAR countless times, and it reminded him of the time he completely tore apart the 1927 Model T in the backyard. Organizing your parts in the order in which you removed them was the key to reassembly. For the first week of training, this procedure was done over and over again until Bill began to perform it automatically. His instructor had one of the Marines blind-fold him and then he proceeded to strip and reassemble a BAR in about three minutes. The act was inspiring and the instructor told them that the blindfold would give them the ability to clear a jam, load, or rectify simple problems in the dark, should it be needed. Ed Susans was in the same BAR class and his tent was not very far from Bill's, and he and Ed would get together with some of the other BAR trainees to help each other with the training. Out of the 200 Marines in Company A, only six would be carrying the BAR.

When the day came to fire the BAR, Bill went over safety procedures and range protocol with the instructor. He was given two 20-round magazines and forty rounds of .30-06 to load into them. They were taught to inspect each round and clean them with an oily rag to aid in the reliability of the firing mechanism, as dirty ammo could foul the action. Bill took his place on the firing line and the instructor told him to load a magazine, making sure that the safety was on. Next, he checked the "fire change lever" to make sure it was on the "slow" position. He was then cleared to fire on the 100-yard standard paper target. His goal was to quickly release the trigger and fire only one round at a time. He aimed the BAR, pushed the safety forward and slowly pulled the trigger. One round fired and the recoil hit him in the right shoulder like a punch. The recoil was similar to the Springfield M1903 but a little lighter due to the increased weight of the BAR. Bill was told to fire two more single shots, then a couple of two round bursts. Next, Bill should try and alternate between three round bursts and two round bursts until empty. Bill's target was shredding as he fired the burst into it again and again, and then the bolt stayed open showing that he was out of ammunition. Bill held the rifle muzzle up in the air and stepped away from the firing line.

Over the next four weeks, Bill fired, cleaned, disassembled, reassembled and carried his BAR. He knew it better than he had the M1903, which he still had to fire occasionally to remain familiar with it. In order to graduate from the BAR training, Bill had to disassemble and reassemble the rifle in front of one of the instructors and pass a rigorous qualification requirement at the range. Bill sailed through the maintenance test and went to the firing line. His belt now contained six twenty-round magazines for a total of 120 rounds. Following strict instructions, Bill would have to fire all 120 rounds into targets at various ranges and from various positions all simulating combat. Bill began the course and he fired three round bursts and several single shots into nearby targets. Then he was directed to hit various targets at 300, 400, 500 and 600 yards. Bill felt quite formidable as he went from target to target

A Marine fires his Browning Automatic Rifle.
(U.S.M.C. Photo)

wielding the BAR. From the "assault position," firing from the hip, Bill directed his fire into each target with only a few missed shots along the way. By the time he finished, he had quite a sweat built up and he enjoyed the workout. Bill's score was not the best, but it was strong. He not only became certified on the BAR, but he was requested to be assigned as an instructor's assistant with new groups coming through. Bill was officially a BAR man.

On a Sunday afternoon, Bill decided to take the train up to Los Angeles to visit Fran McElroy's brother. The "Macs" took him all over Hollywood and then out for dinner. Then they drove Bill up to Lookout Mountain so he could see the lights of Los Angeles at night. Bill thought it was one of the most spectacular sights he had ever seen. There was a little shop in Hollywood where you could make your own record, so Bill and the Macs went in and made one and mailed it home to 454 Simms Street. On another weekend, Bill rode the train up for a visit and the Macs had tickets to see Harry James and his orchestra at the Palladium Ball Room in Hollywood. Bill was amazed at how good the band sounded. He had never heard anything quite like it before. The Palladium had room for about 7,000 dancers and a huge kidney shaped dance floor. The outside of the dance floor was lined with round tables with white linen tablecloths. The place was very classy and Bill heard that a lot of Hollywood stars visited the Palladium, but he didn't see anybody that he recognized other than Harry James. The food at the Palladium was delicious and Bill lost all thoughts of war that night. The Los Angeles and Hollywood night life was like another world to Bill, and it was very exciting.

Bill received word from home that so many things were changing and it would be difficult to write about it all. Al Bennett had made his deal with the Army and reported for Basic Training on May 13th, 1942. After training, he would be attending Officer Training School, which was a good sign that Al might find an administrative position somewhere safe. George Troll had been drafted into the Army and was headed for basic somewhere out east and he had been by to see the Bennetts before he left. Bob Stoner was unbelievably busy training new pilots at Pensacola, and Harley and Dexter had both enlisted in the Army. Richard Turner, Eleanor's widower who lived with the Stoners, had enlisted in the Army Air Corps, so the Stoner house was cleared out of all except for Helen, who was still in high school. Earl "Bud" Dix had gotten married and was working at an ammunition plant in the Chicago area. Bill's neighbor from across the street, Stew Spence, had just gotten married and Bill asked Jessie to pass along his congratulations. Jessie tried to keep up with the enlistment notices from the *Beacon News*, but it seemed that just about every young man in Aurora had either enlisted or been drafted over the past few months. Dick Sheble, Ed Kocjan, Channing Miller, Louis Kuk, Bill Rees, Bob Reder, Bill Johnson and Pete Andrews had all joined the Marines, in spite of Bill's warnings. Steve wrote about how Aurora industry had shifted focus to producing war materials as it was a very serious business. Sam Stoner had left his job with International Harvester's Truck Division and gone to work for Diamond T Motor Car in Chicago. Diamond T had contracts to build heavy trucks for the government and Sam would be working with the War Department procuring the orders. It meant that he would be traveling even more than ever, but he planned on taking Margaret along as much as possible. Bill thought about how much Aurora had changed in six months. If he were still there he might not recognize the place.

33. Shipping Out

Bill had been enjoying his current assignment working with the BAR instruction and he had been able to greatly improve his marksmanship and overall handling of the rifle. He even was able to participate in some of those awe-inspiring firepower demonstrations for the new classes. Everyone in Company A had completed the Advanced Training and had been honing their skills. The Marines had been training on the loading of landing craft called LCVPs, or "Higgins Boats," by climbing down thirty-foot-high cargo nets. The huge wooden structures were called "mock-ups" as they simulated the height of a troop ship. Bill and members of Company A would climb the wooden stairs behind the mock-up, which was like waiting in line at the movies or at an amusement park. When they finally got to the top, they were to grasp the net with both hands and lift a bended knee over the side. They were instructed to not look down over their shoulders, only through their legs to see the progress of the Marine directly below them. Boots would step on the horizontal segments of the net and hands would grasp the vertical segments. This simple rule would eliminate Marines getting their hands stepped on while loading. Platoon sergeants stood on the ground and yelled out "Hands on the verticals only!" over and over. It seemed simple. These mock-ups provided great practice, but could not prepare Bill for the rising and falling of the ship and the LCVPs that would be the reality at sea. War matériel had been flooding into the areas around the docks at San Diego and the word on the base was that the 2nd Division would soon be shipping out. Bill's 1st Platoon was sent to the Quartermaster's to draw combat equipment and visitation to the base had been canceled. Bill phoned Helen and told her the news and they were both hugely disappointed that they would not be able to see each other before

Bill had to leave the United States. No one had any idea where the 2nd Division would be heading, but they were pretty sure that the Japanese would be there when they arrived.

Another sign that things were growing increasingly serious was the inflow of older Marines into the 2nd Pioneer Battalion. Battery G, 1st Battalion, 2nd Marines sent over Private First Class George H. Garcia, along with Privates Bob Stubblefield, Carl Fortenberry, Lester Hellman, Jesse Jeffcoat and John Kleber, who Bill recognized from BAR training. George Garcia was a very humble and gracious guy that everyone liked. He had been in the Marines for several years and had spent 18 months stationed at Guam, being transferred back to San Diego just two weeks before the Japanese attacked the island. Many of George's Marine buddies were killed or captured at Guam. George was from Southern California and his parents lived in Escondido. Should there be time to visit, George thought it would be nice if Bill could meet his family. As it turned out, there would not be.

The 2nd Pioneer Battalion began taking part in amphibious landing drills just off the coast of San Diego. Bill carefully suited up in his combat gear with everything except live ammunition. Jungle green, herringbone twill utilities with U.S.M.C. printed on the left pocket, brown socks with boondockers and khaki canvas leggings with a strap that went under the boot instep for starters. The M1941 backpack loaded with rations, socks, underwear and toiletries had Bill's blanket and shelter half rolled and tied over the top like an upside-down horseshoe. On the back of the pack hung the M1910, T-handle shovel with the handle hanging down. Bill's BAR belt had three large pouches on either side with two 20-round magazines per pouch. This would allow him to carry 240 rounds into combat plus the 20 in the rifle. The belt had a canteen and a K-Bar fighting knife attached to it and the whole belt attached to the backpack straps that acted as suspenders. Under his arm, Bill strapped his gas mask bag and over his right shoulder he slung his BAR. Topped off by the M1 helmet, Bill strapped on roughly 70 pounds of equipment.

1st Platoon loaded the troop ship designated for training and headed out of Port San Diego. Standing on the deck and watching the Navy at work from this perspective was eye opening. Destroyers and cruisers were loading pallets of shells for the big guns, and a pair of aircraft carriers used cranes to load tons of supplies. As far as the eye could see, Americans were loading up for war. Once the ships cleared the port, they swung north and then turned back toward the coast. This was the first time that Bill had been to sea and the sight of the fleet working together was fantastic. Their troop ship formed a line with the others and dropped anchor. The officers organized each Marine platoon into "boat groups." The math seemed pretty simple; each platoon had about 60 men and roughly 30 fit into a Higgins Boat. As the deck officers called out each boat number, those 30 Marines would form two lines with fifteen Marines in each line. There were two nets approximately six feet wide with one dropping down to the front of the Higgins Boat and one into the back. Bill was assigned to boat 5 on this particular exercise and moved to the rail. When they heard the command, "Over the side!" Bill lifted his right knee over the rail of the ship while balancing his top-heavy load of the pack, rifle and other equipment. Since he was first over the rail, he did not have to worry about Marines below him, only above. He looked down through his legs and caught sight of the Navy coxswain (pronounced "coxen") and his two crewmates clutching the cargo net at either end of the LCVP. "Hands on the verticals," Bill told himself. The hands were easy enough, but getting footing on the net as it moved in and out from the ship's sides was a bit of a challenge. As Bill lifted his head from looking down, the back of his helmet banged on the barrel of his BAR and it pushed his helmet forward and a bit over his eyes. He leaned forward and let the brim of the helmet scrape on the net to pull it back up. He didn't dare to let go with one of his hands long enough to right the helmet and take a chance on falling. If he fell, landing in the boat would break bones at the best. Falling into the ocean with the 70 pounds of battle gear strapped to his body would send him to the bottom of the Pacific.

As Bill neared the LCVP, he got the feel for the rise and fall of the ocean swells. The bottom of the boat rose and fell a full four feet and the Navy crew wanted him to let go of the net to meet the boat at the top of the swell. The cargo net went into the boat and the wide edge of the LCVP rose and fell against the net. Bill lowered his feet by using only arm strength on the last three squares of the net and watched the boat bottom as it began to rise. Bill let go and dropped into the boat. Just as his feet hit the bottom of the LCVP, it dropped like an elevator at Macy's and he lost his balance to his left. The Navy coxswain caught hold of his pack and steadied him against the gunwale (pronounced gunnel). The coxswain told Bill to move to starboard and "clear the port side" to make room for the other Marines to drop into the LCVP. The boat pitched and rolled with a "life of its own" apart from the ship. It was a good thing that the ocean was relatively calm today.

Bill craned his neck to watch the last four Marines from boat 5 climbing down the side of the ship. The Marines in the boat were grabbing the boots of the Marines lowering themselves and guiding their feet to the boat's floor. This was far easier than being the first one down the net. As these last Marines dropped in, the coxswain, now at the wheel near the port side rear of the vessel, yelled at his two crewmen to cast off, and they shoved the LCVP away from the side of the ship and the huge diesel engine roared to life. The LCVP swerved away from the ship and plowed for open water while another LCVP moved in for its load of Marines. As the flat front of the LCVP smashed through the rolling ocean, a spray of sea water rained over the front and sides of the boat. Bill was at the front on the starboard side and he leaned his head over the gunwale to see where they were headed. Dozens of LCVPs were circling ahead like confused ducks on a pond. As their craft approached the holding circle, it merged into the flock very smoothly. The rolling of the sea started to take its toll on some of the Marines as the smell of vomit caught Bill's nostrils. A little too much breakfast in some stomachs this morning. Bill had success with eating very little on such days to avoid such an unpleasant event. After what seemed like an hour, the LCVPs broke the holding circles and fanned out into long lines as if a race would soon begin. Another Navy boat appeared on the end of the line with a signalman visible on the side. The LCVPs lined up with this boat as neatly as they could. As the signalman waved a green flag, the coxswain gunned the engine to full speed and the LCVPs roared toward the beach. Bill watched as the shore slowly grew closer. He went over Gabel's orders again and again; "Hit the beach and find a defensive position; simulate locating a target with your rifle; get to your feet and run up the beach. Reassemble into your platoons."

Bill readied his BAR into his hands and waited for the LCVPs to strike the sandy bottom. The craft slammed into the sand and the crewman threw the lever and the cables whined as the huge ramp fell into the surf. Bill followed the ramp like a running back following his blockers through the line and ran into the thigh-deep water. He lifted his knees high as he plowed toward the beach with all of his strength. His boondockers sank into the soft sand below the water and he could feel sand and rocks sucking into his boots. Once his feet were out of the water he sprinted up the beach and then belly flopped with the BAR in front of him. The rattle of machine guns firing blanks filled his ears as he sighted targets on either side. He heard the sound of Marines literally hitting the beach as they plopped onto the sand on either side of him. Bob Swigert appeared on his left and Bill saw him smiling. George Garcia and Gabel crawled up on Bill's left and Gabel shook his head affirmatively that it was time to run up the beach. George stood to run and the rest of the boat load followed, spreading out left to right as to not "clump" and make easy work for those machine gunners. Bill's platoon climbed up the rocks to the road above. As Bill arrived on the road, he looked north and then south and realized that he had just attacked La Jolla Boulevard in almost the exact spot where he had paused to pray on that Sunday morning several weeks ago, while on his way to visit the Cobbs. Hundreds of civilians lined the boulevard and clapped and yelled as the Marines unloaded the LCVPs and headed up the beach. Bill joked that he didn't think the Japanese were going to be that excited to see them. Marine trucks lined the pavement and Gabel found one ready to load. The soaked and sand-clad Marines loaded into the trucks for the ride back to the MCB. Some of the guys waved at the civilians on their way back and yelled out sightings of good-looking young ladies.

June 9th, 1942. 1st Platoon of Company A, 2nd Pioneer Battalion, 2nd Marine Division received orders to move their personal equipment per overseas combat restrictions to the USS President Jackson. Bill placed everything he had into his sea bag with the exception of his combat equipment. Trucks arrived and 1st Platoon piled in for the short ride out to the docks. There was an unbelievable amount of war matériel being loaded at the San Diego docks onto what must have been a hundred ships. The four trucks carrying the 1st Platoon screeched to a halt in front a huge blue-gray ship with the number 37 painted on the bow, the USS President Jackson. Corporal Gabel had the platoon unload their gear and line it up along the dock. He climbed the gangplank with some paperwork and talked to some Navy officers on the deck. The years that Gabel had spent at sea with the USS Maryland had taught him perfect interaction with the Navy and he was clearly the man for this job. He had loaded and unloaded munitions dozens of times while on the USS Maryland before the war and he was the only Marine around who had actually fired at the Japanese. The platoon shouldered their sea bags and weapons and climbed up the gangplank, which was not as stable as they would have liked. Until this moment, most of them had been "landlubbers." Their cabin area was on the third deck and the first thing Bill noticed as he headed down the ship's ladders was the smell and the heat. Gabel explained that their job for the time-being was to "battle load" this ship with all of the supplies that 1st Battalion, 2nd Marines (1/2) would need. Company A would be working with and for 1/2 on this assignment.

The extremely close quarters of a troop transport (APA) ship.

(U.S. Navy Photo)

Corporal Gabel would be working with the Navy officers who were under Commander Charles William Weitzel. 1st Platoon was providing manpower on this project and the Navy would be in charge of every detail. There was, after all, only one way to load this ship, that being the Navy way. There would be thousands of crates, boxes and pallets to be loaded according to the Navy's loading orders. Some of the material was already dockside, but most of it would be trucked in as close to the loading order as possible. The ship had its own crane on board and there were dock cranes that could assist as needed. Each cargo area had to be cleaned and swept before loading and it was dirty work. Down inside the ship, most of the guys stripped to the waist as the heat and humidity were more than uncomfortable. On the deck or on the dock, the breeze and fresh air felt good. Day after day, trucks arrived and were unloaded either by hand, if possible, or with lift trucks. The cargo was placed on pallets to be hoisted by the crane and lowered into the ship's hold. The crew inside the ship would then stack the material in various places according to the demanding Navy officers. Loading food and non-combat provisions was similar to the work that anyone would experience in civilian life, but loading munitions was another matter. Crates of artillery shells, mortar rounds, TNT and small arms ammunition exposed the men to enormous danger. Dropping a load of munitions could cause an explosion beyond comprehension. There would be no smoking in the areas surrounding the munitions at any time and violators would be punished.

    The amount of matériel that they were loading into the President Jackson was staggering to look at. When Bill thought about all of this multiplied by the number of other ships being loaded at the same time, it was nothing short of amazing. Americans were working in factories, shops and plants from coast to coast to manufacture these war materials and the system was working. Now it would be up to outfits like Company A to get the matériel to the exact spots where it would be used to destroy the Japanese Empire. The work of 1st Platoon was frustrating and grueling at times. After loading an entire section of the hold, it was discovered that some of the matériel was loaded out of sequence. The entire hold had to be unloaded and reloaded according to plan, although it would cost two days of work. The Marines learned that Navy regulations would not bend. The Marines of 1st Platoon were also getting a preview of living aboard ship. The sleeping quarters were so cramped and hot that it was only possible to get a few hours of sleep at a time. After a week of torturous nights below deck, the platoon received permission to sleep on the deck. The nighttime air was actually cool and refreshing and Bill got some much-needed sleep.

    The amphibious landing practices continued several days a week with the remainder of the days spent slaving away for the Navy. Once the Jackson was nearly loaded, the ship began taking part in the landing practices. The Jackson would go out to sea, unload her Marines into the LCVPs, then return to dock. Company A and 1st Battalion, 2nd Marines would be dropped off back at the dock after they attacked La Jolla Boulevard.

    Rumors flashed through the ranks that departure was very near. Just about every Marine was standing in a line somewhere to try and call home one last time. Bill had grown used to visiting the Allens whenever he could get away. He had taken Herb Dale along to meet the Allen's and Herb grew fond of Mrs. Allen just as Bill had. Since Mrs. Allen's birthday was only a few days away, Bill and Herb stopped into a shop and bought her a U.S.M.C. pin much like the one that Bill had sent to his mother Jessie. Mrs. Allen loved the pin and she said she would wear it every day. Bill asked her to pray for them whenever she thought of them. Back on the Jackson, Bill had been busy writing letters home. Although there was not much news, Bill didn't know how many more letters he would be able to write. He told Steve and Jessie how wonderful the Allens had treated him and hoped that they could all meet one day. He mentioned that Herb would definitely visit the "Wonder City" when the war was over and they would all be back together again. Bill sat and wrote in the shade beneath the life boats that hung above the deck by the booms. He reflected on how he had found such a wonderful group of friends and his new brothers in Company A. Herb came out on deck and asked Bill if his letters were ready as he was heading into town for a few minutes. He would be happy to get the letters in the mail. Bill licked the last envelope and sealed it up. He tossed Herb a quarter for the stamps and told him that he would haul their bedrolls up from below so that they could set things up for the night.

Since they knew they would be shipping out soon, Bill and Herb decided to spend some money to repay the Allens for their hospitality. They spent Sunday, June 28th with the Allens and went to church with them at the First Presbyterian Church at the intersection of Third, Fourth and Date Streets in San Diego. Bill enjoyed the music and it reminded him of Fourth Street Methodist. The congregation sang hymn 230, "Just as I Am" and Bill sang with his usual gusto. The church then dedicated two new stained-glass windows and Reverend Thomas Law Coyle led everyone in a responsive reading. The choir performed a stirring version of Bach's "Jesu, Priceless Treasure" during the passing of the offering plates, and Reverend Coyle took to the pulpit for the sermon, which was based on Revelation 13:8. After communion had been celebrated, the congregation sang hymn 154, "In the Cross of Christ I Glory," before the final prayer and dismissal. They went to the grocery store and bought supplies for a picnic lunch and then the Allens took them to a park overlooking Mission Bay. The afternoon was glorious with the light breeze coming in from the ocean. This was just how Bill hoped it would be and he was thankful for the role of family that the Allens had been able to play in his life. That evening, Bill and Herb took the Allens into San Diego to the theater to see the new Daryl F. Zanuck movie *This Above All*. The movie was about a young English woman in the service and her love of a hero turned deserter who questioned if the war was worthwhile. There was a marriage proposal over the telephone and a lot of things that made Bill think about his life back home. The soldier decided that the war was worth fighting just before the movie ended. The Allens thought the movie was very good, but Bill and Herb were glad when it was over. They went back to the Allens apartment and spent the night as they had to report back to the Jackson by 8 a.m. the next morning.

Mrs. Allen cooked the fellows a grand breakfast of eggs and bacon in the morning and they all had a good time talking about the previous night and the movie. Herb and Bill looked sharp with their uniforms freshly ironed as they headed out the kitchen door. They told the Allens they would probably be back tomorrow night if all went well. There was no chance of going into town on Tuesday night as usual. On Wednesday morning Gabel told the platoon to prepare for another day of landing drills so every Marine on board donned their battle gear and took their positions as the Jackson's engines reversed and she pulled away from the dock. Mrs. Allen watched the Jackson pull away from the dock at 8:45 a.m. from her kitchen window. They passed the familiar sights of the Navy loading and unloading supplies and maintenance teams welding structures and spraying paint as they passed. The Jackson, along with all of the other troop transports, lumbered west to the place where they would turn north for the landing drills. Company A waited for the 90-degree turn to the north. It seemed somewhat overdue. The ships speakers crackled to life. "All hands! All hands! Now hear this! This is the captain speaking. This ship is now headed for the combat zone. Destination and plans will be given at a future date. Good luck!" Bill looked off the port side of the Jackson and noticed three destroyers turning in with the transports about a mile off their side. He and the guys crowded to the stern to watch San Diego and the hills above slowly fade into the endless Pacific Ocean. Most of them stayed put until the last dark line of the shore sank into the vastness of the deep blue ocean. Bill realized that now even the connection of land itself had been removed between him and what he loved. These ships and these Marines were now all that Bill had left of America. It was July 1st, 1942.

34. At Sea

It was going to take quite some time to get used to being confined while at sea. Since Bill and the other Pioneers from Company A had been on the Jackson for over three extra weeks, they were constantly helping the newcomers to find their way around. Each unit held their own meetings so there was a lot of information bouncing around as to where they might be going. Some of the guys who knew star navigation knew that the convoy was heading southwest in the general direction of Australia, New Zealand or Samoa. No big surprise there, since there were plenty of hostile Japanese in that direction. At the first meeting of Company A, Bill learned that the Company would be divided up into various support roles and not be operating as a team. Bill would be assigned to the 1st Battalion, 2nd Marines, in a combat support role of Pioneer. When 1/2 went ashore, Bill would go along to secure the landing zone, get supplies ashore and make sure those supplies advanced behind the combat troops. Some of the other Pioneers were likewise attached to 2/2 and a few weapons companies. A large group of demolition men from Company A (3rd Platoon) would be working together with Boos, Jarrett, Duke and Ashurst, attached to 1/2, Company B, led by 2nd Lieutenant Harold B. Hayes. The remainder of Company A would be assigned duty as needed with remnants of the 1st, 2nd and 3rd Platoons.

Company A, 1st Battalion, 2nd Marines was led by Captain Paul W. Fuhrhop from Galveston, Texas. Fuhrhop had been a reservist before the war and was quickly promoted after Pearl Harbor. In civilian life, he had been a clerk with the railroad in Galveston, where his wife Nora was waiting for his return from the Pacific. 2nd Lieutenant Byron T. McMichael was Platoon Leader of the 2nd Platoon and Bill would be working directly for him while keeping the line supplied. McMichael was the son of an automobile mechanic from Polk, Texas. Bill had already gotten used to the Texans in the Pioneer's Company A, and he rather liked the confidence that Texans had in general. They wanted to win and nobody messed with Texas. The plans were at first kept vague, and the meetings were organizational and general. Bill understood that his role would put him in harm's way and fighting along with the 2nd Platoon would be part of the job. He would be separated from most of his close buddies, but there was an upside to that; he would be able to better concentrate on the work at hand.

Weapon benches were set up all over the ship so that every rifle, machine gun, BAR and mortar could be checked and double checked. Bill's first concern was for the condition of his BAR. He cleaned and reassembled it every few days and helped quite a few of the younger BAR men with any problems they had. Bill helped Truitt Anderson with some weapons pointers and he noticed that Truitt often asked him for his opinion. Truitt epitomized the young eager Marine and Bill privately liked to try and help the "kids" in any way that he could. Truitt had attended North Side Baptist Church in Akron, Ohio, and he had a strong Christian faith, just as Bill did. The two of them talked about their common beliefs whenever they had the chance. Bill encouraged Truitt to stay away from the pitfalls that were temptations to all of the Marines, and they enjoyed getting together to talk whenever they could. Everyone on board had calisthenics once a day on deck; then the company, platoon and squad meetings, followed by personal equipment time. In the evenings and all night long, card games broke out on every deck. Some of these games were running 24 hours a day if the schedule permitted, and many fellas lost all their money within the first 48 hours. Bill liked to play card games, but not for money; nothing higher than the penny poker type. Some Marines won so much money that they stuffed envelopes and mailed it home to their families. Others produced money belts and actually hired some of their buddies to work security for them in case any other Marines would get the idea to "roll" them for their loot. Bill had squirreled away several copies of *The Upper Room* and he used personal time each day to read and re-read the issues. There were Sunday church services aboard and Bill was surprised that the USS Jackson actually had an organ for the services. Having these services on the top deck with the vast Pacific all around was a beautiful setting and life aboard ship was not too bad.

As the fleet headed farther to the south, the heat and humidity built up to the unbearable. Most Marines on board went shirtless for most of the day, and at night the top deck became covered with sleeping Marines and sailors as the lower decks were too hot for sleep. Everyone was under orders to avoid sunburn and some violators were actually levied fines for "Abuse of Government Property." As the Jackson approached the equator, most of the Marines and sailors were informed by their superiors that they were "polliwogs" that had not been initiated into the Realm of King Neptune. George Garcia explained to Bill and the others from the company that the initiation was for fun and there was nothing to worry about. Of course, George had already been initiated and would be among the few doing the initiating. George assured them that no one would be injured, at least not physically. The next morning, Bill stood in line to join the Realm. He was first blindfolded and had to "walk the plank" which ended in the middle of the dunk tank that had been built on the quarterdeck at the rear of the Jackson. Soaking wet with the blindfold still in place, he was strapped to a table and raw liver was dropped into his mouth like a baby bird receiving a fresh worm from its mother. It was slimy and did not require chewing, so down it went. Next, Bill had to kiss the belly of King Neptune which was actually a fat Chief Petty officer with a greased-up belly. The sound of laughter from the crew was like a large theater audience.

The final phase of the torture would be a blindfolded trip down the "Avenue of Paddlers." Most of the initiators took it easy on the polliwogs, but a few of them really let loose with the paddles causing some pain. Officers tried to oversee this so that it did not get out of hand. Besides the paddles, other initiators used broomsticks and improvised hooks and pokers to irritate the polliwogs as they passed. Once Bill finished the gauntlet, the blinders came off and he was given his certificate, making his trip over the equator and his acceptance by King Neptune official. He could then take his place as a viewer and watch and laugh as Herb, Johnnie Jones and Bob Swigert made their way through the "King's Palace." The day had been a lot of fun; something that most of the Marines would long remember. Overall, the time aboard ship gave Bill a lot of time to read, talk to his buddies in depth, and really get to know some of them. Watching the sun set became a daily show that most of the men didn't want to miss. The sunset at sea was so wide and colorful that there was nothing else like it, with the obvious exception of a sunrise. The colors went from fantastic red and orange, into purple, violet, and even shades of green and blue. It was great to find a place on the rail and watch it slowly happen, the fiery ball of the sun slowly sinking into the Pacific, as if the Japanese had torpedoed it.

July 19th, 1942. The armada of ships arrived offshore at Nuku'alofa, Tongatapu, capital of the Tonga Island Group in the South Pacific. The winds blew across Tonga and out into the ocean so that the fleet could smell the trees and vegetation before they could even see land. The captain announced that everyone would have several hours to stretch their legs on shore at Nuku'alofa. Bill felt as light as air as he climbed down the landing net and into the LCVP without his battle gear. Herb, George Garcia, Bob Swigert, Truitt Anderson, Corporal Gabel and the others were grinning as wide as Bill had ever seen them, as they looked over the gunwales of the boat. The dock was a mass of sailors and Marines and since they only had a few hours, Herb doubted that they would get into town. Nuku'alofa was only about five square blocks in size and didn't have much of anything of interest. The stores were quickly out of soda and candy and there were no bars. Any alcohol on the island was off limits and guarded by armed MPs. The first thing of interest to Bill was that the island was not moving. The guys marveled at the absence of motion and did a few knee bends to get used to it. George Garcia had lived on Guam for 19 months previously and although the customs were somewhat different here, he schooled the newcomers on island life.

They ran into some of the Company A Marines that had been assigned to the USS President Hayes. Manny Bud and Mike Matkovich hired an island kid to show them around the town. The kid was pretty muscular and Matkovich asked him how he became so strong. The kid had purchased the *Charles Atlas Bodybuilding Course* from an American magazine. The guys all enjoyed seeing trees, birds, dirt, flowers and above all else, women. The islanders were particularly defensive about their girls and women as they had been raided and plundered for centuries. After an hour or so, most of the Marines from Company A found each other and compared stories about their ships and their initiations into the Realm of King Neptune. There was Stelzer, Susans, Wysocki, Ellis, Cothran, Montague, Seng, Cabler, Sobolewski, Slowinski, Trier, Crelia and Harold Rice, the Navy Pharmacist's Mate who was the Company medic. For a few fleeting hours that day, Bill and his buddies were nothing more than tourists on a beautiful island in the South Pacific. They found an empty spot on the beach and talked, laughed and smoked cigarettes.

The guys were in a good mood and happy to be on land. Bill looked out at the turquoise waters to the armada of ships anchored off shore. He squinted as the sun reflected off the water and the warm tropical breeze blew back his hair. He thought about home and wondered what everyone was doing at that moment. He wished that he were there, but he found himself farther and farther from the "Wonder City" with each passing day.

35. Final Preparations

As the fleet departed from Nuku'alofa, many more ships became visible on the horizon. Three aircraft carriers, the USS Saratoga, USS Enterprise and USS Wasp, had joined the fleet along with dozens of powerful battleships, cruisers and destroyers led by the USS North Carolina. The Marines now knew that they must be getting close to their target. Another entire fleet of troop transports joined the armada and the news was that this was the entire First Marine Division coming up from New Zealand. It had not been announced where this battle party was headed, but it sure looked like the Japanese were in for some trouble. On July 28th, the fleet anchored near a high arching island called Koro, in the Fiji Islands. Practice landings were planned to begin the next day, so Bill geared up and waited with 1st Battalion, 2nd Marines. As the day progressed, the time table was delayed and then delayed again. Everything was taking longer than expected by the "brass" at the top of the chain of command.

Bill's 2nd Platoon finally got the orders to go down the nets and load the landing craft. As planned, Bill would stay in close proximity to McMichael and they would rehearse looking for good areas to use as ammo dumps. 34 Marines crammed into the Higgins Boat and the coxswain and his crew pushed off as he revved the big diesel engine and churned through the swells. Just like the practices at San Diego, a "control vessel" led the craft out to the holding area where they joined the others in relentless circling. The control boat with the signalmen waved the flags and two dozen Higgins Boats formed a line and moved toward Koro's designated "Blue Beach." The tide was much lower than anticipated and some of the boats struck large coral knobs just below the surface. The coxswain on Bill's boat yelled at one of the crewmen to get up on the ramp and watch the coral; something that could not be done in a combat situation. The coxswain said that they could not afford to lose any landing craft this close to the invasion; there were no more available.

The boat finally struck sand and the ramp cables whined as the ramp lowered and crashed into the surf. Bill followed the backpack of the Marine in front of him and stepped off into waist deep water holding the BAR high and to the left of his helmet. He kept his eyes on McMichael in front as he lifted his knees through the water. Each step became easier as the water depth diminished. Finally, Bill could run and he followed the Marines in front of him to the cover of large rocks between the sand of the beach and the trees at the top of a 20-foot hill. Lieutenant McMichael directed the platoon to their positions and moved them off the beach. He looked back at Bill and told him that this area just behind the large rocks would make a good ammo dump. It was protected from enemy fire by the rocks and it was high enough that the high tide would not swamp it later. Since there was no ammo to load for the simulation, Bill made mental note.

The platoons worked together to navigate as much of the island in front of them as possible and they all got in some very valuable practice wielding U.S.M.C. machetes. Later in the day, Captain Fuhrhop was notified that due to the damaged landing craft and the delays, 1/2 would have to spend the night on Koro and be picked up in the morning. Since this was to be a landing exercise, no one packed rations. The Marines fanned out and found a few abandoned villages as the residents had been evacuated for safety prior to the drills. They had left behind hundreds of chickens and a few goats. By nightfall, dozens of cooking fires appeared above the "Blue Beach" area of Koro Island. Unauthorized barbecues were taking place and Marines stayed up until the early morning hours playing cards and enjoying their first overnight on a South Pacific island.

Sitting around the fire, Bill had a conversation with McMichael and learned some inside info on 1st Battalion, 2nd Marines. McMichael told Bill that Captains Crane and Fuhrop were some of the best Marine captains in the Corps. Coincidentally, they had grown up together in Galveston, Texas, and both joined the Marines together on August 24th, 1936, and had been together almost the entire time. Now they would be leading the first attacks on Japanese-held territory. It was amazing to Bill that even the most "hard-core" Marines had friendly, human sides to them when there was no serious business at hand.

Bill laid his head back onto his backpack and set his helmet next to him as an arm rest. The stars above were more plentiful than anything that he had ever seen and the formations were strange to him. He knew that danger was getting closer by the day and he began to worship in prayer. He prayed through a long list of loved ones as he asked the Lord to watch over each one. Somewhere near the end of the list, Bill fell off to sleep. The next morning, they cleared the fires and waded out to the LCVPs to go back to the President Jackson. Thousands of Marines had clothes to wash out, gear to dry and weapons to clean.

When the fleet left Koro, things were markedly different. Ship lights were limited to red battle lights below deck and there were no unauthorized lights on the deck after sunset. Bill was told that light at sea can be seen over 50 miles away and sometimes farther. There could very well be Japanese submarines in these waters and enemy planes were always on the prowl. Bill and the Pioneers that were assigned to 1/2 went to the battalion and company meetings and were told that their objective would be the Solomon Islands. The 1st Division would attack the largest island of Guadalcanal while the 2nd Division would hit a series of smaller islands called Florida, Tulagi, Gavutu and Tanambogo. Bill's job would be to land with 1/2 on Florida Island with the first wave. Once supplies came in, Bill and the Pioneers would feed ammo, food and water to 1/2 as they attacked and destroyed the Japanese in front of them. Since no one knew exactly what awaited 1/2 on Florida Island, Fuhrhop and McMichael made it clear that their first order of business was to secure a beachhead and get ammunition on the beach where it could be distributed. From there, they would locate forward ammo dump areas and the Pioneers would make sure

An unknown U.S. Destroyer escorts the USS President Jackson near Koro on August 4th, 1942, just prior to the Invasion of the Solomon Islands on August 7th. (U.S. Navy Photo)

that these "forward dumps" were supplied. The 2nd Division had always maintained that they were "2nd to none" in their good-natured rivalry with the 1st Division. As it turned out, the 2nd Division would actually go ashore an hour before the 1st Division, and Bill was excited to hear that the first unit ashore would be Company B/1/2, led by Captain Crane. They would hit the Florida Island beach at Heleta first, followed by A and C at Helavo within 30 minutes. Florida Island would be the first ground that the United States would take back from Japan since the war began eight months earlier.

The next few days were spent cleaning and oiling the BAR and working with dozens of other BAR men to check and recheck the rifles. Bill sat on the deck with Ed Susans and a handful of younger Marines loading BAR magazines. Bill removed the .30-06 rounds from the factory cardboard boxes and oiled and cleaned each round. It was shocking to see how much dirt had attached to the ammunition and the clean rags soon turned dark gray. Truitt Anderson asked Bill if he thought that it would really make a difference and Bill said any advantage was worth taking. He explained that cleaning and oiling the cartridges prior to loading them in the magazines would help the operation by keeping that dirt out of the rifle and the oil would help feed the ammo with less stoppages. This would be true with any magazine-fed weapon. Twenty rounds snapped into each magazine and 12 magazines loaded into each BAR belt. Bill would wear one belt ashore and carry another around his neck for a total of 480 rounds. Once the fighting started, there would be no place to sit and load the magazines. Bill went with about 10 other BAR men to the stern of the Jackson where weapons could be test fired. He loaded a 20-round mag and stepped to the rail when it was his turn. He snapped the bolt back, raised the rifle, pushed the safety forward and let out three round bursts into the vastness of the ocean. He could see where the rounds were hitting the waves and spraying water into the air. The BAR was perfect, and he was ready to go.

Everyone was restricted to sleeping in their bunks below deck and it was truly hard to get more than two hours of sleep in a row. The heat kept Bill's uniform soaked with sweat and their quarters reeked with locker room smells. The daytime temperatures had been about 100 degrees lately and the below deck temperatures stayed over 90 degrees. Cigarette smoke was ever present if not thick. Bill struggled to write a few letters that he knew could be his last. He couldn't write anything descriptive about what he had been doing as it would be cut out by the Navy Censors. Keeping with his commitment, he only wrote positive things and did not give Jessie and the others any reason to be concerned. As far as they knew, "the kid was alright." Bill longed to get back on deck, but it was not possible for the time being. There had never been any privacy in the Marines, but below deck on the Jackson was the worst. The night of August 6th, 1942 was especially tense. Bill attended the Protestant services held below deck and it was packed. With the invasion beginning the next morning, Marines looked around the room with the knowledge that some of them would undoubtedly be dead within 24 hours. The Chaplain's sermon was about trusting the Lord when going into the storm and preparing for death, should this be their last day on earth. Communion was given and Bill reflected in his own heart as to whether he was ready to die. He had not considered such things a year ago when life was so good and he was making the drives out to Sandwich to see Helen or learning about air conditioning from Don. But now, at this moment, literally everything that Bill had in life was stripped away and he had to prepare for the worst. Everywhere Bill went on the Jackson, Marines were either very reflective and quiet or loud and boisterous. There was a lot of talking back and forth about how many Japanese one Marine wanted to kill, or comments about hoping that the first guys ashore would leave some Japanese for the other Marines to kill. Bill was careful to avoid any such conversation as he was not looking forward to killing anyone. In his heart, it saddened him that anyone had to be here to do this grisly task. He also kept in mind that many of these Marines may be spending their last hours on earth. Chaplain Willard worked tirelessly to talk with and pray with hundreds of these Marines. Some of the Christian Marines that had been attending services came to Willard and told him that as Christians, they were apprehensive about killing the Japanese. Willard reminded them of the brutality of the Japanese at Nanking, where they raped and murdered over 100,000 Chinese civilians. He had personal letters from missionary friends that had lived in China that depicted atrocities they had personally witnessed. Defeating the Imperial Japanese was imperative to keep a large part of the world free. Whenever these discussions occurred, the Marines left Chaplain Willard with a clear sense of duty and responsibility.

After returning to the bunks, Bill pulled out *The Upper Room* and his small New Testament and read through a few of the short studies. A young Marine came over and crouched next to Bill's bunk and asked him what he was reading.

Bill told the Marine that it was the Gospel of John. The Marine asked Bill if he believed the stuff in the Bible and Bill told him that he absolutely did. He asked Bill if he were afraid to die and Bill told him that he was; but he knew that if he died tomorrow, that he would be with Christ in Heaven and no longer on the island. Bill reminded the young Marine about the promises that Jesus had made to all of us in the Gospels and explained that Jesus was in fact our Creator that had come to rescue us from our sin. Sin was the only thing that could separate us from our Creator, but Jesus had provided the way for us to be forgiven of our sin through His death on the cross. Just like one Marine would be willing to give his life to save his buddies, Christ had laid down His life for us. Bill prayed with the young Marine before he thanked Bill and went back toward his bunk. Bill stowed his things and laid back on the rolled-up blanket he used as a pillow. He was glad that the young Marine had stopped to talk. He asked the Lord to protect the kid in the coming battle, and he asked for the Lord's protection for himself as well. He closed his eyes and somehow fell asleep.

36. Into the Fray

August 7th, 1942. Bill was jarred from his dreams at 0300 hours and carefully rolled out of his bunk. Only the red battle lights were lit as the Jackson was in very dangerous enemy territory. Bill heard a Marine joking that it was, "Time to wake up and go kill some Japs, you guys!" It was a very sobering way to get out of bed. There had been so many mornings as a Marine, but this one was very different. Today, everything that Bill had learned as a Marine would be tested. Being able to do the job could mean life or death for Bill or the Marines next to him. Bill dressed and tightened his boondockers, and then he laced up the leggings over the bottoms of his pants. Putting on the long-sleeved khaki shirt seemed ridiculous with the sweltering heat below deck, but everyone had to dress prior to breakfast. Bill linked up with George Garcia, Herb Dale, Chuck LaPoint and Fred Ellis, and they followed the sweaty corridors lit by the eerie red lights and fell in line for breakfast. The guys from Company A were all splitting up today and heading in different directions. Bill and Chuck LaPoint would be heading to Florida Island with Sam Herman, Rudy Halazon, Fred Ellis, Bob Swigert and a few others. Russ Jarrett, Henry Duke, Emory Ashurst, Barney Boos and most of the other demolition men were going ashore in the first waves to Florida Island with Lieutenant Hayes, who was leading the way. The "Go to Hell Men" were prepared to show the Japanese their TNT skills. Manny Bud was going ashore with the early waves to a small island called Gavutu and several groups were being held in reserve on the Jackson. Herb Dale, Truitt Anderson, George Garcia and Mike Matkovich would be staying on the Jackson.

Keeping with his usual routine, Bill had a cup of coffee and an apple for breakfast as he did not want to lose a large breakfast on the Higgins Boat later. The guys from Company A said their goodbyes as they headed off to gear up and take their places with their respective adopted units. Bill felt a little like an orphan having to go into battle with officers that were still somewhat unknown to him. Back at the bunkroom, Bill went over the loading of his gear one more time. He had a change of underwear and socks jammed on the very bottom of the pack as padding. He had been issued three days of K-rations which were next at the bottom of the pack. He placed his mess kit on top of the rations with the fork, knife and spoon rolled into a small rag to keep them from rattling in the pack. The New Testament and *Upper Room* were shoved down the side in case he might even find time to read. The pack was ready with his shelter half and shovel firmly strapped on. His Ka-Bar fighting knife was strapped to the left pack strap so that he could unsheathe it with his right hand. Bill strapped on his heavy ammo belt loaded with the 240 rounds of .30-06 for his BAR and two full canteens. He hung the extra ammo belt over the pack. He set his helmet on his head, picked up his pack with one hand and the BAR with the other and made his way toward the deck.

It was a little before 0500 when Bill made his way to the main deck and the cool morning air was refreshing as the breeze blew against his sweat soaked shirt. He made his way to the port side bow area where he was to assemble with 1/2 and report to 2nd Lieutenant McMichael. The Navy was lowering the Higgins Boats by the boom arms that swung out from the ship and the air was already filled with the sounds of dozens of diesel-powered landing craft moving about near the Jackson. The sky was just beginning to show a bit of gray light to the east and tension was high as everyone knew the Japanese were soon to learn that they were due for visitors today. During the night, the naval battle group had split into two groups with the 1st Marine Division forces moving to the south of Savo Island to prepare their assault on Guadalcanal. The 2nd Marine Division forces had slipped to the north of Savo Island to prepare their attack on Florida Island, Gavutu-Tanambogo and Tulagi. At 0610, the sun was bounding off the trees from Tulagi, Gavutu and the other islands within view. The landing area on Florida Island lay out of sight with Tulagi in the line of sight. At 0615 Wildcats and SBD Dauntless dive bombers began attacking Tulagi and this was the first actual combat that most of the Marines had ever seen. Fires were soon in sight on Tulagi and there was a good-sized oil tank on Gavutu that exploded and sent a plume of dark black smoke rising skyward. Destroyers and cruisers opened fire with five-inch guns and Tulagi and Gavutu were soon obscured by smoke. So far, the morning had been very similar to the drills on Koro ten days ago, with the exception of the living Japanese waiting on these Islands. Bill strapped on his pack and spare ammo. A sergeant moved through the ranks of the platoon with an open box of hand grenades and instructed the Marines to take two grenades and place one in each pants pocket. He struck Bill as being reminiscent of a peanut vendor at the ball park. Bill dropped the grenades into his pockets and the thought of what would happen should one of the pins somehow come loose made him quickly grasp at another thought. Across the Sealark Channel, the Navy began pounding the shores of Guadalcanal as the 1st Marine Division was likewise making their preparations to invade there this morning. The huge guns pounded the air and their concussions echoed across the water. At 0640, Captain Crane led his Company B, 1st Battalion, 2nd Marines over the port side of the Jackson and the Higgins Boats began to carry Marines to the designated assembly areas to begin circling. As soon as Company B was over the side, Company A moved into position and began descending the nets into the boats.

Bill stayed just behind Lieutenant McMichael per the plan. McMichael wheeled around and yelled at his 34 Marines. This was their boat. "Hands on the verticals! First guys in guide the feet of the Marines above! Make sure your helmets are buckled and all your gear is secured to your person!" The lieutenant went over the side and Bill went right behind him. The nets were becoming routine and the sea was calm, so loading went smoothly compared to some of the dress rehearsals. As Bill neared the gunwales, he felt two hands grasp his ankles, so he let McMichael guide his feet to the plywood bottom of the Higgins Boat while he lowered himself with his upper body. The boat loaded in five minutes and the coxswain and crew pushed off as the engine roared in its doghouse in the middle of the boat. This was one of the older Higgins Boats without the high sides and the front ramp. When the bow struck the sand of the beach, the Marines would have to jump over the sides to the left and the right at the front. If you went over the side at the back of the boat, the water would more than likely be over your head. The waves were deep blue and the islands were dark green, almost black, with steam hovering within the trees. Had this been a pleasure cruise, the sights were quite beautiful. A light sea spray came over the front as the boat accelerated and it actually felt refreshing.

The control boats appeared and they flagged the landing craft carrying Company B into a line with eight boats abreast, and they started toward the shores of Florida Island toward Heleta. Captain Fuhrop led the eight boats circling with Company A as they broke into a straight line and they were flagged for the run in to Florida Island 20 minutes behind Captain Crane and Company B. McMichael told Bill that they would know by the look of the beach in front of them what to expect. Captain Fuhrop would not have that luxury. The landing wave swung a wide left turn as they passed between Tulagi on their left and Gavutu-Tanambogo on the right. Bill leaned his head over the port side gunwale and he could see the lead boats far ahead with the shadowy mass of Florida Island in front of them. He turned his head to the rear and he could see Company C far behind them. In less than an hour, all 600 Marines should be ashore.

McMichael stepped onto the bracing of the gunwale and raised himself for one last shout at his Marines. He shouted out that he wanted all weapons loaded with the safety left on. As soon as the boat strikes sand, safety off and follow him to the beach. Get to the beach and find cover. Over the drone of the engine and the waves, the snapping of steel became prominent as live rounds were fed into the chambers of three dozen weapons at the same time. The Navy gunners swung their turret-mounted thirty-caliber machine guns as they searched for possible targets on the shore. The faces of the Marines were serious and nervous. There were no jokers now. Catholics were praying and "crossing" themselves, while many had their helmets down and were praying privately. Bill had come to feel that the inside of his helmet was the only private place there was in the Marine Corps. Bill prayed and asked for the safety of these Marines. He committed himself into the Lord's hands and knew there was a possibility he might soon meet the Lord face to face. As the boats approached shore, McMichael watched the beach like a hawk hunting prey and then turned to yell at his sergeant. The beach looked clear and there was no smoke. This coupled with the fact that the Higgins Boat was not being peppered with fire from the shore was a good sign. Bill tensed for the shock of the boat hitting the bottom. It was like a bus hitting the brakes with everyone shifting weight into the ones in front. McMichael leapt over the side and Bill followed into the waist deep water. Searching the beach as he plowed through the water, Bill could not see or hear any signs of fighting. An officer on the beach directed McMichael to the left and was motioning to stay down. The very distinct smells of the tropics were powerful in Bill's nostrils as he ran in a crouching position up the beach toward a group of about 20 Marines who had taken cover behind fallen tree trunks. One of the Marines turned back to McMichael and told him that it didn't look like any one was home.

Old style Higgins Boat loaded for Florida Island, August 7th, 1942.

(U.S.M.C. Photo)

McMichael made sure that his Marines were well covered and he conferred with other officers. Captain Fuhrhop was conferring with his lieutenants about 50 yards east and then Fuhrhop ran in a crouch over to McMichael. He wanted Company A to move off the beach to make room for Company C who were already plowing toward the beach about 500 yards out. Company A moved into the trees and set up a defensive perimeter about 30 yards from the beach. Elements of Company B were out in front of them searching as far as a quarter mile into the jungle. Orders were given to hold all fire unless there was verified enemy activity. Machine gun tripods and mortar plates were snapped into position and the "slit, slit" of T-handled shovels became audible up and down the line. Bill dropped his pack, unsheathed his shovel and began to dig a temporary home between the trunks of two towering palm trees. The surface soil was fairly soft, but he soon hit a lot of root material about a foot down. The dirt and clay had an orange-red color and the smell of rotting vegetation was fairly strong. The sergeant came by and was checking on the positions chosen and had a few Marines move to the left flank instead of bunching up in the middle.

He said that a mortar round could kill men within a radius of about 30 feet and there was no sense in making it easy for the enemy.

Digging a hole three feet wide, six feet long and 30 inches deep with a short-handled shovel was no easy task. Bill worked up a full, dripping sweat as the morning sun was pushing the heat to about 90 degrees already. He piled the dirt from the fox hole in the front towards the jungle and along the sides to act as sand bags, if only they had them. He knelt at the front and sighted the BAR into the trees. He could see fairly well for about 30 feet, but beyond that, the jungle darkened. From out in the trees, Bill heard a voice yelling "Lollipop!" followed by "Second Platoon coming in!" The official password for the Solomon campaign had been selected as "Hollywood" with "Lollipop" being the return. These two words were chosen as they were both nearly impossible for the Japanese to pronounce. Within seconds, Marines appeared as they came back from their hunt. They had not encountered the enemy. The Marines worked tirelessly for the rest of the day setting up and fortifying the defensive positions and Bill worked with Lieutenant McMichael to find and stock a suitable ammo dump. There was a good chance the Japanese who had fled into the jungle would return after dark or at dawn for a counter-attack. Marines from Company A had made it through the jungle to the Japanese seaplane base a few miles away, where they found warm food on the table, but no Japanese. There were ferocious battle sounds emanating from both Tulagi and Gavutu, both just a few miles away. Most of the Marines on Florida were hoping they could get over to these other islands and get into the fight. There would be no fires for cooking so Bill unboxed his first K-Rations in combat. The can had a handful of crackers that were labeled "biscuits," along with lemon candies, sugar cubes and a packet of instant coffee. Some of the guys figured out that they could use a cigarette lighter under a blanket to heat the water in their mess kit cup for the coffee. Bill figured it would be best to drink his at canteen temperature, which was about 100 degrees. It tasted so bad that heating it up would not have made a difference.

Any way you looked at the situation, the lack of Japanese on Florida Island was a blessing. No one had died today, which was certainly not the case on Tulagi and Gavutu-Tanambogo. As night fell, the air began to cool considerably and fog came in from the water. Just after dark, a Marine machine gunner opened fire into the jungle, which started a chain-reaction of all the Marines on the line. Bill fired two full magazines from his BAR before he heard McMichael screaming at the top of his lungs to "CEASE FIRE!" It turned out there were no Japanese in the area and the Marines found out how stupid they could be. One thing that Marine officers ALWAYS stressed was to NOT waste ammunition! This was the first night in a combat zone for nearly every Marine on Florida Island and they all had the jitters. For several hours, the thick fog made it impossible to see more than a few yards into the jungle. The officers ordered quiet so that sentries could listen for signs of a Japanese attack. Bill was assigned the second watch for the night, so he stretched out in his fox hole with the blanket below and tried to get some sleep. Within seconds, an all too familiar sound whined in his ear. It was a mosquito. As soon as he lay still, they seemed to come from everywhere. He unrolled the shelter half and threw it over the fox hole. It soon became so hot that suffocation was a real possibility. He would have to try to cover his face with his helmet and cover all the skin he could and try and get some sleep. Sounds of battle were clearly coming across the water from the various islands with a few naval rounds firing occasionally. Just before 0200 on August 8th, Bill was wakened by the sergeant for guard duty. Bill's job was to watch the jungle out in front of his position and challenge any movement by shouting "Hollywood!" Bill realized that he had numerous mosquito bites on his hands and face and the itching and burning were annoying. The stars were brilliant above and the air had cooled down quite a bit and the fog had dissipated for the most part. Bill struggled to stay awake as he gazed out into the blackness. There were several noises that spooked Bill and the other sentries, but it was probably just animals out foraging. It was easy to imagine the enemy was behind every tree.

Bill was relieved a 0400 and was able to grab another hour of sleep before the 0500 wake up. As Marines ate from their cans and packages, word was being spread around that these 1/2 combat teams would be rerouted to the other islands where Marines were in some tough fighting. Auxiliary units would be coming ashore within the hour to relieve 1/2 and they would leave the island on the same landing craft. Company A, 1/2 would be sent to Blue Beach, Tulagi, just a short trip away. Bill packed his gear and made ready to leave. McMichael wanted to load as much of the spare ammo as they could and most of this could be carried ashore if the resistance was light on Tulagi. The replacements waded ashore and they exchanged news with 1/2 as they waded past to the running Higgins Boats. Bill carried a crate of grenades on his shoulder in addition to the rest of his gear. All 34 Marines from yesterday were accounted for and the Navy coxswain reversed the engine and pulled the hull free from the sandy bottom. The boats made a massive right-hand swing around Tulagi, where numerous fires were burning as Edson's Raiders and 2/5 were locked in a tough fight with the Japanese who were garrisoned to defend the island.

McMichael again yelled the order to load weapons and the snap of the rifle bolts filled the air. Bill pulled the BAR bolt back with his right hand and let it "snap" forward. He checked the safety as it was pushed back into the trigger housing. The coxswain shouted out to stand by, then a short time later shouted, "This is it!" as the hull pushed into what felt like coral. The shock pushed Bill forward into the sergeant who was up against the ramp just as it was released. Sea water sprayed onto Bill's helmet as he charged down the ramp into the waist-deep water. As he pushed forward, the sounds of small arms fire became audible and then Bill noticed something that made his heart sink. There were splashes in the water in front and to the sides of the platoon as they advanced. Although the fire was not heavy, they were nonetheless being shot at by Japanese troops on Tulagi, and getting ashore fast was a necessity. McMichael shouted at the Marines to spread out as they advanced. Bill wanted to run forward, but full speed in three feet of water is horribly slow. At last he could raise his knees out of the water and he powered forward as Marines on both sides churned up the water with equal desire to reach shore and find some cover. There were several groups of Marines on Blue Beach that were returning fire to where they thought the snipers were located. Bill followed

McMichael and the sergeant to where a captain had set up a post behind some trees and rocks. The captain said there were groups of Japanese moving all over this end of the island and he needed Company A to move up the 350-foot hill, and then sweep down to "Sesapi" directly on the other side of the island. The dock area at Sesapi was somewhat secure, so 1/2 would move to the west end of the island to remove pockets of Japanese that they may find.

Bill looked up the 350-foot hill in front of him and realized that this was going to be tough for the Pioneers as they would have to lug ammo and water up the grade as 1/2 advanced. Captain Fuhrhop waded ashore and went over the assignment with the beach captain and McMichael and then passed word that they would move up the hill in search of the Japanese who were firing on the incoming troops. McMichael moved up the hill and Bill stayed to his right and was searching each tree in front of him as he was aware of his heart pounding in his chest. After a 100-yard advance, firing broke out to their left and everyone hit the dirt or took a knee behind a tree. Rifles scanned the trees above, in front and to the rear. The firing stopped and they cautiously moved ahead. McMichael and the sergeant called out, "Bennett!" and Bill took several large strides up the grade and dropped to a knee. There was a depression in the hillside with several boulders on the uphill side. This would be the first ammo dump location and McMichael grabbed two Marines to defend the depression. Bill made his way back down to the beach with four other Pioneers in tow and they each grabbed the extra ammo that 1/2 had just brought ashore from Florida Island. Pushing back up the grade with the 30 lb. ammo boxes on their shoulders, the Pioneers felt the full explanation for why the Corps training had been so vigorous. They reached the depression and deposited the ammo, then quickly made their way back to the beach. The beach captain assigned four other Marines to move the ammo up the hill and they soon had the depression loaded with ammo and several 5-gallon cans of drinking water.

Bill and the Pioneers now pressed forward to find McMichael. Their responsibility would be to locate another dump about 100 yards ahead, then bring up some ammo from the first dump to the second. This would make sure that Company A would not get separated from supplies as they advanced. At the crest of the hill, McMichael sent the 1st Platoon down the ridge moving west as he took 2nd and 3rd Platoons down the opposite slope toward Sesapi. About halfway down the slope, 3rd Platoon was sent west and 2nd Platoon proceeded down to Sesapi. Other Pioneers were split off with 1st and 3rd Platoon, while Bill stayed with McMichael and the 2nd. As they came close to Sesapi, a distant Marine yelled out "Hollywood!" and the sergeant quickly yelled back "Lollipop! First Battalion, coming in!" As Bill came into the clearing above Sesapi, he could see about two dozen Marines from 2/5 who had set up defensive positions to keep the Japanese from taking back the damaged docks and boat ramp. Their main concern was the jungle to the west of them that had not been cleared. They had encountered several attempts by the enemy to attack their positions and there were a dozen dead Japanese littered 20 to 30 yards out from their foxholes. McMichael told their 2nd lieutenant that his men were now on the ridge, the midpoint, and that they would sweep west to clear this end of the island. He would be back here by nightfall to bolster the defenses.

As 2nd Platoon moved out, they passed through the dead Japanese soldiers. The heat had already caused the bodies to bloat and the smell of death made Bill hold his breath as he passed. Thousands of flies covered the bodies and the movement of the Marines caused the flies to rise into the air. Bill was shocked as he saw the damage the machine guns had inflicted on the enemy. Large parts of their bodies were missing and internal organs were strewn about on the ground. One of them was all but cut in half through his midsection. As Bill turned his head away from the sight, he noticed another who looked as though he was about 16 years old, and had died with an awful look of surprise on his face. Seeing these first dead began to verify in Bill's mind what he had already known in his heart; there would be no glory in war. Using the Sesapi defenses as their base ammo dump to move west, Bill went to work to bring supplies forward into the jungle following McMichael. The sound of explosions and heavy fighting were coming from the east end of the island and there was sporadic gun fire up ahead and up the ridge. 1st Platoon radioed McMichael that they had just exchanged fire with the enemy and they had fled down the slope toward 3rd Platoon. 2nd Platoon had the slope covered from the shoreline, uphill at an angle for about two hundred yards and they slowly moved forward as though they were dragging a huge fishing net. Bill fell into the line with the BAR ready and the safety off. He reached into his pants pocket and clipped one of his grenades onto the pack strap.

A large amount of rifle and automatic fire erupted up the slope and it sounded close. Bill took cover behind a tree and sighted the BAR up the slope. The radio crackled and 1st Platoon reported that the enemy they had encountered were working their way downslope and were exchanging fire with 3rd Platoon. What seemed like a few seconds later, bullets whizzed overhead and snapped off tree limbs with loud cracks. Marines began firing and yelling up and down the line. As Bill looked up the slope he saw dark outlines of brown uniforms with mushroom-like helmets running downhill firing as they ran and shrieking unintelligible shouts. Bill's heart pounded as though it was in his throat. He swung the BAR towards the mushrooms and emptied the magazine with four large bursts and the bolt stayed open showing the need for attention. He heard someone yelling "Grenades!" and didn't know if he should throw one or duck from one of theirs. He grabbed the grenade from the pack strap and yanked the pin out, released the lever and threw it out into the jungle. He wasn't sure which grenade was his as several seemed to detonate at the same time. He released the empty magazine and shoved a full one into the BAR, then snapped the bolt back and looked for more targets. Firing continued up and down the line for about 30 seconds before he heard McMichael shouting "Cease fire!" The smell of gunpowder was thick on the jungle floor and Bill noticed that his ears had been dulled by the concussion of the rifle fire. A high-pitched whine was predominant with muffled voices of Marines on both sides.

The radio crackled and came to life again as 3rd Platoon said that they had sent two squads in pursuit of the enemy and they should be making contact with 2nd Platoon. A few minutes later, "Hollywood!" rang out up the slope and the sergeant countered with "Lollipop!" Marines from both units cautiously moved toward each other to probe for live enemy. After a few more minutes, a voice yelled back to McMichael that all was clear. Bill followed McMichael and the sergeant toward the Marine's voices. Scattered up the slope, there were 15 to 20 dead, or very nearly dead, Japanese. Marines were removing weapons and searching for documents that might be handed over to Navy Intelligence. A few of the Japanese were still breathing, but there was nothing that could be done to save them, nor did anyone seem interested. Bill looked at the dead and dying enemy and saw more than their uniforms and their weapons. He couldn't help but think that somewhere in Japan, these men fit into a family just like he did in Illinois. There were wives, children, mothers and fathers that would be getting the news of their loved one's death. Then Bill thought about Pearl Harbor and Wake Island and those Americans that had not asked for war, but died anyway. This framed the dead enemy in his mind. These soldiers were the agents of the destructive ideology of the Japanese Empire, and that was the reason they had died.

Bill helped to collect the weapons and went back to Sesapi with a squad dispatched to bring the Japanese equipment and arms there for safe keeping. The rest of 1/2 pressed on to the west end of Tulagi. When he returned to Sesapi, Bill noticed that more Marines had landed and some were unloading supplies at the small pier. At the end of the pier, Bill spotted a familiar figure as Mike Matkovich of Company A, 2nd Pioneers, was setting up his .30 caliber machine gun. On his way over to the pier, Bill ran into the two corpsmen from Company A, 2nd Pioneers, Harold B. Rice and Roy Ford. They said they had just landed by Higgins Boat about an hour ago and they were told to set up permanent defenses here at Sesapi. Bill was thrilled to see these guys since he had not seen them since the stop at Nuku'alofa several weeks ago. These Pioneers had been on the USS Hayes, which cruised next to the Jackson on the way down. Matkovich asked Bill if he had seen any action yet and Bill gave him the brief description. Some of the guys from 2nd Pioneers were still aboard ship and about 90 had been lent out to the infantry battalions, as had Bill. As Bill was talking to Matkovich, another Higgins Boat appeared heading for Sesapi. As it approached the pier, Bill and Matkovich went to assist tying the boat off when Bill heard his name called with surprise. It was George Garcia and Truitt Anderson looking up from the boat with big smiles. The boat was loaded with supplies and ammo and it had apparently been loaded from the USS Jackson. Bill gave George a hand up to the pier and George said how glad he was to see that Bill was alright.

Bill and George talked briefly, and then he told George and Truitt that he would see them later, probably back here on the island. Bill asked the lieutenant on the dock about getting a hold of some of that ammo. He told the lieutenant that he was a Pioneer for 1/2, and they were busy clearing the west end of Tulagi. He managed to get some boxes of .30-06 rifle rounds and two crates of grenades. George told him to be careful and he would let the other guys on the Jackson know that he had seen him. Bill and the squad from 1/2 all found each other and set out to find McMichael and the rest of the platoon. By the time they caught up with the unit, they had encountered several smaller groups of the enemy and had killed them all. 1st Platoon was ordered to dig in on the west end of the island where there was only about 100 yards of shallow water separating Tulagi from Florida Island. It was highly likely that the enemy who had fled into the jungle the previous day might decide to infiltrate across these shallows. The other two platoons spread out and worked their "net like" advance back toward Sesapi to dig in for the night. Bill went to work with his shovel for the second night in a row and he could feel the sore muscles from last night's dig. Some of the Marines who had first arrived at Sesapi had found sections of mosquito netting but Bill was not fortunate enough to get any. The mosquitoes were equally as bad as they had been over on Florida Island, if not worse. The misery factor took a turn for the worse just as it was getting dark. Rain started to fall.

37. Orphans

Tulagi was a strange place after dark. Everyone knew there were living, stalking, enemy soldiers on the island and they would be active at night. There were still intermittent explosions and gunfire coming from the east end of the island. The 105-degree heat had withered quickly after dark and the rains brought temperatures of about 60 degrees at night. Bill had fallen asleep with the shelter half over his fox hole and he had been tired beyond his own belief. The long day of constant action and lugging ammo and water cans had been far worse than any exertion he had previously experienced. He had fallen asleep and been jarred awake by gunfire so many times that it became torturous. The Marines around Sesapi had imagined they saw the enemy just about everywhere they looked. Mike Matkovich had fired numerous bursts out into the water at the enemy that turned out to be floating logs. The tension turned out to be a good thing when a Japanese soldier carrying grenades rode a floating log to the end of the boat ramp and the BAR wielding sentry sent seven rounds through his Imperial midsection before he could even stand up all of the way. The burst essentially cut the enemy intruder in half.

Bill became so tired that he felt like he was passing out. He must have slept for a good two hours when he woke up to the strangest feeling. His fox hole had about five inches of water on the bottom and he was almost floating in it. He used his helmet to try and bail some of the water out, but the mud was unbelievable. There was no way he could get out of the foxhole as the trigger-happy Marines would probably have shot him in a second. Sesapi was a dangerous neighborhood tonight. As Bill was trying to situate himself to get more sleep, things got even worse. The sky began to light up as though lightning were flashing, followed directly with terrific booms of heavy guns coming in from the ocean side of the island. The flashes and the booms accelerated until they sounded like the grand finale at the 4th of July fireworks. After a few minutes, it became apparent there was a hellacious naval battle underway out in the Sealark Channel. Even those Marines who were dug in on the ridge above Sesapi could not tell who was who out in the channel, and they could only hope that the Americans were getting the best of it. The American troop ships were still anchored out in the channel, and should the Japanese Navy break through, thousands of Americans would die.

The cool temperatures combined with the soaking rain, and Bill began to get the chills and shiver in the cold. This was shaping up to be the worst night of his young life. As he listened to the Navy fighting for their lives, he prayed and asked the Lord to watch over the sailors in the fight and keep the transports safe. There were a lot of fellows he knew out on the transports tonight.

As Bill and the other Marines lay shivering in their foxholes, the two naval forces fired an estimated 1,000 rounds of heavy surface guns at each other. The USS Canberra was hit by a torpedo and heavily shelled by the Japanese, leaving her dead in the water with heavy casualties. The heavily damaged Canberra was evacuated and then deliberately sunk by the U.S. Navy after being hit with 300 rounds from the big guns. The USS Astoria was shredded by enemy fire and was left burning without power. The Astoria finally gave in to the raging fires and sank about noon the next day. Over 1,000 U.S. sailors and officers had been killed with approximately 2,000 wounded. The USS Quincy took direct hits on the bridge, killing Captain Samuel Moore. As the Quincy was sinking, her crew tried unsuccessfully to run her aground on Savo Island. The USS Vincennes took 74 direct hits and sank at 0250 hours. The USS Chicago was torpedoed and shelled and proceeded to steam west for 40 minutes before it radioed warnings to other ships.

Unknown to Bill that night, the U.S. Navy was taking the worst beating in their history. Japanese Admiral Mikawa had brought the Chokai, Aoba, Kako, Kinugasa, Furutaka, Yubari and Yunagi into the channel under the cover of darkness. They surprised the U.S. Navy with their seemingly suicidal assault, but the element of surprise was once again in Japan's favor. Immediately following the naval battle, the U.S. Navy gave orders for the fleet to pull back from the Solomons.

Most of the Pioneers were still spread out across the Solomon Islands or aboard the transports. The transports had 5" surface guns, but they were no match for the larger guns aboard the Japanese destroyers and cruisers. A few of the transports lingered, dangerously, until the early morning hours to allow them to send Higgins Boats with supplies to the various Marines on shore.

When light finally started to arrive, Bill cautiously emerged from his mud hole and tried to organize his equipment. He was soaked to the skin and caked in red mud. He cleared the bolt of the BAR and made sure it would be operational as counterattacks were almost certain. The nearby Marines cursed fluently as they went through the same process with their own gear. Within a few minutes, shouts came down from the ridge above and the radios began to crackle with life. Most of the fleet was already gone and other ships were in the process of pulling out. Word had spread that the Japanese Fleet had torn into the Americans and they were leaving to avoid more losses. Several Higgins Boats made it to Sesapi and the Marines quickly unloaded ammunition as the Navy crews told them of their orders to dump the supplies and "high tail it" back to the ships. The coxswain thought the Navy would be back in a few days. Of the supplies that were dropped off, one thing was obviously missing … food.

By noon on August 9th, 1942, the U.S. Navy was not in sight from Tulagi. The Marines were left on the island with whatever supplies had been brought ashore. All of the members of Company A who had remained on the USS Jackson were gone and no one knew where. Apparently, George Garcia, Herb Dale,

Truitt Anderson and the others were still aboard the Jackson when it fled the area with the fleet. The men were now on day three with their three days of rations and very little food had made it ashore. The heat and humidity were back with a vengeance and the entire island began to reek with the smell of decaying bodies. Everyone on the island was put to work with burial details. The Japanese were buried basically where they fell, while the Americans were brought to a cemetery being dug at the cricket fields near the sandstone bluffs. The bodies had now been exposed to the jungle heat for two days and the burial task was hellish to say the least. Most of the Marines had ditched their gas masks to fill the bags with hand grenades, but any existing masks now became sought after by those who had to carry the dead. Dozens of fallen Marines who had been collected on the west end of Tulagi were brought to Sesapi and then loaded on Higgins boats and taken down the shore nearer the cricket fields.

Seeing these dead Marines was gut wrenching for Bill as their bodies were searched for personal belongings that could be sent back to their loved ones. Letters, photos, jewelry, wallets and cash were sorted by the lieutenants. Their stiff and bloated bodies were moved on stretchers with covers whenever possible. A record of their name, rank and serial numbers were made and charted with the grave number at the cricket fields. Father Kelly and other Chaplains were busy with graveside services as the burials were taking place. Some Marines were able to pause at the graveside of a buddy, but most were buried with no familiar faces present. The Japanese were buried in shallow graves or mass graves and most of the Marines resented having to hand dig graves for the enemy, who they detested. There was no honor in these burials and little or no dignity. Bill was horrified to witness the sadness caused by the loss of the Marines who went into eternity there on Tulagi, but he was also saddened to see the pure hate for the Japanese that some of his comrades exhibited. Bill was just as outraged by Pearl Harbor and Wake Island as any other American, but in his heart, he knew the Japanese were human beings at the very least. He knew that when Christ died on the cross, He had sacrificed for all mankind, even these fallen Japanese.

As the next few days came and went, other members of Company A, 2nd Pioneer Battalion arrived on Higgins Boats as the various units were rejoined. Bill was officially transferred back from 1/2 to his Company A and assigned to the defense of Tulagi at Sesapi. 1st Battalion, 2nd Marines were ordered to Guadalcanal to bolster the pending offensive on that island. Lieutenant Patrick Jones was assigned as Commanding Officer of Company A as the regular company officers were still on the transports headed for who knew where. George Gabel, Charles LaPoint, Roy Ford, Bill Elchuck, Rudy Halazon, Everette Henson, Sam Herman and Bob Kirkpatrick had all been in the vicinity with 1/2 and were already dug in at Sesapi. The reunion was nonetheless refreshing as Bob Swigert, Fred Ellis, George Cothran, Manny Bud, Ed Susans, Charles Montague, Gene Seng, Harrell Cabler, Charles Wysocki and Paul Stelzer all arrived to join Bill, Mike Matkovich and the corpsmen, Rice and Ford. Russell Jarrett, Henry Duke, Barney Boos and Emory Ashurst, all "Go to Hell Men," had ended up on Gavutu-Tanambogo on August 8th, where they engaged in close-quarters combat with the Japanese. Lieutenant Hayes led these men from cave to cave blasting the Japanese out and saving many American lives. Hayes and Boos would later be decorated for their bravery leading this demolition assault. Bud, George, Daily and Ellis had all been on Gavutu and Tanambogo, although they didn't even know that the other side of the causeway was called Tanambogo. There had been heavy casualties there as well, and they had been through an equally hellish burial and clean-up process the day before. There were still occasional snipers being hunted down, but the main fighting on Tulagi was over. A different enemy was about to become all too familiar.

38. Stranded

Work Parties became the order of the day. Due to the intense 105-degree heat, work parties disbanded at noon daily. Most of Company A was assigned to cut a road from Sesapi east to the main areas on the east end of Tulagi. Company A had managed to bring ample TNT ashore during the fight, so they could blast all the sandstone gravel needed for the new roads from the cliffs. Since no trucks had been brought ashore at Tulagi, captured Japanese and Chinese wheelbarrows would have to be used. The task of hand clearing the jungle and laying a road without the use of power equipment proved to be one of the most excruciating forms of labor imaginable. As Bill was working at shoveling and raking the gravel, his dog tags would hang in front of him in the sun. When he stood up, the tags would come back in contact with his chest and burn like a clothes iron. The solution was to wrap a small piece of cloth around the tags or stick them in your pocket; it was against regulation for any Marine to take the tags off in a combat zone. Bill was sent with a work party to clear some rocks in the path of the new road and was involved in the arduous task when one of the Marines from another unit surprised him. As Bill was prying with a pickaxe, he heard the Marine say, "Hey, aren't you Bill Bennett from Aurora?" Bill looked over and saw a familiar Auroran's face, although he couldn't recall the name. It was Stan Boyd, the older brother of Edith Boyd, with whom Bill had graduated. Stan told Bill that he had been present at most of the Tomcat home games during those years, and had even attended a few of the Clippers' games. Stan let on to the guys from Company A that Bill had been somewhat famous in Aurora, but Bill assured them that it wasn't all that. The chance encounter did bring back to mind the fact that Bill had not had a chance to write home or receive letters since they had left the States over six weeks ago.

Besides the obvious work that needed to be done to secure the defense of Tulagi, the most important issue became that of food and water. There were basically no animals left on Tulagi as far as hunting was concerned, so foraging groups were formed either officially or unofficially. Bill paired up with Manny Bud one afternoon as they went down the shore to the west in search of food sources. Bill found conversation with Manny fascinating as Manny was from Chicago and knew a lot about the city and baseball. Manny was a very intelligent guy with wavy black hair and wire rimmed glasses. He and Bill laughed at how they had both joined the Marines on December 8th, 1941 and then wondered what the Marines did while on the way home, even though they had not known each other at the time. If they had only known then what they knew now! Manny recounted to Bill how on that first Sunday in San Diego, the sergeant told the Catholics to march to the right and the Protestants to march to the left. This left Manny standing all alone on the parade grounds. The sergeant got very close to Manny's face and asked him what his problem was. Manny told the sergeant, "I don't have a problem Sir, I am Jewish." The sergeant turned red and walked away to return with another officer a few minutes later. He then informed Manny that there were no Jewish services available, so he would have to clean the latrines while everyone else was at church. Manny cleaned the latrines on Sunday mornings for 12 weeks. After the completion of boot camp, Manny could leave the MCB and attend Synagogue in San Diego.

Manny had graduated from Crane Technical High School in Chicago and had wanted to become a doctor before the war. His father, Anton, worked in retail men's clothing, a vocation with which Bill was quite familiar. Manny was a crack shot with his 1903 Springfield rifle and had qualified as "Expert" on the range at San Diego. Out of a possible 225 points, Manny had earned 205 and only a handful of Marines had a better score than that. Manny was a man of many talents. Marines had been struggling to open coconuts for the water and coconut inside. What seemed like a simple task had proven frustrating and many Marines had taken to trying to shoot open the tropical delicacies, or even blow them apart with hand grenades. Either of these two techniques would splatter the insides all over the area and leave you with nothing but fragments. Manny showed Bill how to set the coconut inside of the steel pot of his helmet, which he held between his legs. Then place the point of a bayonet or Ka-Bar knife into the "attachment seam" of the fruit and tap it with a softball sized stone. The trick was balancing the odd shaped coconut, so having a trusting assistant hold it steady helped the process. The coconut would split open and the helmet would catch the "milk" leaving you with two halves of white coconut meat, all in an edible form. Manny tapped the bayonet twice to line it up and then smacked it full force. Bill felt the liquid start to pool on the bottom of the helmet as the coconut split. Manny inserted his bayonet into the crack and twisted it to widen the crack, then it split wide open into two halves. The coconut milk, which was actually watery coconut flavored syrup, didn't taste as good as Bill had hoped, but was clean and wet. Manny sliced the coconut meat out of the shell and handed Bill a handful. This tasted just like the coconut that bakers used back home and was a good supplement to other foods. Manny also proved himself at locating mango and banana trees and harvesting the fruit. Since Manny was a big fellow, and not exactly a gymnast, he would arrange for smaller athletic Marines to do the climbing. George Cothran and a few other Marines were both pretty good at this.

There were several natives of the Solomons that proved to be extremely helpful in these early days. Most importantly, they showed the Marines how to fish and exactly which fish tasted the best. These "natives" had appearances similar to African tribesmen, but they spoke with British accents. It was not only surprising to the Marines, but hilarious to most of them. Mike Matkovich pointed out that one of the helpful fishermen looked just like Harpo Marx, curly red hair and all. One afternoon, Bill accompanied Manny on a "fishing trip" down the shore about a quarter mile and then out onto rocks protruding into the water. Manny produced a hand grenade from his bag and told Bill to get down behind the rocks. He then pulled the pin and tossed the grenade into the water. The explosion was surprisingly muffled by the water and a small shower of spray came down around them. A half dozen fish floated belly up on the surface and they bagged up the good ones. On the walk back to Sesapi, the supposedly dead fish began to come back to life as they were only stunned by the grenade. "Grenade fishing" became a common activity on Tulagi. One of the Marines hatched a plan to go after a bigger catch and he crafted his tackle from a long boat line, a grappling hook and a gallon jug for a bobber. He baited the hook with a can of C ration corned beef and swam out into the harbor to drop the hook and tie off the line. At first light the next morning, Marines gathered at the shoreline to see the jug being tugged below the surface and moving in erratic circles. The ingenious Marine bravely swam out and untied the line and brought it back to shore. A total of 12 Marines manned the line and fought the creature for about 30 minutes before it splashed near the shore. It was a hammerhead shark about 10 feet long and it wanted to stay below the surface. The Marines won that battle too, and the Master Fisherman finished the shark off with his huge hunting knife once the creature was on shore. The shark was soon filleted into 12 oz. steaks and distributed to fires all over Sesapi. The steaks were a little tough, but they tasted like round steak. It was a culinary treat.

It wasn't all hunting on Tulagi, as Bill was frequently reminded by Japanese air raids several times per day. The roar of engines would send work parties scrambling for fox holes, ditches or caves. The bombs would shake the island and it was quite nerve racking, but they had no accuracy and were more of a nuisance than a threat to life. Another occasional ritual became the shelling of Tulagi by the Japanese Navy from out in the Sealark Channel. They would only come so close to Tulagi as the Marines were manning several 5-inch coastal batteries on the south side of the island. Shells would explode in the water between Florida Island and Tulagi and work their way toward Tulagi as if searching for ships that may be anchored in the natural harbor. It turned out that this harbor was one of the only natural harbors in the South Pacific that was deep enough for the anchorage of full sized naval ships. The Japanese had previously held big plans for Tulagi and did not want to let it go. The Marines were convinced that it was only a matter of time before the enemy would launch a major attack to try and retake Tulagi and Gavutu. Guadalcanal was only 12 miles away and the Japanese had been landing troops on the west end with regularity. It just seemed logical that they would be landing at Tulagi soon as well.

Single Japanese planes would fly over Tulagi high enough to avoid being hit by the small .30 caliber machine guns. These planes were probably taking photographs or just looking for ships or defensive positions that they could bomb later. Mike Matkovich had been complaining about how much he wished he could get his hands on a .50 caliber machine gun that would reach up to these "snooper planes." He eventually got his wish when some Marines told him about a U.S. landing craft that had been hit by the Japanese on August 7th. The craft was partly submerged but the lone .50 caliber Browning machine gun was still on its mount above water. Matkovich and one of his buddies managed the use of a row boat and went out to retrieve the gun. He carried it down the pier like a prized game fish and took it to his gun emplacement and went to work on it. He was sure that he was going to knock some of these snooper planes out of the sky with the prized "50." One problem he faced was that he did not have the proper mount for the .50 cal., so he had to improvise. After he had it set up, the very next snooper plane caused quite a scene as everyone took cover except Matkovich and his gunner's mate. Bill and Manny took cover as near to the gun emplacement as they could and watched carefully as the plane flew within range. Mike had the plane in his sights and he tilted the gun higher and higher until the plane was directly overhead. With everyone anticipating that Matkovich was about to blast the snooper out of the sky, he pulled the trigger. "Click." He looked to the side of the weapon and smacked it a few times. "Click." The uncontrolled laughter of the Company could not be held back. Matkovich was a great Marine and everyone respected him as such, but the scene was just too funny. Matkovich turned every shade of red known to Marine-kind and put on a dazzling display of "south side" profanity complete with hand gestures.

Mike Matkovich kept working on the .50 caliber gun and had it working properly within a few hours. He eventually found a heavy tripod that functioned with the gun, and his fire on low-flying snooper planes and bombers lessened the aerial harassment by the Japanese. Bill liked Matkovich and they had a good relationship as Marines. There was always a connection with the Marines from Illinois as they held some common ground with the Cubs, White Sox or Bears. Matkovich was a south sider who had grown up in a neighborhood where fighting was a way of life. He was a smaller guy but tough and wiry. He told Bill that the day he signed up for the Marines, he was a few pounds under the minimum weight and the sergeant gave him a few dollars and told him to go drink a few milk shakes and come right back. Mike had been in the Marines since 1939 and was assigned to the USS Tennessee where he learned to fire almost all of the Navy's big guns. Machine guns were his specialty and he seemed to know just about everything one could know about them. The machine guns were every Marine's friend as it was much better to strike the enemy at a distance than up close.

Those first few weeks on Tulagi were tough, but not nearly as tough as it would get. The anopheles mosquitoes were relentless. Everyone on the island had suffered hundreds of bites and the worst type were those to the eyelids. Many Marines awoke in the mornings with their eyes swollen closed by the mosquito bites around their eyes. Bill tried sleeping with his helmet over his face; a spare sock or T-shirt would be his pillow. The helmet was surprisingly good at muffling sound, but Bill could hear himself breathing so loudly that it became annoying. Tipping the helmet to one side allowed his breath to ventilate and keep the helmet a bit cooler. Being "inside" of his helmet became about as comfortable as Bill would get for quite some time. The heat and the mosquitoes proved to be a two-edged sword. The best solution found to protect the eyes while sleeping was simply to fold the arm across the face with the elbow bent over the nose. A spare sock or T-shirt over the lips would allow breathing out of the nose. The helmet could then be set over the elbow to act as a small roof over the head. Although Tulagi was devoid of large mammals, there were a host of other creatures that were curious at the least or dangerous at the worst. Huge jungle rats that weighed in at two to three pounds were frequent guests in the fox holes. They were not aggressive and were easily shewed away. Some of the giant rats were given nicknames and thrown useless scraps. At night, giant crabs would come ashore looking for dead things to eat and quite a few of these were machine gunned after being mistaken for the enemy. Giant tarantulas lived in the trees and would drop onto an occasional Marine's back or helmet and cause quite a ruckus. Dark red centipedes that measured 18 inches in length were coated in a substance that would burn the skin if touched. The island was also populated by flocks of large white cockatoos that would screech loudly in the treetops. They were beautiful to look at and one of the few pleasantries to be found.

Bill improved the foxhole situation by digging a diversion trench uphill from his hole. This allowed most of the water running downhill to go to the sides and not into his home. He also lined the bottom of the foxhole with branches that held the blanket off the dirt. The lack of food and water became the biggest concern to the Marines. All existing rations had to be turned over to the Company and they were distributed evenly. Occasional supplies would come over from Guadalcanal, but some of them made no sense, like a boatload of prunes. Holes were dug a few feet from shore that allowed water to slowly filter in through the sand and earth. Water purification tablets could be added to the canteens for as long as the tablets lasted. The Pioneers had water distillation equipment on board the Jackson, but none of it made it ashore before the Navy pulled out. Manny was selected to go with a squad of Marines over to Florida Island to a freshwater spring that scouts had located. He took his Springfield rifle and joined the others at the pier with about 16 empty five-gallon water cans. The Marines loaded the cans onto a Higgins Boat. Bill went out on a work detail hauling gravel to the new road and spent the morning with the usual misery. Later in the afternoon, the Higgins Boat pulled up to the pier and Marines attended to the returning water party. Bill could tell that something was wrong by the look on the returning Marine's faces. They lifted the lifeless body of a Marine into the hands of those on the pier followed by the now full water cans.

Manny walked up the hill towards their foxholes and was visibly upset. He told Bill that they had landed on Florida without any problems and carried the empty cans back into the jungle about a half mile. Apparently, the enemy had been using the spring for their water source but there was no one in sight when they got there. Manny said that he covered the spring while the cans were filled and then carried two cans with his rifle across them on the way back. About two hundred yards back down the trail, the Japanese fired from the rear and one of the first shots hit the Marine behind Manny. The bullet apparently went through his back and hit his heart, killing him instantly. As Manny turned at the sound of the bullet hitting the Marine, he saw him drop the water cans and fall to the ground face first as his helmet rolled off into the jungle. A few of the guys had to cover the others while they carried the dead Marine and the water cans back to the waiting boat. Manny saw the Japanese moving from tree to tree and he fired multiple shots and threw some grenades. He told Bill that it was nerve racking, but he had not been afraid. They backed out most of the way to the boat and then the boat crew fired their .30 caliber machine guns into the jungle. Manny was quite bothered by the Marine being killed. He told Bill that the water they brought back would be the most expensive water they ever had.

3rd Platoon, Company A, 2nd Pioneer Battalion. The "Go to Hell Men," shortly after blasting the Japanese from their caves on Gavutu, August, 1942.

(Photo courtesy of Lieutenant Hayes' private collection)

On August 18th, 1942, Bill got word that Chaplain W. Wyeth Willard, U.S.N.R. had come over to Tulagi from Gavutu. Willard held some services on the other side of the island at Blue Beach, where Lieutenant Colonel Robert E. Hill was in charge of HQ, 1/2 and the defenses at the beach. Regular Protestant worship services were organized and performed by Chaplain Willard aboard the President Adams on the way down to the Solomons. Willard was officially given the rank of Lieutenant by the Navy as a Chaplain, but everyone referred to him as Chaplain Willard. Prior to volunteering as a Chaplain, Willard had been a Baptist minister of a small church near his home town of North Scituate, Massachusetts. Just before leaving San Diego on the Adams, Willard had attended a Bible conference out east where he met a fellow from the Gideon's Bible Society. Willard was asked if he would like to obtain a stock of small, pocket sized New Testaments and in reply, he asked how many Bibles the Gideons had available. After some negotiating, Willard loaded all 2,500 New Testaments and shipped them to MCB, San Diego. The small Bibles were now carefully stowed in the hold of the Adams, wherever it was. Willard was making his way around the island and came down the slope to Sesapi. It was refreshing to see Willard again and know that he had survived the heavy fighting at Gavutu-Tanambogo. General Rupertus had granted Willard the run of the island to hold services wherever possible, provided that it did not interrupt defensive considerations. Bill and about 35 Marines gathered by the beach at Sesapi as Willard led them in worship and it was good for the soul. Chaplain Willard told the guys that he would be staying on the east end of the island near the "Residence" where the British Governor had lived before the Japanese took the island six months earlier. He planned to have regular Sunday services around the island and hoped to post information as soon as he could arrange it. Chaplain Willard was not expected to perform any military duties whatsoever, but he took it upon himself to help in any way he possibly could. He carried a Colt .45 revolver on his belt and two "dummy" grenades on his combat suspenders; one had the name "Mike" painted vertically and the other, the name "Ike."

Willard had begun a well-planned process of interviewing Marines one at a time and then placing the new testaments where need and interest aligned. He also kept copious notes regarding his interactions with these men. When Bill attended the first service with Chaplain Willard, he was very impressed with the effectiveness of the preaching and looked forward to each service after that. After the services, Willard always offered to pray with the fellows as he sat and answered questions and prayed one on one or with small groups regarding personal matters. Bill knew that Willard was genuinely interested in these men and it made it worthwhile to invite other Marines that may or may not be believers. Willard had scheduled Bible studies on weekdays and offered a Wednesday mid-week service. The services became very well attended as Willard's sermons addressed issues of life and death and the uncertainties of combat. Chaplain Willard's presence supplied a highly important connection for the Christian Marines and the beginnings of faith for hundreds more at Tulagi.

Shortly after this, Manny was assigned to be the personal guard for Father Kelly, the 2nd Division's Catholic Priest. Tulagi was still a very dangerous place at this time as Japanese snipers were still being found and some small groups of enemy soldiers were thought to be coming over from Florida Island. Father Kelly carried a Colt 1911 .45 caliber pistol in a hip holster. He joked with Manny about running into the Japanese by saying that he would shoot first and pray later. Manny saw first-hand how much Father Kelly genuinely cared for his men, Catholic, Protestant or in Manny's case, Jewish. Father Kelly was thrilled to compare Judaism with Christianity and pointed out that half of his Bible was the same scriptures that Manny had grown up reading. The only difference was the recognition of Jesus of Nazareth. Jesus claimed to be God in the flesh. Those who believed Him were the first Christians, and those who did not continued along as the Jews had prior to the time of Jesus. Manny knew that Bill had a deep interest in Christianity and had even considered becoming a minister. The two had some deep conversations about religion and Manny relayed his daily experiences to Bill. If there were ever a fellow that had tempted him to "convert" to Christianity, Manny confided that it was Father Kelly. At this point, there were still no Jewish services for Manny or the other half dozen Jewish Marines on Tulagi.

The improvements to the foxholes became a sort of competition as the Marines were trying to bring some sort of comfort to their misery. Some of the guys had ideas about building lean-tos and huts so that they could sleep above ground. These huts were approved by the officers, provided that there were adjoining foxholes and shelter pits for the inevitable air raids. Fred Ellis was a Marine carpenter by specialty, so Bill, Bob Swigert and Manny joined forces with him to build their version of a shack. Finding material was the hardest part, as anything useful to the trio of shack-mates was also useful to the other "contractors." Parts of ammo pallets made a great floor that was leveled with rocks on the hillside. Various boards, panels and boat parts created half walls around the perimeter and two sections of tin roofing from a bombed-out machine shed made a great roof that repelled both rain and sun. Besides his parent's home at 454 Simms Street, Bill figured this was the only roof he had on earth to call home. The new occupants slept quite comfortably above ground and they even had other Marines over to sit around and play cards at night. Considering the level of misery that life on Tulagi had offered the Marines so far, it didn't take much to make them happy.

Lieutenant Jones informed Company A there would be a mail pickup in the near future and they could now write home and notify their families that they were on Tulagi. One looming problem did exist: there was no paper. The island was scoured for suitable paper to write these long-awaited letters. When Bill came back to camp from his work detail, he found that a few of the guys had been over to the Chinese store on the east end and one of them found a pack of what appeared to be rice paper. They distributed the paper until the approximately 50 sheets were gone. Bill was fortunate enough to acquire one. Bill found a shady spot under a palm tree and his mind was filled with Aurora and all his loved ones. He carefully sharpened one of the stubby pencils he had stashed in his pack with his Ka-Bar knife and found a chunk of a board to use as a desk. Bill wrote about how good it was to finally be able to write. He wrote about meeting Stan Boyd and the "little house" he had built with Fred, Manny and Bob Swigert. He wrote that he had "never been better." The last thing Bill wanted in the world was to cause anyone back home to worry more about him than they already were. No matter what he faced, the word going home would always be "fine," "great" and "don't worry about the boy!" Bill was very concerned about his brother Al as he had never heard where he ended up with the Army. Bill assured those at home that, "The Lord is on our side," and signed with, "All my love, Bill." He folded the letter and stuck it in his shirt pocket.

Bob Swigert had not been able to get a sheet of rice paper and the only usable paper he could find was an old paper bag. He opened the bag up, wrote his letter to his mother in South Dakota on the inside, then he folded the bag up as its own envelope. Since there was no glue to seal his letter, he stuck a large black safety pin through the center to hold it together. Bob assured the guys that if the Navy could get this to the States, he was sure it would find Bird and Eva Swigert and his brothers Don and Leo and sister Ila Mae in Oelrichs, South Dakota. Someone acquired a stack of envelopes from the CBs on the other side of the island and the addressed letters were collected and given to Lieutenant Jones to send out on the YP Boat headed for Guadalcanal. Swigert was able to shove the "bag letter" into a proper envelope before it left the island. The Navy censors would have to read the letters anyway, so the envelopes were not sealed. Somehow, George Gabel had slipped half-a-dozen penny post cards into his combat pack back on August 6th, along with a pen. He was all set to write to his girl "Ronnie" back in Chicago. Having been around the Corps longer than most, Gabel was always pretty good at planning ahead.

After the letters went out, routine started to take over on Tulagi, and besides being on the lookout for a possible Japanese counter-attack, the routine wasn't all bad. There were regular shuttle runs of the Higgins and YP Boats and Bill was able to make a few trips over to Gavutu and Florida Island moving some supplies around. After about two weeks on Tulagi, dozens of Marines began to have flu-like symptoms of gut wrenching abdominal cramps, fever and diarrhea. At the first symptoms, the Corpsmen and the doctors were hoping that it was the flu and not what they feared it might be. As the malady spread rapidly across the island, their fears were realized. It was dysentery, an amoebic intestinal infection spread through dirty water and unsanitary conditions. Bill did everything he could to avoid dirty water or coming in contact with those already infected, but he could not avoid it. No one could. The severe cramping left Bill lying in his tin roofed hut in some of the worst pain he had ever encountered. Marines groaned with pain all over the island and most of the work came to a halt. The officers went to great lengths to make sure that any Marine who could participate at all took their turns in defensive positions, as the garrison's ability to defend the island was greatly diminished. The horrible issues with dysentery were that the symptoms were ongoing, and without medication they were prone to continue. The severe diarrhea caused the victims to dehydrate even faster than normal in the tropics. Without a constant source of clean water, it would be nearly impossible to cure. The Marine doctors explained that the outbreak of dysentery was caused by the decaying and bloated bodies which were left in the sun. The millions of flies that bred during those first few days carried the parasites to water and food supplies and then the disease took some time to incubate. The need to quickly bury the dead in these tropical conditions could not have been more strongly emphasized than it was by the dysentery outbreak.

As if things could not have gotten worse, different symptoms of high fever and violent chills began to emerge. No sooner had Bill begun to recover from the worst of the dysentery when he came down with another fever. Corpsman Rice came to check on him and his fever was 104 degrees. There was no doubt that this was malaria. The incessant anopheles mosquitoes had carried the disease to nearly everyone on the island. Compared to malaria, dysentery was an inconvenience. The small amount of quinine that had made it ashore was quickly used up and there was no medication available to assist the Marines on Tulagi. Bill went into a delirium from the fever and he felt as though he was baking from the inside out. Barely aware of the words from those trying to care for him, the pain felt as though his bones were cracking. Bill tried to pray but he could not focus long enough to link words into sentences, even in his mind. At one point, he thought he might die, and for a few days he was sure that he would. The heat built up inside him until he felt he could explode. He lost track of hours and days. Finally, sweat broke from the pours of his skin and the profuse perspiration drenched him from head to toe. Then suddenly, the hellish heat shifted to freezing cold and he began to shake uncontrollably. Several blankets were piled on to try and stop the violent chills, but Bill shook so hard that his teeth rattled. The relief from the baking inner pain caused Bill to show a smile to Manny, Fred and Corpsman

Rice as they checked on him frequently. After 24 hours of chills, Bill's body calmed down and he slept for hours on end. When he finally sat upright, his weakened body ached as though he had been run over by a truck. Corpsman Rice opened a can of crackers for Bill and he ate a few and drank some clean water. A Construction Battalion had landed on the other side of Tulagi and they had brought their water distillation equipment ashore and had been canning drinking water for the past few days. The ingestion of the clean water and the salty crackers brought a relief to Bill's ravaged body that words could not describe. Bill felt as though he had been brought back from death's door and he prayed earnestly and thanked the Lord for allowing him to survive this initial bout with malaria. He had lost 20 pounds.

In the midst of tropic daytime temperatures reaching 115 degrees, Marines were sweating out high fevers, chills and stomach cramps that continued to greatly weaken their ability to get up and walk, much less defend against a Japanese counter attack. The hospital buildings along the south shore of the island were used for the most serious cases of dehydration, but there was little the doctors and corpsmen could do except try and keep the patients hydrated with the cleanest water available. Bill did whatever he could to care for his fellow Marines when they went through their bouts with malaria as his experience had taught him a new level of compassion. Manny, Fred and the others all took their turns with the hellish fever and more than a dozen Marines on Tulagi died from malaria. From then on, the mosquitoes were seen as more than just a nuisance, they were considered killers.

The arrival of the CBs on the south side of the island gave the stranded Marines some hope. Their fresh water was a literal life saver, but the CBs were also a reminder of home. Most of the CBs were untrained as military men and they were in their 40s and 50s. They wore mostly civilian clothes and reminded the Marines of their dads back home. The CBs were remarkably knowledgeable about all things technical and construction and they organized the work parties in an efficient manner. They set up their temporary camp complete with a mess tent and even a barber shop. They were 100 percent supportive of the combat Marines and wanted to lend a hand in any way possible. Their chow was real food and Marines were constantly caught trying to sneak into the lines at their mess tent. The CBs on Tulagi had connections with the CBs across the channel on Guadalcanal so they made trips on the YP boats to negotiate food supplies and the situation on Tulagi began to turn for the better. On Sunday, October 4th, 1942, Bill attended the Protestant Service there on the shore at Tulagi. The Marines had been stranded on the island for almost two months and the sickness and lack of food had ravaged them.

Even cleaned up for church, the men looked shabby as their cotton uniforms were worn and tattered. The constant immersion in salt water had begun to eat the thread in the seams and many Marines had removed the sleeves from their shirts and cut the tattered legs from their pants. The shortages on Guadalcanal had made it almost impossible to get anything but basic medical and food items, let alone luxurious new khakis. On this particular day, most of the men were over their initial bouts with malaria and they had become accustomed to living with dysentery. They all shared one thing in common for which to be thankful to God, they were alive. Passing the cricket fields during normal work activities on Tulagi reminded the Marines that there were quite a few Marines buried there that would never leave the island, in a physical sense. Bill spent the day working around the hut and trying to organize camp life with the other "orphans" from Company A. He passed the time talking with Manny, Swigert, Ellis, Cothran, Montague, Seng, and the corpsmen Rice and Ford. They all shared stories from their earlier years and took turns describing life in their home towns. Montague and Seng had grown up together near San Antonio, Texas. They enlisted together and had been together throughout training in San Diego. They were true Texas cow hands and riding, roping and shooting had been a way of life for them. Montague had been the best rifleman in his county and he was now a machine gunner. He had somewhat of a friendly rivalry with Matkovich over their shooting skills and Montague made jokes about Al Capone being from Matkovich's neighborhood, which was not altogether untrue. Manny had also grown up in Chicago, but he had quite a different upbringing than Matkovich as his Jewish parents would not have approved of street fighting. Manny spent many summer afternoons with his father at Wrigley Field up at Clark and Addison on Chicago's north side. He witnessed Babe Ruth crush a home run over the left-field wall back in 1929. Swigert talked about his years of farming in South Dakota and how he missed his parents and his siblings. Ellis was two years older than Bill, so he was one of the senior enlisted Marines. He had spent his entire life farming in Montana. He had been working side jobs since he was 15 to contribute his earnings toward helping Mom and Dad keep the family farm. The Great Depression had been a stark reality for the Ellis family.

Everybody on Tulagi had a rough go of it and there were signs of mental breakdowns in some of the Marines. A few had even been confined to the hospital and one or two shipped out for mental health evaluation. Sitting around and talking about home was a form of therapy that everyone enjoyed. One of the guys came up with a little song that they sang on many work details just to pass the time. Everyone knew that General MacArthur had a large force of the U.S. Army in Australia and the Marines wondered why they weren't coming to help the Marines in the Solomon Islands. "They sent for the Army to come to Tulagi, but Douglas MacArthur said, "NO!" He said, "There's a reason—it isn't the season, besides, there's no U.S.O.!"

Late one day as the sun was setting on Tulagi, the group set up in and around the tin hut for some card playing and one of the guys had invited a Marine that he met on a work party a few days earlier. Bill didn't catch the fellow's name, but it was not unusual to have Marines from other units over for one of the "bull sessions" at Sesapi. After about an hour of penny poker, Bill noticed that the new guy was acting strangely. He seemed perturbed and nervous; and Manny and Ellis looked at Bill with knowing glances, acknowledging that the guy seemed weird to them as well. Suddenly, the Marine started screaming that he just couldn't take it anymore and that he didn't want to live! He pulled a hand grenade out from under the table, pulled the pin and let the lever fly. The grenade was hot and there were seconds to spare! Manny crashed through the ramshackle door and Bill dove through the panels assembled for the walls as the other Marines sailed out of the shack and into the darkness. Curled on the ground and expecting a shower of shrapnel, Bill heard the "bang!" of a practice grenade. Off in the darkness about 20 yards away, he then heard the voice of the guest Marine yelling, "Suckers!" as he ran off into the night. Several of the shocked Marines started to run after the practical joker, but Manny and Ellis called them back and told them to leave it alone. They were sure that this guy would get what he deserved at some point and there was no sense in giving him the satisfaction of a chase or a fight.

The orphans of Company A settled in for the night and the cool air was refreshing. As Bill lay on the shack floor, he prayed through a long list of requests for his loved ones back in the States, and he began to realize that the past 10 months had already started to seem like years since he had been home. He had not received any mail since he left San Diego four months earlier and almost anything could have happened in that time. What if he received a letter that one of his family or his friends had died over those months? He wondered if Helen was still waiting for him. Being stuck on Tulagi was not something he had expected, but the only thing one could expect in the Marine Corps in time of war was the unexpected. Sifting through his deepest thoughts, Bill began to understand that the only thing that remained from his prior life was his relationship with the Lord. He had an even stronger sense of closeness to God than ever before, and he felt what he could only describe as a "calling" to do whatever he could to help his fellow Marines stay alive and draw closer to God. Manny snapped five .30-06 rounds into his Springfield rifle, said good night to Bill and Fred and went to report for the second watch of the night. Bill thanked the Lord for His sacrifice on the cross, said amen, and drifted off to sleep.

39. The Reunion

Bill was jolted awake at the first light of dawn by shouts coming from the ridge high above their shack. "They're back!! They're all back!! The Navy's back!!" As Bill looked out of the damaged shack, he could see half-dressed Marines hopping into their pants and boots and pulling shirts on as they ran up the slope towards the ridge. Manny sat up and pulled his glasses over his ears as he reached for his boondockers. Bill stuffed the laces inside his boondockers and sprinted up the hill. The 350-foot peak was more than Bill could handle in his weakened state and the sprint quickly turned into a painful hike to the top. When he made the crest of the hill, the morning sun was playing off what seemed like a hundred U.S. Navy ships. The sight was something like seeing the gates of heaven in the Marine's eyes. The U.S. fleet represented security, food, water, news and an overall rekindled spirit of hope. Bill found a pair of binoculars and took his turn eyeing the transports. He couldn't make them out with certainty, but he was fairly sure that one of them was the USS President Jackson and Herb Dale, Truitt Anderson and George Garcia could still be on board. Of course, after two months, they could be almost anywhere in the Pacific. The fleet had arrived in the night just as they had left. The needed supplies would help turn the tide of combat on Guadalcanal and bolster the ailing troops on the other islands. Within a few minutes, YP boats and a few Higgins Boats left the south shore of Tulagi and were headed out to the fleet. Not long after that, the white wakes became visible as launches from the fleet began to head for Tulagi and Gavutu, just to the east.

Back down at Sesapi, the orphans of Company A got into whatever was left of their uniforms and went about their usual routines. About 10 a.m., Mike Matkovich let out a yell from his machine gun position at the end of the pier. There were boats approaching Sesapi on the north side of the island. All work stopped as the stranded Marines scrambled for their defensive positions as it was unclear if the boats were U.S. or Japanese. After someone yelled to Matkovich to clarify, they jumped out of their foxholes and ran to the pier and beach. Two Higgins Boats approached and the coxswains, crew and assisting Marines were waving wildly as they approached the pier. The boats were piled with supplies and Bill joined the ragged Marines to unload them. The sailors and Marines wore immaculate uniforms and their clean-shaven faces were quite a shock to the orphans. There had been no shaving kits on the island for the past two months. Bill looked at the fresh Marines just off the transports and then back at the orphans. Their dirty, tattered uniforms were hideous and their shaggy hair and thick beards gave them the look of hobos living down by the train tracks. Bill had always liked a well-maintained appearance, and he felt somewhat ashamed of his disheveled looks. But he was not alone. There were about 1200 Marines stranded on Tulagi and they all were in a similar condition. As Bill stepped to the edge of the pier, a Marine looked up at him from the Higgins Boat and yelled out, "Bennett!" Bill turned and saw George Garcia looking up at him from beneath his helmet. "George!" Bill shouted as he extended his hand down to pull George up to the pier. George said he was glad that Bill was alive and he had been praying for him for the past two months. He also said how sorry he was to have left Bill behind but there was nothing they could do when the Navy pulled anchor and left. By the looks of the bearded, thin Marines on the pier, George knew instantly that they had been through hell. Before George finished his explanation, Bill heard, "Bennett! Hey! Bennett!" from behind him on the dock. It was Truitt Anderson, and he looked happy and healthy.

Bill showed George and Truitt around Sesapi and showed off the crude piece of real estate that Manny, Ellis, Swigert and he had built. Bill warned them not to drink anything but the water from the ship for the time being as the island was infected with malaria and dysentery. George had to leave with the launch, but he told Bill he would find Herb Dale and tell him that Bill was alive. The rest of Company A would be preparing to land and they would be arriving the next day. George waved back to Bill as the boats pushed through the water and back up the coast and around the east end of the island. The orphans wasted no time opening the five-gallon cans of fresh water, and Bill carried fresh rations up to the shack. He sat on the log near their fire pit and worked the P38 can opener on a can of "Ration, C Peaches" and flipped the jagged top up. He poured the beautiful yellow slices into the tins of Manny and Fred and then poured the last third of the can into his mouth. The peaches tasted delightful and were possibly the best tasting thing Bill had ever eaten;

at least in recent memory. The fleet was back. They felt as though the entire United States had just pulled up to the Solomon Islands, and they had somehow survived the ordeal. As long as the orphans from Company A would live, there were many things that they would never take for granted.

The following morning, two more Higgins Boats approached the pier and they were loaded with Marines instead of crates. It was the rest of Company A. Major George F. Doyle and Captain Donald E. Farkas climbed out of the Higgins Boats and met with Lieutenant Hayes and Sergeant Christiano, who had been in charge of the orphans for the past two months. Doyle explained that while they were away, Farkas had been transferred in from the 2nd Engineering Battalion. He would now take over as the Commanding Officer of Company A. As the rest of the company were unloading on the pier, the officers surveyed the Sesapi area. Bill went to the pier and found George Garcia. George told Bill that he was sorry, but apparently, Herb Dale had been assigned to HQ Company and would not be coming ashore.

Company A's own water distillation equipment would be coming ashore and Captain Farkas would be overseeing its operation as soon as possible. With the return of the Company A officers, there would also be a returned emphasis on Marine Corps protocol. The orphans were treated to several items they had all but forgotten about: soap, deodorant, toothpaste, toothbrushes, shaving soap, toilet paper and razors. Bathing with actual soap, shaving the dark woolen beard and the scent of deodorant made Bill feel almost human again. The arrival of fresh U.S.M.C. "greens" made Bill feel like a real Marine again. The orphans checked their pockets on the rotting uniforms and burned them on their fires. It was good to see them go up in smoke. George Garcia filled Bill in on the past two months as the fleet had been to the New Hebrides Islands where they trained and waited for their chance to return. Bill filled George in on the details of being left behind.

With the return of the Transports and the balance of the Pioneers, all of the missing equipment was finally brought ashore. The Pioneers now had their own water distillation unit and better tools for the road and path improvements. Captain Farkas was from Detroit, Michigan, the son of an automobile design engineer, and he had attended Michigan State University where he studied Engineering before he joined the Marines in 1941. As far as leadership was concerned, Bill had appreciated Captain Joseph R. Clerou and Captain Crouch as leaders. Captain Farkas was younger than the previous captains and not as personable. But he seemed to know what he was doing with the road construction, and Bill decided to give him the benefit of the doubt and be 100 percent supportive. One thing that Bill had learned about the Marines so far was that no matter how good an officer was, somebody didn't like him. It would take the stranded Marines some time to warm up to any new officers that had just arrived from a troop transport. Farther to the east, along the north shore of Tulagi, the Pioneers assisted the CBs, who were expanding and improving roads around the government pier. In order to obtain gravel, cliffs were blasted with TNT by the "Go to Hell Men" from 3rd Platoon. In the process of working with these demolition guys, Bill became interested in the job. Although it was inherently dangerous, there was a thrill in blasting things with TNT that reminded Bill of the firecrackers and cherry bombs that he had used as a boy. The large rocks from the blasting were crushed manually with captured Japanese sledge hammers. Although this work was extremely difficult, Bill used the occasion to exercise and build up his body after the long sickness of dysentery and malaria. The food had improved, the water had improved and Bill's outlook began to improve.

Atabrine tablets arrived to combat the malaria and the Marines all began to take the yellow pills daily, as the supplies allowed. But then a rumor circulated around the island that Atabrine would render the Marines sterile and almost everyone stopped taking them. The doctors and the corpsmen eventually lined up each platoon and monitored the swallowing of the tablets one Marine at a time. After the corpsmen walked away, the sand was spotted with half dissolved tablets that had been temporarily concealed somewhere in the mouth. The doctors finally convinced the Marines that the rumor was false and the Atabrine was in their best interest and the medication was resumed.

The second week of October marked another noteworthy change at Sesapi. The U.S. had developed a high-speed torpedo boat that was 80 feet long and carried a crew of 12. These "Motor Torpedo Boats" were called "PT" Boats for short and they were magnificent machines. These fast-moving weapons could carry two 3,200 lb. torpedoes right to the Tokyo Express. The Navy had planned on setting up a base on Gavutu, but when they inspected the area for a site, there were several drawbacks. One, Gavutu was wide open to the sea, which meant that the Tokyo Express could shell the island at will. Second, the bare island was also wide open to an air attack and there was no place to hide the PT Boats in that case. Third, the Marines had not bothered to bury the 600 dead Japanese at Gavutu and their rotting corpses still littered the island. That being said, General Vandegrift sent the Motor Torpedo Boat Squadron Three officers to see General Rupertus on Tulagi. Rupertus had just the place in mind for this new base. A little inlet with a pier and a boat ramp called Sesapi. The Navy arrived by boat, of course, and Bill and the Marines from Company A knew something was up when the "parade of brass" came by to inspect their makeshift huts. Not long after that, Navy men and a large group of CBs from the other side of the island began to make improvements to some of the destroyed Chinese buildings. The pier was repaired and some new docks were begun as material would permit. Evidently, Sesapi offered a good place of concealment for these boats to operate. Within a week, Motor Torpedo Boat Squadron Three arrived at Sesapi to become Company A's new neighbors. They arrived with five PT Boats that had three 12-cylinder, 1200 horsepower engines per boat. When these boats left Sesapi in a hurry, the rumble was something to hear. The routine developed by the PT Boats was to leave under the cover of darkness, as their main mission was to disrupt the Japanese Navy's nighttime operations.

40. Letters from Home

With the arrival of new supplies, several entrepreneurial enterprises were started in the jungle hills of Tulagi. Mike Matkovich apparently had some home brewing experience from the south side of Chicago, and he used his skills, along with huge cans of raisins, to start a distillery. Of course, this venture only added to the tall tales started by the Texans regarding Matkovich's being from Al Capone's neighborhood. There were several stills being operated on the island, but the best product was coming from the old guys in the CBs, without surprise. One afternoon at Sesapi, Bill noticed a group of ax-wielding officers approaching. They said it smelled as though something strange was cooking and asked Matkovich if he had any idea what it was. Of course, Mike could not smell a thing. Following their noses, the officers hiked up the slope behind Sesapi and located a "raisin jack" distillery, unmanned, but in the process of cooking. A huge clatter erupted as the precious equipment was destroyed. The officers left without a word being said, and the precious liquid was running down the path in a small stream. Matkovich was convinced that the raid was orchestrated by one of his competitors. Nonetheless, any Marines in Company A that wanted any bootlegged alcohol would have to buy it from the CBs for $5 a bottle.

Sunday, November 1st was a day that brought joy beyond belief. One of the old Higgins Boats, without the large ramp on the bow, arrived at the Sesapi pier and a large canvas mail bag was tossed onto the pier. It was all that Sergeant Christiano could do to hold off the hoard of mail-hungry Marines until he could situate himself into a good spot for distributing the mail. The Marines shouted as though they were at an auction and there was no calming them down. Bill shoved himself into the throng as far as was reasonable, but any letters addressed to him would find him in time without forcing his way to the front. As the sergeant read the bundled letters, he bellowed out the addressee. "Cothran ... Cabler ... Seng" and the bundles were passed toward the shouts of "Yo!" from each excited Marine. At long last, Christiano shouted, "Bennett" and Bill fired back his very firm, "Yo!" A thick bundle of no less than six letters found Bill's outstretched hands and he ducked out of the crowd and made a bee line for the shack. Bill sat on the log by the fire pit and untied the string. A letter from Steve Bennett, a separate letter from Jessie Bennett, one from Al, one from his friend Fran McElroy, one from his buddy Ken and one from Helen. He started off with Al's letter as he had absolutely no idea where his brother was. Bill read through four long pages from Al with a full explanation of how he had landed a deal for Officer's Training School with a sure course for some sort of procurement role. The Army had decided that Al's experience with Pillsbury was too great to waste and they wanted to use his skills from civilian life to help the Army find food for the growing Allied Forces. This was such great news. Bill had been rightly concerned about Al being put into a combat unit and having to go through some of the torture that he had already experienced. Al was safely in the States in OTS at the time of the letter writing. How Bill longed for the conversations that he and Al used to have after the lights were out in their room. There were so many things that Bill would like to tell him now, but several things that he wouldn't.

The other letters from home let Bill know that everyone was doing fine, however the war had set many changes in motion. Bob Stoner was still engaged as a flight instructor with Naval Aviation while Dexter and Harley had both enlisted in the Army and were in the states training. Big news from the Stoners read that Harley had married Betty Parker in April and Betty would be living with Sam and Margaret at 211 S. Fourth Street while Harley was away. Bob Stoner had announced his engagement to Marijane Mole, however, the date was unknown as Bob's leave was always in question due to the need to get pilots trained quickly. Bob Reder, Channing Miller, Ed Kocjan and Louis Kuk were probably all somewhere in the States being trained and Pete Andrews, the younger brother from the hat and shoeshine business was already overseas with the 2nd Division. Bill wondered where Pete might be, and decided to keep an eye out for any of these hometown boys. It seemed odd to Bill when he thought about what life in Aurora must be like with hundreds, if not thousands, of these young men gone to war.

As for the Marine enlistments, none topped the charts more that Marian's new husband Perry McIntosh. Perry had decided to volunteer for the Corps instead of taking his chances on the draft. He was headed for basic training at Camp Lejeune, North Carolina. Marian would be living with Steve and Jessie. Jessie was pleased about this as the house was beginning to feel fairly empty with Bill, Al and Jean gone. Little Bobby was all but living at the Bennett's as his mother Bess was working a lot and seriously dating Ed Billstrom. Bill was happy to hear that Bess was moving on, but he still hated thinking about Bobby not being near his father. Bob Bennett and his new wife Sunny had recently moved to California with their toddler Stevie, who the family called "Butchie." Bill knew that this distance would make it even more unlikely that Bob would ever be able to spend more time with Bobby. A photo of Bobby showed that he had grown noticeably since Bill had left for the Marines and Bill became choked up when he thought about how much he missed playing with Bobby. Grandma Phrangle was thinking about moving back to Aurora due to health reasons and she was looking forward to being near to Jessie again. Bill was happy to hear this because it would make it easier to visit with her when he got home after the war.

The letter from Helen was refreshing as Bill imagined her sitting at the dining room table at the house out in Sandwich as she wrote the lines. Helen was fairly absorbed with her job at TWA and she talked about how important their work had become as they flew thousands of service men and women across the country each day. These past ten months had been very stressful but Helen told Bill that it was nothing compared to what he must be going through. She asked a lot of questions that Bill was unable to answer at the time. Very little information could be given and the letters would be censored by the Navy, removing any references to unit identification or size. Helen expressed how she looked forward to Bill getting home and how much he was missed, not only by her but by the family in Aurora as well. Helen was still able to visit regularly with Steve and Jessie, who had even driven out to bring her to Aurora for an occasional weekend. This worked well, as Helen would catch the train on Monday morning for Chicago. The thoughts of life back in Illinois were a stark contrast to Bill's current reality on Tulagi. As he sat down over the coming days to answer these letters, he stayed the course with the decision to only write positive things and not mention any details that might cause any of these loved ones to worry about his safety or condition.

41. Naval Nightmares

Japanese planes continued to pester Tulagi with occasional flyovers, bombings and strafings, which resulted in little or no damage. Since the fleet had returned, more .50 caliber guns had come ashore, along with several larger 20mm anti-aircraft guns. On numerous occasions, Bill would watch the Japanese planes at high altitudes appear as silver x's in the sky. A minute or so after they had been directly above, a high-pitched whine would become audible as the bombs neared the earth. Sometimes these high-altitude bombs exploded out in the harbor and sometimes in the jungle up along the ridge. One morning as Bill was busy working along the shore at Sesapi, three planes appeared over Florida Island, coming in very slow with their wheels down and their landing lights on. It appeared they were U.S. planes, probably looking for Henderson Field over on Guadalcanal. When the planes were about half way across from Florida, just over tiny Makambo Island, the wheels went up and the engines revved as the red "meatballs" under the wings became visible. Everyone scrambled for shelter as the planes were coming straight in for Sesapi. Matkovich jumped behind his prized .50 caliber gun and let it loose just as they passed over. Half a dozen bombs screamed overhead and exploded up the slope toward the ridge. Several U.S. Navy vessels were anchored in the harbor and their anti-aircraft gunners had followed the enemy planes over Sesapi and their rounds were now bouncing all over the camp. It was a good thing the guys had taken cover or several would have certainly been hit by the brainless fire. Matkovich turned his .50 toward the Navy boats and fired warning shots into the water in front of the boats. They got the message and stopped firing toward Sesapi.

Across Sealark Channel, there were daily dogfights between Marine aviators and their Japanese attackers high above Henderson Field. Bill frequently hiked to the top of the ridge with Truitt Anderson, a few other Marines, and a pair of binoculars. The fighter planes twisted and turned while puffs of smoke came out of their wings as they fired at each other. Occasionally, a plane would explode or catch fire and the spectators could follow the plane until it either exploded into the ground or splashed into the sea. There were a few times that parachutes opened and floated back toward the earth. The Marines on Tulagi could only hope that the U.S. pilots were getting the best of it. Truitt watched the dogfights with the excitement of a kid and Bill thought about how a few years ago, Truitt was just out of high school. Bill and Truitt seemed to make good companions and they spent a lot of time talking. The Bennett family intrigued Truitt as Bill told him about life at 454 Simms Street. Truitt was saddened by the divorce of his own parents in 1941 and getting away from home had played a part in his decision to join the Marines right away. Letters from home told Truitt that his older brother Ray had joined the Army, so there was not much of a family left back there. Truitt told Bill that he would like to meet the Bennetts and they agreed that after the war was over, Truitt would come home with Bill and visit for a week on his way back to Ohio.

Besides the aerial battles, nighttime naval battles continued with fury. The PT Boats would wind up their huge engines and roar off to protect the destroyers and cruisers out on patrol. On most nights, naval gunfire would erupt and the familiar flashes in the sky would remind Bill of the summer thunderstorms back in Illinois. When Bill awoke to the rumbling naval battles, he knew our sailors were probably dying as they defended the Marines on shore during their nightly encounters with the Japanese Navy. The Japanese regularly ran a dozen or so destroyers and heavy cruisers into the Sealark Channel in direct naval attacks, or in support of troop transports landing Japanese infantry at Guadalcanal. The Japanese naval attacks were so fierce and so frequent that the Americans nicknamed these ships "The Tokyo Express."

If the naval rumbling lasted for more than a few minutes, some of the Marines would make their way up to the top of the ridge to take in the sight. The night of November 12-13, 1942, was one such night. When Bill arrived at the ridge, there were already several dozen Marines watching in awe as the flashes blazed away across the channel. Huge red flares, called "star shells" hung above the battle, illuminating targets for the huge guns. Shells were striking ships and huge explosions and subsequent fires lit up the sea to the right between Guadalcanal and Savo Island. Bill closed his eyes and asked the Lord for His mercy on those American boys who were in the fight of their lives, especially the new neighbors in the PT squadron. Unknown to Bill that night, one of the American ships he watched burning was the USS Juneau (CL-52), an Atlanta Class Light Cruiser. The Juneau had been hit by a Japanese torpedo and her crew valiantly fought to extinguish the fires. Listing badly to one side, the USS Juneau headed for port at Espiritu Santo to the southwest. At 1100 hours the next morning, another torpedo struck the Juneau in the same spot as the first and she sank in 20 seconds. 687 crew members from the Juneau lost their lives, including the five Sullivan brothers from Waterloo, Iowa. The war brought Bill some bad news that hit closer to him when he found out through the "grapevine" that Captain Paul W. Fuhrhop, who had led him into battle in the first days with A/1/2, had been killed on Guadalcanal.

On Wednesday, November 25th, 1942, the Marines of Company A were just coming in from their various work parties when at just about 1100 hours, eight PT Boats began to arrive a few minutes apart. These boats were absolutely beautiful and in perfect condition, far from the weary hulks that Squadron Three had been using. The new guys were Squadron Two, just out of Panama through Espiritu Santo. None of these PTs had yet seen combat and two of the boats had been delivered directly from the ELCO plant on the East Coast. The first new boat was PT 110, and then Lieutenant Larson arrived with the second new boat, PT 109. The Marines really enjoyed finding time to visit the PT crews and admired their fast boats. Some of the Marines were even invited to go out for short test runs by the mechanics. The PT crews had become "jungle-ized" and many of them stopped shaving, as had many of the Marines. One of Bill's platoon mates, Charles Wysocki, Jr., was visiting the PT base when the Navy guys told him that their bearded and crude looking "Skipper" was none other than the Hollywood actor Robert Montgomery. Wysocki was sure they were pulling his leg, but he maneuvered himself closer to where the bearded Skipper was discussing engine problems with the motormen of his boat, and when he heard the Skipper's voice, he knew it was, in fact, Robert Montgomery. The fact that a famous actor was on Tulagi living with all the difficulties and scourges of this war made the Marines know that this was everyone's war and that no one was above making sacrifices for the country.

Being able to laugh through some things that were tough became a strengthened attribute, and Bill certainly learned a lot about real suffering. He had seen, touched and smelled death up close, and learned some things about life in the process. In the face of hardship, he had not only remained strong in his faith, but he had grown closer to his Creator during this time. By the time Thanksgiving arrived, Bill thought about home and getting off Tulagi most of his waking hours. At this time last year, he was surrounded by his loved ones, watching the Tomcats seal up the best season in their history and working with Don Glossop, learning to be an A.C. Technician. His life had been filled with thoughts about Helen, the future and taking care of the Bennett family. It was all beginning to seem so long ago and so far away, and Bill didn't like it. He was made to be a part of the family and he had been so comfortable in his social circle. The thought that the Bennetts were learning to live without him, that Helen was learning to live without him and that most of his friends back home were headed for harm's way began to bother Bill greatly. He would pull out his tattered photos of "the gang," the Bennetts and Helen, and remember the best days he had spent with them. He recalled the newspaper headlines decrying the aggressiveness of the Japanese and of Hitler's Germany and thinking that these imperialist and fascist dictators would have no effect on his life.

On the night of November 30th-December 1st, another hellacious naval battle brought some of Company A up to the ridge. Evidently, the Tokyo Express was making another visit to Guadalcanal. The exchange of fire lit up the night and the great booms sounded across the water. It was amazing how well these battles could be heard though they were probably 10 to 15 miles away. Bill and the other Marines climbed to their grandstand seats atop the hill and watched the battle. They had no idea how personal this particular battle would become. The following morning, work parties were ordered and sent out and work around Sesapi continued as it had for months now. About 0900, Bill heard shouts from other Marines near the shore and he and others ran near the docks to see what the uproar was about. Coming up slowly from the east was what could only be described as the ghost of a ship. She was a good-sized fighting ship and someone rightly guessed that she was a heavy cruiser. She had two huge gun turrets in front of the bridge with three 8-inch guns in each. The upper turret, closest to the ship's bridge, was facing forward as was the lower turret in front. The forward turret's gun barrels hung out over the water where the deck had been the night before. Twisted steel reached forward in random directions and the gray paint was charred coal black. This was the USS Minneapolis (CA-36), a New Orleans Class Heavy Cruiser. The Minneapolis had taken a Japanese torpedo right in front of the forward 8-inch turret that had blown the entire 60 feet of the bow completely off. The fast work of damage engineers and the watertight doors had kept her from going down. Smaller vessels aided the Minneapolis into position just a few yards off the beach at Sesapi and lines were sent across to attach to palm stumps.

PT 109 bringing in survivors of the night's naval battle to safety at Tulagi on December 1st, 1942.

(U.S. Navy Photo)

As if this scene could not be any more unbelievable, about 15 minutes later, another heavy cruiser appeared from around the bend in the shoreline with even more of her bow blown off. This was The USS New Orleans, and she was missing 150 ft. of her bow. Multiple decks were visible as sailors stood inside the gaping holes above the waterline. The attending vessels had to stop the New Orleans farther from shore as she was sitting very low in the water. There was only one 8-inch gun turret in front of the bridge with the guns cranked 90 degrees to the port side. The other turret had gone down with the bow section. Navy launches went to and from the Minneapolis and the New Orleans for the next hour and more information was relayed to shore. Apparently, the Minneapolis had already unloaded about 35 wounded onto torpedo boats and they were taken to the hospital on the other side of Tulagi. There were about 35 missing sailors who were presumably sealed into the flooded compartments below the surface. Their bodies would have to remain there. The New Orleans had also unloaded her wounded to the Tulagi hospital, but the nature of her damage had left approximately 180 dead on board. On the other side of Tulagi, Motor Torpedo Boat Squadrons Two and Three were bringing in hundreds of sailors that they had fished out of the channel after the battle. One of the PTs loaded with survivors was the brand-new PT 109. She had survived her first encounter with the enemy.

Lieutenant Hayes told the Pioneers that the arrival of these damaged cruisers had altered the work plans for the time being. Some of the work parties would be assigned to help the Navy camouflage the ships. This meant a lot of branches, underbrush and palm fronds had to be cut, collected and loaded into Higgins Boats to be taken and loaded on to the ships. The Navy would take the job from there. The New Orleans was also in need of a burial detail and Bill cringed when he heard that he and Manny had been assigned to this team. The CBs would be digging the graves at the cricket field, but the Pioneers would be assisting the Navy with the collection and transportation of the dead. Bill knew full well this would be a dirty job that someone had to do. Lieutenants Hayes and Henderson explained to the burial detail that the Navy was already in the process of identifying the remains on board. Once they were identified and recorded, the bodies would be loaded onto the Higgins Boats, then brought ashore and carried on stretchers to the cricket field, as the road was in very poor condition. It didn't seem respectful to risk having any mishaps. Bill and Manny joined the team in the Higgins Boat and slowly plowed through the water out to the New Orleans.

As the Marines approached the New Orleans, a slick of fuel oil became evident on the surface of the water. They wondered if it wouldn't be best to take the ship out to deep water and scuttle her. It seemed unlikely that the New Orleans would even be able to move from Tulagi, let alone ever be useful to the U.S. again. Bill and Manny climbed the ladder hooked over the rail on the port side as one of the tending vessels was still moored on the starboard side. Pumps were hard at work near the damage as water shot from hoses like those on a fire truck. The front of the New Orleans was probably sitting five or six feel lower than the stern and it looked like she was sinking. Lieutenant Hayes talked with a Naval Officer and the group descended ladders down to a lower deck and moved forward toward the damaged area. The Naval Officer paused in front of a doorway and warned the Marines that it wasn't a pretty sight inside this area. The lower deck area was putrid with the powerful smell of charred paint, burned rubber and gasoline. Stepping through the doorway, a strong odor of burned flesh was added to the mix. There was a row of dead sailors already lined up on each side of the room and the Marines were told those on the right were whole bodies that were identified and ready to transport. Those on the left were partial bodies and they were still working to try and match the various parts with the torsos. The officer explained that it was their duty to do the best job they could to make sure the remains were buried as complete as possible. The officer could see that the Marines were getting queasy and pointed out several buckets on the floor. Within a matter of five minutes, every man on the detail that had come aboard with Lieutenant Hayes had lost his breakfast into one of the buckets.

The Navy had a stack of blankets brought in and each body had to be laid onto a blanket and set onto a litter covered by a rain poncho. At the grave site, the blanket would be buried with the body and the poncho and litter could be rinsed in sea water before bringing it back aboard. The blanket-covered bodies would have to be brought to the top deck with the use of one of the ammunition elevators just behind the damaged area. Once on deck, a winch was used to lower the bodies into the Higgins Boat. A few of the first bodies looked as though the sailors were sleeping, with the exception of the black soot from the fire. Most had grotesque wounds and most of the bodies were not complete, despite the effort being made. Some Naval personnel were going through the pockets of the dead to see if there were any personal items that could be returned to family. Most were identified by their dog tags, however, headless torsos represented an obvious problem. Other sailors were brought in to try and identify their buddies if all else failed. Seven litters could fit onto the floor of a Higgins

USS New Orleans at Tulagi Harbor on December 1st, 1942. PFC Bill Bennett, PFC Manny Bud and others from 1st Platoon retrieved the bodies of sailors killed in the battle and took them ashore for burial. Miraculously, the New Orleans was repaired and covered the landing of the 2nd Division Marines at Saipan less than two years later.

(U.S. Navy Photo)

Boat, so Lieutenant Hayes went to locate other boats to help with the process. Once the first bodies were ready to go ashore, the coxswain delivered them to the pier nearest the cricket field/cemetery. Stretcher bearers were lined up to carry the dead sailors over to the CBs and their final resting place. Bill's work group assisted lifting the bodies onto the pier, and then returned to the ship. This process was repeated over and over again until dark and then resumed until noon the following day. The heat was once again almost unbearable and the stench increased as time passed. Bill did not attempt to eat a solitary crumb of food during this entire time or for more than a day after it was finished. Bill had been through the initial burial work after the August combat and now this. He was already sure there would be no glory in war, and he had seen things most people should never have to see.

42. Relief

Over the next ten days, the Naval Engineers worked with the CBs to do some amazing things. Coconut trees were felled by the CBs and a makeshift bow that would cut through waves was made for the Minneapolis and a breakwater wall fit into the hole of the New Orleans. Fortunately for the Navy, no Japanese air attacks were ever launched on the crippled ships. The Japanese may have figured that the cruisers were too far gone to warrant the effort. On December 12, the cruisers left Tulagi on their own power and headed for dry dock in Australia. Life returned to abnormal on Tulagi. Just before the arrival of the Minneapolis and the New Orleans, Bill had begun to notice a few hard bumps appearing on his legs below the knees. The bumps began to fill with pus and became quite painful. Corpsman Rice took a look at them and washed them with hydrogen peroxide, but it was not enough to stop the infection. Rice informed Bill that these were the start of tropical skin ulcers. Apparently, bacteria can invade small cuts and insect bites in the tropics, and severe, painful infections can occur. These tropical skin ulcers are commonly called "jungle rot." This was not what Bill wanted to hear. The medications available on Tulagi were not fully capable of reversing the infections; large doses of penicillin would be required. Some of the most severe cases were being evacuated over to Henderson Field and then flown out to hospitals in Australia or New Zealand. Keeping these sores clean became an issue several times a day and the pain woke Bill up in the night.

As Christmas was approaching, Bill wrote some letters home to his parents and asked them to do a few small things for him. He wanted to make sure that Bobby, Stevie, Ginny and her new little brother Billy all got a little something from "Uncle Bill." Of course, Bill relied on Steve to get Jessie a gift and Jessie to pick out something for Helen. With the slow rate of mail delivery, he was fairly sure the letters would arrive some time before Easter. As a Marine, Bill had been faithful, hardworking and competent. Near the end of December, this was recognized, as he was notified he had been promoted to Private First Class. Bill was proud of this distinction which most people didn't quite understand. It was simple, a Private was at the bottom of the chain and a PFC was not. PFC Bennett went about working on Tulagi and as he looked around, the island had been greatly improved from the time they first arrived in August. The camp at Sesapi would be a useful base for those who would be arriving there in the future and the road system would make it possible to deliver supplies by truck.

Bill received more mail from home in mid-December and among the items received was a wonderful miniature newspaper titled *The Stoner Weekly News*. Sam and Margaret Stoner, with the help of Betty and Helen Stoner, still at home, had decided to create the newspaper. With Dexter, Harley, Bob and Eleanor's widower, Richard Turner, all in the service, this would be a "bang-up" way to keep everyone informed. Bill eagerly read his way through the issue dated October 11th, 1942. The main article described Bob Stoner's October 8th marriage to Marijane, at Corpus Christi, Texas. Apparently, none of the other Stoners had been able to attend, but Marijane's family had been there. Bob Stoner wrote some of the description of the small wedding himself and Marijane wrote an article describing their new officer's apartment and the wonderful amenities it provided. Bob was now a U.S. Navy Flight Instructor at Cuddihy Field, Corpus Christie, Texas. What wonderful news. Bill chuckled a little as he thought about how different Bob's life was as a Navy flier compared to Bill's life as a "mud Marine." Bob Stoner had seen this all coming and positioned himself well. The idea of the *Stoner Weekly* was brilliant and Bill looked forward to reading more, should the mail service hold out.

Christmas Eve came on a Thursday. Work parties were canceled until Monday, with the exception of guard duties and defensive measures. Bill walked with a group of Marines over to King George Field on the east end of the island to attend Chaplain Willard's Christmas Eve Service. A large movie tent had been set up and Willard had been using it for such events. That night, 623 servicemen listened as Willard ably described the Creator of the universe coming to Earth in the form of baby Jesus. He then led the group in singing, "Silent Night," "O' Little Town of Bethlehem" and "O Come, All Ye Faithful." As they sang the verses of "Silent Night," Bill imagined being home and attending service at Fourth Street Methodist. He imagined Steve and Jessie in

Picture #1: 1st platoon, Co. A Pioneer Battalion, 2nd Marine Division on Tulagi, Solomon Islands 1942-43

1st Platoon, 2nd Pioneer Battalion, 2nd Marines, Tulagi, December, 1942. Bill Bennett is sixth from the left in the middle row. Truitt Anderson is 14th from the left in the same row. Johnnie C. Jones is seated in the center of the first row. (U.S.M.C. Photo)

the pew together and singing the same song, wondering how Bill was doing. In one thought, last Christmas seemed so near. In the next thought, it seemed so far away. Bill, like all the Marines at the service that night, longed to be home again. As he sang, "Sleep in heavenly peace," tears were forming in his eyes and there were many tears there that were masked by the darkness. After the service, Bill lingered and talked to several of his buddies. As he walked back to Sesapi with George Garcia, Bob Swigert and Fred Ellis, they heard the sounds of a Christmas choir ringing across the island. Chaplain Willard had rehearsed a group of well-voiced Marines and they were now visiting the medical tents to sing carols to the 300 to 400 sick and wounded. As Bill was getting ready to settle in to the shack for the night, he sat on the log to remove his boondockers and gazed up at the brilliant equatorial stars. He thought of how the Creator of that vast array of celestial splendor had lowered Himself to come to Earth as the baby in that manger almost two thousand years ago. He thought about the irony of the peace and forgiveness that Christ had come to offer mankind and the cruel brutality of war that had become familiar in the past year. If only all mankind could know the love and forgiveness of Christ and extend it to others, the world would be vastly different. Bill turned toward the log and dropped to his knees. His folded hands rested on the log, and he dropped his forehead to his hands and closed his eyes in prayer. He thanked the Lord for His coming to Earth, for His teachings and for His death on the cross. He asked for the safety of his fellow Marines as he did not want to have to bury any more of his comrades, but he thanked God for sparing Company A from the losses that some other units had endured. His prayer time ended with considerations given to the Bennetts, Stoners, Cochrans and his friends that were now spread near and far in the service. Bill hoped they would all be together next Christmas in the "Wonder City."

    Christmas Day, 1942 began with the screams of the cockatoos in the trees behind the shack. The morning sun shot sideways across the bay and lit the tree line on Florida Island. The hushed sounds of "Merry Christmas" could be heard as Company A began their morning routines. The Marines all made a big deal of the holiday and some of them gave each other gifts of simple things just to celebrate. Chaplain Willard and Father Kelly held Christmas services that were very well attended. The sound of Christmas music had been good for the soul, but it was somewhat strange to experience Christmas Day in 110-degree, sub-tropical heat. Bill and his friends took turns telling their favorite Christmas stories from back home and describing their mothers' tastiest dishes. Bill had some interesting conversations with Manny about Chanukah and Christmas, and they both learned a few things. Manny enjoyed seeing the other Marines celebrate Christmas and it was really nothing different from his usual Christmas experiences back in Chicago. Bill was aware of the fact that Manny had no support for his Jewish faith on Tulagi, while Bill had dozens of strong, believing Christians for support. Special provisions had been sent out specifically for Christmas dinner and Tulagi now had several well-staffed field kitchens. The cooks put together the finest meal that anyone had eaten in four months. The fare consisted of roast turkey, dressing, snow flake potatoes, gravy, buttered peas and carrots, sliced pickles and olives, apples and oranges, pineapple pie, plum pudding, fruitcake, bread and butter, iced tea and coffee. The Marines that had been left on Tulagi back in August had wondered if they would ever taste such food again. Bill thought about past Christmas Days at home and he wondered if Steve had set the train up for Bobby around the tree. The Bennett place must be awfully deserted this year with Al and Bill off in the service, Bobby sharing time between two houses and Jean and Linc having their own place in Naperville. Bill was thankful that it had been relatively quiet for the time being on Tulagi and he had some time to reflect on the spiritual side of Christmas.

After dinner, 435 Marines and Navy men attended Chaplain Willard's evening service at 1900 hours back at King George Field. The sermon was titled, "Make Room for Jesus," and focused on the individual's need to make room for Christ in their hearts, life plans, schedules, homes and their finances. Willard explained that a lot of people can attend church and never really come to know Christ. They are basically spectators. Bill thought about his own life and whether or not he was as sincere as he could be about his relationship with Christ. He wondered about the other Marines and where their lives might be regarding Willard's questions. The thought crossed his mind about how sad it really was that the Japanese didn't understand Christ or what Christmas represented. Before Pearl Harbor, Bill would have thought about the Japanese in the same way that he would have thought about "non-believers" anywhere else in the world. Christ had taught that believers were to love and seek the lost in the same way that He had when He was on Earth. Now with the complicated issues involved with the war, Bill's job was to kill the Japanese and these two views were hard to reconcile. He knew there was no way he could talk an enemy soldier out of killing him, and he truly was faced with "kill or be killed" when in contact with the Japanese. Although some of the Marines talked tough about wanting to kill or enjoying killing the Japanese, the thought of killing was a bitter pill in Bill's mind.

On Monday, December 28th, 1942, Lieutenant Henderson called 1st Platoon to formation as Major Doyle and Captain Farkas were standing just behind him. Lieutenant Henderson informed 1st Platoon there had been some organizational changes within the Marine Corps. The 2nd Pioneer Battalion had been changed

2nd Platoon, Company A, 2nd Pioneer Battalion on Tulagi, December, 1942. Bob Swigert is standing, sixth from the right. (U.S.M.C. Photo)

henceforth to the 2nd Battalion, 18th Marines, or 2/18 for short, and Company A would henceforth be Company D. The official unit would now be 1st Platoon, Company D, 2nd Battalion, 18th Marines, 2nd Division, U.S.M.C.. Furthermore, Captain Joseph Clerou and Major Doyle would be assigned to the Headquarters Battalion and Captain Farkas would become the permanent Commanding Officer of Company D. Captain Farkas had been in charge of parts of the road construction and water distillation on Tulagi for some time. All the Marines in Company A had known him and none were exuberant about the prospect of having him as the new CO of Company D. This new 2/18 unit would have a sister battalion in 1st Battalion, 18th Marines. Combined, these two battalions would provide the Combat Engineering support for the infantry units of the 2nd Marine Division. Captain Farkas stepped forward to explain the details of the reorganization. He said the paperwork would be completed on December 31st, so the new unit would officially begin on January 1st, 1943. This would mark the end of the short life of the 2nd Pioneer Battalion. The role of "Pioneer" would be carried out by specially-assigned units of Pioneers within the two new Engineering Battalions, so the role of the Battalion would not be changing. New Year's Eve came and for the first time in their lives, Bill and the other Marines hoped there would be no fireworks that night. The Japanese destroyers no longer made their attacks into the Sealark Channel, as the U.S. Navy was engaging them farther to the northwest. The Japanese planes were rarely dropping bombs, as the pilots over at Henderson Field worked with the carrier pilots to engage the enemy raiders before they could get near Guadalcanal or Tulagi.

Over the next few weeks, Bill and his Platoon worked primarily on helping the CBs with building roads and docks at Sesapi, as getting the PT Boat base prepared was a priority. After lunch, Bill would find a place to lay with his upper body in the shade and his leg sores in the direct sunlight. The drying effect was supposed to be good for the healing process. The bad news on the sores was that some of them had gone into the bone, making them worse and much more dangerous. A bone infection could result in amputation or death. The pain worsened and Bill had a hard time walking. Bill did what he could to assist Fred Ellis and the other carpenters, but there were days when there was little that he could do. There had been discussions about getting some of the guys with worsening cases evacuated from Tulagi, but before anything could be arranged, Lieutenant Hayes brought Company D some of the best news they could have heard. They had just been informed they would be relieved of duty on Tulagi and should be shipped out of the combat zone within two weeks. The cheer went up like a football game. Although Tulagi offered tropical scenery similar to a travel magazine, and sunsets and sunrises to match, it had basically become a prison for these Marines and they were just elated by the news. Bill had been on Tulagi for five months.

Company D seemed to come back to life as they made final preparations to leave Tulagi. Bill went through his things and made sure all of his combat gear was in order and ready to go. Some of the guys were packing souvenirs, from Japanese items to the handwork of local natives. Although there were plenty of bad memories to go around, it was hard to believe they were finally leaving. Fleet Transport ships had been arriving and anchoring out in Sealark Channel and the Tulagi Marines were to begin boarding the next morning. Although no one knew where they were going, they all agreed that almost anywhere was better than here.

On January 29th, 1943, the Marines assembled at the cemetery on Tulagi for a memorial service prior to leaving. The service focused on the fallen for giving their lives for God and their country. One officer mentioned that their families would never again welcome these heroes home, or share their lives as they grew old. He then quoted scripture with, "Greater love has no man than this; that he lay his life down for his friends." Looking at the rows of wooden crosses and the neatly raked sand between them, there was barely a dry eye in the formation. The Army would now be taking over the defense of Tulagi and the U.S. Army band played the Star-Spangled Banner followed by the Marine Hymn. When the service was over, Bill again lingered for about an hour as there were numerous Marines he had worked with that he wanted to say goodbye to. No one knew where the units were going, so there was no way of knowing when, or if, they would see each other again. One final night was spent at Sesapi and Bill and the guys talked with excitement before bed. Bill joked that they should have hired a realtor to see what they could get for the old shack, or perhaps they could have rented it to some of the PT Boat mechanics. They had never imagined they would look forward to sleeping in those "comfortable" bunks aboard ship; the bunks that had seemed like torture devices on the way to the Solomons.

January 30th, 1943 began as a beautiful tropical morning on Tulagi. Bill once again awoke to the screams of the cockatoos high in the trees behind the hut. He sat up and rubbed his face and then looked out across the water toward Florida and Makambo Islands. The sun was just lighting the trees and these morning vistas were one of the best parts of being on Tulagi. Then the thought fully registered with Bill that this would be the last time he woke up here. The excitement of departure helped him to get to his feet with some enthusiasm, and then he felt the gauze that had glued itself to his leg sores in the night. He took his canteen to the log by the fire pit and sat down to soak the gauze free from his skin. Getting off the island and having a clean environment would certainly go a long way toward helping these skin ulcers heal. Bill walked with Manny, George Garcia and Fred Ellis down to the nearest mess tent that was now set up near what they called the "Chinese Village," down the shore to the east. Ed Susans was working KP and they served dehydrated eggs, fried Spam, toast with butter, juice and coffee. Everyone agreed that Tulagi was a much better place when you could eat regularly.

Bill spent the remainder of the day helping Fred Ellis and the carpenters finish up some last-minute things around the PT base and he enjoyed talking to the PT crews about their cherished speed boats. Having the wind in your hair seemed attractive enough, but for Bill, Manny and the others that had cleaned up the USS New Orleans, being on any type of ship in wartime did not seem inviting. Of course, the Navy guys did not think sleeping in a foxhole with Japanese stalking you while you slept was much of a deal either. Corporal George Gabel notified the platoon that they should be ready to ship out at the pier at 1800. They were expected to board the USS President Adams at 1900. He joked that anyone not ready to leave at 1800 sharp would spend the rest of their life on Tulagi and should also have their head examined. The guys asked about George Montague who was in the Navy Hospital on the other side of the island with malaria and skin ulcers. Gabel said that Montague would be transferred to the Adams separately, but they could see him in sickbay once they boarded.

As it turned out, Company D was ready to load the Higgins Boats before 1700 and they sat around the pier playing cards, joking and singing songs. They joked with the Army replacements about taking good care of the place. The shack was left abandoned as the Army had brand new tents and mosquito nets to sleep under. It was a shame the Marine Corps didn't foresee the necessity of the mosquito nets before the invasion. A cheer erupted from Company D as a small fleet of empty Higgins Boats appeared around the bend toward the Chinese Village. Their white wakes fanned out as their flat ramps churned up the water. 2nd Platoon formed up and walked to the pier while Corporals Gabel and Slowinski gathered 1st Platoon to formation. All combat gear was in place as Bill pulled his pack straps onto his shoulders then slung the BAR onto his right side. 1st Platoon was called by Sergeant Christiano and Gabel led the way to the pier. George Garcia, Truitt Anderson, Duane Strinden, Gene Seng and Johnnie Jones all moved toward the pier. Along with them walked LaPoint, Slowinski, Sobolewski, Cothran, Cabler, Susans, Banwart, Lieutenant Hayes, Major Doyle, Captain Farkas, Boos, Hermann, Jackman, Kirkpatrick, Jutting, Fuetren, Halazon, and Westover. They all marched down the pier to their waiting Higgins Boat. 1st Platoon was ordered to load and Bill painfully lowered himself into the boat as the coxswain smiled a toothy smile up at him. He was happy to be giving these Marines a lift off the island and hopefully, back to civilization somewhere. The coxswain asked how long they had been on Tulagi and a quick reply of, "Too damn long!" came from somewhere behind Bill. Bill looked at the coxswain and told him, "August 7th." Bill turned to help those behind him into the boat and they filled in around the "dog house" where the big diesel engine was covered. The boots and the gear banged like drums on the plywood deck of the Higgins Boat as it bobbed slightly in the water. Bill leaned back against the rear deck as the crew cast off the lines from the pier. The diesel roared in reverse and the coxswain backed toward Florida Island. The sun was now at their backs as the boat headed back toward the east end of the island. As Bill waved to those still at Sesapi, he noticed a large group of the Army troops standing at attention and holding a salute. Then he saw the PT crews standing on their new docks holding salutes as the weary Marines passed by in the water. Both were given as a sign of respect for the job the Marines had done to liberate Tulagi and pave the way for those to come. Among those who would serve at Sesapi would be a slim lieutenant from Massachusetts named John Fitzgerald Kennedy who would take command of PT 109 on this very dock in April and lead his crew on nightly raids against the Tokyo Express.

As the Higgins Boat made its way along the north shore of the island, groups of Marines, sailors and soldiers waved as they plowed past. One last look as the island passed on the right side of the boat and Bill could see Hill 185 where he had watched some of the naval battles at night, and King George Field where Chaplain Willard had led the worship services, and sadly, the cemetery where he had helped bury so many Americans. His head turned into the sea breeze that now cooled his sweat-soaked Marine utilities. The heat of Tulagi would not be missed. Dozens of transports were anchored in the channel with a variety of cruisers and destroyers nearby. The coxswain followed the other boats toward a huge bath tub of a ship that appeared to be Company D's new home. Their boat circled and came around to the port side of the USS President Adams, where men from the 2nd Platoon were slowly climbing the cargo net. The Adams' faded gray paint gave way to huge patches of undercoat red primer near the water line and she showed signs of wear and tear. On the bow, just behind the anchor was her identifier, P-38. A long row of life rafts was hanging from her sides, a reminder of what could happen at almost any time. Other Marines and Navy crew leaned over the rails and waved at the incoming Marines.

Bill grabbed the wet cargo net and lifted himself to the gunwale of the Higgins Boat and waited for George Garcia to climb up and give him room to follow. He slowly ascended the net and his legs began to burn as he neared the top. A sailor smiled as he reached down and grabbed Bill under his left arm. "Welcome aboard!" he blared. Bill said he was glad to be here. As Bill swung his legs over the side and onto the deck of the Adams, he breathed one of the largest sighs of relief of his life. It felt good to have all this American steel below his boots and the bristling deck guns gave him a sense of security. The Adams would take Company D and the entire battalion out of the combat zone where there were no Japanese planes or ships to worry about. Bill made his way below deck and found a bunk. George Garcia reminded him that the top bunk was the safest, but Bill found a lower bunk that would be easier on his legs. After Tulagi, if someone vomited from above, it wouldn't be the worst thing that had happened to him. The guys spent the next few hours seeing who was nearby on the ship, and the rooms filled with cigarette smoke and card games just like the old days on board the Jackson. In the morning, a good Navy breakfast started the day and more Marines came up the cargo nets. Units from Gavutu, Makambo and a few from Florida Island arrived aboard. Finally, at 1430 hours on January 31st, 1943, the Adams weighed anchor and turned southeast away from the Solomon Islands. Bill and his buddies stood on the deck and watched Tulagi shrink in the distance. After being underway for an hour, the ships ad-

The well-rusted USS President Adams that brought Company D from Tulagi to New Zealand, early February, 1943. An early Higgins Boat without a bow ramp is seen in the foreground.

(U.S. Navy Photo)

dress system crackled and, "Attention, this is the captain," hushed everyone on board. "We welcome our guests from the 2nd Marine Division aboard the USS President Adams. Our destination is Wellington Harbor, New Zealand." A huge roar erupted from the Marines on all decks as some of them literally jumped for joy and shook each other by the shoulders. Some of the guys wanted to make sure that there were no Japanese in New Zealand. Some of 2nd Division had already spent time in New Zealand before the Solomons and they were sure there weren't any Japanese there. The Solomon Islands were now officially in the past and New Zealand, with hope for the future, lay ahead.

43. A Land Down Under

The excitement of being aboard the Adams was beyond the understanding of anyone who had not lived through the past six months in the combat zone. Sleeping in the Navy bunks, eating regular meals, using Navy toilets and sinks with running water were all a part of becoming re-acquainted with civilization. Bill was able to spend more time reading his New Testament and relaxing to allow his legs to heal. The other Marines were generally in great spirits and most were as excited as kids before Christmas. The days went by quickly and the heat and humidity began to dissipate. By the night of February 4th, the evening air on deck felt like air conditioning. On the afternoon of February 6th, land was sighted and the lower decks were clearing out as everyone wanted to see New Zealand approaching. Bill and George Garcia made it to the rail on the port side and watched as the land mass grew before them. Truitt Anderson had been talking to a group of young Privates under a Higgins Boat and came over to the rail next to Bill. He told Bill that he hoped they would be given liberty right away and Bill agreed.

New Zealand consists of two main islands; the South Island was to their left and the North Island to their right. As the Adams came into the Cook Straight between the islands, she turned to the starboard and made way for the mouth of Wellington Harbor. The light green tint of the ocean gave way to the dark green hills that rose on either side of the harbor. Clusters of houses and buildings appeared as white speckles highlighted by the deep green backdrop. Tile roofs came clearly into view and many were vivid colors of red, green, blue and yellow. George commented on the beauty and told Bill that it looked a lot like San Francisco. George had been there, Bill had not. Nonetheless, Wellington was a thing of beauty. As the U.S. ships entered the harbor, New Zealanders waved from every direction. Cars pulled over on coastal highways and even on bridges. Cars honked their horns and pleasure boats came along side at a distance. Marine and Navy binoculars were used handily for surveillance of New Zealand's young ladies waving from shore and these were the first women that many had seen in over six months. Truitt commented on the exuberance shown by the civilians and said he hoped they were still happy when the Marines would have to leave. The bad news was given that the Adams would remain anchored in the harbor and all would remain aboard ship until the following day. The next 24 hours seemed to take forever. Civilization was within site, but no one could touch it!

The morning of February 7th, 1943, brought a warm summer day to Wellington. The temperatures in the mid 80s Fahrenheit would feel quite hot to the New Zealanders, but mild to the Marines. Bill had been given priority to disembark with the sick and the wounded so his combat gear and BAR had to be turned over to the Company. The President Adams lumbered alongside the pier at Wellington and the gangway and hoists were all moved into position. Bill said goodbye to his buddies and was processed off the Adams and into waiting trucks at the end of the pier. As he came down the gangway, the sights, sounds and smells of Wellington brought the sense of new life and adventure. The hills were alive and green and the sounds of the city brought memories of Aurora and Chicago. The gentle breeze brought the scents of food, flowers, soap and a little diesel fuel. New Zealanders had crowded to the dock and cheered as the Marines unloaded from the ships. They cheered as though the Marines were the champion team returning from the tournament. What many of the Americans did not yet realize was that the New Zealanders had been preparing for a final fight against the Japanese in defense of their homeland. The Japanese had been moving closer to New Zealand over the past year. The air field that had been taken on Guadalcanal would have by now been able to launch bombers within range of Wellington. By stopping the Japanese at Tulagi and Guadalcanal, the Marines had literally saved New Zealand and Australia from having the war brought to their shores. The New Zealanders were now about to show the Marines their gratitude.

As Bill was being helped into the waiting trucks, he met several young female volunteers from the hospital near Trentham. As the Marines were loading up, the young ladies repeated, "Good on you, Yank! Good on you!" This turned out to be a congratulatory New Zealand salute for a "job well done." Hearing a woman's voice and smelling their perfume was a sure sign that they had landed in civilization. Many of the Marines had to be transported by ambulance to the hospital since their wounds were so severe. There were a lot of sick Marines in those trucks, along with Marines with missing arms, hands and legs. The 12-mile truck ride became quite uncomfortable for most of them as it took almost an hour at very slow speeds. Arriving at Trentham, Bill was assigned to a ward with many other Marines with similar circumstances. Some of the volunteers brought a cart with cold milk and handed Bill a glass. The glass was empty in three seconds. This was one of the best reminders of home that Bill had experienced in some time. He drank two more glasses. "Getting while the getting was good" crossed his mind. The Marines laughed and talked incessantly in that ward. As soon as the young ladies would leave the room, the comments started flying. There was an abundance of good-looking girls everywhere they looked and the Marines were like kids in a candy store. On the first day in New Zealand, the Marines learned about a curious custom of the "Kiwis," when all work and activity came to a screeching halt at 10 a.m. and 2 p.m. daily. Tea and "biscuits" were served and social conversations were engaged. The "biscuits" turned out to be cookies by American standards, so the Marines ended up with two other reasons to eat each day.

Since Bill could walk, he was able to take his meals in the hospital mess hall or cafeteria. He and the other walking wounded from his ward went to their first meal together and experienced New Zealand's "Steak and Eggs" fare with more milk, fresh bread and mounds of butter. The only warning was that they try not to eat too much. The hospital staff promised them that New Zealand had plenty of food and friendly faces, if nothing else. Bill found George Montague in the mess hall and the two of them were able to spend some time together. While Bill was getting oriented to life at the Trentham Hospital, the other Marines were moving out into the Wellington area. Manny Bud had asked around to find the nearest Synagogue and soon knocked on the door of Rabbi Katz in Wellington. Manny told Rabbi Katz that he wanted to pray and thank God for letting him survive Gavutu, Florida and Tulagi. Rabbi Katz was a very small man, but Manny thought he might be crushed to death by the huge hugs that the rabbi bestowed upon him. The rabbi made phone calls and within 10 minutes there were eight other Jewish men there who had left work to come and pray with Manny. Rabbi Katz then arranged a feast for Manny and he too experienced the abundance of food available in New Zealand. Other members of Company D found "milk bars" in Wellington, where a glass of milk could be had for three cents each, along with ice cream and sodas. The new units of 1st Battalion, 18th Marines and Bill's 2nd Battalion, 18th Marines were gathering just to the west of Trentham to a place called the "Moonshine Valley" at Judgeford. A new camp would be built before any substantial leave would be given. The camp became known as "Camp Moonshine."

Bill was placed on the "new stuff" called penicillin, and ordered to rest as much as possible. Besides having the skin ulcers cleaned out and treated, the doctors also noted that Bill had developed some ruptured veins due to the ulcerations and this would require several surgeries to repair. It looked as though he would have an extended stay at Trentham. To Bill's delight, quite a few of the Company D guys regularly visited the hospital to see how he was coming along. Corpsmen Rice and Ford actually worked at the hospital occasionally, in keeping with their medical training. Bill used the time of rest to read anything he could find and there were plenty of magazines and books to go around. The most frustrating thing about reading was to spend a half hour reading an article in a magazine only to find out it was "continued in the next issue." Most of the time, the "next issue" was missing. Bill began spending more time reading his New Testament and there was plenty of time for prayer.

Getting up early and getting outside to one of the little garden areas was a great pleasure and a very peaceful place to pray. He realized one morning that screaming cockatoos were no longer providing a rude awakening each day. The eventual surgeries were very painful for four or five days, but once the incisions healed, his legs began to feel increasingly strong. Fred Ellis came by with Herb Dale and Manny and George Garcia stopped by several times.

Truitt Anderson came to visit Bill on his way back from a weekend liberty where he had been to the Allied Services Club on Manners Street in Wellington. Truitt was so excited about meeting a girl named Molly Webby. Molly and her friends, Margaret and Nannette Taylor, had invited Truitt, Carmen Yonke and a few other guys over to the Taylor place which was on a hill out in Miramar overlooking the harbor. Molly was an instructor with the Women's Auxiliary Army Corps and she trained women recruits survival swimming and other skills. Truitt said he would be going back to see Molly again and told Bill that he would just have to go along as soon as he could get out of the hospital. Bill asked Truitt if he was sure he wanted to have another drill sergeant telling him what to do. Truitt laughed and told Bill to wait until he met Molly to see what he thought; she was sweet and beautiful, as Bill would see in due time.

There were a lot of things going on with the changes to Company D/2/18, and the guys tried to keep Bill up-to-date. By February 23rd, Bill's skin ulcers and the incisions from the surgeries had healed sufficiently and he was released back to join his Company at Camp Moonshine in Judgeford. The hospital staff and the volunteers had treated Bill and the other Marines like kings and he could not have asked for more. He would be forever grateful for the care that he had received.

44. Company D

Bill said good bye to Montague and the others at Trentham and was given a ride over to Judgeford by a medical shuttle car from the hospital. The scenery from the hospital had been quite nice but it became even more impressive as the car headed west over the bridge spanning the Hutt River. The road then wound up into the rolling green hills, veering northward toward the mountains in the distance. The car passed farms and pastures and what seemed to be thousands of grazing sheep and cattle. As the car came over a rise in the road, Bill could see the camp off to his left, nestled in the valley. There was activity everywhere, as many structures were being erected and the bright fresh lumber reflected the sun. The tires of the car ground to a halt in the gravel at the main gate and Bill thanked the older New Zealand gentleman for the lift. Bill handed the MP at the gate his paperwork, who briefly looked it over, then welcomed PFC Bennett to Camp Moonshine. Bill was directed to an area of row upon row of tents and to his new home with 2nd Platoon. Bill found Corporal George Gabel, who was wearing an extra stripe now, as Sergeant Gabel. He was happy to see Bill return and he took him to a tent where Herb Dale, Johnnie Jones and George Garcia had managed to reserve a bunk for him. Bill set his things on the cot and saw that his sea bag had been delivered. His extra uniforms, dress shoes, underwear and other luxuries were inside. Gabel said that the guys were certainly going to be glad to see Bill back and he asked him how the legs were doing. Bill said he was healing up fine but probably wouldn't be ready for any football for a while yet. Gabel told him there were a lot of things changing with the unit and wanted to bring him up to speed. 2nd Battalion, 18th Marine's new commanding officer was Colonel Chester Salazar, a career Marine and a good leader as far as Gabel knew. Company D's commanding officer was Captain Donald Farkas, as Bill had been told on Tulagi. Captain Bross would remain the second in command with Lieutenants Saylor, Hayes and Simmons. 2nd Platoon was now led by 2nd Lieutenant Barney Boos, who had previously been with 3rd Platoon. 1st Lieutenant Harold A. Hayes, Jr. was in the role of spearheading the reorganization of Company D, and he had sent word that he wanted to see Bill at his tent after lunch. Gabel said that most of the guys were the same from the old Company A and the only one waiting to return was Montague. There had been quite a few Marines rotating in and out of the hospitals at Silver Stream and Trentham. Gabel left Bill to the task of unpacking his things and getting situated before lunch.

A few minutes before noon, Bill arrived at the mess tent where 2nd Platoon would be eating. Sergeant Gabel came in with Mike Matkovich and Charles LaPoint just before the others started to arrive. As the guys poured in from their work details, they made a big deal of seeing Bill again and quite a few of them were interested to hear about the nurses over at Trentham. If Bill thought it was worth it, they were considering injuring themselves to spend some time there. It was all for laughs, of course. Word was that replacements would soon be arriving, but for now, the platoon was basically the old guys from Tulagi. As Bill ate lunch he looked around the tent at the familiar faces. There was Fred Ellis, Dick Reed, George Cothran, Harry Cabler, Manny Bud, George Garcia, Gene Seng, Herb Dale, Truitt Anderson, Joe Sobolewski, Ed Susans, Virgil Dailey, Rudy Halazon, Sam Herman, Jerry Jutting, Russ Banwart, Charles Wysocki, Gerry Graham, Al Slowinski and Carmen Yonke. These were all good, dependable Marines and a great core to rebuild the company. There were other members of Company D dispersed with other duties who would be joining them soon.

As the other Marines were clearing out after lunch, Bill found Lieutenant Hayes and waited for him to finish his conversations. Hayes acknowledged that he was ready to go and turned to walk toward his tent. As the pair walked through the camp, Hayes asked Bill about his origins and his family. Bill quickly went through the basics about Aurora, his family, his girl Helen, air conditioning and sports. They entered the tent and Lieutenant Hayes offered Bill a seat near his make-shift desk. Hayes tapped a cigarette from his pack and offered one to Bill. Bill said no thanks, and the lieutenant lit his and took a long drag before blowing the smoke up to the left as a gesture of courtesy. Hayes went on; there were a lot of changes coming, and coming fast. He was going to need Bill's full effort and cooperation to get through all of these changes. If Bill was on board, it would be good for him as well as the other men. He needed Bill to continue to be a good example as the new guys began to come into the company. Hayes made it clear that he reported directly to Captain Farkas, who reported to Colonel Salazar, but he would always have the men's best interest in mind. That was a promise.

As for changes that would be coming, Hayes told Bill the company would soon be receiving the new M1 Garand rifles to replace the 1903 Springfields. Hayes had fired the M1 and said it was the best rifle imaginable. He opened Bill's service file and placed it on the desk. He said that the M1 loaded eight .30-06 rounds via a preloaded "clip" and fired semi-automatically; one pull of the trigger resulting in one round being fired. Since Bill was a BAR man, he understood what this meant as far as an increase in a rifle squad's firepower. It was a huge leap forward. He said that while Bill would be involved as a BAR instructor in the coming months, he wanted him to draw an M1 as well and become proficient with it. Furthermore, the Marines had learned important lessons in the Solomons and one of the most important was the usefulness of TNT and flamethrowers, especially when used in combination. The Corps was going to need more 533 certifications of demolition experts and Hayes thought Bill was a prime candidate as he was trustworthy, cool headed, didn't drink and didn't smoke. He asked Bill if he would volunteer for demolition training. Hayes would personally assist Bill with anything he needed help with, and Emory Ashurst, from 3rd Platoon's "Go to Hell Men," would be teaching the classes. Hayes told Bill that Ashurst was probably the most knowledgeable 533 in the Marines at that time. Bill agreed to the training and told Hayes he would do whatever needed to be done. As for Bill's legs, he was told that he would be kept on light duty for two more weeks to aid in his recovery. There was just one more thing. Lieutenant Hayes told Bill he was being promoted to corporal, temporarily, and it would be made official in a month or two. He handed Bill some chevrons bundled with a rubber band and told him that he could sew the new stripes on. Hayes told Bill he looked forward to serving with him, then told him that would be all for now. Bill placed his cap on his head and the pair saluted before Bill turned and left the tent.

Camp Moonshine was a great bustle of activity from sunrise to sunset. There was a small stream that ran along the backside of the camp where engineers had dropped hoses from several pumps that were extracting water. The stream descended from the nearby mountains and it was clean enough to drink without purification. Of course, this meant that the stream was strictly off limits "upstream" from the camp. There were no water heaters, as of yet, so showering and washing were going to be extremely cold experiences. Open air wash tables were built for laundry, which utilized buckets, brushes and large bars of laundry soap. Items were scrubbed on the wet tables, then rinsed and hand wrung before being hung out in some fashion back at the tents. There were also ironing stations available for pressing uniforms. There were several mess tents for the enlisted men and one for the officers. The food was high quality with plenty of mutton and lamb cuts, which were often cooked into some sort of stew. Steak and eggs were also plentiful and wonderful cuts of meat could be bought in town for about .25 cents per pound and brought in to the camp for grilling. The cooks would fire up the mess grills late at night and allow Marines with "connections" to grill their custom steaks.

At the first assembly of the battalion, Colonel Salazar awarded Lieutenant Hayes the Silver Star for his actions on Tulagi on August 7th, 8th and 9th of 1942. When 3rd Battalion's "Go to Hell Men" had come up against the enemy embedded in their limestone caves, Hayes had led the way to blast them out. 2nd Lieutenant Barney Boos, 2nd Lieutenant Harley Simmons and Private Clarence W. Roblyer were awarded the Bronze Star for "Meritorious actions against the enemy at Tulagi" on August 10th of 1942. Captain Edgar J. Crane, who led the Marines ashore on August 7th, 1942, was awarded the Navy Cross. Although the battalion was undersized at the time, the marching and the music provided by the 2nd Division Band provided a very impressive assembly and an emotional reflection of what they had been through in the Solomon Islands. In spite of the uplift in morale that the battalion assembly provided, these Marines were a very sick and worn out group of fighting men.

As Bill returned to full duty, he became reacquainted with the 10- and 20-mile marches with full combat gear. He had been getting some strengthening exercises in to help with his legs but new boondockers were always a problem on the hikes. Even though the cooler weather in New Zealand meant no possibility of more jungle rot, he was far more concerned about taking good care of small wounds that could lead to infection of some sort. Bill had not as of yet had any personal interaction with Captain Farkas, but some of the Marines were pointing out that while other captains went on marches with their men, Captain Farkas did not. This began to foster the feeling that Captain Farkas was not willing to endure what he ordered others to do. This assumption may well have been wrong, but it was being talked about within the ranks. Captain Bross remained second in command and the men tried to work directly with him as much as possible. A new rifle range was built near camp and 2nd Platoon's turn came to draw their new M1 Garand rifles. Harkening back to MCB, San Diego, the rifles were issued with a gooey coat of Cosmoline on them. A thorough disassembly, cleaning, oiling and reassembly would be the first order of familiarization. Gunnery Sergeant Christiano led the platoon in the new process. The M1 was "stripped" into approximately 23 parts for a full strip and cleaning. The rifle utilized a "gas" system that routed the explosive gases emitted from firing a cartridge into a tube that forced the bolt backwards to eject the spent casing and reload a fresh round faster than you could blink your eye. Bill had an advantage over the average 1903 Springfield riflemen in that the BAR was also gas operated and very similar to the M1.

For several days, Bill disassembled and reassembled the M1. Then he was called to the range for live firing for the first time. As Bill took his position on the firing line, he was ordered to open the bolt to make sure it was indeed unloaded. Then he was ordered to load the weapon. He pulled one of the eight round clips from his ammo pouch and pushed it down through the open bolt with his right thumb while the meaty part of his right hand held the bolt open. The clip slid all the way down and he let the bolt fly forward, making an impressive snap. He then checked that the safety was pushed back toward the trigger. At the range master's command, Bill aimed his new M1 at the target placed 300 yards out on the range. He located the tip of the "blade" in the front sight into the center of the circle on the rear "peep" sight and held it directly below the black circle of the target. He pushed the safety forward with his trigger finger and then eased it back to gently touch the trigger. Other M1s began to "pop" up and down the line. Bill drew a deep breath and then slowly exhaled. In the middle of the gentle exhale, Bill gently squeezed the trigger and the butt of the stock punched him in the shoulder. Again and again, he pulled the trigger, and the smooth but powerful rifle sent its projectile into the target. When the eighth round was fired, the spent steel clip flew out of the open bolt and sailed behind Bill's head with a noticeable "ping" sound. No doubt about it, he was out of ammo.

The entire company was thrilled about the new M1 Garand and also about the Garand's new "little brother," the M1 Carbine. The carbine fired a less powerful .30 caliber round that had a lethal range of about 300 yards compared to the Garand's 1000 yards. The advantage of the carbine was that it fired a 15 round detachable box magazine, (like the BAR) so that it could fire almost twice as much as the Garand without reloading. Reloading was also very easy as the magazines snapped in and out from the bottom of the weapon as opposed to the open bolt on top. Since much of the Marines combat would be close-quarters jungle fighting, the lightweight M1 Carbine would become very popular. If you wanted more firepower to be delivered over a longer distance, then the Garand and the BAR would be the choice. These weapons were so much more advanced than the bolt action 1903 Springfield that the Marines were sure they would have a great advantage over the Japanese the next time they met each other.

The day came for Company D to qualify with their new weapons and most of the old gang qualified quickly and with high ratings. Bill fired a little better than average, as he had back in San Diego, while Manny once again qualified near the top. The rifle range had a PA speaker that would announce the Marine about to qualify on the range so that their buddies could watch to see how they were doing. As everyone was busy, either preparing to shoot or cleaning their weapons afterward, the speaker announced that Captain Farkas would be the next up on the qualification range. Just about the entire company paused to hear the score. The first shots were announced as misses, then near misses and more misses and the company began to laugh. Farkas, of course, could hear the laughter and was quite embarrassed. He finished his shots and then directly departed the range and went back to his quarters in the hut that had been built specifically for him. His absence on the marches had now been answered by this display of disrespect. Bill and some of the older guys sensed that there would be hell to pay. The next morning the company was ordered on a 30-mile march with full combat gear and their new rifles. Captain Farkas did not go along for the march. On April 1st, George Garcia was given orders to transfer to Company E/2/18, which left a spare bunk in the tent. Although Bill and George were a bit upset by being split up, George only had to move a few tent rows over to join his new company. They would still be able to "buddy around" from time to time.

45. Liberty

Bill had missed out on the initial forays into Wellington and the surrounding towns, but finally got the chance to explore when Company D was given a weekend liberty. The dress uniform was carefully pressed and the shoes shined. Bill was singled out as the guy who would make sure that the other guys looked good. Since Manny and Bill's fathers were both tailors, their opinions mattered more than most. There were so many groups of Marines who wanted to head in different directions that Bill would have his choice. There were those in search of women; Bill had a girl at home. There were those that wanted to get drunk; Bill was not known to drink. He wisely teamed up with Marines that he trusted and they showed him the spots they had found in Wellington. Bill's buddies Dick Reed, from California, and Carmen Yonke from Wisconsin, had been to a dance for servicemen downtown and thought that would be a good place to start out. George Garcia, Fred Ellis, Bob Swigert and Johnny Jones rounded out the adventure team and the seven of them loaded into a truck that would deliver them to the train depot in Trentham, just a few miles away. Al Slowinski was one of the Marines Bill had met back in Chicago on that first morning over a year ago. Al was a master carpenter who had been given the task of building the new brig at Camp Moonshine. Captain Farkas told Slowinski that he could not leave camp for liberty until the brig was finished, so he worked long hours to try and get the new doors and windows installed, complete with bars and locks. Regardless of the effort, Slowinski, or "Ski," as the guys called him, was left behind when everyone else pulled away in the trucks.

The train tracks followed the Hutt River toward the bay through Silverstream, Upper Hutt and Lower Hutt, then across a wide inlet of the harbor and into Wellington. Besides riding through in the medical truck, this was the first time Bill had been out in a city since the night before they shipped out of San Diego. The sights and sounds of the city on a Friday night were exciting and there was everything to see. The guys took him near the waterfront and they walked Lambton Quay and Molesworth Street, where the sharp-dressed lads caught the attention of quite a few of New Zealand's young ladies. One group of young ladies had a camera and asked if they could have their photo taken with a few of the "Yanks." The guys were only too happy to oblige their request. Bill leaned on the rail that guarded the edge of the walkway at the harbor and looked across the light green water to the dark green hills on the other side. The steady breeze coming across from the north pushed rolling clouds over Wellington. The sights, smells and sounds were all refreshing and he felt completely free for the first time in a long time. He had not seen much of New Zealand, but he liked all that he had seen.

The Allied Services Club on Manners Street in downtown Wellington was hosting a service dance and the group went over to give it a try. Truitt Anderson and Carmen Yonke introduced the group to Molly Webby and the Taylor sisters, who they had met at the first dance some weeks earlier. The 2nd Division Band was playing and the songs from home sounded so good to the weary Marines. The Taylors insisted that the group come out to their home in

Miramar. They lived about half an hour by trolley, up in the hills that the USS Adams had passed on the way into the harbor. The trolley took them around the harbor and up into Miramar, exactly the same name as an area just outside of San Diego. The trolley stopped near the winding neighborhood and the group walked up the hill to Number 53 Nevay Road. The girl's mother, Helen Taylor, was a widow that had registered her large house with the government as a "Respite House," where service members could find a place to sleep or a meal to eat, depending on how many were already there. The girls plowed through the door announcing visitors and their surprised mother jumped up from her chair and closed her book, all in one motion. Their mother introduced herself as Helen Taylor and seemed very happy to meet some of the Marines that had "saved New Zealand." Mr. Taylor had passed away almost 20 years ago and Helen had never remarried. She and the girls were able to make a good life contributing to the finances and were very happy. The Marines were made to feel very welcome at the Taylor home, as snacks, drinks, card games and music were plentiful there. This was the first time some of them had been asked into a New Zealand home and it would become common for all of them in the future. Mrs. Taylor invited several neighbors over to meet the Yanks and the night had the feel of one of the old dinner parties back in Aurora. The Taylors told the fellows they should feel free to drop in any time, and bring their friends along.

After two days on the town in Wellington, Bill wanted to make sure he went to church on Sunday morning. He found the Lower Hutt Baptist Church in a convenient location near the train line back to Trentham and joined the morning worship service. While a good number of Marines were waking up with hangovers or worse, quite a few of them made it a point to get to church, as Bill had. The service was surprisingly similar to those in the States and the people were even friendlier. After the service, an older woman introduced herself to Bill as she was thrilled to talk to a Marine. Her name was Lena Mitchell and she told Bill that her son Les was in the New Zealand Air Corps and stationed in Northern New Zealand. Les would be home on leave the following week and she insisted that Bill come to the nearby home for dinner. Knowing how hospitable the New Zealanders were, and being interested to meet Les, Bill agreed to be at their home the following Friday night if he was granted weekend liberty again. When Bill returned to camp, he was surprised to hear what had happened to Slowinski. Apparently, he had finished the brig about noon on Saturday and headed into Wellington on his liberty. After having a "few too many" drinks, he took a swing at some other Marines who had kidded him about missing some of his liberty. "Ski" was arrested by the MPs and returned to Camp Moonshine where he became the first "guest of honor" in his own brig!

While Bill and his buddies had been to the Taylor residence, a huge fight had broken out in downtown Wellington between the Marines and the New Zealand servicemen. Quite a few of the Marines at Camp Moonshine were wearing "battle scars" on their faces and knuckles when Bill came back to camp. Manny and his group of Marines had been drinking at a club downtown when a horrible scuffle was heard out in the streets. The Marines ran to the door and found about one hundred other Marines holding off a force of New

Zealanders, so they naturally joined the brawl. The fight moved through the streets for over two hours and involved well over 1000 men. When the Marine MPs showed up to break up the fight, the New Zealanders pummeled them as well, and the MPs had to join the fight. Manny and his group took refuge in a small alley after being pummeled repeatedly. One of the group had been a nationally-ranked sprinter at Indiana State University and Manny had an idea on how they could use that speed to the Americans' advantage. The speedy Marine ran into the riot and selected a "Kiwi" to punch. He then outran the New Zealander to the alley. When the unsuspecting enemy ran around the corner, the Marines pummeled him and then threw him back into the street. This process was repeated until the fight moved on and the Marines could get away. Some said that the whole thing started when some southern U.S. Marines refused to let the dark skinned Maori soldiers into the Allied Services Club to drink. Manny said it started when New Zealanders and a few Brits made wise-cracks during the U.S. National Anthem at the movie theater. Apparently, the Marines had been respectful during the New Zealand national anthem, but the respect was not returned and the Marines took issue with the Brits. Somehow, one of the British sailors ended up being flung over the balcony rail onto the seats below. The fight then spilled out into the street and in front of the Service Club. However it began, it was a black eye to the Marine's presence in New Zealand and there would be no liberty for several weeks until things cooled down. The fight was never mentioned in the press and it became known to the Marines as "The Battle of Wellington." There was still plenty of work to go around getting the new camp squared away and Marines were now bound to focus on it. His visit to the Mitchell residence would have to wait for a while.

Lieutenant Hayes called Bill back to his tent and had a "work party detail" lined up for him. Bill would be placed in charge of a group from 2nd Platoon who would be responsible for painting a nearby dance hall. The hall was scheduled to be used for an American Servicemen's Dance in a few weeks. The large hall had fallen into disrepair during the Great Depression years, which had greatly affected New Zealand, just as it had the United States and other countries. The paint and supplies were to be provided by the locals and the work party would commute to the site by truck each day until the job was done.

Arriving at the job site, it was much worse than Bill had imagined. There would probably be several days of scraping and caulking before they could even begin to paint. Bill organized the work and had everyone working together to get the job done. There were two Marines that had a history of dislike towards each other, possibly better described as hatred. Bill made sure these two were as far apart as possible. The issue was that the Marine from Texas was under the impression the Marine from Tennessee was lazy and tried to avoid work. The fellow from Texas took it upon himself to agitate the Tennessean whenever he could. After four days of paint detail, irritation was obvious. The locals had been gracious enough to provide very nice lunches for the Marines, which some ladies brought and set up on tables each noon. After lunch, the Tennessean fell asleep on a couch and the other guys were all returning to work. The Texan took it upon himself to grab a spare hot dog from the food table and shove it into the sleeping Marine's mouth. The Tennessean jolted from his nap and let loose with a litany of southern profanity while he grabbed a butcher knife from the table and went after the Texan. Bill knew by the look of the mad Marine that this was no joke this time. The Texan dodged the thrust of the knife and fled towards the exit door with his attacker close behind. Bill threw down his paint brush and ran after the knife wielding Marine. At the door, the Texan again dodged the knife and several of the other Marines were screaming at the crazed Tennessean. Bill caught up to the scrambling pair and dove into the midsection of the Tennessean, taking him full force to the floor. Bill grabbed the Marine's wrist with both hands and pried his thumb back from the knife as they had learned in training. He then threw the knife across the room and picked up the private by the collar and pulled him outside. As much as he hated to do it, Bill reported the incident and let Lieutenant Hayes figure out what do with the Marine. After seeing Bill handle this situation, word got around the company that it would be wise not to mess with Corporal Bennett.

    The old hall looked fantastic when the Saturday of the dance rolled around. The 2nd Division Band was on hand to provide the music and families of New Zealanders volunteered to provide refreshments and friendship. Hundreds of young ladies arrived from near and far and most were accompanied by their parents, as was customary in conservative New Zealand. The hall was decorated with red, white and blue decorations, which were easy to find as New Zealand used the same colors for their national festivities. The American band had a great selection of music and the whole affair was quite a reminder of the States. As Bill mingled with the crowd, he met a member of the New Zealand Air Corps named Stuart Hyde. Stuart asked Bill about his unit and the action he had been involved with in the Solomons. The conversation turned to Bill's home in Illinois, his family and his girl. Stuart told Bill about his home town up north, Shannon, New Zealand. He told Bill it was a small town but it was really "quite a place," and he should pay a visit when he could. Bill wrote down Stuart's name and asked for the address. Stuart said that he wouldn't need an address because his family owned half of the town. Bill only needed to get off the train and ask for Stuart Hyde. He did give Bill the phone number so he could make sure Stuart would be able to meet him in Shannon. A few days after the dance, while Bill was on a detail working at camp, the familiar feel of fever and chills began to creep back into his body. Within hours, he was covered with blankets back in the tent and Corpsman Rice sent for an ambulance. Bill soon found himself in the malaria ward back at the hospital in Trentham, and the ward was filled. After two days, the symptoms were gone and Bill was driven back to camp where he was allowed an additional week of rest.

    To Bill's surprise, the Marine Corps decided to give the Marines numerous extended liberties so they could tour New Zealand and have some much needed rest and relaxation. With back pay coming in from the Solomons Campaign, the Marines hit the streets with a lot of time and quite a bit of cash. Wearing his smartly pressed dress uniform and well shined shoes, Bill caught a Marine truck with Herb Dale over to the train station. Bill pulled the directions that Mrs. Mitchell had given him at the Baptist church from his notebook. The train took them south to Woburn Station where they got off and caught the bus to "Thomas' Store," which was a block away from the Mitchell's house. They hopped off the bus and walked down Fuller Grove, which was lined on both sides by neat looking single-story houses with tile or metal roofs. Each house had a short fence or block wall along the front sidewalk and Bill and Herb eyed the house numbers. Number 14 was almost at the end of the block and they turned up the driveway to the front door. The front door flung open and Lena and Bernie Mitchell stepped out onto the stoop as Mrs. Mitchell welcomed Bill with a hug. Their son Les was around back but quickly came to the front and shook hands eagerly with the two Marines. Several neighbors were out in their yards and they came over to greet the "Yanks." After proper introductions and quite a bit of talk, Bill and Herb were ushered into the house to get ready for dinner. Mrs. Mitchell prepared a wonderful chicken dinner that was competition for Jessie's home-cooked meals. Les had a great sense of humor and a great deal of respect for the combat these boys had been through. Since he was on leave himself, he insisted on being their tour guide and showing them the sights. Bill and Herb were accommodated in the Mitchell's spare room for the night and felt very much at home. Bill inquired of the Mitchells regarding the location of a Methodist church in the area, as he considered himself a true Methodist and wanted to attend services if possible. They looked through the phone book and found a few in the area and Bill wrote down the locations. In the morning, Mrs. Mitchell fired up a delicious "steak and eggs" breakfast and Bill, Les and Herb were off.

Bill's plan was to take the train up the Kapiti Coast to visit the Hydes in Shannon and Les thought that Bill should see the city near Les' base, Palmerston North. Les knew exactly where they were going and pointed out sights along the way. The train ran along Wellington Harbor and then north toward Porirua and over the bridge at Plimmerton, then along the coast at Paekakariki. The view of the green mountains sweeping down into the wide strip of dark brown sand and then into the blue waters was breathtaking. Les explained that this was the Kapiti Coast and the island just off shore was none other than Kapiti Island. This was probably the most visited area of New Zealand's North Island. Fishing and vacationing were the popular activities in this area. The train moved inland again and stopped at Otaki and Levin before coming to Shannon. The travelers went to the ticket window and Bill asked if the agent knew where they could find Stuart Hyde. The agent pointed across the street and told them to try the cinema.

Stuart Hyde, his younger brother Selly and their mother, Eleanor, were all at work in the theater when Bill, Herb and Les walked through the door. Stuart dropped what he was doing and welcomed the trio with strong handshakes. He introduced Selly and Eleanor and said they should all be in for quite a weekend. The Hyde family had quite a unique role in the town of Shannon. Their father Alf had been mayor of Shannon, but had passed away recently. The family owned quite a bit of property in Shannon, including the theater called the "Renown Cinema," the adjacent ice cream shop or "milk bar," the boot shop, furniture shop, book store, town hall, a taxi service and about 16 rental houses. "Stu" was a very intelligent fellow and adept at handling the businesses while 17-year-old "Selly" was a gregarious and funny character.

Bill, Herb and Les took in a movie, "on the house" of course, and had all the ice cream they wanted. As per usual with Bill, he insisted on being of some help with the operation and he helped Selly in the ice cream shop during intermission. The folks from Shannon were a bit shocked to be served ice cream by a U.S. Marine. After the cinema was all "buttoned up" for the night, the Hydes and their visitors went over to the house and cooked a late dinner. They all stayed up late playing cards and telling stories while laughing and getting to know each other. Bill made fast friends with the Hyde family and they insisted that he return to visit them as often as possible.

Stu cooked up a proper breakfast and Bill used the phone book to find a Methodist Church in Palmerston North where the travelers might take in Sunday services the next day. St. Paul's was a notable Methodist church in Palmerston North and Bill jotted down the address in his book. Selly drove the fellows over to the station in a coal-powered taxi. The curious contraption was part car and part locomotive with its belching smoke from the burner mounted above the back bumper. With the rationing of gasoline, coal power had become practical in New Zealand, but it wasn't very dependable and it had to be stoked every 10 minutes. Selly and Stu stood on the platform and gave their guests a proper wave off as the train pulled out of Shannon Station. The half-hour trip up to Palmerston North was through the flattest section of New Zealand that Bill had seen. The farmland to the left went out toward the ocean and looked similar to Illinois, except for the trees, and the plains to the right were bordered by the green hills. Large farms included fields filled with flocks of grazing sheep and vast turnip fields, which Les explained were for the feeding of livestock. The peaceful beauty of the landscape made Bill completely forget about the war for a short while. The train rattled across the trestle bridge over the Manawatu River and into the trees on the far bank. A huge curve to the right took them around the little town of Longburn and Palmerston North was in sight just ahead. As the train slowed into the station, Bill could see the large white and black sign on the platform reading, "Palmerston North."

Les asked a few questions at the station and they found a taxi that would take them to St. Paul's Church. The picturesque red brick church had a beautiful, four-sided steeple rising 50 feet from the street with four smaller spires set on each corner. The top of the black shingled spire had a silver ornament that pointed skyward. The windows were set with alabaster stone frames that contrasted with the red brick and the stained glass. A wide set of stone steps led up to the double front doors and people were moving up the two sets of stairs as the service was about to begin. Bill eagerly made his way up the stairs and shook the hands of the greeters by the front door. The folks seemed happily surprised to see the two Marines and New Zealand airman arriving for the service and the ushers showed them to their pew. The organist was playing an unfamiliar hymn as they took their seats. Bill was surprised that the Methodist services in New Zealand were so similar to those at Fourth Street Methodist back home, though he honestly could not understand all the words the New Zealanders were saying just yet. The Reverend Clarence Eaton delivered a wonderful sermon that was inspirational to Bill and he felt well rested, happy and spiritually strong. Being in a Methodist Church at this particular time

St. Paul's Methodist Church in Palmerston North, New Zealand in 1943. The Reverend Clarence Eaton presided.

(St. Paul's Methodist Photo)

felt right to Bill and he felt like he was with family, in a way. After the service was over, quite a group of New Zealanders gathered around the visitors to welcome them and get an introduction. A dark-haired girl with a lovely smile came up to the fellows and introduced herself as Lorna Proctor. She asked Bill and Herb where they were from. When Bill answered that he was from a town near Chicago, Lorna asked if he had ever seen Al Capone. Herb said he was from Ryegate, Montana, and Lorna asked if he was a cowboy. Herb explained that all the guys in Ryegate were cowboys. Lorna's sisters Daphne, Joy and Bernice joined her and introductions were made to Bill, Herb and Les.

Lorna insisted the Yanks meet their mother Muriel and she towed them over to where several middle-aged ladies were chatting. Muriel was delighted to meet the three lads and asked them if they had any arrangements for lunch. Bill said they had not and Muriel asked them if they would like to come to their house for lunch. It all sounded good to the guys, so they agreed. On the way out of St. Paul's, Bill insisted on introducing himself to Reverend Clarence Eaton and thanking him for an inspirational sermon. Bill explained that he was raised as a Methodist in the States and he had been looking for a church to attend while in New Zealand. Reverend Eaton naturally welcomed Bill back to St. Paul's anytime he could make the trip up from Judgeford. He noticed the visitors had already made the acquaintance of the Proctors and said they would be in good hands.

The Proctors lived about a mile from the church in a beautiful home that their father Charles Proctor had built himself. The family had profited from Charles ability to build and sell houses in succession and he had built several homes there on Florence Avenue. It was a beautiful day as the group walked along the sidewalk and took the right-hand turn onto Florence Avenue. The house was a two-story craftsman style with a plaster first floor and horizontal clapboard on the second story. Gables with small balconies below the window adorned the second floor and the steep roof was clad with steel corrugated roofing. Across the front yard in between two shrub trees were random-sized cut stones, half buried in the dirt along the sidewalk. The drive was made with two wide bands of bricks with a grassy area in the middle, and there was a garage located behind the house. Lorna explained to Bill that Muriel and the girls would be preparing a lunch of trout and rice and hoped the fellows would like it. As the group walked up the driveway, a gray-haired fellow with the look of a weathered sea captain came forth from the garage, where he had apparently been cleaning the morning's catch of trout. Muriel introduced her husband Charles to their guests and he insisted that he give the fellows a tour of the house and yard while lunch was being prepared. Charles could not only give a great tour, he could also tell you the reasons why he had built this feature or that feature as they toured. Herb noticed Charles' fishing gear on the wall in the garage. Herb was an avid fly fisherman in Montana, so he knew about trout. Charles was excited by the subject and Bill could tell by the way his eyes lit up that Charles loved to fish. Bill had more interest in eating fish than catching it, but had been fishing a few times while growing up. As Bill and Al used to joke, it would be hard for Steve Bennett to fish while wearing a tie.

While Bill insisted on making himself useful in the kitchen, Herb was out in the yard getting a fly-fishing lesson from Charles. The girls enlightened Bill about their father and his reluctance to attend church with them. Charles had been in the New Zealand Expeditionary Force during WWI as a machine gunner. His company was holding a hill in France and came under fierce attack from the Germans in the fall of 1917. As the battle dragged on, each member of Charles' company perished leaving him manning a lone machine gun atop the hill. Finally, at long last, Allied reinforcements arrived to push the Hun back and saved Charles' life. He was awarded the New Zealand Military Medal "For Bravery In The Field" and considered to be a hero around Palmerston North. Of course, Muriel and the girls were so very proud of Charles, but he had never explained very much about what happened. Bill had a bit more of an understanding as to why Charles didn't talk very much and relished being alone with a fishing pole. Charles had a connection with these Marines who had been in and would return to combat facing the Japanese. Charles also understood full well that the presence of the U.S.M.C. in New Zealand meant the Japanese would never be able to invade the islands.

Charles and Muriel Proctors home on Florence Avenue, Palmerston North, 1943.

(Proctor/Mitchell Family Photo)

The lunch was expertly cooked and was some of the best tasting fish Bill had ever eaten. Bill and Herb amazed the Proctor girls by rolling up their sleeves and knocking out dish duty after lunch. Muriel protested that it was not proper for guests to do the dishes, but the Marines won the argument. The Proctors had so much fun talking about America and entertaining their guests that they invited them to stay for the night. Although the house was quite full, Joy and Bernice evacuated their room to crowd in with the older girls so that the guests could sleep in their room. As they all sat in the family room talking that evening, Bill looked up and noticed Lorna smiling at him. Of course, he smiled back, but he was a bit concerned about what she might be thinking. He had told her he had a girl at home so he was quite sure there was nothing to it. Charles invited Herb out to fish on the Manawatu River the next morning and Herb couldn't pass up the opportunity to try his skill on the New Zealand trout. Bill and Les would be treated to a tour of Palmerston North by the ladies.

The Proctor Family at home on Florence Avenue in 1943. Left to right: Daphne, Lorna, Joy, Bernice, Muriel and Charles.

(Proctor/Mitchell Family Photo)

If there was only one thing New Zealanders were certainly good at, it seemed to be cooking. The Proctor's breakfast would rival any hotel or restaurant. Scrambled eggs, fried potato cakes, bacon, mushrooms, grilled tomatoes, baked beans and coffee. Daphne told the guys this was more of a weekend breakfast and they didn't always eat like this. Lorna drove the group around the city to show them the sights of Palmerston North, including the radio station 2ZM, 940AM where she worked as an announcer and had her own weekly fashion program. Bill teased her about being a big star and he said he was surprised she would spend time with the likes of him. Back at the house, they reunited with Charles and Herb to hear stories of the "one that got away" and eat a nice lunch of sandwiches. Bill stepped out into the back yard for some air and Lorna followed him out a few minutes later. She told Bill how glad she was he had visited and Bill told her that he had enjoyed the visit a great deal. Their discussion led to yesterday's sermon and Christianity in general. Lorna's viewpoint on deep subjects of faith and commitment greatly impressed Bill, as he had never met a girl of 19 with such insight. As they talked, Bill purposely brought up Helen again, as he wanted it to be clear that he could be Lorna's friend and nothing more. They spent the evening playing cards and Bill tried to familiarize the New Zealanders with his version of Bridge and

King. He became aware of the discrepancy in the rules of card games from one continent to the other. Of course, Les took the Proctor's side on any issues with the rules.

Lorna Proctor behind the microphone at 2ZM 940AM, 1943.

(Proctor/Mitchell Family Photo)

After another great breakfast, the Proctors drove Bill, Les and Herb back to the train station to say goodbye and Muriel and Lorna made them promise that they would visit again whenever they could. They said their goodbyes and the fellows boarded for the three-hour ride back to Lower Hutt and Camp Moonshine. As they talked on the way home, Bill was surprised to hear that Les was interested in coming back again as he had taken a liking to Daphne. Herb told Bill that he thought Lorna seemed to have taken a liking to him and Bill told Herb he had explained his situation well, and Lorna knew it was "friends only." As Bill was lying in his bunk that night, he prayed for those back home and he thanked the Lord for his new friends in New Zealand. In such a short time, Bill had met four families that welcomed him with open arms. There were the Taylors in Miramar, the Mitchells in Lower Hutt, the Hydes in Shannon and the Proctors up in Palmerston North. It felt good to have a new social network outside the Marine Corps.

Whenever the chance for a 24-hour, 12-hour or even an eight-hour pass came along, Bill and Truitt would head over to Miramar to collect Molly and whoever was available to head downtown. The Allied Services Club was open 24 hours a day and had a piano player on duty continuously. Not far from the club was the Majestic Ballroom on Willis Street that frequently had dances with a full band and Truitt and Molly loved to go there. Molly became Truitt and Bill's full time Wellington tour guide and it seemed that they were inseparable. Molly was interested to hear about Bill's "Wonder City" of Aurora and all about Helen Cochran back home. One ingredient that may have made the communication with Molly work so well was that she was military and she understood exactly what the "boys" were up against with their duties. She was also an instructor with the WAAC and carried a lot of responsibility. Molly shared Bill and Truitt's common faith in Christ and understood their desire to live a life that was pleasing to God.

If time permitted, Molly would take Truitt, Bill and the "boys" who may be along over to visit her best friend Doe Marshall and her husband Lesley. Doe and Lesley had a three-year-old son and Molly had stayed with them frequently before she met Truitt. The Marshall family owned a furniture shop and a large residence in Newtown, Wellington, and Molly and her friends were always welcome to spend a night there. Newtown was conveniently located directly on the way from Miramar to downtown Wellington. Since Bill had Truitt's complete confidence and they had plenty of time to talk while on the train to and from their liberty, he could see that Truitt and Molly were developing a serious relationship. Bill felt that he had to be totally honest with Truitt and bring up some of the dangers of allowing himself to fall in love with Molly. As weeks turned into months, there was no question that Truitt and Molly were in love and they wanted to be together. Bill had never seen Truitt so happy or so sure of what he wanted to do.

46. The Stoner Weekly News

As Bill familiarized himself with regular schedules and the luxuries of civilization, mail service greatly improved between the States and New Zealand. Bill was able to send and receive letters on a regular basis and quite a bit of old mail began to arrive. Jessie and Steve had purchased a subscription to the *Beacon News* specifically for Bill so that he could keep up with life in Aurora. Being able to read the news firsthand was wonderful for Bill, even if the newspaper was months old by the time he received it. He could read about high school sports, reports of service men and women abroad and check the prices on groceries and shoes if he wanted. Any letters from home were dear to Bill beyond what others may have been able to understand. As he was now in the midst of his second year away from home, memories were not as sure as they once were and the letters made him feel connected. Since Bill had been socially centered all of his life, not being able to be with his loved ones bothered him greatly. The letters from Helen had not been as regular as they were initially and had become somewhat repetitious. Bill had now been away from Helen for twice as long as he had known her before he left for San Diego. Any type of connection with his previous life was like the breath of life for him.

Back in Aurora, in the brown-brick American Foursquare house on the corner of 4th Street and Avon, *The Stoner Weekly News* was produced with all the intensity of a world-class newspaper. Sam Stoner had taken a key position with the Diamond T Motorcar Company in Chicago. Sam was a Manufacturing Specialist and he coordinated Diamond T's production of heavy trucks for the United States military. When Sam was not on the road or at his office in Chicago, he was the Editor in Chief of *The Stoner Weekly News*. Margaret

Sam Stoner working on an issue of *The Stoner Weekly News* during WW II.

(The Stoner Weekly News Photo)

was the Associate Editor and Circulation Manager and Harley's wife Betty, became the "re-write man." The *Stoner Weekly* mainly contained information about Stoner family activities, but frequently included a line or two about the Bennetts. Bill was delighted after receiving one *Stoner Weekly* edition that verified his letters from Tulagi had indeed made it to 454 Simms Street and described the elation of his parents. The paper also provided detailed information about Dexter, Harley, Bob and now Helen, all in the service. All the Stoners contributed, if even by letter, to the news. Harley was in the Army Corps of Engineers and on his way to the South Pacific, Dexter was in the Finance Corps and near London, England, and Helen had joined the WAVES to do her part and was in San Francisco.

On a typical day at 211 S. Fourth Street, Sam and Margaret were up and eating breakfast before 7 a.m. Margaret would be sharply dressed, with make-up and earrings, each morning before she even started coffee in the kitchen. If Sam were home from being on the road, he would begin the day at his mahogany roll top desk near the window that looked out onto Avon Street. Through his frameless spectacles, Sam would review each piece and prioritize them to the space available. As Margaret prepared breakfast, Sam would make several trips in and out of the kitchen with questions and Margaret would set him straight on the details. Sam would return to the desk and the typewriter would start to clatter. Margaret had letters and information from the week all laid-out and ready for the Editor in Chief to review for column layout. Before Helen went away to the Navy, she coordinated all that she could and wrote up the drafts of the news. When Betty joined the team, she acted as the proof reader and generally helped Margaret with most of the work. Sam had sought advice from some of his associates at the *Beacon News* and purchased a professional little mimeograph machine so that the editions could be "mass produced." Throughout the spare hours of each day, the current issue would take shape and come down to the proof copy, which Betty would then carefully read and correct, if needed. Once Betty had the final copy, Margaret would read it one last time to be safe. Then it was time for the real work. Margaret and Betty ran the mimeograph machine to fulfill a copy for each "subscriber," which totaled about 50 at the high point of circulation. Each copy was then loaded into an envelope, addressed by hand and taken to the post office.

If Sam happened to be home on "print day," he would handle most of the work to give the girls a break, but when he was gone it was an all-female staff. Since Margaret had never learned to drive, Betty would be behind the wheel as they headed down the hill to the downtown area and over to the post office on Stolp Island. The Stoners paid quite a postal bill to mail out the news, but they were happy to do it in order to keep everyone up on the latest. Those little newspapers went out across the country, to the Pacific and to Europe. Sam eventually proclaimed that *The Stoner Weekly News* "covered the globe!" Wherever the *Weekly* arrived, it became a priority to read. The soldiers with Harley and Dexter and the pilots with Bob frequently quizzed their Stoner representative to see if any new issues had arrived. In New Zealand, Bill's buddies felt as if they knew the Stoners personally and looked forward to reading the new editions. As Bill rode the trains in New Zealand, he frequently reread the *Weekly* just to refresh the "in touch" feeling that it gave him. Back at home, Jessie looked forward to receiving her copy in the mail, although she always heard the news from Margaret over the phone or in person before the edition arrived. Jessie would carefully read the issue and share it with the family. Eventually, each issue was folded and set onto the stack of *Stoner Weekly* past issues in the drawer of her dining room wall cabinet, right next to her newspaper clippings.

The effort that the Stoners put into their weekly publication was notable and the dividends it yielded were hard to calculate. For an endeavor that seemed quite trivial at first, the little paper ended up being quite inspirational and meaningful to most of the subscribers. For those overseas, it served as a lifeline connecting them to the lives they once lived back in Aurora; lives that had been unexpectedly disrupted.

47. 533: A New Specialty

While Bill was given plenty of leave to enjoy his new friends in New Zealand, there was serious business to be taken care of back at Camp Moonshine. 2nd Platoon had just been assigned a new officer in 2nd Lieutenant Arthur K. Simonson. Gabel told Bill that Simonson was a good guy and there was nothing to be concerned about. Simonson had been transferred to D/2/18 due to his background with the 2nd Engineering Battalion and had just been promoted. He had joined the Corps in 1940 and gone straight into the Engineering Battalion after basic training. His 2nd Engineering Battalion had been working on a construction project at Pearl Harbor on December 7th, 1941, so he and Gabel held those personal memories in common. He had been a heating and cooling contractor in Portage, Wisconsin, before the war and then trained as a carpenter and a demolition man. They joked that the lieutenant knew how to build things and also how blow them up. Simonson was moving into his new tent and would meet the men in the mess hall at lunch.

2nd Lieutenant Arthur K. Simonson in front of the family home at 810 E. Cook Street in Portage, Wisconsin.

(Photo courtesy of Janet Simonson)

Simonson entered the mess hall and received salutes with a quick return and an "At ease" was given. Gabel and the other sergeants talked to him for a few minutes and then they made their way around the tent. Gabel and Simonson approached Bill, who saluted and then reached out to take the outstretched hand of Lieutenant Simonson. By Steve Bennett's assessment of a handshake, Bill could expect a lot from Arthur K. Simonson. Simonson told Bill that he had heard a lot about him from the men and it was "all good." He asked Bill if he would be able to come with him to his tent after lunch as he wanted to review a few things with him. Bill affirmed that he would wait for the lieutenant. As Bill walked along with Simonson, they exchanged their backgrounds and asked about family. Bill told Simonson that he too, had been a heating and cooling technician before the Marines and planned to get back to it after the war. Simonson had his work cut out for him with getting to know the men, and he wanted to start with his sergeants and corporals, which only made sense. First off, Bill had been assigned to the 533 Demolition training which would start in a few weeks, just as he had discussed with Lieutenant Hayes. Simonson sensed that Bill would make good with this job. Secondly, the final papers had been processed for Bill's official promotion to corporal. Bill was to report to 2/18 Headquarters on June 10th to be officially promoted. Corporal Rudy Halazon would be going with him to receive his promotion to sergeant. Simonson reminded Bill that he needed to depend on guys like him to get things done. As far as being honest, hard-working Midwesterners, they were two of a kind. Simonson was the kind of leader that Bill liked working for, and Bill was the kind of Marine that Simonson wanted to lead.

The Division scheduled amphibious landing exercises for June 20th, 1943, and all liberty would be canceled for two weeks. Bill reported to HQ at Trentham for his official promotion with Sergeant Halazon on June 10th and then headed back to Camp Moonshine to load up the trucks along with Company D. The convoy of trucks wound through the Hutt Valley and rumors were bouncing around about the Yanks' departure. Arriving at the Wellington Docks, Company D boarded the USS Hunter Liggett. The next day, the ship left the harbor while some of the Marines worried they were going back into the combat zone and not to exercises as they had been told. Some of the guys investigated the cargo areas of the Liggett and found that the ship was not "battle loaded" with the supplies and ammunition needed for an assault. The days and nights aboard ship were now miserable as they had all become accustomed to life and liberty on shore. As the days went by, they received word they would be staging a landing on the Kapiti Coast on the beaches at Paekakariki. On the morning of the 20th, the weather was horrible for such an exercise. The high temperature was expected to be in the low 40s, if that, and a 40-mph wind blew in from the ocean driving a steady rain toward the beaches.

As Bill and the 2nd Platoon waited on deck to load the Higgins Boats, they huddled anywhere they could find shelter and used their new rain ponchos to stay as warm as possible. Loading the landing craft was miserable and once at sea, the rough water was torture as sea water came over the sides in buckets. Everyone was soaked to the skin and shivering long before they even started the run into the beach. When the ramp finally came down, the Marines stepped into freezing water and ran for the beach. About halfway to the beach, they were slammed by a huge wave that came from behind and knocked many of them down into the surf. Every swear word known to mankind rang out as they moved up the beach to find their trucks as soon as possible. For all the misery the Marines endured that day, it had been even worse for one of the Shore Party teams that were organizing the drill. As the final Shore Party of 15 Navy and Marine personnel were attempting to get off the beach under darkness at 2315 hours that night, their landing craft could not break through the raging surf. A larger LCM landing craft took the smaller vessel under tow with the use of two large chains. While attempting to break through the oncoming waves, the Shore Party capsized and ten men drowned. When everyone received the news the next day, it infuriated the servicemen and they wondered why the Navy went ahead with the exercises. There were thousands of training deaths during the war and they were all sad. Being killed in a battle that is deemed necessary is tragic enough, but deaths occurring while merely training seemed like a total waste of life.

Lieutenant Simonson was in charge of the 533 Demolitions class and would be working primarily with Emory Ashurst, who had the reputation of being the best "demo guy" in the Marine Corps. Ashurst was a strong Christian fellow and a close friend of Chaplain Willard. He had been born and raised in Fitzgerald, Georgia, the county seat of Ben Hill County. His parents William

A beaming Corporal William W. Bennett shows off his new stripes along with Sergeant Rudy Halazon at Trentham, New Zealand, June 10th, 1943.

(Bennett Family Photo)

and "Lettie" ran the Ashurst Garage, so Emory had grown up with an interest in mechanics. He only had a 9th grade education, but he was somewhat of a genius with mechanical and explosive devices. Ashurst joined the Marines in July of 1940 and spent time at the U.S.M.C. "Powder Factory" at Indian Head, Maryland, where he became proficient with TNT. His smooth southern accent and great sense of humor made him a popular figure with his peers in the Corps. He always seemed to have a smile on his face and was approachable. He had also been one of the "Go to Hell Men" that had blasted the Japanese out of the caves on Gavutu and Tulagi.

Bill reported to class along with Carmen Yonke, George Polson, Charles LaPoint, Chris Paul and Harry Bonawitz; these comprised the demolition men from 2nd Platoon. Alexander Bonnyman and Barney Boos joined the class with a group from 3rd Platoon and there were also some Marines from HQ Company. The primary focus was the proper use of Trinitrotoluene, commonly called TNT. Ashurst pointed out that the whole idea was to blow up what you want to blow up and not blow up what you don't want to blow up. There was a lot of paperwork involved with this class and for obvious reasons. If raw TNT were to be mishandled, it may kill the demolition man, his team, a platoon or everyone aboard a troop transport. They would learn the properties of the explosives, types of explosives, handling of explosives, placement of explosives, sizing the charge of the explosives and detonation of the explosives.

The most common charge was the one-pound block of TNT that was contained in a brown, rectangular cardboard box, which was a little bigger than a stick of butter. The one-pound charge was marked, "BLOCK; DEMOLITION M2, TNT (Tetrytol)." "DANGER" was stamped in red on one end and a line to mark the expiration date. The one-pound charges were generally used in a group of four charges, held together with black electrical tape. The end of one charge would be opened revealing a hole that was formed in the TNT to accept the detonator. A 16-inch fuse cord had a detonator molded onto the end. This detonator was pushed into the hole in the end of the TNT charge and then a small ball of pliable wax was pressed around the fuse at the TNT block. When one charge detonated, it would take the other three with it. Bill learned to form these standard charges with dummy TNT charges that were inert. Ashurst asked for a show of hands of the guys that didn't smoke cigarettes. Bill and a few guys raised their hands. Ashurst smiled and said, "Guess what? ... you do now!" He explained that each demo guy would have to smoke in combat so that he could light the charges. He recommended that they buy themselves a cigarette case to keep the cigs from being damaged and a Zippo lighter. The standard 16" fuse would detonate the TNT in "give or take, 10 seconds." The "give or take" was emphasized because it could burn faster or slower and frequently did.

The Marine Corps had reviewed the use of demolitions in combat in the Solomon Islands, and had concluded that there needed to be a new tactic. The "blast and burn" concept was that emplacements would be hit with a demolition charge first and then burned with a flame thrower or "flame gun" within seconds to neutralize any enemy that may have survived the blasting. Bill learned there were many ways a TNT blast could kill a man. The first was concussion. The severe movement of air would create an impact around a man that would instantly shake him to death. The second, and most dangerous, was shrapnel. The blast would initially send debris of every kind flying at 6,000 feet per second. The bullet coming out of an M1 rifle was only traveling at 2,700 feet per second. The third was being burned by the flash. In a split second, the flash of the explosion could burn a man to death. And the fourth was being thrown by the blast. If someone became airborne from a blast, gravity would surely bring them back to earth.

Another method of detonation was the use of a "blasting machine," which was a portable mechanical device that would generate a short burst of electricity. Charges would be placed with an electric detonator in the TNT block. That detonator was attached to a spool of copper wire that could be run a safe distance from the charge and connected to the blasting machine. The machine had a small generator activated by a twist handle that sent the current through the wire and detonated the charge. This method could be used for blowing bridges and other obstacles where setting the charges would not have to be done while under enemy fire. The blasting machine also gave the technician an almost instant, knowable detonation compared to the fuses that were lit by hand.

As the weeks passed, Bill began rigging live charges made from smaller quarter-pound sticks of TNT that were primarily for training purposes. He had purchased a cigarette case and a Zippo at a smoke shop in Wellington, along with a few packs of cigarettes to get him through the class. He had written home about the need for cigarettes for this purpose and his old boss, Don Glossop, heard about it from Steve Bennett. Don used to kid Bill about being a non-smoker and offered cigarettes to him as a joke when they worked together. He thought it funny how Bill needed to smoke as a demolitionist, so he bought two cartons of Lucky Strikes and mailed them to Bill in New Zealand.

When it was Bill's turn to detonate his first charge, he carefully taped four of the quarter pounders together, inserted the fuse and waxed it. In order to eliminate flying debris, the practice charges were tossed from a pit dug for cover into a pit dug for detonation. Under combat circumstances, the technician may want to hold onto the lit charge for several seconds, making it less likely that the enemy would have time to throw it back. For the first charges, Ashurst directed Bill to light the fuse and immediately throw it into the detonation pit. Bill lit the Zippo and held the flame to the cigarette. He lightly drew some air through the cigarette to light it. A blast wall had been dug into the cover pit in case a charge was dropped. It would be safer to dive behind the blast wall than try and pick up the dropped charge. Ashurst waited behind the blast wall and gave Bill the "all clear." Bill lifted the fuse to his cigarette and it almost instantly ignited. He tossed the charge from the right hand, up over his head and into the detonation pit about 20 feet away, then dropped to a knee. Just about eight seconds later, the ground shook and dirt rained down on his helmet.

The charges gradually became bigger and the targets more interesting. Log structures simulated enemy emplacements, bridges and buildings. Sections of tank tracks were brought out to destroy and even some dilapidated vehicles. Although safety was always emphasized, blowing things up was a lot of fun, and the guys joked through most of the training. Besides the standard "four banger" charge, Bill learned to prepare an eight stick "satchel charge." These charges were assembled into canvas bags made specifically for eight blocks of TNT. There was a supply of self-igniting fuses that had a small red "T" handle at the end of the fuse. There was a connection that used red phosphorus and potassium chlorate, and when the T handle was pulled, the end of the fuse would light much as a common match would. This type of fuse would eliminate the need for the cigarette or cigar in combat.

After mastering the charge preparation and detonation portions of the training, the next phase would closely resemble combat scenarios. Flame gunners were brought together with the demolition teams and they went to work on bunkers constructed on the demolition range. The use of cover pits was employed in every drill and Ashurst taught the guys to consider their cover in combat before they lit anything. He thought it was best that suicide bombing remain strictly a Japanese tactic. During one of these drills, Bill carefully checked the "four banger" in his demo pouch and waited for the "all clear" signal. In another cover pit nearby, a flame gunner from 1/18 sat with his flame thrower ready to go. Bill sat in the pit with the cigarette smoke burning his eyes. The "all clear" was heard and he crawled out of the pit and up the incline toward the side of the bunker. At the wall of the bunker, he rolled onto his side and pulled the charge from the pouch. He brought the fuse to the cigarette and the fuse hissed with fury. Bill looked around the front of the bunker and chucked the charge through the gun slit with a wrap-around motion of his right arm. He instantly dove back down the incline into the cover pit and a few seconds later, the earth shook as his charge detonated inside the mock bunker. As smoke was still pouring from the bunker, Bill heard someone shout, "Okay! Light it up!" and the flame gunner crawled forth from his cover pit and shot a curtain of flame at the opening of the bunker. The heat from the flamethrower was so intense that it made Bill's Marine utilities feel as though they had just been ironed. This combination of force was so lethal that it made most of the participants a bit somber.

Bill completed the certification with good marks and began routine training with the other demolition men, much as the riflemen did on the rifle range. He received a BAR from the company and assisted at the range helping replacements, or those certifying as Automatic Riflemen, learn the use and maintenance of that weapon. As for personal use, Bill was given the choice of the M1 Garand or the M1 Carbine. He practiced with both at the range, but decided on the M1 Garand. It was lighter than the BAR, but fired the same potent .30-06 round, whereas the Carbine was lethal at closer ranges, but seemed a bit of a "pop gun" to Bill.

48. Camp Life

During the months at Judgeford, life at "Camp Moonshine" became somewhat similar to the life that Bill had lived in San Diego before shipping out to the Solomons. Most of the Marines in 2nd Platoon had now been together for quite some time, so they either got along or had learned how to get along. The New Zealand winter runs from June through September, but it is fairly mild. Night time temperatures were generally around freezing, so each tent had a wood- or coal-burning stove for heat. The latrine, shower and laundry areas were fairly crude by any standards, with laundry being done on the wash table using buckets, brushes and bar soap. If it was ever possible to have some laundry done at one of the New Zealanders homes, it was a welcome luxury.

All-new combat gear was issued over the months, including the new 1942 Utility HBT Camouflage combat uniforms. The "jacket" was really a long-sleeved cotton shirt, and the pants were reversible with a green jungle pattern on one side and a brown desert pattern on the other. A canvas helmet cover was also issued with the same reversible patterns. These new combat uniforms were for use at the camps only and not allowed to be worn when away from camp. Matching camouflage rain ponchos and shelter halves were also issued. With the weapon and equipment improvements, the Marines were feeling much better prepared than they had been going into the Solomons.

Company D's somewhat strained relationship with Captain Farkas had not improved with time. Farkas preferred to command the company primarily through other officers, and in 2nd Platoon's experiences, this meant Lieutenant Richard W. Vincent, Lieutenant Wilford B. Saylor, Lieutenant Hayes and 2nd Lieutenant Arthur K. Simonson. These officers were good with the men and good leaders. When the company marched, they marched. When there was a dirty job to do, they took part. Although Bill never had a personal problem with Captain Farkas, he respected Vincent, Saylor, Hayes and Simonson because they had proven themselves to have the men's best interests in mind.

There were a lot of Marines in New Zealand and there was bound to be some trouble. Just as it had been in the States, alcohol had a lot to do with most of the trouble. Bill Poterola had been with Bill since training with Company A back in San Diego, and was a truck driver by specialty. One night, Poterola had too much to drink and decided that although leave had been canceled by Farkas, he would help himself to one of the company trucks. As fate would have it, Poterola dropped the back wheels of the truck off the edge of the railroad crossing headed in to Trentham and couldn't get the truck off the tracks. As the train approached and sounded the whistle, Poterola had to abandon the truck. The train rammed the truck literally to pieces and Poterola was arrested by the MPs. He ended up having to pay for the truck via monthly pay deductions for the next year.

Another Marine that Bill didn't know personally had been a railroad engineer before the war and got himself into some hot water one night. He had been into Wellington and apparently thought he had missed the last train back to Trentham. Spotting an empty train idling on a side rail at the station, he climbed into the locomotive and drove the train up to Trentham. The railroad immediately knew what had happened and they cleared the line for the "phantom engineer," who properly ran the train and sounded the whistle at all crossings. When he stopped the train at Trentham, MPs were waiting for him and took him to the brig to sleep off the ale. According to the story that went around as "scuttlebutt," the New Zealand Railroad officials thought the deed was quite comical, and since there was no harm done to the train or any other property, they did not press charges. Since they didn't, it apparently was not against U.S.M.C. regulations to "borrow a train." On the more serious side, there were two replacements who robbed some New Zealanders at knife point and were arrested. They received a prison sentence of three years and were shipped back to San Francisco. Another pair of replacements managed to go from tent to tent while the entire battalion was out on a march and gathered in over $100,000 dollars in cash. The FBI investigated the crime and eventually nailed the thieves. They were caught in Wellington trying to wire some of the money back to family in the States. They were sent to prison as well, and ironically, the money was not returned, as there was no way of knowing where, exactly, it all belonged.

Money spent at the Post Exchange was saved for a "Battalion Party" that was arranged to be held at a rented dance hall in Lower Hutt, near where the Mitchells lived. Bill started his Saturday night out at the event and it was fairly enjoyable for a few hours. He decided to head over to the Mitchell's for the night and missed out on quite a scene of debauchery from what the guys later told him. As the drinking escalated into the night, the "party" featured beer bottles being thrown into the open grand piano, a foot going through the bass drum and some wise-guy filling the tuba with beer. Suddenly the doors burst open and an enlisted man entered the hall riding a beautiful white stallion. The shining dance floor ended up in need of a refinish due to the horseshoes. At the end of the night, the girls from Wellington were all unceremoniously loaded into Marine trucks for the ride home and some of them told the Marines, "If you ever have another party like this, make sure you call us!"

Overall, Bill knew that he could not have asked for better circumstances at the camp. After all, this was wartime and it was bound to get a lot worse in the future. Most of the Marines were genuine "stand-up" guys that depended on each other and would hold each other's lives in their hands. Bill's mentality remained focused on getting whatever job he was given done well. He maintained a reputation for not complaining and working hard. Another reputation that he had developed was for being one of the only fellows that other Marines had never heard using foul language. For a time, Manny and some of Bill's buddies devised a plan to make him cuss, so they deliberately did some things to try and upset him. Even though they managed to ruffle Bill's feathers a few times, they were unsuccessful. They all had a good laugh when they told Bill what they had been trying to do. There were some wagers won and lost on the affair. Knowing that Bill did not drink brought up another small prank when one of the guys came back to camp carrying a rum cake baked by his New Zealand girlfriend. Manny made sure that he offered a piece to Bill, which he wolfed down. Bill exclaimed at how delicious the cake was and had another piece. When the guys couldn't hold their laughter, Manny told him about the rum. But, the joke was on them; the alcohol burned off during the baking and the cake was delicious. Plus, Bill ended up with two pieces.

49. Sentimental Ties

Anytime Bill was given liberty for more than just an evening he now had a pre-planned route. If he had just one night, he would either head over to the Taylors at Miramar with Yonke and Truitt, as there was always something going on there, or to the Mitchell's place in Lower Hutt. Truitt had been dating Molly for months and went to the Taylor's every time he had leave. Molly would regularly go to the Taylor's house any time that she could get liberty at her base in Miramar and see if Truitt and Bill had been able to make it over. Truitt told Bill that he had fallen in love with Molly and wanted to marry her. There were many reasons to get married and many not to. If they married, then Truitt would have to manage to either come back to New Zealand to live after the war or get Molly to the States. Either choice would require a huge change for the other. If Truitt did not survive the war, Molly would be devastated, but this would be true even if they did not marry. Truitt reasoned that if he did not survive the war, he would rather have been married to Molly if only for such a short time. Molly's mother was not in favor of the marriage and refused to sign the consent letter needed as Molly was only 19. Truitt's dilemma was repeated thousands of times over across New Zealand as relationships had developed between so many Marines and New Zealand's young ladies.

While on extended leave at the Taylor's place, Truitt had a recurring bout of malaria and his fever soared. Mrs. Taylor tended to Truitt as if he were her own flesh and blood and got him through it. After the fever broke, he was so hungry from not eating for days that Mrs. Taylor baked him his favorite: macaroni and cheese.

The extended group which frequented the Taylor house in Miramar became like family over the months and Bill played the role of big brother to many of them. Another Marine that Bill had known since San Diego, Duane Strinden from Minneapolis, had been dating Mrs. Taylor's older daughter Margaret. These two seemed pretty serious, but they were not thinking of marriage. As much as Mrs. Taylor loved her Marines, she did not want Margaret drawn into a relationship that was certain to hurt her in one of many possible ways. Marines Carmen Yonke from Wisconsin and Andy Christopherson from Chicago frequented the Taylor's, along with Andy's friend Paul from the Navy. Everyone called him "Paul the sailor boy." Paul and Bill routinely jabbed each other about the dominance of the Marine Corps versus the Navy. The Marines insisted that they only needed the Navy to give them a ride and the Navy called the Marines their "bell boys." This usually-friendly rivalry would last until the last WW II Marine and Navy man remained alive. Andy was the 2/18 cobbler and also a carpenter. He gave all his friends free shoe and boot repairs and often carried his small satchel of cobbler's tools with him to the Taylor's. A lot of the older Marines, especially the married ones, voiced their concerns about romantic entanglements they were hearing about in the midst of the uncertainties of being combat Marines. In Bill's thinking, it was best to keep in mind that these arrangements in New Zealand were only temporary and the Marines were obviously preparing for further combat missions while there was no end to the war in sight.

As for visiting the Mitchells, if Les was in town, then they would go out, and if not, Bill enjoyed being around the house with Mr. and Mrs. Mitchell. Bill jumped on yard work for the Mitchells as well as kitchen work whenever needed. Mr. and Mrs. Mitchell became so fond of Bill that they began to leave a key under the mat by the back door so he could come and go as he pleased, whether they were home or not. Bill frequently stopped in with either Herb or Johnnie along. With longer liberties, Bill could stop at the Mitchells on Friday night and then ride the train up the Kapiti Coast to visit the Hydes at Shannon and the Proctors in Palmerston North.

Spending time with the Hydes was almost like a party. Bill would arrive in time to do some work around the theater, including cleaning or getting the snack bar ready for opening. Selly taught Bill the ins and outs of ushering and Bill became a standby for the position. At intermission, Bill filled in at the ice cream shop making ice cream cones and sundaes, as well as selling sodas. Bill loved to joke with the customers who began to become familiar with seeing this Marine working at the various jobs with the Hyde family. Bill had a regular place to sleep at their house and Shannon had a very "Midwestern" appeal like the small towns back home. Selly was quite the character and he and Bill laughed so hard at times that they needed to lean on a wall. Selly was mature well beyond his 17 years and he had a great business mind. One might expect that a young man raised with all the businesses around him might take it for granted and become lazy or ungrateful. But, quite the opposite, Selly worked as though he had built the businesses himself, doing whatever needed to be done. Bill respected Selly and thought he would have made a great little brother. Mrs. Hyde became endeared to Bill and frequently said she would adopt him as another son if he weren't already past the adopting age. Over the months, Bill became an honorary citizen of Shannon, New Zealand, and he frequently wrote home with news about his adventures.

Bill's visits to Palmerston North became more than recreational as he began to talk to Reverend Eaton at St. Paul's Methodist Church. Reverend Eaton was a prominent member of the Methodist organization in New Zealand and was known to be an effective evangelist and speaker. He had also been the Director of the South Island Methodist Home and Orphanage in Christchurch and was a firm believer in action-oriented Christianity. His son Owen had been a brilliant young medical doctor who went to China as a medical missionary, only to be shot and killed by bandits who broke into the mission compound in the night. Bill shared his past experiences and his passion for serving the church with Sunday school and the youth group. Reverend Eaton thought it might be a good idea to allow Bill to continue along these lines while away from home. Bill began to fill in by teaching a girl's Bible class one Sunday and then a Beginners and Primary class the next. The kids thought that having a U.S. Marine as a teacher was just wonderful and Bill enjoyed being able to offer the kids some encouragement to their faith. Reverend Eaton was a member of a Christian Men's Guild in Palmerston North that met once a month on Saturdays and he scheduled Bill to speak to the Guild. This was far different from Sunday school and it made Bill a bit nervous. He outlined a speech about what it was like to fully trust God while on Tulagi and how his life had changed now that he had come to be concerned about the well-being of his men. Bill believed that he was gaining a new perspective on what it meant to put other's needs ahead of your own. As he spoke to the Men's Guild, he could see that they were listening intently and he felt as though the Lord was using him to communicate.

Bill explained that before he had left home for the Marine Corps, he considered himself a Methodist and a lover of the church and its activities. He had helped with a religious camp and social activities for young people. Since he had been away from home, he had to learn to rely on the Lord for everything, and when he was on Tulagi, in combat, he learned to rely on the Lord for life itself. He explained that he could see a change in his own heart now, as he was more concerned about his fellow Marines and their well-being than he was about church activities. Bill quoted the first half of the 23rd Psalm, "The Lord is my Shepherd, I shall not want. He maketh me to lie down in green pastures; He leadeth me beside the still waters. He restoreth my soul." He explained to the men that this passage had come to represent peace of mind as far as learning to trust God. He also shared John 6:35, "And Jesus said unto them, 'I am The Bread of Life; he that cometh to me shall never hunger; and he that believeth on me shall never thirst.'" Bill explained to the guild how being hungry on Tulagi and being without water had helped him to fully understand what Jesus was saying in this passage. Then he summarized a passage from the Gospel of John. "If a man is filled with the love of God he will not hunger or long for anything else, but be constantly filled by the Spirit of the Lord." He explained that he had seen all of these Marines, sick and hungry, and how the Lord taught him in the middle of it all that having the Spirit of the Lord living inside was more important than even the food and water the body needs. He then shared a poem he had read in one of the *Upper Room* booklets Jessie had sent to him. This poem by John Oxenham had become quite meaningful to Bill: "Mid all the traffic of the ways, Turmoils without and within, make in my heart a quiet place and come and dwell therein. A little place of mystic grace, of self and sin swept bare, where I may look upon thy face and talk with thee in prayer."

Bill then went through some private thoughts and sayings that had been recently influential to him. From Norwegian Quakers, he quoted, "Pray without getting tired." And, "God will not place us in a more difficult position than He gives us the power to manage." He added, "a lot of people complain about all they have had to give up because of the war," and then he quoted Jesus, "For what does it profit a man to gain the entire world and yet lose his soul?" He then said, "Jesus has the power to transform lives by showing us the things that are worth living for." He went on that "there is a great economic disaster in the world today and also a great spiritual disaster. Many of our Christian friends in Europe and Asia have had a choice to obey God or obey man. A choice between an earthly master that rules by terror and threat of death or a heavenly Master that rules by peace, joy and eternal life." Then quoting from John 10:28-29, "I give them eternal life. They will never perish and no one will snatch them from my hand. My Father who gave me them, is stronger than all and no one can snatch anything out of my Father's hand." Bill told them about the profound truth that came to his mind one night when he was lying in bed at camp. "In this life of mine, I go to bed tired and weary; not of doing the will of God, but of the will of men." This had made Bill wonder what the world would be like if all of mankind went to bed each night tired from doing the will of God. In closing, Bill emphasized how important the prayer of his loved ones at home had been to him. He could feel that he was being held up in prayer. He thanked the guild for their time and thanked them for listening. They stood and applauded and smiled approvingly. As the men mingled and chatted, most of them shook Bill's hand and thanked him for sharing and assured Bill that he would be further remembered in prayer. Some of these men had fought in the trenches during WWI. Bill knew that he was in fine company.

Reverend Eaton was impressed with Bill's ability to teach and communicate so he asked if he might be interested in preaching from the pulpit during a Sunday night service. Bill was both honored to be asked and humbled by the request. He did not feel anywhere near being qualified to do such a thing, but the Reverend told Bill that he should speak from his experiences and from the heart. Bill agreed and Sunday, July 10th, 1943 was selected as the date. The Proctors were so proud of Bill that everyone they knew had heard stories about this amazing young American Marine who had found a home away from home in Palmerston North. Bill had been able to spend just about every Sunday with the Proctors for quite a while and Lorna was extremely helpful to Bill as he wrote outlines for his classes, speeches or sermons. He spent hours at their dinner table or sitting in one of the chairs by the fireplace. Muriel and the girls would usually pick Bill up at the station and drive him over, but occasionally he would walk to save their gas.

Letters from home were almost always full of surprises. Bill's brother Al was planning to get married and Bill's high school sweetheart, Annie Swanson, had her engagement announcement in the *Beacon News*. Of course, Jessie sent Bill the clipping. Annie had met Robert F. Casey at college and Casey was now a Cadet Naval Aviator. Bill wondered if Casey would end up with Bob Stoner as his Flight Instructor. Bess Bennett, Bill's former sister-in-law and little Bobby's mother, had remarried to Ed Bilstrom of Aurora and Bobby would have a permanent home and a man in his life. The thought of coming home to 454 Simms Street without having either Al or Bobby there was upsetting to Bill. Both of them had been central to his life not long ago. A few weeks later more news came that Bill's sister Marian, who he had always called "Pete," was now engaged to Perry MacIntosh, who had also joined the Marines, contrary to Bill's warning. Marian and Perry were now affectionately referred to as "Pete and Perry" by Bill. Bill's old best pal, George Troll, had gotten married in Aurora to his long-time gal Betty. Jessie sent Bill a clipping from the *Beacon*. They were married at the First Baptist Church in what sounded like a big affair. All of the old gang was getting married and Bill was unable to be there, let alone be a part of the weddings or even give them a handshake. George Troll, Bob Stoner and now, Al, Marion and Annie Swanson. Aurora might be in the same place when the war was over, but it would never be quite the same place.

The weekend of July 10th came and Bill arrived at the Proctor's house on Saturday morning and spent the day around the city. Lorna had arranged for Bill to visit the radio station while she aired her fashion show and he was able to watch and listen through the glass. She was very good at announcing and had a very attractive New Zealand accent, which is very similar to the Brits. Having Bill around had made Lorna feel a bit like she had a big brother. Back at the Proctor's, Charles had come back from the coast with a catch of red snapper and they were cleaned and ready for Muriel to perform her magic on them by the time Bill and Lorna returned. The girls had baked a cake during the afternoon, as was common when they had a guest, even though Bill was becoming like part of the family. The next morning, Reverend Eaton was inspirational from the pulpit once again and when he announced that Corporal William Bennett would be bringing the sermon for the evening service, Bill's nerves started to tense.

The evening had finally arrived and Bill and the Proctors arrived a half hour early so that Bill would not feel rushed. Reverend Eaton asked Bill to come into his study and have a seat. He asked Bill if he might pray with him before the service and Bill was relieved to hear him offer. The Reverend leaned forward in his chair and he placed his hand on Bill's shoulder and said, "Let us pray. Heavenly Father, we gather here tonight to worship and praise you because you are a loving God and merciful to us, even though we are sinners. I ask that your Holy Spirit would fill and empower Bill tonight as he brings your message to our congregation. I ask that you would speak through Bill and into the hearts of those present tonight so that your eternal purpose might be accomplished. We do thank you for your great love and mercy in the name of Our Lord and Savior, Jesus Christ. Amen!" Bill said, "Amen," and felt a great feeling of peace come over him. In a sense, he felt clean inside, and close to the Lord at that moment.

Bill went back into the sanctuary and sat with the Proctors. The hymns were sung, the announcements made, the offering taken and a quartet sang. Then Reverend Eaton stepped to the pulpit and welcomed "Corporal William Bennett of the United States Marine Corps to bring the message." Bill rose from his pew and climbed the steps and set his small dark blue note book on the pulpit and looked up at the congregation. The Proctors wore beaming smiles as though he had already succeeded by merely getting to the pulpit. Bill's hand trembled slightly as he scanned the sanctuary and opened his mouth to begin. "Tonight, I would like to talk to you about the need for prayer and faith. I would like to begin by reading to you Psalm 25: verses one through ten."

1. Unto thee, O LORD, do I lift up my soul.
2. O my God, I trust in thee: let me not be ashamed, let not mine enemies triumph over me.
3. Yea, let none that wait on thee be ashamed: let them be ashamed which transgress without cause.
4. Shew me thy ways, O LORD; teach me thy paths.
5. Lead me in thy truth, and teach me: for thou art the God of my salvation; on thee do I wait all the day.
6. Remember, O LORD, thy tender mercies and thy loving kindnesses; for they have been ever of old.
7. Remember not the sins of my youth, nor my transgressions: according to thy mercy remember thou me for thy goodness' sake, O LORD.
8. Good and upright is the LORD: therefore will he teach sinners in the way.
9. The meek will he guide in judgment: and the meek will he teach his way.
10. All the paths of the LORD are mercy and truth unto such as keep his covenant and his testimonies.

"It sometimes takes a lot to make one understand some of the more important things in the Bible. One of the greatest is prayer. I would like to take the attitude that all of us here are devoted Christians. Now our problem is, "how can we help someone else to see the light?" The way that I live my life is helping to paint my neighbor's a picture of God. For me, this brings to mind my life at camp. If others know that I am a Christian, but they don't see a difference in the way that I live my life, then why would they be interested in knowing more about Christ? Consider the way that we live and the things that we do with our bodies. We wouldn't invite people into our home if they were messy, so why would we invite the Lord into our "temple" if we are not fit to welcome him? It is through prayer that we come to know Christ and through prayer that we spend time with him and learn from Him. If we are to make a difference in the lives of those around us, it must be done through prayer." Bill ended his sermon with a quote from Croft M. Pentz, "Prayer is a golden river at whose banks some die of thirst and others kneel and drink."

The Proctors were all very proud of Bill and none more than Lorna. Through her job at the radio station and her friendships across New Zealand, she knew full well what kind of things went on with a large portion of the visiting Yanks. Bill was a young, single, good-looking man who was far away from home. He could be spending his time pursuing a good time and would certainly be popular with the ladies, or he could carouse and drink, as many of his buddies from Company D did whenever they received liberty. Instead of these worldly things, Bill had judiciously sought out good people to surround himself with and found a friendship with Reverend Eaton. Although

Lorna and Daphne were certainly old enough to date, Bill had shown that he wanted to treat them like sisters and he was utterly respectful to them. In addition, Bill would not bring any other Marines to visit the Proctors unless he had affirmed his trust in them. Bill knew that the Proctors had placed trust in him, and he would never think of letting them down.

One fellow Marine that had won Bill's approval was Johnnie Jones. Johnnie made several trips to Palmerston North with Bill on weekend liberties and several on extended liberties. During one such extended liberty, the Proctors invited Bill and Johnnie to come with them to a parcel of land that Charles and Muriel owned, overlooking the beautiful beaches at Paekakariki along the Kapiti Coast. Charles had two large tents and a variety of camping and cooking gear, that when set up looked like a small military camp. Bill and Johnnie made fast work of the tents as they were basically professionals at such things. The coastline offered views to rival the best of California's coast and fishing that was second to none. Charles taught Bill and Johnnie the basics of surf fishing and enjoyed watching them struggle with tasks that he had mastered as a young boy. The two best-tasting fish from the surf would be snapper and moki. The snapper was a stout silver fish that would put up quite a fight, and the moki could be caught in two types, red moki or blue. Bill did what he could to try and assist in the acquisition of fish, but Charles and the girls were far more likely to pull dinner from the surf than he or Johnnie were.

Long walks on the beach were taken and a little swimming in the surf, although the warm summer days had faded long ago. Everyone assisted Muriel as she struggled to keep everything in one place as the wind played havoc with her cooking. Among other things, Muriel had a gift for cooking fish in a way that amazed both Bill and Johnnie. They nicknamed Muriel "The Great Fish Fryer," and spoke of her skill back at Camp Moonshine. As night came at Paekakariki, the Proctors and the guests stoked a healthy fire as the temperatures fell. After hours of talking and laughing and listening to old stories that Charles liked to tell, the Proctors retired to their tents and Bill and Johnnie slept under a tarp where they could see the vast array of South Pacific stars. They talked about how different things had been in the Solomons and how good they had it here in New Zealand. Bill said that he had never even given New Zealand a thought before the war and found it hard to believe what a wonderful place it was. Even better than the beauty of the islands, was the beauty of the people.

50. Broken Hearts

As new "replacements" filled out the ranks of the 2nd Marine Division, orders arrived to have quite a few of the original Marines shipped back to the States for other duties. Within Bill's close group of Marines, George Garcia and Manny Bud received such orders. George had joined the "regular" Marines back in 1939 with a four-year enlistment and his time was up. He would be going back to San Diego, reenlisting and training new Marines. The Marines had not been able to tell their families where they were since leaving Tulagi. Any mention of New Zealand would have been clipped from their letters by Navy censors.

These returning Marines presented a way around that. Once a returning Marine arrived in the States, he was no longer held to the censorship and could write letters directly to parents to inform them of their son's status. George told Bill to write his parents' address on some papers that he was sure not to lose so that he could write them from his home in Escondido, California.

Manny had drawn a new assignment to an experimental photographic unit and would be going back to San Diego to receive his orders. Bob Swigert asked Manny to write his mother in Oelrichs, South Dakota, and Manny had him write down the address. When Manny saw the address, he laughed because it really didn't even need to be written down; "Swigert, Oelrichs, SD" was pretty easy to remember. Having the note in Manny's wallet would serve as a reminder for him, so he wouldn't forget about it after he arrived in the States. Watching these two pack their sea bags to head home was difficult for the other Marines. It looked like these two were getting what every one of them desperately wanted: to survive the war and return home. A group of 12 to 15 Marines gathered around as they said their goodbyes and Bill gave George a hug and a pat on the back. Bill told him that he hoped they could get together again somewhere after the war and George told Bill to be careful, keep his head down and not to volunteer for anything. Bill gave Manny a firm handshake and thanked him for being helpful back on Tulagi. Since the two lived only an hour apart back in Illinois, it was probable that they might see each other again. In addition to loosing Manny and George, the Marines of D/2/18 also had to say goodbye to Lieutenant Hayes. Hayes was ordered back to San Diego to be assigned to various training positions and, eventually, a command of his own. His leadership and well-respected example would be missed by the men but fondly remembered for years.

PFC George Garcia
(Garcia Family Photo)

PFC Emmanuel "Manny" Bud
(Bud Family Photo)

While there were thousands of Marines with serious girlfriends in New Zealand, a considerable number were actually getting married. Two such cases within Bill's circle of friends were Gene Seng from Texas and Truitt Anderson. Truitt and Molly had been planning to get married but had not been able to set the date. Molly's mother was still less than exuberant about the idea and she was stalling the "letter of consent" needed for the marriage.

Bill could see that Molly and Truitt were certainly in love and he knew that Molly meant everything to Truitt now. He told Truitt that he was just going to have to be patient and let it all work out; a discipline that Bill had become all too familiar with in the romance department. The guys kidded with Molly about the fact that she was practically a Yank now, since Truitt had planned to live in the States with her after the war was over. Gene Seng and his Texas buddy Charlie Montague had befriended the McDougall family in New Zealand in much the same way that Bill had befriended the Proctors. Gene had fallen in love with June McDougall and planned to marry her sometime in the near future. The McDougall's loved Gene, and June's siblings called him "brother" and Charlie, "Cousin Charlie." Just as Truitt and Molly had planned, Gene and June were planning to live in the States after the war.

As the months passed by, Bill had become very good friends with his New Zealand hosts and especially close with the Proctors. Bill had been honest with Lorna about his intentions to return home to Helen and he had also been honest with Helen about his friendship with Lorna. He had even sent some photos of Lorna home which Helen had seen, and it did spark some conversation at the Bennett house. Steve Bennett wrote a letter to his son and reminded him that he had a "girl at home" waiting for him to return. Bill had to write back to Steve and clear up the fact that Lorna was not his girlfriend and that he remained faithful to Helen. Bill had seen the mess that some Marines had gotten into and had no intentions of messing anything up with Helen in that way. Bill was actually quite pleased that Steve had been willing to go to bat for Helen in that sense, even though it had been unnecessary in this case.

Bill had been honest on both sides with what his intentions were and straight forward with how he intended to handle himself. His mind was made up and he kept his word. Privately, Bill was quite surprised with the way that he found himself feeling about Lorna. She was such a committed Christian and so sensible. Bill told Jessie that Lorna was so sensible that even if he had changed his mind about Helen (which he had not), "Lorna was far too sensible to go for anything like that." Bill also explained that Lorna was not a "sympathy friend" because he was not in need of anyone's sympathy. He had been happy when he arrived in New Zealand and he remained happy throughout. Lorna had far stronger feelings for Bill than she had let on, and she had determined to respect what Bill had told her and not try to gain his interest any further than she already had. The reality had proven out that both Lorna and Bill were very committed to their Lord and very respectful of each other; perhaps that's why they had become such good friends in the first place.

The Navy and the Marine Corps had been busy planning the most aggressive island campaign in human history. Just as before, the members of 2/18 and 1/18 would be divided up between combat battalions in need of their specialties and their support. During late July and early August, Captain Farkas and his lieutenants attended meetings at headquarters to divide up their 223 men into the needed roles. In the history of the Pioneers and the Combat Engineers there would never be more fateful decisions made. The island that the 2nd division would be assaulting was code named "HELEN" and only a few high-ranking officers knew the actual name and location.

As for the 2nd Battalion, 18th Marines, Company D, it was decided to divide them as follows: 63 men under Lieutenant Vincent were assigned to go ashore at Red Beach 1 with 3rd Battalion, 2nd Marines under the command of Major John F. Schoettle. These men would board the USS Middleton with 3/2 when it was time to head back into the combat zone. The 3/2 Marines were Lieutenant Vincent, Ashurst, Banwart, Baker, Bass, Bowden Campbell, Carlson, Castle, Coble, 2nd Lieutenant Coen, Coloske, Dortch, Duke, Frye, Gravier, Gustafson, Captain Haltom, Hickey, Hudson, Hulse, Jackman, Jarrett, Kinder, Kountzman, Lanning, Larson, Laws, Lazzari, Libby, Lind, Lynton, May, McCoy, McGary, McKinney, Millick, Montague, Naffe, Overman, Pakula, Parsons, Phillips, Quinette, Ralph, Roads, Robinson, Schouviller, Seng, Simon, James Smith, Frank A. Smith, Sobolewski, Stoffer, Thomas, Thompson, Thomazewski, Vollmer, Waltz, Watson, Wetternach, Woods, Wysocki, and Zalut. These 64 Marines were then divided up to support the four companies of 3/2, resulting in teams of approximately 16 Marines to each company. These Marines were primarily the 3rd Platoon of D/2/18.

Another 59 men were assigned to 1st Battalion, 2nd Marines under the leadership of Major Wood B. Kyle. This group would board the USS Lee at Wellington Harbor and go ashore with the first waves at Red Beach 2. These Marines were Achenback, Truitt Anderson, Antonelli, Bittle, Brin, Brock, Burks, Burnett, Lieutenant Comstock, Cordell, Costa, Herb Dale, DeMartini, Dzur, Duffy, Dyer, Elliot, Ellis (James), Floyd, Fowles, Arthur Frank, Galloway, Greer, Grubb, Halazon, Haloway, Harrell, Harrison, Henson, Hoard, Hupp, Jeffcoat, Johnnie Jones, Kerns, Lano, Largo, Lopez, McCuine, Perales, Perry, Redding, Renault, Sewell, Shields, Stone, Al Slowinski, Solberg, Soley, Spencer, Stewart, Strinden, Tharp, Turner, Wallace, Whitely, Woodworth, Carmen Yonke, Young, and Zuchelli. This list was primarily 1st Platoon.

30 men from Company D were assigned to the command of Colonel David M. Shoup and the 2nd Marines Headquarters aboard the USS Zeilin. Most of these men had transferred from company headquarters just for this invasion. These Marines included Adair, Berin, Cates, Craverns, Cullem, Drake, Dunn, Farmer, Fritche, Garafalo, Haaby, Hollingsworth, Kagarice, Maloney, Eddie Nalazek, Polasik, L. Rawling, R. Rawlings, J. Reed, W. Reed, Rehak, Reilly, Renninger, Ringglod, Rockefeller, Sandon, Scott, Ed Susans, Trier and Wharton.

Bill Bennett was assigned with a group of 70 Marines to 2nd Battalion, 2nd Marines under Colonel Herbert R. Amey to board the USS Zeilin and attack Red Beach 2. This group consisted of Andersen (Richard), Bates, Bill Bennett, Bentzen, Bjorneby, Brown, Burke, Cabler, Caldwell, Capra, Chier, Coate, Cothran, Crelia, Daily, Dubuque, DuCharme, Fred Ellis, Captain Farkas, Fertado, Fuetren, Fortenberry, French, Gabel, Glazer, Graham, Guy, Hampton, Hellman, Herman, Hoar, Hunt, Johnson, Lieutenant Jones, Jutting, Karpicky, Keogh, Kinley, Kirkpatrick, Kleser, LaPoint, Landenberger, Lewis, Lore, Luther, Matkovich, McEntee, Morrow, Paul, Peters, Polson, Poterola, Pratt, Price, Dick Reed, Rotramel, Schlef, Scoll, Simon, Lieutenant Arthur K. Simonson, Singer, Snyder, Stelzer, Stogner, Stubblefield, Bob Swigert, Ullen, Webb, Westover, and Wyatt. These men were primarily the 2nd Platoon with the addition of a few others. Captain Farkas would operate with his own group, responsible for oversight of supplies coming in to Red Beach 2. He would keep Bentzen, Bjorneby, Richard Andersen and Hampton with him and the rest would be assigned into three groups. Bill's Pioneer group would be led by Sergeant Gabel with Bill and Fred Ellis assisting as corporals. The remainder of this group would be George Cothran, Jerald Coate, Bill Poterola, Jack Webb, Foch Scott, Ed Cullum, Carl Fortenberry and Lester Hellman. This 11-man Pioneer Team was assigned to Company F, 2/2 under the Command of Captain Warren Morris, Lieutenant Wayne Sanford, 2nd Lieutenant Joseph Barr, 2nd Lieutenant George Cooper, 2nd Lieutenant Laurence Ferguson and 2nd Lieutenant Ray Marion. Company F/2/2's mission would be to land at Red Beach 2, at sector 222, and forge a path across the center of the island with Bill's Pioneer Team supporting them as they progressed.

Company D planned a "live fire" exercise up the road into the Moonshine Valley. Dozens of trucks lugged men and gear up the road and an area was selected for the day's events. The Marines would have to attack against barbed wire emplacements and crawl below wire with live machine guns firing just over their heads. Bill's assignment with the demolition team was to detonate TNT charges in pits in the vicinity to simulate battleground explosions and sound. After several hours had been spent setting up the course, training began and machine guns, rifles, grenades and TNT all combined into hellacious combat noise. As Bill was helping Emory Ashurst prepare and detonate TNT, they heard someone yelling "Cease fire!" at the top of their lungs. The firing stopped and a voice became audible up the hill where the officers had set up their command post. Bill looked out of his cover pit and saw an old man on a swayback horse standing in front of the officers and he was screaming, "Git ooff mai propaty" in a Scottish brogue. Apparently, he was the land owner and no one had cleared the live fire exercise with him. Everything was loaded and put back in order within an hour and the trucks drove the company back to camp.

From the assignment forward, Gabel and the Pioneers traveled back and forth to train with Company F 2/2 so that they could get to know the officers and the outfit. Colonel Amey, who was in charge of 2/2, was a well-respected officer and his men spoke highly of him. Life at Camp Moonshine changed quite a bit as elements of 2/18 and 1/18 were training all over the area with the other units. Being away from camp and seeing how other officers ran things didn't help the strained situation with Captain Farkas back at Moonshine. As the end of September came around, tensions at the camp heightened. The Marines could smell redeployment based on what they were seeing in their training. Everyone received orders to report to their respective ships on October 17th, 1943 for another amphibious landing exercise, this time at Hawke's Bay on the east coast of the North Island. The guys all became anxious over getting liberty just in case they would be leaving for the combat zone again. Farkas ordered additional marches which no one could see the use of at this point. One night just after "lights out" at 2200 hours, a single shot rang out near the officer's quarters. Marines ran out into the darkness in their skivvies while pulling on pants and shirts to see what had happened. Someone had fired a .45 slug through the thin wall of Captain Farkas' shack and missed him in bed by a few inches. Farkas had just laid back with a book he was reading when the bullet came through the wall and just over his bunk where he had been sitting.

An investigation was launched although no one seemed to have seen anything and the only clue was boondocker prints, which 3,000 men on the base all wore. Instead of getting liberty, the company received more marches. The lieutenants tried their best to work things out, but to no avail, and the company was off in the morning on another march. A group of the older Marines began to harass Captain Farkas for the 72-hour passes but got nowhere. Farkas became upset by the badgering and ordered the company to assemble with rifles in 10 minutes. Bill and his friends were all busy with other activities when they heard the orders coming through. They grabbed their gear and headed for the assembly area. Farkas sent them out on a 20-mile march to show them that he had enough of their whining over the passes. He failed to realize that several of the men had wives they wanted to see before shipping out and virtually every Marine had friends they wanted to say goodbye to.

As the company was coming close to the camp at the end of the march, they

Corporal Bill Bennett is on the far left as 2nd Platoon, D/2/18 arrives back at Camp Moonshine, N.Z. 2nd Lieutenant Simonson leads.

(Bennett Family Photo)

were tired and dragging. Some of the lieutenants started running up and down the ranks yelling for the men to "tighten it up" and "look alive." They told them that if Captain Farkas saw them dragging, he would think he had really given it to them. Someone quickly made up new words for their favorite New Zealand marching song, and as they marched through the front gates they were all singing, "Kiss me goodnight Captain Farkas, and put us into our little wooden beds!" As soon as the rifles were stowed and their gear was dropped, dozens of men showed up at the command office demanding their passes. It was already well after dark and Farkas calculated that everyone was tired and they would not leave the base anyway, giving him time to cancel the liberty in the morning if he had second thoughts. But, within 15 minutes, everyone in Company D was gone and the camp was deserted. Bill got on the train to Wellington with the whole gang and he and Johnnie Jones jumped off at the now familiar Woburn Station and made the walk over to the Mitchell's for the night. Tomorrow morning would mark the beginning of the last three days of liberty in New Zealand.

Bill and Johnnie awoke at the Mitchell's house and Mrs. Mitchell cooked them a proper breakfast as Bill asked her about Les' plans over the next few days. She wasn't sure if Les would be home later in the day or not. As they ate, she asked if they had any idea where the Marines were headed and if this was indeed the time for shipping out. The rumors on base were that they would be headed to Wake Island to avenge the death and capture of 250 Marines shortly after the attack on Pearl Harbor. The truth was that none of the Marines knew where they were headed and it was best that way so that the Japanese didn't know either. As Bill prepared to leave, he promised Mrs. Mitchell that he would stop by on the way back to camp to see if Les had made it home, or at least, to say goodbye to her and Barnie.

The pair rode the train down into Wellington and then jumped on a trolley over to Miramar. One last trip to see the Taylors and quite a few friends were there when they arrived. Truitt and Molly were making breakfast with Duane and Margaret when Bill knocked on the kitchen door. Mrs. Taylor shuffled to answer the door and welcomed them with an excited pitch in her voice. Having been a widow for so many years, there was no doubt that she enjoyed the company of all of these handsome young Marines and she gave Bill and Johnnie welcoming hugs. Carmen Yonke, Andy and Paul the Sailor Boy came in a short time later carrying bags of groceries they had just bought at the store. With all of the gang around the Taylor's place, the guys always made sure they brought in more food than they would eat. The air was thick with discussion of where the Marines might be heading and Bill could see the deep concern on the faces of Molly, Margaret and Mrs. Taylor. They were going to be at a loss because the guys were shipping out, let alone the dangers of combat. They had all enjoyed many months of deep friendship and there was a strong sense that it was coming to an end.

When Bill was in the back yard looking over the rooftops down toward Evans Bay, Mrs. Taylor came out to chat. She privately told Bill that he was very special to her and her girls, and she was going to miss him terribly. She wanted Bill to promise that he would come back to visit, but he told her he couldn't make that promise. As she knew, he had plans for Helen back home, and traveling back to New Zealand without the government paying the way was unlikely. She was then noticeably upset, and she told Bill that she had a dream a few nights back which was bothering her immensely. She said that in her dream, she saw Bill and Truitt together and there was terrible fighting going on. She said something terrible happened to Truitt, though she could not see what it was. Although Bill was with Truitt, Bill was unharmed. She asked Bill to do what he could to watch out for Truitt. Bill said that he would, but Truitt had been assigned to another ship and they might not even see each other for quite some time. She had Bill's word that he would do what he could. Tears welled in her eyes and she told Bill she had come to love "you boys" and that Truitt was like "her own flesh and blood."

She also told Bill how much these younger fellows looked up to him and what a fine example she thought he was to them. She said they all spoke so highly of him when he wasn't around. She told Bill she was concerned about Truitt and Molly being able to get married before Truitt had to leave as Molly's mother was refusing to send the letter of consent. Molly already had her wedding dress made by Nan O'Connor's mother and it was hanging in Margaret's closet awaiting the final arrangements. She fully understood the sentiment of Molly's mother, as her own daughter Margaret had fallen for Duane Strinden and she didn't want to see her hurt in any way. The war continued to complicate so many things. Mrs. Taylor gave Bill a warm hug and a kiss on the cheek as she knew this might be the last time they would see each other. Bill went back inside and pulled Truitt and Molly aside to see how their plans were shaping up. The consent letter had still not arrived. Since there would be no wedding this weekend, Bill and Johnnie decided to head up north for, perhaps, one last visit.

Bill and Johnnie hugged the girls as they pulled away from the Taylor's and headed back to the trolley line. The trolley would take them back to Wellington to catch the train for the Kapiti Coast and up to Shannon for a Friday night at the movies with the Hyde family. The weather had been warming nicely as New Zealand headed back into the summer months and the Kapiti Coast was beautiful. As the train ran parallel to the beaches at Paekakariki, Johnnie reminded Bill of the area where 10 members of the Shore Party had drowned in the training accident. They looked at the waves breaking on the beach and were silent. It could have been them. When the train pulled into the station at Shannon, Bill walked past the agent's window and gave him a friendly wave, just as he had every time he visited Shannon since that first day almost eight months earlier.

The "early show" was already in progress when Bill and Johnnie came in, so they made their way to the office. Mrs. Hyde was giddy with excitement as she sprang from the desk chair to welcome Bill with a hug. She was very happy to see Johnnie again as well since he had visited several times before. The guys found Selly and Stuart and then arranged to usher for them so that they could tend to other things for the evening. The patrons got a real treat when they had ticket-taking Marines on both sides of the gate. At intermission, Bill worked with Selly and Mrs. Hyde at the ice cream counter while Johnnie kept on eye on the theater. They had a great turn out for a Friday night and Bill said that he enjoyed working there more than he did watching the movies. After closing up for the night, they all went back to the Hyde's for their usual late-night dinner and played the card game "King," which Bill had taught them. Bill found he was conscious of "taking it all in" on this trip as he knew that this could well be the last time he would experience the warmth of these friendships.

Bill and Johnnie worked side by side with Mrs. Hyde to make a proper "steak and eggs" breakfast in the morning before all six of them piled into the Hyde's car for the short ride over to the station. Selly and Stuart gave Bill firm hugs and Bill felt a tear start to well up, but he didn't let it show, at least as far as he could tell. Then Mrs. Hyde hugged Bill and she started to cry. Bill couldn't hold back the tears. Just in case he would not see them again, he thanked them for everything they had done for him and for how they made him feel so completely at home. He joked that if he needed a job after the war, he now had ushering and ice cream counter experience. Selly told Bill that if he couldn't find a job after the war, he should come back and fill out an application. They all laughed. Bill put down the window on the train and waved back at the platform until the Hydes went out of sight. He put up the window and spun around in the seat. It

Bill's close Marine buddy, Johnnie C. Jones in a photo taken in New Zealand.

(Mitchell Family Photo)

seemed as though he had been in New Zealand much longer than he actually had. He recalled how this familiar route had once been brand new and now he recognized just about every barn along the tracks.

When they got off the train at Palmerston North, it was Daphne and Muriel on the platform as the welcoming party. As much as Lorna would have wanted to be there, it was Saturday and she was working at the radio station until 1 p.m. Once in the car, Daphne hurried to turn on the radio and tune in Lorna's fashion program. She kidded with Bill and Johnnie that if they listened closely they might hear some tips on what all the best-dressed Marines would be wearing this season. It was amazing how different Lorna sounded on the air. She was so professional and articulate and her "soft as butter" Kiwi accent sounded very attractive. After a delicious lunch of sandwiches, cake and tea, Daphne drove Bill and Johnnie over to the radio station to pick up Lorna. Daphne pulled the car to the curb in front of the station and Bill and Johnnie ran in to surprise Lorna at the front desk. She knew they were coming but did not expect to see them in the radio station. She gave both a hug and said she was so glad they made the trip.

Charles returned from the Manawatu River later in the afternoon with a canvas bag stuffed with trout. He welcomed "his Marines" heartily and then went into the garage to prepare the fish for Muriel, "The Great Fish Fryer." The dinner could not have been more satisfying and Bill truly felt as though he had been adopted by the Proctors. After dinner was cleared and all had pitched in on the dishes, they retired to the living room and talked about many things. The rumors of the Marines shipping out were all over New Zealand and even the Proctors thought that the training at Hawke's Bay was probably a ruse to cover the movement. Bill told them that he would know as soon as he saw the transports. Once they were "battle loaded" they would sit low in the water as they had at San Diego.

After quite a while, Lorna rose to her feet and announced that she felt like going for a walk and she was quite sure she would like it if Bill came along. The pair headed down the sidewalk in a direction that didn't matter at all as Bill knew this walk was more for talking alone than exercise. The thought of Bill leaving was bothering Lorna more than she could bear and she did not want to cry in front of her family. But outside in the night, the tears came in abundance as she told Bill she had known this day would come, but had hoped it would not. Bill told her they had both known it would come and there was nothing they could do. She asked Bill if he would ever be able to come back to New Zealand and he knew that he probably would not. Bill told Lorna they had to view their meeting and their friendship as something the Lord gave them for a while and for a reason, even though they didn't understand it all. Lorna hugged Bill and wept for a minute, and then she dried her eyes and was sure she "looked a mess." Bill said that they had better head back to the house and they walked along together.

The next morning at St. Paul's, Reverend Eaton preached a sermon about how God had not promised us ease and luxury, but a chance for service and the reward of eternal life. This was something Bill had often pondered, and he was quite certain that more hardship probably lay over the horizon for him and his Marine buddies. After church, Bill had a brief aside with Reverend Eaton and he thanked him for all he had done for him. Eaton assured Bill that he had not done anything but what the Lord had appointed for Bill. Bill told Eaton that he had been like a father to him while he had been there and this undoubtedly touched the heart of the Reverend. At this place and time, they both had received something that they needed in their lives; a father for one and a son for the other. The whole group went to the train in two cars and made quite a scene on the platform. First the girls started to cry and before it was done, everyone had tears, even the weathered face of the great angler, Charles. Lorna hugged Bill one last time at the train steps and she only let go as the conductor announced the train was about to roll. Inside the train, Bill and Johnnie both let their windows down and waved until the station was gone. Bill shed genuine tears over the Proctors. What a dear family and what a gift from God they had been in his life. He was sure they would all be friends for life. If it had not been for Bill's commitment to Helen back home, Lorna would have been more than a friend.

As they had until 2200 hours to be back to camp and it was only 2015 hours, Bill and Johnnie left the train at Woburn Station and made a quick hike over to the Mitchell's where they found Les at home. He was so happy they had made the stop and Bill said that with the possibility this was "it," he couldn't leave without saying goodbye in person. Bill insisted Les come and visit the States so he could return a small portion of the hospitality he had been given. They both promised to write and write often. Les drove them back to Woburn and they caught the next train up to Silverstream.

Back at camp, there was some very unusual news as Bill got back to the tent. Scuttlebutt had it that the entire 3rd Platoon had headed up to Palmerston North on their liberty and they had wired a telegram to Captain Farkas saying they were "taking an additional week" of liberty and would report back to camp next Saturday. Marines were asking, "Can they do that?" No one was sure, but what should you expect from the "Go to Hell" platoon? Since they were all assigned to other combat companies and would be on different ships, apart from Farkas, they calculated there would be neither time nor inclination for punishment in New Zealand. Besides that, some of them would not survive the coming offensive. For those who would only have weeks to live, the risk was worth it for the whole platoon.

51. A Combat Flier

While the 1st and 2nd Platoons of Company D waited to see when the rebels from 3rd Platoon would return to camp, they prepared their equipment for the "landing exercises" that were fast approaching. Bill had ample time to prepare his gear and caught up on his letter writing. He sent three letters to Helen, one to Mrs. Nix, one to Sam and Margaret Stoner, one to Mrs. Cochran and one to baby Billy Schell, even though he would not be able to read for five more years. He received letters from his brother Al, Steve and Jessie and three back issues of the *Stoner Weekly*. There was a mention in the *Weekly* that Steve and Jessie had "hit the jackpot" when they received two letters from Bill on the same day. It said that Bill was doing fine in the South Pacific. Another article mentioned that Al was now a lieutenant in the Quartermaster Corps, U.S. Army. The *Stoner Weekly* issues also were tracking developments in Bob Stoner's career as he had made a decision to leave his assignment as a Flight Instructor at Corpus Christi, Texas, and join a combat unit.

Unknown to Bill, Bob Stoner had struggled with strong feelings about training pilots for combat but not having to face the danger himself. He had been discussing asking for a combat assignment with Marijane for some time and she was not happy about the idea. In early 1943, about the time Bill had arrived in New Zealand, Bob had asked his Commanding Officer in Texas to put in his request to be transferred to a combat unit. He received the transfer in June and had gone to Jacksonville, Florida, to take training on the TBM 1-C Avenger, the Navy's largest single engine attack plane. The Avenger had a huge Wright Aeronautics Cyclone R-2600 engine that produced 1900 horsepower, carried a crew of three and was designed to deliver bombs, rockets or a torpedo directly to the Imperial Japanese Forces. Bob had adopted the slang of "Pickles" for torpedoes and thus, dubbed the Avenger the "Pickle Lugger." Bob had his hands full with being a student again and making the transition from his beloved SNJ Trainer to the Grumman Wildcat and then into the Avenger. While the trainer and fighter flew almost effortlessly, the huge Avenger was like flying a truck: "heavy on the stick." Bob sat six feet higher in the Avenger seat than he had in his SNJ, and the visibility forward was more obstructed.

Handling the Avenger in the air was much more of a challenge, but all the size and power would mean that the huge plane could deliver one torpedo that could sink a Japanese ship. Bob Stoner had a terrific surprise when his older brother Harley was able to get leave and come to Jacksonville to spend a weekend. Bob had garnered great respect as an officer that provided good

Lieutenant Robert F. Stoner with his first TBM Avenger at Pensacola, Florida, 1943

(*The Stoner Weekly News* Photo)

rapport with his commanders and he was able to manage an Avenger ride for Harley. Just like they had done four years earlier in the little J-3 Cub, the brothers took to the skies of northern Florida as Bob showed Harley the sights. The huge plane soared amongst the cumulus clouds as Harley manned the gunner's turret without ammunition. They communicated via the flight intercom and Bob let Harley feel some G-forces just for fun. After the flight, Bob enjoyed introducing his big brother to the other Navy pilots and both brothers had a very memorable time. They stayed up late and had a "gab fest" like the old days back in Aurora. They talked about all their old buddies and of course, Bill Bennett came to mind. By this time, they had both heard about how tough the Marines had it in the Solomons and they had heard from home about the food shortages and disease.

As Bill read the latest article regarding Lieutenant Robert Stoner, it said that he had successfully completed the transition to the new plane and was due to arrive back in Illinois on September 3rd to begin Aircraft Carrier Training aboard the Wolverine at Great Lakes Naval Air Station, Glenview, Illinois. The Wolverine cruised through the waters of Lake Michigan near Chicago and Bill curled a huge smile when he pictured Bob winging his way over the old stomping grounds of Glenview, where he had reported for Naval Basic Training back in May of '41.

52. The Sable and the Wolverine

Lieutenant Bob Stoner checked his altitude, airspeed indicator and turn-and-bank indicator as he pushed the huge TBM into a bank to the right. As the plane came around to a heading of 260 degrees on the compass, the familiar skyline of Chicago was visible ahead and he could see the curvature of the south shore of Lake Michigan on his left. He continued the bank until he reached 350 degrees and aligned the nose with the USS Wolverine (IX64) just ahead and 1000 ft. below. The Wolverine was a former side-wheel lake steamer that had been converted to the Navy's practice carrier the year before. Four smoke stacks belched a black stream of coal smoke from her left side in front of the 40-foot antenna tower where Old Glory pointed to the south. Bob knew that the Wolverine was cruising about 15 mph, so the flag showed that the winds were probably gusting to over 25 mph out on the lake. With flaps fully extended, he reached forward with his left hand to drop the landing gear and immediately felt the added drag and watched his airspeed drop to 100 mph. At this point, it looked impossible to drop the huge Avenger onto the postage stamp in front of him, but he knew it was possible as he had done it many times. With the prop set at minimum pitch, Bob pulled the throttle back ever so slightly as he wanted his wheels to touch the deck at 85 to 90 mph for a perfect landing. If he dropped the airspeed below 80 mph, the plane could stall and he would be in Lake Michigan. He could now see the Deck Officer with red paddles in each hand showing him the attitude of his wings. His airspeed was 95 mph as he approached the deck. The headwind was blowing out of the north at about 20 mph and some turbulence buffeted the wings with about ten feet to go. The two dashed white lines on the deck were centered in front of him and he braced himself for the touchdown. Bob pushed the stick forward to compensate for the gusting wind but the gust had slowed him to below 85 mph, slower than he needed. The sudden loss of airspeed dropped the Avenger the remaining eight feet to the deck and caused the front wheels to hit the deck much harder than intended. Bob pulled the throttle all the way back to slow the engine. The plane bounced hard before catching the arresting cable which pushed the heavy nose down and pulled the tail up about three feet. The propeller tips ripped into the flight deck and debris flew violently into the air as the plane shuddered and then dropped the tail back to the deck. Bob's quick reflexes had his hand on the kill switch almost instantly. As the engine stopped, Bob could see that the prop tips had been ripped off. The emergency crew raced to the Avenger with fire extinguishers, but there was nothing for them to do but to ask Bob if he was okay. Physically, Bob was fine. Chewing up the deck of the training carrier was not something that a well-respected flight instructor in the United States Navy would choose to do. Dropping the Avenger in at 85 to 90 mph was not an easy task.

 Bob took quite a bit of teasing from the other officers over the next few days, but he was known to have a great sense of humor and the others knew that Lieutenant Stoner could take some kidding. While the deck was being repaired on the Wolverine, Bob was assigned to finish his carrier qualification aboard the USS Sable, the Wolverine's sister ship. Taking off from Glenview Naval Air Station, the Avengers and Hellcats would fly out to find the carrier and then land on her deck. The planes would be turned around and Bob would have to wait hours before he could take off and return to Glenview. Bob was known by all of his friends in the Navy as the only guy whose family had their own little newspaper. He was also one of the only officers who would "shoot the bull" with the enlisted men, and he was frequently in the middle of a bunch of guys who were laughing at his stories. Bob had been able to visit with Sam and Margaret numerous times during these weeks and Margaret made sure that he did not go back to Glenview without some homemade baked goods. The guys in the training squadron and the Sable crew enjoyed Margaret's baking immensely.

The next series of take offs and landings went flawlessly and Bob received his carrier rating with "flying colors," as was expected. Sam and Margaret congratulated Bob, but privately they would rather that he had stayed at Corpus Christi with the instructor's job. That seemed dangerous enough in their eyes. Bob couldn't wait to do his part and he was eager to join his new Composite Squadron, VC-11, out on the West Coast.

Sam had to make an important trip to New York for Diamond T and a defense contract, so Harley's wife Betty drove Margaret in to Glenview to pick up the new carrier pilot. They stopped in at the old homestead in Oak Park so that Bob could visit with his grandparents and then they drove past their old house to see how well it was being maintained. Finally back out to Aurora, Bob relaxed in his old room at 211 S. Fourth Street. He had the run of the place with Dexter and Harley away and Helen now in the Navy in San Francisco. There would be one catch to Bob's visit home and his time off. Sam, the Editor of *The Stoner Weekly News*, asked him to fill in as the "guest editor" for the week, which meant that he would basically have to write the paper. Bob loved to write and he had not really had the chance since he left college where he was a sports writer for the North Central College paper. Saturday morning, September 25th, Bob decided to borrow the car and do some visiting. Wearing his dress whites, he parked the car in front of 454 Simms Street, ascended the porch steps and knocked on the screen door. He pushed his face to the screen and hollered, "Ma Bennett!" into the foyer. Jessie came into sight as she passed through the dining room wondering who could be calling her in that voice. She let out a yell with delight as she saw the dashing Navy man and she swung open the door for a hug and a kiss.

Jessie had so many questions for Bob about his flying, his wife and his plans for the future. Bob wanted to get the war over with as he wanted to start a family. Jessie told Bob how proud she and Steve were of him and how proud they knew his parents were. There were a lot of fond memories for Bob around 454 Simms and he looked out the kitchen door at the back yard where he and Bill had played a lot of football with George Troll, Bob Nix and Bud Dix. He had been looking forward to visiting with Steve as well, but Jessie told him that Steve had been working Saturdays at Schmitz and Gretencort down on Broadway. That suited Bob just fine. He always liked a trip to the men's store. He drove the old Packard downtown and had to park two blocks down in the bank lot as Broadway yielded no available parking spots on a Saturday morning. Bob had a spring in his step as he walked the old sidewalk toward Schmitz and Gretencort. He opened the front door and the familiar smell of the shop made him smile. The shop was busy and Steve was with a customer near the back when he caught sight of Bob and you would have thought the Earth had shaken. Steve set whatever was in his hands on the counter and made his way directly to

Bob. A very firm handshake turned into a full-out hug as Steve was overjoyed to see Bob back in town.

Several customers gathered around them as Bob filled Steve in on the carrier training and his new assignment to VC-11 for combat duty in the Pacific. Bob would join VC-11 out in California and meet the new Commanding Officer. VC-11 would be a "Composite Squadron" made up of FM2 Wildcat fighters and the TBM-1C Avenger torpedo planes. After forming, VC-11 would be assigned to an aircraft carrier for combat duty. Bob then turned the subject to Bill. Steve asked Bob if Jessie had told him about the letters they received from George Garcia. With the excitement of Bob's visit, Jessie had not thought about the letters. Steve filled Bob in about George having been with Bill in the Solomon Islands as well as New Zealand. He had written to the Bennetts to tell them that Bill was fine, as Bill had requested. He had also told them about Tulagi, the lack of food and the disease; things that Bill always failed to mention in his letters home. Steve told Bob that George Garcia had written that the Marines had been lucky to get one meal a day while at Tulagi and Guadalcanal. That was quite a contrast to the fast-paced life that Bob had been living, with dinners, dancing and great bands from time to time. He had heard the stories about the Marines and it made him all the more eager to get out there and get "into it" for the sake of doing some good for those "mud Marines on the ground."

The next day, Bob went to 4th Street Methodist with Betty and Margaret and it was great to see so many familiar faces, including Reverend Dibble. As soon as they arrived home, Bob was at his father's roll top desk loading up the typewriter with paper. There was a deadline to meet and he was the man for the job. The guest editor for *The Stoner Weekly News* had reported for duty! The typewriter chattered all afternoon as Bob brought the *Stoner Weekly* subscribers up to speed on everyone's developments, including dinners, dancing, birthdays and his visit with Steve Bennett at the store. He also mentioned that any civilians who miss having steak and other foods because of the war had nothing to complain about compared to Bill Bennett and his fellow Marines.

With the paper finished and ready for inspection by the regular Editor in Chief, Bob was thrilled to see Sam pull into the driveway just before dinner. He had driven long hours to try and get home to see Bob "off to war" as any red-blooded American father would want to do. They had a wonderful time and the house was filled with laughter as it always had been when Bob and the boys were around. The Stoners were always good for dinner and a laugh. Monday morning arrived as a beautiful day and Margaret prepared a perfect breakfast for Sam, Bob and Betty. They loaded up Sam's car and headed for Glenview to return their favorite Navy flier. Bob said his goodbyes and hugged all three of them tightly. He told them not to worry as he would take care of himself, and they knew that he could. Love was shared in earnest back and forth and Bob pulled away to get inside and check in. As his Dress Whites disappeared through the door, Margaret waved for a few more seconds and then started to cry. Sam put his arm around Margaret and told her not to let Bob see her doing that. Sam felt like a good cry himself.

53. This Is It!

After catching up on incoming and outgoing mail, Bill investigated the possibility of getting out of camp again before heading for the docks. He paid a visit to Lieutenant Simonson's tent and found him struggling with a typewriter, trying to finish some platoon reports. Bill asked about getting a pass at some point, and Simonson said that with 3rd Platoon AWOL this week it was doubtful that Farkas would let anyone out of camp. Bill said that he would be happy with anything, even an eight-hour pass so that he could visit the Mitchell's down in Lower Hutt. Art Simonson knew that while other Marines had been getting drunk and fighting on weekends, or chasing girls all over Wellington, Bill had been preaching sermons, working at a cinema and doing yard work at the Mitchell's house. He had no problem letting Bill out of camp, so he made Bill an offer which was the best he could do. Since the company was pulling out for the amphibious landing training on Sunday, he would give Bill an eight-hour pass on Saturday from 1100 hours to 1900 hours and Bill would keep it quiet.

Bill took the pass and slipped out the front gate late on Saturday morning. He rode the train down to Woburn Station, crossed the footbridge over to Pohutukawa Street and headed west to the intersection of Whites Line East and Whites Line West. The intersection was very busy that time of day and Bill had to be cautious to get across safely. He was sure that Lieutenant Simonson would be pretty upset if Bill got himself run over and missed the training exercises. Once across, he headed down Whites Line West a few blocks and made the familiar turn onto Fuller Grove. Fuller had become the closest thing to Simms Street that Bill had known in the past two years and several neighbors waved and yelled, "Hello Bill!" as he approached the Mitchell's at number 14. Disappointed that no one was at home, Bill lifted the corner of the mat by the back door, retrieved the key and let himself in through the kitchen door. After a cold chicken sandwich and a glass of milk, Bill sat back to relax for a few minutes and thought that he might take a nap. The spring weather was so nice outside that he could not bring himself to stay indoors, so he went out to the yard to see how things looked.

The grass had been growing quickly over the past week and there were a lot of spring weeds popping up. He knew that Mr. and Mrs. Mitchell worked very hard and would no doubt appreciate a manicured lawn when they got home, so Bill retrieved the reel mower from the garage. Harkening back to his years of mowing his neighbor Bessie Hemm's yard and others in the neighborhood, Bill cut, trimmed, pulled and pruned the entire property from front to back. It was a first-class job. As he was washing up with the garden hose, the Mitchell's arrived home and they were thrilled to see Bill as well as his gardening work. Mrs. Mitchell asked Bill what time he needed to be back and then she spun into her work preparing a sheet of "humble pies" for dinner. The little pies had a wonderful crust filled with steak and cheese with a potato top all baked in the oven. Bill ate his with "tomato sauce," known as ketchup in the States. This was one of Bill's favorite home-cooked meals and she knew how he loved them.

The three talked over dinner, cleared the table and washed up the dishes. Nearing six o'clock, the Mitchells drove Bill over to Woburn and had one last goodbye. Bill told them that if the exercise turned out to be training, he would be back in a few weeks, if not, then, it was anyone's guess. He told the Mitchells he would write them as soon as he could and he said he loved them like family. He asked that they give his regards to Les when he came home. Bill waved as he headed up the foot bridge and then turned to cross the tracks. Mrs. Mitchell cried.

54. Tarawa

The following morning was Sunday, October 17th and the Marines visited the mess hall as usual and then went back to their tents to shave and get their gear together. Bill packed his sea bag with all his non-combat belongings and parked it on his empty bunk. He then went over his combat gear to make sure he had not missed anything. He strapped up his combat pack with the rain poncho and the T-handled shovel and pulled out his helmet liner to tighten up the new camouflaged cover. Most of the new jungle camouflage gear was reversible with a green side and a brown side. Orders were given to show the green side only for training exercises. Johnnie Jones and Herb Dale came by Bill's tent to see how he was coming along, but mostly to say goodbye to him. Johnnie and Herb had been assigned duty to 1st Battalion, 2nd Marines and would be boarding the USS Lee at Wellington Harbor later in the day. Bill had been assigned to 2nd Battalion, 2nd Marines and would be boarding the USS Zeilin at Wellington. Lieutenant Vincent would be with yet another group attached to 3rd Battalion, 2nd Marines which would load aboard the USS Middleton that afternoon. Truitt Anderson and Duane Strinden would be on the same ship as Johnnie and Herb so Bill knew he would miss joking around with all of them.

Bill was upset that Truitt would not be going with him as he had hoped to stay with him if at all possible. Truitt had been trying desperately to get a pass for the weekend as Molly was still trying to secure the marriage license and was waiting for him at the Taylor's house in Miramar. It seemed as though the plans for marriage would have to wait.

At 0900, Company D assembled on the parade grounds and divided into their respective combat groups while Lieutenant Vincent and Captain Farkas addressed them briefly. Trucks would be loaded with a sequence of 1st Battalion, 2nd Battalion and 3rd Battalion for the trip to the docks. After orders to fall out and prepare to load the trucks, groups of Marines mingled to say a final goodbye to their friends. The boys from Texas, Charles Montague and Gene Seng, found Bill and Fred Ellis and told them how they wished they could be together on this one. The pair at least had each other as they had since they were kids. Gene and Fred had developed an "older brother/younger brother" type of relationship, just as Bill and Truitt had over the past year. The guys all said things like, "Keep your head down!" "Save some Japs for me if you get in there first," or "See you on the beach," before they parted ways. Gene Seng told Fred to remember what he asked him to do, then he said goodbye to Bill as he and Montague returned to their group. They were going in with a great group of guys led by Lieutenant Vincent and Bill and Fred knew they were in good hands. Bill asked Fred what Gene meant by what he said. Fred told Bill that Gene always gave his mother, back in Austin, Texas, a white carnation on Mother's Day. He asked Fred to make sure that she was sent one next Mother's Day if Gene got killed. Fred smiled at Bill and said that he was sure Gene would be sending the carnation himself.

Bill and Fred went over to Lieutenant Vincent to say goodbye and did the same with Jarrett, Kountzman, Waltz, Millick and a few others. Some of the guys from 3rd Platoon joked with Bill and Fred about having to be on the Zeilin with Captain Farkas, but Bill and Fred would now be under the command of Captain Warren Morris with F/2/2, who seemed to be a stand-up guy. The call came for the 1st Battalion group to load up and Bill gave Truitt, Johnnie, Duane and Herb a final wave as he passed their loading line. The group loading for 2nd Battalion was under the command of Lieutenant Robert C. Jones, Jr. and Art Simonson was standing with him conferring about their loading procedure. Bill and Fred joined Gabel, Kinley, Cothran, Webb, Scott, Coate, Poterola, Fortenberry, Collum and Hellman as they were ordered to form up in lines for truck loading. Simonson came down the line and called roll one more time. Each man bellowed out, "YO!" as he heard his name called. A row of six heavy trucks pulled to a screeching halt and Sergeant Gabel stepped to the tailgate of the second truck and yelled to Bill and Fred to "Load it up!" Bill climbed in the back and Fred handed up the sea bags. Bill reached down and gave Fred a hand up and then all twelve from their team loaded likewise until the truck was crammed with Marines, combat gear and sea bags.

The weather was beautiful and the open trucks provided a breezy trip through the green hills and valleys. Bill wondered how the company that made these trucks managed to make sure they gave the occupants a jarring ride even when the roads were smooth. Cigarettes came out, were lit, and the guys knew they were saying goodbye to Judgeford, more than likely forever. Crossing the bridge at Silverstream, the trucks pulled onto the main thoroughfare down to Wellington and they saw the familiar rail lines and stations that had taken them to their destinations while on liberty so many times. At one point, Bill looked over to get a last glimpse of the Woburn Station where he had left Mr. and Mrs. Mitchell only hours before. New Zealanders and American servicemen, alike, waved as the trucks went past and the Marines waved back.

As the convoy wound through the Wellington streets out to the docks, the transports came into view. Turning onto the long dock, Bill caught his first sight of the large, blue-gray bathtub, the USS Zeilin. Winches and cranes aboard the Zeilin were hoisting supplies to the main deck and lowering equipment down into the holds. As the team was unloading the truck, Bill looked over at the water line on the Zeilin. From what he recalled from loading the USS President Jackson at San Diego, the Zeilin was sitting pretty low in the water already. His suspicion that this was no exercise was holding up. The ship appeared to be in good shape and she was clean down on the decks. Gabel talked to the Navy and found the location of the bunk room where the Pioneer team would be located and then they all found empty bunks. Even though Manny had gone back to the States, Bill still remembered his advice to take the top bunk. Bill smiled to himself, but took a bottom bunk just the same. Vomit doesn't rise, but heat does, as do noxious odors.

The USS Zeilin, APA-3 would carry Corporal William Bennett to Tarawa along with 2nd Battalion, 2nd Marines Combat Team. *TIME* magazine Reporter Robert Sherrod would share the ride aboard the Zeilin and go ashore with Bennett in the fourth wave.

(U.S. Navy Photo)

On Monday, October 18th, Molly went to the post office in Miramar to check her post office box and, much to her amazement, found her mother's letter of consent waiting for her. With Truitt already aboard the ship and all leave canceled, there was no apparent way the wedding could take place. But there is an old saying, "Love will find a way," that put Molly's keen mind to work. She "rang up" Reverend Lawrence North, a Baptist minister she had kept in mind per Truitt's wishes to be married by a Baptist, and he was open for an 11 a.m. service at his home near the Wellington docks. Next, she rang Doe Marshall and told her of the plan. Molly would send word through military connections to the USS Lee and the USS Zeilin to tell Truitt and Bill to make all effort to be at 26 Aurora Terrace, Wellington, ready for the ceremony at 1100 hours. Molly would arrive at Doe's house at 1000 hours, they would get dressed quickly, and then head for Reverend North's residence. Molly went back to the Taylor's and collected her dress and Margaret and they both headed into action. Molly decided that for the sake of time and accuracy, she would deliver her notes directly to the USS Lee and the USS Zeilin while she was still in uniform. She went to the deck officer of each ship and handed them the messages in New Zealand military envelopes and asked that they be delivered immediately.

The girls then headed for the Marshall's house to go on from there in the Marshall's car. The worst that could happen would be that the groom would not show up. Aboard the USS Lee, a very surprised PFC Anderson was handed a note that told him to report to the Commanding Officer of 1st Battalion, 2nd Marines. Truitt had to quickly locate the staff of Major Wood B. Kyle and find out what this was all about. Arriving at Major Kyle's quarters, a 2nd lieutenant with a big smile showed Truitt the note and said, "Apparently someone wants to marry you!" It turned out that Truitt's buddy, Corporal Loren Karchner was assigned to 1/2 as a company clerk and decided that he might "need some help" delivering some bags of mail to the post office in Wellington. Quickly changing into their dress uniforms, Truitt and Corporal Karchner went down the gang plank with bags of mail and a one-hour pass.

Just a few hundred yards away, Bill was working with Lieutenant Simonson aboard the USS Zeilin squaring away company equipment according to the "Navy way" when a note arrived to Simonson. He handed the note to Bill and told him that there was no possible way he could get liberty. Bill had been looking forward to this wedding for some time and he appealed to Simonson's mutual concern for Truitt "Andy" Anderson. Truitt was one of the guys in the company that everybody liked and the thought of him being married with no one there to stand up with him was unsavory. Bill and Lieutenant Simonson put their heads together and Simonson agreed to write him a pass that would get him off the Zeilin, but may not be able to get him back on without trouble. The pass would state that Bill was on his way to another ship carrying correspondence. Once the correspondence was "delivered," then Bill could "take the long way home" via the Reverend North's house about a half mile away. Simonson emphasized that if Bill was caught downtown with this pass his butt would be in a sling. Simonson would have to deny having any knowledge of Bill's intentions. Bill donned his dress uniform and dodged 20 questions as to where he was going. He picked up the envelope from Simonson and made his way down the gangplank.

Bill walked along the dock until he was out of site from the Zeilin and then turned left toward Manners Street. By the time Bill found 26 Aurora Terrace, it was 1057 hours and a woman who he assumed was Mrs. North let him in the front door with a huge smile on her face. There in the living room was Molly in her wedding gown and what a beautiful sight she was, to be sure. Margaret Taylor and Doe Marshall were assisting Molly with adjustments of her veil and headdress. Bill found Truitt and Loren Karchner in the kitchen along with Reverend North. Truitt lit up when he saw Bill and asked how he managed to get away. Bill told Truitt that Simonson said to tell him he owed him one! Bill said he was supposed to be running a message over to the USS Lee. Truitt and Karchner laughed as they told Bill that they had to drop mail bags at the post office on the way over.

The men were summoned into the parlor and shortly thereafter, Molly arrived to stand by Truitt's side. Reverend North read from 1st Corinthians, chapter 13, and then briefly described the Biblical establishment of marriage as being between one man and one woman for the duration of life. The ceremony was short and sweet and the rings were exchanged and at long last, Truitt was able to kiss his bride, and Molly her husband. The wedding party of six thanked the Norths and headed over a few blocks away for a lunch reception at a nearby hotel. Along the way, Molly noticed that the "boys" seemed quite nervous about seeing U.S.M.C. Military Police walking the streets and she decided not to ask them exactly how they managed to get off the troop transports. Bill and Karchner chipped in with Doe and Margaret to cover the bill for lunch and they had a wonderful time. At 1400 hours, Bill and Karchner headed back on foot to the docks while Doe drove Molly and Truitt back to her house, then on to drop Margaret back at Miramar. Doe had set things up to allow the newlyweds to have a private afternoon at the Marshall residence. Bill walked up the gangplank of the USS Zeilin at about 1430 hours, handed his pass to the deck officer and not a word was said. Karchner, of course, was the Company Clerk and there was no suspicion whatsoever over at the USS Lee.

Doe and Lesley Marshall lent Molly the car to drive Truitt back down to the USS Lee just after 1900 hours and the newlyweds shared their first goodbye kiss as a married couple. Molly promised Truitt that she would write his mother back in the States and mail a copy of their wedding photo as soon as she got them back from developing. They promised to write often and Truitt told Molly that he would come back to her as soon as he could and would be thinking of her until then. Truitt got out of the car and came around to the driver's side window and gave Molly one last kiss goodbye. Their hands held until their arms outstretched and their fingers slid apart. Molly watched as Truitt went up the gangplank, handed his "pass" to the deck officer, then turned and waved to Molly from the deck. Molly returned the wave and blew Truitt a kiss before driving away. Molly smiled as she drove back to the Marshall's and looked at the wedding band on her finger. She was now officially Mrs. Truitt Anderson, and a happily-married woman.

Molly and PFC Truitt "Andy" Anderson, October 18th, 1943.

(Anderson Family Photo)

There was a lot of gear coming to the Zeilin, and when pallets of ammunition, including mortar and artillery shells were seen coming aboard, there was no doubt that this would not be a training exercise. Word had gotten around quickly that there would be some real business to take care of soon. On October 31st, there were a lot of jokes about "trick or treating" aboard the Zeilin and the Marines were sure they were likely to get a "trick" over a "treat" from the Marine Corps. They also joked about how every Marine was wearing the same camouflaged costume. Without notice, at about 0100 on November 1st, some Marines broke the silence when they heard the engines start up and then felt the Zeilin moving in the water. Truitt went to the deck and watched off the starboard side as the lights of Miramar passed from his sight. How he longed to stay near Molly who was now his family. Under the cover of darkness, the convoy of troop transports headed out of Wellington Harbor and out into Cook Strait, then swung north. The trip up to the exercises at Hawke's Bay would take 24 hours. By 0300 of November 2nd the Zeilin was still churning north and it was official; there would be no exercises at Hawke's Bay.

After dark on November 6th, old sailors aboard the Zeilin told the Marines they could "smell land." Sure enough, the island of Efate in the New Hebrides was off the starboard side when the sun came up. The transports made their way into Mele Bay and dropped anchor. Already moored in Mele Bay were about a dozen U.S. Navy battleships and heavy cruisers; another sign that something big was brewing. Mele Bay was already much hotter than New Zealand and the landing teams made several practice landings over the next five days. The Marines had learned that the Higgins Boats were fine machines if the ocean was calm, but in choppy waters they were far worse than the trucks on land. Some of the fellows even tried talking their boat mates out of eating prior to practice to avoid the inevitable lost breakfast. The heat had been building back up below deck and the Marines once again began to sleep on deck whenever possible. Gabel, Ellis and Bill took turns sleeping in the bunkrooms so there would be someone with rank around if needed. They also liked to have at least one member of the team there to discourage any thieves from pilfering their sea bags.

Sitting on the deck of the Zeilin, Bill opened up a piece of blue "V Mail" that he had gotten from the Navy and thought to write to "Pete and Perry." He explained that he was at sea, so there would not be many letters received from him for a while. Perry, who Bill also called "Mac," due to his last name of McIntosh, was now a Marine, and Bill wondered where he was based. He told them to tell everyone not to worry about Bill Bennett because he was fine, although it didn't pay to make plans anymore. He knew that the two of them were in the same boat, as the Marines would dictate everything about life for the time being. They had asked Bill if he needed anything and he replied that he didn't need a thing. He folded up the little one-page letter into an envelope and slid it into his pocket. A quick trip below deck to the USS Zeilin Post Exchange and the letter was off to the Navy Censor's office.

On November 12th, the whole fleet pulled out of Mele Bay and continued northward, and each day was hotter than the last. On the 13th, a rumor spread through the fleet that the Marines were on their way to Wake Island to avenge the Marines killed there just after the Pearl Harbor attack. The commanders marveled at the speed at which the rumor traveled from ship to ship. This was made even more amazing by the fact that it was false. On the morning of November 14th, the brass gave the word to unveil the plans to all of the Marines. "Helen Island" was a small coral island at one end of the Tarawa Atoll in the British Gilbert Islands. The island was only two miles long and 700 yards wide and about 6 to 10 feet above sea level. Officially named "Betio," the island was now the home of 5,000 highly-trained Japanese Marines who called the island "Betitu." The Americans would long remember the island as Tarawa.

A few days out of Efate and about half way to Tarawa, Lieutenant Simonson informed Bill and the Pioneer team that there would be a battalion meeting the following day and 2/2 would be addressed by Colonel Amey. This would be a good chance for the guys to get the "straight dope" directly from the colonel. The deck of the Zeilin was crowded with nearly 1,000 Marines from the 2nd Battalion. A few captains and lieutenants stood to speak when the meeting began and then Amey was introduced, as if there might be someone who didn't already know who he was.

Lieutenant Colonel Herbert R. Amey was a black-haired, black-mustached Marine officer who was thought to look like a Hollywood movie actor. As dashing as he was, he was very shy and disliked having to make speeches to the men. He basically had decided to just talk as though he were addressing a small group and talk from the heart. Amey was raised in Pennsylvania and moved to San Diego when he became a Marine in 1935. He was now in his mid-30s and had become a very popular leader with his men and fellow officers. As he began his outline of the operation, he said he could now refer to the islands by their real names, but he couldn't pronounce them correctly. Laughter was heard among the men. Amey said he would use the island code names since all the Marines knew them better anyway. Bill noticed a lean fellow wearing Marine utilities sitting near the front taking down serious notes onto his yellow legal pad. He had seen this man around the ship for several days and the guys told him that his name was Bob Sherrod, a war correspondent from *TIME* magazine. As Colonel Amey spoke, Sherrod's pen was at work.

Amey continued to outline how "Helen Island" would be mercilessly bombarded by air and sea and said that the amount of shelling would be unprecedented by any military force on earth. Just before the invasion, every Japanese airfield within range of Tarawa would be hit by American air power to make sure that no enemy planes would make it over the island. He was sweating so profusely that he had to pick up a towel to dry his face from time to time. The Colonel summarized his points and added that the Marines might just walk ashore and finish off the few Japanese that survived the bombardments, but there was no way to be sure. As he finished his speech, Lieutenant Norvik took his spot and talked to the battalion about the "Gilbertese" civilians that might be encountered on Tarawa. He said that they were very friendly people, many of whom spoke English. They probably didn't care for the Japanese any more than the Marines did. If encountered, their heads were not to be touched as it was a religious taboo for them. They would be very jealous of their women and there is a native drink that makes men go insane and want to kill. The drink should be avoided. This drew some sporadic laughter from the Marines as they were known to have a few drinks, and they were definitely in the killing business. When the natives were being addressed, they would probably sit down as this was their way of showing respect to the speaker. The elevation of Tarawa was only about six feet, so when digging or using pits for cover one would likely find water. This water would be brackish and should not be used for drinking until such a time as the engineers could test it.

Colonel Amey stood up and said he had forgotten a few important things. He wanted the men to drink very little water at first and to carry two canteens ashore. Water would be scarce until they could get barrels ashore and anyone caught stealing water would be shot by the MPs if needed. Amey then encouraged the officers to hit the Japanese fast and hit them hard before they could recover from the bombardment. The meeting was dismissed and Bill stood with Gabel, Simonson and Ellis as the effectiveness of the bombardment was discussed. Most of the older Marines thought the fight would be worse than anyone had said as the shelling would only kill a few of the enemy and not enough to make a huge difference. Either way, the only smart thing to do would be to expect the worst.

For this assault, the Marines would be coming ashore onto four different beaches: Green Beach, Red One, Red Two and Red Three. The map of the island had been divided up into 38 "sectors" to clarify exactly where units were supposed to go. The main Assault Regiments consisted of the 2nd Marines, 3rd Marines, 8th Marines and the 6th Marines. Each of these regiments was divided into battalions and the battalions divided into companies. The small island had the appearance of a cardinal lying on its back with its leg sticking up in the air. The "leg" was actually a 700-yard long pier jutting northward out into the lagoon. The center of the island was completely taken up by an airfield which was the primary objective for taking the island from the Japanese. Shortly after the announcement of the objective, large topographical maps appeared on the deck of the Zeilin and paper assault maps were passed out to every platoon. Bill's team was called in to be briefed by Captain Warren Morris, commander of Company F. Sergeant Gabel's Pioneer team would be fighting with Company F when they hit the beaches and red pencils went to work on the new maps. Aerial photographs taken on October 20th, 1943, were the latest images of the defenses on Tarawa. As Captain Morris reviewed the aerial photos, the teams took notes on their individual maps that they would carry ashore during the assault. Bill listened intently and looked on with Gabel and Fred Ellis. Gabel asked for an additional copy of the map for Bill and they were handed an extra copy from a stack nearby. Bill opened up the map and noticed that it had belonged to Captain Barrett of Company F 2/8, but his name was now crossed out in pencil. Bill re-folded the three-piece map and stuck it under his arm. He would find a place to study it later.

Bill's Pioneer team would come ashore in the "fourth wave" comprised of Higgins Boats that would follow the first three waves of Amphibious Tractors. These tractors were officially called Landing Vehicle Tracked, or LVTs as the Marine Corps acronym. Capable of carrying 15 to 20 combat Marines, the LVT was a boat powered by tracks with large blades that acted as propellers while in the water and tank tracks while on land. Instead of dropping the front ramp and having Marines wade through the surf, the LVT would drive right up on the beach and the Marines would jump out over the left and right sides. The LVT had a .50 caliber machine gun mounted on the front right side and a .30 caliber gun on the left front side, to cover the Marine's deployment to the beach. This was a big improvement over the Higgins Boat. About 25 minutes after the first waves would hit the beach, the Pioneers would arrive to support F/2/2 in their move off the beach. The goal was to move to the other side of the island as quickly as possible to cut the island in two.

Some of the joking subsided among the Marines, but not all of it. Everyone became focused on preparation of equipment and the training to effectively use it. Bill recalled the feelings that he had experienced over a year earlier when he prepared to land at Florida Island and Tulagi; the feeling that these could be his last days. Everyone knew there was a possibility Tarawa would be heavily and desperately defended. The maps and models showed a small island that was crowded with bunkers and pillboxes, and bristling with artillery and machine guns. If the Navy's big guns could not clear away these emplacements, there would be a lot of dirty work for the Marines once they got ashore, if they could get ashore. Bill met with Lieutenant Simonson, Sergeant Gabel and the lieutenants of F/2/2 to talk about their battle plans. 1st Lieutenant Wayne Sanford from Shelby, Michigan, 1st Lieutenant Joseph Barr from Wood River, Illinois, 2nd Lieutenant George F. Cooper, 2nd Lieutenant Lawrence Ferguson from Duncanville, Texas, and 2nd Lieutenant Ray Marion from Worcester, Massachusetts, all gathered around a three dimensional diorama of the island. They pointed out where they planned to land in sector 222 and how they meant to work their way through the defenses, cross the airfield and establish a position on the south side of the island. It would be up to the men of the Pioneer team to make sure that the advance had the supplies it would need to get the job done. The first, second and third waves should have the beach defenses knocked out by the time the Pioneers in the fourth wave made it to shore. As Company F moved in from the seawall, the Pioneer teams would keep them supplied with ammunition and water.

It felt good to know what to expect when they got to the beach and it helped to focus on the plans. Conversations broke out about the effectiveness of the bombardment and many thought that the Marines would walk on to an island loaded with dead Japanese and just have to clean up the mess that the Navy made. Others were cautious and reminded the optimists of the failure of bombardments and air support to kill off the enemy in the Solomons. It was true that Tarawa was much smaller and the fire should be concentrated, but there would, in all likelihood, be living, fighting Japanese onshore when the Marines arrived. Bill grabbed some free time to sit under a Higgins Boat on deck and write a letter to Steve and Jessie. He set some of the new "Semper Fidelis" letterhead, that he had gotten back in New Zealand, on top of the folded battle map and wrote, "Nov. 17th, 1943, High Seas" in the upper right corner. "Dear Mother & Dad, today your son is in the best of health. He is at the present thinking of home and wishing that he could see the two most lovable people in the world. Well, now that I have left New Zealand, I would like to have you write to some of the swell folks that did so much to make me happy. I'll give you their addresses and something about them. First there is the Mitchell Family; Mom and Pop and Les..." Looking up occasionally to ponder his next line, Bill scanned the horizon and an armada of ships stretched out as far as he could see. Every few minutes, three or four Navy fighters would roar over the Zeilin as they patrolled for submarines or stayed at the ready for an enemy air attack. Bill knew that he couldn't write anything about what the next few days would bring, nor would he want to upset his parents. His thoughts were that if this was his last letter home, he wanted his friends in New Zealand to be known to Steve and Jessie. He also wanted to send Helen a present and entrusted Jessie to pick out something nice. At the bottom of

The New Zealand One Pound Note signed by the Marines of D/2/18 on November 19th, 1943, the day before the Battle of Tarawa.

(Photo courtesy of Dean Laubach)

the fourth page, he signed off with "Love and prayers, Bill" and folded it into the envelope. During the dinner mess hall, George Gabel had a New Zealand One Pound Note that the guys were passing around for the men of Company D to sign; just the names and nothing else. This ritual was known as making a "short snorter," although Bill had no idea how it had been started. It was a good idea though, as the finished note would make someone a great souvenir if they survived the battle.

55. Getting Ready

The Zeilin now moved deep into the combat zone and smoking was only allowed on deck during the day. Below deck, the ships interior was lit by red combat lights that gave off just enough light to see where you were going. The Marines' mood remained somber for the most part, although the loud bragging about the number of Japanese that the Marines planned to kill was inevitable. As Bill worked his way along the red corridors, he noticed Bob Sherrod standing in an open area talking with a few officers and taking notes on that now-familiar legal pad. Rumor had it that Sherrod was not only writing a magazine story, but he was going ashore with the fourth wave and he was attached with 2/2. Some of the guys thought that anyone going ashore that didn't have to must be nuts.

Most of the Marines had stopped shaving a few days earlier and there was no good way to thoroughly wash. The 100-degree temperatures had rendered the decks below a sweaty, smelly world of locker room odors. Just getting washed up and past a urinal was quite a job and Bill was looking forward to getting back to his bunk. George Gabel came by and asked Bill if he needed anything and wanted to make sure that everyone knew where to go for tomorrow's final day of combat preparation. Bill said that he was all set and thanked George. Likewise, Bill asked the sergeant if he needed him to help with anything. As Bill lay on his bunk, he tried hard to ignore the talk of nearby Marines as he prayed and tried to spiritually prepare himself should he be killed in the coming battle. He earnestly asked the Lord to prepare his mind to do the job that he was trained to do. He asked for forgiveness of anything that he might have done contrary to the Lord's will, even if he had been unaware of it. Bill was aware of the fact that the nature of his prayers seemed to have changed quite a bit over the past year, and he felt as though he were actually in God's presence now as he prayed. Bill asked for the safety of his fellow Marines and mentioned quite a few by name. He also prayed for his family back home and his friends that were in the service. Bill felt close to the Lord and he knew that if he were killed, he would join Christ in eternity.

November 19th, 1943, would be the last day of preparation before going ashore at Tarawa. Bill joined the other demolition men on deck in a designated area to prepare his TNT charges and review last minute details regarding charge placement on the fortifications that they were probably going to encounter. He carefully taped four sticks together and inserted the fuse and formed the wax around the fuse base. A Marine walked nearby with a lit cigarette in his mouth and a wave of profanity flew from the demo guys telling the Marine to get that cigarette away from the area or prepare for some dental work. The Marine quickly turned around when he realized he had wandered into a dangerous situation. Getting blown up the day before the invasion was not on anyone's "to do" list. Bill went back to work putting his charges together and packed extra TNT, fuse cord, wax and tape into a second demo bag. All of his prepared charges went into his BAR ammo belt that hung over his shoulders and buckled around his waist. Bill had decided that the BAR belt offered him the best support for the charges as he could carry them and run without a shoulder bag bouncing around. He put an extra pack of Lucky Strikes into the pouch on the belt and slid his metal cigarette case and the Zippo into his pants pocket. Lighters could not be stored with the TNT for obvious reasons. He wrote "BENNETT" on the bag and the belt with a grease pencil and turned them in to be locked in a fireproof container on deck until loading time tomorrow. Moving to the back of the Zeilin, Bill found dozens of BAR men oiling their weapons and he set about to check on the young guys to make sure they were ready. He sat with a few of the BAR men under a Higgins Boat and wiped the .30-06 rounds with an oiled white cotton cloth to clean and lubricate each round prior to snapping it into a 20-round magazine. The stacks of magazines were then loaded into belts to be carried ashore. Bill could see most of the kids were nervous, while some of them seemed excited.

After taking care of the demo kit and BAR duties, Bill turned his attention to his own M1 Garand and oiled and checked the action. He sighted through the peep sights, exhaled and squeezed the trigger to hear the click of a dry fire. Everything seemed good and he felt light without the old BAR. Bill returned to work on his ammo belt and checked the 10 eight-round clips that he had in the pouches. He wrapped eight more clips in a cloth and stuffed them into the bottom of his pack with extra socks and underwear: both luxuries that he had wanted on Tulagi, where he was taught that there was no way to know what to expect. He filled and attached two canteens to the back of his belt and checked the position of his Ka-Bar knife on his right hip. The M1 bayonet went into the pack so that the handle would be accessible from the top with his left hand. Then, he attached the T-handle shovel onto the back of the pack and Bill pulled it on to see how the pack hung over his ammo belt. A few adjustments on the pack straps and everything felt ready to go. He would have to adjust it all after the demolition belt and bag were retrieved tomorrow morning. All of the packs for the team would be stored with Lieutenant Simonson until the following morning, so Bill went to add his to the pile. The last detail was to make sure that all of his non-combat gear was stowed into the sea bag so that the Navy could store them after the men left the ship. Bill paused at the stacks of letters from home that were now held together with rubber bands. He looked through the stack of photos that frequently reminded him of home: Helen, the Bennetts and "the gang." None of them had any idea where Bill was or what he was about to do. He dropped the photos into the large dog-eared envelope and set it in between two books halfway down into the sea bag. He had thoughts that this could be the last time he ever saw the photos or the letters.

The heat on deck became unbearable in the afternoon and officers prowled the deck to make sure that everyone had their skin covered. They didn't want anyone failing to do their duty because of sunburn received through negligence. In fact, Marines getting severe sunburn would be fined $15 for "Abuse of Government Property."

The Protestant worship service was planned for the evening and Bill eagerly attended with Bob Swigert and several other guys that he knew from 2/2. The deck felt cooler as the sun had slid to the western horizon, but the humidity was still fierce. There must have been 1,000 Marines on the deck for the worship service and every face looked as though it meant business with God. There was no doubt whatsoever that this would be the last church service that a number of them would attend on this earth. Chaplain M. J. MacQueen delivered his sermon, driving home the need for each man to make his heart right with the Lord. He highlighted how Jesus had done the work of redemption on the cross and how a man must trust in Christ's work, receive forgiveness and receive the gift of eternal life. The Chaplain explained how God's very Spirit was promised to come into the lives of those who believe in Christ's work, and the Holy Spirit was given as a deposit guaranteeing that which was yet to come: eternal life. Bill fervently prayed and asked the Lord to reach the hearts of other Marines who may soon die and come before Him. As they sang hymns, Bill looked at Bob Swigert and he could see the look of deep concern on his face. The reassuring words of "A Mighty Fortress" seemed to sooth the concern. The Chaplain then offered communion and a line formed completely around the Zeilin. Bill and Bob waited for what seemed like an hour for the wafer and juice that symbolized the body and blood of Jesus Christ. Bill noticed several photographers and a motion picture camera on the deck as there were quite a few members of the press on board. The service concluded and Marines steadily descended below deck to their bunks to try and get a few hours of sleep. Bill went through the process of washing up, brushing his teeth and getting through to "the head" to relieve himself. Everything was ready to go. As Bill was getting back to his bunk, his mind went over the plans for the following morning. Upon waking, the 12-man Pioneer team would gather with Lieutenant Simonson and stay together until the battle was over; that was the plan. At about 2030 hours, Bill finally got into his bunk and tried to get some sleep. He knew that he was going to need it.

November 20th, 1943. There was quite a bit of movement and scuffling from time to time and Bill woke up numerous times covered with sweat. In the darkened bunkroom Bill could see several glowing orange embers as nervous Marines puffed on cigarettes. At 0130 the red lights went on and an officer ordered everyone to get up and dress for breakfast. Bill swung his legs out of the bunk and toweled his head and shoulders to try and dry some of the sweat. He quickly moved through the urinal line, then stopped at a sink to splash some water on his face and dry off with the towel. Each Marine had a fresh set of utilities set aside as orders were for clean uniforms to help fight infection in case of wounding. Deodorant went on just out of habit as it was probably going to be quite insignificant. Bill opened his cigarette case and looked at the nicely aligned Lucky Strikes, snapped it shut and dropped it into his right front pants pocket along with the Zippo. As he was buttoning his shirt and rolling up the sleeves, Simonson and Gabel came to his bunk to see how he was progressing. Within a minute or two, all thirteen Marines were together as they merged into the corridor and moved to the breakfast line.

Bill realized the nervousness he felt and it was similar to pre-game football jitters, only worse. Everyone seemed extra quiet as they contemplated what lay ahead for them. At about 0215 the loudspeaker came to life: "Target at 112 true. 26,000 yards ahead. Blackfish 870 yards. Blackfish 1,000 yards. Blackfish 900 yards." "Blackfish" was the codename of the transport in front of the USS Zeilin. Someone on the Zeilin's bridge was monitoring the distance as they followed them in to Tarawa. As the team approached the wardroom at about 0245, groups of combat-clad Marines from the first wave crossed through the line on their way topside. All the Marines in line yelled out, "Good luck!" or "Give 'em hell!" as they passed. It was a sobering thought that these would be the last few hours of life for many of these guys. Once inside the wardroom, the chow line was moving like a conveyor belt in a war plant. The Navy cooks didn't smile or joke with the Marines as they had days ago. Even they were hushed by the gravity of the situation. Bill slid onto the bench next to Fred Ellis and they went to work on their steak, eggs and fried potatoes, and then downed two cups of coffee. Bill knew that it would be hours before the fourth wave loaded the boats and had decided to take the chance on keeping his breakfast down. He would need the energy for later.

Simonson led the group back through the corridors to the bunk area where they went to work as a group to get ready to go topside themselves. Bill slid his feet into the leggings, pushed his pants down over his socks and laced the leggings up his calves. He checked the size of his ammo belt and buckled it around his waist, then twisted from side to side to see how everything sat. It felt secure and everything was within reach. He lifted his pack and George Cothran grabbed it from behind to help Bill slide his arms through. Bill adjusted the straps and wiggled a bit to get the pack into the center of his back. He picked his helmet up from his bunk and set it on his head. He adjusted the strap so he could secure it on the front of his chin, just below his lip. The helmet stayed secure in this fashion and he could pull it completely under his chin when he needed to run. The last piece of equipment to strap on would be his M1 Garand. He extended the sling a bit to allow some slack and slipped it over his right shoulder. The entire bunk area clicked, snapped and clunked with the sounds of Marines gearing up. Outside of the Zeilin's hull, the whining of the cables and hoists could be heard as Higgins Boats were being lowered for the first wave to load. The Higgins Boats would deliver the invaders to a rendezvous area where they would meet the LVTs for the ride into the beach. The first three waves would ride the LVTs, while the fourth and later waves would take the Higgins Boats all the way into the beach. Lieutenant Simonson asked if everyone was ready and each man affirmed his readiness. Sergeant Gabel looked at his watch. It was nearly 0400 and time for the team to get up to the deck. Lieutenant Simonson told Sergeant Gabel to take roll call. Gabel called the names from memory. "Bennett, Ellis, Kinley, Cothran, Webb, Scott, Coate, Potorola, Fortenberry, Cullem, Hellman." Each Marine answered with their typical roll reply of, "YO!" Gabel looked at Bill and asked if he would say a prayer. Bill bowed his head and asked the Heavenly Father for protection and strength in the face of the enemy and he asked that each man would be granted the strength to do his job, and then he said, "Amen." It sounded as though the twelve others all chimed in on the "Amen." Simonson told them it was time to go and turned to move down the dimly-lit corridors to the ladders topside. It took nearly 30 minutes to get from the bunk area up to the deck. As Bill was still 10 feet below the deck, he could feel the cool air pouring down the hatch and everyone groaned with relief from the sweltering heat and stench of sweating bodies. The steak and eggs breakfast had also begun to contribute smells that made the confined spaces all the more unpleasant.

 A little past 0430 hours, the team emerged onto the deck of the Zeilin and stepped into a hive of activity. Combat teams from the second wave were now going over the sides and down the nets. A bright half-moon moved in and out of scattered clouds and provided just enough light to find one's way across the crowded deck. Simonson led the team to a holding area and then dismissed Bill to find his way back to retrieve his demolition kit from the lock-up. As Bill moved through the Marines on deck he could feel the cool breeze hitting his sweat soaked utilities and it felt strange to almost shiver. Arriving at the demolition locker, he had to wait behind a few other demo guys and then a sergeant asked him which bags were his. The sergeant handed Bill both of his bags and told Bill to open them and check them now before he found out something was missing on the beach. Bill went through his gear and acknowledged that it was all there. He pulled the cigarette case and the Zippo out of his pants pocket and pushed them into one of the large pouches on the front of the demolition belt and snapped it shut. As Bill was fastening the large demolition belt around his chest, there arose a commotion on deck that forced Bill to look toward the bow of the Zeilin. Several miles distant, a large red flare spiraled into the sky above Tarawa. The entire fleet now knew for sure that the Japanese were aware of their presence. The flare was an alarm to the 5000 Japanese preparing to defend their island.

Bill pressed his way back to his team in the holding area and Gabel asked him if he found his "firecrackers" okay. The pent-up energy on deck was palpable. At 0505 hours, a huge, flaming explosion shattered the darkness as one of the fleet's battleships let loose with a lone 16" shell toward Tarawa. The Marines snapped their heads toward the flash and then watched in awe as a huge glowing ember lofted through the air toward the enemy. About halfway to the island, the enormous "BOOM" rang out across the water. The red ember then dropped out of sight and a distant thud was heard seconds later. The shell had landed in the ocean on the other side of the island. One minute later, there was another flash as the second shell was fired, and it too lofted through the air and fell into the ocean. Within three minutes, another 16" shell was fired and Bill watched again as it arched through the dark sky toward Tarawa. As it neared the horizon, a huge explosion erupted sending a wall of flame over 500-feet into the sky. The Marines and Navy men on deck let out a cheer as though their team had just scored the winning touchdown in the championship game. Other explosions erupted and it looked as though the third shell had found an ammo dump on Tarawa. The battleship had been probing the range for the fleet. One minute later, four 16-inch shells were fired at the same time and they streaked into Tarawa setting off more fires and explosions. Now another battleship joined in and minutes later some heavy cruisers with their eight-inch guns, followed by the six-inch guns of the light cruisers. The concussion of each shell fired could be felt in the Marine's chest and they seemed transfixed by the sight and sound. Within minutes, the ocean around the Zeilin was almost as bright as noon as the fleet poured their deadly shells into enemy positions. Bill and the Pioneer team cheered loudly every time a shell found its mark and erupted in flame. Within 10 minutes, it seemed as if the entire island was on fire.

The Marines that could pay attention to the bombardment thought that every Japanese soldier on Tarawa must have already been killed by what they were seeing. None of them had ever imagined that such a barrage was possible. As the bombardment continued, the eastern horizon began to lighten as sunrise crept closer. At 0545 the call went out across the deck for the landing teams in the fourth wave to assemble above the cargo nets. Simonson yelled for his team to follow him to the loading area. Once in position to load, the Marines were ordered to take four hand grenades from the open crates along the staging area and put them into their pants pockets. They were not to hang on pack straps or belts until they were safely down the nets and into the Higgins Boats. Bill passed on taking the grenades as he was already weighed down with the demolition kit. He would have to rely on the riflemen to carry some of the firepower ashore. Suddenly, the Navy's bombardment stopped. As the sky lightened, they were expecting the carrier planes to attack. The team moved ahead and they were next in line to go over the side at the second net on the starboard side of the Zeilin. Bill looked down the net and watched the last Marines drop into the loaded Higgins Boat below. The boat bobbed up and down on the water and bumped into the sides of the ship as a dozen men tried to hold it close to the Zeilin's sides. Then the coxswain revved the engine and it pulled away as an empty boat churned up the water to take its place below.

Sergeant Gabel turned toward the team and once again shouted the roll call. "Bennett! Ellis! Kinley! Cothran! Webb! Scott! Coate! Potorola! Fortenberry! Cullem! Hellman!" Each Marine again confirmed his presence and Simonson shouted, "Over the rail!" and swung his legs over the net. Bill grabbed the net and swung his right leg over the side and his boot searched for a toe hold. Then the left leg followed and he looked straight at Fred Ellis. As he descended the net, the diesel fumes from the Higgins Boats became quite strong. The net was always a moving target as Marines above and below placed their weight onto the heavy ropes. Looking through his own legs, Bill could see that Lieutenant Simonson was already in the bobbing boat and looking up at him to guide his feet to the safety of the floor. As Bill's boots stretched for the floor, it quickly rose several feet and he landed in a squatting position with Simonson bracing him from behind. Since Bill had the extra weight of the demolition bags, Simonson told him to move to the port side of the boat and he would guide the others coming in. Ellis, Cothran and Gabel pressed in near Bill as they all looked up to see the final Marines from the 2nd Battalion nearing the boat. Several of the last Marines wore radio sets on their backs and there was also a machine gun team. About 30 Marines and their combat equipment were now crammed into the craft. The coxswain waved his arms to the attendants looking over the side and the crew pushed off the side of the Zeilin as the diesel engine revved to get under way.

As the Higgins Boat cleared the Zeilin and made a left turn toward the assembly area, large amounts of water began to spray over the front ramp. Bill had to push his way toward the back of the boat to try and keep his charges dry. Everything was supposed to work even though wet, but there was no sense in getting it soaked if it could be avoided. Water dripped from his helmet and his shirt was pretty well soaked already. The breeze and the water combined put a chill into the Marines, and within a half hour most of them were shivering. It seemed odd that hours ago they were trying to sleep in 100-degree heat and now they shivered in the cool, wet morning air. The sunrise was now in full force and the sky looked like a painter's dream. Red, orange and purple rays reached across the sky and melted into shades of green and blue. As Bill looked skyward, five or six Navy planes appeared heading for the island. Then several dozen appeared and soon there were hundreds. The Marines watched as planes in groups of three, four, five and six dove down toward the smoking cauldron and dropped bombs or fired their machine guns at the enemy below. The explosions created a constant roar like summer thunder that would not cease. Arriving at the rendezvous area, the Higgins Boat joined others of the fourth wave in the circles of the holding pattern.

From the rendezvous area, they could see the first three waves of LVTs lining up for the nearly two hour push in to the beaches. At 0650, 42 LVTs of

2nd Division Marines descending the cargo nets on their way to Tarawa on November 20th, 1943.

(U.S.M.C. Photo)

the first wave received the signal from the control vessels and headed for the beaches. A few minutes later, 24 LVTs forming the second wave moved out and ten minutes after that, the 21 of the third wave. Bill could see the two white "rooster tails" of water churning up behind the LVTs as all 87 of them moved toward the island. Control vessels gave the fourth wave the go-ahead to move up to the line of departure and at 0730 the Higgins Boats were released to the beaches. Tarawa now lay straight ahead and the noise remained a steady roar even from miles away. As Bill leaned his head out over the gunwales, he could see the first wave churning far up in front of them. As he looked around inside the boat, other Marines nodded their heads positively and a few even smiled as they were glad to finally be underway. Most of them had adopted the attitude of getting the job done just to get it behind them.

56. The Gauntlet

The first wave hit the beaches between 0910 and 0922 and the second and third waves came in 10 to 15 minutes behind them. Bill hoped they had the beaches under control by the time the fourth wave arrived. About 0940, Japanese shells began landing within the ranks of the fourth wave. As Bill looked to the right, the boat two over from theirs received a direct hit and boat parts mixed with body parts flew into the air. Pieces of debris bounced off the side of the Higgins Boat and Simonson yelled out to "Keep your heads down!" There were definitely live Japanese on Tarawa and they were fighting back. An airburst went off directly over their Higgins Boat and hot sand rained down on them. Had the shell been adjusted properly, there should have been deadly shrapnel instead of pulverized, sand-like material. The coxswain again yelled for everyone to keep their heads down and Simonson gave the order to "Load weapons!" Bill opened the first pouch on the right side of his belt and pulled the clip out, pulled the bolt of his M1 back and pushed the clip down with his right thumb. He let the bolt snap forward and then pushed the safety back toward the trigger. He pulled the second clip out and pushed it over his shirt above the top button. It would be ready in a hurry if he needed it. More artillery bursts were exploding near their Higgins Boat and several pieces of shrapnel blasted through the front ramp without striking anyone. The faces onboard held looks of concern at this point. As they were nearing the end of the 700-yard-long pier, Gabel swung his head over the side near the ramp. He quickly moved back toward the coxswain and Simonson.

"Something is wrong!" he shouted. None of the Higgins Boats were moving over the coral reef. The tide was lower than the Navy had expected and the boats needed three feet of water to clear the reef. Suddenly, their boat slammed into the reef and everyone went forward causing groans from those being crushed up front. The coxswain reversed the engine and tried again, but the reef would not let them move forward. Simonson and another lieutenant went to the front and scanned the reef left and right. Some of the other boats were being blasted out of the water and Marines and parts of Marines were in the water. Within minutes, an LVT driver pulled up alongside and shouted that things were bad on the beach. They need men and ammo right away. He yelled for half of the men in the Higgins Boat to "get in!" Arms reached across and grabbed the LVT as Simonson yelled for the Pioneers to go first. As Bill went over the side, he noticed machine gun fire splashing in the water nearby and it was moving toward the LVT. The driver yelled to "get down!" just as bullets "pinged" off the sides. Poterola and Cothran came in last, followed by a machine gun team and one of the Marines with a radio on his back.

The LVT roared to life and the rooster tails of water shot up from the rear. Just to the right there was a freighter that had been wrecked on the reef and its rusty bow pointed slightly upwards. The driver took a route veering slightly toward the pier on the left. Bill knew that the team needed to get to Red Beach 2, just to the right side of the pier. The LVT stayed about 100 yards to the right of the pier and Bill could see hundreds of Marines in the water trying to find cover beneath or alongside the pier. There were flashes from under the pier and machine gun bullets banged off the left side of the LVT. There were several Japanese hidden under the pier! About 200 yards in from the end of the pier and 500 yards from the beach, the LVT driver turned and shouted, "This is as far as I go! You can make it from here! I need to go back and get the others!" The LVT jerked to a halt and Simonson screamed, "Over the side!" Bill rolled out on the left side and dropped into waist-deep water. His first thought was to hold the demolition bag up with his left hand and the M1 with his right. He looked up as the rest of the team rolled out of the LVT. Someone fell out and went completely underwater, then quickly stood up cursing. Looking to the right, Bill could see hundreds of Marines wading in the waist-deep water toward the beach that was 500 yards away. Machine gun fire raked the lagoon, splashing up water like rain drops on a lake during a thunderstorm. There were dark shapes floating in the water. Bill shouted at the others to get moving. Cannon fire and mortar explosions erupted in front and behind them. Machine gun fire seemed to zero in on them and some of the team went under to try and avoid being hit. As they caught up with other Marines, Bill began to lose track of Simonson and Gabel. Cothran and Ellis were still in view and Bill shouted for them to stay together. Bill ran into something in the water and glanced down. There was a Marine face down in about three feet of water and he had a huge hole through his back. Bill noticed hundreds of dead fish floating in the lagoon that had been killed by the bombardment. Moving a few yards ahead, he watched for the machine gun tracks to approach again as the Japanese gunners swung their weapons from left to right to sweep the approaching Marines. As the splashes came near, he had to decide whether to move side to side or stand still and take the chance that they would miss him. Two nearby Marines had been hit and they flailed in the water. Other Marines converged on the wounded and began to drag them toward the pier. Bill went to another Marine he had seen get hit and pulled his head out of the water, but the Marine had been hit in the abdomen and part of his insides had been ripped out. He must have died instantly. Bill let him go and he rolled face down again.

Bill dug deep and moved his powerful legs with increased intention to get to the beach. Dozens of other Marines were drifting over toward the pier to seek cover, but Bill knew there were enemy guns on that side as well. He decided to move straight in to the beach. Looking back toward the reef, he saw Ellis and Cothran were falling behind. He waved his M1 over his head and motioned for them to follow him. Oddly, the closer he moved to the beach, the less enemy fire he encountered. He constantly bumped into dead fish and had to push his way past dead Marines. He didn't want to look at them, so he just kept his eyes open for machine gun splashes. Several bursts of machine gun fire whined and zipped past like mad hornets. The bullets that passed just over his head snapped like a firecracker. He was used to this from the "live fire" drills in training, but these bullets were meant to kill, not train. His knees splashed up water and some of if got into his mouth. The stale, salty water reeked of fish and algae and the thought of human blood in it was repulsive. Bill wanted to get to the beach as he knew he didn't want to get hit out here in the water. The thought of being killed was bad enough, but he knew he didn't want to die in the water with the others. Over to the right, there were several LVTs blown apart and burning with charred Marines draped over the sides. More dead Marines lay in the shallow water surrounding the wrecked craft. Now about halfway to the beach, Bill encountered concrete and barbed wire obstacles in the water. He decided to stay to the pier side of these as he recalled Simonson telling him that these obstacles were there to feed targets into machine gun lanes. The bodies of several Marines were snagged on the barbed wire and they bobbed in the water as the others passed by. Bill could now see Red Beach 2 directly in front of him and he reckoned that sector 222 was just to his right. Mortar explosions wracked the beach area and Bill could not see many Marines standing. They all appeared to be huddled behind the coconut log seawall about 20 feet in from the water's edge. Marines were running in a low crouch in either direction along the beach and corpsmen were frantically working on the wounded just about everywhere he looked. Bill looked back and could not see either Ellis or Cothran now. There was no way he could go back to look for them. He was sweating profusely and his legs ached and wanted to rest. Similar to some of those hot August football workouts with Coach Thompson screaming to keep moving, Bill plowed ahead.

With about 200 yards to go, the machine gun fire had completely disappeared, as the elevation of the island kept the guns from shooting into the water near the beach. The first three waves had knocked out most of the machine guns along the shore. The Japanese machine guns that were still active 20 to 30 yards in from the beach were occupied as the Marines attacked their bunkers.

Bill had caught up to a group of slower moving Marines and one group moved like they were on a Boy Scout hike. As Bill passed them, he encouraged them to step it up and get into the beach. Bill then started to pass a group of five Marines and as he did, one Marine turned his head and said, "Bill! Hey Bill!" Startled to hear his name, and from a familiar voice, Bill turned his head to see Truitt Anderson looking out from beneath his helmet. Bill was elated to see Truitt and know that he was still alright. Bill asked him where his unit was and Truitt told Bill that everyone had been scattered by the machine gun fire. Several of the Marines from Truitt's LVT were now submerged beneath the water with machine gun wounds. Nearing the beach, Marines who had waded in along the pier now merged over to their right and Bill ended up in a fairly large group for the last 100 yards. Bill asked Truitt if he wanted to stick together until they found their respective units and Truitt seemed more than happy with the idea.

The water was now knee deep and Bill could take larger strides. About 50 yards from the beach, he went through another group of dead Marines and some of them had been eviscerated. Several Marine officers caught Bill's attention as they were yelling for those wading ashore to stay low as they came in to the beach. All of the wading Marines that were lugging ammo and other equipment struggled on depleted legs to keep a low profile as they came onto the beach. Bill's legs burned as he finished the last few yards and dropped to his knees on the sand a few steps from the water's edge. Truitt plopped down next to him and they looked at each other quite wide-eyed as they surveyed the surreal scenery on Red Beach 2. Bill gulped air for about a minute before he could even talk to ask a question. The noise was deafening as machine gun, artillery and rifle fire were thick in the air. As Bill raised his helmet to look inland, two Navy fighters dropped bombs on what must have been the other side of the island. When they exploded, he could feel the sand shake beneath him. He looked at one of the officers directing traffic next to him and shouted that he was, "Looking for Company F, 2/2. Where is Colonel Amey?" The officer replied that Amey and Doc Welte were both, "dead in the water" and pointed to the bodies that Bill and Truitt had just passed about 50 yards out. "You just came around them!" He then advised Bill to get up nearer the seawall and dig in to stay alive. Bill asked if he knew where Company F was. The officer shouted back that he didn't know. Everyone was all mixed up. Bill shook his head and headed toward the wall. There was no spot to dig a fox hole. There were dead and wounded Marines so close together that he had to step on some of them in order to move. According to Bill's recall of the map, he was now in sector 220 and he needed to move to his right to find sector 222 and Company F.

As he crawled through Marines while asking for Company F, one Marine told him Captain "Lefty" Morris had been wounded but he thought there were some Company F guys up ahead. Bill kept an eye out for Cothran and Ellis but did not see them anywhere. Marines laying low in the sand with their helmets on tend to all look the same. Bill crawled past a wounded Marine where two corpsmen were working to stop his bleeding. The corpsmen had blood up to their elbows and they paused in their work to cover the wounded Marine with their bodies as sand and debris rained down from a mortar explosion. As Bill crawled along, Truitt stayed right behind him. Bill asked again about Company F and a Marine shouted back and pointed to a group huddled up against the four-foot-high log wall about 20 yards ahead. As Bill approached, a lieutenant, who had bloody gauze wrapped around his upper arm, saw him and yelled out that he needed demolition men. Bill crawled over to him and the lieutenant eyed his gear. He asked if he had TNT and Bill nodded his head. The lieutenant put his helmet right up against Bills and yelled into his ear. He said they needed to get off this beach and there were pillboxes about 20 yards inland that needed to be blasted. He pointed to a flame gunner and said he had everything scouted out. He told Bill there were rifle pits just over the wall that had already been taken out. They could go over the wall into one of the pits and then they could see the pillboxes from there. Bill noticed an opening, or "embrasure" in the wall where a Japanese machine gun had welcomed the first wave. There were four dead Marines lying on the sand in front of the opening. They must have died trying to silence that gun. The lieutenant told Bill he needed him to follow, stay behind and get the charges ready to hand to him once at the target. Bill nodded his head, opened one of his demo pouches and pulled out a Lucky Strike. He put the cigarette to his lips as he stripped off his bulky equipment. He kept his M1, demo belt, cartridge belt and one canteen. He set the rest of his gear against the wall and asked Truitt to keep an eye on it and not go anywhere so he could find him when he got back. Truitt nodded his head affirmatively. Bill lit the cigarette with the Zippo and noticed that his hands shook like an old man. He puffed the cigarette to life and stuffed the pack and the lighter back into the pouch. He opened the other pouch where he had one of his charges stored and showed them to the lieutenant. He shouted to the lieutenant that these were "six second fuses." The lieutenant smiled and shouted, "Perfect!" The lieutenant had six other Marines ready to go, one being the Engineer with the flame gun. For cover to clear the wall, four Marines pulled pins on grenades and waited for the lieutenant to give the signal. They then threw all four grenades over the wall to try and get them in front of the pillbox. As soon as they exploded they all went over the wall and into the rifle pits. As Bill rolled into the pit, he came face to face with two Japanese soldiers that had died from a grenade. They were splattered against the wall of the pit and the floor was soaked with their remains. At the other end of the pit, there was the body of a Marine that had probably been killed by his own grenade, or he may have been entering the pit when another Marine threw the grenade. As the dust was clearing, the lieutenant showed Bill the route they would take to the pillbox. The riflemen would give covering fire on the pillbox while they crawled to the end of a neutralized bunker to gain cover from a rubble pile. Then the riflemen would lob two grenades at the opening which would cover their crawl to the side of the pillbox, just out of sight of the Japanese gunners. The "pillbox" was barely visible to Bill. It appeared to be nothing more than a mound of sand about three feet high with a shoe box-sized hole at ground level. Bill set his M1 aside and left the reserve demo bag and his ammo belt in the pit.

Two Marines readied grenades and chucked them in front of the pillbox. When they exploded, Bill followed the lieutenant to the cover of the first bunker. The bright white sand had been pulverized by the shelling and the top layer was about the consistency of baby powder or Portland cement. It stuck to the sweaty skin and soaked uniform and made a paste-like substance. The dust was in his eyes and in his nostrils and he could taste it in his mouth. Bill felt his heart pounding again as he watched the lieutenant signaling back to the riflemen. Smoke and dust floated through the air and it was difficult to see more than twenty or thirty yards. There were piles of rubble and parts of palm trees everywhere he looked. The island appeared to be a smoking junkyard, but a junkyard would have been much more organized. The lieutenant looked at Bill and said that after the charge detonated, he needed to get right back to the rifle pit because the "Zippo" was going to "light it up." Bill recognized this slang for the flame gunner's part of the assault. The lieutenant said he was going to crawl over to the pile of rubble on the left side of the pillbox under covering fire. Then the riflemen would lob grenades at the opening; as soon as the grenades went off, they would crawl to the side of the pillbox and feed them the TNT. Bill pulled one of his four-stick charges from his belt and checked the fuse; all looked good. The lieutenant again told Bill to stay right behind him. He asked if Bill was ready just as the pillbox began to spew machine gun fire toward the lagoon and the Marines trying to wade ashore. The lieutenant waved at the riflemen and they lobbed two more grenades. Bill and the lieutenant hugged the sand as the grenade fragments shot overhead. The riflemen fired into the embrasure and the lieutenant shouted, "GO!" Then he crawled through the dust toward the pillbox as Bill stayed on his heels. A bullet struck the sand just to the side of the lieutenant and he looked up at the trees behind them, then back at the pillbox. The white sand above the seawall was far hotter than the sand on the wet beach. The heat felt as though it were burning right through his cotton utilities as the surface must have been well over 120 degrees in the sun. Bill brought the TNT up to his face and the lieutenant shouted, "Fire it up!" Bill pulled the cigarette from his mouth with his left hand and handed the charge to the lieutenant who pointed the fuse back to Bill. Bill set the cigarette to the fuse and it instantly ignited. The lieutenant spun toward the embrasure and with about three inches of fuse left, chucked it through the hole. Bill buried his face into the sand and held onto his helmet as he felt the lieutenant dive on top of him. The ground rocked as the charge went off inside the pillbox. The lieutenant jumped to his knees and pulled Bill by the shirt. "GO! GO! GO!" he shouted, and Bill sprinted through the cloud of dust back to the rifle pit, and jumped in. The lieutenant crashed into the pit alongside Bill and they both tried to get the dust out of their eyes and their mouths. The lieutenant looked at Bill and said, "Good job!" Just as the words came out of his mouth a huge flash erupted in front of them as the flame gunner blasted a stream of flame through the gaping hole in the pillbox.

A Japanese soldier emerged from the back side of the bunker in an attempt to make a run for it. The flame gunner caught him in the withering stream and he seemed to just explode in flames as he flailed onto the ground. The flame gunner cut the flame and wobbled back to the safety of the pit. That machine gun would not be used to kill any more Marines.

Bill followed the lieutenant back over the seawall and they caught their breath for a minute. Bill told him that he was part of the Pioneer team and pointed over to Truitt. The lieutenant seemed even more pleased. He said he would be moving men of Company F through this path toward the airfield just ahead. He would need Bill to "Pioneer" them as they advanced so he should try and get some other guys to help him. Bill said he would find some men for the job and he left his charges with the lieutenant, who would be going back to more enemy bunkers. Bill put the rest of his gear back on and washed his mouth and eyes out with water from his canteen, then took a quick drink. He left his pack against the seawall to mark the spot. As Bill and Truitt made their way back down the beach toward where they had come ashore, they heard someone shout, "Bennett!" up ahead.

Bill looked up and saw Ellis and Cothran waving for him to come over to them. Bill was glad to see them both alive and told them so. To top that off, they had run into Bob Swigert and he came crawling over to them. Bill told them he had found Company F and they were needed to help get the assault off the beach. The five of them crawled back toward sector 222 to find the lieutenant. Bill asked Truitt if he had heard where E/2/2, was and Truitt said that he had no idea. It was all such a mess and he had not been able to find any officers from Company E. Bill told Truitt and Bob that they were pushing inland with Company F just up ahead and Truitt instantly said that he would come with Bill. Swigert smiled and nodded his head, and all five Marines from Company D crawled back toward the lieutenant.

Bill led the group back to where he had left his pack and waited for the lieutenant to return from blasting another bunker. Sniper fire peppered the beach and corpsmen were attending the wounded and trying to set up some form of an aid station. Bill told the Pioneers that if anyone was separated they should meet back at this point. The lieutenant and some of his men rolled back over the seawall and panted for air after their dash back through the sniper fire. Bill got his attention and said that the Pioneers were reporting for duty. The lieutenant pointed at a knocked out LVT down the beach and told Bill and a few others to follow him over to it. Along the side of the LVT, the lieutenant took off his helmet and pulled a battle map from his shirt. He pointed to the position where he had been going over the wall. He said he now had Marines in the pillbox Bill had helped him take out and they had knocked out two more bunkers to the left and the right. He pointed to an area inside a large triangle in the middle of the airfield and said he wanted to move to that position as fast as possible. He told Bill he wanted him to find a spot along the wall where his guys could gather and stack ammunition and water. They needed M1, BAR, carbine and .30-caliber light machine gun ammo, grenades, demolition packs and lots of water. The first dump would be the pillbox they had blown and they would move it up as they progressed.

As Bill looked at the map with the lieutenant, a bullet "zipped" in and hit Bill in the right thigh, halfway between the hip and the knee. He rolled up against the LVT, grabbed his leg and said, "I'm hit!" A corpsman was working on some wounded behind the LVT and was with Bill in seconds. The corpsman put his fingers into the hole in Bills pants to stop the bleeding and then pulled his fingers out with a puzzled look on his face. He tore the hole in the pants open to look inside and then felt again. There was no blood. The corpsman looked at Bill with a huge smile and shouted, "It didn't break the skin! This must be your lucky day!" then returned to the back of the LVT. The lieutenant shook his head and asked Bill if he was alright. Bill massaged the purple welt on his leg and said he was fine. Evidently, the rifle round must have been fired from quite a distance away and was out of effective range. Bill moved back to the seawall with the lieutenant and filled Fred Ellis and the others in on the plan.

They looked a few yards to the west and Fred found a place where there were two good-sized shell craters just beyond the seawall. They could actually push supplies over the wall and into the crater for cover. Then they would have to move over 25 yards of open ground to the blown-out pillbox. At the

Marines collect ammunition and supplies from the bodies of the dead in the early hours of the battle for Tarawa.

(U.S.M.C. Photo)

Betio Island, Tarawa Atoll, November 20th, 1943; Red Beach 2 looking east in the approximate location where Bill Bennett operated the small ammo dump along with Ellis, Swigert, Anderson and the others. The 700-yard long main pier is to the left while Navy Hellcats overfly the beach on bombing runs.

(U.S.M.C. Photo)

base of the seawall, about 10 feet in front of the logs, Bob Swigert and Truitt Anderson went to work marking out a 10 by 10 square-foot area and digging in with their shovels. They piled the sand around the perimeter to use as cover for themselves and the ammo they would put into the hole. Bill decided to put George Cothran over the wall and into the shell hole to make sure no Japanese could approach unseen, or that other Marines moved in with other plans. The first order of business was to gather material that Company F was going to need. Fred and Bill went to work retrieving ammo and water from the dead on the beach and depositing it in the dump they were digging. Some of the dead Marines had .30-caliber machine gun belts draped around their head and shoulders. Others were BAR men with ammo belts around their waists and almost every dead or wounded Marine still had grenades in their pockets or clipped onto their gear somewhere. Just as valuable as the ammunition were the two canteens of water that each dead Marine had brought ashore. Within 20 minutes, they had collected quite a pile of supplies.

Just a few yards away, the lieutenant had assembled remnants of Company F that had already taken about 50% casualties and had every officer wounded. Some of the officers had to be evacuated by LVT while several were still in the battle with wounds wrapped in bandages. They really did not want to leave their boys. Bill brought them several demolition bags he had found and handed them to the lieutenant. He looked at the officer and yelled, "Remember. Six seconds!" Groups of six to eight Marines crawled over the wall and into the rifle pits, and then moved out to pre-planned locations to the left and the right. All in all, Bill thought there must have been about 70 Marines going over the wall. Bill and Fred, who were both corporals, thought it would be best if Truitt and Bob Swigert kept scouring the beach for equipment and ammo. They were to keep an eye out for any LVTs that might be landing more ammo. They would need to get to the ammo and speak up for Company F. Bill told them about the stray bullet and reminded them to find cover if possible as there were snipers killing Marines up and down the beach. Before the lieutenant went over the wall, he ran over to Bill and pointed down the beach to-

"Going over the wall" at Red Beach 2 on November 20th, 1943 just about noon. PFC Charles Wysocki, Jr. from Milwaukee, Wisconsin, a member of D/2/18, is against the wall left of center looking at the camera. Anyone that went over the wall had a matter of seconds to live without finding cover. Bill Bennett and his Pioneer team were bringing supplies over this wall in support of F/2/2 as they advanced across the island. (U.S.M.C. Photo)

ward the pier. "Colonel Shoup is ashore now and he has set up his command post right down there and about 15 yards beyond the wall. He has given us orders to get to the other side of the island to cut it in two, so keep the stuff coming. We will supply ourselves out of the pillbox until we can move you up with us later. Got it?" Bill answered "Yes sir!" as the lieutenant ran back, checked his carbine and went over the wall.

57. The Whisper

Privately, Bill was concerned about Truitt and he thought about his new wife Molly back in New Zealand. He wished that he could put him on an LVT and get him out of there, but Truitt was a Marine and he wanted to do his job as much as Bill did. Bill and Fred went to work heaving boxes of ammo over the wall and into the soft sand of the crater. Bill had stashed most of his equipment, but kept his M1 cartridge belt and the canteens. He held his breath, and rolled over the wall into the crater. The ground around the craters had become treacherous, as tree roots had been blasted out of the ground and were now exposed. This made for some difficult running. Cothran told him he had taken some fire from snipers that were probably in the palm trees a few hundred yards toward the airfield. Bill lifted a case of hand grenades and told Cothran to watch the trees. He climbed out of the crater and ran for the pillbox. The embrasure that the lieutenant had thrown the TNT through had been widened by other Marines so that it could be used as a door. Bill pushed the grenades in first, and then he crawled through. The room was three to four times larger than Bill had expected it to be and it smelled of charred flesh. There were the remains of two Japanese soldiers that had literally been blown to pieces and then charred by the flame gunner. On the left side of the room was a Japanese light machine gun that had been bent into a u-shape by the blast.

Bill's inspection was interrupted by a case of .30-caliber ammo bouncing into the pillbox followed by Fred Ellis. The bunker was made from huge logs like those of the seawall and they were covered by several feet of sand on the outside. At the back door, the log structure was evident. Nothing but a direct hit from the Navy could have taken this fortification out. They decided to stack the ammo near that door. Back at the opening toward the beach, Bill waved to get George's attention so that he could watch for snipers on the way back. Bill bolted from the hole, sprinted toward the crater and made a nice baseball slide into it. He grabbed his M1 and turned to help George cover Fred's return. As Fred ran across the open area with his loping Montana cowboy gate, two rifle bullets sprayed up sand just behind his feet before he crashed into the crater. Bill and George had both seen that the rifle fire came from a coconut palm about 100 yards back behind the pillbox. Fred retrieved his M1 and George pointed out the tree; fourth from the right. They all "got a bead" on the center of those palm fronds and on the count of three put nine or ten .30-06 bullets into it. Palm fronds floated to the ground, but nothing else moved. The Japanese were known to tie themselves into the trees.

After several trips back and forth, Bill wanted Fred to have Swigert help him lug boxes to the pillbox while Bill ran up to find the lieutenant and let him know that the dump was full. He told Fred to let Truitt guard the dump on the beach as it would be safer for him. Truitt was a married man now and Bill didn't want him to take unneeded chances. Bill took four canteens of water, put a case of grenades on his shoulder and went out the back door toward the airfield. There was another knocked out pillbox about 15 yards to Bill's left and he headed toward it for cover. As he came to the mound of sand, bullets began slapping the sand as there was machine gun fire coming from the far right. He ran to the far side of the mound and dropped the crate. A voice yelled out, "You gotta watch those machine guns from your right. We're hoping some other guys are working on those for us." Bill looked to his left and there were three Marines looking out from between the remnants of two large blockhouses. Bill asked if they were Company F and they affirmed it. Bill picked up the grenades and the canteens and ran over to them. There were 10 or 12 Marines in that alley, about 10 yards long, and they had a machine gun set up behind a pile of rubble at the other end, where they could overlook the airfield. Bill asked for the lieutenant and they told him that he had been hit again and had to be evacuated. He caught one in the leg and they had to help him back to the beach. A 2nd lieutenant was now in charge and he was in a similar alley on the other end of the building to the left. Bill told a sergeant that he could send guys back for more ammo as it was stacked in the pillbox about 50 yards back. The sergeant yelled for a Private to go back with Bill. Bill left the canteens and the grenades and went back to the opening. He peered through the smoke and then ran for the cover of the sand hill with the Private on his heels. Looking out from behind the sand hill, there was no apparent enemy fire, so Bill pointed out the pillbox to the Private. Bill gave a three count and they headed back toward the pillbox. They attracted no fire this time, but Bill ran around to the other side of the pillbox as the back door was a clear shot for those machine guns. He told the Private to only use the beach side to go in and out as the back wasn't safe. He also recommended that he change course a bit while running, to keep the snipers guessing.

The afternoon sun was now in full force and it was over 100 degrees. Bill took a minute in the pillbox to take a few swallows from his canteen and he asked the private where he was from. He was from Texas and Bill thought he must be tougher than he looked. All of the kids he knew from Texas were tough. Bill told him that he would cover him with his M1 as he left and that he should follow the path back to the sand hill for cover. The kid wanted to carry two .30-caliber boxes, but Bill talked him into just taking one so that he could run faster. Bill told him that if he carried two and got shot, then he would have to come out there and pick them both up. The kid laughed at Bill's humor and said "Thanks for thinking of me." They went out the blown-out embrasure and Bill took a look around the backside of the structure. He told the Private it was okay and he headed out with the load on his shoulder and his carbine in his right hand. He disappeared through the smoke and Bill turned to see George back in the pit. Bill pointed toward the beach so that George would know he was heading over, then ran right for the wall and jumped down to the beach. Fred and the guys had been busy and had gathered quite a pile of supplies. Bill told them where he had been and thought they should probably start moving some of the ammo from the pillbox to the alley themselves. Bob Swigert took the first shift with Bill and they headed back for the pillbox. George moved his cover to the back door of the pillbox so that Bill and Bob could pause and wait for his signal on each trip. He could also cover them on their return. The Company F Marines from the alley had knocked out two more pillboxes in front of them and advanced another 15 yards. Bob waited as Bill crawled out to the 2nd lieutenant in charge to talk about moving the dump. As he crawled through the sand he came upon two Marines that had just been killed by a machine gun and their blood was already drying in the heat of the sun. One lay face down in the sand with his hands at his sides and the other had died looking up into the sky. His eyes were still open and he had a look of surprise on his face.

    A mortar round landed about 30 feet away and Bill tried to crawl into his helmet as shrapnel and debris flew past. He approached two teams firing their .30-caliber machine guns while two others tossed grenades, then hit the sand for cover. Bill crawled over to them and asked who was in charge. They pointed to a group of Marines behind a pile of debris and one yelled, "Lieutenant Barr is over there!" Bill crawled toward the lieutenant as incoming machine gun and rifle fire zipped above his head. Lieutenant Barr was trying to figure out where some of this fire was coming from, but it was nearly impossible to see. Bill grabbed his sleeve and he turned his head as if surprised. Barr had white coral dust on his face that had mixed with his sweat and caked like mud. He also had dried blood on his face and neck from shrapnel wounds incurred in the LVT on the way in. As he was wading in to the beach after his LVT had been destroyed, he was shot through the shoulder and had dried blood on the front and back of his utility shirt. His shoulder was wrapped with dirty, bloody gauze. Certainly, he could have been evacuated back to a ship but he had refused to leave. Since Captain Morris had been seriously wounded and evacuated, 2nd Lieutenant Barr now led the Company F advance along with Lieutenant Sanford. Every officer in the company had been wounded by this time.

    Bill told Lieutenant Barr that he wanted to move the ammo dump up to the space between the block houses now and Barr nodded his head affirmatively with three emphatic bobs. He told Bill they were going to take an entrenchment a few yards to the right that would lead them up to the taxiway. He wanted to get across that airfield today if there was any way possible. He told Bill to keep the ammo coming and that the guys needed water desperately. Bill said there were Pioneers on the beach trying to acquire water and he would bring it up right away. Bill crawled back to Bob Swigert and they made their way back to the beach. The pillbox would no longer be needed as they began to lug the ammo directly over the seawall and move to the new dump between the demolished bunkers. Truitt told Bill that he wanted to come along on a run. Bill's instinct was to protect the younger guys, especially Truitt. Bill told him to stay on the beach and he could see the frustration in Truitt's eyes. Bill relented and told Truitt to pick up as many canteens as he could carry. Bill led the way with a box of machine gun ammo on each shoulder. Truitt waited at the new dump while Bill carried some canteens as he crawled out to Lieutenant Barr to check on their progress. He passed the bodies of three dead Japanese that had begun to stink terribly after baking in the sun. The smell was sickening and Bill held his breath as he passed. Bill found Lieutenant Barr and told him they were stacking supplies in the new dump and his guys could grab what they needed from there. Bill handed Barr a canteen. He looked like he needed it. Barr said he was moving up to the trench along the taxiway and that would be where they would locate the next ammo dump. Bill nodded his head affirmatively and said, "Yes sir!"

Once over the seawall, U.S. Marines advanced on Japanese strongholds. Pioneer teams advanced along with these units and shared in the front-line fighting.

(U.S.M.C. Photo)

Bill and Truitt made it back to the seawall and they decided that Bill and Fred would work as one team and Truitt and Swigert would work as the other. This way, they could keep the ammo moving with "fresh horses" each trip. Truitt and Bob went on the next run as Bill and Fred kept an eye on the ammo dump. Bill watched as Truitt and Bob disappeared into the smoke. All the smoke and dust made it difficult to see at times, but it also gave them cover from the Japanese machine guns still firing from the left. While Truitt and Bob were gone, three LVTs made their way onto the beach with ammo aboard, so Bill and Fred went to grab what they could. The LVT was a magnet for Japanese fire and they had to take cover behind it as bullets slammed into the sides. Catching a ricochet off armor plating was basically the same as a direct hit in most cases. They were able to get two more crates of hand grenades and several boxes of carbine and M1 ammo. Several mortar rounds fell in that general area of Red 2, but they had been coming in all day. Corpsmen carried wounded men on stretchers and Bill and Fred went back out to the LVT to help lift them over the side. Back at the seawall, Bill and Fred waited anxiously for Truitt and Bob's return. Bill was just about to go look for them when they came running around the rubble pile about 25 yards from the seawall. Bill and Fred smiled as Truitt and Bob came rolling over the coconut logs.

Bob told Bill the boys in Company F were solid in the trench on the west side of the taxiway now and they were sending scouts across to take a look at a low spot on the other side. He also said they took some sniper fire from the block house alley out to the trenches where the next dump was started. They had to crawl and drag the ammo out to the trench. Bill set a crate of grenades and a box of carbine ammo up on the coconut log wall and Fred grabbed some machine gun ammo and a five-gallon can of water. Bill had his M1 slung over his back and Fred had his carbine. Bill asked Fred if he was ready, Fred said, "Let's go!" and the pair headed out with their heads as low as possible. It was 1400 hours.

Back at home at 454 Simms Street, it was Friday night, November 19th, at 9 p.m. It had been a long day for Steve and Jessie and they sat in the parlor reading and listening to some soft music on the radio. Whenever news came on the radio, they would pause and Steve would turn up the volume. Al had married Eunice May Hampson earlier in the day at Camp Lee in Petersburg, Virginia. Al wanted to tie the knot before shipping out and had to settle for a service conducted by Army Chaplain Captain Jotham F. Norton at the camp chapel. Al and Eunice had phoned earlier so they could share in the moment, if only by long distance. Steve and Jessie knew where Al was, but they had no idea as to Bill's whereabouts. According to George Garcia's letters from last summer, Bill was in New Zealand and that was the last they had heard. Even though they had received letters from Bill since then, the letters could not contain his location.

Steve had just finished a long week at Schmitz and Gretencort, and they were both getting tired. Before Jessie went upstairs, she closed her book and took some time in prayer. As was her custom, she prayed for all the Aurora boys that she knew were in harm's way and then for her two boys. How she longed to have them both home again and her heart ached. She sensed that Bill was particularly at risk since his job was to face the Japanese in combat. The family had tried to conceal the news of Marine battles in the Pacific, but she read the paper and listened to the radio during the day herself. She would get numerous phone calls during the week from friends who had heard that the Marines had fought at one place or another and asked when they had last heard from Bill. She knew what the deal was and she knew Bill. She knew that if he was near a fight he would want to be in it.

Bill and Fred were both starting to feel deep fatigue as they dropped their loads behind the sand hill and caught their breath for the run over to the alley. As they lay on their backs, four Grumman Wildcat fighters roared over the north side of the island as their machine guns emptied into the Japanese emplacements below. Barely audible above the roar of the ground battle, the Wildcat's guns sounded like grease popping in a frying pan. The planes pulled up and banked north, out over the sea. At the very least, the Marines had air cover whereas the Japanese had nothing going in their favor. Inside the alley, there were six more Marines that were coming up to find Lieutenant Barr. Bill looked out the front of the alley from behind the rubble pile and he could see a dozen or so Marines advancing across the taxiway far to the left. These must have been elements of 2/8 that had landed at Red Beach 3. It was good to see that others were also pushing across the island. Other than what they could see in front of them, most Marines had no idea what the big picture was looking like. Bill put his left elbow into the sand and grabbed the metal ring handle on the ammo case with his right hand and started to crawl out to the trench. The sand was burning hot in the sun and the heat had to be 120 to 130 degrees on the ground. Bullets hissed overhead and they seemed to come from all directions. If Bill would have lifted his hand up, it would probably have been shot off. He looked back and Fred was crawling behind him with the canteens. Another Marine was behind Fred with the case of grenades. One by one, all three slithered into the trench. Bill went to the north end of the trench to find Lieutenant Barr and there were half a dozen dead Japanese up on the edge of the trench. Bill assumed that these were the previous occupants. Lieutenant Barr told Bill they were going to make a run for the other side but this trench would remain the primary dump until he heard otherwise. The machine gunners would cover the riflemen on their way across the open taxiway, then once across the riflemen would return the favor for the machine gunners. The supplies had kept Company F going; the Pioneers just needed to keep it coming. Barr was probably the dirtiest, sweatiest, bloodiest Marine that Bill had ever seen. Bill patted the lieutenant on his good shoulder and said, "You're okay lieutenant, God be with you!" and went back to Fred.

These Marines are advancing to the airfield on Tarawa just as Lieutenant Barr and F/2/2 did during the early part of the battle. The midday sun baked the weary Marines in 105° F. heat.

(U.S.M.C. Photo)

Bill thanked the Marine who had brought the grenades over as he and Fred crawled out of the trench and back toward the alley. As they ran for the cover of the sand hill, they once again drew machine gun fire and they had to dive to the ground. The smoke had cleared and Bill could see two hundred yards to the west, and apparently the Japanese could see 200 yards to the east. Bill told Fred he would go first and draw fire, and that he should wait about five seconds and then follow him. Bill took off with as much of a sprint as he had left in him, and he rounded the corner of the blockhouse. As he was about even with the pillbox, he saw Truitt and Bob smiling and waving him on as they knelt next to the ammo dump. Suddenly, in the midst of the great cacophony of war, Bill heard a soft voice whisper his name, "Bill!" Although it was a whisper, the voice was louder in Bill's ears than the battle around him. Startled, Bill turned to look behind him thinking that it might be Fred.

Fred was not yet in sight. As Bill's head was turned and looking back, his foot caught on strands of palm root that had been blasted out of the ground. He tripped over the roots and went head first, on his back, into one of the shell craters just above the seawall. He barely managed to keep a grip on his M1 with his right hand as he plunged. As he impacted the bottom of the crater, a huge explosion rocked the ground and the concussion sucked the air out of his lungs. Smoke and fire billowed over the crater and debris began to rain down. Bill's gut ached as he tried to start breathing again and then he was suddenly horrified. Where were his men? Bill crawled up the crater side to the coconut logs and looked through the smoke. Where the ammo dump had been, there was now a smoking crater. He rolled over the wall and crawled toward the dump. He saw a dark mass on the right side and stood to run to it. It was Bob. He was obviously dead, and his shredded uniform had white smoke coming off it. Bill turned to look for Truitt. He found him on the other side of the crater and he was sitting up with his feet out in front of him and his head and helmet were looking down at the ground. Bill raised his head and yelled, "Andy! Andy!" Truitt's eyes were wide open and his skin was grayish in color. His uniform and his helmet cover were smoking, but not on fire. Bill grabbed Truitt's face and tried to get him to snap out of it. Bill was terrified, exhausted and partially in shock. As he looked around, he started screaming, "Corpsman!!" At that time, a corpsman happened to be working his way down the seawall, and Bill caught his attention. As the corpsman came closer, he saw the situation and yelled back to Bill, "He's dead!" Bill told the corpsman that Truitt was still alive and wanted his help. The corpsman, exhausted, snapped profanity back at Bill and said that he had other Marines to help. Uncharacteristic of Bill, he snapped with rage at the disrespectful attitude of the corpsman. He charged the smaller corpsman, grabbed him by the collar with his left hand and stuck the barrel of his M1 in his face with his right hand. Bill then dragged the wide-eyed medic through the sand and dropped him at Truitt's feet and ordered him to "Check him out!" The corpsman felt Truitt for a pulse, and then looked into his eyes. He laid him on his back and felt his chest. The corpsman looked up at Bill and said, "Sorry, sir, but he's dead!" Bill did not answer the corpsman and just dropped to his knees beside Truitt. The corpsman was more than happy to put some space between him and Bill, and ran off down the seawall. Bill closed Truitt's eyes and pulled his helmet over his face.

As Bill tried to think, he remembered what Helen Taylor had told him about her dream before they left New Zealand; she said that she had seen Truitt hurt in her dream, but Bill was unharmed. Then Bill thought about that sweet girl Molly and how happy Truitt was to have found her and married her. Of all the boys on this beach, why did it have to be Truitt? Then Bill looked over to Bob Swigert's body and he thought about his mother in Oelrichs, South Dakota. The three of them had been together for such a long time, and they were like brothers. Bill looked at the seawall, and suddenly Fred came back to his mind. He had been right behind Bill when he heard … that voice. Suddenly, Bill was chilled to the bone although his body was overheated. How did he hear that voice? It was all more than he could take in at the moment and he headed back to the seawall. As he looked over, he saw Fred limping toward him. Fred said, "I'm hit!" and Bill helped him down from the wall. Fred said that when the explosion went off, he just happened to be running past a coconut stump and the stump screened him from most of the shrapnel. He had caught some in his left leg and the left side of his back. He pulled up his shirt and there were several bullet sized holes in him. Then Fred saw the crater and the bodies and he said, "Oh no, no, no! Not Swig and the kid!" Fred started to cry as he went over to Swigert and touched his body. He asked Bill what he thought happened and judging from the crater and the blast, it had to have been a mortar round that dropped straight down. The mortar hit their ammo pile and neither one of them had a chance. Truitt had been killed by the concussion. There were no visible wounds on his body; it was just the force of the blast of air that killed him instantly. Another corpsman came along and patched Fred up. He recommended that Fred evacuate, but Fred was not having any of it. He said he would be fine and they could pull the metal out of him later. As hard as it was to focus, the two corporals knew they still had work to do. The battle was raging and it looked like they might lose. For Bob Swigert and Truitt Anderson, the war was over. If the Japanese mortar men had delayed dropping that round by a few seconds, it would have been Bill and Fred there on the ground as well.

Area of Red Beach 2 from which Corporal Bill Bennett's Pioneer Team operated on November 20th, 1943 at Tarawa. As the battle has moved inland, a high tide has washed Marine bodies to the coconut log seawall.

(Official U.S.M.C. Photo)

58. Hell on Earth

One eight-pound mortar round, a few clicks of adjustment by a Japanese mortar man and timing that would always be beyond explanation; there was no place to even begin to sort out an event like this. With Fred wounded and Truitt and Bob dead, Bill had to get back to Lieutenant Barr and let him know what happened. One more trip ensued through the smoke, debris and enemy fire. By the time Bill reached the lieutenant's last location, he had gone across the taxiway into the wide-open ditch within the triangle between the taxiways and the runway. Six Marines were still holding the trench position with two .30-caliber machine guns and a stack of ammo and grenades. They pointed out Lieutenant Barr's location. Bill waited for covering fire and raced across the open taxiway and slid into the ditch on the other side. He found Lieutenant Barr and told him the dump had been lost and he currently had nothing to supply from this point on. He told him that he had just lost two good friends. Barr said he was sorry, but it looked like everyone in the 2nd Division was losing friends today. He said they had better kill these bastards as fast as they can and get off this damned island. Bill said he would see what he could do to get more supplies but they should not count on anything. Barr asked for volunteers to go back with Bill and finally came up with two. Bill and the volunteers sprinted across the taxiway and made their way back to the beach.

Once at the beach, Bill checked on Fred and encouraged him to take the evacuation and get out while he still had the chance. Fred promised Bill he would go if he couldn't stand the pain or thought he couldn't do his job. Bill, Fred and George moved Truitt's body next to Bob Swigert's and they would keep an eye out for stretcher bearers who could take them both to the collecting point near Colonel Shoup's command post. Bill set a hand on Truitt's arm and bowed his head to recite the 23rd Psalm from memory:

> The Lord is my Shepherd, I shall not want. He maketh me to lie down in green pastures: He leadeth me beside the still waters. He restoreth my soul: he leadeth me in the paths of righteousness for his name's sake. Yea, though I walk through the valley of the shadow of death, I will fear no evil: for thou art with me; thy rod and thy staff they comfort me. Thou preparest a table before me in the presence of mine enemies: thou anointest my head with oil; my cup runneth over. Surely goodness and mercy shall follow me all the days of my life: and I will dwell in the house of the Lord for ever.

Bill prayed like he had never prayed before. He had seen death many times before, but never in such a personal way. His eyes filled with tears as he thought about how close he had come to death. He asked the Lord a difficult question, "Why did you take them and allow me to live?" The reality of Truitt and Bob being with the Lord now, while they had been here only minutes before, was mind numbing for Bill. He had never been so aware of his own frailties. The sounds of battle were still deafening in Bill's ears. He lifted his head and looked east along Red Beach 2 toward the pier. The beach was littered with dead Marines and rows of wounded waiting for an LVT or a boat to take them to safety. Lieutenant Barr was right. There was only one thing to do; win this battle and get off this island. Bill set out with Fred and George to gather more supplies and find a way to get them up to the Marines still fighting their way across the island.

More Marines had come ashore at Red Beach 2 so Bill, Fred and George teamed up with others trying to retrieve and consolidate equipment and supplies. Lieutenant Colonel Irvine Jordan had come ashore as an observer but had been forced to take command when Colonel Amey was killed before reaching the beach. Colonel Shoup was putting together functional teams from the scattered Marines on the beach. Father Kelly had made it ashore and was beginning to organize burial of the dead Marines. Some of the Marines killed in the first waves had been lying in the sun the entire day and the smell of death was becoming overpowering. These early burials were being done in an area near Colonel Shoup's command post. Stretcher bearers were carrying dead and wounded in both directions on the beach and many of them became casualties themselves. Standing upright while carrying a load on Tarawa was a very dangerous business.

Navy planes continued to blast the Japanese positions and the island shuddered frequently. The vibrating ground caused sand to get into Bill's boondockers and he had to remove them to empty the contents many times. As the sun started to lower in the western sky, the task of digging into defensive positions became the primary concern. Just a few yards from the destroyed ammo dump, they began staging a new dump and dug deep fox holes for those guarding it, just in case it would be hit by another mortar round. Stretcher bearers arrived and Bill and Fred assisted with setting the bodies of Bob and Truitt onto the stretchers. Bill followed them down the beach toward the command post and watched as they laid them in a row of gathered dead alongside one of the bunkers. As Bill watched the stretcher bearers remove the bodies, he heard a familiar voice shout, "Bennett!" Bill turned to see Lieutenant Art Simonson running over to him. Simonson and most of the others had crossed under the pier to avoid machine gun fire on the way in and ended up on Red Beach 3 with 2/8 and Major Crowe. They had worked their way back over to Red 2 during the day and were looking for F/2/2. Bill explained that he had found F/2/2 and supplied them all day until the dump was blown and Swigert and Anderson were killed. He pointed to their bodies. Simonson cringed at the news and told Bill how sorry he was to hear it. He commented that those were two of the nicest fellas in the outfit, and Simonson painfully recalled Truitt's wedding just a month ago.

Simonson retrieved Gabel, Poterola, Fortenberry and the others and Bill led them to Cothran and Ellis at the new dump. Simonson reorganized the team by having some of them acquiring and stacking ammo and then setting up a defensive perimeter for the night. Shoup had ordered that all units set up as strong a defense as possible and hold their fire for the night. Knives and bayonets would be their weapons in the darkness as he wanted no positions revealed due to muzzle flashes. There was no doubt that Japanese Commander Shibasaki would organize a strong wave of counter attacks before dawn and it would not take much to overrun the 50 to 70 foot wide defenses along the beach. Besides the penetration by F/2/2 and three or four similar advances, the Marines clung to a surprisingly small beachhead for the night. Bill gave Gabel and Simonson a quick tour of the craters, pillbox and subsequent path they had used to supply Lieutenant Barr, who was likewise digging in for a hair-raising night out on the airfield. Concentrations of enemy fire continued to come from the right side where other Marine units were facing heavy resistance in an area that would later be known as "The Pocket."

Since Bill and George were uninjured and knew the area, Simonson had them dig in near the corner of a bunker about 20 yards out from the seawall.

Fred was able to stay on the beach due to his wounds, but he had already come to realize that being on the beach did not equate to safety. Hellman, Collum, Fortenberry and Poterola were positioned in the craters and Coate, Webb and Kinley were set up behind the seawall at various points. Bill found a pile of BARs stacked on the beach and grabbed one along with several BAR belts containing 20-round magazines. He carried the BAR along with his M1 and other gear out to the corner of the bunker where he had a view of the open area looking across to "The Pocket." When the counter attack came, it would more than likely be from that direction. He pulled the shovel from the sheath on his pack and went to work "digging in." George came up to the position carrying a crate of grenades. The two dug a foxhole more than wide enough for both of them and their gear and piled the sand to the front to create more cover. They buried concrete chunks inside of their sand pile to stop the larger 13mm Japanese machine gun rounds from punching through. Bill loaded the BAR and leaned it against the front of the pit and set the ammo within grasp behind him. He and George set the crate of grenades between them within easy grasp, if needed. The position was heavily armed and if the Japanese were able to advance at all, they would pay the price for coming across at this point. Up and down Red Beaches 1, 2 and 3, Marines dug in and readied themselves for what looked to be a long night.

At all the positions, the orders were for one to sleep while one kept watch and to keep fresh eyes at the machine guns. As complete darkness engulfed the island, the American firing ceased. One thing the Marines had proven to be very good at was controlling their fire. They did not tend to waste ammo or give away their positions unless necessary. George took the first shift and Bill lay on his back up against the sloped front end of the foxhole. He set one of the BAR belts behind his head and pulled his helmet down over his eyes. There was a smell of leather and sweat inside the helmet that was reminiscent of his football helmets, and somehow Bill felt at home with it. Being inside his helmet was the only privacy he could get. He was so exhausted that his body was shaking. He was spent both physically and mentally, and just wanted to sleep. Bill took the chance to collect his thoughts and open his heart in prayer. He thanked the Lord for getting him through the day and he poured his heart out over the death of Truitt Anderson and Bob Swigert. He realized that Truitt would not be coming home to Aurora with him after the war, and he cringed when he thought about what would happen to Molly when she received word of his death. He knew that the Swigerts, in their little town in South Dakota, would be devastated to learn that Bob would not be coming home. Nor would he buy land or have a wife and family. He was overwhelmed when he thought about the hundreds of families that those dead Marines all represented and the heartache that would ensue when letters began to be delivered to homes across the nation. He asked God for the safety of those left fighting and for victory over the enemy. Even now, Bill felt no hatred for the Japanese. He just wished they would surrender when there was no way for them to win. He knew Marines would fight to the death if they had to. Bill asked for the Lord's Spirit to be with his brother Al, wherever he was, and also with Bob, Harley and Dexter Stoner. He summed up his prayer by acknowledging that all of this was somehow in the Lord's plan and that Bill's role was, as always, to trust the Lord. He finished by asking God to take care of his mom and dad and Helen and her parents out in Sandwich. Somehow, Bill fell asleep inside his helmet as red flares from mortars illuminated the sky and effeminate-looking pink tracers from Japanese machine guns tempted the Marines to return fire.

Bill was jarred from his dreams by the whine of an air raid siren as several Japanese planes swooped in to bomb the Marine invaders. It took him several seconds to mentally grasp where he was as the memories of the previous day painfully erased his dream. The tension of the approaching planes proved to be the worst part as their bombs fell wide of American positions and either hit the Japanese on the other side or fell into the ocean. Bill swung himself around and told George he would take over, just like two motorists driving straight through the night. Bill crawled out of the hole and then along the back of the bunker to relieve himself, and then took two gulps of water from his last canteen. George said he had not seen anything and told Bill to wake him up when the pancakes were ready. George was soon asleep and Bill stared out across the debris of Tarawa as the flares continued their eerie light show. For the rest of the night, Bill waited for the counterattack or one of the now famous Banzai charges, but they never came. Bill mused that perhaps the Japanese had decided to win the battle by "out sleeping" the Marines and there would be hell to pay in the morning.

November 21st, 1943. At dawn's early light, Bill opened a can of K-ration from his pack and enjoyed some curious beef substance, a few crackers and some lemon drop candies. This was the first food he had eaten in almost 30 hours. After George came to his senses and prepared to defend the position, Bill made his way over the seawall to talk to Simonson. Fred was very sore from his wounds, but they seemed to be all relatively superficial, as he was doing quite well. The tide had come in during the night and swamped most of the beach, so everyone ended up either wet, up against the seawall, or both. Bill was learning that there always seemed to be a new level of misery. The Navy and the Marines had been bringing in supplies at the pier head during the night and were continuing now during the early light. Simonson was conferring with other officers regarding tactics and support for the coming day. It was decided that the Pioneer team would remain in support of F/2/2 and move supplies in toward the airfield. Company F would be crossing the main runway to establish a position on the south side of the island in an attempt to cut the island in two. E/2/2 would be crossing over farther to the west and E/2/8 farther to the east.

As soon as there was enough light to make out targets again, firing began in earnest from both sides. Some of the bunkers and pillboxes that had been blown the previous day were once again populated by living Japanese and some had to be blown out and burned again. Bill and the Pioneer group took the arduous task of lugging ammo and water forward and trying to stay alive during the process. At 0630, a wave of Higgins Boats attempted to land companies from 1/8 to reinforce Marines on Red Beach 2. The apogean neap tide was actually lower than the previous day and the boats again snagged on the reef.

The Japanese had moved up ammunition and reinforcements in the night and they could not believe the Marines were, once again, coming straight in at Red 2. Shore guns zeroed in on the Higgins Boats and began blasting them into the air. Bill and the Pioneers turned toward the reef in disbelief as 1/8 was being cut to ribbons. The Marines on the reef took to the water and began wading toward the beach and the Japanese machine-gunned them mercilessly for the next hour. The Japanese had set up machine guns in the wreck of the freighter Saidu Maru overnight, and had the Marines caught in a triple cross-fire. Steadily, the Marines plodded toward either Red Beach 2 or the pier to find cover. The tide was so low that the coral flats actually began to dry in the sun leaving no cover whatsoever. The carnage was so bad that Marine photographers opted not to use their cameras. As what was left of the Marines from 1/8 neared the beach, Marines from Red 2 ran out into the fire to help them ashore. When it was all over, there were over 300 bodies lying out on the coral flats.

Wounded Marines tried to find cover for hours in most cases. Navy salvage boats appeared near the reef and they exchanged fire with the enemy holed up within the Saidu Maru and risked their own lives pulling wounded Marines out of the water. The crew chief of one of these heroic salvage boats was Lieutenant Eddie Heimberger, known by many as Eddie Albert, who had left a decent acting career in Hollywood to join the Navy after Pearl Harbor. Ironically, before Hollywood Eddie had lived in Aurora with his uncle and worked at Ward and Jones Furniture on Broadway, just a block away from Bennett's Men's Store at the time. Watching these Marines being cut down by the Japanese machine guns infuriated those already in combat and units moved off Red 2 with a vengeance to try and silence the guns that were decimating 1/8. The Pioneers began moving up with these units and the blasting and burning of emplacements and pillboxes sparked hellacious combat that lasted, again, until the sun had set. As elements of 2/2 had now made it across the island, the Pioneers were spread out from the beach to the airfield and some were diverted to duty near the base of the pier as supplies had begun to make it down the pier to the beaches. Some good news arrived as some water barrels came in from the Navy. The bad news was that they had once been filled with gasoline and the water tasted of gas. The Marines drank it anyway, but belched out a gas flavor. They joked about staying clear of the flame gunners so they would not ignite. On the beach, other horrors were delivered to the Marines as supplies came in at a heavy cost. Crates of spent ammunition that had been meant for salvage were accidentally sent ashore along with brooms, mops and other useless items instead of what was needed. It was tragic that some men may have lost their lives attempting to move some of these useless supplies ashore.

The heat and dust seemed worse today than it had yesterday. Bill's hands and the back of his neck were painfully sunburned and his lower lip was cracked and bleeding most of the time. His hands had taken a beating as he had many small cuts and scrapes that had gone unnoticed due to his other more serious problem of staying alive. Every pile of rubble and every palm tree seemed to have a Japanese soldier within it. The Marines had the difficult task of trying to locate the exact positions from which the rifle fire was emanating; usually at the cost of other Marines becoming casualties. The 10th Marines had brought their 75mm

Pack Howitzers ashore in pieces and then assembled them. They were now set up by the beach and they began to shell the Japanese in "The Pocket" and elsewhere. Ten "medium" Sherman tanks had made it ashore and a half-dozen of them were still running. The Shermans were a great advantage, provided they had adequate infantry support so that they did not get over run by the Japanese. A handful of the lighter Stuart tanks were also ashore and trying to navigate the pock-marked landscape.

The smell of death came to the point of permeating the entire area as bodies left in the equatorial sun bloated and burst. In all but a few areas, trying to remove bodies could still be fatal so Marines lay where they fell. Bill witnessed corpsmen moving to aid wounded Marines without any thought of their own wellbeing. Several of these corpsmen had been killed while trying to administer aid. Bill recalled his treatment of the corpsman the previous day and thought there might be a courts martial in his future. There was so much death and destruction on the second day that Bill resigned himself to the fact that it was only a matter of time before he would be killed as well. The thought occurred to him that since he was basically dead already, he would do everything he could to help others survive. Being able to now see the ocean on the other side of the island, Bill knew they had cut the island in two and they now had to tighten the noose around the main concentration of Japanese.

Bill and his team set up a new forward dump out near the airfield and dug in for the night to defend it. The fatigue Bill felt after another day of fighting was beyond anything he had ever experienced. The darkness was welcomed as the ability to get even an hour of sleep was badly needed. Bill settled into a shell hole with Gabel and Ellis and they took turns sleeping while the others expected the counter attack that had failed to show up the night before. When it was Bill's turn to sleep, he rolled on his side and pulled his helmet over his eyes. He wanted to pray before he fell asleep, but he didn't have anything left as he closed his eyes.

59. A Bitter Farewell

November 22nd, 1943. News was received first thing in the morning that the 6th Regiment had landed on Green Beach on the far west end of the island and they would be advancing to the east. This was in an area where F/2/2 had seen nothing but the enemy, so they needed to watch out for Marines coming from that direction. At about 1000 hours, the Pioneers were relieved by some fresh Marines and allowed to go back to Red Beach 2 for other duty. The beach was still far from safe as mortar, artillery, machine gun and rifle fire plagued the entire area. Lieutenant Simonson found work for the team organizing supplies as they reached the base of the pier. Bill was shocked to see the entire pier had now been lined with wooden crates on either side so Marines could move safely up and down it. Boats waited in line to offload ammo at the pier head.

The 6th Marines, under Major Jones, were attacking from the west behind a wall of well-placed naval gunfire, as the 10th Marines continued to pound Japanese positions with their little 75mm Pack Howitzers. The Navy was also shelling the east end of the island and the ground continued to shake under

Bill's feet. Burial details had begun to form and hundreds of Marines were being laid to rest in trenches dug by a bulldozer. As the breeze came from across the island, the pungent smell of death became overpowering in places. As hungry as the men were, they could not eat and keep food down. The ongoing battle, the intense heat and the abundance of decomposing bodies had turned Tarawa into a degree of hell on earth. Chaplain Willard, who Bill had met on Tulagi, had made it ashore the day before and had been working non-stop to minister to the wounded and the dying. He had taken it upon himself to see to the burial and recording of the dead Marines. As the dead were lined up in rows, Willard hand wrote in his notebook the name and location of each body. He also wrote the names of the wounded that he talked to and comforted. At times being under fire, Willard was seen walking upright and shouting at the Japanese, "I am Chaplain Willard and you cannot shoot me!"

Unknown to Bill at the time, Lieutenant Alexander Bonnyman, who had been Bill's Athletic Officer for Company D before transferring to F/2/18, had been killed near Red Beach 3 that afternoon. Bonnyman, who had landed on the pier head as a Shore Patrol officer on the first day, had taken it upon himself to lead assaults for the past three days. There remained a large pyramid-shaped bombproof bunker full of Japanese about 50 yards in from Red 3. Preparing multiple demolition charges, flamethrowers and about 50 Marines, Bonnyman led the assault up the sloped sides of the huge bunker. Using demolitions, flame and even gasoline, Bonnyman's Marines flushed out nearly 100 Japanese from the bunker and eliminated them. During the fighting, Japanese fought their way towards Bonnyman's men and he held them off with grenades and a rifle before he was mortally wounded and died atop the bunker. Alexander Bonnyman would posthumously be awarded the Congressional Medal of Honor for his actions on Tarawa.

As the day grew late, Simonson announced that the Pioneer squad would move back toward the airfield for the night to carry supplies and reinforce the defenses. Starting from the same area where Truitt and Swigert had been killed, Simonson and Gabel led the group over the seawall. Bill slung his M1 over one shoulder and lifted a crate of hand grenades on the other. They carefully picked their way through the rubble and carnage, out past the destroyed bunkers where he had met Lieutenant Barr. They found the trench where Marine machine gunners watched over the center of the airfield. Lieutenant Barr and the remnants of F/2/2 had been relieved by the advancing 1/6 earlier in the day and they had moved back across the airfield to the trench area. Lieutenant Sanford had been shot through the jaw by a sniper and half of Company F that made it across the airfield had been wounded. There were only 30 of the original Company F men left. Marines moved in and out of the trench as they hunted snipers and rooted out "dug in" Japanese that had been bypassed earlier. As darkness fell, the heat began to die down and defenses were readied for another night. Even when sleep was attainable, it never lasted for more than 15 or 20 minutes, and the constant smell of rotting flesh made any kind of comfort impossible.

Darkness brought relative calm to the battle of the previous days, but at 2130 hours, all kinds of fire erupted to the east of Bill's position, where

1/6 had dug in for the night. Everyone was awake in the trench and binoculars peered through the darkness as the flashes and tracers were being exchanged across the airfield. The voices of Japanese soldiers charging into the lines of A/1/6 and B/1/6 could be clearly heard several hundred yards away. No one knew how many Japanese were attacking or whether or not they would come across the airstrip. The combat lasted for about an hour, gradually calming down. Bill took his turn to get some "shut eye." He was jolted awake at 2300 when another Japanese attack was launched into the same area. As the Japanese screamed and clanged empty canteens against their helmets attempting to intimidate the Marines, the sounds of hand grenades, bursts of rifle fire and hand-to-hand combat could be heard across the field. The Marines in the trench wanted to cross the field to assist 1/6 but had strict orders to hold their position. Had they left their position exposed, they would have endangered other Marines who were counting on them to defend their post.

November 23rd, 1943. At 0300, the Japanese attacked both Companies A and B of 1/6 again; this time, they fired heavy machine guns into the Marine positions. This lasted about 20 minutes and the guns were silenced by several explosions. At 0400 Bill was again jolted awake by the cries of a substantial force of Japanese screaming, "BANZAI!" as they charged into the lines between A/1/6 and B/1/6. The 75mm howitzers of the 10th Marines opened fire from Red Beach 2 and the shells buzzed overhead and into the Japanese. Shells began raining down from another battery to the east and then naval gunfire erupted out at sea to the south. The entire area where the attacks had been originating became entirely engulfed with artillery explosions. The ground shook and Bill put his fingers in his ears. He could clearly see Lieutenant Simonson and the others in the trench from the light of the artillery explosions. If there had been any Japanese heading toward the trench, they certainly would have been stopped by the shelling. It was amazing what concentrated fire could do when everything worked properly.

As dawn broke on the fourth day, word came to the trench that A/1/6 and B/1/6 had taken a lot of casualties in the night. Fighting hand to hand, they held their lines until C/1/6 and D/1/6 could come up and help them. PFC Pete Andrews, who Bill had known from back in Aurora, had manned his thirty-caliber light machine gun with D/1/6 throughout the night, repelling the repeated charges from the desperate Japanese. The Marines were about to press on to the east end of the island. The Pioneers made their way back to the base of the pier at Red Beach 2 and assisted in organizing and moving supplies inland, in the direction of "The Pocket" at the west end of Red Beach 2. By 1100 hours there were only three areas of combat still active on the island, not counting the snipers that could still appear almost anywhere. The Marines of 1/8 moved through The Pocket, 3/6 made its way to the tail of the island on the east end and 2/8 finished off the last emplacements in the area where Lieutenant Bonnyman had died the previous day. At 1312 hours on the fourth day ashore, Tarawa was declared "secured."

Lieutenant Simonson located Captain Farkas, who had been working at the pier area with the Shore Party. Farkas gave orders to begin to assemble the remnants of D/2/18 so they could leave Tarawa as a unit. Bill's landing team had miraculously survived the last four days relatively unscathed, with the exception of Fred Ellis' shrapnel wounds, which were now being looked at by medical personnel. Members of 2nd Platoon slowly gathered late that afternoon as Gabel and Simonson took a roll call. Members of 1st Platoon, those assigned with Farkas, and those with Shoup's Headquarters unit, arrived as well. Seeing the members of Company D who had been in the thick of it for four days was shocking. Beards had grown and it was hard to imagine that humans could be this dirty, smelly and foul. Bill's utilities had grown stiff with sweat, coral dust and the blood from the wounded that he had assisted. The island itself smelled so bad that no one noticed the individual body odors. As small groups arrived, there were mixed emotions as the men were elated to see others alive but saddened at the news of those who had been killed. Bill told Johnnie Jones and Herb Dale the bad news about Truitt and Swigert and the group sat silently, as though at a funeral. Bill told them that Truitt and Bob had been buried two days ago over by the command post. Some of the guys shouted, "He's coming in! Look at that!" and Bill looked up to the west where a lone Navy Hellcat was approaching with his wheels and flaps down. The Construction Battalion, or "CBs," as they were called, had already repaired the craters in the runway and the first American planes were beginning to land. It was a strange sight since there were still Japanese snipers and hold outs all over the island. Corpsmen and Medical Assistants handed out burn cream for severe sunburn on hands, necks, faces and lips. Bill smeared the cream on his cracked and bleeding lips and it stung at first. The white cream made the guys look as though they were wearing big smiles with pure white teeth showing. Nothing could be further from the truth at this point. Simonson sent George Cothran and Carl Fortenberry out to try and locate members of 3rd Platoon, to get word to them to assemble at the base of the pier. As Company D settled in for another night on Tarawa, there still had not been any contact with 3rd Platoon, and the guys that had gone ashore at Red Beach 1.

November 24th, 1943. When morning came on the fifth day on Tarawa, Cothran and Fortenberry came back to the pier area with Emory Ashurst and Joe Sobolewski from the 3rd Platoon. The guys were emotional to see them and they looked like they had been through hell. They *all* looked like they had been through hell. Bill, Fred and Lieutenant Simonson greeted them with hugs and Simonson asked where the others were. Sobolewski said they had seen some of the other guys and they should be coming along, as word had gone around for them to rejoin Company D near the pier. Simonson asked if they had seen Lieutenant Vincent and his men that went ashore with K/3/2. Ashurst and Sobolewski were silent and Ashurst rubbed his face and they started to sob. "They're all dead," Sobolewski mumbled. Fred asked, "What do you mean 'All'? Seng, Montague, Roads?" Sobolewski nodded his head affirmatively. "We found them on Red 1 this morning on the way over. They are all lying right where they died. They never even got off the beach the first day." Fred said, "We sure as hell can't just leave them laying there; we've got to give those boys a proper burial." Bill agreed as he thought about Gene Seng's new wife, June, back in New Zealand; another tragedy beyond description. Bill squinted hard as he pulled tears from the corners of his eyes. "Let's go," he said to Fred. The two were already grabbing shovels as others were getting the news.

Company D was scheduled to load Higgins Boats at the pier for the trip back to a transport this afternoon. This left little time for what they had to do. As they were grabbing some shovels and gear to go, Simonson reminded them to take their rifles and ammo belts as there were still snipers all over the island hiding in debris piles. Nearly the entire Pioneer squad headed down Red 2 to the west with rifles and shovels in hand. As they walked along, there were burial parties picking up the dead on Red 2 and the carnage was ghastly. Many of the burial party had finally found a use for the discarded gas masks. The masks protected them from the unbearable smell that was excruciating at close quarters to the dead. There were damaged LVTs all along Red 2 and Marine bodies floated in the gentle waves. The men of Company D walked along in total silence as no one dared to speak. At the west end of Red Beach 2, the shoreline took a 90-degree turn to the left where the east end of Red Beach 1 began. The beach ran south for about 150 yards before curving back to the west, creating a large, arcing cove. The area to their left was "The Pocket," where smoke still rose from smoldering rubble and the battle had ended about 20 hours earlier. As the beach rounded back to the west, Bill took a good look at a knocked out LVT that had "#15, Worried Mind" painted on the side. Three dead Marines lay on the sand next to it. Sobolewski broke the silence when he turned to the others and said, "They are right up ahead; before you come to the privy piers."

All eyes now looked 50 yards ahead as Bill focused on clumps of bodies on the sand. Sobolewski came to the first body; it was Lieutenant Vincent. The men fanned out in groups of three or four and began identifying them. Bill heard, "Here's Larson," and "McKinney is over here," from the others. He and Fred walked directly to a pile of five Marines slumped over a .30-caliber machine gun. They were all facing up a slope in the sand that rose three feet to a somewhat level beach. Their boots were only 10 feet from the water. Bill grabbed the shoulders of the Marine who was directly behind the gun and rolled him on his side. It was Charlie Montague. It was all Bill could muster to get the words, "Here's Montague" out of his mouth. He looked at Fred and they both seemed to know who was next to Charlie in the position of Gunner's Assistant. They rolled over the next body and it was Gene Seng. One by one they called out the identities, "Kountzman, Jarrett, Lyntton, Parsons, Watkins, Waltz, Lanning, Castle, Roads, Millick." One dog tag was removed from each body to be turned over to the main burial team back at headquarters. As Bill looked up, he noticed the *TIME* magazine reporter, Bob Sherrod, standing about 30 feet down the beach with another Marine. Sherrod was almost unrecognizable but for the yellow legal pad in his hands. Bill thought that surely, no one could possibly understand what Tarawa had been like. There was nothing known to mankind with which one could compare it.

Up the small slope and about 50 feet from the water's edge, they measured out a 60 foot by 10 foot rectangle, paced out a grave every five feet and began

Fallen United States Marines on Red Beach 1 as the battle for Tarawa winds down. Bill Bennett and the men of D/2/18 buried Lieutenant Vincent, Charles Montague, Gene Seng and the rest of Vincent's Pioneer team just above the beach between the small piers visible in the background.

(U.S.M.C. Photo)

digging graves, roughly 30-inches wide, six-feet long and three-feet deep. Looking through the equipment strewn about, they located rain ponchos and began to lay out the bodies for burial. They decided that Lieutenant Vincent should be buried in the first grave to the east, as he was their leader. Unknown to any of the Marines, including Vincent, he had been promoted to captain a week before his death. He would have made a good one. He led from the front and died in the process. One by one, they carried bodies from the water's edge to the fresh graves, wrapped them in the brown and green ponchos and placed them in the sand. Some of their bodies had to be bent back into a suitable shape for burial and at best, they only slightly resembled the living Marines that their friends remembered. Shovel loads of sand began to plop onto the ponchos as the 15 members of Company D became one with the sands of Tarawa. The Marines buried were Lieutenant (Captain) Richard William Vincent of Westfield, Massachusetts, Corporal Hazen Burdette Lanning of Nowata, Oklahoma, PFC Charles Montague of Bandera, Texas, PFC Gene Gustav Seng, Jr. of San Antonio, Texas, PFC Russell Lloyd Jarrett of Vandalia, Illinois, PFC Ralf Clement Kountzman of St. Louis, Missouri, PFC Samuel Roy Parsons of Boston, Massachusetts, PFC Arnold Richard Millick of Ely, Nevada, Navy Corpsman H. F. Watkins, Private Wayne Alfred Larson of Sacramento, California, Private Robert Coleman McKinney of Fergus Falls, Minnesota, Private Max Lyntton, Jr. of Oakland, Illinois, Private Merlin Wilbur Waltz of Monroe, Michigan, Private James Scott Castle, Jr. of Dungannon, Virginia, and Private Addison Blanchard Roads of Denver, Colorado. Bill's tired body was drenched with sweat as he threw shovel after shovel of sand over his comrade's bodies in the sweltering heat. The sand mounds were evened out and shaped into somewhat symmetrical shapes above each Marine and the rectangle began to take the appearance of a cemetery.

The others had been gathering suitable wood splinters to tie into crosses with twine cut from some of the log structures nearby. "Gus" Gustafson used his woodworking skills to put together the crosses with a variety of knives as his only tools. One large cross was fashioned in the same way to mark the cemetery in general. The name of each Marine was scribbled in grease pencil, as well as could be expected onto the crude crosses, before they were pounded into the sand with the back of a shovel. Emory Ashurst gathered everyone in front of the graves and led them in an eloquent and heart-felt prayer that brought tears to every Marine's eyes. Bill found the idea of a 15-man funeral overwhelming. Ashurst prayed, "Dear Heavenly Father, we thank you for the lives of these, our brothers, that we have laid to rest here today, and we ask that your Spirit will be with their friends and families as they learn of their loss. We thank you for your many blessings and your gift of eternal life through the blood of our Savior, Jesus Christ and we thank you for keeping those of us standing here alive through this battle. We thank you for this victory on this island and for your victory over death itself; help us to never forget these men who died here on this island." He then asked the others to join him in reciting the 23rd Psalm. Their voices murmured the familiar words that seemed so appropriate this day. Although most of the men present, like Bill, had learned the 23rd Psalm years ago in Sunday school, they now realized that they had, in fact, just gone through the "Valley of the shadow of death." The entire group knelt behind the graves as one Marine with a camera took one last photo of the living as they left behind the dead.

The men of Company D picked up their gear, set their helmets on their heads and began the long walk back to the pier. As Bill and Fred walked along, Fred reminded Bill of Gene Seng's request that Fred send a white carnation to his mother back in San Antonio for Mother's Day if he were killed. Bill noted that he had a letter to write to Molly Anderson back in New Zealand as well. At this point they still had no idea how many men Company D had lost at Tarawa. Looking across the island, the CBs were already working with heavy equipment they had brought ashore and bulldozers and road graters were moving debris and piling up dead Japanese for burial. Fred made the comment that he didn't understand how God could allow such things to happen. Bill responded firmly that what they had just been through had been caused by the actions of men, not God. Bill said that God can use all things for good, but he was sure God had not been the architect of what they had been through here at Tarawa.

In order to make room for the reinforcements coming ashore, Command wanted to start getting the combat Marines off the island and out to the transports as soon as possible. By 1400 hours that afternoon, Lieutenant Simonson had the remnants of 2nd Platoon lined up at the pier head to load Higgins Boats out to the USS Monroe. Everyone wondered why they were all going back to a different ship and how they would get their sea bags, but all of Company D would eventually end up on the Monroe. Bill noticed that the smell of the island was far weaker out on the pier head with fresh ocean air blowing in toward them. He also noticed that his own smell and the smell of the others, was now far worse than he had imagined. Bill dropped off the pier and hit the bottom of the boat with about 30 others from Company D and the crew pushed out from the pier as the coxswain revved the large diesel and the prop began to push the boat out toward the transports. The breeze was much cooler out over the water and the spray coming over the ramp was welcome now; it had been uncomfortable on the morning of the attack.

Bill looked back as Tarawa thinned with distance, and its shattered palms reached skyward. The thought of Truitt Anderson, Bob Swigert, Gene Seng, Charlie Montague and the others being left there forever overwhelmed him. Bill lowered his head and went into his helmet and real tears started to flow. He knew that life would never be the same. He knew that he would never be the same.

Corporal Bob Swigert prior to leaving San Diego in 1942.
(Photo courtesy of Leo and Jackie Swigert)

60. Tarawa: The Aftermath

Dozens of transports were anchored in an area several miles offshore from Tarawa. As the Higgins Boats were approaching the transports, it soon became evident where they were headed. The slender gray ship with "A 104" painted on her bow must be the USS Monroe, as the coxswain paralleled his boat and slowed up to a long cargo net hanging over her starboard side. All of the hands on the port side of the Higgins Boat grabbed hold of the cargo net and began the long climb upwards. Their loads were light as most of the gear had been used up, lost or deliberately left on Tarawa. Bill shouldered his M1 and pulled the chinstrap of his helmet below his chin and began his climb. As he came up and over the rail, the faces of the Navy crew members were not what he was expecting. The sailor who gave him a hand over the rail had a solemn, almost sickly look on his face. As Bill's feet planted on the deck, he looked up at the other Navy men looking down from the gun platforms and the rails above and near the bridge. Each face had a look of shock and surprise that took a minute to understand. The Marines were already used to seeing and smelling each other throughout their ordeal ashore. The Navy crews had seen them in their brand-new utilities with clean rifles and exuberant attitudes when they had left the transports five days ago. Now, what they were seeing were the bearded, filthy remnants of the survivors of combat. As the Marines moved past the crew on their way to find quarters and showers, many of the Navy men turned to vomit from the pungent smell of death that was clinging to the Marines. Captain George D. Morrison realized the Marine's condition and hailed his subordinate officers immediately. He ordered the Marines to wait on deck and ordered towels brought up to meet them. The combat gear and the utilities were going to have to come off on the deck and lines formed for the salt water showers as a first order of business. Bill peeled off his equipment and rubbed his head. His hair felt like steel wool. His hands must have had two dozen little cuts on them. He sat down on the deck and untied his boondockers and pried his feet out of the soaking wet, stinking boots. His socks were worn through on the heels and the balls of his feet, and he had bloody spots where the constant friction of sand had rubbed through his skin during the last five days. His beard and mustache had grown to be a quarter inch long and the whiskers irritated his cracked lips. A shave would be heaven. Sailors arrived with bales of clean towels and were distributing them to the Marines. Bill got out of his utilities and skivvies and wrapped a towel around his waist. He felt the deep bruise on his right thigh where the spent bullet had hit him that first day. Bill had been sore and beaten before, but never to this extent. He knew that had the battle lasted another day or two, he would have been finished. Fred now had to be placed into the care of the ship's doctor who would have to remove several small pieces of shrapnel from his leg and back. A few days in the infirmary would be a good start at recovery.

The Marines began to pile their uniforms on the port side of the Monroe. Lieutenant Simonson shouted for Marines to check their pockets for anything they wanted to keep because it was all going overboard. Sailors with shovels began to heave the offensive uniforms over the side as the Marines headed below for the showers. Usually, the showers were loud and obnoxious places but not today. There wasn't a sound besides the water jets. Relief poured over Bill as the soap began to wash the smell of death from his body. The water on the shower floor ran a deep gray to the drains and almost every Marine had healing cuts and abrasions visible somewhere. Bill scrubbed his ears and he felt grit packed inside and behind. The sunburn on his neck burned in the hot water and the pain matched the pain of his bloody feet.

Outside the showers, in the sink area, dozens of shaving kits were set out and Bill found a sink to share with Lester Hellman. Even though the blades were new and sharp, they tugged at the now week-old beard that had been toughened in the heat. The men in the mirrors were starting to once again look civilized. Piles of U.S.M.C. "Greens" were stacked in the dressing area along with underclothes, socks and Navy shoes. As soon as they were dressed, lines formed for food. Clean drinking water that did not taste of gasoline was on the menu, along with Bill's old favorite, cold milk! Sandwiches and oranges were handed out and the sailors watched the famished Marines inhale food like there would be no tomorrow. Marines were suddenly realizing there was no one shooting at them and they could relax. After eating, Marines went straight to the bunkrooms to catch up on sleep; something they had lived without for almost five days. Bill crawled into a bunk, rolled over to face the wall and hugged the pillow. He slept for 10 hours.

The showers stayed open for the Marines 24 hours a day as multiple trips were needed just to start getting rid of the smell. The barber shop was opened to the Marines as it was determined that their hair now retained the smell of death. The Navy bent over backwards to give the Marines whatever they needed, including privacy. Sailors noticed the "1000 yard stare" which men who have been in combat frequently exhibit. They were under orders to refrain from asking questions about the battle. The food tasted better than anything the men had eaten previously and they drank gallons of water and milk. The obvious issue bothering all the Marines, and specifically Company D, was the missing friends. Captain Farkas called a meeting of his lieutenants, minus Lieutenant Vincent, and they went over the muster rolls. Of the 235 men in Company D, 120 had been assigned to assault companies. 32 had been killed on Tarawa and more than that wounded. Those who had been assigned to Shore Party with Captain Farkas had been fortunate, as had those who were assigned to Colonel Shoup's Headquarters Company, although they had all been in danger just by being on the island. None had it as bad as the Pioneers assigned to K/3/2, along with Lieutenant Vincent.

Having lost track of the days in battle, the men were reminded when they awoke on Thursday, the 25th of November, that it was Thanksgiving. Bill went to see the ship's Chaplain and asked for a Bible. He went and found a shady spot on the deck of the Monroe and opened up to the Gospel of John. There were some things that he needed to get done. The first order of business was grief. Besides the physical beating of his body, Bill was in the midst of emotional trauma that only the survivors of such carnage could understand. In addition, he had just begun to grieve over the loss of many of his friends and comrades. As Bill sat still and tried to think, he could only put his head down and cry for the loss of Truitt, Bob Swigert, Gene Seng, Charlie Montague and Lieutenant Vincent's team. His memories of friendships that were shared, for almost two years, made it hard to grasp that they were no longer on this earth. Bill remembered how Truitt was planning on stopping off in Aurora on his way back to Akron when the war was over and how interested he had been to meet the Bennetts and taste Jessie's cooking. He recalled how they had shared stories of growing up in church with Bill at Fourth Street and Truitt at his North Side Baptist. They had shared so much as Americans, Marines, and brothers in Christ. Now, all that remained was Christ. In an instant, mortar rounds and machine gun bullets had taken all earthly concerns from those men and their spiritual readiness for eternity was all that really mattered in the end. Bill had wanted to protect his friends and especially Truitt, who was like a younger brother to him. How did Bill survive the blast that had killed Truitt and Bob, only feet away? The memory of that loud whispering voice sent shivers up his spine. There was no explanation other than divine intervention. But why had the Lord let Bill live while the others died?

As his thoughts worked through these things, Bill was compelled to pray. He poured out his heart of sorrow to the Lord and asked that His Spirit would comfort Molly and Truitt's loved ones when they received the news. He prayed for the Swigert family, for when they received the news of the loss of their son and their brother. He prayed for the Sengs and the Montagues in Texas and for the Vincents in Massachusetts. Bill thanked the Lord for sparing his life and he was bold enough to ask why. In the stillness of Bill's heart, he was comforted by the presence of God, as he clearly understood that God had a plan for Bill's life and it would be revealed to him with time. God wanted Bill to trust in Him and believe that He was working out the details beyond what Bill would be able to understand. This aspect of Bill's relationship with the Living Christ had never been so clear as it became at this time. In the midst of physical shock, emotional stress and almost unbearable grief, Bill felt healing beginning in his soul as the Lord was touching him. As Bill finished his prayer, he realized that he had just received from God the very thing that he had been asking be supplied to the loved ones of those killed. The Lord had touched his soul and allowed healing to begin. There was no bitterness in Bill's heart after what he had been through and the losses at Tarawa. He had an understanding that evil had brought the war to be and that God would work all things together for ultimate good for those who love the Lord. Romans 8:28, "And we know that all things work together for good to them that love God, to them who are called according to His purpose."

The Navy cooks aboard the USS Monroe pulled out all the stops in preparing Thanksgiving Dinner for the crew and the Marines. Roast turkey, mashed potatoes and gravy, stuffing, sweet potatoes and canned cranberry sauce contributed to a meal that tasted like heaven. The men of Company D began to talk about what they had been through and the shared memories of their fallen comrades. Bill and Fred sat and talked about all they had been through and how thankful they truly were just to be alive. The Monroe remained at anchor, and Bill and the others frequently went to the bow to look at that wretched island as they waited for the last Marines to come aboard. Finally, on December 3rd, 1943, the USS Monroe raised anchor and set sail for Pearl Harbor. There was literally nothing to do during this trip but rest, read and play cards. It was a welcome reprieve for the men who had been busy preparing for Tarawa for eight months prior to the landings. As the Monroe pushed east to Hawaii with the fleet, Bill wondered what would be next. There were rumors that some of the Marines would be rotated "stateside." Bill could only hope that he would be one of them. As long as the Marines of Company D would live, they would never forget those five days at Tarawa. Nearly six thousand men on both sides had died in those four days and almost two thousand more had been wounded. The aftermath of Tarawa would send shock waves through the American public as they were confronted by the barbarity and the carnage of war.

61. Blue Hawaii

As the Monroe sailed northeast, the equatorial heat and humidity subsided and some of the nights became cool. Standing along the deck rails at night, some of the Marines just enjoyed the absence of the heat, and the cool sea air was refreshing. On December 12th, the island of Oahu came into view and the Monroe, along with the other transports, brought the 2nd Division into an American Territory for the first time in 17 months. Bill stood at the rails as the transports passed submerged hulks of battleships that had been sunk by the Japanese two years earlier. Hundreds of sailors' and Marines' bodies were still inside some of these ships. It was a solemn sight and it helped justify what they had just done to those 4,000-plus Japanese soldiers on Tarawa.

The Monroe docked and the Marines were given four hours to walk about in the dock areas before loading onto the USS Polk at the end of the pier for the next leg of the trip. As the guys from 2nd Platoon talked at the bottom of the gangway, Mike Matkovich was talking to Bill Poterola about catching a cab over to the Post Exchange Bar on the other side of the base for a few cold beers. Matkovich had been stationed at Pearl Harbor before the war, so he knew his way around. Poterola, not known to turn down a beer, decided to go along even though several of the guys tried to tell them otherwise. Matkovich seemed to have a way of stretching the rules which kept things interesting from time to time. Bill spent his time with the others talking to sailors on the docks and finding out where many of them had been throughout the Pacific. Of course, the public had learned some of the details regarding Tarawa and the sailors were eager to hear any firsthand accounts. As ordered, 2nd Platoon arrived at the gangway of the USS Polk to board; all of them with the exception of Matkovich and Poterola.

Lieutenant Simonson found Bill after Sergeant Gabel had reported the two missing. Bill explained that they had hopped a cab to a bar and probably lost track of time. Simonson cursed Matkovich and told Bill that he could not hold up the entire ship for the sake of two beer-guzzling Marines. They would have to let the chips fall where they may. Simonson hated the thought of two combat Marines getting themselves into hot water over something so unnecessary. The USS Polk pushed off from the pier and fell in line in the harbor as the transports prepared for the short trip over to the big island of Hawaii. Bill and Fred went to the rail at the stern with a group of 2nd Platoon men and they pondered what would happen to Matkovich and Poterola. As they were headed out of the harbor, one of the guys yelled out to take a look at the harbor launch gaining on them from the rear. Bill looked slightly to the right and saw the wake of a small craft planed out at full speed. As it came closer, they could see a sailor at the wheel and there were two Marines holding on tight just behind him. "It's Mat and Motorola!" as were their common references within the Platoon. The group moved over to the starboard side and began to yell, whistle and cheer as the speed boat came along side. The deck hands had just started to haul up the last cargo net as Matkovich and Poterola grabbed hold and started climbing up to the deck. Their platoon members pulled them over the rail while rubbing their heads and laughing hysterically. As they moved back to the stern, Lieutenant Simonson walked up to Matkovich and said, "Say Mat, I'd swear that one of those Marines who climbed aboard looked just like you." Matkovich smiled and said, "Is that right sir?" as he kept walking and made a bee line for the anonymity of the thousand Marines below deck. The story, it turned out, was that the pair had lost track of time at the bar and by the time they got back to the dock, the USS Polk had sailed. Matkovich found a sailor tuning up the engine on a Navy launch and offered him the wad of 20-yen notes that Mike had found on

Tarawa. Not being able to turn down such a terrific war souvenir, the sailor agreed to catch the Polk as it was getting under way. The Marines had their beer, the sailor had his souvenir and Simonson had gotten his Marines back. Everyone was happy.

The USS Polk moved out of Pearl Harbor at Oahu and headed for the "Big Island" of Hawaii distinguished by the snow-covered peaks of the Mauna Loa and Mauna Kea volcanoes. The Polk and her companion transports came into the harbor at Hilo, Hawaii, on the island's east shore. The light-colored buildings of Hilo set off a contrast with the rich green hills rising up behind it. The single large pier that protruded into the bay from the center of town was reminiscent of the pier at Tarawa. The volcanic peaks rose up to soaring heights in the distance. This would be the first civilization the Marines would be turned loose in since New Zealand.

Bill's sea bag had been loaded onto the Polk and getting it back meant a lot to him as it did to all the Marines. The things inside the sea bag were as close to home as he could come. While waiting to disembark the Polk, Bill went through his stacks of letters which were bundled with rubber bands, put on his dress shoes and overseas cap, shirt, tie and belt. He pulled out his New Testament which he had marked with red and black tabs while in New Zealand. Lieutenant Simonson came by and told Bill that most of the Marines on the transports would be heading across the Big Island to a new camp at Parker Ranch, but 2nd Platoon, Company D/2/18 would be sent to a camp near Hilo so they could do some unloading work at the docks. The news garnered groans from 2nd Platoon, and rightly so. Although they did not know it at the time, the new camp at Parker Ranch was a pile of supplies that would take weeks of hard labor to turn into an actual camp. The weather in Hilo was warm and relaxing whereas the weather at Parker Ranch would be below freezing at night with highs around 50 during the day. Staying in Hilo was definitely an upgrade.

2nd Platoon was trucked to the new camp that had actually been built to be a Japanese POW camp. The problem was, as the Marines knew all too well, the Japanese would not surrender. Therefore, the camp was empty. The camp was an odd place as it was built on irregular bumps of lava flow so that some huts were at one level and other huts and tents at other levels. They soon learned that if one fell on the black lava, your uniform and your skin could be cut to shreds.

Bill was elated to share a tent with Johnnie Jones and Herb Dale at the new camp and they traded stories about Tarawa. They had both been assigned to 1/2 under Major Wood B. Kyle and had gone in with the 4th wave on Red 2. They were fortunate to still be alive. Herb had been a Pioneer with Company A who had lost Captain Bray to wounds and three of their five lieutenants had been killed in action. Herb had gone over the seawall with Lieutenant Armstead Ross and ended up in a shell crater right in front of a Japanese pillbox. Ross ordered Herb to a frontal attack on the pillbox and Herb told the lieutenant that pillboxes need to be taken out from the sides. Ross told Herb that he was just being a coward and proceeded to leave the cover and head straight for the machine gun. He didn't even get ten feet before the machine gun cut him to pieces. Bill shared the details of losing Truitt, Swigert and the others and it was hard not to shed tears again.

Work began at the docks right away as there were two transports that had not been properly "battle loaded" in New Zealand. The matériel was in such disarray that they had not been able to off-load the supplies at Tarawa and now much of it had collapsed into trash heaps. Since Lieutenant Simonson had "battle loaded" two ships successfully, his platoon was assigned the task to unload the problem ships. Bill could now clearly see why the Navy was always so particular about loading. A negligent job could have cost many lives had the battle gone differently. The dock work was enjoyable as the weather was so nice. The platoon fell into regular work hours as though they had full-time civilian jobs. Bill drove the lift truck and loaded Herb Dale and Bill Poterola's trucks to transport material away from the dock. Some of the guys teased Poterola and asked him if he had the truck from New Zealand paid off yet. After all that 2nd Platoon had been through, there were very few complaints about their assignment.

Liberty was available on most nights and weekends and the layout of the small town of Hilo began to become familiar. On the first weekend, Bill and Herb sought out a church service and found that the Hilo Center on Kamehameha Avenue not only hosted the U.S.O., but a Protestant church service as well. The church service was organized by a local Pastor, Shannon Walker, and his wife Helen. The couple had three children: David, 15; Elizabeth, 12 and little Dunham who was six. Shannon Walker was about 40 years old and was a tall, slender and handsome guy with a little gray starting to show at his temples. His sermon dealt with the seriousness of war and death, yet he used some humor a few times and the laughter felt good. Bill and Herb talked to Shannon after the service and they were introduced to Helen and the children. David was a sophomore at Hilo High School and enjoyed playing basketball, as did his dad. They mentioned getting a game together at the Hilo Center in the coming week. The Walkers invited Bill and Herb over for dinner and Shannon offered Bill their address. Bill pulled out a notepad he had received from the U.S.O. and Shannon wrote the address for him. In the coming months, the house at 92 Kamakahonu Street would become like home to Bill.

Bill talked to Lieutenant Simonson about writing a letter back to New Zealand regarding Truitt Anderson's death and it was decided that Bill would do the writing since he was a close friend. Knowing that this letter may be the first notification Molly received of Truitt's death was a burdensome thought. Bill wrote the letter to Helen Taylor so she could break the news to Molly. There was no way around the harsh facts and Bill wrote how sorry he was to tell her that Truitt had been killed. He explained they were together at the time and he had tried to help, although Truitt had died instantly. Bill reminded Molly of Truitt's commitment to Christ and the fact that he was now home with Jesus. He also wrote of how Molly had meant the entire world to Truitt and how he had talked about her since the night they first met at the Allied Services Club in Wellington. Bill said he had never known a fellow that was so head over heels in love with a girl. He promised Molly she would remain in his prayers. As he wrote the letter to Helen Taylor, his heart raced as he recalled the last night he was with her as she told him of the dream where she saw Truitt in peril while Bill was safe. This whole scenario would have been hard for Bill to believe had he not lived through it all.

On the other end of Bill's letters to New Zealand, Helen Taylor breathed a sigh of relief when she pulled the envelope from the post box at 53 Nevay Road. Molly had informed Helen of her receipt of a telegram from the Marine Corps telling her that Truitt was missing in action. Since that time, Molly was holding out hope that there was a mistake and that word would come from Truitt that he was fine. She had been calling the War Office in New Zealand to check on the information for weeks when another telegram came notifying her that Truitt had been killed in action at Tarawa. Molly had still not believed the news and had been staying with the Taylors and frequently waking at night and calling Truitt's name. Mrs. Taylor's heart was broken over Molly's grief, as well as her own. She had loved Truitt by her own description as "almost flesh and blood to me," the Kiwi phrase for "like my own flesh and blood." After Mrs. Taylor read what Bill had written, she called Molly to the parlor and presented the letter to her. As Molly began to read, she broke down in tears and fell to Mrs. Taylor's shoulder. Molly then proceeded to read Bill's words, and they seemed to finally settle things in her soul. Knowing Bill was with Truitt in his last moments on Earth and that Bill had watched the corpsmen carry Truitt to his burial was enough for her to accept the loss. Her grieving could finally start. Mrs. Taylor sat down later to return a letter to Bill to thank him and explain what life had been like for them all since the Marines had shipped out almost four months earlier.

During this time, Bob Swigert's Mother, Eva, received word at her farm outside of Oelrichs, South Dakota, that there was a telegram waiting for her at the Oelrichs train depot. She waited until her teenage son Don returned from farm chores that afternoon and he drove her the four miles to the depot in the Swigert's gray 1936 Studebaker. The depot was just up the street from the grain elevators and the station manager also ran the Western Union desk. Eva went inside to retrieve the telegram and brought it back out to the car. She opened the telegram and put her hand over her mouth as she read the words, "Regret to inform you …" Bob had been officially listed as "Missing In Action." Don drove a few blocks over to the two-story brick school and they both went in to get the youngest Swigerts, Leo and Ila Mae, released from class. Eva told them the news and emphasized that Bob was only missing in action, there was no certainty that he was dead. Perhaps he was taken prisoner or there was some other mistake. Eva informed her husband, Bird, of the telegram and all anyone could do would be to pray.

Several weeks later, another notification came to the house and the drive was repeated. The worst had been expected and the worst was revealed when Eva tore open the Western Union telegram. This time, there was no room for hope. Corporal Robert Swigert had been killed in action on November 20th, 1943 while engaged against enemy forces in the Pacific. No information was given as to the location of his body or details of his burial. The truth was, no one knew.

Regular mail service started again after settling into camp at Hilo and Bill received a lot of backed-up mail from home. Several letters from Helen described her life at home in Sandwich, as well as her visits to the Bennett home in Aurora. Helen also explained to Bill that she was doing very well with TWA and there was a possibility she could be promoted soon. With Bill being gone for so long now, work had become Helen's main focus. She was very good at what she did and work kept her mind busy. All of her friends and coworkers routinely asked her if she had heard from "her Marine" and she would share the news if there was any. Bill's brother Al had finished all his training and was by this time a 2nd lieutenant with the United States Joint Procurement Bureau (U.S.J.P.B.), specializing in acquiring food supplies for the war. The big news in this letter was Al's plan to marry his girl Eunice as soon as she could arrange travel to Virginia. He was still in the States, but could be sent overseas soon. Bill had a hard time imagining Al being married and he thought back to his last night at home and their talk in the dark. That was the end of a long and very enjoyable era for Bill. He was happy for his brother, but devastated that he would not be able to be at the wedding. Aside from the war, missing Al's wedding would have been unthinkable. It was all academic at this point, as Al and Eunice had already been married for well over a month by the time Bill read the letter. As it turned out, Al and Eunice had been married in Virginia at the same moment Bill had been wading in to Red Beach 2 at Tarawa. Bud Dix had quit his job at the munitions plant and enlisted in the Army. He was now overseas in England, as were Dexter Stoner and Sergeant George Troll, who was in the 745th Tank Battalion serving as Intelligence Officer. Bob Nix and Jack Morey were both in the Navy somewhere in the Atlantic. Harley Stoner was a sergeant in the Army Engineers serving somewhere in the Pacific, and Lieutenant Bob Stoner had joined his new Navy Squadron. It seemed as though everyone Bill had known was at war, and everyone he knew would be married by the time he returned. Aurora's population had been about 42,000 before the war and there were now almost 9,000 of those residents in the service.

The grueling work of unloading the transports and clearing away the mess lasted for several weeks. The small town of Hilo became comfortable as everything was within walking distance from the pier and liberty was available on a regular basis. When Bill had time off on the weekends, the Walkers took him swimming at some of their favorite beach spots, and the coastal scenery was some of the most beautiful Bill had ever seen. Shannon asked Bill how long it had been since he had driven a car and Bill said he really couldn't recall. Bill drove the Walker family as their chauffeur, and attended some youth meetings where Shannon asked him to share his story with the younger believers. Bill was thrilled to be alive and to be able to let others know what God had done in his life. Making each day count and focusing on yielding his own will to God's will became a constant desire.

Camp life began to resume some of the familiarities of life back at New Zealand, but the work schedule kept the company from any extended liberty or chance to travel around the island. Hilo had a movie theater downtown called the Palace Theater, and Bill and the others frequented it as much as possible. Mike Matkovich introduced some of the 2nd Platoon guys to Lee Powell, from Company HQ, who shared their camp. Powell had the distinction of having been a Hollywood actor before the war, when he most notably portrayed the first Lone Ranger in 1938. Ironically, the Lone Ranger film was being shown at the Palace Theater in Hilo during this time. Matkovich made a point of taking other Marines to the shows along with Powell and then announcing to the kids afterward that this particular Marine was none other than the Lone Ranger that they had just seen in the movie. The kids would line up for autographs and all the Marines had a great time with it.

At Parker Ranch, between the two volcanic peaks, the rest of 2nd Division was not having as good of a time as D/2/18 or Company HQ at Hilo. When they had arrived at the site of the new camp, there was nothing there except piles of supplies. The new camp was named "Camp Tarawa" in memory of those fallen in the recent battle, however, the camp would have to be built by those who were to live there. The weather was colder than anticipated with snow on the peaks and nighttime temperatures well below freezing. The first order of business in the mornings would be to break the ice in the water buckets. The Marines had no warm clothes or blankets. The civilians on Hawaii donated what they could to help until supplies arrived. One huge problem was there were no winter items available in the Pacific Theater, because there was almost no place to use them, with the exception of where the 2nd Division had chosen to make the new camp.

62. Disillusion

Unloading of the transports was finally accomplished and the ships made their way back to Pearl Harbor for reassignment. Company D received orders to move to "Camp Tarawa" to rejoin the 2nd Division. Everything was loaded into trucks once again and they all lamented moving up to the chilly elevations of Parker Ranch. The truck ride over the lava fields on "Saddle Road" was 65 miles long, dusty and jarring. Some of the Marines complained that they would rather get out and walk than have their kidneys damaged by the truck ride. The lava had been ground to black dust that settled on the Marines in the trucks and looked like coal dust. The fine black dust got into everything. Once near the town of Kamuela, the road turned tolerable until the trucks turned and drove through the new gates of the camp. Bill and 2nd Platoon were able to move into small cabins equipped with stoves and warm blankets, so they did not have to endure the same discomfort others had initially. The terrain at Camp Tarawa was cool and dry, the perfect place to heal malaria, dysentery and other tropical diseases. So very different from the coast at Hilo, Parker Ranch had the look of the western U.S.

To celebrate the completion of Camp Tarawa, 2nd Division planned a rodeo and barbeque for February 12th, 1944. The Parker Ranch was a huge working ranch and one of the perks was the presence of beef. Since there were thousands of seasoned farmers and ranch hands in the 2nd Division, it made good sense to let them compete in a real rodeo and put on a real western barbeque. The ranch also had dozens of professional cowboys working the place and they would team up with the experienced Marines to fill out the competitors list. Since Fred Ellis, Gerald Coate and Herb Dale were all from

Montana, they were quite enthused about being able to work on the ranch and have their hands into preparation for the rodeo. Bob Stubblefield also knew his way around livestock with his experience back in Texas. Sadly, Bill knew that Bob Swigert, as well as Charles Montague and Gene Seng, would have greatly enjoyed the rodeo events. By this time, the absence of Truitt Anderson's conversations and sense of humor greatly bothered Bill.

When the day arrived, the festivities kicked off with the 2nd Division Band playing in and around the nearby town of Kamuela and the barbeque beginning at the ranch at 1100 hours. At 1230, a rather large parade began, led by General Edson and the Chief of Staff, followed by the U.S.M.C. color guard. The Queen of the Rodeo, Mrs. Marjorie Wilson, followed, riding a dazzling white stallion with full rodeo regalia. Behind her came the cowboy contestants with equally impressive regalia, and then the Marine contestants with toned-down horses and tack. The 2nd, 8th, 10th and 18th Marines all had entered contestants, as well as the "Special Troops" regiment. A dozen brand new "Water Buffalo" LVT-2s roared past at the end of the parade.

The scheduled "Greased Pig" event had to be canceled after the local cowboys went out and roped a huge wild boar for the event. The Division Recreation Officer, Captain Todd, ordered the boar to be greased. The Marines with the grease were relentlessly attacked by the boar, who also took on one of the broncos. The bronco won the fight with a hoof to the boar's snout and they somehow got him back into the cage. Captain Todd drove the cage out to the flats to release the uncooperative guest, but the boar immediately attacked Todd, who had to climb a nearby fence to survive. The boar then destroyed the cage and trotted off toward his wild home in the hills.

Bill spent the entire afternoon with Fred, Herb and Gerald, who explained the details of the rodeo competitions. There was the "Pony Express" race, put on by the professional cowboys, who passed a leather bag in a full-out relay race. The dust flew and the crowd cheered as many were surprised by the raw speed and agility of the horses. The Marines participated in a steer-riding competition, followed by a roping exhibition by the Hawaiian professional cowboys. The Marines roared with laughter at the "wild cow milking competition" before the roping and bulldogging began. Another comedic event ensued with the "mule race," where Marines learned that there were creatures more stubborn than their commanding officers. At 1615 hours, the ultimate event began when the Marines competed in the bronco-busting competition. The guys from 2nd Platoon all cheered wildly for their contestants, PFCs Clark and Sultonfus, from the 18th, but to no avail. At the end of the day, General Julian Smith handed out the prizes to the winners. The day was like no other during Bill's time in the Marine Corps. As they were all enthralled in the rodeo events, most of them, at least for a time, did not even think about the war.

Bill looked forward to any mail from home with the utmost enthusiasm. He received two letters from Jessie at the same time and he eagerly found a place to sit and tore open the envelopes. He put the letter to his nose to try and get just a whiff of the air from 454 Simms Street. The letters did smell like his mom, or perhaps he just imagined they did. All seemed well on the home front and Jessie told Bill that Al and Eunice had been married on Friday, November 19th, 1943. Bill knew there was about a 17-hour difference in time zones between Tarawa and Virginia, which meant that his brother Al was getting married just about the time he hit the beach at Tarawa. There would be even more catching up to do when he got home. Next, he opened two long letters from Helen's mother, Carrie Cochran. She filled in details of life in Sandwich, Illinois, and the routines of Helen, Wally, Phyllis and their new grandson. Wally had become good friends with Bill's father, Steve, and they shared their business knowledge in detail. Wally was now having thoughts about opening a men's store out in Sandwich, in addition to his "Sanitary Cleaners" business. The letters were so enjoyable and he could tell that Carrie thought so highly of Bill and his service to the country. He couldn't help but think about what a great mother-in-law Mrs. Cochran might make some day. As he finished the letters, Bill was a little disappointed that Carrie had not mentioned anything about Helen and Bill in a future sense, she only mentioned Helen's work and how she had been promoted and they had big plans for her. Bill was not sure what big plans might mean for a TWA employee, but for the first time, he began to wonder if he and Helen would be heading in the same direction when and if he ever made it home. Bill also knew something that no one else back home could have known; he had been changing since he left for the war, and he was more determined than ever to live a life that put God first above all else. He wanted to have a family, but he knew that if he were to trust the Lord, he would have to allow all his plans to be arranged by God, and that included marriage and family. It had now been more than two years since Bill had left home and the thought came to mind that it may not be fair for him to expect Helen to continue to wait for his return. He sensed that Helen's career at TWA would be her main focus in life. Helen had been to Kansas City, St. Louis and Phoenix on work assignments by now and it was only natural that her career had become very important to her. The Marine Corps, the airline and the war had all worked together to push them in different directions.

    Bill told Shannon about his disillusion with maintaining the long-distance relationship with Helen back home. When Bill had left home, he was certain he wanted to marry Helen when he returned. Over the past two years, Bill had changed as he had grown closer to the Lord, and this had changed his outlook on the future. Getting to know Lorna in New Zealand had helped Bill to see his future in a different light. Any woman he could consider settling down with would need to love God and place importance on the work of the church. He had a great respect for Lorna along these lines. Shannon asked Bill straight up if he had fallen in love with Lorna. Bill thought about it, but said he didn't think so. Being practical, Bill also cited that even if he did have feelings for Lorna, it would not make sense as they would end up 8,000 miles apart after the war. Bill enjoyed New Zealand, but he knew he was a hometown boy and wanted to live in Aurora, where he felt he belonged. Shannon encouraged Bill to consider that neither Helen nor Lorna seemed to be right for him and this was going to be a situation he would have to release to the Lord. Shannon told Bill he was sure he would find the right woman and be absolutely certain when he did.

Rev. Shannon Walker at Hilo, Hawaii, in 1944 with an unknown Marine.

(Walker Family Photo)

63. The Meeting

Not long after the rodeo, Bill had the chance to go into town at Kamuela and was walking down the sidewalk looking for a shop to buy some gifts. As he walked along, he noticed an Army soldier walking towards him who looked familiar. As the two approached each other, they stopped and studied one another for a good four seconds. Bill said "Phaxton?" and the other fellow said "Bennett?" Then they both started to laugh and shook hands. Phaxton had gone to school with Bill's brother Al way back when and had frequently been a visitor at 454 Simms Street. They shared a few stories about where they had been and Bill promised Phaxton that he would mention the meeting in a letter to Al.

The following day, Bill and the guys were going to the mess tent for dinner when Bill found a familiar face in a crowd of Marines. Just as Bill saw Bob Reder, Bob saw him and the two Aurorans shouted at each other and made straight for a very firm handshake. Bob Reder was with another East High friend, Duane Burkhart, who was a Chief Cook and had just gotten off duty. Bob asked him if he knew about any other Marines from Aurora, but Bill had only heard a few things and had not run into any of them. Bob told Bill that he and Duane had been looking them up in their spare time and they were planning on playing some baseball. They were going to have about eight of the Aurora Marines over to Bob's tent the following night and Bob wanted Bill to be there. Bill wanted in and they exchanged platoon info so that they could find each other again. Bill was very excited, as finding these old friends was like receiving a living letter. Getting together with the guys would be a real spirit lifter.

The following evening, Bill headed across camp to locate Company A/1/18 and Reder's tent. Bill asked a few Marines for directions and they pointed out Reder's tent down the line. Due to the chilly weather, the flaps were down and smoke puffed out of the stove pipe. Bill flipped the flap saying, "All right you guys, let's keep it down in here!" He was shocked to see his old high school buddy, Dick Sheble, who, in turn, was equally surprised to see Bill. The two shook hands wildly, then exchanged bear hugs and patted each other on the back. The good times they had shared flooded to mind and they were both thrilled beyond words. Reder and Burkhart were already there and the others were expected soon. Bill ribbed Dick Sheble about getting him into all of this in the first place. Back on December 8th, 1941, Dick was the fellow who told Bill that the line at the Marine Corps was short and they could get him right in. Dick admitted that he had no idea what the Marines did at that time either!

As the four of them laughed and reminisced, the flap flew open and Louis Kuk *(pronounced* cook*)* stepped into the tent. Louis' dad owned the East Side Body Shop and he had been a good body man himself before the war. Louis had played basketball at East High, and he and Bill had frequently played some pick-up games together around town. Ed Kocjan and Bill Johnson came along and they had both played football with Bill at East High. They laughed about having the largest overseas gathering of Tomcats in history, and that may well have been true. Ed's dad owned a liquor store up on High Street in Aurora and the guys couldn't help but ask him if his dad had recently shipped him anything they could drink. Bill Johnson had played football with Bill and he was one tough guy. Pete Andrews and Channing Miller arrived, and the tent was so loud the neighbors were probably about to complain. The other seven Marines buffeted Pete and Channing with pats on the back and shoulders and firm handshakes. There were now nine Tomcats in the tent. Bill had not seen Pete since one of the last days in Aurora when they ran into each other downtown. Pete's dad owned Main Hatters and the shoeshine business on Main Street. There was a lot of catching up to do in the tent that night. Pete's older brother, George Andrews, was in England with the 101st Airborne Division while Pete was with A/1/6 in the 2nd Division. Pete's battalion had first come ashore at Guadalcanal in January of 1943 and led the final offensive that pushed the Japanese off the island. Pete was in charge of a four-man M1919A4 light machine gun crew and had gathered a lot of experience. D/1/6 came ashore at Tarawa on Green beach and pushed along the south shore and once again led the assault that all but eliminated the Japanese resistance. Pete's unit had been one of those defending the Banzai charges which Bill witnessed from across the airstrip that night in the trench. Pete had been with Company D/1/6 at Tarawa and recently transferred to Company A/1/6. The 6th Marines had earned the nickname "Pogey Bait 6th" because their battalion was known to eat more candy than any other outfit. Bill was impressed with the younger Andrews as he had been in the thick of the fighting and done well.

Channing Miller had been a strong football player and an outstanding catcher in baseball. After high school, Channing worked as a solderer at the Stoner Manufacturing Company, (no relation to Bob Stoner), that made vending machines in Aurora. He also was the catcher for the 129th Club's men's baseball team, and considered to be one of the best catchers in the league. He had an arm like a rocket. Bill found out that Channing had been with 1/2 at Red Beach 2 on Tarawa, only two hundred yards to the west of where he had been fighting and lost Truitt and Bob Swigert. Herb Dale and Johnnie Jones had been with Channing's outfit, but they didn't know each other. Channing had been hit by shrapnel inside the LVT before he got to the beach and then received a gunshot wound to the arm but continued fighting. He had been awarded a Purple Heart for his wounds. Channing was a focused competitor and he transferred that into combat. Channing viewed his sole purpose as a Marine Squad Leader to kill Japanese so that he could go back home. Bob Reder was a flame gunner with A/1/18 and he had gone ashore with the first wave at Tarawa, landing on Red Beach 1 with 3/2, where so many Marines had been killed all around him. Bob had spent three days taking out Japanese positions with demolition men and his flamethrower. He told Bill the only reason he could ponder as to how he survived it all was that he promised God he would never miss church again. Reder was also a great athlete back home and played football, basketball and baseball in high school and in some men's leagues. He loved baseball.

Some of the guys brought their *Beacon News* copies along and they began taking turns reading newsworthy stories or joking about things they thought to be funny. Together, they put together a pretty good picture of what had been going on back in Bill's "Wonder City."

In the weeks that followed, Bill regularly got together with Reder and the Aurora Marines to play softball games which Reder had arranged with other Marine teams. The competition was fierce and Reder proved what a great strategic thinker he was when it came to baseball and softball. They won most of their games. Reder loved to read the sports section in the *Beacon-News* and he had the idea to sit down and write the new Sports Editor a letter. The *Beacon News* not only enjoyed getting the letter from Reder; they printed it. This is how it appeared weeks later:

Marine Writes Letter to the Sports Editor

A letter has arrived from Robert Reder, former star catcher for several softball teams in Aurora, who just got off Tarawa island but who had been able to keep up with local sports via the Aurora Beacon-News.

Reder mentions five other boys who were with him in the second Marine division that battled at Tarawa. Among them were Bill Bennett, who used to play a great tackle for East High, Louis Kuk, who was a cage star at the same school, Channing Miller, who caught for the old 129th Vets Baseball Team, Ed Kocjan and Bill Johnson. Following is Reder's letter:

Dear Eddie: You will undoubtedly be surprised to hear from me, but I have been noticing that you have been taking over George Eisenhuth's job on the sports column and must say that you are doing a pretty swell job. You also did a good job when you operated those baseball, diamond ball and boys basketball leagues back in Aurora. I am looking forward to playing ball again after this old war is over.

I've traveled quite a bit since I left Aurora for the Marine Corps. I was also in the initial landing on Tarawa and consider myself lucky to get out of that without a scratch. It's not like playing ball and it isn't as interesting, but a guy sure puts all he's got into it. There are a few of us from Aurora in this division. Channing Miller, who used to catch for the 129th Club, Ed Kocjan, Bill Johnson, Bill Bennett, who played football at East High, and Louis Kuk, who played basketball at East Aurora. Have been playing a little ball lately to keep in shape for the time I can get back. I know you are probably pretty busy these days but I thought you might like to hear from one of the boys who was usually in your hair when you umpired a baseball game or refereed a basketball game.

I see that LaVoy broke the conference scoring record; that's swell dope. Well Ed, I'll close now, wishing you lots of success as a sports writer.

Bob.

Reder's address is PFC Robert J. Reder, Co. A, 1st Bn., 18th Marines, 2nd Marine Division, Care of Fleet Postmaster, San Francisco, California.

    During the remaining days of February, Bill settled in to camp life at Camp Tarawa. Having the other eight Marine buddies from his hometown to talk to, in addition to the close friends from Company D, provided a solid social set up for him. Any time he could gain liberty to make the 65-mile trip over to Hilo, he would take it to visit the Walkers. There were several times that Lieutenant Simonson needed a work party to drive to Hilo to bring back supplies and Bill was always eager to be a part of it. Since the Walker's house was a short distance from the docks, he could ask the driver to stop for a few minutes. Shannon was frequently at the Hilo Center, which was even closer to the docks. Similar to the relationship that Bill had enjoyed with Clarence Eaton back in New Zealand, he engaged in long conversations with Shannon and they made a habit of praying together whenever they met. Bill shared his grief over the death of his friends at Tarawa. He also became convinced that sharing his faith in Christ with other Marines was more important than ever after seeing the 36 from Company D killed in action.

    March 2nd, 1944. The 20-minute long documentary film, "With the Marines at Tarawa," was released in theaters within the United States after requiring special permission from President Roosevelt. After news of the Marine Corps losing over 1,000 Marines at Tarawa had hit the newspapers and radio, there was a public outcry claiming that the Corps had been reckless with the lives of these Marines. Since the footage of "With the Marines" was actually shot on Tarawa during and after the battle, the public was able to see, for the first time, what the horrors of war looked like. Back home in Aurora, the Bennett family made a special effort to see the film, as did many more of Bill's friends and relatives. For those who knew that Bill had been at Tarawa, it was a sobering realization of what he had survived.

64. Replacements

Toward the end of March, the first arrivals of what would amount to thousands of new recruits began to settle in with the 2nd Division. There was a stark realization at the apparent youth of most of these new "replacements." Compared to the weathered and worn appearance of most survivors of the Solomons and Tarawa, the replacements looked like high school kids, and many of them should have been. The veterans referred to the replacements as "kids," "boy scouts" and "new guys." Of course, the replacements were made up of many good new Marines who knew their jobs and were dependable, but others were immature, annoying and had strong illusions about the glory of war. Company D was in need of approximately 60 replacements in order to bring it back up to the fighting size of 200 men. Near the first of April, 1944, Lieutenant Simonson reorganized the 2nd Platoon and paired Bill with Sergeant Charles "Chuck" LaPoint from North Swanzey, New Hampshire. Bill and Chuck had been together since San Diego, and Chuck had scored well on the sergeant's exam. The two "Montana Men," Gerald Coate and Fred Ellis, would round out the Pioneer team as corporals. Sam Herman, Carl Fortenberry, Lester Hellman and Bill Poterola completed the line-up for the "old timers." Assistant cook and carpenter Philip Trier came over from Headquarters Company along with the six new replacements: PFC William Taber, from Chicago, Basic 521 rifleman. PFC Anthony Di Gennaro from Greenwich, New Jersey. Di Gennaro was an assistant cook whose dad worked at a munitions plant back home. PFC William C. Walzer from Virginia, Basic 521 rifleman. PFC Harold G. Bonawitz, a 533 demolition guy from Billings, Montana. Bonawitz had been trained with the new C3 plastic explosives, which Bill had not. PFC James R. Clodfelter, from North Carolina, who was a Basic 521 rifleman. PFC Bennie Urioste *(pronounced* yoo-ros-tay*)* from Boise City, Oklahoma. Bennie's dad was of Bolivian descent and worked for the WPA. Lieutenant Simonson brought the replacements in for a talk with the platoon. His most important piece of advice for the new guys was, "Do NOT get killed."

The new replacements heard every kind of horror story imaginable and they had a lot of questions for the veterans. Bill worked with all of them to try and instill survival skills as best he could. In addition to Simonson's sage advice of "Do not get killed," Bill advised them to "Never volunteer for anything." He reasoned that if an officer is asking for volunteers, it is either something he is afraid to do himself or he figures your chances of survival are slim. If you volunteered to do it, he won't feel as bad when you get killed trying. Bill knew that in combat your chances of getting killed were plenty good without volunteering. The officer's job was to know what needed to get done and pick the best men for the job. Following orders was a must, volunteering was not. Bill spent a lot of time with Bonawitz and unofficially learned how to use C3 and accessories. Bonawitz was a tough Montana kid that had lived with his uncle in Billings and worked as a ranch hand. Ellis and Coate welcomed the new "Montana Man."

Bennie Urioste had a personality that fit with Bill's and he was respectful and eager to learn. Once he understood what Pioneers do, Bennie decided to train for the 729 Pioneer classification so he would be more useful than just a 521 Basic Rifleman. Bennie soon found out about Bill's serious devotion to Christ and he wanted to know why Bill prayed so often. Bill took Bennie to church with him and Bennie decided he wanted what Bill had in his life. Bill made sure he was available to pray with any of the Marines that had concerns. Some of the older Marines had never thought much of Christians before the war, but they had to admit that Bill practiced what he preached. As April 14th came and went, Bill had now spent three birthdays in the Marine Corps and away from home.

The mail call on April 18th, 1944, was an unusual one. Lorna had baked Bill two-dozen "Anzac" cookies made with oatmeal and raisins and sent them to him in a tin box. When he unwrapped the tin, there was a card attached with a short message written in her beautiful calligraphy. "To Bill, A little parcel for you to remember me by. Love & best wishes, from Lorna." The cookies were delicious and he allowed only the most endeared Marines to share them. Bill cherished the memories of New Zealand and the friendship of the Proctors. Eating cookies baked in their kitchen could not have brought the memories back with more force. He second guessed his decisions at times, but keeping his word to Helen and not exposing Lorna to the devastation that many New Zealand brides had to endure were good choices. For as much as the New Zealanders were grateful to the American Marines, they would pay a price for the actions of men who were not as virtuous with their daughters as Bill had been. In addition to the cookie delivery, Bill received the *Beacon-News*, a *Stoner Weekly* and several birthday cards from friends at 4th Street Methodist Church. *The Stoner Weekly News* gave Bill the breaking story that Harley's wife Betty had given birth to 7 pound, ¾ oz. Barbara Jane Stoner. Harley was somewhere in New Guinea and was probably getting the news about the same time Bill was. Lieutenant Robert F. Stoner and his wife Marijane had moved out to California as Bob was in the process of putting together the new squadron. *The Stoner Weekly* also mentioned Steve and Jessie Bennett coming over for an evening of food and a game or two of Bridge; no news about Bill getting home any time soon; Al Bennett was heading to San Francisco. That could only mean Al was headed to the Pacific.

Having been away from home for 28 months with no relief in sight, Bill came to the conclusion that he should no longer expect Helen to wait for him. He had to be honest with himself and with her; they had not really known each other well enough to be able to endure such a long absence. Helen had her hopes fixed on her career with TWA and it didn't sound as though having a family would be important to her anytime soon. There had been several men interested in dating Helen while Bill was gone, but she had kept her promise just as she said she would. Bill had been honest with Helen about his friendship with Lorna, and he had fully intended on coming home to Helen. If there were to be anyone to blame for ending the romance between Bill and Helen, it would have to be the Japanese. No one had foreseen a three-year separation and no one could expect them to survive it. There would be relationships that survived separation, but they tended to be the exception and not the rule. Bill arranged to make a phone call from the Walker's house in Hilo one Sunday night and it took a half hour to connect to the Cochran residence out in Sandwich, Illinois.

Mrs. Cochran answered the phone and she was so excited to hear Bill's voice. Helen came to the phone immediately and the two talked about their current situation as much as they could. Finally, Bill got around to his thoughts. He told Helen how sorry he was that the war had taken him away for so long. She knew that even if he had not volunteered he would have been drafted by now. Her father Wally had overseen the drafting of hundreds of men in their small town. Bill told Helen he wanted her to feel free to date and he would no longer hold her to her word to wait for him. He made it clear to her that nothing had happened between Lorna and him other than friendship and that he did not have plans to return to New Zealand. Helen told him she had an offer from TWA to transfer to Phoenix and she really wanted to give it a try. Considering what Bill was telling her, she thought she would reconsider the work option if it was still available. They exchanged apologies for any disappointments there might have been on either side and they agreed that they shared mutual respect for each other. Bill knew she deserved his respect for waiting so long. Helen had been learning that Bill's service to the country may have involved more than most could imagine. She had read accounts of Tarawa and knew that Bill had been there. They said goodbye and Bill placed the handset back on the receiver. It hurt to know it was over, but he knew he had done the right thing.

Bill was glad he had found the friendship of Shannon Walker and his family during his stay in Hawaii. Shannon had helped him through the aftermath of Tarawa, and had helped him in trusting the Lord with his future. The home-cooked meals and family interaction had been exactly what Bill had needed. The last weekend that Bill was able to spend in Hilo was one of the best. On Saturday, they went for a drive along the coast with the top down on their convertible and Bill drove most of the time. It was a warm day and they stopped at a secluded and very natural beach and spent about an hour swimming in the surf. Seeing Shannon and Helen interact with their children confirmed in Bill's mind that he wanted to be a family man. Bill related to David as a teenager and he hoped the war would be over before he reached draft age. "Lizzy" thought Bill was one of the nicest people she had ever met and little Dunham reminded Bill of Bobby back home. The Walkers decided to stop in to visit some friends near the beach and they all ended up staying for dinner. The hosts had a wonderful record player and a great collection of popular music. They literally rolled up the carpet in the living room and danced for hours. Bill danced the feet off little Lizzy.

The next morning Bill attended church with the Walkers, and as usual, had a nice lunch at their home. Bill went with Shannon and David to the Hilo Center for a pick-up game of basketball, where there were always plenty of servicemen looking for a game. Before Bill left for camp that evening, he made sure he properly said goodbye to the Walkers as he knew the 2nd Division was once again preparing to ship out. When that time came, there would be little or no time for goodbyes. The family gathered around Bill at the door and Shannon led them all in prayer as he asked the Lord to keep His hand of protection on Bill and to guide his path through life.

65. USS Nehenta Bay, CVE-74

Lieutenant Robert F. Stoner's attention was miles away as he looked through the window of the dining room at Club Del Mar and out to the Pacific Ocean. His attention was brought back to the table by the voice of his lovely wife Marijane. She had just asked Bob if the officers who had just been seated across the room were from his squadron, VC-11. Bob looked and saw that they were not. Bob and Marijane had been on a whirlwind tour of the U.S. since Bob left the Flight Instructor assignment at Corpus Christi, Texas, for preparation and assignment to the new Composite Squadron, VC-11. After the squadron had come together in Seattle late last year, they had trained in Oregon, several bases in California and were now in San Diego for their final shakedown cruises aboard aircraft carriers. VC-11 had just completed their cruise aboard the USS Altamaha, CVE-18, off the coast of San Diego and they were waiting for their cruise aboard the USS White Plains, CVE-66. Bob had completed torpedo training and "glide rocketing" training and the squadron looked as though it was coming together as a first-class operation. Once the shakedown cruises were finished, VC-11 would be assigned to the brand-new escort carrier USS Nehenta Bay, CVE-74, currently on her own shakedowns out in Hawaii picking up damaged aircraft for delivery back to San Diego.

The commanding officer of VC-11 was Lieutenant Commander Onia Burton Stanley, known as "Burt" Stanley. Stanley had led one of the Wildcat groups aboard the USS Lexington back on February 20th, 1942, when the Lexington was attacked by a large force of Japanese bombers near the Solomon Islands. Two four-engine flying boats had spotted the Lexington and were running for home when Stanley and his wingman shot one of the huge Japanese planes down. Stanley's counterparts, Lieutenant Butch O'Hare and Lieutenant Jimmy Thatch, teamed up over the next three hours to defend the Lexington from almost certain destruction. For shooting down three Japanese bombers and damaging a fourth, Butch O'Hare was awarded the Congressional Medal of Honor and became a national hero. Chicago's new international airport would be named in his honor in 1955. Stanley and Thatch received the Distinguished Flying Cross.

When Bob found out that Stanley would be his commanding officer, he couldn't have been happier. Stanley was a no-nonsense, by the book commander who could fly instinctively. The fact that he had been one of the heroes that saved the Lexington was an inspiration. Stanley was known to be somewhat cold as a leader, but he seemed to like Bob in a personal way, as Bob's personality was difficult to dislike. Bob had been a well-respected instructor at both Pensacola and Corpus Christi, and Stanley knew that he was a good pilot. Once the squadron began training together, Bob Stoner proved his abilities quickly. Bob took the initiative to find and solve any problems affecting the squadron in the air and he coached the other pilots on combat tactics and procedures. When it came to hitting targets with torpedoes, bombs or rockets, Bob led the way with his training scores. Since Bob was

Lieutenant Commander Onia Burton "Burt" Stanley, Commander of Composite Squadron VC-11 aboard the USS Nehenta Bay. Stanley was a tough "by the book" commander who became friends with Lieutenant Robert F. Stoner. (Official U.S. Navy Photo)

Lieutenant Senior Grade Robert Fraser Stoner, United States Naval Aviation, 1944. (U.S. Navy Photo)

An unknown flight of TBM-1C Avengers fly from an aircraft carrier somewhere in the Pacific.

(U.S. Navy Photo)

a Lieutenant Senior Grade and a skilled pilot, Stanley learned to rely on him as a leader of the TBM section of the squadron. It would only be a matter of time now and VC-11 would complete these shakedowns and finally go to sea aboard the Nehenta Bay. Then the real work would begin.

66. "Island X"

Once the 2nd Marine Division replacements had arrived and become acclimated to the new units, serious training began once again. Maps were handed out for the next objective, "Island X." There was a large sugar cane plantation on nearby Maui that became a frequent training area. Units would load Higgins Boats and make landings at the plantation and then perform simulated combat maneuvers. No one knew where "Island X" was, but it was obvious there would be cane fields. As for Company D, the time at Camp Tarawa had been much more peaceful as far as Captain Farkas was concerned. Liberty was not nearly as frequent on Hawaii and the losses from Tarawa may have softened the captain's view of the need to discipline the Marines. If he appeared heavy handed with the old guard, the replacements would not think well of it as they idolized the veterans. 1st Lieutenant Wilford Saylor and 2nd Lieutenant Simonson did a great job easing tensions between Captain Farkas and the men. Robert C. Jones had been promoted to captain, and shared some of the work load with Farkas.

On the training field, Bill worked with the demolition teams, and for the first time the Pioneer team had three demo guys: Bill, Sergeant LaPoint and PFC Bonawitz. If they needed to blow something up, they would be quite capable. The demolition teams trained hand in hand with the flame gunners again and they updated the tactics used at Tarawa. Besides the back-pack type flame guns, there was a new fearsome weapon, the Sherman M4 Flame Throwing Tank.

The assignment in the coming campaign would be different from previous ones. Instead of Company D being "farmed out" to other combat units, they would go ashore as a unit under the command of Captain Farkas. D/2/18 would land on Red Beach 2 with Bill's 2nd Platoon going in with the first waves. The 1st and 3rd Platoons would arrive the following day to move supplies forward to elements of 2nd Battalion, 2nd Marines and 2nd Battalion, 8th Marines. Red Beach 1 and 2 were directly south of a good-sized town on the battle maps. There were towns shown on the "Island X" maps and it didn't take a genius to equate towns with civilians. In the previous attacks, there had been a very limited amount of non-combatant civilians.

Bill spent time on the BAR range helping the replacements fine tune their technique and maintenance skills. He was issued a brand new M1 for his own rifle and he cleaned and oiled it daily. As for the rest of his combat gear, he prepared almost the exact equipment combination he had taken ashore at Tarawa. The only camouflaged piece of gear that remained was the helmet cover, as standard green utilities once again became the assigned combat uniform. If the need arose, Bill felt he was proficient with the .45, the carbine, the M1 and the BAR. During the first week of May, the 2nd Division held a massive dress rehearsal that involved over 10,000 Marines, dozens of Navy ships, hundreds of new LVTs, dozens of Higgins Boats and hundreds of Navy and Marine Corps aircraft. Company D went through several landing rehearsals on a little island called Kahoolawe, near Maui, prior to the big show, and then landed again with masses of Marines during the "dress rehearsal." The 2nd Division moved across the huge plain below Mt. Mauna Kea as Marine Corsairs and Navy Hellcats flew low overhead on their way to unload live fire on the hills up front. Rows of tanks led the way with new Sherman M4s fitted with flame throwers. Looking across the entire plain, the men and machines arrayed for battle were impressive. It didn't look as though anything could stop the 2nd Division. Combat teams took their turns attacking mocked-up pillboxes and bunkers. The Engineers had built an entire town out of crates, lumber and just about everything imaginable. Marines assaulted the town using live machine gun, mortar and 75 mm artillery fire. As the day wore on, they entered the town and cleared buildings going door to door. Officers barked out orders with unprecedented zeal as they looked for anything out of order or any Marine not doing their job properly.

When the massive maneuver was over, Company D went back to Camp Tarawa and cleaned and repacked all their combat gear. The division command only waited a few days before orders came that they were shipping out, and that this was "not a drill." Lieutenant Simonson went over the plans with Sergeant LaPoint, Fred Ellis and Bill. The 15-man Pioneer section would load onto the USS Sheridan the following day at the Hilo docks. They would be aboard the Sheridan for a while before the task force shipped out to Pearl Harbor. Bill, Fred and Gerald Coate went over their own gear with a clear mind that combat was coming and then went over the gear of the new guys one more time. As Bill spent the last night in the little cabin, he was glad he had said his goodbyes to the Walkers a week earlier, as there would not be time for it now. Although Bill could not imagine combat being any worse than it had been on Tarawa, he knew that facing the Japanese on the much larger "Island X" would mean a longer, more drawn out ordeal and it would cost many Marine lives to win it. Bill prayed for his fellow Marines and God's protection. As he fell asleep, he was imagining what everyone at home was doing.

Monday, May 8th, 1944. LaPoint told Bill and Fred to keep the team together while he went to find Simonson to check on the truck schedule. Dust rose from Camp Tarawa as everything that wasn't nailed down was being loaded for the docks. When LaPoint returned, he told the team they would have to walk across the camp to a staging area where trucks were lined up for loading. Each man had his full combat gear, as well as his sea bag; literally all they owned as Marines. Hours went by before they loaded a truck, and then getting all 15 Marines and their gear aboard was difficult. Everyone was checking with the Marine next to him to see if there might be a few more inches of room available somewhere. The 65-mile trip along "Saddle Road" to Hilo took much longer than usual and then getting the truck through to the docks to unload was like finding a parking spot at the state fair. Everyone munched on rations as they waited to unload at Hilo Pier 1. The USS Sheridan was moored with Pier 1 on her port side with the stairs dropped down to the dock. The Sheridan was a beauty as far as transports went, with dark gray paint and the white "PA 51" painted on her bow. The Sheridan was only a year old and the guys were glad they didn't get another rust bucket. The team went up the stairs and registered with the Naval Officer waiting on deck. A Navy Ensign directed them below to the bunkroom where they settled in for the duration of a long journey.

For nearly two days, Bill and the team watched crowds of Marines and equipment funneling through Hilo to the docks. At 1649 hours on May 10th, the Sheridan shoved off from Pier 1 and headed out to sea with the USS Doyen, USS Comet and USS Oak Hill. They made way to Honolulu Harbor where they moored at Sand Island for a few days before heading over to Maui to wait at anchor. The boredom of life aboard ship returned, but at least they had the Hawaiian weather on deck and the Navy food was always pretty good. On May 19th, the Sheridan made way to Pearl Harbor to take on fresh water and fuel oil and they steamed past Kahoolawe Island where they had made practice landings weeks earlier. As the Sheridan steamed through the islands, the scenery was about as good as it could get.

There was a momentary bit of excitement when PFC Hoyer, from the 2nd Assault Signal Corps, was showing his buddies how sharp his Ka-Bar knife was by cutting through a bar of soap. The Ka-Bar went through faster than Hoyer must have thought as it also made a six-inch laceration in his thigh. The wound was not life threatening, but it left a lot of blood on the deck. Simonson talked to the team and asked them if he really needed to say anything about knife safety.

On May 20th 1944, the Sheridan followed the USS War Hawk into Pearl Harbor and moored at berth X-17 in the East Loch, just offshore from Pearl City. Bill watched from the deck as Higgins Boats, Navy Launches and barges of every size moved matériel around the harbor. He imagined what it would have been like to have been here when the Japanese had attacked. Lieutenant Simonson made some jokes about keeping an eye on Matkovich and Poterola in case they got thirsty again and went AWOL over to the Post Exchange Club. Matkovich had been trying desperately, for over a month, to get an emergency leave back to the states to see his mother who was seriously ill. He certainly was on his best behavior. All the transports were taking on their fresh water and fuel oil while the LSTs (Landing Ship Tank) were across the harbor in the West Loch area loading hundreds of new LVTs (Landing Vehicle Tracked) for the planned invasion.

On the afternoon of Sunday, May 21st at 1508 hours, Bill was on deck with Bennie Urioste, Fred Ellis and a few other Marines relaxing in the shade when they heard a huge explosion from the west. They hurried to the rail to see a

The USS Sheridan carried Corporal William Bennett from Hawaii to the invasion of Saipan on June 15th, 1944. (Official U.S. Navy photo.)

black plume of smoke rising hundreds of feet into the air. Flames could be seen at the base of the smoke and then several additional explosions erupted that shook the Sheridan. At first, Bill thought it was some sort of attack, but there were no planes in the air. It must be an accident. After several minutes passed an explosion that defied description rocked the entire harbor and sent a shock wave across the deck of the Sheridan. A huge, mushrooming fireball rose a thousand feet in the air and Bill could actually make out LVTs and parts of LVTs flying through the air. Even more horrifying was the sight of bodies twisting high into the air. Debris showered down everywhere. From the deck of the Sheridan, they could not see the ground where the explosions were occurring because there were two land masses between them. They could see debris splashing into the water as far away as the Middle Loch. Word spread onboard the Sheridan that LST 143 was "afire" and the Sheridan's doctor departed in a launch to head to the area.

The fire and explosions continued throughout the night and the fires raged for most of the day on the 22nd. When it was over, six LSTs of the 2nd Division, which had just been loaded at Hilo, had been destroyed. There were at least 400 men injured and another 175 dead or missing. The invasion fleet was held at Pearl Harbor until another six LSTs could be brought in and reloaded with the surviving 2nd Division Marines. Bill thought back to his days of combat loading the transports and how careful and meticulous the Navy had been. Their description of what could happen if one spark or cigarette landed in the wrong place was nowhere near the actual horror of what 50,000 servicemen had just witnessed. Here had been hundreds of Marines concerned about being killed in the coming combat and they never even made it out of the harbor. Remarkably, the LSTs were replaced within a few days and the slower craft exited the harbor to get a head start on the rest of the fleet.

Unknown to Bill at the time, Bob Stoner's VC-11 Squadron had been assigned to duty aboard the USS Nehenta Bay CVE-74 on May 20th at San Diego, California. Bob and Marijane had spent a wonderful week together attending dinner and dancing at the Del Mar Club with the other officers and their wives. They managed to get up to Los Angeles for a few days and even managed to secure a pair of tickets to the Ice Capades. Since VC-11 would be at sea for an undisclosed period of time, Marijane would be going back to Chicago to share an apartment with her twin sister, Marjorie. Bob was looking forward to finally "getting to work" with VC-11, but he had mixed emotions about leaving "Mare," as he called her. The Nehenta Bay was leaving port on May 28th, so he thought to make the most of the nights that the two had left to share. Bob rationalized the sadness of separation with the thought that thousands of servicemen had done the same thing all over the country and now it was just his turn. He knew that he and Mare had things better than anyone could have asked. The Navy hosted a dinner for the officers of the Nehenta Bay and VC-11 aboard the aircraft carrier. The hangar deck was decorated in red, white and blue bunting and rows of tables supported brilliant white tablecloths. Hung on the hangar bulkhead was a large painting of the new VC-11 emblem and mascot. Walt Disney Studios had created an "angry ape" clutching twin machine guns with his feet while holding three aerial bombs in each hand. A patch of this new mascot would be sewn onto the flight jackets of all the VC-11 fliers and crew. A dance band played favorites as Bob and Marijane mingled with the officers and their wives. Lieutenant Commander Burt Stanley toasted the men of VC-11 and their coming tour of duty. The officers and their wives raised a glass in salute to VC-11 and their brand-new aircraft carrier. Captain Butterfield gave a speech about patriotism and winning the war. He said he was certain the men of the USS Nehenta Bay would do their part. In a matter of days, the carrier would leave port and sail for Pearl Harbor and then the Pacific beyond. Privately, in the darkness of their quarters at Del Mar, Bob stayed awake to pray about his departure and Mare's well-being. Bob earnestly looked forward to having a family after the war and he knew he

Shoulder patch of VC-11 Designed by Walt Disney Studios.

Poster of Lieutenant Commander Stanley and his pilots, made upon the assembly of Composite Squadron VC-11, 1944.

(From the archives of Lieutenant Commander Onia Burton Stanley)

would more than likely be in harm's way soon. Just as he had done his entire life, Bob placed his life in God's hands and went to sleep.

On May 31st, just past noon, the USS Sheridan weighed anchor and got underway for the harbor entrance following the USS Bolivar, USS Monrovia and USS Cambria. Just as they were nearing open water, Lieutenant Simonson announced a mail call and 2nd Platoon huddled on the bow to get mail from home. Bill had several letters from Steve and Jessie that had caught up to him and he went to sit in the shade to read them. Nearby, Mike Matkovich was reading through a letter from his sister in Chicago when he became visibly upset. His mother had taken a turn for the worse and died. He became furious and wanted to know the whereabouts of Lieutenant Saylor. He stormed to the officers' ward room, walked directly to Lieutenant Saylor's table and in a loud voice asked for permission to speak. Saylor gave him permission and Matkovich let go a tirade over not getting the emergency leave. He stated that over the past month he had plenty of time to get home and still rejoin the company. Saylor told Matkovich he had planned to promote him to company sergeant after they made the beach assault. Matkovich told the lieutenant that he could respectfully deposit the promotion into a bodily cavity and asked to be dismissed. Lieutenant Saylor told Matkovich he was sorry to hear about his mother and sorry about the whole affair. Matkovich saluted, turned and stormed out of the ward room. Quite a few of the guys from 2nd Platoon conveyed their condolences to Matkovich over the coming days and some of them thought it was best to leave him alone. The Sheridan turned to head west, leaving the mouth of Pearl Harbor behind. Four days later, Lieutenant Robert F. Stoner, aboard the USS Nehenta Bay, would make that same turn into Pearl Harbor on his way to the combat zone.

67. The Marianas

No sooner had the transports lost sight of the Hawaiian Islands, when an announcement was made that the Marines were now on their way to the Marianas Islands, some 3,000 miles to the west. The attack they had been planning would be on the island of Saipan, followed by another assault on the island of Tinian, just a few miles away. Saipan would actually be closer to Tokyo than it was to Hawaii. Strict combat-zone rules went into effect and the eerie red lights began to light the ship's corridors after dark. The card games and gambling became the entertainment and books and magazines were highly sought after. At the planning meetings on deck, "Island X" now had a real name. Saipan would be defended by an estimated 30,000 Japanese soldiers and sailors, and there were an estimated 40,000 civilians on the island. 33,000 of the civilians were Japanese or part Japanese while another 3,000 were indigenous islanders called Chamorro and 1,000 Carolinians. The Japanese had also transplanted 1400 Korean war-slaves to Saipan as laborers. The Marines could expect the Imperial Japanese soldiers and sailors to fight to the last man, but no one knew what the civilians would do. It was assumed that the Chamorro, Carolinian and Korean population cared for the Japanese about as much as the Marines did. Saipan was 12 miles long from north to south and

5.6 miles wide. The total landmass accounted for approximately 45 square miles which included jungle, farms, towns, hills, caves and the 1550-foot high Mt. Tapotchau in the center.

As Bill and the Pioneer team were standing in the chow line aboard the USS Sheridan on June 6th, 1944, just a little after 1700 hours, the captain's voice came on the intercom. He announced that Allied Forces had landed at Normandy, France, a few hours earlier and were advancing inland. A terrific roar was heard throughout the ship. Surely, this was a sign that the world was one step closer to the end of the war. On June 8th at 1905 hours, enemy planes were spotted about 40 miles away from the task force and General Quarters was sounded. Any Marines that had been trained as naval gunners were to report to battle stations while the rest had to wait helplessly below deck. This was a terrifying spot to be in on a ship. After 15 minutes, the alarm was canceled, but it was better safe than sorry. The next morning the fleet arrived at Eniwetok Atoll for fresh water and fuel. The following morning, 2nd Lieutenant Simonson, Captain Jones and Sergeant Gabel took 25 Marines from Company D and left the Sheridan to load onto an LST, as they would go ashore with the third wave. Simonson's team would prepare the beach for Bill's Pioneer team coming in minutes later in the fourth wave. Hopefully, things would go better in the first hours on Saipan than they did in the first hours on Tarawa.

On June 14th, the fleet rendezvoused with the flagship USS Rocky Mount about 100 miles from Saipan. Bill went over final preparations with the team and had his gear ready to go. There was a Protestant and a Catholic service held on deck, and Bill attended with most of the Marines of the Pioneer team. As they were preparing to try and get some sleep, Bill asked Bennie and the younger guys how they were doing. They were nervous and quite honestly scared. Bill told them they were all normal and reminded them to listen to LaPoint, Ellis, Coate and himself and they would all get their jobs done. They didn't have to win the entire battle; they just had to take care of the business in front of them. At 2100 hours, General Quarters were again sounded and this time it was a Japanese submarine. Now everyone had the same, helpless feeling. There is not much anyone can do about an enemy submarine at night. The fleet ran zig zag patterns on and off. The only harm done was the interruption of what little sleep may have been available.

Inside their two-story family home in Garapan, Saipan, eleven-year-old Setchan Akiyama prepared to run for her life. Her father, Tomomitsu Akiyama, had given Setchan a stack of important family papers that she was to carry to the family farm in Iliyang, along with her younger brothers and sisters and her stepmother. Setchan's father was a Japanese surveyor who had married her Chamorro mother when he came to Saipan to make maps during the 1920s. Setchan's mother had died when she was five and her father had remarried. Her father had to go to the north of the island and he told Setchan and her stepmother to stay off Beach Road by using the beach as they fled. He would come and find them at the farm as soon as he could. Setchan's 13-year-old brother, Shiuichi, had been out in the countryside with his friends when the shelling had started two days earlier and he was now missing. Her father had been out looking for him without success. They would later learn that he had been killed. Tomomitsu asked his next-door neighbor to watch over his family before he departed. As Setchan scrambled to get ready to leave, gunshots rang out from the house next door. A few minutes later, the Chamorro housekeeper from next door burst into the Akiyama's house in a frenzy. The neighbor's son was a Japanese soldier and he had just killed everyone in the family. Fearing they would be next, Setchan placed her youngest brother on her back, picked up her sister in her arms along with the stack of papers and headed out the back door with her stepmother and her siblings. They hurried away from the Garapan neighborhood, careful to avoid Japanese soldiers who might kill them, thinking that they would "save them from the Americans."

As they made their way out of Garapan, they walked along the beach just to the south of town. In the dim light, Setchan could see Japanese soldiers on the beach burying land mines in the sand. Suddenly a huge roar ripped through the sky and the ground shook as the Americans began shelling the island again. The small band of refugees crawled in between some large boulders along the beach. Setchan and her stepmother laid their bodies over the younger children who cried with fear. Setchan clutched her hands over her ears as the shells pounded the earth around her. When the shelling moved away from them, they got up and ran inland. Her stepmother decided to change their course and head for her family farm farther inland at Aslito instead of Iliyang. Moving through the light of dawn, they avoided any contact with others and only stopped to avoid the shelling.

At 0200 hours, the bunk room was awakened, but Bill had been awake for some time watching the orange glow of a cigarette brighten and then fade across the compartment. A quick trip to the head, a splash of some water on the face, a good tooth brushing and some deodorant was all that was needed before getting his utilities on. LaPoint waited for everyone to get dressed and then led them to the chow line for the now usual "steak and eggs" breakfast. The somber faces of the Navy cooks told the story of what was expected to happen today. By noon those same cooks would be carrying wounded aboard the Sheridan. Bill told the young guys not to overdo it on the chow as they would be loading the landing craft in a few hours. At 0433 they heard the sounds of the cables and winches lowering the Higgins Boats into the water; by 0453 the job was done. LaPoint led the Pioneers onto the deck and the demolition men went to retrieve their explosives while the riflemen loaded up with hand grenades. As soon as Bill came back with his demolition belt secured, it was time to go over the side. LaPoint shouted out roll call: "Bennett! Coate! Ellis! Clodfelter! Bonawitz! Walzer! Herman! Fortenberry! Taber! Poterola! Hellman! Urioste! De Gennaro! Trier!" Each team member bellowed, "YO!" as his name was called. Their team would be with a group of 75 Higgins Boats that would feign a landing north of the city of Garapan, to freeze the Japanese battalions at that point. In order to get into position, the boats had to get an early start, so it was nice to avoid the long line this time. Bill went over the side first and watched his hands to keep them away from Urioste's boots just above. Once his feet hit the bottom of the boat, Bill reached up and grabbed Bennie by the ankles and guided his feet inside. The

Marines loaded the boat in a matter of minutes and the crew gave the signal to the deck that they were ready to go. The eastern sky was just starting to show signs of light as the coxswain gunned the diesel and pulled away from the Sheridan at 0545.

Once out in the open water, the Higgins Boats amassed and headed north. The battleships and cruisers opened up with their pre-invasion bombardment and 16-inch guns belched smoke and fire hundreds of feet out over the water. The concussion of the guns was so great across the water that Bill could feel the air move on his face. Admiral Spruance had purposely positioned battleships that had been damaged during the Pearl Harbor attack to pour fire into Saipan. Japanese Admiral Chuichi Nagumo, who had led the surprise attack at Pearl Harbor, was caught on Saipan without an escape. The rebuilt USS Pennsylvania, USS Tennessee, USS Maryland and USS California poured Pearl Harbor revenge into the Japanese positions onshore. The thunderous 16-inch guns seemed to rock the very earth. Among the ships firing over Bill's head, but unknown to him, was the rebuilt heavy cruiser, USS New Orleans. 18 months earlier at Tulagi, Bill had helped remove the dead crew and take their bodies to burial on Tulagi Island after the Japanese had blown 150 feet from her bow. Now the guns from the deck of the New Orleans fired vengeful shells into Japanese positions. Sergeant George Gabel pointed out the USS Maryland as she sent her lethal explosives toward the Japanese command center. The Maryland had a special place in Gabel's heart and it was good to see her back in action. As Navy guns fired in unison, Bill surveyed the faces of the Pioneer team, both young and veteran. He could see the concern on the Marines faces and a few of the team deposited their steak and eggs on the floor of the boat. The sea spray slowly soaked everyone in the Higgins Boat. Wiping his breakfast from his mouth, Bennie looked up at Bill, who smiled slightly and said, "Welcome to Saipan!" The Higgins Boats plowed through the water to a distance just north of Mutcho Point north of Garapan. They made the turn toward the beach at 0745 and were right on time. The Japanese defending Tanapag Harbor watched but held their fire and their positions as the boats came nearer to shore. As soon as the Japanese opened fire with their shore batteries, the coxswains all turned the boats in a tight circle and headed back out to sea. The job was done. It would take hours for the Japanese to bring the troops north of Garapan down into the battle.

Just after daybreak, Setchan and her family arrived at the family farm and home of her uncle, William S. Reyes, at Aslito, where her uncle's family and her grandmother planned to hide from the coming battle. For several hours, her uncle and all who could help dug two pits beside the house and covered them with logs and dirt to make bomb shelters. After the pits were finished, a squad of Japanese soldiers came and told the family to get out of the shelter as they set up a machine gun in their place. The family had no choice but to seek shelter in the shallow crawl space below the house.

The Higgins Boats now headed back toward the line of departure for Red Beach 2, arriving at the control vessel at approximately 1030 hours. They were placed into a circular holding pattern to await the arrival of an LVT to take them into the beach. Most of the Marines in the boat caught up on a bit of sleep during this time. The scene on shore bore some resemblance to Tarawa with its palls of smoke rising high into the air. Dozens of Navy and Marine planes flew in low to bomb, rocket and strafe Japanese positions just inland from the beaches. The first waves of Marines met heavy enemy fire on the beaches, but they fought their way through and were pushing the Japanese back 100 to 300 yards. Bill could see burning LVTs across the lagoon as the Japanese mortars and artillery had been surprisingly accurate during the first waves. Focusing on the job at hand, Bill thought about getting to the beach and supporting the assault troops as they moved forward. He at least *hoped* they could move forward. Around noon, the Pioneer Team transferred from the Higgins Boat to a Water Buffalo LVT-2. The 15 of them and the driver were all that would fit. The LVT maneuvered to the line of departure and circled for another hour waiting for the other LVTs to bring their loads. Finally, at 1310 hours, the driver received the signal to head for the beach. After five minutes, artillery splashes began to send up geysers of water within the formation of LVTs. Several were hit and exploded and sank. Bill looked over the side for a second, just to get an idea of how far out they were. He knew this was not the smartest thing to do as there was a lot of metal flying around out there. LaPoint yelled at Bill and Fred and told them to "load weapons!" They turned and passed the order to the team. Bill pushed an eight-round clip into his M1 and let the bolt snap. The sound of M1s loading could be heard over the roar of the LVT's diesel. As they drew closer to the beach, machine gun and small arms fire began to ping off the LVT. LaPoint moved to the small opening in the forward armor and then exchanged shouts with the driver. LaPoint was trying to see where the best place to unload might be. Due to the LVTs on either side, the driver was telling him that they had to go straight ahead.

The LVT jarred as the tracks made contact with the sandy bottom and the speed increased twofold. There were so many Marines lying on the beach that the LVT driver had to stop about 30 feet from the sand. The driver shouted, "Everybody out!" and LaPoint immediately echoed the command with, "Over the side!" Bill swung his legs over the side with his M1 in his right hand while his left hand shoved his body away from the LVT. He splashed into the knee-deep water and ran for the beach while in as low of a crouch as possible. There were splashes of small arms fire and the LVT was getting hit with sporadic shots, but all fifteen men made it to the sand without getting hit. As Bill plowed into the sand on his belly, he looked back to see the rest of the team hitting the beach behind him. He crawled up behind the Marines in front, who were deeply dug into the sand. The beach rose up about eight feet in front of them, where grass, shrubs and trees lined the edge of the beach. LaPoint told Bill they needed to find Simonson and Matkovich. Bill took Poterola and headed south while Ellis took Herman and headed north. Find them or not, they were to be back to this point in 10 minutes.

The beach was all too familiar as Bill and Poterola crawled along looking at the faces of the dug-in Marines. There were dead Marines lying on the beach and parts of Marines covered in sand. The Japanese, as expected, had the beaches "zeroed in" with their artillery and mortars and it was life or death to get everyone off the beach as soon as possible. The fighting on Red 2 had now been raging for over five hours and the combat teams had pushed inland about 100 yards. U.S. tanks were at work up over the berm taking on Japanese armor trying to push the Marines back into the sea. Bill went as far down the beach as he could in five minutes, then went back to the team. When Bill and Poterola found LaPoint, the team had already headed north to where Ellis had found Lieutenant Simonson. The three of them moved out in that direction.

Teams of D/2/18 arriving at Red Beach 2, Saipan, around noon on June 15th, 1944.

(U.S.M.C. Photo)

    They located the Pioneer team and the command section from Company D about 50 yards north of where they landed. It was good to see familiar faces looking out from under their camouflaged helmets. Bill spotted George Cothran and crawled over to him. Bill asked Cothran where Matkovich and Simonson were. Cothran pointed up the beach and Bill turned to "duckwalk" in that direction. Bill located Matkovich and Simonson and LaPoint arrived a minute later. Simonson explained to LaPoint that they were actually on the southern edge of Red Beach 1 as the LVTs had veered somewhat north under fire. They should have been closer to where Bill and Poterola had been a few minutes ago. They would stay put for now. Bill dropped his pack and unsheathed his shovel. He and LaPoint went to work digging in to one of the only open spaces left in the proximity as they needed to get below ground fast. The beach sloped up toward the trees at a fairly steep angle and Bill dug extra deep on the front to try and make room for keeping his head down. The plan was to move forward about 30 yards as soon as they could and start piling ammo in a low area in the sandy hills just beyond the beach. Matkovich had brought a 4' x 10' canvas sign, complete with poles and ropes to set up on the beach. When they arrived under fire, they threw it over the side of the LVT and ran for cover. The sign had a black crescent moon painted on it to signify the location of food delivery. Matkovich had taken a ribbing over carrying his "outhouse sign." Simonson had retrieved the sign and was waiting for things to settle down on the beach before setting it up. At this point, he didn't want to give the Japanese anything else to shoot at. It looked as though the entire 2nd Platoon had made it ashore unscathed and had managed to assemble on the beach. Lieutenant Simonson took a rifle team and crawled up and over the sand dunes to recon the area above the beach.

Marines digging in on Red Beach 2, Saipan June 15th, 1944. Recovering water and ammunition from dead Marines became a priority of survival.

(U.S.M.C. Photo)

As Bill crouched in his foxhole looking up the grade toward the tree line, a Japanese artillery shell exploded down the beach behind and to his left, about 75 yards away. The sound of shrapnel hissed through the air as another burst and another began "walking" right up the beach in his direction. Some of the shells were airbursts that exploded above ground to rain down lethal shrapnel. Every Marine in 2nd Platoon hugged the bottom of their foxhole or lay flat on the beach as the sand shook beneath them. Two shells landed just behind Bill's position and it felt as though the explosions would throw him right out of the foxhole. Sand and debris rained down on Bill's helmet and seemed to fill half of his foxhole. As soon as the explosions subsided, the shouts of Marines were coming from everywhere. Bill clearly heard, "I'm hit!" coming from nearby and rose to his knees to survey the smoking beach. LaPoint, Ellis, Cothran and Gabel all came crawling toward the shouts as Bill moved on his elbows over to Matkovich's foxhole. Matkovich lay on his side clutching his left buttock where his pants were partly blown away and blood was soaking the area. Gabel was screaming for a corpsman. Matkovich cursed at the Japanese as Gabel told him to lay face down as he tore open a package of bandages to apply pressure to the huge wound. Bill came around to Matkovich's face to tell him that he would be okay. Matkovich asked Bill to see if he could find his wallet, which had been in his left back pocket. Bill looked around as did several of the others, but the wallet was not to be found. Matkovich cursed fluently as he explained that he had forty dollars in his wallet, more than a month's pay. He again cursed the Japanese for blowing his rear end off. Some poor Marine's intestines had landed next to Matkovich and some of the guys quickly buried the gore in the sand.

Corpsmen went to work up and down the beach as several Marines had been hit by shrapnel from the artillery shells. Lieutenant Simonson crawled back over the sand dunes to assess the situation. He carefully came to his knees just behind the corpsman as he was attempting to dress Matkovich's wound and stop the bleeding. Matkovich needed more work and the corpsman was afraid he might go into shock. He jabbed a syrette of morphine into Matkovich's arm and tied a cardboard tag onto his shirt stating that he had been given morphine. Another LVT arrived with ammunition a few minutes later and the corpsman told Simonson they could move Matkovich. Bill lifted Matkovich by the shoulders as Gabel and Ellis carefully lifted from the knees to place him on a stretcher face down. Marines pulled the ammo boxes out of the LVT as they ducked for cover when rifle fire pinged off the sides. Once the LVT was emptied, they lifted Matkovich over the side for a ride back to the ship. There was no doubt that the war was over for Mike Matkovich. Bill turned his head to see the LVT grinding back out to sea and asked the Lord to watch over Matkovich. Lieutenant Simonson now shouted out orders to "Get these men off the damn beach." They immediately moved 2nd Platoon off the beach and into the trees to dig in and start setting up the supply dump.

Marines loading wounded into an LVT-2 Water Buffalo at Red Beach 2, Saipan, on June 15th, 1944.

(U.S.M.C. Photo)

For the next several hours, the Marines from Company D pulled ammunition and water cans from incoming LVTs and started to stockpile a dump just over the first hill in the cover of the brush. Bill made sure that the guards dug foxholes as far from the ammo dump as possible, a lesson well learned on Tarawa. Bill and Fred went forward with Lieutenant Simonson and located a lieutenant from 2/6. Simonson made arrangements to push supplies into their company as they advanced. Lieutenant Saylor was now on the beach organizing the off-loading of ammunition and water and getting a flow going up to the supply dump. Lieutenant Simonson was running from the beach to the dump and then forward to make sure supplies were moving ahead to the Pioneers and then on to the front line. The Shore Party was able to set up the canvas marker on the beach to show their location to the incoming LVT drivers. The Marines from 2/6 pushed inland and over Beach Road, which was about 50 yards from the beach. Cothran and the Dump Marker Section located the next dump just in front of Beach Road, which would allow them to move supplies up and down the road once the area was secure. 18 riflemen, all PFCs, made up the Security Section from which Bill and other team leaders could pull additional Marines to station as needed. The Pioneers stayed busy bringing supplies up to 2/6, in the front line, from the nearest dump. Bill left most of his equipment, including his demolition charges, at the Beach Road dump and carried his M1 on the sling as he ran ammo cases and crates of hand grenades up to 2/6. Bonawitz carried his C3 explosives, should they be needed. The fighting was hellacious all afternoon and there was a steady flow of wounded and dead Marines coming back from the line of 2/6. Sergeant Gabel positioned the Security Section out on the flanks, about 30 yards north and south. Several small groups of the enemy appeared out of nowhere and exchanged rifle fire and grenades. The Japanese were killed without any Marines being wounded. The biggest problem continued to be the relentless shelling by the Japanese from the high ground far inland. The Navy was punishing the hills with their big guns, but the Japanese were very good at digging in and protecting their positions. Just offshore, and behind D/2/18, the USS California was sending 16" shells into the hills. The boom from those guns could be felt in Bill's chest and the shells shrieked overhead with a sound that had to put the fear of God into the enemy. At 1630 hours, three Sherman tanks roared up over the sand hills and crashed through the brush just to the north, effectively making a new road as they went past. Seeing all that steel going up in front was a good feeling. The Japanese had a lot of armor on the island and there was no doubt the Marines would be seeing it soon.

A little after 1900 hours, as the sun was sinking in the west, Colonel Richard Nutting brought in company headquarters and a rifle company from 2/2 to the beach directly behind Company D. Nutting set up a command post and the riflemen came up through D/2/18 to dig in for the night. Bill moved up to the front line with LaPoint and half the Pioneers while Coate and Ellis dug in on the east side of the road with the other half of the team. 2/6 had pushed inland about 500 yards and then swung north to face Garapan for the night. They were expecting the counterattack to come from this direction. 2/6 set up listening posts out in front about 100 yards with radio communication back to the lines. The Pioneers dug their foxholes near the 2/6 command post. Supplies would continue to be brought in under the cover of darkness. Nearly 8,000 Marines were already ashore spread out over four miles of beach. The combat teams had pushed inland as far as 1,000 yards at several points, and as little as 300 yards in others.

Just a few hundred yards to the south, out in front of the center of Red Beach 2, Pete Andrews dug in his light machine gun crew with Company A /1/6, under the command of Captain Charles R. Durfee. Pete had an assistant gunner, who carried the gun, and two riflemen who carried ammunition and guarded the flanks of the machine gun position. Pete carried the tripod so that he could direct the position of the gun. The assistant then set the gun on the mount so that Pete could load and fire while the assistant supported the in-feed belt. The position for the night consisted of the large fighting pit for the two gunners and two smaller pits for the riflemen about 10 feet on either side. The riflemen were also loaded with hand grenades. Pete had selected a spot that gave him a good view over 200 yards of mostly flat terrain. No one planned on getting any sleep tonight.

Out at the family farm at Aslito, Setchan Akiyama lay on a blanket under her uncle's house as she huddled with her younger siblings to try and keep them quiet and as happy as possible. She could hear the Japanese soldiers just a few feet away talking about how they planned to fight the Americans when they arrived. They would try to catch them by surprise when they were out in the open, kill as many as possible, then move back into the hilly jungle behind the farm and set up the machine gun again. Setchan's uncle was quietly worried about the presence of the soldiers as it would definitely attract unwanted trouble to the house. Setchan's Chamorro side of the family were devout Catholics and they prayed for the best. She checked the papers that her father had given her inside the bundle of extra clothes she had brought and she placed it under her head for a pillow. It had been a long, hard day and it was easy to fall asleep. Tomorrow would be worse.

68. Counterattack

After digging a foxhole worthy of saving his life, Bill rolled in and opened his pack to pull out two cans of cold C rations. The day had been a long one and the fighting was brutal, but the guys who had been on Tarawa could not complain about the temperatures that had been in the upper 80s. Word had gone out from the command post to "buddy up" for the night and have one awake while one sleeps. Bill and LaPoint traded shifts of sleep until midnight, when one of the listening posts radioed in that there was movement approaching them. The Japanese unleashed a hellacious artillery barrage that began to pound the ground and Bill felt as though the explosions might "shake his teeth out." There was nothing that could be done except stay in the foxhole and keep one's head down. After about fifteen minutes, the barrage stopped and all was silent for a minute or two.

The captain radioed an offshore destroyer and ordered star-shell illumination, and within one minute Bill heard the naval guns boom behind them. The huge red flares lit up the sky and the ground in front of them, and a mass of humanity could be seen moving toward them. A few hundred yards away, Pete Andrews looked down the barrel of his Browning .30-caliber machine gun at the mass of Japanese, lit by the dim red light. He heard Captain Durfee order the listening posts back to defensive positions. About 500 yards in front of the Marine lines, the Japanese stopped. Shouting and singing broke out and some of it sounded intoxicated. Then a single Japanese tank clanked its way to the front of the hoard and the turret opened as a lone bugler stuck his head out. A Marine out front shouted back toward the command post, "Tell the Colonel that the 'kitchen sink' is here!" referencing Colonel William K. Jones, the commanding officer of 1/6 who was nearby. Pete couldn't help but chuckle in spite of the biting nerves that had him on edge. The muffled laughter of Marines could be heard across the line.

Within seconds, the bugler sounded the charge and the shouts of 1,000 Japanese soldiers cried "BANZAI!" as they sprinted toward the Marine lines. The Marines held their fire until the enemy was within 200 yards and then the full fury was unleashed. Pete put the front sight on the nearest attackers and let a full belt of 50 rounds fly. He moved his tracers slowly from left to right to cover a wide area across the Japanese front line. Without waiting to see the results, he opened the breech and set another belt in place, snapped the bolt back and fired in 10 round bursts at the oncoming Japanese. Back at 2/6, Bill and the Pioneers left their foxholes and filled in on the line as the Japanese screamed and charged. Trying to pick out any individual enemy was nearly impossible as they fired into the dimly lit human mass as it rolled across the undulating field. After eight pulls of the trigger, Bill's M1 ejected the steel clip and the bolt stayed open. He shoved another clip into the breech with his thumb and let the bolt snap forward. Machine gun tracers poured into the enemy lines and lit up the night sky. Additional star shells burst overhead and Bill could see the Japanese falling by the score. Mortar shells exploded and a few bazooka rounds shot toward the advancing enemy. It was slaughter. After fifteen minutes of sheer chaos, the Japanese retreated and cease fire was called across the Marine lines. Not one Japanese soldier had reached a Marine position.

At first light, Colonel Jones sent a recon team out front to assess the damage to the enemy. The lone tank had been hit by a bazooka round and the bugler was slumped over the turret. A single rifle bullet had gone straight up the stem of his bugle and blown the back of his head away. The 6th Marines counted over 700 Japanese bodies that morning, indicating that the attack had been at least a battalion strong. Bill and the Pioneers spent the second day on Saipan helping 2/6 reorganize and resupply, while Pete Andrews with 1/6, did the same. 2/6 had lost so many men on the first day that Command had sent in Lieutenant Wood B. Kyle with 1/2 to relieve 2/6. Fellow Auroran Corporal Channing B. Miller dug into the Saipan soil less than 100 yards from Bill and the Pioneer team, but neither knew that the other was nearby. Command wanted to strengthen their current positions before extending themselves too far to the front. Colonel Jones of 1/6 was adamant about not allowing any unit to push ahead of the battalion. In his experienced opinion, that was the fastest way to get good Marines killed. The battalion had to advance together in order to defend each other's flanks. The day would be spent preparing for another counter attack and bolstering defensive positions. The Japanese rained down artillery and mortar rounds most of the day. More Sherman tanks would come ashore to strengthen the line. When Bill went back to the dump at Beach Road, he told Fred Ellis about the night they had spent and the successful repeal of the counterattack. Fred had hunkered down during the artillery barrage and then watched the fire-fight from a distance. He was upset that he had not been there. He asked Bill to agree that the two of them would not separate again as long as they were on the island, and Bill agreed.

69. Collateral Damage

Not long after the first light of morning, Setchan and her family heard the Japanese soldiers outside in the pits talking quietly, but excitedly. Weapons clicked as though readying themselves for battle. One of Setchan's cousins peered out through a gap in the foundation toward the fields at the front of the house and the tree line several hundred yards away. He turned and reported that he could see soldiers in the tree line and he thought they must be Americans. Setchan's stepmother held her baby brother and took him behind a post to shelter him while Grandmother picked up little sister Elpedio and joined them. Uncle William whispered loudly as he told everyone to get down and stay down. Younger sister Teruko and younger brother Jose were across the crawl space near Aunt Carmen.

Suddenly, the Japanese machine gun opened fire just a few feet outside. Setchan could hear boots on the floor of the house and then rifle fire just above them. The Japanese were shooting out of the house as well. Setchan put her thumbs in her ears and her fingers over her eyes as her father had taught her to do when in danger. Loud "zips" began to smash into the house and foundation and dust and debris flew into the crawl space. One of her cousins crawled past and said, "Look, they are fighting right outside!" The machine gun continued to fire and explosions were heard out across the field. The Japanese were dropping mortar rounds from far back behind the house into the field where the Americans were trying to cross. Setchan opened her eyes to look across the crawlspace and she saw her younger sister Teruko crying and sitting up. Setchan thought to crawl to her to comfort her. Before she could finish the thought, a blinding flash seemed to explode in the middle of the crawl space and Teruko disintegrated in the midst of it. Setchan's breath was sucked from her lungs and her ears deafened with the blast. As she tried to sit up from beneath the debris, it was suddenly bright where she was. She looked above her and the house was gone from its foundation. One of the American Sherman tanks had made quick work of the poorly-built farm house.

Setchan's back was numb in places, her eyes, nose and mouth were filled with dust and she could barely make out sounds. She crawled to the post where her stepmother had been. Her baby brother's head was opened wide with gore and his lips quivered with a sucking motion. Her stepmother's arms were moving slowly and she was bleeding from many places. Setchan found Grandmother, who was also wounded, and little Elpedio who seemed unharmed and was screaming frantically. Setchan instinctively crawled for the safety of the pits outside and slid into the first one. The dazed Japanese soldiers were preparing to make a run for it. One of the soldiers looked at Setchan and told her, "I am a soldier. I am supposed to die! You can come in." As he turned his head to pick up the machine gun, Setchan saw that part of his face was missing, and the huge festering sore was crawling with maggots. The Japanese jumped from the pit and "zips" of gunfire from the Americans peppered the ground around them as they fled into the trees. Setchan's younger brother was trying to run to the pit and one of the bullets hit him squarely in the chest and knocked him flat on his back. Setchan reached for him and grabbed his shirt and pulled him into the covered pit. He was not breathing. He had a hole in his chest and she rolled him over. His back was shattered. Two of Setchan's older female cousins crawled into the pit. The first had four or five bullet holes in her shoulder, torso and leg. She was bleeding profusely. She took off her clothes to try and stop the bleeding and Setchan tried to help. Her cousin cried and said she was getting very hot. Then she leaned back against the wall of the pit and died. Her other cousin had a horrible wound to her abdomen and she was holding her intestines in with her dirt- and blood-covered hands.

U.S. Marines using a flamethrower to attack a Japanese position near a farmhouse on Saipan.

(U.S.M.C. Photo)

Setchan crawled back to the wreckage of the house and brought Elpedio to the pit. She then went back and somehow managed to drag her stepmother and Grandmother to the safety of the pit. When she returned with Grandmother, her cousin with the abdominal wound had died. Setchan and Elpedio seemed to be the only ones unhurt. Setchan did not realize that she had several pieces of shrapnel lodged in her back. She sat for a period of time trying to think of how she could get help for her family. She could hear shouts outside the pit and then two or three loud explosions that shook the ground. Suddenly, there was a roar and then a flash of flame blew into the pit. She instinctively turned and tried to cover her face. She felt the flame searing her back and she screamed wildly. The flame stopped and she heard men yelling outside the pit. A rifle barrel came through the opening and she expected immediate death. Then the barrel pulled back and an American Marine peered into the hole. He immediately began to yell in words that Setchan could not understand. Then the logs that formed the roof began to lift and Setchan could see many Marines above working to uncover the pit. A Marine with a medical bag jumped into the pit and quickly looked at Setchan and Elpedio, then lifted them up to the arms of the Marines above. As Setchan's head hung face down, she could see that everything around the pit had been burned black. The Marine quickly carried Setchan to the other side of the house wreckage to gain shelter from possible Japanese fire. Soon Grandmother and her stepmother were carried over and laid next her. As the medic was checking their wounds, several other Marines stopped to assist him. Setchan noticed that all of the Marines had very concerned looks on their faces. Her stepmother's arm was badly broken but she kept trying to reach for Elpedio. She cried out for her baby, but Setchan told her that he was dead. One of the Marines put his hand on Setchan's forehead and smiled at her. He nodded his head as though saying yes and told her something she did not understand. Setchan's body shook with pain and fear. A tank rolled past the house followed by many more Marines as they went to pursue the Japanese.

A Navy corpsman and U.S. Marines treat a wounded Japanese girl on Saipan. She had been told that the Marines would torture and eat her.

(U.S.M.C. Photo)

The medic gave Setchan, Grandmother and her stepmother a syrette of morphine and drinks of water that he poured into a metal cup from his canteen. Another Marine held Elpedio and tried to get her to stop crying. Soon a group of Marines arrived with stretchers and they loaded the three badly wounded civilians onto them and carried Elpedio in their arms across the field. Beyond the tree line, many more Marines were digging holes and moving equipment where they came to a truck with a red cross. The stretchers were placed into the truck and it bounced along the dirt road. The ambulance arrived at an area of tents near Lake Susupe, where Setchan, Grandmother and her stepmother all underwent surgery at the hands of Marine Corps and Navy surgeons. Eight members of Setchan's family lay dead at Aslito.

70. The Long Haul

On June 17th, 1944, Captain Farkas recalled all three platoons of Company D to an area just to the east of Beach Road. The Company unloaded water distillation equipment at Red Beach 2 while experiencing occasional artillery fire from the slopes of Mt. Tapotchau. Captain Farkas had the equipment brought to a clear area near the road so that the distilled water could be loaded on trucks to be delivered north or south. The orders given were all regarding the organization and assembly of the equipment without anything being mentioned about security. Somehow, orders to dig in and set up defensive positions were overlooked in the rush to move the equipment. The sounds of battle raged in the areas nearby. Bill had teamed up with Johnny Jones and they were bolting up a support structure when Japanese shells began exploding in the midst of Company D. Shrapnel buzzed so close to Bill that he could feel it move the air. Captain Farkas screamed, "Get in your foxholes!" Bill and Johnny ran with their heads down toward a large banyan tree with a huge tangle of roots at its base. Bill dove in between the roots and buried his head into his helmet as the ground shook with fury.

The shelling continued for about three minutes and then stopped abruptly. As Bill and Johnny crawled from the banyan roots, Johnny looked at Bill and said, "Foxholes? What foxholes?" Bill started to laugh and then Johnny started to laugh and a few others began laughing nearby. As the smoke cleared, so did the laughter and fortunately, Captain Farkas did not hear the guys laughing at his order to take cover into the non-existent foxholes. Bill did not dislike Farkas, but he had yet to see him tried in combat and it was hard to trust him completely. Apparently, in the haste to set up the distillation equipment, Captain Farkas had overlooked digging new defensive positions. Any chuckling about the orders halted quickly as shouts for a corpsman rang out from the trees across the clearing. PFC Wysocki had been hit by shrapnel in both arms but he was conscious and seemed in good spirits as two other Marines held pressure on his wounds. There was another Marine on the ground near Captain Farkas. As Bill moved through the smoke and dust, he could see the Marine had his helmet off and a corpsman was applying pressure to a wound on the back of the fellow's neck. Blood had soaked the back of the utility jacket and it looked pretty bad. When the Marine asked the corpsman "How bad is it?" Bill immediately recognized the voice as belonging to Lieutenant Simonson. The fact that he was still talking was a good sign. The Navy corpsman held pressure on the three-inch gash until he could have Simonson take over the pressure for himself. The corpsman thought that the shrapnel bounced off Simonson and was not lodged in his neck. Captain Farkas assigned two nearby Marines to help get Simonson back to the beach to catch an LVT for the USS Bolivar for treatment. Simonson got to his feet, put his helmet on his head and began to head for the beach. Dozens of Marines said, "Good luck lieutenant" and "Take care sir!" as he passed by. Most of the company thought Simonson may have the "million-dollar wound" that would send him back to the States. Bill knew Simonson's presence as a leader could not be replaced. Another corpsman was able to stitch PFC Wysocki right there in the field and he stayed in the fight. The distillation equipment was a total loss.

A short distance away from Company D/2/18, to the north and a half mile from the beach, Channing Miller led his recon squad across open ground. Channing paused every 15 yards and surveyed the terrain ahead for the enemy. He knew they were there, but he couldn't see them. Silently, he waved to the left and right and the 12 Marines came back to their feet, crouched low to the ground, and slowly advanced. Suddenly, Japanese machine gun bullets zipped past Channing's head and he heard the sickening impact on human muscle and bone. Before he could even scream, "Get down!" two of his men dropped to the ground dead. Channing looked forward and spotted the fire from a well-hidden machine gun nest. Two machine guns were firing on them from the same fortification. He needed rifle grenades or a bazooka, but the squad had neither. Channing told the squad to stay put and headed back to the line to get the right tools. He crawled through grass and brush until the ground became bare, then jumped to his feet and ran a zig-zag pattern across open terrain. The Japanese machine gunners splashed bullets into the dirt in front and in back of him.

Coming upon a shell crater, Channing slid to the bottom to take a few breaths before continuing his sprint back to A/1/2. As he approached the line, he waved his arm above his head and shouted "Miller!" Channing shouted that he needed rifle grenades and TNT. He quickly filled a bag with four rifle grenades and grabbed a satchel charge and sprinted back to the squad. Instead of going back to his pinned-down men, he ran to the east for the cover of heavier brush and a tree line. He ran low to the ground and crawled through open areas to come around the back side of the covered fortification. On the left side of the pillbox, he encountered two Japanese riflemen guarding the enemy's flank. He dispatched them both with his M1. Coming around to the back of the pillbox, Channing attached a rifle grenade in place and fired it through the open door of the emplacement. Smoke and dust blew out the door as the grenade exploded, but a few seconds later, machine gun fire spewed through the opening. He clicked another grenade in place and fired through the smoldering door. The second explosion was followed by silence. Channing approached the door from their left flank and fired into the two riflemen he had previously dropped to make sure they were dead. Then he pulled the igniter on the satchel charge, threw it through the opening and took cover. The satchel exploded and almost completely destroyed the pillbox structure. Channing ran back to his men to find two dead and three wounded. Forward elements of A/1/2 advanced to the site of the blown-out pillbox, moving their lines forward by 500 yards. Corporal Channing B. Miller would later be awarded the Silver Star for his "conspicuous gallantry." In Channing's estimation, he was just six Japanese closer to going home.

Later that afternoon, Captain Farkas notified Company D that they were going to be separated into combat groups and attached to nearby battalions. Sergeant LaPoint was assigned to the beach area due to his Construction Foreman rating, while Bill, Fred Ellis and the rest of the Pioneer team were assigned to the familiar F/2/2 as regular combat "support troops." Bill and Fred gathered the team together to tell them what was happening. Bill explained that he did not know any of the current officers in F/2/2 and he told the team he and Fred would not let the team be split up if they had anything to say about it. Being under the command of lieutenants who were unknown to the men could have serious setbacks. The Pioneers of 2nd Platoon had all come to know and trust Lieutenant Saylor and they didn't want be attached to another unit. The new guys were very nervous about the development and some of them double checked with Bill to make sure he was going to stay with them. Bill told Bennie Urioste he would do everything possible to keep him close, and then he told the replacements not to wander off from the team. Bill and Fred then led the team out to find the command post of F/2/2 to report for duty. They first reported to Lieutenant Cooper, who told Bill that 2nd Lieutenant Barr was now a 1st lieutenant and Captain "Lefty Morris" was still in charge of Company F. Bill and Fred breathed a sigh of relief knowing these were the same officers they had fought alongside at Tarawa. Cooper and Morris had been evacuated at Tarawa, but Lieutenant Barr remembered them well. Lieutenant Barr had the group from D/2/18 dig in about 50 yards from the command post, and they settled in for the night.

The night ahead would set a pattern for many nights to come. Bill and Fred tried to have half the team sleep, while the other half remained alert and watching for encroaching Japanese. Intermittent firing was heard all across the line in spite of orders not to shoot at anything you couldn't see. As Bill peered out from under his helmet into the darkness, he knew the Japanese were not more than 100 yards away. The enemy soldiers would occasionally shout out insults in very poor English. "Hey Marine," (which sounded like "Hey Ma-leen") "I drink your blood," and "Tonight you die." Some of the nearby Marines couldn't help but make wisecracks out loud, usually followed by a sergeant telling them to, "Pipe down." When Fred woke from his two hours of sleep, he traded the watch with Bill. Bill pulled out his toothbrush from his gear and took a sip from his canteen. Brushing his teeth before he went to sleep was one of the only habits from home that he was able to continue. Bill was awakened by Marines firing after an illumination round exposed movement out in front of the line. Everyone remained on high alert until dawn. A scout team was sent out at first light to see what damage had been done to the Japanese attackers during the night. They found a group of dead civilians, including women and children that had apparently been trying to move under the cover of darkness. All of the Marines were sickened by this revelation as the news spread through the company. This was a part of war they had not experienced before, but it would become all too familiar over the next two weeks.

June 18th, 1944. PFC Pete Andrews had set up his machine gun team to cover members of A/1/6 as they pushed up a small hill at the base of the foothills to Mt. Tapotchau. The Japanese were dug into the hill and putting up stiff resistance with machine gun fire. Pete watched for signs of the enemy locations, and then poured a fifty-round belt into his target. The key to staying alive was to move the gun frequently and the team had quickly become capable with their entrenching tools, also known as shovels. The company advanced half way up the hill and became pinned down by enemy machine gun fire. Captain Durfee radioed for Sherman tank support, and about 30 minutes later two Shermans rolled up to the base of the hill. Durfee was loved by his men and they considered him a true leader. He was the type of captain who would not ask you to do something he wouldn't do himself. Durfee exposed himself to machine gun fire and ran to one of the tanks. He climbed up on the back of the tank and talked to the tank commander, pointing out the machine gun positions. The tank fired on each position, destroying them with one shot of its 75mm gun. Durfee then dismounted the tank and picked up the handset at the rear of the Sherman and continued to direct the crew in the destruction of the deadly Japanese positions. Company Clerk PFC Wendell V. Perkins found himself at Captain Durfee's side as they advanced behind the tank. Suddenly a Japanese sniper-shot caught Durfee square in the chest and he fell into Perkins. Perkins called to his captain, but the bullet had killed him instantly. The tanks continued to pour cannon fire into the hill and Company A overtook the positions and eliminated the Japanese. Several Marines carried Captain Durfee's body to find cover and PFC Perkins waited there with the beloved captain until stretcher bearers arrived to carry him to the rear for burial. Lieutenant Albert Wood took over the temporary command of A/1/6 per the orders of Lieutenant Colonel Jones via the radio. Jones climbed the hill himself to find the body of Captain Durfee and found that Wood had also been wounded. Jones forced Wood to be evacuated and installed Captain William E. Schweren as commander of A/1/6. Schweren had been reprimanded by Jones in the past for pushing his unit ahead too fast and jeopardizing their flank and rear. He emphasized again to Schweren that Company A must move forward with the other companies. Schweren was called "Wild Bill" by the Marines, as he was known to be a fast-moving, somewhat reckless leader. Schweren refused to wear a helmet and always wore his garrison cap instead. He carried a single Colt 1911 pistol in his belt.

As Bill and his team advanced northward, one day blended into the next and there were times when he wasn't even sure what the date was. Marines who were old enough to grow beards already showed eight to ten days of growth and Bill now had a stubby full beard. Some of the younger guys had grown out their "goat whiskers." Taber and Urioste were both from Oklahoma and they schooled the rest of the team on why you really would not want to visit that state. They had to admit that it was far superior to Saipan though. Clodfelter and Walzer were both southern boys and they reminded some of the Marines, using crude language, that they were southern gentlemen. Verbal jabs were traded about the South being on the losing end of the Civil War, but Clodfelter explained how it was a good thing the Yankees had boys who knew how to shoot out here now.

The rough terrain had shredded their Marine utilities and bare knees and elbows generally sported scabs or fresh blood from the coral and rocks. They all smelled so bad that they really couldn't smell the other guys. Bill made an effort to remind the guys to "say their prayers," and even offered to pray with them from time to time. Whenever he could, he talked to each one to see where they were spiritually. Most of them had church backgrounds and they knew where Bill stood. As far as Bill knew, there were no atheists in these foxholes.

Just after dawn, as they were trying to eat what they had left for food, Japanese mortar rounds began to explode within their lines. Grabbing his M1 and pack, Bill looked out in front and saw the Japanese flooding out of the tree line across the field. Marine fire began to pour into the Japanese ranks, but the enemy was advancing quickly. Bill fired two clips from his foxhole and decided to move the team to their right toward the command post. He yelled to Fred and waved the team to follow him. Mortars were exploding and Japanese bullets zipped past as they moved out. Just as Bill looked behind him, a bullet hit PFC Bonawitz and a red mist exploded from his shoulder as he spun and crashed to the ground. Bill turned back and told the others to keep moving. Fred brought up the rear and grabbed Bonawitz by his good shoulder as Bill lifted him by the waist. Bonawitz groaned in pain as Bill reached down and picked up the C3 explosives and the demo bag. Aided by Bill and Fred, Bonawitz stayed on his feet until they brought him to the cover of Marine foxholes and called for a corpsman. Fred had both of his hands on the gaping wound in Bonawitz' left shoulder. The bleeding was under control and Fred told the kid he was going to be alright. The corpsman arrived and took over the pressure and assessed the situation. Bonawitz received a syrette of morphine to calm him down. Bill and Fred told him they would see him later and took the team back into the fight.

The Japanese retreated back into the tree line leaving bodies all over the field. The day's fighting had led them farther to the west as they followed several lieutenants throughout the day. Realizing they had become detached from F/2/2, Bill became concerned. It was too dangerous to go back to find Lieutenant Barr, and he had no idea who was in charge of the current company. They were not the only Marines who were somewhat lost, as there were men from 1/2, 2/2 and 1/6 all mixed together in this area. They dug in for the night on a high area overlooking a sugarcane field below. Bill dug his foxhole just to the right of a huge banyan tree where he could see several hundred yards down a slight slope. He set out his M1 with two clips, and laid the C3 outside the foxhole near his feet. Before he fell asleep, he set out a can of K-ration so that he could grab it if he wanted it in the night or in the morning. Being awake on and off during the night, Bill had not paid any attention to the K-ration can, but when he sat up in the morning it was gone. He asked the guys who the joker was and wanted his food back. Everyone denied any knowledge of the missing rations. Bennie Urioste laughed a bit and told Bill that if he was going to steal food, he would take it from one of the smaller guys, and not Bill. Bill looked at all of them with suspicion. Food was scarce and stealing a fellow Marine's food during combat was a good way to get a fat lip, or worse. There were no orders to move ahead during the day. They were waiting for the 8th Marines to catch up with the advance, as they were far to the east on the end of the "swinging gate."

As night fell once again, Bill set another can of K-ration on the ground just outside of his foxhole. This time, he planned to listen closely and grab the hand of the perpetrator as he reached for the food. A relatively quiet night for Saipan ensued and Bill caught several hours of deep sleep. When he awoke, the food was gone. He crawled over to Fred's foxhole and asked him if he was playing a prank on his good buddy. Fred seemed clueless. Bill asked the rest of the team and some nearby Marines about the missing food. As Bill went back to his foxhole, he paused to take a long look at the ground. There appeared to be some dragging marks in the dirt, as though someone had crawled to his foxhole and then crawled away. With his M1 in hand, Bill followed the marks around the banyan tree until they disappeared beneath the root mass. Fred, Walzer and Poterola had become curious as to what Bill was hunting and were looking over his shoulder. It seemed to Bill that some type of large varmint may have burrowed down in the banyan roots. Poterola handed Bill a flashlight and Bill shined it into the deep hole with the sights of his M1 trained on the light beam. Bill's blood ran cold in his veins as he looked into the dirty face of a Japanese soldier peering up at him from the hole. Walzer shouted, "Blast him!" but Bill did not squeeze the trigger. The enemy yelled back, "WATASHI O UTANAIDE KUDASAI!! ONEGAISHIMASU!" (Please do not shoot me! I beg of you!) Bill yelled out, "Hands!" to the enemy, who must have understood some English as he showed his empty hands to Bill. One of the guys behind Bill yelled out, "TE WO AGERU!" which meant "Hands Up!" in Japanese. Bill handed the light to Walzer and motioned the Japanese "food thief" to come up out of the hole. The Marines stepped back as the filthy enemy came forth shaking with fear, hunger and fatigue. He said, "Watashi o utanaide kudasai!" again. Keeping the M1 on the prisoner, Bill asked Fred to frisk the shaking enemy who Bill thought looked to be about 18 years old.

A 2nd lieutenant came to the tree and told Bill that he would take charge of the prisoner. Bill told the lieutenant he would escort the prisoner back to the nearest command post with his permission. Bill had pity for this kid, as he saw him as a hungry human being. He also realized that this enemy could easily have stuck a knife in Bill's neck while he was sleeping and run off with the ration. This kid was more interested in staying alive than he was in killing. Bill wanted to return the mercy and make sure the new prisoner did not get shot on the way to the command post. He knew that most of the "Japs" taken prisoner never made it to the camp, as angry Marines would rather shoot them in the field instead of risking their own lives to cross terrain that still held hidden enemy combatants. Bill wanted to make sure this prisoner stayed alive. He smiled at the prisoner and told him it was "Okay" and motioned for him to start walking. Bill used the barrel of his M1 to tell the prisoner left or right and to remind him that he was in fact a prisoner. Bill brought the prisoner into the command post and turned him over to a lieutenant. A Marine was called over, who began to speak Japanese to the prisoner, who then responded with a flurry of speech. He looked at Bill and said, "Go shinsetsu ni, arigatou gozaimasu!" The interpreter looked at Bill and said, "He is thanking you for letting him live." The interpreter told Bill that they might be able to get some information on the location and strength of the enemy. Bill left the prisoner and went back to the line. He would never know if the food bandit made it to the camp at Susupe alive, but he would remember him for the rest of his life.

Later that day, the unit that Bill's team had found themselves attached to received orders to move out. Moving across a large open area, U.S. artillery pounded a small village ahead where the Japanese had undoubtedly taken up defensive positions. As the Marines came within 200 yards of the demolished buildings, Japanese mortar rounds began to explode across the open area, followed immediately by heavy machine gun fire. Fortunately, the field was pock marked with shell craters in all directions. The advancing Marines occupied the shell craters and waited for orders to attack. No orders came. The sergeants and corporals spread the word as night fell to toss a small rock into the next crater and announce one's self before dropping in during the night. This was intended to lessen your chances of being shot or bayoneted by your

Marine brothers. During the night, dozens of Japanese infiltrators crawled out to the craters and attacked the sleeping Marines with knives and bayonets. Bill heard hand-to-hand struggles in craters so close that he could hear the knives slicing into human flesh. He maintained his habit of sleeping with his Ka-Bar knife clutched to his chest by his right hand. Mortar rounds continued to fall during the night and Japanese snipers were active at all hours. By morning, there were many dead Japanese littered about the positions and several dead Marines.

Throughout the day, the Marines baked in the sun as they kept a sharp eye on the village to their front and surrounding wooded areas to the left and right. Occasional mortar and sniper fire kept them in their holes as they waited for orders to move out. Bill and the Pioneer team grew restless as they saw no point of staying out in the open and wanted to move out to find cover. Still, orders did not arrive. As the sun began to set, the Marines prepared for another night of infiltrators. A 2nd lieutenant moved from crater to crater to check on the defenses and slid into Bill and Fred's crater trailing communication wire and an EE-8 field telephone. Bill asked the lieutenant who was in charge and the lieutenant said that there was a captain and 1st lieutenant to the rear about one hundred yards or so who were in charge. The 2nd lieutenant then told Fred he wanted him to take a field phone toward the village about 100 yards and set up a "listening post" for the night. He was to go alone. The lieutenant would be on the other end of the wire and wanted Fred to report in if the Japanese were on the move, then head back to the line.

After the 2nd lieutenant scrambled out of the crater, Bill told Fred he would go with him. He thought there was no good reason to send one Marine out to a listening post alone. Bill reminded Fred they had promised not to split up. They checked through their gear, took a few extra grenades and waited for darkness. Bill told Poterola that he would yank on the wire in the morning to let him know they were headed back. Poterola should give a yank to let them know he was expecting them. Fred went out first and quietly stalked forward with his M1 at the ready, while Bill came behind about 20 yards with the field phone and trailing the wire. About 100 yards out, Fred found a suitable shell hole and dropped in to wait for Bill. They quietly moved to the edge of the crater which faced the village and set up for the night. In order to listen well, one of them would have to keep his helmet off and his head above ground level. After two hours, they decided to take turns getting some sleep and Bill took the first watch. Fred lay on his side with his Ka-Bar knife clutched in his hand and quickly fell asleep. Bill stuck his Ka-Bar into the dirt just to his right and gently placed his M1 across the crater edge in front of him. He knew there were Japanese within 100 yards and was expecting them to start screaming and charging at any second. On the other hand, they might be quietly slithering up to him at any moment. Staring out into the darkness, it was hard to concentrate as his tired mind wanted to play tricks on him. He thought about home and held onto a thread of hope that he would see it again.

The adrenaline could only keep him awake for so long as his head began to nod after about two hours. He reached over and placed his hand on Fred's wrist that held the Ka-Bar and shook him. This made sure that Fred would not stab

Bill by reflex as he awoke. Bill leaned close to Fred's ear and whispered that all was clear. Fred moved into watch position and Bill rolled on his side, grabbed his Ka-Bar and drifted off to sleep. The pair traded off throughout the night without incident. As soon as the sky in the east began to lighten, Bill took the field phone and removed the wire. He pulled out the slack and then gave it several yanks. About five seconds later, he felt two yanks coming from the other end. He placed his helmet on his head and pulled the strap below his chin. He nodded at Fred and Fred nodded back. They made their way back to the lines and dropped back into the crater with Poterola, who was already pulling in the wire. Walzer and Clodfelter asked Fred and Bill if they had heard anything out there and Bill told them it had been quiet as a cemetery. They all expected to move forward and take the village shortly.

The tropical sun began its horrid work on the dead and by the end of the second day they began to bloat and stink of death. The high temperatures were well over 90 degrees with humidity at about 80%. No one could stand upright to carry the dead without becoming a target of the Japanese snipers. Marines that had any food finished it on the second day and water had begun to run low. Salt tablets were consumed until gone and the sun felt as though it was roasting the Marines alive. It became evident to the Marines that if they stayed where they were, they would die. Bill waited for orders but none arrived. On the third day, the stench of the dead became almost violent and Marines dry heaved as they had no food to vomit. Flies and maggots covered the dead and it was horrific to think that these Marines were being left out there for no apparent reason. Bill waited for darkness to fall, and then began crawling from hole to hole, asking, "Who's in command?" and, "Where's the captain?" It took about half an hour of looking before Bill was pointed to the command crater several hundred yards behind the front line. Bill slid into the crater and announced himself as "Corporal Bennett looking for the captain." Bill saluted the officer sitting in the bottom of the crater until he was saluted back. Bill then instinctively stuck out his hand to shake the captain's. There it was: a "dead fish" handshake. Bill knew right off not to expect much.

Bill launched into his speech about needing orders and the men needing food, water and relief from the rotting corpses. The captain said he was waiting for word from Command and the radio had been damaged. Bill told the captain that Command probably had no idea where they were or what their situation was and that he needed to lead these men. Bill emphasized that the whole unit was in danger of being killed if they did not make a move soon. The captain told Bill that he was overstepping his rank and he would not be told how to command. Bill could see that the captain was afraid to come out of his protected hole and lead the men. The captain was what Bill and his friends had called "a chicken" growing up. Bill's anger flared and he lashed out at the captain. He said exactly what was on his mind. "If you don't get out of this hole and lead these men, I will make sure that your superiors know exactly what you did out here as soon as I can find them. I am gonna tell them you were a coward who was afraid to lead your men!" The captain and his lieutenant were so surprised by what Bill said that they didn't say a word as he climbed out of the crater and headed back to the line.

About two hours later, a runner came from crater to crater asking for Corporal Bennett. He slid into Bill's crater and said he had orders from the captain. Bill had been ordered to take two of his men and go recon the enemy positions in the village at dawn. Bill told the runner he understood and the runner crawled away. Fred and members of Bill's team overheard the orders and several of them soon dropped into the crater. They all said they would volunteer to go with Bill. Bill insisted he would go by himself and would take none of them. He then scolded Bennie Urioste for volunteering, as he had told him never to volunteer. Fred told Bill to disobey the order, as it was obvious the captain was trying to get Bill killed to protect himself. They all knew the recon order was a death sentence. Bill sat in the dark of the crater and prayed for his protection and went through things he thought necessary between him and the Lord, should this be his last night on Earth. Bill felt comfort from his prayer time and he held a strange peace that he would be alright no matter what happened. He then thought of home and especially of Jessie. He thought that he would never see his family again.

Bill was awakened by a small rock hitting his helmet a few hours before dawn. Three members of Bill's team slid into the crater to tell Bill they were on their way to drop a grenade into the captain's shell hole. Bill was furious with them. He grabbed the spokesman by the jacket and said they were NOT going to do any such thing, and NOT for his sake! Bill told them he appreciated the loyalty they were showing but he would rather die than know that they murdered the captain and a lieutenant to save his skin. They left the crater and the incident would never be discussed by any of them again. Just as light was appearing in the eastern sky, Bill prayed and asked the Lord to receive his spirit unto heaven should these be his last minutes alive. He fastened his helmet strap for running, checked his M1 safety and his ammo belt, and then took two hand grenades from Fred. As Bill peered out of the crater, he could not see any movement through the slight mist ahead. He laid his M1 across his forearms and crawled toward the Japanese positions. He crawled into a shell hole about 20 yards out from the first crumbled stone wall and lay silently to listen. All he could hear was his pounding heart and his own breath. He crawled the final 20 yards to the cover of the half wall and then listened again. He waited for a full five minutes thinking that one of the Japanese might cough, sneeze or knock over a piece of rubble, but all was silent. Bill took off his helmet and raised it above the wall on his bayonet; still quiet. He then rolled over the wall and moved behind the remains of the corner of a small building. On the other side was a pile of spent Japanese shell casings and empty ration cans. He moved through the rubble finding multiple signs that the Japanese had been there, but no Japanese. At some point in the night, they must have moved out fearing an attack or another shelling from the Marines.

Bill went back to the rubble of the small wall and looked back towards the Marine lines. He waved toward Fred Ellis and saw Fred wave back with his helmet in his hand. Bill rolled over the wall and ran from crater to crater on his way back. As he slid into the crater with Fred, Bill told him that the enemy had pulled out. Fred said he would send someone with the news as it was better for Bill that he stay away from the captain. Bill was not afraid to go face the captain again because he had fully meant what he had said earlier, but he agreed with Fred. Fred found some Marines nearby and handed one of them a pencil-written note that said there were no Japanese present in the village to the north. The Private headed off toward the captain's position. A few minutes later, mortar rounds began exploding again and machine gun fire began coming in from the wooded area to the east. Japanese infantry ran from the trees toward the stranded Marines and Bill did not wait for orders. He shouted for the Marines around him to head for the cover of the shattered village where he had just been. Thirty or forty Marines from the immediate area headed toward the rubble, including all of Bill and Fred's original team. Moving from crater to crater as they went, they exchanged rifle fire with the attacking Japanese. They could see Marines moving in two other directions as well, back south and to the west. The Japanese retreated back to the wooded area and the Marines with Bill worked their way west to try and find a unit from 2/2. Bill had no idea where the cowardly captain had gone, and he never saw him again. By this time Bill's beard had grown unbelievably thick compared to the others in his team and Jimmy Clodfelter started referring to him as "Moses." As they headed off in search of 2/2, the younger Marines joked about keeping their eyes open for the enemy and "to just keep following Moses to the Promised Land."

One of many disconnected and tattered groups of Marines on Saipan during late June of 1944.

(U.S.M.C. Photo)

Within a few hours, Bill and the lost Marines found the lines of Company G/2/2 just to the south of the city of Garapan. They were able to draw some water, but there were almost no rations, as supplies had not reached Company G for days. Bill inquired as to the location of F/2/2 in order to try and find Lieutenant Barr or Captain Morris, and moved the team farther west. They dug in for the night with food and survival on their minds. Early the next morning, Bill borrowed Fortenberry's binoculars and went to a spot where he could see down the slope to the beach. There were Higgins Boats unloading supplies onto trucks about a mile away and Bill hatched an idea. He took Bennie Urioste with him and they made their way down to the beach. There was a 2nd lieutenant in charge of the Shore Party unloading the supplies and Bill approached him with Bennie in tow by the shirt. Bill said, "The captain is tired of this screw-up and thinks that a work detail might do him some good. Can you put him to work on one of those trucks?" The lieutenant agreed and Bill told him he would be back in a few hours. Bill then went back up the hill toward their unit but stayed within sight of the beach. Per Bill's instructions, Bennie located a case of food and threw it off the truck each time it went around a curve on the way to the supply dump. After four trips in the truck, Bill reappeared to collect the "screw-up" and he and Bennie disappeared. Later, they both arrived back at the team with peaches, beans, Spam and K-rations on their shoulders. After three days without food, the weary Marines thought they were in heaven. They all loaded the extra cans of food in every possible pack, bag and pocket and moved on to find F/2/2.

When they finally located the command post for F/2/2, seeing Lieutenant Barr again felt like a family reunion for Bill and Fred. Bill told Lieutenant Barr what they had gone through. They had all been officially listed as "Missing in Action" for the past nine days. The team looked "like hell" according to Barr, who barely recognized Bill with a full beard. Lieutenant Barr noticed that Bill's team seemed to be well stocked with canned goods as they were handing some of it out. Fred smiled and handed Barr a can of Spam and said, "This one is on us, sir!"

Since the team was officially assigned to F/2/2, they asked if there had been any mail while they were away. They found the Executive Officer who had charge of the mail and found that letters had come in for these men from 2/18. They eagerly grabbed their mail and turned to open it. There was only one letter for Bill. He walked away from the others and eagerly tore the envelope open. Any word from home would be very refreshing to him as he had not had a letter in over a month now. He unfolded the letter and began to read: "Dear Mr. Bennett, we thank you for your past support of the YMCA. As the summer months quickly approach, we are looking forward to the operation of our Summer Camping Program. As you know, there are many young, disadvantaged boys in our area who would not have the opportunity to attend a summer camp without the donations of supporters like you. Please consider making a generous donation at this time to help send a needy boy to summer camp." At first Bill's eyebrows scrunched low with disappointment, but then he started to chuckle, and then he started to laugh. Poterola gave Bill a quizzical look and asked him what was so funny. Bill handed the letter to Poterola and he started to laugh and then handed it to Fred. As the letter went around, they all had a good laugh.

Bill asked permission from Lieutenant Barr to take the guys down to the beach to wash in the salt water. Lieutenant Barr agreed, but he told them to make sure they posted guards because there had been some Marines killed at the beaches while washing. On the way down to the beach, Billy Walzer came alongside Bill and said, "Hey Mr. Bennett, will you send me

Ragged, battle-weary Marines receive a welcome "mail call" on the front lines of Saipan.

(U.S.M.C. Photo)

Marines washing off combat filth just south of Garapan, Saipan.

(U.S.M.C. Photo)

to summer camp?" and started to laugh; then they all started to laugh. For a few minutes, they were like a bunch of kids on their way to the swimming hole. Once at the beach, Bill and Fred stood guard while the team dropped their gear, stripped naked and fell into the water. Their uniforms were so grungy that they didn't even lay flat on the beach; they almost stood on their own. The uniforms all went into the waves and everything was scrubbed as well as possible, without soap. Fred asked Poterola and Fortenberry to stand guard so that he and Bill could wash up. Bill dropped his gear and his boondockers and just walked into the waves with his utilities on. Feeling water on his body was almost as good as the Spam feast they had earlier in the day. It was good to have a reprieve, but there was a lot of fighting left to live through. Bill had carried some stationery with a beautiful island girl on it and a pencil in his pack since they left the USS Sheridan. He knew that if mail was coming in to the command post that it meant it would also be going out. He sat under a tree and quickly wrote a short letter to his mom and dad telling them he was in good health and there was little else he could say at this time. He had to mention the letter he had just received from the YMCA. Steve and Jessie probably wouldn't see the humor in it the way Bill did.

71. The Silver Star

Tuesday, June 27th, 1944. PFC Pete Andrews and his machine gun team, with A/1/6, worked their way along a narrow road in the hills about halfway between the top of Mt. Tapotchau and Garapan. Company A had been rapidly pushing back Japanese resistance and they were making a large advance; too large, in fact. Captain Schweren ordered the company through a narrow ravine and wanted to take a hill in front of them to gain the high ground. Lieutenant Wood told Schweren he was concerned that they had lost contact with the other two companies from 1/6, against Lieutenant Colonel Jones' orders to keep the companies tight. Schweren ignored both Woods' concerns and Jones' orders and drove the company ahead. Once the company cleared the ravine and started up the hill, Japanese infantry attacked them from all sides closing off the ravine they had just moved through. Company A moved up the hill under enemy fire and Pete found a spot flat enough to set up the tripod and return fire. Company A was cut off from the other units and completely surrounded. The fight ensued throughout the night as Pete had to be judicious with his targets, move the gun frequently and not give his position away unless necessary.

Wednesday, June 28th, 1944. About 0300, the Japanese went silent and word was passed through the Marine lines to expect an all-out attack at dawn. Pete and his team took turns sleeping and keeping watch until first light, when every Marine was awakened. Just after dawn, mortar rounds rained down as enemy machine guns opened fire, followed by a rush of Japanese infantry moving out from the trees. Pete used three-round bursts to keep the Japanese at bay for about 15 minutes, which seemed like hours to him. As he was loading a fresh 50-round belt, a Japanese bullet tore through his right arm. The assistant gunner took over the trigger as one of the ammo carriers tore Pete's sleeve open and wrapped the tear through his triceps with a bandage. Pete yelled for the team to relocate the gun and they picked up their gear and moved up the slope. The Japanese were coming up the slope behind them. Pete reset the gun and opened fire, taking down six Japanese pursuers. Marines tossed grenades down the hill and blasted the oncoming enemy. Pete could see that the Japanese were coming in faster than he could shoot them down and he yelled to the assistant gunner to move the gun once more. The assistant slid his hand into the asbestos mitt and grabbed the smoking barrel and Pete grabbed the base and followed him up the hill while the ammo carriers covered them both with their M1s. As Pete climbed the hill, a bullet tore through his left thigh and another struck him in the back, knocking him down face first. He got back to his feet and set the base down, then rolled out of the way to allow his assistant to position the gun. The assistant lifted the breech and placed a fresh belt, then snapped it shut and pulled back the bolt. Pete rose behind the gun and told the assistant and the ammo carriers to leave the ammo and get up the hill to find a better position. They did not want to leave Pete alone. Pete had now been hit three times and was losing blood quickly; he knew that he did not have much time left. He yelled at his three long-time buddies and told them to go.

Pete began firing down the hill in short bursts to maximize his ammunition. He successfully pinned down the attackers allowing his team and other Marines to ascend the hill to relative safety while he continued to fire and reload. As he opened the breech to load the third belt from this position, Pete was hit with automatic rifle fire from the base of the hill which killed him instantly. The other Marines from atop the hill fired on the Japanese as they over ran Pete's position. Sergeant Michael Convertino from HQ/1/6 reported to Lieutenant Colonel Jones that Company A had been cut off and was now surrounded. Jones fumed that Schweren had ignored his orders and driven the company too far ahead. Now good Marines were dying. There were no communications available with Company A as the telephone wire they had been trailing had been cut by the Japanese. Convertino had actually seen Company A heading for the ravine and told Jones that he could get through if he went alone. Convertino, who had been a star running back in high school, hefted a spool of wire and a SCR-300 heavy walkie-talkie and ran off into the jungle. The command post monitored the radios and an hour later they

Private First Class Peter Nicholas Andrews of the First Battalion, Sixth Marines, 2nd Marine Division, U.S.M.C. Pete's decisive action in aggressively repelling a major Japanese attack and allowing his comrades to escape to find cover, cost him his life on Saipan. He was awarded the Silver Star posthumously for his actions.

(Andrews Family Photo)

heard Convertino's voice calling out for, "Billy Red One, Billy Red One," in his unmistakable Brooklyn accent. Convertino had somehow managed to run through the Japanese and up the hill to find the remnants of Company A. Jones grabbed the radio and told Convertino to put Tom Carroll, the Executive Officer, on the line, as he did not even want to talk to Captain Schweren. Carroll asked for an air strike at the bottom of the hill and an artillery bombardment. Jones ordered both, and then put together a rescue unit to retrieve what was left of Company A. By the time the company could be reached, 39 had been killed, and about the same number had been wounded. The radioman, PFC Billy Laird, had been killed and his radio destroyed. The land wire had been cut numerous times. When Convertino returned to Jones, he had numerous bullet holes in his shirt but was not seriously injured. It was almost miraculous that the entire company had not been killed. Lieutenant Colonel Jones heard the story of what Pete Andrews had done to save his fellow Marines and recommended he be posthumously awarded the Silver Star. The young Auroran, whose family had left their native Greece for a better life in America, not only volunteered to defend his country, but he had given his life for it. At the time of Pete's death, his older brother George was in combat somewhere in Normandy with the 101st Airborne Division. Their father Nick was trying to run the store on Main Street without either of his boys.

72. The Combat Zone

Bill and his team from D/2/18 had been fed, watered and bathed. Their tattered uniforms became pliable once again and much less offensive in aroma. They drew water and ammunition from the F/2/2 command post and rejoined the front lines as they made preparations to enter the southern end of the city of Garapan. Bill's team went with a platoon directed to enter Garapan from the east. It was unknown as to how many Japanese were holed up within the city. Bill chopped at the ground with his "entrenching tool" to make a safe place to sleep. He wondered how many holes he had dug over the last two years and marveled how this short little shovel had become one of his most important tools. It was just another night sleeping in a foxhole; a can of beans ready for breakfast and his Ka-Bar knife on his chest. He prayed for the safety of the 2/18 group in the coming attack and prayed for his long list of loved ones at home and in the field. Before he fell asleep, he remembered when he thought that his cot and tent in San Diego had been crude accommodations. There always seemed to be a lower level of misery.

The attack began early the next morning with an extended naval bombardment that was joined by the 75mm Pack Howitzers of the 3/10 and 4/10 Marines. Bill shared binoculars with the other Marines as they marveled at the devastation being dealt into Garapan. The ground shook beneath them as they waited for orders to advance. They had passed columns of Sherman tanks the evening before on their way over, and these tanks would now lead the way into the city. The orders came to move out and Bill and the team moved north, out in the countryside, in order to come into the city on the east flank, about a quarter mile ahead. As they moved north, the road narrowed between hills where trucks and tanks had been stopped by huge boulders that had been blown onto the road by the bombardment. As Bill approached the scene, Captain Warren Morris, the F/2/2 commander, spotted Bill with the demolition bag over his shoulder. He shouted out, "Corporal!" to get Bill's attention. He jogged over to Morris, saluted and said, "Yes sir!" Captain Morris asked Bill if he thought he could move these boulders with his explosives. Bill answered affirmatively and told the captain that everyone should take cover. Bill surveyed the slope of the road and calculated that he could blast the largest boulder on the upslope side causing it to roll down and off the road. He pulled a chunk of plastic C3 off that was about the size of a brick and pushed it against the boulder. He pressed in a blasting cap and a 24" fuse, and then made a quick trip around the boulder yelling, "Clear!" several times. Bill lit the fuse with his Zippo and ran for the ditch yelling, "Clear!" one more time. The explosion rocked the ground and sent stone fragments flying in all directions. The huge boulder rolled off the road. When the dust and smoke cleared, the tank commander told Bill that he thought he could push the smaller boulders aside with his tank and proceeded to do so. Captain Morris saluted toward Bill and the vehicles began to roll north.

U.S.M.C. 533 Demolition Men destroying a Japanese position on Saipan.

(U.S.M.C. Photo)

As Bill entered Garapan, he was not surprised to find the Japanese were not only there, but putting up a good fight. The wreckage of the city was reminiscent of Tarawa with the exception of paved roads and the absence of coconut log bunkers. Another difference they found in short order was the inability to "dig in." The team had to find cover rather than create it, which meant that their entrenching tools could only be used to pile up debris for cover. The smart tactic in Garapan became the use of radios working with the Sherman tanks. If the tanks could not reach the targets, then Marines would go in and get the job done. By the end of the first day, the Marines were covered in concrete dust, sweat and blood. As the team hunkered down into defensive positions for the night, Bill realized how soft a freshly dug foxhole could be compared to rubble. Some of the Marines located blankets and even mattresses in the rubble, which made life much better. Just about everything in Garapan had been burned to uselessness.

As the USS Nehenta Bay steamed toward Saipan, Lieutenant Robert F. Stoner was working long hours organizing and leading anti-submarine flights with Composite Squadron, VC-11. Bob had become the right-hand man of Lieutenant Carlson and due to his extensive experience as a flight instructor, Lieutenant Commander Stanley trusted him with overseeing flying procedures and tactics. Bob had actually been the flight instructor at Pensacola and Corpus Christi for several of the navy pilots flying with VC-11. As the heat and humidity built up heading into the combat zone, some VC-11 pilots began to sleep in the reclining chairs in their "ready room," as it was one of the only places on the carrier that was air conditioned. The pilots spent hours sharing stories and discussing just about everything one could imagine. The squadron became interested in reading *The Stoner Weekly News* when it arrived in the mail. On their way to Eniwetok, one particular letter of notable elation came to Bob aboard ship. After a recent trip to her doctor in Chicago, Marijane wrote Bob with the news that she would be expecting their first child in January of 1945. Bob shared the news with the other pilots and a celebration ensued. Stanley invited Bob to his quarters with Lieutenant Carlson and they enjoyed cigars at Stanley's expense.

Bob was not only interested in his duties as a flying officer, he was also interested in every aspect of the operation aboard the carrier. The crew of Bob's TBM-1C Avenger was filled out by AOM2c Gunner Owen P. Stenson, a former firefighter from San Francisco, and ARM2c Radioman Paul W. Palmer from Atlanta, Georgia. Bob was very good to his crew and wanted to make sure they had the things that were needed. He relied on them and they relied on him. Bob let them know he was interested in them by making sure he associated with them at times other than official Navy "business." In the evenings, when the light was still sufficient and the temperatures had cooled down, the mechanics and technicians gathered on the catwalks of the Nehenta Bay to smoke and "beat their gums." The crew members did the same. Officers did not ordinarily frequent such gatherings, but Bob found the companionship of the enlisted men refreshing and reminiscent of the old days in Aurora. The men became interested in Bob's funny stories of his brothers Dexter and Harley and the quips that he shared from *The Stoner Weekly News*. Bob frequently visited the crew chiefs of the TBMs to discuss maintenance issues and understand exactly what was happening with the planes. He became very familiar with one crew chief named Armand Blackmore, who hailed from Michigan. Armand was as passionate about maintaining the TBMs as Bob was about flying them. Bob and Armand discussed every part of the TBM from the prop to the tail. If Bob had any questions or concerns, Armand put them at the top of his list. Whenever Bob had time to spend with the guys, Stenson, Palmer and Blackmore were usually there.

A typical anti-submarine patrol would have six TBMs in the air to cover an assigned zone along the perimeter of the task force. The planes would fly a half-mile apart so they could cover a two- to three-mile path on each pass.

Most of the spotting work was done by the radioman who had a perfect downward view out of the ventricle window below and aft of the radio compartment. The pilot also kept an eye out, although the wings and his attention to flying somewhat inhibited his ability. Each shift of ASP duty would keep the TBM in the air for about two hours and it was extremely boring work. The gunners scanned the skies for Japanese planes which rarely appeared. Bob was excited to finally be taking part in actual combat activities. He now had a sense he was doing something to directly defeat the Japanese. The routine was monotonous, but the discipline and organization of the entire operation was quite remarkable. On July 2nd, 1944, the USS Nehenta Bay arrived 40 miles off the coast of Saipan and assumed anti-submarine patrol duty and orders to standby for air support over Saipan if needed.

Meanwhile, back in Garapan, Bill worked his way, step by step through the rubble of what was once a neighborhood. Most of the civilians had fled Garapan, but a few remained. The Marines were making grizzly discoveries of families that had gathered closely together to commit suicide with hand grenades rather than be captured by the Marines. Captured Japanese soldiers had explained to interrogators that the civilians had been told the Marines would torture and abuse the children and the women if captured. Many were even told that the Americans were cannibals. The Emperor of Japan had supposedly written a letter to the Japanese civilians telling them that if they committed suicide, they would be able to enter the same level of "heaven" as the Japanese soldiers. After finding several families that had killed themselves, and learning of the lies they were told by their own government, Bill burned with anger against the Japanese. He wondered how human beings could be so cruel, thoughtless and barbaric, but he reasoned that evil had flourished where God's love had been absent. He saw these dead children and they brought tears to his eyes. He wondered how a mother could blow up her own children. Among all the horrors of war that Bill had seen, these dead Japanese and Chamorro civilians were the worst. The sight and thought of these killings made him sick to his stomach. Some of the Marines tried to rationalize that the Japanese were not human and this might have helped them deal with the carnage and the killing, but Bill knew better. The adult Japanese, especially the government and military leaders, may have deserved what they had coming. They made decisions that led the world into war and had committed atrocities against others throughout the Pacific, but these children had no say or responsibility for what went on around them. The children had just been caught up in the immorality of war.

Farther south at Camp Susupe, built near Lake Susupe, 11-year-old Setchan Akiyama's wounds had been healing well. Five pieces of shrapnel, probably from the 75mm shell of the Sherman tank, had been removed from her wounds while her severely burned back had been well tended by the Navy surgeons and burn team. Her stepmother, grandmother and little sister, Elpedio, were all improving. When Setchan was able to walk around the camp, U.S. Marines would often come to the fence and give her and Elpedio Hershey Bars and sometimes a bunch of wild flowers. She was surprised that most of the Marines had been so kind to her. Some of the Chamorro survivors in the camp knew Setchan was half Japanese and they forbade her to speak Japanese in their presence. Some called her "Tojo" and other hateful names. Each day, she went to the fence and waited for her father to arrive. He had told her that he would come for her. The family heard rumors that her father had arrived at their farm at Ilyang not knowing they had pressed on to the farm at Aslito. Setchan loved her father and remembered the bicycle races they used to have on Beach Road by their farm at Ilyang. She had lost the important papers on the day her family members had been killed and now it seemed she had lost her father as well. She longed for his embrace and his warm smile when he came home from work. Her entire world had been shattered.

Several times, as they fought through Garapan, Marine officers tried to split up the D/2/18 team. Bill and Fred had come close to insubordination by arguing their case with a 2nd lieutenant and a lieutenant. They reasoned that all these Marines had left of their original unit were these 12 other guys. If they were split up, someone like Bennie or Walzer would just be an 18-year-old kid that no one else knew or cared about. If they stayed together, Bill, Fred and Gerald Coate could watch over them and make sure they did not get killed needlessly.

The Japanese in Garapan were fighting to the death, just as the others were, in the hills. The Marines improvised loud speakers that were manned by Japanese-speaking Marines or civilians that had volunteered to try and save lives. They called out in the streets that if the soldiers or civilians would come out and surrender, they would be well treated and given food, water and medical care. Once this practice was started, many more civilians began to come out of hiding. Some of the most painful moments were after a fire fight with Japanese hold-outs; a Sherman tank would blast the ruins where the machine gun fire was emanating. Once the Marines were inside, they would find the bodies of several Japanese soldiers and a dozen civilians. How foolish it seemed for those soldiers to attract the Marine's fire toward civilians. If they were all thinking it was a glorious way to die, then it would not matter what the Marines tried to do. It was probable that if any civilians had tried to run to the Marines, the Japanese would have shot them down anyway. It seemed as though every building in Garapan had been roofed with corrugated tin sheeting. The bombardment had blown the roofing sheets all over the ground so that large areas were covered with them. The Japanese soldiers would find holes in the ground and cover themselves with a piece of the tin roofing so that they were invisible. As the Americans advanced on a street or rubble field, the enemy would pop up from the hole with a light machine gun or hand grenades to kill a few Marines before being annihilated. The safest route through Garapan became to follow a Sherman tank, but there were a limited number of them. Bill and the team continued to fight their way through on foot with 2/2.

Monday, July 3rd, 1944. After five days of pushing through Garapan, sleeping in rubble and broken glass and dodging sniper fire, the team followed a lead platoon up the main street. A huge steel box about seven feet long and three feet by four feet was lying on its side in the street. Bill let four guys go up the street on either side about 40 yards and then signaled them to wait. He and Fred went over the box and realized that it was the vault from the Garapan Bank across the street. Apparently, the big Navy guns had hit the

U.S. Marines fighting their way through Garapan, Saipan, late June, 1944.

(U.S.M.C. Photo)

Wreckage of Garapan, Saipan, looking east toward Mt. Tapotchau. Photo taken by 2nd Battalion, 18th Marines. The endless pieces of tin roofing made good cover for Japanese snipers.

(U.S.M.C. Photo)

bank squarely and blown the massive safe out into the street. There were huge bolts on the back with brick and mortar still attached. It looked like other Marines had tried to open it with hand grenades or by shooting the dial and hinges. For some reason, this safe fascinated Bill. He looked at Fred and with a mischievous smile asked him if he would like to open it. Bill pulled a block of C3 from his demo bag. Fred called the team closer and told them to take cover because Bill was going to blow the safe open. Bill stuck a chunk of C3 on each hinge and then a larger chunk onto the dial and bolt. He quickly wired the three together and then ran his spool of wire behind a block wall. He looked up and down the street and yelled "Clear!" He twisted the crank on the blasting machine and the C3 rocked the street. The door blew up and over the safe and bounced on the street. Bill ran out to look inside and there were bundles of now useless "island money" and some bundles of Japanese yen, which had no value outside of Japan at the time. Bill looked at Fred and had another idea. He said, "Fred, tell the guys to line up. It's payday!" They were all in the mood for a diversion from the past few weeks and they lined up with their helmets held out as receptacles. Bill gathered up an armload of cash and began to drop a handful into each helmet. He said, "Now I know you haven't been paid in a while, but I want you to know you are all doing a mighty fine job out here. Keep up the good work and I will make sure you all get a big, fat promotion!" They laughed so hard that some of them bent in half. The story of Corporal Bennett blowing the safe would be told and retold at many U.S.M.C. card games in the future.

73. Banzai!

July 4th, 1944. As the Marine units of 1/2 and 2/2 cleared the northern end of Garapan, the shore turned 90 degrees to the east and then north again. There was a large Japanese seaplane base at this point, with a gigantic four engine flying boat that had the engines blown off and more holes in it than anyone could count. At this juncture, the Marines from 1/6 and 3/6 had also swung to the western shore so the remnants of four battalions all came together. About 0900 hours, someone yelled out, "Hey! It's the Fourth of July!" The best part of having the battalions coming together was that the seaplane base was a port with an intact dock and tons of supplies were coming in to resupply the battalions directly. The U.S. Army's 27th Infantry Division had come up from the south and then swung over to the west to take over the front lines for the time being. There were a lot of things the Marines needed but at the top of the list for Bill was a pair of pants. His pants had been in tatters before entering Garapan, and the salt water wash seemed to eat at the seams that remained. For the past few days, the only way Bill could retain his dignity was to wear a towel around his waist held in place by his cartridge belt. This was one time he was literally, "out of uniform." Fortunately, he was able to find a pair his size by asking the Shore Party.

On July 5th, 1944, elements of F/2/2 went north with the Marine Artillery from 3/10. 3/10 was led by Major William L. Crouch, who had been Bill's captain back in San Diego during the early days of Company A, 2nd Pioneer Battalion. Bill and Fred's team went up to 3/10 with a platoon assigned as forward security for the 75mm artillery teams. This seemed like better duty than trying to blast the Japanese out of the caves up ahead. The defensive positions were dug in and they even had the luxury of sand bags that had been delivered. The battle lines were now a half mile to the north, so any kind of attack seemed unlikely. The "75s" blasted barrages ahead, on and off, throughout the 5th of July, and as darkness fell, everyone was hoping for a quiet night.

At 0100 hours, Bennie Urioste rousted Bill from a dream saying, "Bennett! Bennett! You better wake up!" As Bill tried to remember where he was in the darkness, Fred slid over to him and said it had been going on for about a half-hour. As everyone quieted down, Bill could hear what sounded like a pep rally off in the distance. There was a large group of men singing a song with unintelligible words. Then there were other songs from other directions. Poterola made a crack about the Japanese having a glee club. The truth was, the Japanese were known to have a drinking party just prior to a suicidal

Banzai charge. Word came from the 3/10 command post for all Marines to be awake, alert and armed to the teeth. Bill told the younger guys to make sure they had all the grenades they could find in front of them and plenty of .30-06 clips for their M1s. There were heavy and light .30 caliber machine guns set up 20 yards to the left and 20 yards to their right, so the area in front of them would be well covered. 60 mm mortars were 50 yards behind them zeroed in on the open areas out front. 100 yards in back were the Pack Howitzers. There were no Sherman tanks in the area to Bill's knowledge.

Just before 0230 the singing stopped for about a half-hour. The silence was just as eerie as the singing had been. A few minutes before 0300, the silence was broken once again as distant shouts of, "BANZAI! BANZAI! BANZAI!" were heard. Hearing what sounded like thousands of men cheering, as though at a football game, in the darkness was unsettling. Knowing that they were about to sacrifice their lives to take yours was frightening. Suddenly, mortars, machine guns and rifle fire broke out and the sounds of battle spread across the landscape in front of them. Flashes from explosions, machine gun tracers and illumination rounds lit up the sky. If the term, "All hell broke loose," ever applied, this was the time. Within the drone of fire, the shouts of men could be heard as a backdrop. For 20 minutes or so, the defenders in front of 3/10 watched as the flashes and sounds grew closer, like a slow motion tidal wave. And then, out in front of the line, lit dimly by illumination rounds, Bill could see the mushroom helmets and flashes of bayonets moving toward them. It was unthinkable, but the Japanese had found a gap in the lines and they were headed right for 3/10. Marine lieutenants on the left and right shouted at the top of their lung capacity to hold fire until ordered. On they came, screaming and running. Bill could see a Japanese officer waving a sword as he ran and he held his M1 sights on the figure as best he could. At about 150 yards out, a Marine officer screamed, "FIRE!" and all the M1s in the foxholes began to fire clip after clip. The machine gun tracers crisscrossed the field in front of them with a flow of deadly yellow light. 60 mm mortar rounds exploded one after the other, as screams could be heard from the enemy wave.

The Banzai charge came to within 30 yards and Marines up and down the line pulled pins on grenades and let them fly. The grenades exploded in rapid succession and took down the wall of enemy soldiers. A few Japanese closed to within 10 yards before they were shot down by M1s or carbines. More Japanese tried coming over the first wave and the machine gunners had reloaded. As the onslaught continued, dead fell upon dead until the bodies were three or four deep and still they tried to crawl over the pile to get to the Marines. Flame throwers were brought up from the rear and they shot torrents of flame onto the dead and dying Japanese. The flames lit up the night so that Bill could see the horror on the faces of his team. The breeze blew the horrid smell of burning flesh back onto the Marines. Ammunition in the Japanese pouches and rifles began to detonate and everyone hunkered down into their foxholes. Grenades on the Japanese belts exploded and blew the dead and burning bodies into the air. Japanese that were still alive stood, trying to escape the flames, only to stumble and fall again or be shot by Marine riflemen. Nothing that the Japanese did made any sense to Bill. Why did they fight and waste their lives like this? They knew there was no possible way for them to gain victory, but on they came. It seemed as though they were possessed by an evil spirit.

Bill was alerted to the fighting behind him as many of the Japanese had gotten around or through their defenses and attacked as far back as the command post to the rear. The firing back in that area lasted for about 10 minutes before it went silent. It seemed as though they had stopped the attack. When Bill checked the time, it was 0420 and all they could do was to stay in their foxholes and wait for dawn. No one could sleep a wink, not after what they just been through. As dawn arrived, the sky over the hills to the east lightened and Marines moved out to look for survivors within the hundreds of dead Japanese. The 3/10 command post had been over run and there was hand-to-hand fighting within the tents. Commanding officer Major William L. Crouch was killed in the fighting. Bill had always thought highly of Major Crouch and was upset to hear he had been killed in his own command post. He was well liked by his men. Marine squads and platoons moved out into the countryside to look for Japanese that survived the Banzai attack and had taken cover elsewhere. By coming out of the caves, the Japanese had taken a toll of 45 Marines killed and 82 wounded, but there were over 1500 dead Japanese counted on July 7th and another 1,000 on the 8th. Engineers brought in bulldozers to bury the decomposing Japanese and the Marines were laid to rest down at the 2nd Division cemetery. The final count of the dead Japanese from this Banzai charge ended up being 4,311. One could not call the charge a failed attempt as they had accomplished what they intended to; they went into eternity in a blaze of glory. The sight and smell of 4,311 dead Japanese soldiers in the path of their Banzai charge would remain beyond the scope of description for Bill and the other Marines who witnessed the attack and the clean-up. It was by far the largest Banzai charge of the war.

Hundreds of dead Japanese litter the beach near Tanapag, Saipan, on the morning of July 6th, 1944. Bill and the Pioneer Team fended off the onslaught a few hundred yards from this location. (U.S.M.C. Photo)

On July 8th, Lieutenant Bob Stoner flew an anti-submarine patrol (ASP) off the coast of Saipan with Stenson and Palmer along as his crew. Stanley had assigned Bob to divert to "Isely Field" on Saipan to pick up VC-11's newest member; one Lieutenant Roberts. Roberts had made the trip from Eniwetok on a Navy transport plane and arrived the day before. The field was known as "Aslito Field" when it belonged to the Japanese a few weeks earlier. A U.S. Navy pilot named Isley had been killed while bombing the field, and it had been renamed in his honor. As Bob made his approach into Isley, he dropped below Mt. Tapotchau directly in front of him. As he came over the end of the strip, he couldn't help but glance at the intact Japanese Zeros along the east edge of the field. These "fly boys" from the Nehenta Bay were actually flying right into a combat zone. As the wheels touched down on the strip, a huge cloud of white dust rose up behind the TBM as Bob worked the brakes and turned toward the hangars. Grungy Marine guards became visible as they were stationed every 50 yards along the perimeter. Coming closer to the hangers, Bob taxied past two long rows of P-47 Thunderbolts belonging to the 19th Squadron of the U.S.A.A.F. The Thunderbolts looked dirty and worn from their past weeks of "ground pounding" at Saipan and elsewhere.

Bob parked the TBM along the west taxiway and shut down the engine. A bearded Marine climbed onto the right wing and stayed in a crouch beside the cockpit. He recommended that Bob and the others exit the plane on the right side and stay behind the plane as they had been having sporadic sniper fire from the direction of the left wing. Bob's hopes of finding Roberts and making a quick take off were dashed as the sun was already sinking low in the western sky. Bob, along with Stenson and Palmer, would be spending the night on Saipan. After finding Roberts, the Navy men were given boxes of rations for dinner and shown into a sandbagged tent for the night. Stenson and Palmer engaged in several lengthy conversations with the Marines guarding the field and they had their first news of the horrors of the battle still underway to the north of the Island. Bob knew that if Bill Bennett was still alive, he would be out there in the night. It felt strange to know that a friend was so close and have no possible way to know where he was. The Marine guards told Bob that a lot of the Marines on Saipan probably didn't even know where they were. As he lay in the tent, the night was filled with the sounds of rifle fire and occasional explosions in the distance. The Navy fliers all had their .45s at hand as they slept. Toward dawn, there were several close cracks of rifle fire followed by Marines yelling at the top of their lungs across the airstrip. After a breakfast of black coffee and some crackers, Stenson and Palmer stuffed Lieutenant Robert's bags into the aft compartment of the TBM as Bob brought the engine to life. The TBM rumbled down the debris-strewn runway, lifted into the air and banked west out over the Pacific. As he flew up the west coast of Saipan, Bob looked out over the right wing and thought about the story he would have to tell Bill Bennett the next time they saw each other.

Corporal Channing Miller of Company A/1/2 was eager as usual to hunt the Japanese after the Banzai charges. Company A went out the morning of the 7th and tracked and killed the hold-out Japanese. On July 8th, Miller's squad cornered a group of Japanese and engaged in a close-quarters firefight in which all of the Japanese were killed. In the course of the fight, Miller received gunshot wounds to the head, chest and left hand and was evacuated by boat to a hospital ship offshore. The wounds were serious but Miller survived. He would spend two weeks aboard the ship. Bill and the team from 2/18 moved north and helped to push the remaining Japanese units to Marpi Point, at the northernmost tip of Saipan. On the 7th, 8th and 9th, there was an increase in the number of loudspeakers and Japanese speaking translators trying to talk civilians and Japanese soldiers out of suicide. One Marine unit witnessed a Japanese officer behead four of his own soldiers before the Americans could gun him down. Other Japanese officers machine gunned their own units to keep them from surrendering. At the cliffs of Marpi Point, mothers threw their children to their deaths and then jumped after them. Families huddled in caves, pulled pins on hand grenades and held them to their children. In the midst of this, brave Marines entered caves to try and save children and the translators were able to talk hundreds of civilians out of suicide. Some Marines had become so upset by the civilian deaths that they gathered up living civilian children in their arms, dropped their weapons and began walking south to the refugee camp. After all the killing, the thought of being able to save a life became more important than orders.

At 1615 hours on July 9th, Admiral Turner declared Saipan "secured." It would be almost two months before the Japanese stragglers would be cleaned out. Starting with the Banzai charge of July 6 and 7th, the last four days of the campaign had nearly pushed Bill and his fellow Marines over the edge mentally. The carnage they had witnessed for 25 straight days of combat had left them exhausted beyond words. The thousands of dead Japanese bloating in the sun and being buried by the bulldozers was a throwback to the situation on Tarawa, almost a year earlier. As Bill looked at the "new kids," Clodfelter, Walzer, Taber, Urioste, Di Gennaro and Trier, he realized they all looked at least 10 years older than they had on the day they came ashore. Inside, they had all aged more than that. When they had asked questions about what combat was like back at Camp Tarawa in Hawaii, there was no answer that could have even begun to describe what they had seen and done in these past 25 days. As for Bill, Fred, Coate, Fortenberry, Herman and Poterola, it was getting difficult to remember what life had been like before all of this started. In the middle of combat they didn't have a view of the "big picture" around them, only the situation within view. Bill had sorted out in his mind that when the fighting started, the goal was to stay alive and help your buddies to stay alive. He had to focus on the job at hand. The Pioneer team had made it through one of the bloodiest battles in United States history without losing a man.

On July 10th, the 2/18 team was released from their 2/2 combat assignment and ordered south to the new camps to rejoin Captain Farkas and the rest of D/2/18. A column of trucks arrived to drive the tired Marines south about eight miles to the Susupe area. Bill was reunited with his buddies Johnny C. Jones and Herb Dale. They had been spared most of what Bill's team had endured and worked with the Shore Party on supplies, as did a good number of Marines from D/2/18. Bill found that 2nd Lieutenant Simonson had healed from his neck wound and returned to lead 2nd Platoon along with Lieutenant Saylor. Simonson's wound had been dangerously close to severing vital nerves in his neck and he was lucky to be alive. The guys were astonished at the changes in the southern areas over the past three weeks. The construction battalion had built new camps with barracks, showers and mess halls. There were crushed rock and coral-paved roads that didn't even exist before the invasion. Farther south, Isley Field was now home to the 19th Squadron of Army Air Force P-47 Thunderbolts. These large fighter planes were capable of hitting ground targets with remarkable power. Nearby, 155mm Howitzer batteries lobbed fire onto the nearby island of Tinian, just three miles across the water from Saipan. At the new camp, Bill turned in every piece of equipment he had left for a shower, shave, food and a new uniform. After the experience of taking an actual shower with actual soap, Bill looked in the mirror at a thin, bearded, older man. Scissors took off the first inch of beard before he could even think about lathering up to shave. He had almost forgotten what it felt like to touch his smooth face. Barber shops were set up without charge and within hours Marines began to look civilized once again. Hot food was served and bunks issued. Sleeping in relative safety was as foreign to Bill that night as Saipan had been the day he arrived. He thought about how he might ever be able to tell friends or family about what he had been through here on this island. He could not think of how that would even be possible. He was not sure he would even want to tell them.

A bearded and bushy-haired Corporal Bennett reunites with Marine buddy Herb Dale on Saipan just after the island was declared secure. It would be months before the Japanese hold-outs could be rooted out. The beard earned him the title of "Moses" as he led the team.

(Bennett Family Photo)

The list of wounded from D/2/18, as far as Bill could find on July 11th, was as follows: Wounded in Action: PFC Harold Bonawitz, PFC Richard M. Fertado, PFC Robert G. Haak, PFC Alphee DuCharme, Corporal Robert E. Stubblefield, Sergeant Mike A. Matkovich, 2nd Lieutenant Arthur K. Simonson, Harris, Sloan, Knifer, Rogers, Sullivan, Hickok, Quigley, Johnson, Tucker, Sukennik, Brislan, Lombardi, Ellas, Captain Robert Jones, Benoit, Lea, Gannon, Moody, Fowles, Dombrowski, Wight, Brown, Bruhnke, House, Willett, Tullos, Tamsy and Wallace. Rittenhouse and Schweitzer were missing in action. The total was 35 wounded and two missing, but none confirmed as killed in action.

Corporal Channing Miller had earned his second purple heart of the war and was recuperating from surgery on a hospital ship offshore, and PFC Peter

Nicholas Andrews had made the supreme sacrifice on that hill east of Garapan. 3,100 Marines, Navy and Army personnel had died; another 13,100 were wounded. 24,000 Japanese soldiers had been killed and 5,000 more committed suicide. Over 20,000 civilians had died on Saipan, including the suicides. The island and its airfields were now in American hands. Little Setchan Akiyama was well on her way to healing and getting used to life at Camp Susupe. A total of 10 of her close family members had been killed, including her father Tomomitsu and older brother Shiuichi, whose bodies were never found. Approximately 52,000 people lost their lives during the battle for Saipan. The exact number would never be known.

74. Recuperation

Company D/2/18 had about one week to recuperate before word came that they were to prepare to re-enter combat on the nearby island of Tinian. 9,000 Japanese soldiers had been expecting an attack for the past month. One afternoon, as Bill was chewing the fat with his buddies and staying out of the midday heat, a PFC from F/2/2 brought Bill a message saying his presence was requested by Captain Lefty Morris. Bill scratched his head and had no idea why this captain would want to talk to him. He set off across the camp looking for the F/2/2 area and then asked where he could find Captain Morris. When he arrived at the tent, Morris was meeting with some officers and Bill had to wait until they were done. The staff sergeant showed Bill in to see the captain as the other Marines were leaving. Morris sat behind a makeshift desk as Bill saluted and waited for the reply. Morris saluted and told Bill to stand at ease. He shuffled through a pile of files on the end of the desk and finally spun one around and looked at the name for a few seconds. Morris asked Bill if he remembered him and Bill answered affirmatively. Bill was dreading hearing the words, "Bank vault." Morris had been with the blocked column outside of Garapan when Bill blasted the boulders out of the road. Morris explained that he had been thinking of putting Bill up for a commendation for his actions that day, so he was looking through his file from D/2/18. A problem arose when Morris could not find Bill's qualification for C3 Plastic Explosives. Bill had been trained for TNT and not C3.

The captain's demeanor became slightly terse as he asked Bill why he misled him into believing he was a certified C3 Demolitions man. Bill answered Morris by saying he had not misled the captain but had only answered his questions. The captain had asked Bill if he could clear the road with explosives and Bill had told the captain he could. Morris shook his head and told Bill he could very well reprimand him over the occurrence, but his record was immaculate and he knew Bill was a stellar Marine. He told Bill he was glad to see he had gotten through the ordeal of the past three weeks without being wounded, thanked him for clearing the road that day, and dismissed him. Bill saluted, about faced and made his way back to his tent. Everyone wanted to know what the "dope" was on the visit with the captain and Bill told them that he had come close to having his tail in a sling. The ordeal was comical to most of Bill's buddies who knew how straight-laced he was.

The following day, Bill was at his tent in the late afternoon, enjoying a few hours of doing nothing, when Fred Ellis came back to the tent. Fred had been down at the brand-new mess hall where they had erected a large corkboard for notices and general information. Fred asked Bill if he had seen the board this afternoon and Bill said he hadn't. Fred couldn't help but smile a bit and he suggested Bill get over there right away and check it out. Now Bill, with his curiosity piqued, told Fred to just tell him what he was talking about, but Fred, with a chance to grill his good buddy just a little, would not say more.

Bill headed out for the board with Bennie and Walzer in tow, as their curiosity had gotten the better of both of them. Once at the board, Bill scanned the dozens of posts for a clue as to what Fred had been talking about. On one end of the board, below the heading of "Specialist Training Schedule" was a flier posted that read *Introduction to 533 Demolition, Instructor: Corporal William W. Bennett, D/2/18. July 15th, 0700, Training Pavilion 2. General use of TNT and C3 Plastic Explosives.* Apparently, Captain Morris had set this class up for Bill and he must have cleared it with Captain Farkas. Simonson looked into it for Bill and affirmed that the assignment was legitimate, and he couldn't help but smile at what Bill had gotten himself into. Bill still thought it might be a joke and Simonson was in on it. It was no joke. Bill found Harry Bonawitz, who had recently rejoined the Company after he had been shot in the shoulder shortly after they came ashore at Saipan. Bonawitz had some additional training material on C3, but not all of it. Hurrying about the camp, Bill managed to locate the books and material that he needed for the class and went back to the tent to prepare. After gaining permission to keep a light on and a supply of coffee, Bill worked into the wee hours of the morning. With a few hours of sleep, he was up again at 0430 to get some chow and mimeograph the class outline for his fast-approaching "students."

At 0650 hours, Marines were appearing at the Training Pavilion and Bill stood at the table in the front organizing his papers and training materials. Roughly 30 Marines attended the class, wanting to become Demo men for a variety of reasons. Bill's thinking at that point was the opposite. He had been through enough and had no interest in blowing anything up in the future. He was so ready to get the war over that the thought of swimming due east had occurred to him. The class seemed to be a success, much to Bill's surprise, and after the second day, Bill was relieved by the actual instructors who would finish the training regimen. The incident ended up being a good diversion from the aftermath of another round of combat for Bill. Captain Morris had the satisfaction of letting Bill know that there were still rules in the Marine Corps without exacting unnecessary punishment.

As Bill sat alone before "lights out" in his tent, he prepared to pray and searched his soul for a few minutes. He was aware how each step of his combat experiences had been changing him. He could see and feel in his spirit the growth that the Lord had caused within him. Seeing the death and destruction of military men on both sides of the war had been a shock that had to be dealt with, and Bill thought he had done well. However, the death of these civilians on Saipan had been an entirely different matter. Trying to reason as to why little boys and girls, and mothers nursing babies, had gotten into the middle of this kind of destruction was an impossible task. As Bill read his New Testament and prayed over the coming days, he felt that the lesson he was being taught was one of mankind's consequences. When humans set evil into motion, there will be consequences to pay. These consequences will not only consume the guilty, but will also affect the innocent who may be nearby. When a man robs and kills another, the robber has set evil into motion. The victim, who was killed, was innocent of the crime, but greatly affected.

The Lord seemed to settle Bill's spirit with the understanding that the Japanese had put this evil into motion. The Marines had brought the consequences home to Saipan and many innocents had perished along with the guilty. Japanese Admiral Chuichi Nagumo had led the Japanese attack on Pearl Harbor, even though he personally did not agree with the attack. He had studied naval warfare in America years before, and the thought of a sneak attack did not sit well with him. Nagumo had been unable to flee Saipan due to the surprise arrival of the American fleet. On the night of July 6th, 1944, as the Banzai attack was being organized, Nagumo shot himself in the head to avoid being captured. His body was found the following day by Marines. Admiral Nagumo had faced the consequences of his actions.

75. Tinian

Company D/2/18 had 190 Marines on active duty on July 16th at Saipan. A few were wounded and out of the war and several had already rejoined the company, as had Harry Bonawitz and Arthur Simonson. Unbelievably, not one Marine from D/2/18 had been killed on Saipan, although Schweitzer and Rittenhouse were missing, now presumed dead. Mike Matkovich's wound had been very serious and he was back in Hawaii starting a long road of recovery that would eventually take him back to Chicago. The corporals and sergeants of 2nd Platoon took the lead of organizing the new equipment and making sure that everyone was once again battle ready for the coming invasion of Tinian. Inspections and short marches ensued, but Captain Farkas did not see any reason to inflict hardship on his battle-tested Marines. There had not yet been a time where the company had come out of combat and then returned to combat so quickly. Bill did not look forward to more combat as he was conscious of his now long history of avoiding a serious wound.

Quite a few of the younger Marines had come to respect Bill and they asked his advice on numerous things, both Marine Corps and personal. Bill emphasized to each of them the importance of putting the Lord first in their lives and trusting Christ to lead them according to His will. His reasoning was that if God Himself has put together a path for your life, why would you want to live it any other way? It was not that the Lord's path would be easy or painless; it was that God knew the best path and men do not. Bill used the passage from Proverbs 14:12, "There is a way which seemeth right unto a man, but the end, thereof, are the ways of death."

On July 23rd, 1944, Bob Stoner attended the Sunday Worship Service aboard the USS Nehenta Bay. Chaplain John R. McLain conducted the service which was attended by several hundred officers and crew. It was vitally important for Bob to maintain his relationship with Christ and everyone that knew him also knew that about him. Although he was an officer and a respected pilot, Bob managed to keep a sense of humility about him because he knew he was no better than any other in God's eyes. He had always tried to conduct himself in a way that would honor the Lord and not shame Him. He and Bill Bennett held this deep conviction, as well as their common interest in becoming pastors earlier in their lives. Bob loved the camaraderie that he had within the Navy and he was always aware of the fact that others would be looking to him as an example. Being a good officer, a great pilot, a friend to all and a man who loved God, summed up who he wanted to be.

Around 2300 hours, Company D/2/18 loaded aboard LST-131 (Landing Ship Tank) at Charan Kanoa, Saipan and headed offshore a few hours later at 0330 hours on the 24th. The LST was much smaller than the troop transports but it would accommodate Company D nicely. LSTs had huge doors in the bow that would allow the ship to push right up to a beach and let the entire company out at once. They had sufficient guns to cover such a landing if the beach was not heavily opposed. Generally, the LSTs held about 17 LVTs that tracked out of the bow several miles at sea and the LVTs delivered the Marines to their beaches. It did not make sense to expose an LST to fire from shore. The good news for the 2nd Marine Division was the primary beach assaults would be handled by the 4th Division at White Beach, while the 2nd made a feint landing toward the heavily guarded Blue Beach at Tinian Town, on the island's west coast. The strategy here was to hold the Japanese at Tinian Town while the 4th Division made it ashore at the northwest part of the island. Once the 4th was ashore, the 2nd would pull back and head north to follow the 4th Marines at White Beach. By the time the Japanese realized the attack at Tinian Town was a fake, it would be too late for them to defend the true assault at White Beach. No one had any idea how hard the 9,000 Japanese on Tinian would fight, but no one dared underestimate them. Gone were the notions that Marines would wade ashore and finish their work in a few days. The Navy, Marine airmen and Army Air Forces had been pounding Tinian for weeks prior to this invasion, so lessons were being learned and implemented. The Marines would still need to go in and get the dirty work done.

The USS Nehenta Bay steamed toward Tinian after refueling and resupplying at Eniwetok and supporting Fleet Operations at Guam. The ongoing anti-submarine patrols kept the pilots and crew extremely busy with long hours for everyone aboard. Pilots of VC-11 logged near record flying hours for the month of July.

Lieutenant Bob Stoner knocked on Lieutenant Commander Stanley's door and asked if he could have a word with him. Stanley sat at his desk with a stack of flight reports and a cigarette. He asked Stoner to have a seat. He sensed what the visit was about. Stoner sat down and began to explain that he wanted more flying time as he felt his value to the squadron was in the air, not organizing flight activities. Stanley knew what Stoner wanted as they had discussed the topic several times. Stanley had no doubt Stoner was one of the best pilots he had, but he also had organizational and leadership skills that were highly valuable to Stanley and the squadron. Stoner told Stanley that he joined the Navy to defend his country and he wanted to do so directly. Stanley had taken a liking to Stoner and he wanted to allow him the combat missions, but he wished that Stoner could just be happy overseeing flight operations. He assured Stoner that when it came down to it, he would get his share of the missions. Bob nodded his head affirmatively, thanked Stanley, and headed back toward the ready room.

Bob decided to take one of his diversionary visits down to the hangar deck and watch the mechanics work their magic on the VC-11 birds. There was something about the hangar deck that Stoner found exciting. It was probably the "smell of aviation" that lingers in all hangars: a mix of oil, fuel, rubber, solvents and paint. The activity was intense on this deck. The sound of tools clanging, air tools chattering and men yelling reminded Bob of the garages back in Aurora where his father Sam had sold cars and trucks while he was growing up. Each plane was under a different scrutiny as the teams of mechanics worked against the problems, the solutions and the clock to get their plane ready on time. Each of VC-11's aircraft had been assigned a "plane captain" who stayed with that particular aircraft 24-7 with as little sleep as needed. One of the plane captains was 19-year-old Carl Lee Davis from Kentucky. Davis had to make sure that every detail on his TBM-1C Avenger was perfect and ready for the pilot when it came time to launch the next mission. Bob stood back and watched as Davis was showing a small leak of hydraulic oil to Crew Chief Armand Blackmore, whose mechanic team had been assigned to work over Davis' TBM, "Number 92." Blackmore was certain that there was not a problem with the small amount of oil he was seeing, but Davis insisted that it be checked again.

Bob had gotten to know both of these men while visiting the mechanics on the adjacent catwalks to the hangar deck. Davis was a soft-spoken fellow who took his job as plane captain about as seriously as a man could. This was a trait that the pilots liked to see. Davis had been given the nickname "Mouse" by his shipmates, not because he was soft-spoken, but because of a narrow escape he had made not long after leaving San Diego. Davis made a habit out of watching the planes being "recovered" (landing) after missions, and stood in a safe place just aft of the superstructure on the flight deck. The plane captains were actually part of the flight deck crew, so this was allowable. On this occasion, the pilot of a FM2 Wildcat bounced the plane off the deck, missed the arresting cable and went out of control directly toward Davis. With no apparent escape, Davis spotted a small hatch opening and dove through it into an ordinance room below deck. Those who witnessed the escape saw Davis disappear into what seemed to be "thin air." Upon inspection of the opening through which Davis had thrust his body, his buddies concluded that "only a mouse" could have pulled off such a feat.

Two mechanics stood on rolling platforms as they worked on the exposed Wright Aeronautics R-2600 radial engine. The engine oil was being changed, which meant pumping out the 20 gallons of oil with a hand pump attached to a waste-oil barrel on the platform. Blackmore and Davis noticed Stoner watching them and gave him a "Good evening, sir" greeting. Bob returned the sentiment with a smile and moved on to the other TBMs. After dark, the hangar deck was closed up tight so that no light would leak out to the open ocean where Japanese planes and ships might spot it a hundred miles away. All the mechanics worked with a pair of rubber-soled shoes, shorts and their dog tags. Their skin was shiny with sweat as the large round thermometer on the wall showed a temperature of 105 degrees. The work that went on during the night would partly determine whether pilots and crew lived or died. A single-engine aircraft over the ocean has few options if the engine dies. This was serious business. In the morning, long before dawn, the plane captain and the crew chief would oversee their TBM to the deck elevator and the two of them would ride up with the plane. Once their TBM was in its determined spot of the launch order, the planes would be armed with the assigned ordinance by the armorers.

Approximately 20 minutes prior to launch, the engines would be started by the plane captains while the crew chiefs stood by to listen to the engines. If any problems were detected, the plane would be scrubbed and the "spare" brought up from below. Davis and the other plane captains would check all the indicators in the cockpit and look for problems. While the TBMs were warming, the gunner and radioman would appear in their flight gear and climb aboard to get situated. Five to ten minutes before launch, the pilots would climb onto the wing and the plane captain and the pilot would trade places. The plane captain would then assist the pilot with getting strapped in with helmet and goggles in place and double check the radio and intercom. Once the pilots and crew were in place and launch was imminent, the deck officer would appear off to the side of the first plane where the pilot could clearly see him. The crew chief and plane captain would both give the deck officer a "thumbs up," meaning that their jobs were done. The deck officer would then wait for a "thumbs up" from the pilot. Once received, the deck officer would spiral his index finger upwards, telling the pilot to achieve the required RPMs for launch. A second "thumbs up" from the pilot started the countdown. The deck officer would then bring his hand up near his head, and extend it straight with one finger. Then his hand would come back to near his head and he would extend two fingers. Back to the head a third time, and with three fingers extended, he turned and pushed his hand toward the bow of the carrier. This was the signal for the catapult lever to be pulled, which sent the plane forward with an 80 mph assist from the steam-powered piston below the deck. The plane captain and crew chief always stayed on deck until they saw their plane safely in the air. With all the props spinning, the ordinance being loaded, the waves and areas without guard rails, the carrier decks were dangerous places to be.

The plan at Tinian called for D/2/18 to load LVTs aboard LST-131 and participate in the "feint landing" at Tinian Town. Once again, Sergeant LaPoint led Bill, Fred Ellis, Gerald Coate and the Pioneer Team to load their LVT down on the "tractor deck" of the LST.

A few minutes before departure, the diesel engines of the LVTs were all started and the blue-gray fumes began to fill the deck. Finally, when Bill felt that he couldn't take any more fumes, the front doors swung open and the LVTs began to waddle down the ramp and splash into the ocean like huge, mechanical waterfowl. As their LVT hit the doorway, fresh ocean air relieved the smell of the putrid diesel fumes and it was good to break free of the LST. The nerves of the Marines were nothing like before as everyone knew they were just there for show to the Japanese. A Naval bombardment ensued, followed by the planes coming in low to strafe and bomb the beaches. Everything looked and sounded just like it did on Saipan five weeks earlier. The waves of LVTs made their run for the beach and began to draw enemy fire about 800 yards out. At 400 yards out, the lead LVTs received the radio message to turn it around.

Deck Officer aboard USS Nehenta Bay launching Plane Captain Carl L. Davis' number 92 TBM-1C. Lieutenant Stoner flew this plane at times. It is not known who the pilot is in this photo.

(Photo courtesy of Carl Lee Davis)

The armada of LVTs swung to the north as Navy and Marine planes flew low overhead and pounded targets onshore. Bill had become used to the Hellcats and Avengers after Tarawa and Saipan, but he found the F4U Corsairs to be remarkable as they flew over with their gull-wing design. It made the Marines feel better to look up and see those hunters overhead. The super-charged engine of the Corsair created a substantial "whine" as it went overhead and the Japanese soon referred to the new plane as "Whistling Death." The team spent hours getting up to the White Beaches and into the circular holding patterns before heading in to land. The Marines had been ordered to pack very light for this attack, which made for a little more room in the LVT. Some of the guys were able to crouch or even sit and catch some sleep as they bounced around in the waves. At long last, they were given the go ahead to land at White Beach 1 just behind and in support of 1st Battalion, 8th Marines. The feint landing at Tinian Town was masterfully done and it allowed the 4th Division to flood ashore at White 1 and White 2. They were already pushing deep into the island to the east and to the south. There was hardly any fire to speak of on the way in and the LVT lurched onto the sand and came to a jarring halt. The new LVT had a rear gate that dropped down so the Marines did not have to expose themselves to fire by crawling over the side. The team piled out onto the sand and Shore Party officers waved them forward off the beach. It was 1630 hours.

Lieutenant Simonson had his 2nd Platoon organized to receive and supply 1/8, and due to the rapid advance, trucks were available to move supplies forward. Bill and the Pioneer Team moved forward to the northeast toward the prized Ushi Airfield. The terrain was surprisingly different from Saipan in that it was fairly flat with huge fields, almost like Illinois in some places. The huge P-47s from Isley Field on Saipan came from behind and were dumping bombs far up ahead which roared into huge fireballs and sent palls of black smoke high into the air. As the Thunderbolts flew over, the Marines in the trucks and on the ground cheered, waved and pumped their fists into the air. The pilots were dropping a new mixture of explosive for the first time; a blend of diesel, gas and metal powder called napalm. By 1900 hours, 1/8 was ordered to dig in for the night and the Pioneers made plans to create and supply the dump. As Bill chopped at the dry ground with his shovel, he reasoned that this was just one more island and one more foxhole. Bill wondered how many more holes he would have to dig. Foxholes were better than graves, and as long as he and his team were safe, there really was nothing to complain about.

Experience had taught the Marines there would be a counterattack on the first night ashore and 1/8 made serious preparations for that possibility. At some time in the darkest early morning hours, the attack came down from the north and off to Bill's left. The tracers and mortars lit up the sky and the Marine 75mm Pack Howitzers from 1/10 delivered defensive fire into the Japanese lines. Star shells fired from destroyers offshore lit up the night with an eerie red hue. The Marines in the line braced themselves to repel the attack if it reached them, but the forward defenders held fast. The Japanese were still too fresh to mount a suicide attack and they retreated to reform for tomorrow's battle. Intermittent firing and fighting continued throughout the night, and sleep was difficult, if not impossible. Because of the rapid advance and the use of trucks and jeeps, having supplies was a refreshing change from the earlier campaigns.

When cans arrived with clean water in them the following morning, Bill knew the Marine Corps had been learning some lessons. 1/8 was once again fast on the move and heading east toward the airfield. Opposition from the Japanese was light but the advance of equipment and supplies was tough work. On the third day, the Marines swept over the airfield with very few, if any, casualties. As the advance moved into the low ledges and plateaus, approaching Tinian's east coast, it became apparent that the Pioneer team had outrun their intended usefulness. There was no need for Pioneer combat specialists to bring up supplies behind the rapidly advancing infantry and armor in open country. Bill, Fred and the team were ordered to return to the rest of D/2/18 near White Beach 1.

The returning trucks bumped and slammed the Pioneers as they made their way back to Lieutenant Simonson and Captain Farkas. Farther south and along the forward lines of the Marines advance, TBM Avengers from the USS Nehenta Bay flew air support missions against targets that were called in by ground troops. Lieutenant Robert F. Stoner's request had been granted by Lieutenant Commander Stanley and Stoner was on his second mission. As he overflew the Marines on the ground, he knew the 2nd Division was ashore and his old buddy Bill Bennett was somewhere down there in the thick of it. He had mentioned to the pilots and crew, numerous times, how important their jobs were to the Americans on the ground. The pilots of VCV-11 who were familiar with *The Stoner Weekly News* had read about Bill Bennett and the tough going the Marines had experienced. For the first time, the VC-11 TBMs and FM2 Wildcats were making direct contributions to the combat on the ground.

By the time the Pioneers rejoined 2nd Platoon, Simonson told them they had orders to board another LST the following day, as they were being taken toward the southern tip of the island to be reinserted into the battle as necessary. The rapid advance would necessitate the landing of combat supplies on beaches to the south as the Marine lines moved in that direction. During the night, near White Beach 1, guards remained alert watching for infiltrators, but the mood was much lighter as the battle lines were now miles away. The guys even joked a bit and they were all very happy to be going back aboard an LST. Some of the veterans noted that most of the guys didn't even have any holes in their utilities yet. When morning came, there were rations and even hot coffee. Simonson came by and told everyone to get it together quick. The remnants of a typhoon were approaching, so they moved up the loading of LST-130 to 0900. This would allow the LST crew to get off the beach and out to sea before the rough stuff arrived.

At White Beach 1, LST-130 sat with her bow and the gaping doors open on the sand. Company D marched aboard through the doors and onto the tractor deck and spread out into every available space on the small ship. Bill had always thought the APA transports were somewhat ugly vessels, but they were beauties compared to the homely LSTs. Calling an LST a gray bathtub would be a compliment. Bill and Fred found bunks in one of the troop areas and went up to the main deck with Johnny Jones and Herb Dale. Dark clouds were rolling in and the wind was churning the sea. The LST's captain, Lieutenant John E. Collins, and the crew moved about the ship with a display of efficiency and speed that impressed the Marines. LST-130's deck vibrated as the twin General Motors 900 horsepower diesel engines powered the ship to reverse her off the sand. The LST stayed in reverse as she moved about a half mile from the beach. Hundreds of ships and boats were visible along the coast and far out at sea. Large floating platforms had been bolted together to form a floating pier and the waves were already raising and lowering it somewhat drastically as they passed. LST-130 turned and swung her bow out to sea to head south. Rain started to come down with the 30 mph wind and Bill and the guys took refuge below deck. Company D had gotten on and off the island without any casualties. Compared to the outcome on the previous islands Bill had fought on, Tinian had been quite tolerable.

76. Bulls Eye!

On the afternoon of July 27th, 1944, the flight deck had been cleared aboard the USS Nehenta Bay and the plane captains had their planes safely below on the hangar deck. The tail end of the typhoon lashed the fleet with 35 to 40 mph wind gusts and heavy rain, but nothing the large ships were concerned about. The hangar deck buzzed with activity as the mechanics carefully worked over their birds for tomorrow's mission. The word was that the weather would clear and the mission would be flown. Lieutenant Stoner came down from the ready room to check on Carl Davis' TBM, which he would be flying in the morning. The engine cowling of number 92 was off and mechanics were testing the magnetos and adding engine oil. Davis was examining the tail hook after what seemed to be a hard landing during the last recovery. Stoner bent low under the horizontal stabilizer and looked in on Davis and the crew chief. Davis explained that he wanted the hook replaced since it had been somewhat mangled, and according to his "better safe than sorry" philosophy he had learned on the farm in Kentucky, the hook would be replaced.

Davis and the mechanic team were ready to take a break and they gathered on the catwalk on the port side, where there was shelter from the wind. The best part about being grazed by the typhoon was that the temperatures had dropped into the 70s, which felt like cold air to those used to 110 to 120 degrees on the hangar deck. Most of the crew even wore shirts today. The crew was eager to hear about the missions over Tinian and Stoner answered their questions. Even though they worked on these planes every day, the thought of flying over a combat area and seeing Marines and Japanese on the ground firing at each other was a wild tale. Stoner wanted the crew to know how important their jobs were and that these planes could not do the job without them. He explained how many of his friends from Aurora, Illinois, were now Marines on the ground and how eager he was to help them from the air. He mentioned that his dad back home sold the heavy Diamond T trucks he had seen at work on Tinian, and he couldn't wait to tell his dad he had seen them in action. He could not only talk about the Navy, but he knew his sports as a football and basketball player throughout his life. To Armand Blackmore, Lieutenant Stoner was a rare officer and pilot, in that he was a genuine fellow that showed an interest in the enlisted men. They didn't know the Stoner family or the parents behind this lieutenant, but they could see the product of a great upbringing. Lieutenant Bob Stoner was known as a thorough and capable pilot who even served on the Courts Martial Board at times for disciplinary action, but he was also a regular guy with some great jokes and stories.

All of the planes were ready earlier than normal and Carl Davis, Armand Blackmore and Lieutenant Stoner all enjoyed some hours of sleep before their wake up calls.

Friday, July 28th, 1944. Plane captain Carl L. Davis climbed out of his bunk and dressed for duty in the dim red lights of the bunk room. Several other crewmen were in various stages of the same process. Moving to the "head," Davis shaved without a mirror, navigating his face by memory and feel. Getting ready to hit the chow line, Davis caught up with his buddy Danny Thomas and they enjoyed a few minutes catching up on the "latest dope" from around the carrier. The chat had to be cut short as Carl needed to get down to his plane to meet up with the crew chief and get old "92" up on deck. Lieutenant Bob Stoner was rousted from a dream at 0330 hours and shaved and donned his khaki flight uniform before heading to the officer's mess for breakfast. Stoner sat next to Lieutenant Commander Stanley as they worked on their toast, dehydrated eggs and bacon. They drank down several cups of coffee from their white Navy china, emblazoned with blue anchors. The amenities in the officer's mess were quite a few notches above the chow line where Carl Davis had been served. Stoner and Stanley finished up their coffee and headed for the ready room to get into their flight gear and go over the day's mission.

Stanley maintained contact with "Commander Support Aircraft" directly from the ground on Tinian, while Stoner went over the plane assignments for VC-11's mission. Stoner noted he would be flying "92" today and he felt confident she would be ready to go. CSA gave Stanley the coordinates for roughly the center of Tinian near the west coast, not far inland from Tinian Town. Late on the previous evening, Marines had run into a Japanese stronghold of several bunkers surrounded by anti-aircraft guns and multiple machine guns. They had been unable to destroy the stronghold with artillery and they had lost too many Marines with ground assaults. VC-11 would have to try and hit it from the air.

At 0430 hours, Carl Davis and the crew chief escorted 92 up the elevator to the flight deck. She would be taking off in the number two spot right behind the Air Coordinator, Lieutenant Commander Stanley. Working in almost total darkness, the crew prepared the six TBMs and eight Wildcats. Davis climbed onto the left wing of 92 and dropped into the cockpit. The crew chief came within view on the right side of the plane and they exchanged hand signals. Carl used a pen light to view the dozens of gauges, switches, levers and buttons on and around the control panel. He made sure the prop was set to "full low pitch" and turned on the battery switch. He set the Fuel Tank Selector Valve to "Center Main," turned on the electric fuel pump to get the line pressure up to 7 to 9 pounds per square inch. He made another quick hand signal to the crew chief and energized the starter for a full 15 seconds. Next, he activated the electric primer and set the throttle to 1/3 open. The crew chief gave him the "prop clear" signal and Carl turned the starter as the engine began to rotate to life. After four or five seconds of the whining starter, the R-2600 engine "popped" and sputtered, then "poppity-pop, popped" until it rumbled to life while shooting out huge plumes of grayish white oil smoke across the deck. The huge Avenger vibrated beneath Carl's seat as he monitored the throttle to 1100 rpm. He motioned to the crew for the clear signal to unfold the huge wings and then reached the wing folding lever and watched the stowed wings swivel into their flight positions. The crew chief walked under each wing and set the wing locks manually, then gave Carl a "thumbs up." Carl ran the engine up to 1400 rpm for a few minutes and then shut the engine down.

The TBMs were attended by the armorers who were fitting each plane with two 500-pound bombs, one under each wing. Stanley's plane would not carry any bombs. At 0510 hours, Carl dropped back into the cockpit and repeated the sequence to restart the engine. The starter whined and clunked and the engine quickly came back to life and roared up to 1400 rpm. Stoner's crew emerged from the ready-room door and approached 92 from the starboard side. Carl felt the plane rock as they boarded through the crew hatch and climbed into their positions. Owen P. Stenson, AOM1c, U.S.N.R., climbed into the turret behind the greenhouse glass and situated himself with the .50 caliber Browning machine gun to the left side of his head. Paul W. Palmer, ARM2c, U.S.N.R., sat himself into the radioman's seat and checked that his .30 caliber Browning was properly stowed for launch. Stenson was a veteran gunner and a former San Francisco fireman and Palmer was a soft-spoken southern boy from Atlanta, Georgia. They had been out on the first two missions with Stoner and were very impressed with his flying skills. Knowing that Stoner had a reputation for being one of the best pilots in VC-11, as well as a seasoned flight instructor, had set them both at ease. They both carried a .38 revolver in a shoulder holster, just in case they had to bail or ditch in enemy territory. Partly out of respect and partly out of protocol, they both referred to Stoner as "The Skipper." Stoner liked the sound of that since his dog back in Aurora was named Skipper. They plugged in the neck mics and checked the intercom with Davis. "Gunner checking in," came into Carl's ears, then, "Radio checking in." Carl replied, "Roger, check in received."

A few minutes later, Stoner appeared from the ready room and climbed up on the wing. Carl stepped out of the cockpit and Stoner dropped in. Carl reached into the cockpit and sorted the shoulder straps of the parachute harness for Lieutenant Stoner. Stoner then lifted his hands above his head and Carl snapped the four clips into the buckle over Stoner's waist. Carl then plugged in Stoner's head set and got a "thumbs up" back from Stoner. Carl's work was finished and he crouched at the lower edge of the wing and jumped down. Stoner pressed his mic and greeted Stenson and Palmer, asking them if they were all set back there. They both replied affirmatively.

Farther up the line, the engine noise droned to full throttle as the Wildcats roared into the air. The fighters began to double back and fly along the side of the deck as they formed for security while the TBMs got airborne. Stoner ran through his own check list leaving nothing to chance. Check fuel, mixture-rich, low blower, set prop, wings locked, cowl flaps, check trim tabs, tail wheel position, fuel selector switch, oil pressure, manifold pressure; all looked good. Stanley's Air Coordinator TBM was connected to the catapult and launched into the wind. The deck officer motioned Stoner forward and 92 was connected to the catapult. The deck officer spun his finger upward and Stoner revved the R-2600 engine up to 2600 rpm and kept his eye on the DO's fingers. One finger was shown and held, a second finger displayed and Bob gripped the control stick; his feet gently rocked the rudder pedals back and forth anticipating the wind resistance on the rudder in mere seconds. The DO showed Bob the third finger and thrust his hand toward the bow of the carrier. The catapult lever was thrown and TBM 92 shot forward, pushing pilot and crew back in their seats and off the carrier deck like a shot. Bob felt the heavy wind on the control stick as he worked to trim the flight controls. He turned his head and caught a glimpse of the USS Nehenta Bay already dropping away like a toy boat. Stenson always had the best seat in the house on takeoff as he could watch the TBM ascend while looking rearward.

As the final TBM was launched from the deck, Stanley had the Avengers form into an echelon formation off his right wing. The FM2 Wildcats formed into two groups of four, one on either side of the TBMs. As Air Coordinator,

Stanley began communication with the ground forces on Tinian. It was now 0615 and they would be near the target in 15 minutes. Arriving offshore and out of range of anti-aircraft guns, Stanley turned the formation over to Stoner and dove away to survey the target area. Marines on the ground marked their forward lines with white smoke so the Navy pilots could see them. Artillery fired red smoke rounds into the target areas and Stanley soon had the picture. He swung in across the target area and attracted some anti-aircraft fire so that he could locate it for the Wildcats. He radioed the flight leaders of the Wildcat wing and then watched them dive into action strafing the enemy position with their deadly .50 caliber guns. Stanley watched the attacks at a distance, noting the origins of the anti-aircraft fire, then directing the Wildcats to fire on those locations. Target spotters on the ground directed Stanley's attention to an area of enemy bunkers with truck-mounted anti-aircraft guns and well-defended machine gun positions. This was the main reason they had called in the air strike. Stanley had the area marked again with red artillery rounds and called in the TBM Avengers to drop their 500-pound bombs, referred to as "quarter tonners."

The first two TBMs dropped their bombs wide and deep and left the emplacement unscathed. The enemy fired glowing red balls of anti-aircraft at the TBMs and it was the first time the pilots had faced heavy anti-aircraft fire. It was unnerving. Stanley, wanting to reserve some of the "quarter tonners," called in Lieutenant Stoner to take care of this target. Stenson came on the intercom and said, "Lay it on 'em Skipper." Stoner pushed his rudder pedal and nudged the control stick forward to the left to drop the TBM toward the target area. Banking now to the right, he lined up the target and began to dive from 2000 feet. His airspeed rose as the altimeter dropped and he gripped the bomb release lever with his right hand. The red balls of the anti-aircraft fire began to ascend toward the Avenger like crazed fireflies trying to swarm over him. The only thing to do was to focus on the target and ignore the anti-aircraft fire. Reaching 300 feet above the ground, with airspeed of 230 mph, Stoner waited for the precise time to release the bombs and pull up. He could see the Japanese moving about as he rapidly approached. He yanked the release lever and felt the 1000 pounds drop from the airframe as he pulled the stick back and began to bank to his right. The intercom crackled to life with wild screaming from both Palmer and Stenson and all he could make out was, "Woo-hoo! Bullseye Skipper! Bullseye!"

As Stoner banked the Avenger to rejoin the squadron, he looked right and dropped the wing to see the huge pall of smoke rising up from the enemy fortification. Stanley's voice came into his ears over the radio and said, "Direct hit! Nice work Stoner!" Bob felt great; he had effectively dropped the "pickles" right where he wanted them. The Marines of the 4th Division on the ground immediately overran the enemy installation and finished off the stunned survivors of Stoner's bombs. There was no doubt on the ground or in Command's estimation that Stoner's accuracy saved the lives of many Marines. Palmer and Stenson continued to celebrate on the way back to the carrier and Bob tried to curtail his exuberance, although it was difficult to hide. Bob lined up the TBM with the flight deck, extended the flaps and dropped the landing gear. The steady ocean wind lent itself for a good landing and he set the wheels down at 85 mph and the tail hook grabbed the arresting cable and jarred number 92 to a halt. Carl Davis watched from along the starboard edge of the flight deck, and he was glad to see that his plane had no apparent damage. Once the pilots had climbed out of their planes, they began to congregate around 92 to congratulate Bob and his crew. Stanley and several other pilots had witnessed the bombing from the air and they were all smiles about seeing the perfect placement of those "quarter tonners." Bob maintained that he "was just doing his job," but he couldn't hide the smile. Stanley approached and shook Bob's hand and told him what a great job he had done. The handshake and those words coming from Lieutenant Colonel Stanley meant more to Bob than anything. Unknown to Bob, Stanley went back to his quarters to complete the After Action Reports, and later that day wrote up a recommendation for Lieutenant Stoner to be awarded the Distinguished Flying Cross for his actions.

One of the seven TBM-1Cs from USS Nehenta Bay over Tinian on July 28th, 1944. There is a one-in-seven chance that Lieutenant Robert F. Stoner was the pilot in this photo.

(U.S. Navy Photo)

77. The Unthinkable

Bill Bennett and Company D/2/18 returned to shipboard routine with the exception of watching the battle from the rails of LST-130. Of special interest to the men were the close support air attacks by Navy, Marine and Army Air Force pilots. The Marines referred to these attacks as the "air show" and just about everyone stopped what they were doing to watch the attacks.

Weapons were stripped and oiled and gear was laid out to dry and repack. Lieutenant Simonson warned they would be landing somewhere south of Tinian Town with little notice and they needed to be combat ready as soon as possible. Even though this would be their second landing on Tinian, the situation going ashore would probably be far worse than the first landing. The LSTs carrying elements of the 2nd Division were now anchored about a mile offshore from Point Lalo off the southwest coast of Tinian. Bill went over a map of Tinian with Lieutenant Simonson and the beach they would be headed for this time was Blue Beach, just north of Point Lalo, where terraced bluffs rose up from the ocean. This type of terrain promised to have almost endless caves and crevasses in which the industrious Japanese could wedge themselves. Getting them out would be a difficult job. Being aboard the LST was a good place to be for a few days. The Navy chow was pretty good and sleeping on a bunk was a luxury compared to the muddy foxholes that other Marines slept in on Tinian. Several inches of rain had fallen from the tail end of the typhoon and vehicles and men had been mired in misery.

July 29th, 1944. Corporal Channing R. Miller had been released from the hospital ship and returned to Saipan for duty. He had been brought over to Tinian on the 27th, just in time to catch the misery of the typhoon. On Saturday morning, July 29th, he reported to Captain Kyle's Company A/1/2, as they were advancing southward on the east side of Tinian near Marpo Point. The terrain in this area was changing from flat farming country to rising cliffs and plateaus where the enemy had dug in to resist the advancing Marines. Channing Miller rejoined familiar faces from Company A and moved out to scout the enemy positions that lay ahead. It didn't take long to find them. Machine guns opened up on the patrol and pinned the Marines down in the red mud. Channing moved from cover to cover to try and get an angle to advance on the enemy position, but they were in a bad spot. Raising his head to survey where the fire was coming from, the bullets cracked overhead, indicating their close proximity. One of the bullets hit Channing on the right side of his head, creasing his skull and opening up a six-inch slash just above his ear. Dazed and in the mud, he crawled to the rear to find help. A Navy corpsman found him and tried to temporarily close the wound and bandage it so that Channing could be evacuated. Channing placed his helmet back on his head and snapped the chinstrap so that the helmet would hold the bandage in place and crawled back through the mud to his men. Refusing to evacuate, he then spent the next two days leading patrols against enemy emplacements.

On the evening of July 29th, Lieutenant Bob Stoner visited the quarters of Chaplain John R. McLain aboard the USS Nehenta Bay. The following morning would be Sunday and Stoner would have an early mission over Tinian which would cause him to miss the Chaplain's services. The two Navy men had spent many hours discussing all sorts of subjects and they had developed mutual respect and admiration for each other. Bob had told the Chaplain that he had never gotten into a plane without praying and acknowledging to the Lord that his life was in His hands. He had told McLain he had considered becoming a minister before joining the Navy and had not ruled it out as a possibility after the war.

Bob was excited about the baby scheduled to arrive around the end of January. He hoped the war would be over by then so that he could be back in the States with Marijane to welcome the new arrival. McLain told Stoner about his sermon for the service the following day as he was still finishing it up. Bob asked Chaplain McLain to pray with him before he left and the two bowed their heads and took turns praying for a few minutes. Bob shook Mc-

Lain's hand and thanked him for spending the time with him, then headed back to the ready room.

Lieutenant Stoner checked the TBM assignment for the following day and saw that he was scheduled to fly TBM-1C, bureau number 16951, assigned to Crew Chief Armand Blackmore. As usual, he headed down to the hangar deck to see how the plane was progressing. The hangar deck was "buttoned up" as the mechanics poured over the planes with the usual flurry of activity. Rising temperatures, along with the humidity left in the wake of the typhoon, had the thermometer on the wall reading 105 degrees. There were no shirts on the mechanics as they dripped sweat onto the planes and the deck. Bob found Armand examining the turret controls and stuck his head in through the crew hatch. Blackmore noticed the lieutenant and said, "Evening sir!" Bob asked him how she was looking and Blackmore told him that she would be as good as new. They had just replaced a relay to the turret that had shorted out intermittently on the previous mission and it was now working perfectly. Bob knew that Stenson would appreciate a perfectly working turret. Bob told Blackmore he appreciated his work and would leave him to it as he wanted to get some sack time. Bob returned to his quarters to get ready for the mission, then went back to the ready room and settled into one of the reclining chairs to get some sleep. The ready room was filled with pilots sleeping in the cool air-conditioning.

Sunday, July 30th, 1944. The pilots in the ready room were awakened at 0330 hours and they went to the head. Some of them shaved before they ate breakfast, brought in from the galley. Lieutenant Commander Stanley talked by radio with Command Support Aircraft from their Task Force 52 Flagship, to get the details of today's mission over Tinian. Lieutenant James J. Darling and Stanley then called for the pilot's attention at the front of the ready room for their briefing. The ground troops had now advanced to a line that was just south of Tinian Town (Sunharon) on the west coast of the island. Enemy troops had concentrated in a wooded area just below the rising bluffs to the south and their artillery and anti-aircraft had become a problem firing from these heights. Stanley had ordered the TBMs loaded with two 500 lb. bombs and eight HE (high explosive) rockets; four under each wing. Stanley would fly as the Air Coordinator, as usual, and carry only the rockets. The FM2 Wildcats would be armed with 3400 rounds of .50 caliber machine gun ammo. The P-47 Thunderbolts would open the show from their land base at Isley Field on Saipan and strafe the area at 0700.

Armand Blackmore watched closely as TBM 16951 was towed over to the flight deck elevator and then backed into position. As he came into the opening, the cool morning air descending to the hangar deck felt refreshing, if not a bit chilly. Once the plane was positioned behind Stanley's TBM, the plane captain went through the routine of starting the engine as Armand took his position and exchanged hand signals. The engines coughed to life all up and down the deck and the noise was soon deafening. 16951's wings unfolded and Armand stepped under each wing to set the lock pins. He then went through the crew hatch and climbed into the gunner's turret to check the controls. Everything worked fine. The engines were shut down and the armorers went to work loading the bombs and rockets on the Avengers. Armand thought how appropriately these planes were named as they were bringing death to the attackers of Pearl Harbor. Four of the huge red-tipped rockets were carefully hung under each wing and then the 500 pounders were rolled up on the ordinance carts.

A TBM Avenger crew chief making final preparations before a mission. Armand Blackmore was frequently a crew chief for the TBM of Lieutenant Robert F. Stoner.

(U. S. Navy Photo)

TBM Avengers being loaded with 500-pound bombs on the carrier deck.

(U.S. Navy Photo)

At 0515, the plane captains once again started the engines and checked the controls. Stenson and Palmer arrived at the plane and entered through the crew hatch. Lieutenant Stoner fastened his Mae West and adjusted his shoulder holster as he prepared to step out into the wind of the flight deck. The carrier was producing a 25-mph wind, coupled with the 15-mph actual headwind. This would account for 40 mph of the airspeed required for takeoff. The catapult supplied nearly 80 mph, which should give the pilots about 120 mph at the end of the deck; more than enough. Bob's pant legs flapped in the wind as he stood on the wing of 16951 and steadied the plane captain as he relinquished control of the cockpit. Bob smiled at the captain for doing a fine job and stepped onto the seat before lowering himself into position. The plane captain straightened the parachute straps and clicked the buckles in at his waist. The cord to the headset was plugged in along the port side and Bob turned up the volume knob to check the intercom. "Pilot to crew; how are we doing?" Stenson came back with, "Good to go Skipper!" and Palmer's soft drawl returned, "All set here Skipper!"

At 0530 hours, with the sky beginning to show signs of the sun in the east, the USS Nehenta Bay was located 45 miles from Tinian at coordinates 15 degrees, 20 minutes north, and 145 degrees, 15 minutes west. Beautiful cumulus clouds floated above at 6,000 feet. Stanley revved his R-2600 engine to full throttle and the catapult shot his TBM Avenger off the deck. The catapult cables were attached to TBM 16951 and Bob turned his attention to the deck officer. He called back to Palmer and Stenson to "standby to launch." He pushed the throttle forward and held the brakes while the deck officer showed him the single index finger, then two, then three! Release of the brakes and the catapult jolted the Avenger forward and off the end of the carrier. Pulling the stick back, the huge plane began to climb away from the deck. As Bob banked away to the left, he looked back to see the huge white 74 painted on the deck.

TBM Avenger as catapult cables are attached; armed with high explosive rockets for ground attack.

(U.S. Navy Photo)

The Avengers once again formed into echelon formation with Stanley in the lead. The two groups of FM2 Wildcats formed above on their right and below on their left. As they headed for Tinian, the sun broke the surface in the east at 0558 and sprayed the most beautiful sunbeams across the Pacific. The spectacular sunrise would have made it easy to forget they were going to war. Bob could clearly see Stanley on the left side and Lieutenant Healey on the right. Palmer and Stenson commented via the intercom about the fantastic sunrise behind them. Stanley led the squadron into a holding pattern a few miles off the west coast of Tinian and then dove away to go take a look at the target areas.

Aboard LST-130, Bill Bennett had been awakened at 0430 and prepared for whatever the day ahead might bring. He went to the galley for breakfast at 0500 and enjoyed powdered eggs, toast and coffee with Fred Ellis, Johnny Jones and Herb Dale. Since it was Sunday morning, Bill wanted to get up on the deck and read his New Testament and have some prayer time, if possible. He came up on deck about 0545 and noticed the sky in the east was about ready to dawn a beautiful day. At 0558, the sunrise burst over the horizon and the sun shot through the cotton-like clouds drifting above. It was a picture that could have been on the cover of a church bulletin. Explosions began to emanate from Tinian and smoke began to rise. In the midst of God's beauty, there was a reminder of man's ugliness. Word had spread that Company D was to have an inspection at 1000 hours to make sure they were ready for the landing. At 0700 hours, the P-47s from Saipan were lining up over Tinian and Marines began to line the port side rails for the "air show." Bill found some of the fellows from 2nd Platoon and took his place on the rail. The Thunderbolts carried eight .50 caliber guns, and they were probably the most fearsome ground interdiction aircraft in the war. They took turns shredding the wooded area with machine gun fire. As the Thunderbolts neared the ground for the pullouts, blazing red balls of anti-aircraft fire would rise to meet them. The anti-aircraft fire was much heavier than what the Marines had seen before, probably due to the Japanese being concentrated into the southern tip of Tinian.

Stanley flew offshore watching the P-47s rake the wooded area with machine gun fire and re-directed their fire as he saw necessary. His flight path was taking him almost directly over LST-130 below. At 0720, the P-47s left the area and headed back to Saipan to reload and refuel. Stanley ordered his FM2 Wildcats to resume the strafing and directed them to areas where he had observed anti-aircraft fire. Marines on the ground marked their position with white smoke and fired red smoke into the noted enemy positions. The Wildcats made their runs from 5,000 feet with pullouts at about 1,000 feet. With airspeeds reaching just over 300 mph, they made difficult targets for the Japanese anti-aircraft guns. Each of the eight Wildcats made two runs at the target and then turned out to sea.

Stanley had intended on having the Avengers drop their 500 lb. bombs next but changed his mind when he saw how close the Marine positions were on the ground. Even though he would have liked to believe differently, the pilots were pretty wild with their bombing accuracy. At 0735 he ordered the TBMs to begin their HE rocket "glides" into the target area. One of the TBMs did not have rocket rails, so it stayed back in the holding pattern with the Wildcats. Lieutenant Stoner heard the order over his radio and told Stenson and Palmer that they were going in to release the rockets. Stoner brought the Avenger down from 7,000 feet to 6,000 feet as they approached the target area. Coming in from the north, the first Avenger pushed into a shallow dive called a "glide," and set his sights on the red smoke marking the chosen targets. He was starting with the target nearest the west coast and the following planes would move their target slightly to the east to cover the full area. At 3,000 feet the first Avenger began firing the rockets and they hissed away from the wing. All eight of the rockets hit inside the wooded area as gray smoke erupted on the ground. Suddenly, heavy anti-aircraft fire rose up from the ground to the east and zipped past the Avenger as he pulled up to bank back to the north. Stanley radioed the location of the anti-aircraft fire and noted it for destruction as soon as possible.

At the rail on LST-130, Bill watched the Avengers line up for the attack. The rockets were an amazing weapon and the Marines were glad that the Americans had them and the Japanese didn't. From the vantage point of the LST, the red balls of the anti-aircraft fire seemed to rise in slow motion toward the planes. On the bluffs, the Japanese anti-aircraft batteries were firing their Model 96, 25mm, dual-purpose guns at the slow-flying Avengers. Following the faster P-47s and Wildcats, the Avengers, in an attack glide, were flying a little over 200 mph. With their larger size, they must have seemed like dirigibles to the Japanese gunners. Lieutenant Stoner was fourth in line for the rocket attack and nosed the Avenger downward at 6,000 feet to begin the descent. He could clearly see the Avenger in front of him firing the rockets and then pulling out amidst the shower of anti-aircraft fire. Bob selected his target and shifted his path a bit to the left while flipping the cover up over the trigger switch. There was nothing the crew could do but ride out the attack. At 3,000 feet, Lieutenant Bob Stoner fired his HE rockets and he could feel the wings shuddering as they left their racks. White trails of smoke followed the rockets off the wings as they sped toward the ground targets. First two, then four, then the glowing red balls of the Japanese Model 96 gun began to rise through the rocket trails; then six and then all eight were away. At the exact instant the last rockets left the rails, the glowing balls of anti-aircraft fire came directly at the Avenger and Bob thought to try and dive to the right. There was no time. A 25mm explosive anti-aircraft shell slammed into the right wing of 16951 and the fuel in the wing tank erupted in a ball of flame. In a split second, most of the right wing disintegrated and the Avenger rolled over to the right pinning both pilot and crew to the left side. At 1500 feet, there was little time to react. Bob tried to use the intercom to order Stenson and Palmer to bail out but the swift rotation of the plane created strong G-forces which made any action impossible.

As Bill watched from the deck of LST-130, the Marines gasped when the wing of the Avenger was suddenly blown from the aircraft. Huge chunks of the wing trailed back through the air. The Avenger began to spin wildly as the building airspeed created a haunting screech and black smoke trailed behind the plane. Bill and the Marines held their breath as they hoped to see parachutes. At 0745 hours, the out of control Avenger slammed into the water about 100 yards off Point Lalo and exploded into a fireball as the fuel tanks and bombs erupted. Fire, water and steam created a huge cloud, and then two seconds later, another huge explosion followed by yet another. The Marines on deck stared in utter silence realizing that they had just witnessed the death of the three-man TBM-1C Avenger crew. Bill closed his eyes and thought, "Oh, dear Lord, be with the families of those men." He had no idea that he had just witnessed the death of one of his dearest friends.

From the air, Lieutenant Healey had been watching Lieutenant Stoner's Avenger from his vantage point behind and above. Healey watched the anti-aircraft tracers come straight up to and then through Stoner's plane. The debris from the exploding wing actually passed Healey's plane and he had to abort his rocket run and go around for another pass. Stanley was horrified by the sight and dropped down to overfly the crash site on the water. A thick black pall of smoke rose more than 1,000 feet into the air from the surface of the water and the surface was aflame with gasoline. Stanley's heart was in his throat as he pulled up from the scene. He directed Healey to follow him in and he repositioned to attack the site of the anti-aircraft emplacement that had downed Stoner and his crew. As Stanley climbed for the attack, he radioed Command Support Aircraft and requested that the P-47s from Isley Field return to join in the attack on the anti-aircraft emplacements. Stanley dove his Avenger toward the anti-aircraft guns and the red balls began to ascend toward him. He held his glide and fired all eight rockets into the area before rolling out to his right. Lieutenant Healey now fired all eight of his rockets into the smoke created by Stanley, thereby totaling sixteen rockets to silence the guns.

Stanley moved back into position as Air Coordinator and directed the P-47s to decimate the entire area with their powerful guns. As the P-47s worked over the Japanese on the ground, Stanley contacted the Navy offshore and ordered a naval bombardment from the heavy cruisers. The P-47s exhausted their ammunition and headed back to Saipan. The Navy cruisers pulled into position and let loose with their five-inch guns. The entire bluff area from which the anti-aircraft guns had been firing erupted with 100 rounds of fire. After the smoke began to drift away, Stanley over flew the area to draw anti-aircraft fire; there was none. The crew on LST-130 watched with binoculars as two Higgins Boats probed the crash site. They retrieved nothing. All the men aboard had witnessed men being killed in one fashion or another, but the sight and sounds of the Avenger slamming into the water would never be forgotten.

LST-130. Corporal Bill Bennett and the men of D/2/18 watched the final attack of Lieutenant Robert F. Stoner from the rails on July 30th, 1944 at 0745 hours just off Point Lalo, Tinian. (U.S. Navy Photo)

Stanley led VC-11 back to the carrier and the radios were silent. No one would say an unnecessary word for days. Stanley circled the Nehenta Bay until all of his planes were aboard. A slight delay was experienced recovering the planes when one of the Wildcat pilots forgot to lock his landing gear, which collapsed upon landing. His prop chewed the deck somewhat, but not too seriously. Carl Davis and Armand Blackmore watched the planes being recovered and realized that a TBM was missing. Carl's number 92 had returned, but Armand's 16951 did not. He inquired with the other crew as to whether Stoner and his crew were able to get out and heads just shook. After landing, Stanley jumped from his wing and walked silently to his quarters. Word quickly spread on the carrier that Stoner and his crew had been shot down and killed. Those who knew him grieved and thought of his wife Marijane and their unborn baby back in the States. They also thought of his family with their faithful little newspaper that had kept them entertained. How heartbreaking it would be for the Stoner family. Hours after the death of Lieutenant Robert Fraser Stoner at Tinian at the age of 25, his paternal grandmother, Josephine Stoner, the matriarch of the Stoner family, passed away in Oak Park, Illinois, at the age of 83.

July 31st, 1944. After fighting for two days with his wound held together by his helmet, Corporal Channing Miller was evacuated back to Saipan. His wound was cleaned at the base hospital and his head sewn up with more stitches than his friends could count. Due to the rapid advance on the south end of Tinian, which was partially due to Lieutenant Commander Stanley's personal vendetta against the anti-aircraft battery that killed Lieutenant Stoner, D/2/18 was not recommitted to the battle on Tinian. On August 1st, LST-130 arrived back at Charan Kanoa, Saipan, and unloaded Company D/2/18. Bill settled back into the new camp and the Marines were relieved that they once again had survived an offensive campaign against the Japanese. Bill went to find Bob Reder over in A/1/18 to see how the Aurora Marines had fared. Reder told Bill that Pete Andrews had been killed on Saipan and Channing Miller had been wounded twice. Bill and Reder went to see Channing in the hospital with his head bandaged up and Channing was in good spirits. It was hard to believe he had earned three Purple Hearts and a Silver Star. Channing was nothing if not energetic.

August 1st, 1944. Back home in Aurora, Steve and Jessie Bennett were getting ready to drive to Oak Park, Illinois, to attend the funeral of Sam Stoner's mother, Josephine Stoner. The funeral was planned for 2 p.m. and it would take over an hour to make the drive, which was practically as far as Chicago. Just a few blocks away at 211 S. Fourth Street, Sam and Margaret were getting ready to head out the door at their set time of 10 a.m. Harley's wife Betty, who had been living with them and helping in every way imaginable, would be going along. Sam had been out and about earlier in the morning and had pulled the Packard up in the driveway so that the ladies could get right in. He had gone back inside to see if Margaret needed any assistance as she double checked her purse and the bag she was bringing. Betty stepped out on the porch and waited as Sam and Margaret came through the door and Sam turned to lock the front door with the key.

Betty spotted a yellow taxi cab approaching slowly as though looking for an address. The cab came to a stop in front of the house. Sam and Margaret turned to see the cab and thought the fellow must have gotten the wrong address as they had not ordered a taxi. The cab driver approached with an envelope in hand and climbed up the steps to the porch. "Mr. and Mrs. Sam Stoner?" he asked. Sam said, "Yes sir?" The cab driver replied, "I have a telegram for you," and he handed Sam the envelope. Sam studied the envelope as the cabbie returned to the car and drove southward on Fourth Street. He looked at Margaret and they both had a look of grave concern. They had received many telegrams bearing good news, but they had many loved ones at war. Sam opened the seal on the telegram and began to read, "THE NAVY DEPARTMENT DEEPLY REGRETS TO INFORM YOU THAT YOUR SON LIEUTENANT (SG) ROBERT F. STONER HAS BEEN KILLED IN ACTION 30 JULY WHILE …" At these words, Margaret let out a shriek of grief and began to buckle to the porch. Sam reached for her arm as Betty grabbed her at the waist. As tears began to well up in Sam's eyes he tried to console his wife. Margaret could not help but to scream out, "NO! NO! NO!" Sam hugged Margaret as best he could, and read the remainder of the telegram, "… IN PERFORMANCE OF HIS DUTIES AND IN SERVICE TO OUR COUNTRY. DUE TO EXISTING CONDITIONS THE BODY CANNOT BE RETURNED TO YOU AT THIS TIME. IF FURTHER DETAILS BECOME AVAILABLE YOU WILL BE INFORMED. TO AVOID AIDING OUR ENEMIES PLEASE DO NOT DISCLOSE THE NAME OF HIS SHIP OR STATION."

Betty was heroic in her attempt to console Margaret on the porch, but it was useless. Margaret's grief over the tragic loss of Eleanor five years earlier was now compounded with the sudden shock of losing her youngest son, and the news coming on the way to Josephine's funeral was more than she could bear. Her continued screams of grief echoed up and down the block on Fourth Street and neighbors knew immediately that one of the Stoner boys had been killed. Betty and Sam guided Margaret back inside the house to try and regain some composure and think out what they needed to do. Sam decided that he needed to make several phone calls, including one to Steve and Jessie Bennett. After 15 minutes had passed, they once again left the front door and began the drive to Oak Park.

At just about the same time, a Western Union delivery boy rang the bell at the apartment shared by Marijane Stoner and her twin sister Marjorie at 10 S. LaSalle Street in Chicago. The girls, like Sam and Margaret, were getting themselves ready to attend Josephine Stoner's funeral in a few hours. Marjorie answered the door and received the telegram. There had been so many telegrams received from Bob over the past few years that neither of the girls thought the worst as Marijane opened it and began to read. She could not finish reading as the words "REGRET TO INFORM" and "KILLED IN ACTION" hit her like a hammer and she began to shake frantically. Marjorie guided her to the sofa where they both cried and consoled each other. Phone calls went out to Marijane's family and common friends.

Later that afternoon at the funeral home in Oak Park, the atmosphere was surreal. Most of the friends and family arriving for Josephine's funeral heard for the first time that Bob had been killed in action and on the same day that his grandmother had passed away. Josephine's funeral became a joint memorial service with the news of Bob's death. Josephine Stoner had been such a devoted follower of Christ that her family considered the joy the Lord must be experiencing just to have her home. They also talked about what it must have been like for Josephine and Bob to find each other there when arriving in the presence of Christ Himself. Sam and Margaret's main concern had instantly become Marijane and the baby. Anything and everything that could be done to help her through this incredibly great time of sorrow would be done. They shed tears not only for their current grief and loss, but also the realization that Bob and Marijane's child would be deprived of such a wonderful father.

Front porch of 211 S. Fourth Street where Sam and Margaret Stoner received the telegram informing them of the death of Lieutenant SG Robert F. Stoner on August 1st, 1944.

(Author's Photo)

August 4th, 1944. Lieutenant Commander Onia Burton Stanley sat at his desk aboard the USS Nehenta Bay; the same desk where he had sat and had many conversations with the young and impressive Lieutenant Stoner. As he placed the empty page on his desk, he looked at the empty chair where Stoner had been seated just a few weeks before when they talked about his desire to fly more combat missions. There was a lump in his throat and he fought back the urge to shed more tears. He pondered the best way to approach this letter to Sam and Margaret, who he had become familiar with through *The Stoner Weekly News*. His pen wrote these words:

Mr. and Mrs. S.D. Stoner
211 S. Fourth St.
Aurora, IL

My dear Mr. and Mrs. Stoner;
    I deeply regret to confirm the death of your son, Lieutenant Robert Fraser Stoner, A-V(N), U.S.N.R., in action against the enemy on the morning of July 30, 1944 at approximately seven forty-five o'clock.
    He was leading his division in an attack when heavy and accurate anti-aircraft fire so damaged his plane that control was lost. The resulting crash

in the sea was instantly fatal to him and his two air crewmen. His courageous attack and that of his squadron mates effectively destroyed their target.

Bob was one of the outstanding officers of the squadron. His ability and friendly manner earned him the respect of every officer and man of the group. It is rare that a man is so universally liked and trusted. He occupied and performed well the duties of an important and responsible office within the squadron. My faith in his ability as an officer and as a pilot as well as my personal admiration and friendship for him helps me to feel and understand the great pain that his death brings to you.

Bob was an exceptionally able officer and a gentleman. The Squadron and the Navy can ill afford to lose so valuable a man.

I realize that no words of mine can in any way compensate for your great loss, or ease the shock caused by the news of his untimely death, but please be assured of my deepest sympathy and that of his fellow officers to you.

Very sincerely yours,

(signed)

Lieutenant Cmndr. O.B. Stanley, Jr.
U.S. Navy, Commanding

Just down the corridor aboard the carrier, Chaplain John L. McLain thought to send Sam and Margaret a letter of his own. It read, in part:

We remember your son at all times, but especially do we think of him and his brave comrades when we celebrate aboard ship The Sacrament of The Lord's Supper and repeat the closing prayer, "Eternal Light, Immortal Love, we bless Thy Name for all Thy servants who have kept the faith and finished their course and are at rest with thee. Help us to abide in their fellowship and follow their Christian example that we, with them, may sit down at the Marriage Supper of The Lord, which is in heaven, Amen.

The Lord bless you and keep you, The Lord make his face to shine upon you and be gracious to you, The Lord lift His countenance upon you. Peace, both now and in the life everlasting, Amen."

With the loss of Lieutenant Robert Fraser Stoner at the young age of 25 years, his loved ones mourned the loss of one of the most loving, intelligent, thoughtful and funny people they would ever know. America lost one of her best and brightest that would certainly have enriched the lives of countless others had he lived on. Bill Bennett lost a childhood friend, a fellow believer and one of the most respected young men he would ever know.

78. The Homecoming

The new camps at Saipan had continued to grow and the Construction Battalion at Isley Field had been converting the ramshackle airfield into a gigantic bomber base. Some of the Marines went about the island to see the new developments, but the safest thing to do was to stay around the camp. Groups of Japanese hold-outs were still coming out from their hiding places and attacking sentries and camps during the night. Special platoons were organized to hunt, root out or kill the straggling Japanese. Bill realized he had nearly reached his wits end with combat and the war in general, and had convinced himself he would probably never get home. As Company D/2/18 began to reorganize and clean their gear after returning from Tinian, Bill was called in to see Lieutenant Simonson. Simonson said a lot of good things about Bill and thanked him for being so dependable over the past years. At first, Bill thought Simonson might be setting up to ask Bill to do something he wouldn't want to do, but the lieutenant got around to the point. He told Bill the Marine Corps had come up with a "point system" that would fairly rank a Marine's service and allow "high pointers" to be rotated back to the States. The good news for Bill was that he was one of the "high pointers" and he was scheduled to head for Pearl Harbor on August 7th and then on to San Francisco. Bill couldn't believe his ears. He asked Simonson how sure he was about all of this and Simonson smiled and told Bill that he could count on it. Simonson and almost all of the original D/2/18 Marines would be leaving at the same time.

Word quickly spread and Fred Ellis, Gerald Coate, Herb Dale, Johnnie C. Jones, as well as Poterola, Herman, Stubblefield, Hellman and the others, celebrated the long-awaited news. There would probably be no more combat for any of them and they would probably survive the war. For the first time in over two years, Bill could actually allow himself to think deeply about getting home and even dare to plan on it. One of the hardest parts of the past 32 months was that Bill could never really plan anything. The Marine Corps did all the planning and anything that he wanted to do would be quickly overridden by the Corps. He would still be a Marine until the war was over, but being a Marine in the States was a far cry from being a Marine in a foxhole. In addition to celebrating with the old guard, Bill spent some time with the replacements who would have to stay and fight elsewhere before the war was over. Bonawitz, Walzer, Urioste, Taber, Clodfelter and DiGennaro would all be reassigned into the new 2nd Engineer Battalion as D/2/18 would be dissolved. As much as Bill relished getting home, he realized that the news was bittersweet. For the past 32 months, these Marines had been his family. He encouraged the replacements to pass along the tradition of watching out for the new kids who would be coming along, and *NEVER volunteer for anything!*

Bill turned in his combat gear to the company equipment officers and repacked his sea bag for the journey. There were dozens of Marines that he wanted to stay in touch with and he used a small address book he kept in his sea bag to record home addresses. Most of the guys from Company D that were heading stateside would be traveling together all the way back to San Diego, so they would have time for goodbyes later. Uniforms were updated and unit citation awards and campaign awards were handed out so others would be able to see what these Marines had been through. On the morning of August 7th, 1944, Bill and the "high pointers" of Company D boarded trucks and were driven to the docks at Charan Kanoa, Saipan, to board the troop transport for Pearl Harbor. Unlike other troop transport journeys, this one was special. The others had been taking the Marines into the unknown, into danger and away from home. This time, the transport was taking them toward the known, toward relative safety and toward home. All the Marines on board were far more jovial than they had been in years. There were times when they may have almost forgotten the horrors of the war they were leaving behind; almost.

Coming in to Pearl Harbor was, in itself, a great relief. The threat of running into a Japanese submarine would be greatly diminished from here on in and Honolulu had everything that most American cities had. The most precious sight of all was the civilians. Regular Americans were wearing street clothes and living normal lives, an existence the Marines had all but forgotten. The guys from Company D had a few nights of liberty at Honolulu before getting orders to board the United States Army Transport Sea Barb, on September 1st, 1944. There was just enough time to get everyone aboard and get settled in before the Sea Barb got under way for San Francisco, California. The next port would be special; it would be the mainland. Now Bill began to think of home in earnest. The Marines would certainly let him go home for a visit after all this time, wouldn't they?

Life aboard the Sea Barb was almost monotonous. There was no duty for the Marines to speak of, although they did help the crew out at times if needed. The Sea Barb ran with a transport group escorted by light cruisers and a Casablanca-class aircraft carrier, much like the Nehenta Bay. The aircraft kept watch for submarines, just to be safe, and they also guarded against air attack, should a rogue Japanese plane appear almost miraculously.

On September 7th, 1944, after seven days at sea, the USAT Sea Barb entered San Francisco Bay beneath the Golden Gate Bridge and all the Marines were on deck to shout at the top of their lungs. Seeing the U.S. again after all they had been through brought tears to the Marines' eyes. As Bill shouted and hugged his beloved Marine family, he noticed there was not a dry eye among them. They had all lived with a hidden fear they might never see home again, and "home" had never looked so good! For those who had not been to San Francisco, seeing Alcatraz Prison was of particular interest. As Bill looked at San Francisco with the houses overlooking the bay, he recognized the similarities with Wellington, New Zealand, just as George Garcia had told him. Once they were off the Sea Barb, many of the Marines got down on their hands and knees and kissed the ground of the "good ole U.S.A." Bill had been gone from the U.S. for exactly 800 days. San Francisco was a beautiful sight to see.

Naval operations were extensive, and ships were being built and repaired, all within view. After what the Marines had seen of the Navy, there was no doubt they would make fast work of the Japanese and end the war. The Marines moved quickly through San Francisco and boarded a train for San Diego. While waiting for the train, Bill managed to get a collect call through to the house at 454 Simms Street. It was 11:30 p.m. in California and 1:30 a.m. in Aurora. Steve rolled himself out of bed and made his way down the staircase and over to the phone table in the foyer. He had not heard his son's voice in two years. Steve listened as Bill told him that he was actually at the train station in San Francisco. Steve handed the phone to Marian, and went to get Jessie. Marian was so excited to hear that Bill was on his way home. Jessie came to the phone and had tears of joy as Bill told her he was in the States. He was on his way to San Diego, where he would have to stay for seven days before heading back to Aurora. There was unspeakable joy on both ends of the line. Bill told Jessie that he hoped to see Grandma Phrangle while in San Diego, if they could arrange it, and asked her to call Grandma to set it in motion. He promised that he would let her know when he would be home. He told Jessie how much he loved her and Steve and said he would be hugging her again soon. As a special treat for Bill, Steve went and woke little Bobby who was visiting from Chicago and four-year-old Virginia who was also spending the night at Grandma and Grandpa's house. The phone call was just the thing for Bill. He hung up feeling as though he was coming back to life, and it was exciting.

The train ride to San Diego was relatively short and it was good to be back in familiar surroundings. Everyone was waiting for their orders to come in and it seemed like most of them were being assigned to training battalions at Camp Lejeune, North Carolina. After three days at Marine Corps Base, San Diego, Bill received a message to report to the main gate at once. He had a suspicion as to the reason, and sure enough, there was Grandma Phrangle with a huge smile and a very strong hug for such a little woman. Bill savored the hug and kiss from Grandma and it was so much more meaningful than before. At long last, he had reunited with family. Bill received permission to leave the base and he took Grandma out for lunch in downtown San Diego. It was just like two years earlier, only Bill had been to war and he was glad that it was all behind him now.

Back on the island of Saipan, Channing Miller had been released back to Company A/1/2 and promoted to sergeant. The hold-out Japanese continued their attacks, and the Marines were taking needless casualties. Units were selected to hunt down and kill the remaining Japanese as quickly as possible. There was essentially no difference in this duty and the combat that most Marines had been through during the main battle for Saipan. As a sergeant and a squad leader, Channing soon found himself back in the thick of it as he hunted down and rooted out the tenacious enemy. A/1/2 moved up into the hills and caves of Mt. Tapotchau and primarily blasted the Japanese from their caves. On September 11th, 1944, Channing's squad came across a large cave protected by machine gun fire and a firefight ensued. Demolition men made it to the mouth of the cave and threw satchel charges inside. The charges rocked the ground and even caused some of the cave entrance to crash in on the inhabitants. After letting the smoke clear for several minutes, Channing had the Japanese-speaking Chamorro interpreter shout into the cave, "Dete ki te! Anata wa yoku atsukawa remasu! Watashitachi ni tabemono to mizu ga arimasu!" (Come out and surrender! You will be treated well! We have food and water!) There was nothing but silence. Channing led two other Marines cautiously into the cave with a flashlight and his carbine in hand. As they moved 25 feet inside, shots rang out from the rear of the cave and the Marines opened fire in return. Channing emptied the magazine and turned for cover. A machine gun fired from the rear of the cave and several bullets tore into Channing's back and he went down on the cave floor. The other Marines returned fire and grabbed Channing by the shoulders and dragged him outside to a corpsman. Channing was alive but bleeding profusely from his wounds. The corpsman tried, with all that he knew, to slow the bleeding, to no use. The Marines poured rifle fire into the mouth of the cave and brought up the flame thrower to roast those who had shot Channing. He was stretchered down the hill, but he died before they could get him to an ambulance. The patrol brought up enough TNT to collapse the cave and leave whoever may be alive inside to suffocate. The next time they came to a cave, there would be no plea for the Japanese to surrender. Channing Miller had earned his fourth Purple Heart and lost his life in the process.

On Thursday, September 14th, Bill and a large group of Company D Marines left San Diego for Chicago and followed the same tracks they had taken almost three years earlier to get back to the Midwest. Before boarding the train, Bill ducked into the Western Union office and sent a telegram to Jessie. It read, "ARRIVING HOME SUNDAY NIGHT. ORDER EXTRA MILK FOR MONDAY." Bill spent a lot of time on the train with Alex Slowinski and Joe Sobolewski, just as he had on the way out to San Diego back in 1942. He had met them at the train station in Chicago within the first few minutes of arriving there. They had been through a lot together and lived to tell about it. Slowinski had been in 1st Platoon with Herb Dale and Johnny C. Jones, so Bill had kept up with him the whole time. Sobolewski had been in 3rd Platoon. Simonson and Wysocki were on their way back to Wisconsin through Chicago and they would all meet in a few weeks down in North Carolina. George Gabel was not only glad to be going home, but he was also on the way to make good on his promise to marry his girl "Ronnie" Otto in Chicago. The Japanese had delayed the wedding by 34 months! Fred Ellis, Herb Dale, Gerald Coate and most of the westerners had taken trains in different directions to get home. Bill and his old buddies talked about some of the good times and also some of the hell they went through. It was hard to believe there was no longer a Company D/2/18; it had been a good outfit.

The closer Bill got to Chicago, the better he felt. Sunday morning on the train, he found a place somewhat alone and read the new edition of *The Upper Room* that he had picked up in San Diego. He thumbed through his little New Testament with the red and black thumb tabs that he had made while in New Zealand. He spent some time in prayer thanking the Lord for saving his life so many times and for allowing him the blessing of going home without an injury. As Bill looked out at the Missouri countryside, he was taking a close assessment of his life. He was 25 years old, had no idea when he would get what was left of his life back from the Marine Corps, and he had no girl in his life. Things had not turned out as he had planned. He then thought about

Truitt Anderson, Bob Swigert and the other Marines he had seen killed. Bill felt compelled to dedicate himself to the Lord's will and live a life that those who had died could not. As Bill prayed, he felt a closeness to the Lord he had not felt since the time just after Tarawa. Coming back to Aurora, Bill knew he was not the same. He wondered if others would see it as clearly as he did.

One of the oddest things about the trip home was that the train had to go through Aurora to get to Chicago, but it would not stop there. Bill joked about jumping out as the train passed through. Coming in from the west, Bill saw Somonauk and Sandwich, and then Plano, Bristol and Montgomery. As the train churned over the Fox River, Bill caught a glimpse of the Leland Tower down on Stolp Island and then the factory buildings on the south side. The huge spire of the First Methodist Church stood guard over the valley like a giant sentry. Bill watched out the right side of the train and looked up the hill toward Simms Street. He realized that his mom and dad were just up that hill, and tears came to his eyes. The people of Aurora were bustling to and fro, just as they had been the day he left. Bill had lived to once again cast his eyes upon the "Wonder City."

Arriving at Union Station was like a gigantic party. Reporters from the Chicago papers were there with photographers and there were signs welcoming the "Heroes of the 2nd Marine Division" home. There were hundreds of pretty girls and a band playing the Marine Hymn. Strangers shook the Marine's hands and patted them on the back. The girls gave out kisses and some people even handed the Marines dollar bills. People had gone far out of their way to make sure these Marines were thanked for what they had done for the country, and they deserved all of it and more. Bill said goodbye to the Wisconsin contingent as they had to move to the track headed north and Bill headed for the tracks headed back west. Checking in for the last train home, Bill noted the train would arrive in Aurora at 8:30 p.m. The train to Aurora was a bit strange as he was the only Marine in sight while aboard. Several older men asked him where he was headed and Bill proudly said, "Home!" They could see by the bars on his chest that he had been in combat, and his 2nd Division patch would tell anyone who paid attention to the war about Tulagi, Guadalcanal, Tarawa, Saipan and Tinian.

On the way in on the train, Bill hatched a plan for arriving at home. They all knew he was coming Sunday night, but they didn't know the exact time. The train slowed for Aurora and came around the curve by the CB&Q Round House, then along the elevated line where he could see down on to Broadway. The lights were all lit by this time and it was a beautiful night in his home town. The train rolled along the platform with the concrete roofs above and came to a stop. That was it. He was home. As Bill stepped off the train and set his feet firmly on the platform, he drew a long, deep breath of air from the "Wonder City." Bill shouldered his sea bag and made fast work of the stairs down to the underground and then back up to the terminal. As he walked across the station, people sat reading newspapers and smoking cigarettes and a little boy's screams echoed across the terrazzo flooring. The thought came to Bill's mind about how he and Truitt Anderson had once planned on coming to the Bennett's place together the first chance they were given. Had Truitt lived, he probably would have been with Bill tonight. There should have been two Marines walking through the terminal. Outside, along the curb were four waiting taxis and Bill threw his bag into the first one. "Where to?" asked the cabbie. "454 Simms Street!" was the answer, and off they went. The cabbie was curious about Bill's exploits, and his questions were answered as well as could be. Driving up Fourth Street, Bill passed the Stoner's house and Fourth Street Methodist. He had the cabbie stop at the alley that ran behind the Bennett house and he jumped out to pay the fare. The cabbie asked Bill if he was crazy, and said there was no way he would take any money from a combat Marine. He then said, "Welcome home and enjoy your milk!" as he drove away.

Bill walked down the alley in the dark and saw the lights on in the house. Coming across the back yard, he hoped no one would spot him. He crept up the wooden steps to the back porch, carefully set down his sea bag and looked through the curtains on the door window. Jessie was in the kitchen with Marian, a much taller Bobby, and little Ginny. He just watched them for a minute or so waiting to see what happened next. Marian, Bobby and Ginny left the kitchen leaving Jessie alone. This was the moment he was waiting for. He slowly turned the doorknob and tried to keep quiet, but Jessie heard something and turned around. Then she screamed a scream like he had never heard before. They reached for each other and hugged as Bill kissed her on each cheek repeatedly, saying that he owed her so many kisses.

Everyone flooded into the kitchen, and Bill hugged and kissed his way out into the dining room. Bill hugged Steve and thanked him for all the letters and the wise advice. He picked up little Bobby, who had grown a full foot, and squeezed the air out of him. Bill asked him if he had taken care of grandma like he was asked to. Then Linc brought little Ginny to Bill and asked her if she would give him a hug. Bill grabbed her up and held her close, seeing Jean holding little Billy Schell. Jean looked at Bill and said, "I am sure you know who this is!" Bill lifted little Billy high in the air and then tickled him lightly. Bill thought these were the most beautiful children he had ever seen. Marian had hugged Bill in the kitchen but couldn't help but hug him again and again.

Dozens of cookies were on the table and the girls had baked a cake as well. There was still some milk in the ice box and Jessie assured Bill that several extra bottles would arrive in the morning. Bill pushed a freshly baked chocolate chip cookie into his mouth and noticed his mother's violets in the dining room window. He hoped this was not a dream. Bobby and Ginny hovered for the attention of their Uncle Bill. Jessie stood back and watched Bill with the children and how he paid attention to Bobby. She could tell Bill was different. It was hard to nail down, but he had matured greatly. He had seen a lot and she could see it in his face. She was beyond measure with joy; one of the greatest moments of her life. Bill's presence was an answer to hours and hours of prayer while he was away. Jessie had taken hold of heaven for Bill's safety and had not let go. Seeing Bill at her dining room table was more than joyful; to her it was a miracle.

Sunday, September 17th, 1944. Bill slept until 8 o'clock for the first time since he could remember. Steve, Jessie and Marian joined him for breakfast and they chatted and laughed their way through. Jessie told Bill the family had planned a "Welcome Home" open house for the following Sunday and they were sure there would be quite a crowd. The Stoners were mentioned and Bill asked if they had heard from Bob recently. There was a stunned silence. Jessie turned from the dining room cabinet where she kept the issues of *The Stoner Weekly News* and gently handed one to Bill. She said there was no good way to tell him. There on the cover of the August 4th, 1944 edition was a photo of Bob Stoner standing on the wing of his Avenger wearing a Mae West jacket and flight gear. The headline read, "Notify Parents Lieut. Stoner Is Killed in Action." Bill could not read on. Bob had been killed over six weeks ago and since Bill was on the move, there was no way he could be notified. It just didn't seem right to Jessie and Steve to tell him over the phone since he was so excited about getting home. No one wanted to ruin the joy of Bill's homecoming, but it had to be done. Bill asked about Bob's body and Steve told him that Bob had crashed into the sea. Bill's sadness deepened as he thought of Sam and Margaret and the pain they felt at the loss of their second child within five years. Jessie told Bill it had been hard, but they were holding up. Bill stepped out on the back porch and looked at the yard. There were many memories there, including the younger years with the gang. Bill was always tough, but little Bob Stoner was fast. There would always be a hole in Bill's heart whenever he thought of his childhood and his pal Bob, who never came home.

Corporal William Wesley Bennett holding his nephew, Billy Schell, in front of 454 Simms Street on September 17th, 1944. Bill had returned from combat in the Pacific the night before. This was the day he learned of Lieutenant Bob Stoner's death.

(Bennett Family Photo)

Monday, September 18th, 1944. Bill ironed his dress uniform and wanted to borrow the car for an hour or two. He stepped out back and was welcomed by Art and Ida Lipke and Bessie Hemm. Mrs. Spence from across the street saw the commotion and came running over as well. The news was out; Bill was back. Bill drove the car up Fourth Street to Smely's flower shop and went in to buy two bouquets of cut flowers. He then drove up Fourth Street to Marion

Avenue and parked along the curb. He walked in to Fourth Street Methodist Church and asked the secretary to see Reverend Dibble. Dibble heard Bill's voice and came out to greet him. He hugged Bill and grabbed his shoulders. He said that Bill looked pretty tough and Bill laughed. Bill said he wanted to talk to the Pastor later as he had to do some things this morning. Bill drove two blocks west and passed Bardwell School where he and Bob Stoner had gone to school together. He had fond memories there of the many games of basketball, baseball, tag and kickball. He turned onto Lincoln Avenue and then down to make a right onto Avon. Coming back to Fourth Street, he made another right and parked the car in front of 211 S. Fourth Street. Bill got out of the car with one of the bouquets and made his way up onto the front porch and rang the doorbell at the bottom of the mail box.

It was a beautiful morning and the door was partly open to the screen. As Margaret Stoner pulled open the door, she had the surprise of seeing Bill. She gasped as she opened the screen door and said, "Oh Bill! Welcome home!" Margaret gave Bill a warm hug as she invited him in and sized him up to see what shape he was in. She had never seen him in uniform. She explained that Sam was on the road with work this week and he would be disappointed to know he had missed Bill's visit. There was still a war on and the government needed those Diamond T trucks. Bill handed her the flowers as he told her he had just found out about Bob's death yesterday. Margaret, who was always the picture of composure and properness, began to cry and hugged Bill once more. Bill knew her anguish was deeper than he could understand and she knew she owed Bill condolences for losing his friend. They both found themselves in tears. She told Bill that Bob was so excited about being a Navy flier and he was doing what he wanted to do. She and Sam had wished that Bob had stayed in the States as an instructor, but he wanted to do his part. She told Bill that Bob often spoke of the hardships Bill was facing in the ground fighting and he wanted to make a difference.

Margaret offered Bill tea and cookies and he accepted to be polite. He followed her into the kitchen as she heated the water and plated some cookies. She asked Bill how it felt to be home again and of course, she already knew. Bill mentioned the open house that Steve and Jessie had planned for the coming Sunday and Margaret smiled affirmatively. She told Bill that she and Sam had discussed attending the open house and had thought it might be best if they did not attend. Bill looked puzzled. Margaret explained that everyone who would be at Bill's open house also knew that Bob had been killed in action. If they attended, Sam and Margaret feared this would cast a shadow over the event and dampen the celebration for a well-deserving son who did come home. Bill politely disagreed with Margaret and told her it would mean a lot to him if she and Sam would attend. He reasoned that if Bob were alive and in town, he would definitely be there.

The teapot whistled and Margaret poured the water and headed to the family room with the tea tray. Bill followed her with the plate of cookies. Margaret asked Bill about Helen Cochran and whether they planned to see each other again. Bill said he had planned on seeing her, but only as friends. Margaret asked Bill if he had heard about Marijane expecting a baby this coming January, and of course, Bill had heard this through *The Stoner Weekly News* and a letter from Jessie while he was at Saipan. This brought the conversation back to Bob Stoner. Bill asked what they had heard from the Navy about the circumstances of Bob's death. Margaret got up from her chair and went to Sam's roll top desk where he edited the *Stoner Weekly* and retrieved a folder of papers and brought them to Bill. These were the letters and documents they had received from the Navy.

Margaret Fraser Stoner, 1940.

(Stoner Family Photo)

She showed Bill the Western Union Telegram they had received on August 1st, and then the letters from Stanley and Chaplain McLain. Bill was not surprised that these men thought so highly of Bob, as the qualities noted were all things Bill had seen growing up. Bill began to read a Navy document that was an official notification of death with more detail. The report stated that Bob was killed while flying a mission over Tinian. His mind snapped back a few moments to the Stanley letter. He read the letter again. Stanley stated that Bob had died on July 30, 1944 at 0745 after being hit by "heavy and accurate" anti-aircraft fire, then "crashed into the sea." He went back to the report, then back to the letter. He glanced over at Sam's desk as he tried to assess what he was reading. Bill's mind went back to that Sunday morning aboard LST-130 and the sight of the wingless Avenger spiraling into the sea. There was only one plane that went in at Point Lalo that morning; he had been there the whole time. It was an Avenger; Lieutenant Bob Stoner's Avenger! Bill pondered whether or not he should speak. He had a lump in his throat and found it difficult. It seemed impossible, but it was true.

He looked at Margaret and tears came back to his eyes. He said, "This is incredible ... I can't believe this." Margaret was not sure what he meant. Then Bill explained that he had been aboard LST-130, just off Point Lalo, on the morning of July 30th and had seen the entire attack from start to finish. He told her he had seen the anti-aircraft fire hit Bob's Avenger and then watched it spiral into the sea with the right wing blown off and burning. Margaret was in shock and without words and she began to sob. She asked Bill if he could be sure, and he looked at the dates again and told her that he was certain. Bill was just as shocked as Margaret and they both cried together. Bill hugged her and told her what a great mother she had been to Bob and how all the Stoner kids spoke so highly of her for as long as Bill had known them. Bill then purposely asked about Dexter, Harley and Helen, just to get Margaret's mind on another subject. Before Bill left, he again stated that he wanted Sam and Margaret to be at the open house as it would not be the same without them. He hugged Margaret at the door, put on his hat and headed down the concrete steps. Driving down 4th Street to Simms, Bill realized that he was emotionally stunned. He pulled the car into the drive and grabbed the other bouquet of flowers and went inside to give them to Jessie. He told Jessie and Steve what he had realized during his visit with Margaret and they were shocked. Steve asked Bill how he could be sure and Bill gave him the details. There was absolutely no doubt that Bill had witnessed Bob Stoner's death.

Bill Bennett holds Billy Schell while Linc Schell keeps a father's hand on Ginny Schell aboard the work horse. Taken September 21st, 1944, at the Schell farm on Jericho Road. Bill had just arrived home from combat in the Pacific.

(Bennett Family Photo)

    Bill spent the rest of the week visiting friends and family all over town and catching up with the old gang. Mary Anne Swanson had married a Navy flier, George Troll was in combat in Europe with the 745th Tank Battalion and Bud Dix was somewhere nearby with an attached infantry company. It did seem, and was basically a fact, that everyone had gotten married but Bill. Bill phoned Helen Cochran and left a message with her mother Carrie. Helen phoned back and told Bill that she would be at the open house on Sunday, and she wouldn't miss it for the world. Bill went to a Kiwanis dinner with Steve, celebrated his Aunt Mary's birthday and had a "sandwich date" with his old friend "Frannie" McElroy. Jean and Linc invited Bill and Jessie out to their farm on Jericho Road for the day on September 21st and Bill had a long conversation with Linc about some of the things he had seen in the war. Linc told Bill that everyone sensed he had been in the worst of it. Bill spent a large part of the time carrying little Billy around and playing with four-year-old Ginny. Linc sat Ginny on one of the plow horses to have her picture taken with Uncle Bill. Bill laughed as he told Linc about having to learn to drive the Marine tractors and how he had thought of Linc at the time.

    Bill walked in to Schmitz and Gretencort and every set of eyes locked onto him. Steve asked his customer to give him a minute and Mr. Schmitz came down from the upstairs office. There was soon a group of eight or nine men around Bill, both employees and customers alike. Bill had been to the places that they had only read about in the papers or heard about on the radio. Most were gracious with their questions, but someone usually asked something awkward about killing Japanese or seeing "action." Bill knew that if he told the truth, he could probably make half of them vomit and the other half run away. The details of what he had seen would not be told, except to a select few. Bill recalled Bob Stoner's mention in his last writing in the *Stoner Weekly* about his visit to Steve at the store, and he recalled how much Bob had loved Schmitz and Gretencort. As Bill was telling Steve that he would see him at home, one more thought came to his mind. He walked around the corner to Main Street and turned into Main Hatters and the shoe shine shop. The Marine uniform once again grabbed the attention of those in the store. Nick Andrews recognized Bill instantly. Bill told Nick that he had spent time with his son Pete in Hawaii and played some softball with him. He told Nick how sorry he was to hear Pete had been killed at Saipan. He told him he had been on Saipan as well and Pete was a great Marine. Nick thanked Bill with tears in his eyes and then Bill shook his hand and left.

Sunday morning came around and Bill was excited to attend a service at Fourth Street after such a long absence. Reverend Dibble preached a sermon just the way Bill liked it and with the church filled with friends and family, Bill felt truly at home. Back at the house, Bessie Hemm and the Lipkes sent a beautiful bouquet of gladiolas and chrysanthemums, and the McElroy's sent zinnias and marigolds. Marian, Jean and Jessie had decorated the place with red, white and blue streamers and a "Welcome Home Corporal Bennett!" sign. Jessie set out a scrap book for the visitors to sign. Reverend Paul Dibble and his wife Marie arrived, as did the Lipkes, Bessie Hemm, the Spence, Dix, McElroy, Swanson and Nix families. The "west side" Bennetts, Phrangles, Moreys and Trolls arrived and on and on it went. Nearly 150 visitors filled the house and yard at 454 Simms Street. In the midst of the great hustle and bustle, Bill turned to see the front door open and in walked Helen with her sister Phyllis and her father Wally Cochran. Helen was a sight that he had longed to see for over two and a half years, and she looked fantastic. Bill made a beeline for Helen and gave her a great hug and thanked her for coming. Helen told Bill that he didn't need to thank her and she wouldn't dream of missing this day with him. The Bennetts, after all, had opened their home to Helen and allowed her to stay with them during the week when she started working in Chicago and she had become very good friends with Al and Marian.

After signing the guest book and getting some punch and a snack, Bill asked Helen if he could talk to her outside for a few minutes and they found a spot on the side porch. They agreed it was fantastic to finally see each other face to face, although the meeting had not turned out to be quite the movie scene they had once envisioned. Bill thanked her for the faithful letter writing and told her how important those letters and photos had been in helping him through it all. She said she appreciated the letters, flowers and gifts he sent. She told Bill she had waited just as she said she would and wanted him to know that. She continued to say how happy she was that Bill was home safe, and she hoped he would not be sent back. Helen had accepted her transfer to Phoenix with TWA and would be leaving in two weeks. She was sure this was the right thing to do for both of them. Their parting in this way was bittersweet, but not painful. They agreed that they had barely begun to know each other before the war and they had both changed a lot over the past three years. Bill would always think highly of Helen and she would always think highly of Bill. As the afternoon passed and the time approached 4 p.m., the guests began to leave and Bill stood on the front porch shaking hands and hugging dozens of people. As Helen, Phyllis and Wally came through, Bill walked with them to their car along the curb. He shook Wally's hand and hugged Phyllis and Helen and then waved goodbye as they drove away. Bill would never see Helen Cochran again.

79. Swamp Lejeune

October 20th, 1944. Bill's wonderful 30-day furlough had come to an end. He had been able to do far more than he had imagined while at home. He even found time to play a round of golf and put in a few days of work with Don Glossop. Don had a job lined up that included tearing out an old furnace and installing a new one. The day had now come to get back to being a Marine. The Bennett gang drove Bill to the train station where they said their goodbyes. Bill assured all of them that there was practically no way he would get sent overseas, given all of the points he had accumulated. He had high hopes he could be home again for Christmas, so the seriousness of this goodbye was not anywhere near the first one. The train ride down to Camp Lejeune had none of the hijinks and camaraderie of the first trip to San Diego. The trains headed south were filthy and the tracks were bumpy. Bill became extremely sad as he thought about having to leave home again and his homesickness seemed far worse than ever now that he had been there to refresh his memory of how good he had it.

As Bill was stretching his legs at Raleigh, North Carolina, he spotted a familiar face in the crowd. It was Fred Ellis switching trains on his way down from Billings, Montana. It had only been a month since they had last seen each other in Chicago, but still, Fred was a welcome sight. The last 100 miles of the trip went by like a snap as the two old pals caught up on their furloughs. Upon arrival at Lejeune, Bill was assigned to Company C, Engineering Battalion FMF, (Fleet Marine Force), Specialist Training Regiment, Training Command. Bill was sent to become a Demolitions Instructor, but he complained that he no longer wanted anything to do with demolition work. They sent him to Blacksmith School to get his 024 Blacksmith rating. The daily regimen was working on the anvil from 0700 to 1145, then back again from 1245-1700. One night a week he had Infantry Training from 1700 to 2100 hours. Regarding those days, he would say, "The days were long but you didn't have to worry about planning anything." Bill was near a lot of the old Company D Marines, including Herb Dale, who got a job that he loved, driving a truck all over Lejeune. Herb had such a lead foot that he got a ticket from an MP for going 30 mph over the limit on base. Herb was found guilty and had to pay a fine of eight dollars. Sergeant Gabel had been promoted to Warrant Officer and was assigned to the Roads and Forestry Department at Lejeune, a job which he greatly enjoyed. He had married his girl "Ronnie" in Chicago while on leave. 1st Lieutenant Art Simonson was also at Lejeune and had been assigned to lead the Pioneer school. A new breed of Marine Pioneer was being trained by someone who knew the job well. Simonson was now the last member of the D/2/18 "old breed" to remain a Pioneer.

Sergeant George P. Gabel and his bride Verona "Ronnie" Otto on their wedding day, October 17th, 1944. The war caused them to delay their wedding by 34 months.

(Gabel Family Photo, restored by Belle Peterson)

One day when Bill had to go over to the Regimental Head Quarters office, he heard someone say, "Hey Bennett!" When Bill turned around, it was Manny Bud, who had left Company D back in New Zealand for the special photographic job in the States. That job was with the Engineering Battalion at Camp Lejeune. Manny, who Bill still called "Bud," had gotten married to his Chicago sweetheart, "Niki," after coming back from the Pacific and the two of them lived in a tiny trailer at the edge of the base. Manny invited Bill over to meet Niki and have some spaghetti and meatballs for dinner. Niki's maiden name was actually Thelma Sladnik, but she had never been too fond of it. She used the "nik" from Sladnik and became "Niki." After marrying Manny, she became Niki Bud. Bill ended up getting along wonderfully with Bud and Niki, even though they tended to drink quite a bit and Bill did not. Manny still laughed about the fact that while he and other Marines were involved in the biggest bar fight in history, Bill was at church. He was referring to "The Battle of Wellington." Dinner turned out to be so much fun that Bill returned every Wednesday for the same menu. Manny and Niki had a great sense of humor and they helped Bill get his mind off the monotony at Camp Lejeune.

Upon arriving at the trailer one Wednesday, Manny told Bill that Niki had gone over to the PX to pick up some groceries and the two old Marines had some time to talk openly about their experiences in the Pacific. Before Niki arrived back at the trailer, Bill and Manny revisited some of the tough times back on Tulagi, like the USS New Orleans detail and the initial combat on Tulagi and Gavutu. Manny asked about Captain Farkas and some of the other old timers. Bill told Manny what had happened to Truitt and Bob Swigert on Tarawa. This was extremely upsetting to Manny since he had sent the letter to Mrs. Swigert letting her know that Bob was fine in New Zealand. Swigert had been the epitome of a nice guy in the Marines. Bill explained how Seng, Montague and Lieutenant Vincent had landed into a cross fire at Tarawa and the entire team had been killed. Bill recalled how Slowinski, Ellis and he had helped bury them. It was difficult for Manny since he knew what he had missed, but also in knowing that he might be headed back.

Alcohol was not officially allowed on base, with the exception of the Base Clubs and Officer's Clubs. Manny liked to have some adult beverages around for entertaining guests at the little trailer, and on one occasion, he asked Niki to go to a liquor store off base and buy some bottles. When Niki was coming back through the security gate, she saw the MP searching some parcels and became very nervous. She began to shake with fright thinking she would be discovered and the bottles began to clang inside the bag. The MP approached her and put his hand on the bag to silence the bottles. He then leaned close to her ear and whispered, "Next time, tell them to send someone who's not so nervous."

Bill insisted on doing some of the cooking, so Niki enjoyed the visits more than ever when he would show up with a bag of groceries and take care of dinner. This fantastic social connection only lasted for about five weeks when Manny ended up shipping out to the Pacific with the 4th Division. Since Manny had missed Tarawa, Saipan and Tinian, he did not have the combat points needed to stay in the States, so he was sent back to the Pacific. Niki headed back to Chicago to live with Manny's parents until he came back. Bill wrote their Chicago address in his book and planned to get together with them when they got home.

 Although he was able to see the old Company D members, there were none in his actual company and the new camp and training life seemed hollow compared to the days in the Pacific. Bill took to letter writing as an escape and wrote home frequently and to many people he had met over the years, including Selly and Stuart Hyde from New Zealand. Bill struggled with keeping a good attitude, as most of his superiors had never been in combat. It was hard to respect an officer who had never been to war bossing battle-hardened Marines around. Bill had to bite his tongue on many occasions as he knew that his main purpose was to bide his time until the war was over.

Bill was able to go to a real football game on November 19th when Bainbridge came to play the Marine Chevrons at Camp Lejeune. As Bill watched the first quarter he saw a familiar face on the field in number 63 for Bainbridge. A quick look in the program showed that Bill had a good eye. It was Elwood Gerber who used to play offensive guard on the Clippers with Bill in 1940. Gerber was from Naperville and was currently in the Navy and the captain of the Bainbridge team. He had gone from the Clippers to play in the NFL in '41 and '42 with the Philadelphia Eagles under legendary coach "Greasy" Neale. Bainbridge "swamped" Lejeune 33-6. After the game was over, Bill shouted out to Gerber and the two got together and talked for a half hour or so. Bill thought that Gerber had certainly had it nice during the war. He mailed the program home to Marian.

Bill was given liberty one weekend and he went with a few Marines into Wilmington, North Carolina, to see the sights. The only problem was there really were no sights to see. They ended up going to a movie and then arrived at a home the U.S.O. had lined up for them for the night. The next morning, Bill went to church with the family and then the group headed back to Lejeune. The Lejeune Chapel was having a young people's meeting that night so Bill went to listen to a guest speaker who was a young minister from the Congregational Church. As the fellow spoke, it sounded as if he was more interested in helping people into the Congregational Church than he was in helping them into heaven. Someone actually raised their hand and asked if he had gone into the ministry for the money or to win souls? The fellow answered that he was not the "soul-winning type" but just wanted to help people, and the church seemed like a good place for that. A Netherlands Marine, who was at Lejeune for training, chimed in that he once thought about the ministry because he wanted to help people too. He then decided that it wasn't enough to just want to help people because the Christian church's mission is to win souls. You could have heard a pin drop in that room. The guest speaker told the Marine that he accepted his criticism with humility. Bill wanted to shake the Dutchman's hand.

Bill graduated from the 024 Blacksmith School and was so impressive that he was assigned permanently as the class instructor. Although camp life was mostly drudgery and he really did not like some of the officers, he knew he had it pretty good compared to where he had been. He resigned himself to looking at his situation as though he had a job to do and just get through it. News swept the company that there would be Christmas liberty given. Then the news changed; liberty would be in the middle of January. Finally, Bill received official word that he would be given liberty December 20th through December 26th. He was so excited about getting home for Christmas that he could not even write a legible letter to tell Jessie and Steve. On the 20th, Bill boarded a U.S.M.C. bus for the trip up to Washington D.C. and then boarded a train to Chicago. Jean and Linc picked Bill up at Union Station and drove him out to Aurora on the evening of the 21st. He would only have 70 hours at home before heading back on Christmas Eve. Orders were to report at Lejeune by 1000 hours on the 26th. It seemed ridiculous that someone could not have set up liberty so the Marines could have been be home for Christmas instead of near Christmas.

In spite of the hurried schedule, Bill had a wonderful time buying presents and being in the snow. He even set up the train around the Christmas tree with little Bobby. Sam and Margaret came over to see Bill on Christmas Eve and Bill had a great time, one he would always remember. Bill helped Jessie in the kitchen just like the old days and he must have hugged her 100 times. Word came through a letter from New Zealand that Bill's brother Al had arrived there. He had visited the Mitchell family in Lower Hutt as well as the Proctors up in Palmerston North. Bill got quite a "kick" out of knowing that

Al was sitting in the same kitchens he had sat in and was enjoying the friendships of some of the friendliest people Bill had ever known.

Jean and Linc drove Bill back to Chicago to catch a 6 p.m. train back to D.C. There was some winter weather and the train arrived on Christmas Day over four hours late. The U.S.M.C. buses back to Lejeune had all departed and the late Marines had to wait for another bus to be brought over. Bill knew they would not be on time, so he crafted a letter stating the situation so an MP could sign it. The replacement bus finally arrived and the tardy Marines headed out overnight for Lejeune. The next morning, about 100 miles from Lejeune, the replacement bus broke down and they sat along the highway waiting for a "replacement-replacement" bus to arrive. Again, Bill had an MP sign his letter. There was no way he was going to spend time in the brig for this messed-up trip. The bus finally arrived and it looked to be in worse shape than the one they were leaving along the side of the road. They finally made it to Camp Lejeune around 1845 hours on the 26th of December, over eight hours late. No one ever said a word about it.

In addition to his duties as the Blacksmith Instructor, Bill had to maintain his infantry readiness, which meant drills once a week and some time helping out at the range with the BAR specialists. During this time, Bill realized the firing at the range brought back memories of combat and it made him a bit jumpy. During his early days of training, they were trying to get him prepared for the sounds of combat, and now he was more interested in forgetting the sounds of combat. Bill thought about how he once stood at the shore in San Diego and knew the Japanese were somewhere out in the Pacific waiting for him. Now he was able to look out over the Atlantic and know American G.I.s were across that ocean fighting the Germans. The news from the European Theater had been promising, as both the Americans and the Russians were driving toward Germany and Berlin. They would soon have Hitler in a noose.

Out in the Pacific, and unknown to Bill, Manny landed on the black sand at Iwo Jima on February 19, 1945. Manny, now a sergeant, fought through some of the heaviest fire in Marine Corps history as he climbed up the sloping beach from the water's edge. Some of the units that Manny fought alongside in taking Hill 425 suffered 135% casualties during the first few days of battle. After six days on Iwo Jima, Manny was one of three Marines left from his platoon that hit the beach. On March 5th, Manny was assigned seven Marines and two .30 caliber machine guns. His orders were to move up from the line about 700 yards, dig in and fire at the Japanese throughout the night. The strategy was to pull the Japanese out of their fortifications and toward the machine gun position. At precisely 0700 the next morning, Marine artillery would rake the entire area with fire and the Marines' line would advance on the Japanese. The attack would come from three directions with the 3rd Marines attacking from the south, the 5th Marines from the west and the 4th Marines from the north.

Under cover of darkness, Manny led the patrol out to a ridge where they could fire and stir up trouble. No one had any idea if they would live through the night or even be killed by their own artillery in the morning. They dug in the guns and started to randomly fire. Within minutes, the Japanese returned fire and the game ensued all night long. Manny was relieved when the sun began to rise and he kept an eye on his watch. At 0650 he ordered the slowest three Marines to head back to relative safety of the line. At 0655 he ordered the next three to make a run for it while he kept a track star from college behind with him to fire the gun. Manny then told the speedy Marine that it was only fair he leave last because he was fast and Manny was pitifully slow. Manny left the fighting pit and made a dash for the line, running a zigzag pattern as Japanese machine gun bullets zipped by his head and smacked at the ground. He made it about forty yards before his right thigh exploded as a round passed through it and made a 19-inch split in his femur. Manny crashed into a shell hole and clutched his shattered leg. Within a few seconds, the last Marine dove into the hole and gave Manny bandages. Manny told him to get the hell out of there and not to send anyone until after the barrage had lifted. The Marine headed out just as artillery shells began to shriek overhead and pound the entire area where they had been throughout the night. Manny lowered his helmet and kept pressure on his leg as the earth rocked with the explosions.

After 20 minutes, the artillery fire stopped and Manny heard the sound of advancing Marines. A corpsman dropped into the hole and took charge of Manny's wound and administered morphine. A few minutes later four African American Marines from a Support Battalion slid into the shell crater with a stretcher. The stretcher bearers were all fairly small guys and one of them sized up the 6 ft., 200-pound Manny, looked at his buddy and said, "How come we never get the little Marines?" Manny never forgot those four stretcher bearers as they were fired on while they carried him out of danger. They risked their lives to save his. Manny was quickly evacuated to a hospital ship and ended up back at Pearl Harbor where he underwent the first of many surgeries. Several months later, he was shipped back to Great Lakes Naval Hospital, near Chicago, so he could be close to Niki and his family.

On April 14th, 1945, Bill spent his 26th birthday doing his daily routine at Camp Lejeune. It was his fourth consecutive birthday away from home. Spring arrived at Lejeune and the weather along the Atlantic coast was mostly fair and beautiful.

On May 8th, 1945, it finally happened: word spread across the base like wildfire, as truck horns honked and sirens rang out. Hitler was presumed dead and Germany had surrendered! Bill's blacksmith class was canceled for the day and celebrations were happening everywhere around camp and in nearby towns. The war effort would now be focused squarely on Japan. The newsreels showed America's fearsome B-29 Superfortress bombers pounding Japan daily from the new bases at Saipan and Tinian, and Bill could clearly see that the U.S. strategy was working as planned. These bombers were protected over Japan by P-51 Mustang fighters that were able to reach Japan from their new base at Iwo Jima. It had been costly to the Marines to take these islands, but their struggle had not been in vain. Japan was being crushed by the American war machine.

80. Home at Last

Bill's letter writing kept him busy with the small amount of spare time he had. He focused on reading and prayer time, which would usually happen at night before falling asleep. There were a lot of things Bill could share with his family and friends, but there were other things that only Marines who had been there could understand. There were things at the very core of his soul that he knew only the Lord could understand. There were times when he prayed for five or ten minutes and there were times when time seemed to slip away and he would find he had prayed for almost an hour. As Bill read the scriptures, there were times when the words seemed to come alive on the page and times where he suddenly understood something that he had read before. In all of this, Bill became aware that God's Spirit was teaching him things and changing him from the inside out. He became aware that prayer was actually a two-way communication and not just Bill going through a list of things that he wanted from God. He actually took the time to be still and ask God what he wanted him to do. At the same time, he noticed that his patience for the Marine Corps nonsense had grown and he was better able to handle difficult people. Bill's heart seemed to soar as he found passages in scripture where Jesus described the type of life that Bill was experiencing. Although Bill loved church activities and the fellowship of other believers, these activities were no longer the driving force behind his "religion." The driving force had become his direct and personal interaction with the God of the Universe through the person of Jesus of Nazareth and the miracle of the Holy Spirit. Bill completely understood that he didn't need religion because he was able to deal directly with his Creator.

Corporal William Bennett, U.S.M.C. after returning from the Pacific. Probably taken at Camp Lejeune in early 1945.

(Bennett Family Photo)

Bill spent some long periods of time at Lejeune where he would describe himself as "blue." He had begun to have vivid dreams where a Japanese infiltrator would look down on him while he was in his foxhole and then jump down with knife in hand. Bill would wake up with his right hand raised as though it still clutched his Ka-Bar fighting knife and his heart would be pounding out of his chest and his shirt wet with sweat. Most of the combat veterans had similar dreams and even worse issues to face. Some were experiencing paranoia and even wetting the bed from what would come to be known as "post-traumatic stress disorder." At the old age of 26, one of Bill's longings was yet to materialize; that of being married and having a family of his own. He had given this longing over to the Lord as he reasoned that it would have to work out according to His plan, whenever it would be. During this time, there were no plans on the horizon and Bill didn't have any idea who he would ask out on a date, whenever he did get home. He just came to the point where he tried not to think about it.

On Sunday, August 5th, 1945, while Bill was attending service at Camp Lejeune Chapel, Colonel Paul Warfield Tibbets was going through his pre-flight checklist aboard his B-29 Superfortress, "Enola Gay." The Enola Gay sat on a hardstand at the new North Field base on Tinian, Marianas Islands. North Field was developed on the site of Ushi Airdrome, which Bill and the D/2/18 Pioneer team had helped remove from Japanese hands on July 27th the year before. While Bill was enjoying the afternoon off, and trying to stay cool in the summer heat, Tibbets lifted the B-29 and its top-secret weapon off the runway and headed west toward Japan. As Bill was getting ready to head back to the Chapel for the Sunday evening young people's meeting, Tibbets dropped the first atomic bomb, "Little Boy," from 30,000 feet above Hiroshima, Japan. The bombardier had aimed the bomb at the crossroads of the Aioi Bridge in the heart of Hiroshima. The bomb exploded 350 feet above the bridge and instantly killed 60,000 Japanese. It was 0815 hours, August 6th, 1945 in Hiroshima, and exactly one year since Bill had defended against the suicide Banzai charge on Saipan.

The Monday morning newspapers at Camp Lejeune and Jacksonville carried headlines about the new master weapon that had hit Japan. President Truman vehemently called for Japan to surrender but they did not respond. Back in Aurora, everyone had been "glued" to the radio as they waited for news about the possible surrender. Three days later, while Bill was just finishing up his letter writing prior to "lights out," Major Charles W. Sweeney dropped the second atomic bomb over Nagasaki, Japan, at 1058 hours local time. 33,000 more Japanese perished. The August 9th newspapers and radio newscasts told of the second atomic bomb and the world waited for Japan to respond.

Finally, on August 14th, Emperor Hirohito intervened and demanded that the Japanese War Council surrender unconditionally to the Americans. At 7 p.m. EST on Tuesday, August 14th, 1945, Bill Bennett, Fred Ellis and Herb Dale gathered around a radio at Camp Lejeune to listen to a special news conference called by President Harry S. Truman. Truman confirmed to the world that the Empire of Japan had acknowledged their acceptance of Unconditional Surrender. The Marines went wild. World War II was over. For the next 24 hours, drinks were poured, girls were kissed, horns were honked and streamers were thrown. From coast to coast in America, countless millions swarmed the streets of all major cities and celebrated like they had never done before.

To Bill, this meant he would finally be going home for good. His agreement with the U.S.M.C.R. was for the "duration of the war plus six months." This did not mean he had to be kept in for six months after the war was over, it meant six months was the maximum he could be kept active. On September 2nd, General Douglas MacArthur officially accepted the Japanese surrender aboard the Battleship USS Missouri, anchored in Tokyo Bay. On September 17th, Bill stood in line at Camp Lejeune to turn in all he had left of his infantry combat equipment: his pack, his ammo belt and his mess kit. He was officially transferred to the 3rd Processing Company to await discharge. On September 28th, 1945, Bill stood in line to be officially discharged from the Marine Corps. Papers were stamped and 2nd Lieutenant, Walter L. Sullivan signed the discharge. Bill Bennett was a free man. Now he just had to get home. Making good on their plans over the past four years, Bill, Fred and Herb all boarded the train for Chicago. The entire trip on the train was filled with "Whatcha'gonna do now?" questions, and most of the answers had to do with women, jobs and fantastic meals. Every car on the train was filled with homeward-bound servicemen and this was probably the most exciting trip of their lives. Fred decided to continue on from Chicago as he was anxious to get home, so he and Bill exchanged a hug and one heck of a handshake on the platform at Union Station in Chicago. They promised each other to keep in touch and somehow see each other again. Bill and Herb caught the CB&Q line out to Aurora where the Bennetts waited for their hero to arrive.

Monday, October 1st, 1945. Marian, Jessie and Steve met Bill and Herb at the train station and Bill greatly enjoyed introducing Herb after four years of talking about him in his letters. Bill walked through the front door and the stained-glass window over the stair landing welcomed him home. He glanced up the stairs which turned to the left and then looked straight ahead into the dining room. He and Herb took their sea bags upstairs and Bill showed Herb the room where he and Al lived before the war. Herb would get the honor of sleeping in Al's bed. Jessie had a pot roast cooking in the kitchen with carrots and potatoes and the house smelled like heaven to the Marines.

For the next three days, Bill took Herb around town and showed him everything from the Athletic Field to Schmitz and Gretencort. They stopped in at Woolworth's for milk shakes and pie and met just about every family Bill knew. Bill was glad to have Herb visit and he thought about Truitt from time to time. The Bennett's car had been running poorly and Bill and Herb broke down a few blocks from home. They walked home to get some tools and Herb knew exactly how to fix the problem. Two minutes later, the Ford was running and they drove it home. Herb proceeded to tune the engine and had it running like a top.

Herb's brother had ended up living in Chicago and Herb planned to live with him for the time being. Bill drove Herb to his brother's apartment and the pair of Marines filled his brother in on their adventures for several hours. Upon shaking hands and giving Herb a heartfelt farewell, Bill headed back toward Aurora with the mindset that it was at long last, time to get his life started. Once back in Aurora, Bill headed over to Spencer Street to see Don Glossop. Don and Helen were so glad to see Bill finally home and wearing civilian clothes.

Don had tried to enlist three times during the war and each time he was a year too old. They raised the age limit throughout the war, but the limit stayed just below Don's age. Don was a very capable twin-engine pilot and mechanic and he repaired and ferried aircraft for the Navy. Planes that had engine problems would land at Aurora Airport where they could be serviced on their way to Great Lakes Naval Training Base. Essentially, Don had found a way to fill a military role without actually being in the service. His business had suffered because of the war, as there were no new houses being built. Bill came in to Don's office and had a seat. Don asked Bill if he was ready to get back to work and Bill said that he was eager.

Don had sheet metal work and air conditioning work lining up, but he also had an idea for a new business in mind. When he had bought the shop building on Spencer, it had previously been a canvas awning shop and the large sewing machines were still back in the corner. Don had contacted the woman who had run the machines for the previous business and made a deal for her to sew for him. She did not want anything to do with working with customers or measuring, she just wanted to sew in the shop. That is where Bill would come in. Don proposed a business called Bennett & Glossop Canvas and Awnings. Don already had the first orders going and just needed Bill to jump in. Bill didn't even have to think about it and the firm handshake was made across Don's desk.

Don had a huge job working in the shop for Camp Quarry Ledge, downriver near Oswego, Illinois. Some of the awnings were ready to be installed and Bill agreed to work with Don the following day to get oriented with the work. There were over a dozen awnings that needed to be installed over the windows of some of the cabins, dining hall and office. Bill jumped right in and began hanging the framework for the canvas with Don. As they worked together, Don asked Bill quite a few questions about the war. Don had taken an interest in Bill's campaigns and knew quite a bit about Tulagi, Tarawa, Saipan and Tinian. He knew something about what Bill had been through and he admired Bill for what he had done. Bill told him some of the better parts, but kept the details light.

81. A New Beginning

Sunday, October 7th, 1945. Bill had been working hard with Don Glossop all week and he was looking forward to attending church again with the family. Steve had taken Bill's dress uniform to the cleaners and it was looking about as perfect as it ever had. Most of the returning servicemen and women continued to wear their uniforms in public as America was still in a lingering mode of celebration over the war's end. Bill planned to work down at camp Quarry Ledge later in the day, but would grab lunch at home with Jessie, Steve and Marian. Jessie beamed over the sight of her youngest son in his dress uniform and this would be a special day of thanks between her and the Lord. The war was over, Bill had his honorable discharge and Jessie had him seated in the pew next to her at Fourth Street Methodist Church. Sam and Margaret Stoner had been attending First Methodist Church for quite a few years but had recently made a decision to return to the smaller Fourth Street Church with Steve and Jessie. Jessie knew all too well the anguish that her best friend Margaret had endured over the loss of her son Bob, and it made her deeply grateful to have Bill home. The church was filled to capacity as the choir sang, announcements were read and Reverend Dibble came to the pulpit. He prayed a prayer of thanks for the return of our servicemen and women and named those present whom he recognized, including Bill.

After closing prayer, Bill became very busy with dozens of friends who shook his hand, hugged him and welcomed him home. As Bill was talking to Marie Dibble and a few others, he glanced to the back of the church where folks were filing out. A young lady in a navy-blue dress with a white collar caught his eye. He had not seen her before and she seemed to be with a few friends. She turned her head and smiled at Bill and he smiled back. Suddenly very distracted, he listened to Marie for a few more seconds and then excused himself as he headed to the back of the church. Trying not to be totally obvious, he moved closer to the beautiful young lady and introduced himself. She smiled and told Bill her name was Edna May Ulferts. She already knew who Bill Bennett was. Edna May was strikingly beautiful and her smile and manners were very attractive. Bill wondered if she were somehow "attached," as it was improbable that he was the first fellow to have noticed her. Edna had been visiting the church with her friends, as she lived just a few blocks away on Maple Avenue.

Edna stayed behind while her friends went outside as she and Bill continued talking. By this time, Jessie had been watching Bill as he chatted with this beautiful young lady and decided to help things along. She approached the pair and Bill immediately introduced Edna to his mother. Jessie said how lovely it was to meet her and how glad she was that she had been able to visit the church. She looked at Bill and then back at Edna. Jessie then asked Edna May if she had any plans for lunch. Since she did not, Jessie informed her that the Bennetts would love to have her over for some sandwiches. Jessie said she was sure Bill could drive her home on his way to work after lunch. Bill was quite certain he could accommodate the plan. Edna told her friends about the invite and then headed to the Bennett's car. Edna was introduced to Steve and Marian and they made the short drive over to 454 Simms Street. Over lunch, Edna answered many questions and explained that she had moved to Aurora with her family from Oregon, Illinois, in 1940 and graduated from East High with the class of 1941. Her family had lived on Jackson, but now lived at 450 Maple Avenue, which was two blocks away. Her father Henry and mother Bessie had three other girls: Erma, 20; Margaret, 15; and Frannie, seven. Edna had been working as a clerk for the CB&Q Railroad for the past two years. She was full of personality and had a good sense of humor, which Bill knew she would need if she were to spend time with him.

Time had flown by and Bill needed to get to Camp Quarry Ledge to work on the awnings for a few hours. He politely told Edna he would drive her home. Then, quite unexpectedly, Edna asked Bill if he could use an extra pair of hands with the awnings. Bill was sure she was just being polite and told her that she wasn't dressed for it. Edna told Bill that if he could give her five minutes at home, she could change into her work clothes. This was definitely an offer that Bill couldn't refuse. Bill went up to the door of the Ulfert's home with Edna, who quickly introduced him to the family. Henry and Bessie were very friendly and the middle girls seemed to size Bill up as they were surprised at his sudden appearance at their door. Little Frannie was curious about Bill and he made her feel at ease by joking around with her. Edna appeared with her "ready for work" clothes on and Bill was struck by the fact that she looked just as good as she did in the dress.

The awning work went well, although it was difficult for Bill to concentrate on the measurements as he found himself wondering how all of this had happened in the past few hours. Here was this gorgeous 22-year-old woman helping him install awnings out of the blue. Don Glossop would not believe this story! Edna was not only good looking, but she could get some work done as well. Bill was impressed by her helpfulness, good nature and quick thinking. She would end up making some lucky guy a great wife.

A very young and beautiful Edna May Ulferts caught Bill Bennett's attention after Sunday service at Fourth Street Methodist Church on his first Sunday back from the Marine Corps.

(Bennett Family Photo)

When Bill dropped her off at home, he thanked her for the help and then asked if he could take her out to eat tomorrow night to reciprocate. Edna smiled and said she would love to. The night out went wonderfully and it became evident to Bill that Edna May was as interested in him as he was in her. When he left her at the door that night, they parted with their first kiss. After arriving home from the war, it had taken Bill two weeks to get busy with work, start a business and find a great girl. He thought about how quickly his life was getting put back together. It seemed that there was a supernatural hand at work. Edna May began to occupy Bill's mind more and more, and the fellows he worked with at Glossop's became familiar with her name. Bill filled in on sheet metal work and teamed up with Jack Kane, a heating and cooling specialist, who had been in the Navy during the war. He tried to work on Don's heating and cooling jobs during regular hours and install the awnings on the weekends. After a few weeks, Bill and Don went to the Aurora National Bank and opened a business account for "Bennett and Glossop" with an original balance of $150.

As Bill settled into the beginning of his new life in Aurora, he took special note of where his friends had been during the war, as many of them were returning home during the first few months. Marian's husband, Perry McIntosh, returned from the Marines and for the first time ever, Eunice, Jean and Linc, Marian and Perry, along with Bill and Edna, got together at the Bennett house. If Bob and Sunny had not lived in California, they would have been there as well.

On Thursday, November 22nd, Bill and Steve began a new tradition on Thanksgiving. The two of them, along with Perry and Linc, attended the East Aurora vs. West Aurora football game, while the girls opted to stay home and prepare the Thanksgiving dinner. Little Ginny Schell sat between her uncle Bill, who rooted for East, and her Grandpa Steve, who rooted for West. When West made a good play, Grandpa would pick her up and cheer and scream. When East made a good play, Uncle Bill would pick her up and cheer and scream. West edged the Tomcats 6-0 in a hard-fought defensive battle and Steve thanked her for helping West win. She was indifferent as to the outcome, but had a memorable time. Later at the family gathering, Bill had a blast playing with the children by giving them "horseback rides" all over the house and swinging them in Uncle Bill's Marine blanket.

Three days later on November 25th, 1945, the Commandant of Great Lakes Naval Base presented PFC Peter Nicholas Andrews' Silver Star medal to his father, Nicholas Andrews, during a ceremony held at the Leland Tower in Aurora. Pete's older brother, George, had returned home safely after being in extended combat in Europe with the 101st Airborne Division. Bill read the article in the *Beacon News* on Monday the 26th, and he told Steve and Jessie how he had hung around with Pete in Hawaii and played softball. In a similar ceremony, Bessie Miller, the mother of Corporal Channing B. Miller, was awarded his Silver Star for his heroism in taking out the Japanese pillbox on Saipan on June 17th, 1944. Bessie Miller also received her son Channing's Purple Heart medal with three oak-leaf clusters; he had been wounded four times, perhaps the most of any U.S. Marine during the war. Ensign Wayne Warren, who had been the captain of the Tomcat's football team during Bill's senior year, was awarded the Bronze Star for bravery at Tarawa. Warren wore the number 14 and was seated on Bill's left when their 1937 Tomcat Football photo was taken. How ironic, six years later, they would both find themselves trying to survive the hell of Red Beach 2 on Tarawa. Warren repeatedly drove his LVT into the beach with Marines and supplies under heavy enemy fire on November 20, 1943. While Bill was ashore with F/2/2 on Red Beach 2, Warren had been one of the LVT drivers coming and going just yards away from where Bill and his Pioneers were moving supplies over the seawall. On that same day, 1st Lieutenant Bonnie A. Little from nearby Batavia, Illinois, was killed at the controls of his LVT going in to Red Beach 2. Little had been promoted to captain a few days earlier, but never knew it.

Bill's old best friend George Troll had been awarded the Bronze Star for his role with the 745th Tank Battalion and their actions on D-Day at Normandy and the fight across France and Belgium. Bud Dix had a late start in the service but made it to the European front just one day before the outbreak of the Battle of the Bulge. He enlisted in the Army in June of 1944 and received his Basic Training at Fort Hood, Texas. Upon completion, he was sent overseas as a replacement and assigned to Company B, 55th Armored Infantry Battalion, 11th Armored Division, 3rd Army. He served his country well and was awarded the Combat Infantry Badge, a Bronze Star, Purple Heart with Oak Leaf Cluster (wounded twice), the ETO Medal with three Battle Stars, the German Victory Medal, the Medal of German Occupation, and the Good Conduct Medal. Bill Rees, Louis Kuk, Bob Reder, Ed Kocjan and Duane Burkhart all returned to Aurora from the Marine Corps. Elmer Renner, who had played on the Clippers with Bill, had been lost at sea in the Pacific as a lieutenant in the Navy. Renner somehow managed to survive over a week at sea holding onto a broken life raft with no food or water, and was eventually rescued. Sharks ate some of his friends and others just died holding onto the raft.

Walter Truemper had been a fairly quiet guy when he went to East High, along with Bill, and graduated in the class of 1938. Truemper's father had been an Alderman and Street Commissioner in the city. Truemper enlisted in the Army Air Corps and became a navigator on a B-17 crew. Prior to leaving for England, Walter phoned his sister and had her place their disabled mother, Fredericka, in her wheel chair in her favorite window overlooking the back yard on North Avenue in Aurora. His sister had their mother in position at the precise time and date Walter gave her. He then directed his pilot's course to bring the shadow of their B-17 directly over that window and his mother's face three times before heading for the east coast. He said that it was his way of saying goodbye.

On February 20th, 1944, Truemper and the crew of their B-17G, "Ten Horsepower," flew a bombing mission over Leipzig from their base at Polebrook, England, with the 351st Bomb Group. Luftwaffe fighters attacked and badly damaged the plane, killing the co-pilot and severely wounding the radioman and pilot, who was unconscious. The plane was out of control and the other six members of the crew bailed out to become POWs. Truemper and the flight engineer, Sergeant Archibald Mathies, moved the pilot and co-pilot from the cockpit and took over the controls of the crippled bomber. Making it over the English Channel and back to Polebrook, they flew the plane over the tower to allow a damage assessment from the ground. They were ordered to bail out and let the plane crash. Truemper told the tower that the pilot was still breathing and he did not want to leave him to die. Upon the second order to bail out, he replied, "Sir, if that's an order, then okay, but I'd rather try to bring her in. The pilot is still breathing." He was given permission to land the plane. On their third attempt at an open field belly landing, the B-17 cartwheeled and crashed, killing all three left aboard. Truemper and Mathies were awarded the Congressional Medal of Honor, our nation's highest award for their actions. On July 4th, 1944, Fredericka Truemper received Walter's Medal of Honor in a ceremony in their front yard at 807 North Avenue in Aurora. Since she was unable to travel, the Army Air Forces came to her.

The population of the city of Aurora, Illinois, was nearly 40,000 during WW II. Nearly 10,000 residents served in the Armed Forces with 298 losing their lives. At Fourth Street Methodist Church there were approximately 500 members and 104 served in the military during the war.

82. Like No Other

Christmas of 1945 arrived and Bill was able to enjoy the entire holiday season for the first time since 1941. It was wonderful, as he was able to spend time with the family and his new sweetheart, Edna May. Just as his sister Marian had somehow become known to Bill as "Pete," Edna May took on the nickname of "Eddie." He also spent time with Edna's family and they were becoming quite fond of Bill. As Bill was recognizing that he was falling in love with Edna, he looked back over the past few years and the journey that he had been on spiritually. The years he had spent longing for a relationship and having his life disrupted only to be disappointed had left him wondering if he was on the right path. Coming back from the war with no idea which way his life was leading or whether or not he would find the right girl had been troublesome. Now things were completely different. Edna seemed to really understand Bill and he was able to be completely honest about how he felt about serving God and making Him first in his life. Edna had never been as enthusiastic about spiritual things as Bill had, but being around Bill had caused her to reexamine exactly what she believed. Bill made it clear to her where he stood and that following Christ would be first in his life. He was willing to have Edna occupy second place if she would have him.

While working at the Burlington office, Edna had picked up the habit of smoking cigarettes. Bill liked everything about Edna; well, almost everything. One night while dropping her off at home, he explained that her smoking was a great concern to him and he didn't think he could continue with their relationship if she wanted to keep smoking. Edna was more than a bit surprised by the revelation, but Bill asked her politely to think about it. After Bill drove away, Edna had one last cigarette outside the kitchen door and then put it out in the ash tray and threw the pack into the trash. Bill was exactly what she was looking for in a man and she was not going to let a cigarette get in the way.

In early 1946, Al Bennett finally received his discharge and made his way home from New Zealand. It was a reunion that Bill had waited for since the day he left home in January of 1942. Al looked good and he had done a great job as a Procurement Officer with the Army. They had a lot to catch up on and Al brought greetings for Bill from their friends in New Zealand. Al and Eunice had a lot to catch up on as they had not seen each other for two and half years. Eunice was finally able to introduce their two-year-old daughter, Donna, to her daddy. Now, at long last, the family was home and together. Bill had not seen Al in over four years and they had both missed those bed time chats. Al had caught up on the battles that Bill had been in and he was relieved to hear that his little brother seemed to be handling everything so well. He was also glad to meet Edna and see that Bill was so happy.

During 1946, Bill and Edna both worked hard at their jobs and saved money for the future. They did not have focused plans for marriage yet, but they had been discussing their future and they both knew they wanted to be together. Bill was becoming a part of her family and she was becoming part of the Bennett family. Bill was able to travel out to Oregon, Illinois, with Edna, to visit with her aunt and uncle on several occasions. Bill met Edna's childhood friends and the pair began to socialize with Edna's best friend Bev Parker and her husband Gerry. While some guys were hesitant about getting married, it was what Bill had wanted for his life. He just wanted to make sure that Edna was the one, and at some point, in 1946, he was sure; so was she. Edna discussed Bill with her parents and they agreed that they thought the world of Bill Bennett. Every man that Henry Ulferts mentioned Bill's name to, had the same answer, "He's quite a guy!" Bill and Al became just as involved with church as they had been before the war and they had reputations of being genuine Christian men. The Bennett and Ulferts families seemed well suited for each other as well. Jessie sent a special lunch invitation to little Frannie, just to let her know she was special. Bill treated Frannie like she was his own little sister and she came to love him like a big brother.

In April of 1947, just after Bill's 28th birthday, he bought a diamond ring and asked Edna if she would marry him. She said yes. When Bill brought Edna home that night and drove away, she waved good bye quite reservedly. After the door closed, she began to scream with excitement and her sisters thought she was being attacked. She hugged her parents and showed all of them the ring. Edna then headed upstairs to Frannie's room, as she had somehow remained asleep. Frannie sat up in bed as Edna showed her the engagement ring. From what Frannie understood about the engagement, it was a pretty good deal. She would be gaining a big brother.

Bill and Edna decided not to wait to marry and had a very small private service followed by a reception at the church. They were married by Reverend Paul G. Dibble at the church parsonage on Marion Avenue in front of a small group of family. Gerry and Bev Parker attended Bill and Edna as best man and maid of honor and then drove them to Chicago for their honeymoon. The reception followed on Saturday at the hall in the church basement. The reception at Fourth Street was filled with well-wishers per the usual Bennett celebrations, and Mr. and Mrs. William Wesley Bennett began their new lives together as man and wife. Gerry and Bev were unable to attend the reception as Bev gave birth to their first child, a girl, named Judy, on that very day. Bill was exuberant about being married and he would never have imagined that he could be so in love. He considered God to be an active partner in a marriage between a man and woman and he considered that he had made his vows not only to Edna, but also to the Lord. Edna viewed marriage in the same light.

Since Bill was the only one living with his parents now, they invited him and Edna to live there until they could put a down payment on a house. Bill and Edna worked and saved their money for their future. Living at 454 Simms Street was easy for them as Steve and Jessie loved having them there. Bill and Edna, in turn, were able to help Steve and Jessie with just about everything that would come up. Life was so enjoyable for Bill during this time as he finally had a mate. They had some wonderful times with Al and Eunice, Jean and Linc, and Marian and Perry. Al and Eunice now had two children, Donna and "Bert." Jean and Linc had two with Ginny and Billy, and Marian and Perry had their first child, a son named Tosh.

Bill continued to love playing with his nieces and nephews and looked forward to the day when he and Edna would have children of their own. When Bill and Edna's first daughter, Sarah May Bennett, was born, the entire family was thrilled. Bill could not believe he was holding his own little daughter and he was truly filled with joy. Between work, church, family and taking care of Sarah, life was busy, but life was good. Bill's life seemed complete to him as he and Edna looked to the future together. There was not much time to take it all in, as Edna was quickly expecting their second child.

Edna May and William Wesley Bennett on their Wedding Day, May 14th, 1947.
(Bennett Family Photo)

Bill and his bride cutting their cake at Fourth Street Methodist Church on May 17th, 1947.
(Bennett Family Photo)

Bill had been in contact with Bob Reder from the Marine Corps days, who had found a good job with Stephens-Adamson Corporation in Aurora. Reder told Bill about the great benefits the company provided. Bill looked into working there and was offered a job. The hard part would be telling Don Glossop he was leaving after all Don had done for him. Bill talked to Don and explained everything. Don knew better than anyone what the difficulties were in running your own business and balancing that with raising a family. Don told Bill that going to Stephens-Adamson was probably a smart move and he was very gracious about the whole thing. Privately, Don really hated to see Bill go as he had been such a great guy to have around. The two would remain friends for decades to come.

Bill took the job at Stephens-Adamson and started as a receiving clerk, working with incoming materials. Stephens-Adamson manufactured conveyor systems for all sorts of manufacturing. The large plant used every type of metal-working machinery one could think of, so they had a multitude of materials coming in on a daily basis. With Bill's previous experience at All-Steel, air conditioning and sheet metal, along with his engineering and blacksmith experience in the Marine Corps, he made a great hire for the company.

83. Challenges

William Wesley Bennett, Jr. was born 11 months after his big sister Sarah and there would be no doubt that it was time to buy their own house. William Jr. would be called "Wes" for distinction, and both Bill and Edna were thrilled about the birth of their second child.

By the second day of little Wes' life, it became apparent that something was wrong. He was having difficulty taking nourishment, and when he did, he could not keep it down. The doctor immediately ordered testing to be done, as they were not sure as to the cause. It seemed that he had a difficult time eating, a possible sign of a neurological problem, but even when tube-fed, Wes could not keep the nutrition in his stomach. The doctors, perplexed by the problem, told Bill and Edna there was nothing they could do. Wes would not live unless he could hold nourishment within a few days. Bill and Edna held little Wes in the hospital room and prayed fervently for the child. Word went out to Fourth Street Methodist via Jessie and Steve and soon hundreds of Aurorans were praying for Wes.

Bill went home and got down on his knees and took the situation to God. Bill reasoned with the Lord over Wes' life and he recalled all the times He had watched over Bill and kept him alive. Bill acknowledged that the Lord knows all things and He knew exactly what was wrong with Wes. Being the Great Physician, He could surely fix the problem that had the doctors confounded. Bill had seen death, and far too much of it. He told the Lord he would be glad to exchange his own life for his son's if it were acceptable. He knew God was not looking to make any deals, but if it might save Wes, then it would be worth it.

Bill was filled with a sense of trusting God's will, whichever way things went. Bill had learned that trusting in God's will doesn't always mean you get what you want; it means you trust God to work all things for the best, according to His will and acknowledge that He is ultimately in control. The fact that God is in control does not mean humans can't do things contrary to His will. Humans have been granted free will by the Creator, and because of this granted freedom, God works in the overall sense to create good out of bad. Wes had been born with a potentially deadly problem, and Bill was asking for God's help where there was no other possibility.

Bill examined his own life and found areas where he had not been as humble as he might have been, or as committed to following Christ as he could have been. Perhaps there were some areas with his relationship with Edna that might be handled better. In every aspect of his life, Bill made a promise to the Lord that He would be first in all things at all times. Bill did not want to run his own life as he saw fit, he wanted to live each day as God saw fit. Bill had come to the realization that God's Holy Spirit had come to actually dwell within him and that transformation was very real after Tarawa. Now the Lord had brought him to another place where he dealt with giving himself completely over to God as though he were dead. Scriptures that came to mind were Romans, 12-1, "Therefore I urge you brothers, in view of God's mercy, to offer your bodies as living sacrifices, holy and pleasing to God—this is your spiritual act of worship." Matthew 10, 38-39, "and anyone who does not take up his cross and follow me is not worthy of me." John 12: 25-26, "The man who loves his life will lose it, while the man who hates his life in this world will keep it for eternal life. Whoever serves me must follow me; and where I am, my servant will also be. My Father will honor the one who serves me."

Bill's realization was that he had not given all of himself to the Lord and that he needed to render himself as dead to the world and dead to sin in order to truly be alive in Christ. Just as Christ had delivered Himself to the cross and then rose again, so the believer must die to his life of sin and self-centeredness, and come to spiritual life in Christ. As a believer, it was now Bill's "act of worship" to allow God's Holy Spirit to live in his life while rendering his sinful nature as dead. This would allow the Lord to live through Bill and touch the lives of others. Bill had never felt so close to the Lord, and, perhaps, he had never been so close. Coming out of prayer, Bill had a renewed sense of trust for Almighty God and he knew that Wes was in God's hands whether he lived or died.

Over the next two days, Wes began to eat and digest nourishment. Just as there was no understanding of why the problem existed, there was no understanding of why it disappeared. Little Wes was taken home and he strengthened and progressed as a normal, healthy baby boy. Bill and Edna thanked the Lord for allowing Wes to live and they never forgot about it.

It was time for a home of their own and they found and purchased a small bungalow on Aurora's west side at 609 View Street. Within a few months, Edna was once again expecting and they made plans for the arrival of their third child in as many years! Between working a new job, the new house, the new family and the new bills, life took on a hectic pace. At some point, just after buying the new house, Bill talked to some other Marine buddies from around town who had re-enlisted in the Marine Corps Reserve as a way of earning extra money for their bills. All they had to do was report one weekend per month and two weeks a year in the summer and it seemed very unlikely that they would ever get "called up" for active duty. This seemed like the thing to do and Bill re-enlisted on February 12th, 1949. The duty of the Marine Corps reserve was light, tolerable and even enjoyable at times.

Bill was very concerned about Edna's stress level with two babies and all that went with it. He tried to relieve her whenever possible and she knew that he was looking out for her. On December 30th, 1949, Edna gave birth to their third child, Carol Ann Bennett. Hundreds of thousands of servicemen and women were going through the very same thing across America as they began families and started their careers. Just across the river in Aurora, George Andrews, the older brother of fallen Marine Peter Andrews, was one of them. On October 23rd, 1949, George's wife gave birth to their third child; a baby boy who they named Peter G. Andrews, in honor of PFC Peter Andrews, who died defending his fellow Marines on that hill on Saipan. Within the Bennett family, the birth went unnoticed, although this new arrival would one day become very significant to the Bennetts.

Bill and Edna's first home at 609 View Street on Aurora's West side.

(Bennett Family Photo)

By the summer of 1950, Edna was pregnant with their fourth child. On June 25th, the North Korean People's Army crossed the 38th parallel into South Korea. Suddenly, the United States was at war again and the Marine Corps needed experienced Marines. By the end of July, Bill had been called to active duty and ordered once again to report to the Chicago Court House on September 11th, 1950.

Edna was devastated by the news. How was it possible that she would be able to keep the house running with three very small children and another on the way? She also did not see any reason why Bill, having given four years of his life for the country, would need to give any more. Before Bill even reported, Edna began to research and write letters to keep Bill out of active service.

Without a current option, Bill hugged and kissed Edna, Sarah, Wes and baby Carol and reported for active duty. He was immediately shipped to the guardhouse at the Marine/Naval Base at Philadelphia. Assuming guard duty was not a bad assignment, and Bill knew how the Marine Corps operated. While Edna continued her letter writing and kept in close touch with Bill, he carried on as a well disciplined and exemplary Marine.

Edna's letters reached the Commanders of the U.S.M.C.R., as well as congressmen and senators. There were thousands of U.S.M.C. veterans without dependents available and many others who were still in the Corps. Others volunteered to act as instructors. Bill's record was reviewed and his lengthy combat performance considered. By the end of October, 1950, Bill was notified that he would be once again Honorably Discharged from the Marine Corps. On October 27th, 1950, he packed his sea bag for the last time as a U.S. Marine, said goodbye to his new-found buddies, phoned Edna May, grabbed a ride to the airport and headed for Chicago. As the four-engine, DC-6 winged its way closer to home, Edna arranged for her little sister, Frannie, to baby sit the kids. Jean and Linc came by with Billy and Ginny to drive Edna to Midway Airport to retrieve her handsome Marine. The small entourage parked the car and found the arrival gate and waited patiently for Bill and Edna's U.S.M.C. ordeal to end. The plane finally roared to the gate and Bill appeared through the doorway and made a beeline for Edna. Once again, Edna noticed how dashing her Bill was in his dress uniform. Billy and Ginnie had always thought the world of their Uncle Bill and seeing him in his uniform was very impressive.

Arriving back in Aurora, Linc pulled the car up the driveway to let Bill and Edna out by the back door into the kitchen. Bill retrieved the sea bag from the trunk and waved goodbye to Jean and Linc. Bill opened the kitchen door and saw little Wes looking up at him. He set his sea bag on the kitchen floor and bent down to lift Wes up to his chest. Father and son embraced and felt each other's warmth. Bill knew this was where he needed to be at this point in his life, and this would become the first lasting memory that Wes would have of his father. Bill returned to a "workaday" life and being a family man; he said goodbye to the Marine Corps forever. Months later, March 24th, 1951, Kathy Jo Bennett was born and Bill and Edna May had quite a family in that little house on View Street.

84. Terry Allen

An older couple from Fourth Street Methodist had decided to sell their large two-story frame house at 310 S. LaSalle Street and Bill and Edna May bought it. They were given a great deal as it was in need of minor updates. The house came complete with a turn of the century carriage house that faced the alley behind them. This returned Bill and Edna to the east side of town where Bill was happy to send the kids to Bardwell Elementary School. The Bennett family was again set to grow as number five was expected in May. On May 28th, 1952, Terry Allen Bennett was born at Copley Memorial Hospital. Bill was thrilled to have another boy arrive, and of course, Edna was pretty tired. Terry had red hair and Sarah and Wes were old enough to know that they both had a new baby brother. During Terry's second day of life, abnormalities were observed, including a slight fever. As a precaution, several tests were ordered and conducted. Terry was having a difficult time eating, just as Wes had years before, but now the problem was identified. Terry Allen Bennett was diagnosed with infantile poliomyelitis.

Terry's doctors explained to Bill and Edna that there was no cure for infantile polio, although there were things that needed to be done to treat the symptoms. For as much as what was known about the disease, Terry held a 50/50 chance of survival at that time. Of the 50% that lived, a percentage of those would have life-long disabilities from the disease. Terry remained in the hospital after Edna was released. Although Bill and Edna did not want to leave Terry alone at the hospital, they did have four little children at home that needed them as well, so family and friends rallied to help the Bennetts get through. As summer vacation had just begun, Ginny Schell and Frannie Ulferts were available to rotate as baby sitters for Sarah, Wes, Carol and Kathy. Bill would have to leave for work about 6:30 a.m. and Edna would get the kids up and ready for the day. Frannie would come over to the house at 8 a.m. and then Grandma Ulferts would drive Edna to the hospital for the day. Bill would come to the hospital after work and spend a few hours there before he and Edna went home to relieve the sitter. Ginny would rotate with Frannie, and Edna worked it out on a daily basis with Jean Schell and Bessie Ulferts.

The Bennett Home at 310 S. LaSalle Street in Aurora, Illinois.

(Bennett Family Photo)

Once again, people prayed for the Bennett's baby. As the summer months wore on, Bill and Edna were held together by the love and support of their family and friends. Terry was allowed to come home for a few days during that summer and the family managed to get a few photos of Bill and Edna with all five of the Bennett children. By the middle of August, Terry's condition was deteriorating and he had to be moved to Children's Memorial Hospital in Chicago. The same routines applied with much longer driving distances. Edna, without a driver's license, was driven into Chicago every morning by a volunteer and then Bill would drive in directly after work unless something was needed at the house. The Bennett children were moved to Steve and Jessie's house so that Jessie could help Frannie and Ginny full time. Bill and Edna would arrive from Chicago after dinner and have some time to play with the kids, get them ready for bed and pray with them. These prayers always asked God to make little Terry better. Bill and Edna would head home to get some sleep and start the whole schedule over again in the morning. Many of these nights, Edna would say good bye to Bill and sleep at Jessie and Steve's house.

During the first week of September, paralysis began to set in and Terry had very little time left. Bill and Edna stayed with Terry around the clock.

On September 6th, 1952, Terry Allen Bennett breathed his last breath as Bill and Edna held him close. This earthly battle had been lost, but from previous lessons learned, Bill and Edna would trust God and they prayed and thanked the Lord for the time they had with their son. Phone calls were made and Bill and Edna headed home to tell their children. When they arrived at 454 Simms Street, Jessie had all four little Bennetts out on the front porch and Bill and Edna came up the steps to hug them and tell them that baby Terry had gone to be with Jesus. There were a lot of tears shed on that porch and Bill and Edna consoled each child as well as Jessie and Steve.

Terry's funeral was held at Fourth Street Methodist Church and Bill and Edna planned the service and spoke to those in attendance. It was decided the children would not attend. Bill selected 2nd Samuel 12:22-23, where King David said, "While the child was still alive I fasted and wept. I thought, 'Who knows? The Lord may be gracious to me and let the child live.' But now that he is dead, why should I fast? Can I bring him back again? I will go to him, but he will not return to me." Also, Romans 8:28, "And we know that in all things God works for the good of those who love him, who have been called according to his purpose." Bill also read Matthew 18:14, "For even so, it is not the will of your Father which is in heaven, that one of these little ones should perish." Bill prayed and thanked the Lord for the short time the Bennetts had with baby Terry on this Earth. He acknowledged that they would one day be rejoined with Terry when they too, came into the presence of Christ. Edna rose to the podium to share a poem she had selected by Annie Johnson Flint:

WHAT GOD HATH PROMISED
God hath not promised skies always blue,
Flower-strewn pathways all our lives through;
God hath not promised sun without rain,
Joy without sorrow, peace without pain.
God hath not promised we shall not know
Toil and temptation, trouble and woe;
He hath not told us we shall not bear
Many a burden, many a care.
God hath not promised smooth roads and wide,
Swift, easy travel, needing no guide;
Never a mountain rocky and steep,
Never a river turbid and deep
But God hath promised strength for the day,
Rest for the labor, light for the way,
Grace for the trials, help from above,
Unfailing sympathy, undying love.

Bill and Edna May buried Terry Allen Bennett in the family plot that Steve and Jessie had purchased, located in the Lincoln Memorial Cemetery in Aurora, Illinois. It had been a very difficult time in the lives of their young family, but their faith and their trust in a Loving God had held them together. That night, Bill took the task of getting the four little Bennetts ready for bed and had them tucked in.

The Bennett family in 1951.
(Bennett Family Photo)

Terry Allen Bennett with the entire Bennett family.
(Bennett Family Photo)

There had been a lot of talk the past few days about Baby Terry going to heaven and going to be with Jesus. When Edna came to kiss the kids goodnight, Wes consoled her by saying, "I just want you to know that I am not going anywhere."

85. The Good Life

As the years moved ahead, life was a busy blur of work, school, church, family, birthdays and holidays. For Bill and Edna, with their four children, there were not many "days off" of which to speak. Money was pretty tight in those years and Bill was a master of repairs of all kinds. Edna believed that Bill was so good at repairing things that he could even repair things that should not be repaired. The children eventually all became enrolled at Bardwell School and they even had some of the same teachers that Bill had when he went there almost 30 years earlier. The Bennett kids were now fifth-generation Aurorans on the Phrangle side and fourth-generation Aurorans on the Bennett side.

Aurora was a great place to raise a family during the Eisenhower years and the Bennetts took full advantage of the good things. Bill and Edna were very attentive parents and they marveled at how different each child was. Just as Bill had done with the other children in his earlier life, he made a point to get to know what made each of them tick. At one point, seven-year-old Sarah had enough of her mom and dad's rules and thought the whole setup was unfair. She did not want to live there anymore and decided to pack a bag and head for Grandma Jessie's house. If they could not see things her way, she was going to "run away." Bill told Sarah that he would help her pack and did so. Sarah lugged her little suitcase out the door and headed down the street with dad secretly keeping a close eye on her. Bill followed her in the car, just out of sight, for a few blocks, until she approached a busy street. He then turned the corner, opened the back door and said, "Are you ready to come home yet?" Sarah burst into tears and climbed into the back seat.

One thing that Bill and Edna very nearly perfected during these years was a "united front." If there were any disagreements between the two of them on disciplinary measures, they were good at talking about it privately. The Bennett home was run in an orderly fashion and manners, decency and respect were modeled and expected.

Bill had moved up through several jobs at Stephens-Adamson over the years, moving from Receiving to Expediter to Pattern Custodian to Storekeeper. Occasionally, Bill would find Bob Reder in a place where they could chat for a few minutes and they caught up on their families, work and things around town. Bob Reder had jumped right back into baseball and softball after the war, and was always busy coaching or playing during the warm months. They talked about the "ghosts" of combat, and how strange it was at times to live with people who couldn't possibly understand what those islands had been like. Most of the movies made about the Marines were almost funny compared to reality, and Bill would point out that you can't smell a movie. Bill would run into other Marines around town from time to time.

The Bennett clan in 1953: Steve on left with Bill, Edna, Carol and Wes. Jean holds Kathy Jo; Bill Schell is kneeling. Across the back: Linc, Marian, Perry, Eunice, Al, Bobby, Jessie, Sunny and Bob. Stevie is in front of Bob with Grandma Pfrangle to his right and Sarah in front of Grandma. Standing in front of Marian, is her son Tosh (cowboy shirt) and daughter Bonnie; Al and Eunice's son Burt and daughter Donna. Ginny Schell is at the far right holding baby Craig, son of Marian and Perry. (Bennett Family Photo)

He had some long conversations with Bud Dix, who had been in the thick of horrific combat during the Battle of the Bulge while in the Army. Bud had been wounded twice and awarded the Bronze Star for bravery in combat. Bud and his wife were members of Fourth Street Methodist and members of the young married couples group called the Macabeans. The Macabeans consisted of about 12 couples that regularly gathered for potluck dinners and fellowship at the church. There were usually quite a few playpens in the room when they met. The Macabeans hosted an annual chili supper as a fund raiser for the church, as well as ham-and-bean suppers and an annual rummage sale. All of these couples socialized with each other and Bill and Edna had one or two couples over for dinner every month. Edna loved cooking and was notably good at it. She also loved to have folks over to the house for just about any reason. The children grew used to having the other couple's children over to play.

In 1956, Bill's highly respected high school football coach, Glen Thompson, was hired at Stephens-Adamson. The coach was a clerk in the office and Bill was able to stop by for a chat from time to time. How Bill loved Coach Thompson. The coach had taught Bill some hard lessons about "gutting it out" back in those football days; lessons that helped him through the war, now that he had time to think about it. Thompson had been dealt a hard blow by the school board when they refused to hire him back after he had been drafted in 1942. He had served four years in the Coastal Artillery in the States and then had to find another job when he was turned down by East Aurora's District 131. He later found a job as a teacher and coach at Marmion Military Academy. Thompson was never bitter about the snub as it would have been hard to put the current coach out of a job. Most east-siders thought that it would have made sense to hire Thompson back and allow the current head coach to have the assistant job. It was ultimately ironic that the coach who inspired the "Tomcats" name could not get his job back after serving his country. Thompson always had a high level of respect for Bill, and he knew what Bill had done during the war. Thompson moved up to Expediter with the company and was put in charge of plant safety and the social club. Another old-time player, "Hack" Zilley, worked at Stephens-Adamson as well, and it made for a great talk when all three of them ended up in Thompson's office.

Bill Bennett with his four children, in front of their home at 310 S. Lasalle Street, Easter of 1957.

(Bennett Family Photo)

Bill would check the mail box when he came home from work and sort bills, junk mail and letters. Every once in a blue moon a letter from an old buddy would show up. He received letters and photos from Johnnie Jones, Fred Ellis, Herb Dale and Art Simonson. All four were married and had children of their own and the letters would usually have a photo or two enclosed. Bill and Edna reciprocated and sent letters and photos back. Johnnie was back in Oklahoma City, Fred had his own farm out in Basin, Wyoming, Herb had been back to Ryegate, Montana, and then moved to Seattle and Art Simonson was once again living in Portage, Wisconsin. Bill got to thinking about the old days and especially how he and Fred promised that they would get together. One night he picked up the phone and made a long-distance call to Basin, Wyoming. Fred's wife Donna answered the phone and she was excited to hear Bill's voice as she had heard so much about him. She quickly had Fred on the line and it was great to finally hear his voice after 13 years. Fred said that Art Simonson had been out last summer with his girls on vacation and they stayed for a couple of days and had a great time. He told Bill that he should think about doing the same thing. This planted a thought in Bill's head as he thought about how his Uncle George Phrangle lived out in Meeteetsie, Wyoming, and the Bennetts could visit him on the same trip. Bill had heard from quite a few other families that a trip out west was quite the thing to do with kids.

In the summer of 1959, Bill bought a brown 1958 Ford Country Squire Wagon with "woody" sides and a top carrier and used his upholstery skills to make some cushions for the flat area in the back. He managed to buy an 8mm movie camera to take along as he wanted to make a "documentary" of the trip. He and Edna worked out dates for the trip and coordinated things with Fred and Donna Ellis and old Uncle George. Looking at the map, Bill found that he could pick up Route 20 just west of Elgin, Illinois, and stay on it all the way to Basin, Wyoming. Uncle George and Aunt Phoebe only lived about 35 miles farther in Meeteetsie. The trip was planned and the Bennett kids were excited about getting out on the road and seeing the Wild West. Bill loaded the suitcases and bags onto the top carrier and covered everything with a tarp and rope to keep it dry and bug free. Wes took the front seat between Bill and Edna and was in charge of the maps. The girls had the back seat and the back end with the cushions where naps could be taken.

There were parts of life from the Marine Corps that would always be a part of Bill's life, and getting an early start was one of them. Edna and Bill woke the kids up and helped everyone organize into the car at 0500 hours, where they fell back asleep as Bill drove west to Illinois Route 47 and then north to U.S. Route 20. By the time the sun was heating up the car and the kids were awake and asking questions, the Bennetts crossed the long bridge at Dubuque, Iowa. The vista looking north over the mighty Mississippi and the buildings on the bluffs overlooking the city was a sign of the beautiful scenery to follow. When the westward bound Bennetts passed over the Cedar River at Cedar Falls, Iowa, they crossed, at some point, the actual trail taken by Steven and Betsy Bennett and their six children 105 years earlier. The Bennett pioneers, with their two prairie schooners and oxen, had followed the Cedar River north toward where the modern town of Floyd now exists. The modern Bennetts, with their 8-cylinder wagon with woody sides sped west at 60 miles per hour.

Keeping the trip within budget was a priority and stops for lunch at a general store or a local market would help keep things in line. A loaf of bread and a package of bologna and chips made an inexpensive lunch that could be eaten at a local park. Breakfast, likewise, would often be a gallon of milk, a box of cheerios and a box of donuts. Bill made Sioux City in good time and the family checked into the Sheraton-Warrior Hotel downtown. This was a true "downtown hotel" with doormen, bell hops and eleven stories. The rest of the trip would be spent in motels and cabins along the way. Sioux City, in those years, was almost the end of civilization heading west.

The next day, Bill made a longer haul over to Casper, Wyoming, and Wes admired his dad's ability to drive almost endlessly. Bill and Edna kept the kids attentive and civil by playing games as they drove. Bill had made four small clip-boards with pads of paper attached so each Bennett child could write their observations from the games Bill had picked out. There was the popular "license plate game," where family members call out plates from various states and a score is kept. They also "spotted" various animals and birds to see who could find the most. Bill tried to coordinate bathroom breaks with gas station stops, but there were ultimately more bathroom breaks than he had imagined. The Bennetts were also subjected to the never-ending array of "See the Sights!" billboards, and they managed to decide which places to see and which ones to avoid. In order to keep the kids interest as they drove, Bill made up wild stories that were told from the perspective of a character he made up called "Wild Bill Bennett." "Wild Bill" rode through the Wild West on a donkey, since everybody knew donkeys were far better than horses! The kids laughed for hours as Bill told them about catching bad guys, putting out fires and rounding up cattle. All of Bill's stories had a moral or little lesson hidden inside. Even Edna had to laugh, as she had never known that Bill was capable of hosting his own TV show for children.

Coming into the Bighorn Basin area, Bill was able to see the beauty that Fred had described to him so many times in foxholes, bunkrooms and mess halls. Fred had been born here on the 100-acre farm that he and Donna now owned. Just as Bill had fought to stay alive and return to Aurora to have a family, so had Fred fought to return to Bighorn Country. Bill followed Fred's directions along the river and spotted the farm on his left. As he turned onto the gravel drive, he saw the familiar form of Fred Ellis waving from a spot near one of the buildings as he made his way toward the house. As they drove up the lane, three boys ran from the front door of the house, followed by Donna wearing a bright white summer dress. Bill put the car into park and shut off the engine, threw open the door and he and Fred bear hugged each other as they laughed and told each other how good they looked. Then they turned towards their families and exchanged introductions of wives and children. It was hard to believe the blessings of life that were evident at this moment compared to the hardship and uncertainty their lives had been filled with 15 years earlier. Fred and Donna's oldest son Bruce was about the same age as

Sarah and their twin boys Brent and Brian were about the same age as Carol and Kathy. Fred told the boys to show the Bennett kids around the farm and the adults did the same, but at a much slower pace.

The farm was mainly supported by crops of sugar beets, navy beans, some corn and a small herd of beef cattle. Fred also maintained a sizable chicken house which allowed him to supply eggs locally as well as chicken for the family. Donna worked as a hospital administrator, which helped the farm income greatly. After touring the farm, both families sat down to a pot roast dinner and fresh baked apple pies from Donna's oven. After dinner, Bill walked with Fred out through the pasture to check on a few calves. Fred said that the farm was running along very well and things were a lot better than the old days when he was growing up here. Bill recalled the story Fred had told him while they were on Saipan about the farm. Back in the early days of the Great Depression, Fred had taken a job at the "bean plant," about three miles back up the gravel road toward Basin. The family was in danger of losing the farm and being the only son with three sisters, Fred took the job for 13 cents per day. The only way he had to get to and from the plant was a rickety old bicycle. The long hours at the plant, combined with the ride to and from work and his regular chores at the farm, had worn Fred down. One day on the way to work, Fred hit a pot hole in the gravel road and the front wheel of the bicycle collapsed. Fred threw the bike off the road and just sat down and cried. That junky old bike was the only luxurious part of his life at that time. Now he would just have to walk to work and back.

Corporal Fred Ellis and his wife Donna at their farm in Basin, Wyoming, 1959.

(Ellis Family Photo)

Bill greatly admired Fred for being such a gracious man despite the hardships he had been through. Perhaps he was so gracious because of those hardships. In all the situations they had been in together during the war, Fred had always shown great judgment and dependability. It was impossible to measure it, but these men had probably both saved each other's lives several times over.

The conversation went back in time to training at San Diego and the day they first met. They recalled that they had no idea what they were headed for and hoped the Japanese would just surrender when they saw all the ships arrive. How wrong they had been about that. They recalled the disease of Tulagi, the good times of New Zealand, the hell of Tarawa, the cold of Hawaii, more hell on Saipan, Tinian and then the boredom of Camp Lejeune. It was all an adventure to say the least. Then Bill thought of Bob Swigert and Truitt Anderson and Tarawa. Bill and Fred had both been spared from death at that instant; Bill by the shell hole and Fred from the palm trunk. They found this was something that each of them thought about almost daily. There was no doubt in either of their minds that God had spared them, but they both wondered why. They looked toward the farmyard at the seven children running around exploring and playing together and noted that Bob and Truitt never had the chance to see what they were seeing. At one point, Bill asked Fred about the dreams. Fred knew all too well what Bill was talking about. It would have been impossible to live through what they had without having such issues and memories. These were mostly things they didn't want anyone else to know about. Talking to each other was safe because they both understood.

They watched Donna and Edna walk along chatting and they both agreed that their wives were the best things that ever happened to either of them. Fred had known Donna during the war, but he had no idea he would marry her. The Ellis and Bennett kids seemed to hit it off just fine as Bruce gave the city slickers inside information on farm life. Fred saddled up their lone old mare and the Bennetts took turns riding around the farm at a very slow pace. It all went fine with the exception of Kathy falling off and having the wind knocked out of her. Sarah ran for help thinking Kathy might be seriously injured, but Bill and Fred checked her out and she was soon running with the herd. Despite Fred's warnings to the boys to not disturb the hens, Wes inadvertently ran through the chicken house during a game of tag and chickens and feathers flew everywhere. It took quite some time for the chickens to begin to settle down and even then, they remained on high alert for Wes. The following morning the results of the "hen-raising" were realized when there were no eggs laid. Knowing that the eggs were part of Fred's income. Bill opened his wallet and wanted to cover the cost of the loss. Fred, of course, would have none of that as he gently pushed the money back toward Bill and said, "Now Bill, boys will be boys."

After a two day visit at the Ellis farm, the families bid each other farewell and the Bennett wagon headed north along Route 20 until it curved west onto Highway 14 towards Meeteetsie. Bill pulled the Country Squire into the drive at George and Phoebe Phrangle's place, where they would get a home town taste of life in the west. Uncle George had moved to Meeteetsie over 40 years earlier and had spent his career working at the King Ranch. He knew real cowboys and lots of them. Uncle George decided that Wes needed a proper cowboy hat and took him to a local shop. It was a swell hat and Wes fit right into the Meeteetsie landscape. George wanted to buy Wes a pair of cowboy boots, but Bill decided that they were too expensive and would not approve. Wes and George tried Bill's position on the boots several times to no avail.

Uncle George decided he would introduce Wes to some real cowboys and quench his own thirst at the same time. He asked Wes to come with him in the car, without telling anyone else, and they drove into town to the saloon. This was an old Wild West saloon with swinging doors, a long bar with a mirror behind it and a piano. The bar was lined with cowboys drinking beer and shots and a big, burly cowboy lifted Wes by the armpits and set him on a bar stool. The bartender snapped the cap off a little bottle of Coke and set it in front of Wes while Uncle George had something a bit stronger. Wes sat and listened to the old cowhands exchanging stories for about an hour and he thought he had somehow ended up in "cowboy heaven."

George had lots of information about their trip over to Yellowstone, and he recommended they stop by the Buffalo Bill Museum in Cody. Between Meeteetsie and Cody, one of Uncle George's old cowboy pals ran a horseback riding stable and set Bill up with the directions. Bill agreed with Uncle George that riding horse-back was an essential part of the quintessential "wild west" road trip. The riding operation was quite nice as they had well-maintained horses and tack in a large enclosed area where the customers could ride freely. Each one of the kids carefully selected their horse and managed an enjoyable ride around the dusty pasture. This was about as close to being a real cowboy or cowgirl as a kid from Aurora could get. After the kids had ridden around for a while, Bill decided to take a ride for himself. He handed the movie camera to Edna with a few reminders on how to operate it and found a horse he liked. Bill took the reins from the hitching post and checked the girth and bridle before throwing one of the leads over the horse's head. Edna noticed that he seemed to know what he was doing. He then threw a leg over the saddle and yanked the horse's head around to head out into the pasture. He took the white mare through a few trial trots to see how she handled, then turned her around and dug his heels into her ribs. The mare bolted across the pasture as Bill exhibited perfect control with an experienced horseman's form. Wes and the girls were amazed at how well their dad could handle that horse. When they commented on the display of horsemanship, Bill asked them what they expected from "Wild Bill Bennett?" It was just too bad that the stable didn't have a donkey!

The family enjoyed the Buffalo Bill Museum as no one could have imagined how many things old "Wild Bill" had collected during the years of putting on his famous show. Quietly, "Wild Bill Bennett" gathered ideas for future adventure stories while behind the wheel. Yellowstone was a marvel of natural beauty, wildlife and geothermal activity. The kids were spotting wildlife almost nonstop and it was hard to referee who had seen what first. They saw bear, buffalo, elk, deer, bighorn sheep, cranes, hawks and the very friendly ground squirrels. The Bennett kids were so excited to see all of this natural wonder, including the bubbling hot springs and the timely blasts of Old Faithful. Bill and Edna not only enjoyed seeing it all, but they greatly enjoyed watching the kids experience it. Exploring Yellowstone was an experience that none of them would ever forget and it would be talked about for years to come. Bill took in some of the highlights with his movie camera so they could look back on the trip and share some of the fun with family back home.

The Bennetts spent several nights around Yellowstone and they had never seen so many stars at night. Leaving Yellowstone, Bill headed back east on Highway 14 toward Basin.

No trip to the west would be complete without a visit to Mt. Rushmore and the kids wondered how anyone decided to carve that mountain so far out in the middle of nowhere. A trip through the tightly-wound roads of the Badlands pushed carsickness to the limits and it was becoming apparent that the girls' close proximity to each other in the back seat had about run its course. As with all long road trips, the Bennetts became as eager to get back home as they once were to leave. The countryside slowly began to turn green again as they neared Minnesota and came back into corn country. After life on the road for two weeks, there was no place like home and probably no one who appreciated it more than Edna. Bill and Edna had pulled off the epic wild-west vacation and the family had made memories for a lifetime. There would be more trips like it in the coming years and Wild Bill Bennett would lead the way.

Edna with "Wild Bill Bennett" in front of their home during June of 1961.

(Bennett Family Photo)

Bill's nephew, Billy Schell, had grown up on the various farms with Jean and Linc and his older sister, Ginny. He had become not only a fine young man, but an All-State football player as well. Bill Schell had gone off to college at Illinois Wesleyan University in Bloomington, Illinois, but after the fall semester of his sophomore year, his college money had run out and he had to come back to the family farm in Yorkville, Illinois. He landed a job at the Seaboard Seed Company in nearby Bristol. The pay was low and the work was hard as he loaded and unloaded seed bags through a brutal Illinois winter. Bill was deeply saddened to see his nephew have to leave college and wanted to see him get to finish school with his football team. Bill came up with an idea for a business, and undoubtedly inspired by his old boss, Don Glossop, made his nephew Bill Schell an offer. Bill would buy a trailer-mounted stump grinder and an old Ford pick-up truck to tow it. Bill would then endeavor to line up work for the business and let Bill Schell do most of the grinding and assist as needed. By April of 1962, the business was a reality as the two Bills operated under the name Bennett Family Stump Grinding with assistance from Wes.

Bill and Edna Bennett with their children during 1962.

(Bennett Family Photo)

    Bill's method for finding business was nothing short of genius. He kept in touch with the City of Aurora Street Department as they worked their way through the city cutting trees along the streets. Every time a tree was removed, a homeowner had an unsightly stump in the front yard. Bill would usually find an older couple in the middle of the block and offer them a half price discount of 50 dollars with the agreement that they not tell their neighbors how much they were charged. The regular price of 100 dollars would be charged to the others on that block. If Bill found a widow in the middle of that block, she would get her stump removed for 25 dollars and if she was a war widow, the stump was ground for free, but the agreement to not disclose their discount was always part of the deal. Bill would get the work lined up and Bill Schell and Wes could grind away while Bill was at work at Stephens-Adamson. Wes was no stranger to his dad's work ethic and he enjoyed the hard work offered by the stump grinding. He also noticed the admiration and respect that Bill Schell had for his Uncle Bill, and vice-versa. Bill Schell could see that Wes had a desire to please his dad and win his approval; the standards were set incredibly high, which caused Wes some frustration at times. One advantage of the work arrangement was that Wes had no shortage of role models.

    After a few months of towing and backing the grinder with the old Ford pick-up, Bill decided that it would better to have a shorter truck. The problem was there were no shorter trucks available. The old Ford went into the Stephens-Adamson machine shop one weekend where some of Bill's buddies from work dismantled it, shortened it by three feet and rebuilt it ready for service. This may well have been the first "short bed" Ford pick-up truck known to mankind, but the world didn't notice. The two Bills were able to drive the shorter truck through and around a wider variety of obstacles. Business was good, and Bill Schell was soon able to return to college and play football again. He could not have been more grateful to his Uncle Bill. After another year in college, he was drafted into the U.S. Army and ended up going to Vietnam. His Uncle Bill ran him through "the ropes" of military survival, including never volunteering for anything. Bill Schell had a successful tour in the service and returned to Illinois Wesleyan College in the fall of 1967.

As the years accumulated, Bill and Edna soon had a house full of teenagers and busy schedules that go with the territory. Edna went to work for Ginsberg's Clothing Store in downtown Aurora and all four Bennett kids eventually had a job there, once Wes began as the elevator attendant. Wes had taken to football and baseball and Bill tried to make sure he passed along all he knew about both. Uncle Perry McIntosh was the head coach at Dundee High School and he was also an inspiration to Wes.

In the late spring of 1965, Bill received a letter from Les Mitchell from New Zealand. Les was starting off on a worldwide trip for his company and would be through Chicago during August. Bill and Les worked things out so that Les could take a few days off over a weekend and visit both Bill and Al in Aurora. The red carpet was rolled out at the Bennett house as Les arrived and was treated as royalty. Les was able to finally meet Jessie and Steve, who thanked him endlessly for the kind treatment the Mitchells had provided for both of their boys during the war. Bill and Al took Les to Soldier Field in Chicago for an All-Star football game and then showed him all around the "Windy City." Sarah picked out a blouse at Ginsberg's for Les and Lorna's daughter Allie, and Les packed it away in his bag to take home. Word got out about the New Zealander's visit and a reporter and photographer from the Aurora *Beacon News* stopped by for the story. The photo appeared in the newspaper showing all three war veterans grasping hands with enormous smiles.

Al Bennett, Les Mitchell and Bill Bennett shake hands in Aurora, Illinois, during Les' visit in 1965.

(Aurora Beacon News Photo)

Bill and Edna knew that the world was changing rapidly during the 1960s, and not for the better. They were not only concerned about their own children, but also for their friends. Wanting to keep the teenagers focused on their purity, integrity and spiritual course in life, the Bennetts began a weekly Bible study at their house on LaSalle Street. Bill fashioned the structure after the youth meetings from the past and Bill and Edna's hospitality and friendliness drew many young people to the house. At several times during these years, Bill and Edna even brought in a young woman or young man that was having a hard time at home and allowed them to live with them until things worked out. Bill and Edna had several talks about their ability to lead these Bible studies and they agreed that they sometimes felt inadequate for the task. Considering work, school, church, parenting, social activities, sporting events, family gatherings and their personal relationships, Bill and Edna had the reputation of being a couple that worked together on everything. Within the privacy of their own home, the children saw how loving Bill was toward Edna and the respect that Edna had in return for Bill. It was not that they automatically agreed on everything or that Edna did not have a say; in fact, the kids noticed at times that Edna seemed to have the ability to send Bill a message with nothing more than a look. When Edna decided that she should get her driver's license at long last, Bill set out to teach her, and in much the same manner that he had taught the four kids. The Marine Corps and football had taught Bill one basic instruction style that worked for Marines, athletes and even his kids, who knew how to accept Bill's programs. But, it quickly became evident to Bill that this was not going to work with Edna. He decided that if he wanted Edna to succeed and maintain the same address as his, he was going to need help. He arranged for one of his friends from work to teach her to drive.

    With all of the Bennett kids attending East High, school activities became a huge part of family life. District 131 had built a large modern high school building on Fifth Avenue, right next to the former Athletic Field, renamed in honor of Roy E. Davis in 1953. The East Aurora Tomcats no longer had to make the long walk from the old school over to the field on game nights. Once Wes was old enough to play at Davis Field, Bill was bursting with pride. With the exception of the clothes and the cheers, the night games under the lights brought back fierce memories. Grandpa Steve still came around for the East-West games during those years, but he openly rooted for West even though his grandson was wearing red and black. Wes enjoyed the social connections of being a high school athlete and carried a desire to deserve the approval of his parents. It seemed as though just about everyone he associated with either knew Bill Bennett or knew of him. Admittedly, Wes had been born with huge shoes to fill. Wes was a popular guy at school and there were plenty of pitfalls available should he stray from the straight and narrow. His respect for his parents, and partially, the fear of shaming his dad, helped to keep his head on straight.

    In 1966, Sarah headed off to school at Southwest Missouri State College in Springfield, Missouri. Bill began to make regular trips down and back to the college and soon had other students at the college coming and going in the Bennett station wagon. Bill was working in Shipping and Receiving at Stephens-Adamson, and he soon located several suppliers along the route and arranged to pick up reasonably-sized materials on his way back to Aurora after dropping Sarah and her college mates off at school. It seemed that no matter what Bill did he found a way to streamline and network to everyone's benefit. Sarah didn't seem to mind when Bill dropped students off, then followed directions to a bearing plant or machine shop. Bill was always upbeat and if anyone needed to hear a story along the way, he would have one ready.

Early in the fall of 1967, one of Wes' school buddies, Pete Andrews, walked beneath the stands at Davis Field with a group of friends. The boys stopped to briefly talk to some girls, and Pete noticed a good looking, dark-haired sophomore among them. After the girls walked away, Pete asked his buddy about the dark-haired girl, and was surprised to find out that she was Kathy Jo Bennett, Wes' little sister.

After talking to Kathy at school a few times, Pete decided to ask Wes if he thought his sister might "go out" with him. Wes told Pete he had no idea and he should ask Kathy directly. Pete decided to phone Kathy and stop by the house for a visit. Kathy asked Pete into the kitchen and introduced him to Edna, who Pete thought seemed very nice. A few minutes later, Bill came into the kitchen and after looking Bill in the eye and getting the classic Bennett handshake, (with a little extra pressure for young suitors) he briefly wondered if this had been a good idea. As it turned out, Pete and Kathy ended up spending a lot of time together and Pete grew to greatly admire both Bill and Edna. The closeness of the Bennett family and the open affection between Bill and Edna was encouraging to young Pete and their Christian example began to have a life-long effect on him. Pete recognized the "see the job, do the job" mentality which Bill lived by, and the Marine Corps showed through on just about everything Bill did. Pete knew a little about the Marine Corps since his uncle, PFC Peter Nicholas Andrews, had been killed in action on Saipan. Every Memorial Day was a solemn event at the Andrews house as his Uncle Pete's memorial flag was hung on the front of the house.

During this time, Bill had undertaken an engine overhaul on the old Pontiac station wagon. One evening after dinner, Bill announced to Pete that he was finally ready to fire up the engine and asked Pete to assist out in the barn. As Bill tightened down the air cleaner and attached the vacuum hoses, Pete noticed a pile of engine parts lying on the work bench. Bill looked up from under the hood, looked at the pile of parts and said, "Don't worry about those! We won't need any of that stuff!" The engine impressively roared to life and the car went back into service. When Wes had commented about how nice it would be to have a car that had some "cool" to it, perhaps a "muscle car," their Buick Skylark mysteriously appeared with a new rear "spoiler" that had been made by someone with some sheet metal experience. Pete soon found himself attending Bill and Edna's Bible studies at their house and he learned that Bill and Edna were the genuine article; they practiced what they preached.

454 Simms Street remained a center for the Bennett family throughout these years as the teenagers routinely stopped by to see Grandma Jessie and Grandpa Steve before dances and the family regularly gathered for dinner. The Bennett kids knew every inch of that house just as Bill had when he was growing up. Bill and Wes had played ball in the back yard many times over the

years, which invoked rich memories for Bill of "the gang" from days gone by. As it sometimes happens with memories, Bill could clearly recall the faces of George Troll, Bob Stoner, Bob Nix, Bud Dix and the others. Those were wonderful years for all of them, long before the winds of war arrived to change life forever.

With Vietnam exploding into a full out war, Wes became "draft age" and decided to enlist before being drafted. Since his dad and his Uncle Perry had both been Marines, he naturally thought that he would join the Marine Corps as well. Nothing doing! Bill and Perry both put the hammer down on the idea. Bill knew all too well that the Marines would be the sledgehammer in any type of offensive and he had seen more than his share of dead Marines. He did not want Wes to become one of them. Wes adjusted his direction and joined the Air Force. Bill made it very clear to Wes that he should never volunteer for anything. Bill told Wes to respect officers but to not necessarily trust them. As hard as it was to see their son go into the Air Force, Bill and Edna both felt a lot better knowing that he was not headed for the jungles as a Marine. Wes soon found that being raised by his father had prepared him for the military; in fact, the Air Force was a piece of cake in many ways.

Sarah had been dating a young man named Dick Brauer who had worked at Stephens-Adamson and then Northern Illinois Gas. Sarah and Dick were married on July 25th, 1969. With Sarah moving out of the house and Wes away in the service, a quieter life appeared at 310 S. Lasalle Street as Bill and Edna now had only Carol and Kathy at home. The two younger girls graduated high school and began to work full time. Kathy continued to date Pete Andrews and Carol dated a young man named Nolan Foreman, who she had known for years at Fourth Street Methodist. When Kathy hatched a plan to drive to Colorado with one of her girlfriends, Bill made sure she had a course in road safety. The thought of one of his girls out on the open road without him was a bit hard to handle. The correct procedure for changing a tire was demonstrated in the driveway and then Kathy was drilled to repeat the procedure while her dad watched closely to make sure her ability would be sufficient. Kathy ended up making the trip without a flat tire, but she drove with the confidence that she could handle things should there be a problem.

Bill had to say goodbye to his beloved mother, Jessie Jean Bennett, after several years of failing health, on April 23rd, 1970. Bill had been blessed to live 51 years with a wonderful mother. He knew he would not have become the man that he was, were it not for her influence. The family grieved the loss of a woman who they all agreed was one of the most Godly, loving people they had ever known. For Bill, it was a sobering event that was made tolerable with the knowledge that Jessie was now with the Lord, and Bill knew he would certainly see her again one day. Jessie had lived 87 years. Bill had maintained a very close relationship with Al, Jean and Marian, and had a much-improved relationship with his oldest brother Bob, who was still out in California. The entire Bennett family gathered to lay Jessie to rest in the Lincoln Memorial Cemetery, as they recalled the immeasurable love and sacrifice that this Godly woman had poured into each of their lives. Bill knew that his mother's prayers had played a huge role in his life. She had started

Bill's spiritual journey by introducing him to Christ at an early age and then demonstrated a Christlike life over her remaining years.

Wes married his girlfriend Linda while he was based at Rantoul, Illinois, and half the Bennett kids now had their own families. Bill and Edna continued their Bible study in their home, and they enrolled in a Moody Bible Institute night study program in Elgin, Illinois. They began attending classes two nights per week and studied the Bible as well as numerous related Christian subjects. Their organization of the Bible study, as well as classes at church, became very effective, and others relied on them for advice and insight into Biblical issues.

Kathy married Pete at Fourth Street Methodist on March 31st, 1973 and Carol married Nolan on August 31st, 1974, at the same church. For Bill and Edna, this ended a 27-year span of raising their family. The Bennett nest was now officially empty, and they enjoyed days where their activity was primarily based on what the two of them would like to do. To offset the quieter days around the house, birthdays and holidays became even busier affairs as the family now had new members. Bill enjoyed his new relationships with Dick, Pete and Nolan and the extended family remained very close. Wes had decided to make a career out of the Air Force and was only able to visit back in Aurora on occasion.

86. Full Circle

Sunday, May 25th, 1975. Carol and Nolan made a decision to become members of Claim Street Baptist Church, and Bill and Edna made an effort to occasionally attend church with them. Bill recognized the energy at Claim Street and enjoyed the sermons delivered by their Pastor Adamson. On this particular Sunday, Bill and Edna met Carol and Nolan in the parking lot on the west side of the building and they were greeted by a dozen or more people on the way to their seats, about halfway up on the right side of the sanctuary. Dorothy Scroggins played an ascending prelude on the huge organ that rose to fill the auditorium with heavenly chords. It was a beautiful morning and the fresh air flowed through the open windows on either side of the church. The sound of the organ and the 500 attendees greeting each other created the anticipation that something big was about to take place. The organ crescendo came to an abrupt end that left only human voices audible for a few seconds before Pastor Adamson welcomed the congregation and led them in prayer. He then led the congregation in the singing of two hymns and voices filled the room with energy. One of the deacons arrived at the pulpit and read through the weekly announcements and prayer requests.

Pastor Adamson eventually came back to the pulpit and announced that in observance of Memorial Day, the church wished to recognize those in attendance that had served our country in the various branches of the service. He asked that those who were serving, or had served, would stand when their respective branch was called so they could be recognized. He called out, "Army!" and quite a few veterans stood up. "Navy!" and about a half dozen stood. "Air Force!" and three or four stood. When he called out, "Marines!" Bill quickly rose to his feet and let out a very audible bellow of "YO!" which rang out across the auditorium. Heads turned toward the lone figure of the man who had sprung to his feet. There was a slight burble of laughter that washed across the room, a reflex from the exuberance Bill had just shown for the Marine Corps. For the rest of the congregation, the recognition was a regular formality to honor servicemen and women. For Bill, it was the memory of disease, hardship, death and destruction. In Bill's soul, he lived on to represent Lieutenant (SG) Robert F. Stoner, PFC Truitt Anderson, Corporal Bob Swigert, PFC Gene Seng, PFC Charles Montague, PFC Peter Andrews, Sergeant Channing Miller and other fine Marines that had died for the country in which he now enjoyed freedom and family. The stern look on Bill's face and the seriousness of his soul did not go unnoticed. Across the room on the left-hand side of the church, a 12-year-old boy who had come to church that morning, alone, locked his eyes on the former Marine. The sight of the stern look on Bill's face and the honor with which Bill still represented the Marine Corps would leave a lasting impression.

Bill and Edna were very busy that year planning a trip to the Holy Land which ended up being one of the finest times of their lives. Not only did they have the chance to visit the ancient sites that Jesus himself frequented, but they were also able to experience it together as they looked to the future. Bill felt that no man had ever been more blessed by a wife than he had been and Edna loved and respected Bill immensely. After years of raising their family and seeing each Bennett child marry, this trip made a perfect reset. Once the pair returned home and shared the details of their adventure and the photos showing the highlights, the Bennett family realized they had probably never seen Bill and Edna so entirely enthusiastic about their faith, their family and their future.

Bill and Edna considered how they might serve the Lord in the coming years. They committed themselves to reaching out to people that had yet to understand who Jesus was and why His death on the cross was vitally important to them.

Sadly, 1976 became a year of loss as Samuel D. Stoner passed away in April at the age of 86. Bill and Edna took the elderly Steve Bennett to the funeral and consoled Margaret, Dexter and Harley. Bill was reminded of how much he loved to be around Dexter and Harley and they could have talked for hours that day. Four months later the visit was repeated as Margaret Fraser Stoner passed away in August at the age of 83. Two months later, Dexter and Harley returned the visit as the Bennett family lost their patriarch when Stephen Robert Bennett passed away at the age of 96. Steve had been a great father to his children and he had been one of the best friends that Bill would ever know. Bill had realized throughout his life what an enormous blessing he had been given in his parents. Bill had always carried a burden to honor his parents and he hoped he had been able to do that. When Steve Bennett died, the family not only lost a father, grandfather, great grandfather and uncle, the entire city of Aurora lost a pillar of the community. Steve was buried in Lincoln Memorial Cemetery next to his beloved Jessie Jean Bennett. Bill, Al, Jean, Marian and Bob laid to rest the man who had been the leader of the Bennett clan as long as they could remember; the young man who had come to Aurora as a teenager from the family home out on the prairie of Iowa.

The stark reality of this being the end of an era came next as Bill and Edna worked with Al and Eunice, Jean and Linc and Marian and Perry to clear out the house at 454 Simms Street and then put the old homestead up for sale. This structure held so many memories for the family that letting it go would be hard for all of them. Bill and Edna sorted through the papers, photos and newspaper clippings that told the stories of the Bennetts, whose lives had centered around this home for almost 50 years. Bill boxed up a lot of his keepsakes from his school years and the war years and moved the items to their attic on LaSalle Street. The house was cleaned and eventually sold. As Bill and Edna left the house for the last time, Bill paused to recall a lifetime of memories that would always be alive for him within that house. As he backed out of the front door for the last time, he noticed the colors in the stained-glass window above the stair landing and recalled countless times when coming in that door meant the relief of home, the love of his parents and the laughter of his family and his friends. He pulled the door shut on a big part of his life, walked down the front steps to the sidewalk where little Bobby used to roller skate, turned to look at the front porch, and then he and his Eddie drove away.

In September of 1982, the children of Steve and Jessie Bennett posed for this photo with their spouses. From left to right are Marian "Pete" and Perry McIntosh, Linc and Jean Schell, Eunice and Al Bennett, Edna and Bill Bennett with Sunny and Bob Bennett seated in front. (Bennett Family Photo)

Over the next seven years, Bill and Edna attended Claim Street Baptist more and more frequently until they shared services almost evenly with Fourth Street Methodist. During this time, the Methodist Church had been going through a tumultuous time of "liberalization," which had caused division within the church on several vital issues. Bill and Edna felt very strongly that the church was in danger of making the huge mistake of toning down the Gospel of Christ in order to make the church more attractive to new members. The cultural revolution that had ravaged America during the '60s and '70s was now making an impact on many churches. Christianity, according to Bill and Edna, was far more than the Methodist Church or any other human organization; it was a relationship with the Living Christ through the miracle of the regeneration of His Holy Spirit. They believed that all humans are born into an inherited state of sinfulness and separation from God, who alone is Holy.

God, our Creator, came to Earth in the body of Jesus of Nazareth and made the necessary sacrifice, a price that only He could pay, on the cross at Calvary, outside of Jerusalem. The shedding of His sinless blood opened the way for those born into sin to receive full forgiveness for their sin and receive the presence of God's Holy Spirit, as it combined with the spirit of man into a new creation. This is the act of "the regeneration of the Holy Spirit" and what Jesus himself described to Nicodemus as being "born again" in the third chapter of the Gospel of John. From Bill's perspective, being forgiven and having a personal relationship with the risen Christ did not give him superiority over those who did not. In fact, Bill recognized the great sacrifice and enormous grace the Lord had extended to him and it made Bill realize he needed to do the same for others, and even be willing to die for those still "lost" in their sin. If, in fact, God's Holy Spirit had actually come to live in a believer, then there would be evidence in that person's life of God's presence. The Bible refers to this spiritual evidence in a believer's life as "fruit of the Spirit," which is described as, "Love, joy, peace, patience, kindness, goodness, faithfulness, gentleness, and self-control" in Galatians 5:22-23.

In May of 1983, Bill had accumulated 35 years of service at Stephens-Adamson and had just turned 64; he decided that it was time to retire. Edna and the family threw a retirement party at Sarah and Dick's house which was now filled with grandchildren and excitement that reminded Bill and Edna of the old days when their children were young. Edna retired from her job at Lyon Metal, and after 36 years of marriage, they could finally do whatever they wanted. Bill and Edna had rented a trailer for some of their road trips years ago and Bill now had some ideas about buying their own trailer to see the country. After researching trailers in depth, they decided to buy a Winnebago that would tow behind their car. Some of their friends from the Macabeans at Fourth Street Methodist owned trailers and they introduced Bill and Edna to the trailer club that met in nearby Amboy, Illinois. The trailer club not only camped together locally, but they also planned annual trips cross country and traveled in a caravan to and from these destinations. Bill took to the technical aspects of trailering and had his systems and procedures down pat. Edna enjoyed putting the finishing touches on the trailer that would make it home away from home. The best thing about Bill and Edna's retirement was that they had each other. After all of their years together, the pair had remained remarkably affectionate. Each of their children knew that their father and mother held a deep love and respect for each other.

As plans were being made for the first winter road trip with the trailer, Bill received a letter from his Marine buddy Johnnie C. Jones from Oklahoma City. He and his wife Chris had retired a few years earlier and had been spending the winters in Arizona in their own trailer. Bill made a phone call to Oklahoma City and there was a familiar voice that he had not heard for a very long time. Since Bill and Edna were planning a trip with the trailer club down to Arizona, they would stop by the trailer park where Johnnie and Chris were based and spend a few days together.

In early January, 1984, Bill and Edna headed west toward Denver and then south toward Albuquerque, New Mexico. They enjoyed hours upon hours of talk time as they discussed their family and recalled both fun and difficult times in their lives. Moving west on I-40 in New Mexico, Bill recalled the terrain exactly 42 years earlier as he sat on the train headed to San Diego. The Marine recruits were all so innocent and naïve at that time and they had no idea of the horrors that awaited them out in the Pacific. Bill picked up I-17 south toward Phoenix and then Highway 101 around the east side of the city and out to Apache Junction. As Bill drove north on North Signal Butte Road, he mentioned to Edna the irony of today's date of January 9th. It was on this day 42 years earlier that the train had arrived in San Diego at the Marine Recruit Depot.

Slowing to read the sign, Bill made the right-hand turn into the Trails West Mobile Home Park and pulled up in front of the office. He paid for four nights and was directed to the spot that Johnnie and Chris had reserved for them next to their trailer at the back of the park. Bill's heart raced with excitement and a bit of nervousness as he pulled up to the spot and got out of the car. As he went around to open the door for Edna, Johnnie and Chris hurried out to meet them. Johnnie and Bill made a bee line for each other and the extended hands blended into a strong bear hug. The familiarity of a friend that Bill had not seen in 38 years was astounding. With the exception of the gray temples and a few wrinkles, it seemed that time had stood still. They quickly introduced Edna and Chris to each other and then Chris invited Edna inside to freshen up while Johnnie helped Bill back the rig into place and get the Winnebago braced. Chris had plans for dinner at their trailer that evening and the four retirees spent hours discussing their lives and raising their families.

Edna and Chris realized that Bill and Johnnie were going to need some time alone to reminisce and they graciously planned their time accordingly. Chris drove Edna to town to do some shopping a few times while the guys sat in the warm Arizona sun to reminisce. At first, they talked about meeting when they came into Company A, back in 1942, and the life they led in San Diego. When Bill had gone ashore at Tulagi, Johnnie had remained aboard ship and avoided being stranded with Bill and the others. Johnnie knew how fortunate he had been to miss those months when Bill, Fred, Manny and the others had suffered.

That night, the two went outside to sit by the fire pit while the ladies watched TV in the Jones' trailer. New Zealand became the topic and they both had very good memories of that time. Johnnie, of course had a life of his own at New Zealand, but he had also traveled extensively with Bill up to the Proctor's place in Palmerston North, the Hyde's in Shannon and spent many nights with the Mitchells in Lower Hutt near Woburn Station. Johnnie asked Bill if he knew whatever had become of Lorna and Daphne, and to his surprise, Bill told him that he and Edna had been writing to both of them in New Zealand for some years. Les Mitchell had actually married Lorna and they had three children together. Les had visited Bill and his brother Al in Illinois back in 1965, but unfortunately Les and Lorna had divorced some years later.

From New Zealand, the conversation naturally went toward Truitt Anderson and his wife Molly and the gang from out at the Taylor's house in Miramar. They recalled how Truitt and Bob Swigert had been killed and this brought tears into Bill's eyes once again after 41 years. Johnnie hadn't thought about Helen Taylor's dream for a long time, but it still raised the hair on the back of his neck. Bill elaborated on how the Lord had saved him from the mortar round and how it had been made clear to him. Johnnie had witnessed the hell of Tarawa from his vantage point just about 200 yards down Red Beach 2. Johnnie recalled Lieutenant Vincent and the team he led into the crossfire on Red Beach 1. Bill's memory brought back the feelings from burying all 15 of them there in the sand. Both Bill and Johnnie had held a high level of respect for Lieutenant Vincent and had been friends of Seng, Montague and the others who died there.

Many of the other occupants of Trails West heard about the meeting of the two former Marines and someone thought the local newspaper might be interested in the story. To Bill and Johnnie's surprise, a young reporter named Wendy Derzawiec arrived the following afternoon and asked them for an interview. Just as the old Marines were always gracious to any one they shared war stories with, they gave Wendy a fun interview and left most of the horrors out. They did mention the sadness of recalling some of their fallen buddies. Johnnie told Wendy about how he had decided to join the Marines in 1939 when he was plowing snow up in Wyoming for very little pay. A car came up behind Johnnie's plow and began flashing the lights and honking the horn. Johnnie stopped to see what the problem was and it was a Marine recruiter who invited him to sit in the car and have some bourbon. The recruiter made the U.S.M.C. seem like the best thing going for a young man and Johnnie bought the pitch. He went back and told his boss at the Highway Department that the Marines were going to give him "uniforms and everything!" His boss told him, "joining the Marines would end up being the biggest mistake of your life." Johnnie reflected on the hardship of war and reckoned his old boss was right. Bill told Wendy he joined the day after the Pearl Harbor attack; he "just couldn't sit still." Bill never acknowledged that joining the Marines had been a mistake; difficult perhaps, but not a mistake. He told Wendy about one of his best buddies who was already in the Navy when the war broke out; it made Bill want to do his part. Wendy sat and listened to Bill and Johnnie talk about the old days and snapped some photos of the pair sitting in their folding chairs between their trailers in the late afternoon sunshine.

The following day, there was a half-page story in the paper and it was quite the center of conversation around the trailer park. Bill and Johnnie had gotten together to quietly visit about the old days and never thought anyone else would be interested in their meeting. There were very few people who fully understood the memories these Marines carried and spending time together was hard to arrange. As they parted ways, they both knew there was a bond between them that time would never erase.

Bill Bennett (left) and Johnnie C. Jones sit and reminisce in Apache Junction, Arizona in January of 1984.

(Wendy Derzawiec Photo)

This trip to Arizona would set the pattern for many trips for Bill and Edna in the future and the trailer suited them just fine when they were away from home. Now that both were retired from their jobs and the children were busy with their own families, Bill and Edna became focused on what they could do to serve God full time with their lives.

Unfortunately, the changes in the Methodist Church had been giving them second thoughts about which church they would spend the rest of their lives serving in. Considering leaving the church where Steve and Jessie had met, married and raised their children was very unpleasant to say the least. The entire church family was considered to be friends of Bill and Edna's. Bill had long ago dealt with the issue of where his true allegiance lay. He was first and foremost a follower of the Risen Christ and any church organization would have to come after that. In 1984, the Methodist Church made some decisions that Bill and Edna felt they could not support. Since they had been spending a lot of time with Carol and Nolan at their church, they decided to leave Fourth Street and become members of Claim Street Baptist Church under the leadership of Reverend W. Ted Harmon.

87. Getting to Know Bill Bennett

My family attended Claim Street Baptist church at the time of my birth. When my mother was a young girl, Miss Lucille Vickroy came to my grandparent's house and asked if she could take my mother and her two younger brothers to church. My mother became a follower of Christ in Lucille's Sunday school class and Miss Vickroy always held a legendary status in our family history. Lucille taught the young ladies Sunday school class for 48 years. My mother was a primary influence in my faith as a boy and Lucille was one of my favorite customers on my paper route. I held her in high esteem. Our family ended up going to other churches while I was growing up, but I somehow ended up attending Claim Street again when I first saw Bill Bennett on that Memorial Day weekend, and then again at the end of my high school years. By the early 1980s, my wife Belle and I had become members, and were very active in the church with our young son. I had seen Bill and Edna around the church for so many years that I just assumed they had always been members. I had no idea of their exodus from Fourth Street Methodist until later.

Belle and I became familiar with Bill and Edna at large gatherings of the church body when we would have a dinner of one sort or another. Bill and Edna both had a sense of humor, and there always seemed to be laughter emanating from their table. I had noticed that Bill wore a U.S.M.C. belt buckle since first seeing him back in the '70s. To no surprise, he still wore it proudly. In 1982, I ventured to the men's breakfast one Saturday morning and I went early to work in the kitchen. When I arrived, the assistant pastor was assigning work stations and he pointed to Bill and told me to, "Give Bill Bennett a hand with the pancakes." I reported to Bill and he greeted me with that famous Bennett handshake and then showed me how he had things set up. We were expecting about 75 men for the breakfast (roughly a full platoon) and we needed to get the batter mixed. He knew the formula and I stirred the bowls until the lactic acid was burning in my arms. Bill could pour that batter out on the griddle in nearly perfect rows of exact sized cakes. He would pour out 12 cakes on the griddle and then I would count roughly to 90; then they had to be flipped rapidly as we reset our unseen clock to about 90 seconds. We would have to lift a few edges to check the color. Then those cakes came off and onto the tray, covered with foil, and a new batch poured out. He had enough batter ready for about 200 pancakes, or about 15 batches off the grill. Bill mentioned that this was the procedure he had learned in the Marines. I thought his system was pretty interesting.

I had learned from my years of associating with veterans that some were open to talking about their experiences and some were not. Usually, those men who had been in combat were far less likely to identify with their military experience than those who had not been in combat. I barely knew Bill, so asking him about it was out of the question. He could have just worked in the kitchen while in the Marine Corps for all I knew. One thing I had learned while growing up was never to assume that older men and women had just sat around most of their lives. I knew some of them had done some amazing things and there was always something I could learn from them. From the way Bill Bennett could grill hotcakes, I had a sense that he had a history of getting things done.

Looking back, I believe I may have earned a bit of respect from Bill that day. I was one of very few young men who showed up that morning (actually, the only young man) to work and I had kept up with him. I also liked to laugh and he and I did plenty of that. I had grown up next door to my maternal grandparents and had been very close to my Grandpa Fred. I learned from that relationship that age mattered very little in friendships. A young child can find commonality with an elderly person if they have similarities in their soul. It was very near the time of this men's breakfast that my grandfather passed away suddenly. Bill was about the same age as my grandfather.

During these years, my wife was making more of an effort to devotionally follow Christ than I was. I had no problem with any of it and I would have told you that I was a Christian without question. Adventure had managed to gain control of most of my attention as I had become an avid skydiver, among other things.

In early 1984, I had an unexpected experience that changed my life completely. I came to the realization I had placed earthly things in front of my relationship with the One who gave Himself on the cross for my mistakes. Quite unexpectedly, the Lord made it vividly clear to me that He had a plan for my life. If I were to follow Him and pursue His path, it would cost me everything. I got on my knees and gave Him all of it. I felt pure love for the first time in my life. No human being had a part in what happened within my soul that day, and living my life to allow Christ Himself to live and love through me became my identity.

Belle and I began to volunteer to teach children's Sunday school and ended up working with the junior high and then the high school youth at our church. We both ended up working on other projects as needed and we had a close group of church friends at Claim Street. By the late 1980s, Belle and I were both working with the AWANA (Approved Workmen Are Not Ashamed) children's club at church, which met on Wednesday evenings. The AWANA kids memorized Bible verses, sang songs, watched videos and played some very exciting games. It was a lot of work, but many children benefited from these activities over many years. The structured interaction that this Christian club provided was a good influence on both "churched" and "un-churched" kids alike.

On a wintry Wednesday in 1990, I came into the church basement to get ready for the meeting. I had two regular helpers with the 3rd through 6th grade "Pioneer" group. As the start of the meeting drew near, neither of them had arrived. We would have anywhere from 15 to 30 boys in Pioneers and handling them all alone would be a daunting task. A few minutes before starting time, our Assistant Pastor, Dean, came by and saw my need. A few minutes later he came back and told me that Bill Bennett would come down in a few minutes to lend me a hand. There were times when some of the older guys would come down to help me and I was a bit concerned about how they would view my somewhat unorthodox club environment, but I was pretty sure that I would be okay with Bill.

When Bill arrived, he came over to me and asked what I needed him to do. We went from one activity to the next and he worked like he had been doing the same things for years. We split up the boys and listened to their Bible memorization and marked their books and handed out the awards that were earned. We ran through our games and Bill helped referee and ran the stop watch. At the end of the games, we had about 15 minutes of old fashioned "dodge ball" and Bill seemed a little surprised at how hard the ball was being thrown; but he just shook his head and laughed. At devotion time, I gave the boys a talk on how the Holy Spirit works and what it means to live a life that demonstrates the "fruit of the Spirit." We ended with our usual prayer requests and then a short prayer time where the boys took turns praying out loud for each other's requests, and then I closed with a short prayer. The group picked up their books and some boys high-tailed it for their parents or waiting cars, while a few stragglers talked here and there. My own two boys, Ben and Brandon, found our dodge ball and had a scaled down pick-up game with a few other boys at one end of the basement. Bill and I piled up the supplies into a few boxes and then went to work folding the tables and chairs.

Whenever I worked with Bill, I could sense his "get it done" attitude and it made me feel somewhat energized being around that "old Marine" mentality. As part of my life-long habit of reading WW II history, I had spent the past year reading several books about the U.S.M.C. campaigns of the Pacific and had just finished a book about Saipan a week earlier. Bill picked up three chairs under each arm and headed for the rack and I followed behind him. "I just finished a book on Saipan last week," I casually informed him. I wondered if he knew anything about that battle. He set the chairs onto the rack and turned and looked me squarely in the eye. He had a deadly serious look in his eyes that stopped me cold in my tracks. Bill firmly stated, "I was there! We lost a lot of good men on Saipan." I could see that his eyes were beginning to well up and I apologized. "I'm sorry I brought it up Bill, I…." He cut me off and said, "Oh, no. You don't have to apologize. You're one of the only young people that I know who knows about Saipan, I was just surprised by it." I brought up the fact that 50,000 people died there during the three weeks of battle. Bill's face grew troubled and he pulled off his glasses to rub the corners of his eyes. "We did everything that we could to save those civilians. We had Japanese-speaking translators with loud speakers and everything. They were committing suicide and the Japanese were killing them too, thinking that they were doing them a favor." It was at this very moment that I realized how special Bill Bennett really was. Living through an ordeal like Saipan set him apart from most other people and certainly most other Americans.

I told Bill that I greatly appreciated what he had been through and what he had done for our country. He said he had only done what he had to do. I then told him I would be very interested to hear his story and find out what he had done during the war, provided he wanted to talk about it. He said "That would be fine," as we went back to the task of stacking the chairs and then folding the tables. I shook Bill's hand to thank him for filling in and as he turned and walked away I remember feeling a huge amount of respect for him. I knew from my reading what some of the Marines from WW II had gone through and I now knew that Bill had been in the thick of it as a combat Marine. I felt genuine humility during our brief discussion that night.

The following Sunday morning, just before church, Belle and I ran into Bill and Edna at the back of the church and exchanged the usual pleasantries of such a morning. Bill asked me for my phone number and I wrote it in on a corner of the church bulletin and tore it off for him. At some point in the middle of the week, he called me and said he had been thinking about his years in the Marines and a few stories had come to mind. He told me about San Diego, Tulagi, New Zealand, Tarawa, Hawaii, Saipan and Tinian. Overall, he had been in the Corps for 46 months, and 27 of those were spent overseas. He said he had a lot more that I might be interested in, but we could get together and talk more later. The words "Tulagi," "Tarawa" and "Tinian" immediately broadened my understanding of Bill's war experience and I knew he had to have been with the 2nd Marine Division. I focused my reading on their history during the war and made a point to read all I could so I would be able to understand where Bill had been.

Later that year, the Bennett family suffered the loss of both Lincoln Schell and Perry McIntosh when they passed away within a few hours of each other over October 24th-25th, 1990. Both men had suffered extended illness, and Bill and Edna tried to be as supportive as possible to both Jean and Marian. Linc had been an example of hard work and kindness to Bill and taught him how to ride a horse like an "old hand." Perry had been a close friend, a voice of reason and a fellow WWII Marine.

Our church began to explore the possibilities of moving out of the neighborhood where it had been for almost a century. The church had been a bastion of support for overseas missionaries since its founding. Some members found it strange that such a church would pick up and leave because the neighborhood had become a challenge. I had been asked by the church leadership to explore the possibilities of finding a Hispanic congregation that would be suitable and interested in the Claim Street Baptist Church building, should the congregation actually go through with the move. I began to visit Hispanic churches in Aurora with retired Reverend Paul Johnnaber, who spoke fluent Spanish. Bill was involved with the board of Deacons at this time, so we had to attend some of the same meetings. I offered to pick him up so that we could talk in the car and this gave us some time for Bill to get into more detail about his experiences. At these meetings, I was vocal about the irony of a missions-minded church fleeing the neighborhood that had now become a mission field. The opposing argument was that there was little a "mostly white" congregation could do to reach out to a mostly Hispanic neighborhood. We had well over a dozen Hispanic boys from the neighborhood attending AWANA Club and I had visited their homes and seen first-hand what the challenges were. I was sure that the God who made the heavens and Earth was big enough to reach out to this neighborhood, regardless of the cultural differences.

After one of the meetings, Bill told me he completely understood everything I was saying and he happened to agree. He then told me there was something I didn't understand about the situation. I asked him to explain. He said the real problem with the church wasn't the neighborhood at all. The real problem with the church was that the people did not want to do the job of reaching out, and because of this, the job would go undone and the people would not be reached. He saw it clearly that the white European congregation needed to get out of the way of what God needed to do in this situation. As much as I disliked the stark reality, I knew that Bill was right. I stopped opposing the move and Paul and I helped Reverend Victor Mendoza of the Iglesia Bautista Emanuel move into a dialogue that eventually saw them purchase the building at 742 Claim Street. The old congregation moved to the west side to become Morning Star Community Church. Bill's wisdom ran very deep, and I began to see how he lived his life with a closeness to the Lord which I had seen in very few people. Our age difference meant nothing to me as I felt a common bond in our faith. There were things I had experienced since giving my life to Christ that Bill talked about and I could identify with him. At different times and in different circumstances, we had both come to know the Living Christ and it was like talking about someone we both knew in a personal way.

At some point, shortly after Bill and I began our discussions about his Marine Corps experiences, their granddaughter Audra was diagnosed with leukemia and began treatment. I believe that few men have ever out prayed Bill Bennett and few couples have ever out prayed Bill and Edna. They were no strangers to the rigors of dealing with a sick child and they played a key role in supporting both Audra and her parents, Sarah and Dick. The closeness of the Bennett, Brauer, Foreman and Andrews families was tried and tested during this time and they rejoiced when remission arrived and hope showed signs of returning to Audra's future. The holdout of hope was eventually dashed when it was determined at a regular check-up that the leukemia had returned. Audra May Brauer lost her battle with leukemia on March 15th, 1995 at the age of 23.

As with so many situations in Bill's life, there were no apparent good answers to hard questions regarding the loss of a young, beautiful girl like Audra. In Bill's mind and acquired understanding, there are times when believers have to look above the pain and suffering of this world and look into the face of Christ and trust Him with all of our ability to do so. A tragedy such as this has the power to partially or fully destroy us if we become bitter and angry. When we trust God through it and hand the grief and bitterness to Him, He can and will use the pain to strengthen, heal and ultimately bless those left behind. There are some things we cannot understand while we are here on this Earth, and the loss of Audra would remain one of them.

During these years, I would occasionally call Bill and he would occasionally call me. I would pick up the phone, and he would ask how the family was doing, then tell me he had more memories to share.

He told me the stories from Tarawa; about wading in from the reef and how the Pioneers were dragging supplies into the front line and crawling under machine gun fire.

He also told me about hearing his name whispered in the heat of battle, and falling into the shell hole as their ammo dump erupted from the mortar shell, killing Anderson and Swigert. I was speechless when I heard Bill recounting this story and I could see well that God's hand had been on him throughout his life.

At another time, he told me about his friend Bob Stoner and how he had looked up from the deck of LST-130 and watched Stoner's plane explode, spin out of control and smash into the surface of the water. He was emotional when he told me this story and I could see it in his eyes. He described the red balls of anti-aircraft fire coming up from the ground and rising to hit the plane as it fired the rockets.

He told me of coming home and finding out it had been Bob Stoner flying that plane. Bill looked at me and said, "What are the chances that I would be at war on the other side of the Earth and look up and see a kid I grew up with get killed like that? I was 7,000 miles away from home and hadn't even seen him in years!" That story sent a chill up my spine.

Bill filled in details over the years and added some funny stories to offset the horrific ones. He also liked to tell me about his family and especially his grandkids. He would often recount his morning bike rides when I called. He rode about six miles a day when the weather permitted. He talked about Edna as though she were his girlfriend, calling her "My girl" occasionally. He and Edna had a wonderful life together and it was full of all the good things that a couple works so hard to achieve. I never felt like I needed to go out of my way for Bill because he was so physically well maintained and had so many loving people in his life. I, like they, was blessed just to have him as a friend.

Bill and Edna at their granddaughter's wedding. Their warm personalities and great sense of humor attracted friends and relationships of all ages. There was usually laughter emanating from their location.

88. To Japan

In November of 1995 I began to make a number of trips to Japan, and immediately began to study the Japanese language and culture. A friend arranged for me to meet a former exchange student from Japan, Kenji Tsuji, on the first trip. He and I remain close friends to this day. The Tsuji family invited me to stay with them while in Japan and they became like family to me over the years.

Kiyoshi (Tony) Ito and I became friends as well and that friendship grew far beyond our business deals. Mr. Ito invited me to his home where I ended up staying on a regular basis. His family and his staff became dear friends also. Being a "people person," I encountered countless Japanese through business, travel and friendship. My experiences in Japan were life-changing for me and I learned that people are pretty much the same wherever you go.

Bill was very interested in my travels to and from Japan and he became very inquisitive about my interaction with Japanese people in particular. He called me on several occasions just to talk about the Japanese I had met. He told me he had only known the Japanese as the enemy, and had always wondered what they were like as individuals. He asked me about the "older generation," "Surely, they must hate Americans?" I told him I had not experienced or even sensed any animosity toward me or other Americans whatsoever. Bill found this fascinating. He asked me about my friends and what it was like to stay with a family. He asked me about the food and if I had eaten sushi. I explained that after swearing to never eat sushi, I finally relented and it was now one of my favorite foods. He asked me about their religion and I told him about the experiences and conversations with my friends, including visits to their Shinto temples.

I became aware of the reason why Bill was so interested in hearing about the Japanese. He lived with memories of the enemy he had killed in combat and those he had seen killed. Even though these men were the enemy at that time, as a Christian he was aware of God's love for them. If the political landscape had been different prior to the war, Bill and his family may have been supporting mission work in Japan during the early 1940s instead of fighting them in the Pacific. Bill knew the Japanese soldiers had mothers and fathers and wives and children. He knew families mourned when each Japanese soldier died. In his mind, Bill had struggled to find a balance that allowed him to move on from the atrocities of war and live his life as an example to his family and his loved ones. Many men who went through the same experiences self-destructed after the war and became abusers of all sorts. I know that Bill's closeness to Christ made the difference in his life after the war. As Christ taught, His followers must consider others more valuable than themselves and a person who is separated from God still has immense value. Bill's entire focus in life was centered on helping others find the truth of Jesus Christ and it was difficult to bring his heart into alignment with his memories of the war.

One night as I was dropping Bill off at his house, we talked in the car for a few minutes before he got out. We had been discussing the woes of American youth and how many of them just didn't seem to care about anything but themselves. He said, "You know, in a way, I have more in common with the Japanese that I fought against than I do with a lot of Americans today. At least the Japanese believed in something they would fight and die for. They had honor and dedication and held a commitment beyond what most young Americans could understand." Although the Imperial Japanese committed atrocities and evil beyond belief, Bill was talking about the soldiers he faced. I knew what Bill meant. For those of us who were raised either by or around some of these "Greatest Generation" patriots, it is not uncommon to have a hard time relating to "modern" Americans.

89. The Enemy Has a Face

My experiences with the Japanese broadened the bond that I had with Bill, as we now had the Japanese people as a common interest. I told Bill about the night Kenji and I took his father to climb Mt. Fuji by moonlight. Kenji and I arrived at the summit about 3:30 a.m. and fell asleep. Hours later, as the red sun began to lift out of the Pacific, I was startled to hear thousands of Japanese voices shouting, "BANZAI! BANZAI!" in unison from the top of the volcano. As we climbed the eastern face of Fuji that night, several thousand Japanese soldiers climbed the trail on the northwest side of the mountain. They were amassed about 200 yards away when the shouts erupted. I immediately thought of Bill at that moment, as he was the only other human

I knew who had heard such a sound from Japanese soldiers. In my setting, I was in no danger and it was an interesting thing to experience. In Bill's setting, it would have been horrifying. The soldiers on Mt. Fuji were shouting a traditional cheer which can have several meanings, and on this particular morning it was a salute to the sunrise.

Kenji and I talked like brothers when we were together and I told him of my friendship with Bill. Kenji had a lot of interest in WW II and had learned a lot while he was in the U.S. as an exchange student in 1987. He assisted me in many ways during my trips to Japan, and his parents were equally gracious. His maternal grandmother lived with the family and she lived for her gardening. I loved coming into their house and talking to her. She had osteoporosis so badly that she could not stand upright and she was very hard of hearing. Kenji would straighten out my Japanese so that his grandmother could understand. Kenji and I would frequently stay up late to watch Japanese game shows after the rest of the family went to bed and we almost always had some conversation going on at the same time.

One such night, Kenji asked me to follow him into another room of the house where he opened a dark wooden cabinet that held urns and photos. I had asked Kenji about his grandfather earlier. Kenji handed me a photo of a young Japanese Cavalry Soldier in dress uniform holding the reigns of a horse. "This is my grandfather," Kenji said. "He was killed in the war." I was speechless. My mind immediately connected the possibility that Bill and Kenji's grandfather had been foes on an island so many years ago. It turned out that Kenji's grandfather had been killed when the troop transport ship he was on was torpedoed by an American submarine. He was on his way to the Philippines at the time. This also meant that Kenji's grandmother had lived through the loss of her beloved warrior long ago and raised their daughter without a father. She worked in a steel plant which was frequently bombed and had to scrounge for food to feed herself and her baby. The enemy suddenly had a face. The enemy suddenly had a family. I shared this new information with Bill when I got back home and he found it interesting to say the least. In a round-about way, Bill now knew about the family of one of his long-ago enemies.

Tony Ito's mother and father lived with Tony and his wife, Yoshie, in the original wing of the large family home in Hazu, Japan. Tony's father was an elderly, small-framed man when I met him, and he too, had a large garden just across the road from the house. I think he was surprised when I told him I wanted to get up early and help him with his gardening. I wanted to learn about Japanese gardening and I also wanted the elder Mr. Ito to know that I was interested in knowing him. One night as I was talking to Tony about the many common interests he and I shared, he told me this story: His father had been an aeronautical engineer and designed fighter planes for Sumitomo during the war. As the Japanese defeat became inevitable, his designing services were no longer needed and he was invited by the Emperor into the Kamikaze Pilot Program. He completed the brief pilot training and was sent to an airbase to await his final flight. He completed his Shinto cleansing ceremony to prepare for death and then had to wait in a hut along the runway until his plane was prepared. This wait was usually a few days, and in his case, Japan surrendered before the plane was ready! Tony's summary of the story was, "Maybe one more day and no Papa. No Papa, no Tony!" I shared this story with Bill, and it opened up another thought about the Japanese. Like the Germans during WW II, the average Japanese man had very little to say about serving in the armed forces. To dissent or refuse to serve would have been a death sentence or worse. I believe most Japanese were caught up in a movement that had gone so far out of control that it could only have been stopped in the way it had ended. I was introduced to the Ito's neighbor Tsugiko, who made work gloves for a living in her house. I joined Tony's mother and "Tsugi" for many morning walks where they told me of watching the skies fill with silver B-29 bombers when they were school girls and then seeing the lights of the fires as Nagoya and Toyohashi burned. They knew they were fortunate to have lived in an insignificant fishing village called Hazu.

I shared the essence of a message with Bill which I read at the exit of the Hiroshima Peace Memorial Museum in 1999. The mayor of Hiroshima stated that the Japanese people acknowledge Imperial Japan had caused the death and suffering of millions of people throughout Asia between 1936 and 1945, and that these actions were responsible for bringing about the horrific bombing of Hiroshima and Nagasaki. Bill was astounded that the Japanese would feel this way. The Japanese he had known would never have made such an admission.

Bill and Edna on the front porch of their family home at 310 S. Lasalle Street, approximately 1999. To say that this home was a lighthouse to the community would be an understatement.

(Bennett Family Photo)

90. Losing His Girl

At some point in 2001, Bill told me that Edna had been battling cancer. Since Bill and I called each other a few times a year, and we weren't attending the same church regularly, there were times when we weren't up to speed on the latest developments in each other's lives. This became more the norm than I would have liked during these years, but church is a bond between people, and when you aren't there regularly it impacts friendships. After feeling increasingly tired and "run down," Edna's doctor began testing her for sources of the fatigue. Eventually, things were narrowed down and the diagnosis was non-Hodgkin's lymphoma. I told Bill how sorry I was to hear this news and I told him that I would be praying for both of them. He referred to Edna as his "girl" many times and I remember him saying, "The most important thing for me right now is taking care of my girl." I knew that he would be thinking this without saying it. This was a part of Bill's soul.

I didn't know Edna like I knew Bill. We talked occasionally, but most of the time I spent with Bill was based around "guy stuff." Bill told me later that Edna was getting worse and I didn't want to bother him during this time. As Edna grew weaker, their children pushed for them to move from the old two-story at 310 S. LaSalle into a newer ranch house on Aurora's west side on Candleberry Drive. The old place on LaSalle Street was cleaned out and antique dealers and garage sale enthusiasts aided in the effort of trimming down Bill and Edna's belongings to fit into the smaller house. In October of 2001, Bill and Edna moved to the new house, which was much easier to get around in and maintain. It was a difficult move, in that the old house was the center of years of wonderful memories for the Bennett family. As the months passed, Edna weakened and by early June she was placed into hospice care. The outlook became dire from a human perspective. Although Bill felt as though his heart was being torn from his body, he managed to not let Edna see his tears. His children and grandchildren were aware of Bill's grief, but he did not want Edna to see it. He emphasized that she was going through a hard-enough time without having to be concerned about him. As Edna neared the end of her life, she came in and out of consciousness and it appeared to their granddaughter, Jessica, that Edna was holding on for Bill's sake. On June 7th, 2002, Jessica urged her grandfather to tell her grandmother that it was okay for her to give up the fight and go to be with Christ. This was probably the hardest thing that Bill Bennett ever had to say. Jessica's insight appeared to be accurate, as a short time later Bill's "Eddie" slipped from this world into the arms of God. She had been the center of Bill's life for 55 years and 24 days.

Bill had been no stranger to death during his life, but Edna's death was decidedly different from the others. He had been making decisions and plans with her for so long that it just didn't seem possible that he could have a life without her by his side. If there was one thing that Bill did not want to think about, it was the prospect of being lonely. The blessing that Bill and Edna had been to their family for all of their years together paid dividends for Bill during his time of grief. His children and grandchildren supported and loved him to an extent that was hard to imagine. The Bennett family had been in good hands for years thanks to Bill and Edna and their close reliance on the Lord, and now Bill found himself in the good hands of his loving family.

Being away from church and living out of town, news did not reach me as it should have at times. I did not hear of Edna's death until several weeks had passed. I called Bill to tell him how sorry I was for his great loss and also for not attending Edna's funeral. I felt like I had let Bill down as a friend. Bill always emphasized to me that he had a great family, and his relationships with his children and grandchildren were beyond precious to him.

Bill had always been a very able-bodied guy. I reason now, looking back, that had Bill needed help with ordinary things, I would have wanted to help him more. Even though his years were advancing, I never thought of Bill as old, but he had just lost the person who had been the center of his life for 55 years, and things would never be the same for him. As if things could not have gotten any worse for Bill, his brother Al, arguably his best lifetime friend, passed away on July 18th. The loss of two of the most important people in his life marked a difficult chapter for Bill and he mourned deeply. I made it a point to call Bill more often after Edna's passing and I know that dozens of his loved ones did the same. Bill and Edna had planted a lifetime of love and commitment and Bill was blessed with the rewards during this time.

Bill and Edna with their children and their spouses: 1997.
(Bennett Family Photo)

At Edna's funeral, as Moses and Ann Cheng went through the receiving line, Bill made the comment to them, "Don't forget about me." This especially resonated with Ann and she made an effort to invite Bill over to their house for dinner with the family. The Chengs soon became endeared to Bill, and he to them. Bill's love for football brought him over to the house to watch games that following season and his interest and attentiveness for the Cheng's daughters soon earned him the honorary title of "Grandpa Bill." Bill's love for people and his ability to forge new friendships was as relentless as ever.

Now at the age of 83, Bill's love for the bicycle had not diminished in over 75 years. Each morning, weather permitting, Bill would set out at 0530 hours on a six-mile ride. After losing her grandmother "Eddie," Bill's granddaughter, Jessica, determined to ride along with Bill on as many of these early morning rides as she could. Jess would have to ride a considerable distance from her apartment to meet her grandfather at an early hour. She soon found that an 83-year-old former Marine with a one-speed bike could maintain a speed that she could not match on her modern 10-speed. There were many times when Bill recounted those precious morning bike rides with his granddaughter.

After Edna's passing, Wes would stay with Bill when he visited from Wyoming, and the two enjoyed time between father and son. After a day of visiting with family, the pair would find themselves talking for hours at bed-time and solving the "world's problems." Even though they had lived far apart for many years, there remained a need for understanding and acceptance between them. Bill sensed the need to help his kids start to heal the hole left in their hearts by Edna's absence and they, in turn, knew how lonely Bill was. Bill had to make a choice after losing Edna, whether to feel sorry for himself and become inactive, or to focus on living each day for the Lord and invest his remaining years into the lives of others. He chose wisely. If Bill had any chance at all to wake up and serve God, then the day would be worth living.

91. Reliving Saipan

2004. I had been attending Blackberry Creek Community Church on West Galena Boulevard in Aurora for about eight years. During this time, I had become friends with a man named Ed Pavek through some activities around the church. Ed knew I had worked in Japan from time to time and mentioned that his mother-in-law was Japanese. One night after Ed and I had been to a church function together, he told me that his mother-in-law would be with them at church the following Sunday and I decided to make it a point to meet her.

After the service the following week, I found Ed and his wife, Vicki, and approached the woman sitting next to him, who I assumed was his mother-in-law. I spoke Japanese to her just for the sake of surprising her. I said, "I am Ed's friend, my name is Brent. Thank you for coming here today." She was shocked to hear Japanese. I asked for her name and where she lived. She said her name was Vicky Vaughn and she was from Saipan. We switched to English; I told her that I was very familiar with Saipan because of the terrible battle that was fought there. She suddenly began to cry and I felt like I had just run her toes over by accident. I tried to back things up and I apologized for bringing up Saipan's horrible past. She said that it was alright and she would be okay. She said she lived through the battle and most of her family had been killed. Her childhood name had been Setchan Akiyama. I told her that a very good friend of mine had been there as a U.S. Marine. She jerked her head back slightly as if something had really caught her attention. She asked me if I still knew him and was in contact with him. I said yes. She hesitated for a few seconds and I could tell she was turning a thought over in her mind. Then she said, "I have wanted to meet one of the Marines that were there on Saipan my whole life. Do you think you could ask him if he would meet with me?"

I thought about Bill, and knew he would at least listen to the request. I wasn't sure what he would think. I told Setchan that I would ask Bill and then I would give Ed a call to let her know Bill's answer. This certainly was an unexpected development and I thought about how I would present this to Bill. I knew Bill struggled with memories from Saipan and I didn't want to impose anything uncomfortable on him. I reasoned that it was not actually my request but Setchan's, so there was no reason for Bill to be upset with me either way. I dialed Bill's number. I explained the unusual meeting to him and told him that Setchan wanted to know if he would meet with her. He said, "Really?" in a suspicious tone. "Do you have any idea what she wants?" I told him that she had always wanted to meet a Marine who had served on Saipan. There was an unusual silence and I could tell this was uncomfortable for him. Then he said, "Oh, I don't know. Those people went through an awful lot back then. I can't imagine what she wants. Maybe she wants to yell at me or stab me or something?" I told him that she was maybe 5 feet tall and didn't look very dangerous to me, and he chuckled a bit. I told him I completely understood if he was not comfortable with it. He said he would rather not meet her.

For some reason, I didn't call Ed right away and decided to let it sit for a few days. Three days later, on Wednesday night, my phone rang and it was Bill. He said, "You know, I really didn't want to go talk to this friend of yours, but I decided I had better pray about it for a few days. I did, and I think He wants me to go. Can you still set it up?" I told him I still had not given Setchan his answer, so I was sure it would be okay. Then he asked me if I would go with him. I told him I would be honored to go. Then Bill said he needed a few days as he wanted to find some things he thought he should bring along. He had mentioned a box of war relics, but had never gotten around to bringing it down from the attic. Now that he had moved to a single-story house on the west side, he knew approximately where his relics were. I called Ed and set the meeting up for the next week and then I called Bill back. I told Bill I would pick him up when we went so we could talk on the way.

I remember being pretty excited about this meeting because getting two people together who were present on Saipan with such different perspectives had to be quite unusual. I wanted to hear more from Setchan if she were willing to share her story. I pulled up in front of Bill's house about 6:30 p.m. and ran up to the door. Bill answered, and I stepped inside. He went back into the kitchen and put a few things away quickly, then pulled on a windbreaker. On the way to the front door, he went over to a chair to pick up a wooden box about the size of a shoe box. He motioned to the box and said, "There are some interesting things in here." As soon as we started out, Bill went back over the events of the past week and was apologizing for changing his mind and not just saying yes right away. He asked me why I had not told Setchan that he did not want to meet her. I replied that I thought he would probably rethink his answer and waiting a few days would not make any difference if he still decided to decline. I told him not to even think about it again as it was all understandable. I was still a bit surprised he had changed his mind.

Bill and I pulled into Ed and Vicki's (Setchan's daughter) driveway and went to the door. Ed answered the door wearing one of his usual Hawaiian shirts and Vicki was right behind him. "Hi! How are you doing? C'mon in!" and as we came through the door I saw Setchan smiling as we approached. I introduced Bill to all three of them and Setchan said, "So nice to meet you, thank you for coming." Ed showed us over to a couch with a coffee table in front of it and we sat down with Bill and me on one side of the table, Setchan off to our right and Ed and Vicki across from us and to the left. Bill asked Setchan about her home still being on Saipan and how long she would be visiting on this trip. Bill told them about his family and how he had lost Edna recently. Setchan told us about her family and how she traveled to see her kids. They asked Bill some questions about how he came to the Marine Corps and he told them his story.

Then Bill picked up the wooden box from the floor by his feet and set it on the table. He lifted the top with both hands and pulled out a folded piece of yellowing paper, then carefully unfolded it. He handed it to me and said, "This is Saipan, isn't it?" I took one quick look and said, "No, this is Tarawa." He looked closely through his glasses and asked, "Are you sure?" I said, "I'm sure Bill, see how this looks like the shape of a cardinal?" Then I showed it to Setchan and she said, "No, that's not Saipan." Bill pulled more maps out of the box and I opened one and there it was, Saipan! The curious thing about these maps was that none of them had any names on them, only military markings of various types with a legend on the bottom. Bill said, "These are the battle maps that I carried in my shirt when I was there." The thought that these were his original maps was amazing; to think of how many times these had been pulled out while Bill and his Pioneers had been finding their way through battle. We literally unfolded history. These were some of the items that Bill had told me he would pull out of his attic for the past 15 years. Bill placed the map on the coffee table and he asked Setchan if he should go first. She said, "Yes." Bill pointed to the spot where his landing craft had approached the beach just south of the town of Garapan. He described the heavy gunfire and how some of his company had been wounded on the beach by the Japanese artillery. After fighting their way inland a few hundred yards they started to turn north toward Garapan and that was where they dug in for the night. The Navy had left them hundreds of handy shell craters to sleep in. The Japanese came out that first night with a huge counter attack and the heaviest concentration of combat ensued.

Bill showed approximately where the 2nd Division had pushed to the north through Garapan, Tanapag and up to Marpi. This was the first and only time that I saw Bill explain this with a map in front of him and I was glued to that map as he described it. Then Bill pushed the map over in front of Setchan and he said, "Do you remember where you were?" She said, "Oh yes!" She explained how her house was in Garapan and that they knew the invasion was coming ahead of time, just not when. Her father had to ride the "sugar train" up toward Marpi the next day, so he gave her instructions to carry some important papers to the family farm in Iliyang, about one mile to the southeast. For the next 30 minutes, Setchan told us her story in great detail and with unequaled emotion. She explained to Bill how grateful she was for the Marines saving her and her family members lives, and that she wanted to thank Bill on behalf of those Marines. Bill started to cry and this made Setchan cry even more. Vicki and Ed were both crying and several tears rolled down my cheeks as we passed around a tissue box. Bill explained how the Marines tried so hard to help the civilians on Saipan and how difficult it had been to watch them committing suicide because of the lies they had been told. Bill was clearly touched by the horrible story that Setchan was telling him of the carnage at her aunt and uncles farm at Aslito. Bill then talked about his fellow Marines who had died on Saipan. These stories were exchanged for another hour and it was one of the most emotional scenes I have ever witnessed.

Setchan (Victoria) Akiyama with her beloved father Tommomitsu on Saipan in 1936. Her older brother Shiuichi (Jesus) is on the left and Mitsunori (Maximo) is on the right.

(Akiyama-Vaughn Family Photo)

After the stories were exchanged and the tears subsided, Bill pulled out a few other things he had stored in the wooden box, including several bundles of "island money" he had blown from the bank vault in Garapan. Setchan knew exactly what it was. There was some laughter about Bill's bank robbing career. As we got up to leave, Setchan gave Bill a huge hug and thanked him several times for coming. Bill thanked her for the invitation and said how glad he was that he came. I knew I would never forget this meeting. Once we were in the van and on the way back to Bill's house, he told me how thankful he was that he had changed his mind, and he thanked me for setting it up. I told him it was amazing to be there and I was glad to be a part of it. I had a very strong sense I had just witnessed God doing something amazing, but I wasn't sure exactly how to describe it. I pulled up in front of the house and Bill said goodnight and thanked me again as he shut the door and headed towards the front door with his little treasure box. As I drove through the countryside in the dark, I kept the radio off and just thought about the stories I had just heard. The thought crossed my mind for the first time that this meeting was more than a coincidence. When I got home, I tried to describe what I had just experienced to Belle, but I am sure the description didn't even come close. I had a new appreciation for what both Bill and Setchan had endured on Saipan and I hoped their meeting would be good for both of them in the long run. I thought others should hear their story. Years later when I would tell friends this story, some would tell me they could feel the hair on the back of their neck stand up while they listened.

Setchan Akiyama (Vicky Vaughn) in her later years.

(Vaughn Family Photo)

Setchan's daughter told me that Setchan also had five shrapnel wounds to her back. It is assumed she dragged her family members from the burning house into the fighting pit that had been occupied by Japanese soldiers. The Marines then assaulted the position with hand grenades and a flame thrower, not knowing wounded civilians were now inside the pit. As far as the Marines had known, the pit had contained Japanese machine guns that were firing at them as they approached hundreds of yards out from the house. The machine gun position needed to be destroyed.

92. Marine Corps Monument

Ed and Vicki Pavek planned a trip to Saipan in 2005 to help Setchan prepare to make a permanent move back to Illinois. Bill wanted me to ask Ed if he would visit the Marine Monument on Saipan and take photos of the names engraved there. Bill had said earlier that seeing this monument would be one of the only reasons he would want to return to Saipan and these photos would certainly save him a long trip. After their return from the island, Ed brought copies of the photos to my house and I called Bill and told him them they had arrived. I asked him when he would like me to drop them off, and we agreed to the next night.

For those of us who have stood in front of a war monument at least once in our lives, there is a long list of names without a meaningful connection. Sometimes the length of the list is astounding just by the sheer number of names listed. It's hard for us to wrap our heads around a scenario where thousands of people are dying violent deaths in a short period of time. Only the ones who lived through the events that the monument immortalizes can fully appreciate the monument. I wondered if one of these names was the 18-year-old replacement who died in a crater next to Bill one night, or one of the Marines killed in the Banzai charge. I knew Bill would see these names differently from the rest of us. I always had a sense of excitement when I was on my way to visit Bill and this evening was no different.

I pulled into his driveway and noticed his front door was open with just the storm door closed; a sign he was expecting company. I rang the bell and he was at the door in seconds to welcome me inside. He was just putting some things away in the kitchen and I followed him to the table and sat down. I asked Bill if he was still riding his bike every day and he answered, "Six miles a day, every day that I can!" Bill was now 86 years old and showed no signs of slowing down. He told me he still rode with his granddaughter Jess occasionally and he really enjoyed it.

Bill finished up his kitchen work and set the dish towel on the counter, then he pulled back a chair across from me at the table. As he was sitting down, he reached for the manila envelope containing the monument photos and slid it over. "Well, let's see what you have here," he said with a serious, low voice. He slid the photos out of the envelope and adjusted his glasses a bit as he started to read the names on the first page, then shuffled to the second. He stopped his finger at a name and said, "Oh my ... I remember him." Then he slid back the chair and went over to a drawer and pulled out a pen. He circled one name, then another, and then looked through several more pages. "There are so many here," he said. "I will look these over more carefully later so that I can spend more time thinking about it. It's been such a long time now and it's harder to remember some things." Ed had also included many photos of Saipan as it appeared now and the vivid color photos seemed to really jog Bill's memory of the island. Bill told me to make sure to thank Ed and Vicki for getting the photos for him and said this was something he had wanted to see for a long time. Then he asked me how Setchan was and if I had seen her. I told him she was fine and I thought she may be moving to Aurora soon. He said he thought it would be nice to see her again sometime.

We moved out into the living room and talked about all kinds of things for about 45 minutes. He told me some things about his old friend Bob Stoner and he recalled the Mitchells, the Proctors and the Hydes from New Zealand. He said he used to have thoughts about visiting New Zealand but now he thought himself too old. I told him that I would go with him if it would encourage him to go. Then he wondered how many folks he had known were actually still alive there. He told me he wanted to get out some old photos and letters from the war and go through them some night when I had more time and I told him I would love to see them. Bill and I walked to the front door and then out to my minivan in his driveway. We talked through the rolled down window for a few minutes after I closed the door. Bill stooped a bit with one hand on the roof of the van so that he could see me inside. I heard a woman's voice call to him from a distance. I turned to see an older woman standing in front of the house next door holding her storm door open. She said she needed help moving a table. Bill told her he would be over in a few minutes, and she went back inside. Bill stooped back down and said in a lowered voice, "I think she just makes up stuff for me to do so that I'll come over." I told him it was nice of him to help her out. He said, "I think she is looking for some male attention." I couldn't help but laugh and I told him I would give him a call later and told him to be careful. Bill stood watch as I backed out into the street. As I started to pull away, he started jogging down the sidewalk towards the neighbor's house, and then turned up the driveway. Here was an 86-year-old Marine running next door to move a table! Perhaps an unusual sight, but not for those who knew Bill. The thought of Bill as an 86-year-old eligible bachelor had not occurred to me, but if Bill was right about her motive, who could blame the lady. I called Bill about a week later and he told me he didn't know the names of most of the Marines that he saw die, but he had nevertheless recognized several names in the photos.

93. A Historic Record

2007. Bill had turned 88 and he was still amazing. He mentioned to me that his family had been trying to convince him to give up the morning bike rides, but he wasn't ready to. He said he would know when it was time for that. I offered to video tape Bill's stories several times over the years, but he always declined or politely said, "Let me think about it," then never brought it up again. I offered again and told him that someday his family would probably like to have a record of his stories; not just the war stories, but life stories in general. He said, "I know that a lot of guys are doing that, and I just don't like the idea for some reason." Bill leaned forward in his chair and said, "I told you all of my stories. When I am gone you can do anything you want with them." It turned out that his granddaughter Jess had actually bought a tape recorder for the very same reason and left it with Bill. Years later when she found the recorder, the only thing audible on the recording was Bill saying, "This stupid thing doesn't work!"

I could not entertain the thought of a day when Bill would not be here. Just knowing that Bill, and men like him, were alive on the planet somehow made me feel safer. There are things that human beings go through that strengthen them for life. A combination of the Great Depression, the hell of war, raising a family and being touched by God's grace forms a list of unique ingredients. The Earth may never again see a generation like Bill's. On the way home that night, I knew that I would one day write Bill's stories.

Bill told me that meeting Setchan had been very good for him and he was glad he went that night. He told me that for all those years before, he had thought the civilians on Saipan had probably been hateful of the Marines. Meeting Setchan, and hearing how the Marines had worked so hard to save her and her family's lives, and her subsequent gratitude, had changed those feelings for Bill. It wasn't that Bill had been tortured by his memories, because his closeness with his Creator had been sufficient to heal any emotional scars left by the war. But God had also placed a compassionate love for others into Bill's heart, and that compassion caused him sadness when he remembered the plight of the civilians from Saipan and Tinian. Seeing how one of those little girls had survived the carnage to live a long, fruitful life with her family was a gift Bill needed. When Setchan wanted to thank Bill on behalf of the Marines who saved her on Saipan, she honored Bill as both a Marine and as a human being. Bill enjoyed hearing of my friendships with Kenji and Tony Ito. I think it made him feel good to know that Japan was filled with gracious and friendly souls who did not harbor hatred and resentment about what took place on those islands years before. Bill had never actually hated the Japanese people; he fought against an evil empire and did what he had to do to survive.

94. A Historic Flight

When Bill went to renew his driver's license at the age of 90, he learned he would have to take an actual driving test. He was horrified when he failed the test and was told he could no longer drive. Bill's daughters did a wonderful job explaining to Bill that it was not the end of the world, as they would all chip in and take him wherever he needed to go. This all sounded very nice, but Bill had another idea. He talked to one of his old friends who told him about a driver's license facility in a small town nearby where the examiners were far less stringent. Bill's old buddy drove him out to the small town the next day and Bill came home with his renewed Illinois driver's license! Bill had agreed to hang up his bicycle, but the car was going to stay.

During early 2010, Bill had begun to have some unusual pain and was feeling more tired than usual. At first, he believed it just went with the territory of being over 90. Eventually, his doctor began to look for the reason for the lower abdominal pain and the added fatigue; the diagnosis was determined to be cancer. Bill's doctors assured him that it had been caught very early and they were sure that with him being in such good health, he could survive it. Treatments of radiation were begun and Bill's strength was sapped even further. For the first time in his life, Bill began to have second thoughts about going out to family events such as birthday parties, cookouts and holidays.

A wonderful group of people in Chicago began an organization called "Honor Flight Chicago." It was formed in order to raise funds to provide aging WW II veterans a chance to fly to Washington D.C., visit the monuments and fly back home the same night. Bill had talked to several vets who had taken the trip and they all agreed it was one of the most wonderful days they had ever spent. Bill was reluctant to fill out an application as he said he did not need to be thanked or fussed over as he just did what he had to do. A further deterrent was his failing health and complications that went along with the treatments. Bill's family encouraged him to apply for the trip and thought it would be wonderful to see him go to the WW II monument and the U.S.M.C. Iwo Jima monument, among others.

Bill gave in to the throng of encouragers and his application was approved; his flight date was to be July 14th, 2010. Bill had to arrive at Midway Airport at 0500 hours and he met a group of 92 other WW II vets for breakfast at the gate. They listened to three very talented young ladies singing WW II era songs in the style of the Andrews Sisters. Bill was placed in the care of his assistant for the day, Herschel Luckinbill, from Montgomery, Illinois, who volunteered his time to work as an escort for the flights. Herschel would have to push Bill in a wheelchair for most of the events as the cancer treatment had left him depleted and unable to walk for long distances. Southwest Airlines Flight 2371 pushed back from the gate at 0730 hours and lifted off for Washington D.C.'s Dulles Airport for a 1010 arrival. With Herschel's help, they navigated the airport and the bus and arrived at the Iwo Jima Memorial at noon. Bill had seen the memorial on TV and in photos countless times, but being there in person was a sobering experience for him. Those giant-sized Marines lifting the flag atop Mt. Suribachi now represented every Marine who served in WW II. For Bill, those larger than life bronze statues carried the names of men like Truitt Anderson, Bob Swigert, Peter Nicholas Andrews and Channing Miller. All of Bill's memories swelled to the surface as he viewed the memorial. Sights and sounds of battles long ago once again filled his mind as he thought of those left behind on those islands.

The bus pulled up to the WW II monument and Herschel wheeled Bill closer to the enormous structure. Bill surveyed the walls and found each meaningful inscription from the Solomons, Tarawa, Saipan and Tinian. A ceremony was held in remembrance of those fallen long ago and a bugler played a beautiful rendition of "Taps" that rang out against the marbled walls. Bill, as well as the other 92 Vets with him, knew in their hearts that this would, in all likelihood, be the last time they would be able to attend such a ceremony, and certainly not ever again at this site. It was a somber remembrance and a somber acceptance that life was now in its twilight. As the group of aged warriors boarded the plane to head back to Chicago, "Mail Call" was announced and Bill surprisingly received 70 letters and cards from friends and family. This would have been a "dream" mail call back in 1942 when he was longing for any letters at all from the "home front" that he had left behind. As Bill began to open letter after letter, he read some of the kindest and most heartfelt words that he had ever read in his long life.

Bill opened a note from his daughter Sarah that read, "We love you, we're proud of what you've done to help keep Americans free. We are PROUD to call you our Dad. Lots of love, Sarah and Dick." Kathy wrote, "I've always been so proud to introduce you to my friends and bring them home with me as I was growing up. You were always so welcoming; even now my friends always ask how you are doing. The more I hear and learn about WW II, the prouder I am of you. The sacrifices you gave to serve our country are great and I am so glad that you are able to go on this trip and be honored in such a way." Carol wrote, "I am and always have been proud of you. You have always been my hero. But even before I was born you were a hero for what you did in the service of our country. With your faith in God, you got through the difficult times and I'm sure that you were an inspiration to the men that you served with. Thanks Dad for the steadfastness in all you do. You are a father that I can be proud of!"

As the plane flew into the sunset towards Chicago, Bill opened letter after letter and several tears found their way down this old Marines cheek. He read a moving letter from his son-in-law Pete Andrews and cards and notes from his grandchildren and great-grandchildren. There was a warm note of thanks from the Cheng family and his church mates including Ron Olson. There were letters from his nieces and nephews which honored the great example Bill had set for the entire family over a lifetime. Of all the beautiful and heartfelt letters that Bill received, one in particular seemed to squarely summarize the impact that Bill's life had on so many others around him:

Dear Bill,

We pray this has been a great day for you as you traveled to Washington. Thinking of the times we have spent with you and the blessings that you and your family have been in our lives causes us to be thankful.

Over the years we have known you, your wife and your children, we have been encouraged by the stand that you have taken for our Lord and Savior, Jesus Christ. He has done wonderful things in your lives and ours as well. Thank you for being faithful to Jesus Christ and working to build a Godly marriage and family. You have given good examples that we have been able to see and have been encouraged in our own walk with Christ.

We have only heard a small amount of your time in the military and serving in the Pacific. Thank you for standing firm as a Christian in the military and for your courage to fight for the wonderful nation God has raised up. You literally put your life on the line for us—thank you.

One request we have of you. You have fought your battles well. Pray for us that we may fight our battles well and bless the next generations. You know the battles we are facing today will determine our course and destiny. May we humbly walk with God, listening to his voice, and obey it without hesitation.

God's rich blessing on you.
In Christ's love,
Dick and Ruth Ann Miller

    These letters were so touching to Bill; and he did indeed feel honored by the very solemn and kind words he read in letter after letter. Bill had tried to live his life in a way that would honor the Lord. Perhaps it had made a difference in some of the lives around him. Bill tore open a card from a familiar address in Arizona; it was from Tom and Jean Lewis who had trailered with Bill and Edna years ago. Tom Lewis had been a Navy man back during the war and he and Bill had carried on the age-old rivalry in a light-hearted way for years; this card would be no exception. Bill began to read ...

Bill—I know how frustrating it must have been for you to not get into the U.S. Navy. The Army and Marines needed some men too. We in the Navy saw to it that you "Few Good Men" got to your many destinations in good order; whatever mischief and hi-jinx that you got into once we delivered you was up to you. Don't blame the Navy; we did our part! I guess that the Navy is not so choosy anymore-so next time, try us again. You might even like the Navy-the food is great!

Thanks again,
Tom.

P.S. I just can't thank you enough for your service in the U.S. Marines 68 years ago. A lot of prayers were answered to bring you home safely.

If Tom had only known how right he was about the prayer involved for Bill's sake during that time in his life. As Bill continued with his final "Mail Call," he came to a letter written by his son-in-law, Pete Andrews:

You are one of the only people that can honestly say, "I have fought the good fight, I have finished the race, I have kept the faith." Yes Willie.....THANK YOU.... You are my HERO who I love very much. I hope that this day is one of the very best days that God has blessed you with. You deserve it.

As you receive thanks from many others on this day, I also know that someday you will look forward to hearing these words ... the very best words of thanks that any of us could ever hope to hear: "William, my son; Well done my good and faithful servant; thou hast been faithful over a few things; I will set thee over many things; enter into the Joy of The Lord."

Thanks for being like a "Dad" and for the positive influence that you have had on my life. May God bless you always.

With love,
Peter G. Andrews.

As the 92 weary warriors made their way back through Midway Airport in Chicago, they were guided to the lower level and the baggage claim area. The sounds of a military band and throngs of people cheering wildly broke the usual sounds of the airport's busy interior. Herschel pushed Bill forward as Bill held the ceremonial encased American flag that had accompanied the group to Washington. The room was filled with American flags, red, white and blue decorations, balloons, and signs of welcome and thanks. People lined both sides of the pathway and they cheered and smiled as the veterans were quite astonished at all the "hoopla." Coming around a curve in the path, Bill spotted his family waving American flags and smiling and cheering as he approached. Pete and Kathy were there with their daughters Jess and Jennie, as well as Bill's nephew Bill Schell and his wife, and Moses and Anne Cheng with their daughters Katie, Stephanie, Natalie and Allison. Kisses and hugs and photos abounded as Bill was greeted and honored by his family. A handmade sign that read, "Thank You Bill Bennett" was waved with enthusiasm and handed to Bill so that a photo could be taken. Pete Andrews looked on with a smile as Bill was welcomed by his loved ones. Pete carried an encased memorial American flag in his own arms. Pete had brought this special family flag along as a way of representing his father George Andrews and his fallen uncle, Peter Andrews, who was killed in battle on Saipan. PFC Peter Nicholas Andrews, like so many others, had not lived to have his own children and grandchildren, or be able to see what Bill was seeing as he was honored for his service; but he had not been forgotten. Bill had his picture taken with everyone who had come to welcome him home from the Honor Flight and he thanked them all from the bottom of his heart.

As Bill made it home and settled in for the night, it was amazing to think of all that had transpired in one day. It reminded him of those days of long ago when travel was just a part of life in the Marine Corps. Life itself had been an amazing journey for Bill, filled with more good things from the Lord than he would have had the mind to ask for. In Bill's estimation, he had not given up anything through his efforts to serve Christ during his lifetime; quite the opposite. His life had been filled with so many good and wonderful things that he would fall asleep tonight while trying to thank the Lord for all of them.

95. The Arms of God

Belle and I were in the habit of going back to visit Morning Star Community Church from time to time and we decided to go on a Sunday in early September of 2011. The largest group of the former Claim St. Baptist Church congregation was still at Morning Star and it was good to see them. As we came to the front door, we were greeted by several young people that I didn't recognize. They welcomed us with smiles and handed us the bulletin for the service. We soon found our old friends Ron and Darlene Olson and made arrangements to sit with them during the service. Ron and Darlene had been missionaries to Argentina for 42 years, after Ron had taken several years away from Bible College to fight the Germans with the 9th Infantry Division in Europe. I turned my head back toward the door just in time to see Bill walk in and he saw me at the same time. We walked towards each other and exchanged a handshake and a quick hug as we had not seen each other in a while. He asked me if I minded if he sat with us. That was a rhetorical question. He looked around and said that he had a couple of people he needed to talk to briefly. I told him that Belle and I were sitting with Ron and Darlene and I would save him a seat.

As the band started to play their prelude, I saw Bill appear on my left and he made his way down the row to the seat I had saved for him. As he sat down, he set his Bible on the floor under his chair and as he came back up, he squeezed my arm pretty hard and said, "Thanks!" Even though I have always been an advocate for modern praise and worship music, the traditional hymns stir my soul, especially when I am in a service with the older generations. As we sang that day, I had my wife next me to with the Olson's on her right and Bill on my left. As we sang "A Mighty Fortress," the volume of the voices rose as the older folks responded to something so familiar. I could hear Bill boldly belting out the old familiar hymn and I am quite sure he didn't need to read the words projected onto the wall. Looking back on that day, I am quite sure I have never been in the presence of a better group of people.

After the service was over, Belle and I talked to quite a few old friends and Ron and Darlene's granddaughter, Amy, came by to chat with Belle, who had been her Sunday school teacher many years before. Bill came back to where we had been sitting and said he wanted to ask me about something. I had previously informed Bill that Setchan had been undergoing treatment for cancer and he had been praying for her, so he had opportunity to mention his treatment to me; he did not. He asked me how she was and I told him I thought she had come through the treatment and was okay. He then asked, "I was thinking it would be nice to see her again, do you think you could see if that's possible?" I told him, "Sure, I will ask Ed about it the next time I see him and let you know." I thought it was awesome that Bill was still interested in Setchan and thought she would certainly be glad to see him again. Bill and I shook hands and I told him I would call him later. Bill was now 92, and that was the first time I had noticed that he had slowed down a bit.

The reason Bill looked a little tired that Sunday was because he had been undergoing more treatment for cancer. It would have been out of character for Bill to call me just to tell me he was sick, but I wish he would have. I didn't know Bill's family well enough at the time for any of them to realize I would want to know what Bill was going through, or they may have thought I knew. It was just one of those things that slipped through the cracks. Bill had actually been through radiation therapy and he had been weakened even more than it showed that Sunday. Within a short time, Bill went to live temporarily at "Jennings Terrace" nursing facility on Aurora's east side at 275 S. LaSalle Street. The idea was for Bill to have a chance to strengthen for a while and then return home. For several days, Bill seemed to be gaining strength and Sarah, Kathy, Carol and their families were confident that Bill would be home in a short time. They relayed the good news by phone to Wes who was living in Wyoming. Over the next few days, Bill suddenly weakened and his doctor knew there could be no further therapy without it taking Bill's life. Bill was placed in hospice care and he and the family were told that he only had a short time to live. In spite of the bad news, Bill remained humorous, as was his norm. The nurses and hospice care workers learned that Bill was not afraid to die but that he viewed the news as though expecting a homecoming. He had lived his life to honor the Lord and it was Bill's heartfelt belief that the Lord had guided him along life's long path and soon he would meet Jesus Christ Himself when he left this Earth. How many people were directly impacted by Bill Bennett's last days will never be known.

As suddenly as Bill had taken a turn for the worse, he had several good days and everyone was encouraged that he might be turning around. Wes, who was receiving updates in Wyoming, was even encouraged by what he had heard and decided it was not necessary to leave for Illinois in a hurry.

By November 13th, Bill had again taken a quick turn for the worse and even told the nurses that he didn't want any company. When granddaughter Jess arrived and was told about the request for no visitors, she would have none of it and went in to see her Grandpa Bill. The two talked just as they always had, but Jess could tell that Bill was slipping fast. Pete and Kathy came to stay with him on Monday, November 14th and when they left Bill, it seemed like he was hanging in there and they planned to be back the following day. The hospice caregiver checked in for the night and Bill weakly chatted with the fellow for a few minutes before he said he wanted to get some sleep. Per

Bill's life-long habit that was instilled into him by his loving mother, Jessie, 87 years earlier, on a street not too far away, Bill prayed and thanked the Lord for yet another day of life. He closed his eyes and drifted off to sleep. The night shift for the caregiver was usually one of silence as he sat nearby to Bill with a dim light reading a book.

At 2:30 a.m. on November 15th, 2011, Bill suddenly woke from his sleep and caught the caregiver's attention. He set his book on the table next to the chair and went to see what Bill needed. Bill looked up at his caregiver and said softly, "It's time to go … I've got to go now." At that, Bill put his head back and breathed out his last breath. His caregiver pressed the alarm for the nurse and checked Bill for a pulse; there was none. At the age of 92, Bill Bennett left his earthly body and stepped into the arms of God. Even though he lived his last years on the west side of Aurora, he died only a few hundred yards away from the house where he and his beloved "Eddie" had raised their family and spent so many years together working on heavenly things and helping others come to know what Jesus had done for them on that cross long ago. At the bottom of the hill were the train tracks that had carried him to the war in the Pacific and home again. Close by was the Hurd's Island athletic field where a young Bill Bennett trained as a member of the Aurora Clippers football team. He had lived and died in the community where he had invested his entire life.

Bill's family laid him to rest next to his Edna May and Baby Terry, in the all too familiar Lincoln Memorial Cemetery on Route 30 in Aurora, Illinois. Wes came back from Wyoming and all four Bennett children were able to find solace in the lives that both of their parents had lived and how they had, in every way, honored the Lord with their time on Earth. Friends and family reminisced about the model that Bill and Edna had been to so many for so long. Just the thought of Bill being gone left most who had known him with some big shoes to fill.

William Wesley Bennett, Sr. with his great grandchildren, Kendall and Jack.

(Bennett Family Photo)

One afternoon in February 2012, I dialed Bill's number and planned to apologize for taking so long to get back to him regarding his request to meet again with Setchan. The phone rang once or twice and then clicked into the familiar recording of, "The number you have dialed has been disconnected. No further information is available." My heart sank as there was no good scenario which would have Bill's phone disconnected. Had he become sick or have an accident? Maybe he moved in with one of his kids? I quickly looked up Nolan and Carol Foreman's number and dialed it. Nolan answered and I told him why I called. "Here, I'll let you talk to Carol," he said. In a few seconds, Carol came to the phone. I said, "Carol, I just called your dad and his phone is disconnected. Is he okay?" She said, "Oh ... Brent ... he passed away in November." I was shocked. How could he have died and I hadn't heard about it for three months? I asked Carol what had happened. She told me that he had been under treatment for cancer and it had progressed very quickly in the end. I told her how sorry I was for her loss and I thought that her dad was a great man and I had the utmost respect for him. She thanked me for calling and we hung up the phone. It was very hard for me to process that Bill was gone. I had never even seen him in sickness or frailty. Maybe that was the way it was meant to be.

I laid the phone down on the counter and just let myself feel stunned for a few minutes. My thoughts went to the fact that Bill had gotten sick and died without me even knowing about it. Had I not waited so long to get back to him on his request, I am sure I would have found out that he was suffering and could have at least been able to say goodbye to him. I considered myself to be Bill's friend, but I wasn't there for him, as a friend should be, at the end of his life. I knew that Bill's family had been there with him, and he had everything a man could want during that time. I also knew that because of what Christ had done for Bill on the cross all those years ago, and Bill's acceptance of that great sacrifice, Bill's spirit was now with Christ for eternity. Because Bill and I had this in common, though I would miss him for the rest of my life, I would certainly see him again one day. I told Belle that Bill had died and I then went and sat in the garage and prayed and cried at the same time. There have only been a few times in my life when I have been acutely and suddenly aware that the world had changed and would never be the same; this was one of them.

96. Memorial Day

May, 2017. My dad had participated in dozens, if not hundreds, of parades over the years, by driving his WW II vintage Jeep set up with a full array of combat gear. In 2016, he completed a three-year project of restoring a 1942 Ford-manufactured Jeep and invited me to drive the "new" Jeep during the 4th of July parade in my old home town of Aurora. One might think this type of municipal parade had become outdated and poorly attended in the enlightened age of social media and streaming television, but not in Aurora, Illinois. The crowd was huge and appreciative. The following year, I was asked to drive the 1942 Ford, again, in the Memorial Day parade, and

I agreed. Thinking about all that Memorial Day means and those we are to remember on this holiday, caused me to think deeply about Bill Bennett, Bob Stoner, Peter Nicholas Andrews, Channing Miller and other veterans from Aurora. I decided these were the heroes that Memorial Day was all about and they deserved to be remembered.

I made a few 10" x 20" placards with the names and awards for Stoner, Andrews and Miller, as well as a listing for Bill and his 2nd Division Marine buddies from Aurora. There were many other notable figures from Bill Bennett's life like Truitt Anderson and Bob Swigert, but this parade would be just for the hometown boys. Another placard noted that 9,834 men and women from Aurora served in the U.S. Armed Forces during WW II; roughly 24% of the city's population of 40,000 at the outset of the war. 293 gave their lives and there were 470 Purple Hearts awarded to Aurorans. I called Pete and Kathy Andrews and asked them if I could borrow one of Bill's original 2nd Division patches and a pair of his "Globe and Anchor" insignias. I attached the red patch, featuring a hand holding a yellow torch with the number 2 and five white stars, to the left arm of my khaki shirt and set the small insignia into the chest pocket. The large insignia went into my pants pocket. Belle helped me refold an eight-foot by five-foot, 48-star American flag I had bought at a garage sale when I was a ten-year-old back in Aurora. This flag has always been special since it is not only a WW II era flag, but is also the same size as those used during memorial services and then given to the family of the fallen.

May 29th, 2017, dawned clear and bright and a finer day for a parade had never been gifted to mankind. I put out our American flag on the front of the house and a smaller one out front next to the mailbox and had a great breakfast and chatted with Belle for a while. I drove to Aurora and turned from my usual route to head north on South Fourth Street and took the turn on to Simms Street. I slowed down to take a long look at the old Bennett place at 454 Simms and marveled at how similar it still looks to the old photos from the 1930s and '40s. Every time I see that house, I think about how badly Bill wanted to see it again back during the war years; how he longed to turn the front door knob and hug his family. I also think about Jessie Bennett's faithfulness in prayer for her son and how Bill eventually did have that blessed homecoming. Jessie had indeed filled the air between that house and heaven with constant prayers. I arrived at my dad's house where he had the two Jeeps and a trailer already staged for departure. We drove the Jeeps downtown and found our place in the staging area for the parade. I set a WW II Marine helmet on the passenger seat in front of the tightly folded 48-star flag and attached the six placards to the trailer. There was a lot of hoopla going on in the staging area, as there always is, as I attached the placards. Just about 50 yards away from me, the East Aurora High School Band was going through their warm ups and they blasted out "Wave the Flag of East Aurora" as well as I have ever heard it played. My thoughts went back over 80 years to a young Bill Bennett in a Thanksgiving Day parade; how proud he had been to carry that East Aurora flag. I walked up the street and watched the band. The red and black uniforms were modern and very sharp looking. There were a dozen or so "color guard" members carrying a variety of flags including several East Aurora flags. I wondered if those kids had any idea how much heritage there was in the flags they carried. I doubted it. I wondered if any of the 200 kids in the band had ever thought about the dozens of their alumni who had died for their country 75 years ago. I doubted that, too.

It's hard to imagine that fine men like Stoner, Andrews and Miller, (among many others) who walked the halls of the school, graduated from the ranks and then went on to serve their country and lose their lives, have been completely forgotten.

I started the Jeep and waited for the instruction to move ahead as the parade started. I took the Globe and Anchor insignia from my pocket and set it on the seat next to the helmet. This detail was just for me. The helmet and the flag represented the fallen men of D/2/18, as well as PFC Peter Nicholas Andrews and Sergeant Channing B. Miller. No one else would know, and only a few would catch the meaning of the folded flag in the seat. As the parade began, I kept my attention forward and did not wave, look or smile at the huge crowd that had gathered along Benton Avenue. As the parade stopped and started, I could tell that some of the people were reading the placards and seeing the statistics of the large sacrifice of Aurorans from the Greatest Generation. Applause would erupt intermittently as we wound through downtown.

New generations of Americans were seeing the names of real heroes on that trailer and maybe they were thankful for the sacrifices that were made long before they were born. I hoped at least a few had such thoughts. We passed the old post office where Bill Bennett had walked with Dick Sheble to enlist on December 8th, 1941 and then turned north on Broadway past where the old Schmitz and Gretencort men's clothing store used to be. This was the town where Bill Bennett grew up with Bob Stoner, George Troll, Bob Nix, Bud Dix, Dick Sheble, Bill Rees, Ed Kocjan, Louis Kuk, Duane Burkhart, Pete Andrews, Channing Miller, Bob Reder, Bill Johnson and so many others; long before they were called to defend their country and the freedom of future generations. All of these men were gone now and memories to but a few friends and family. Their faces are gone from the crowds that line the streets for parades and they are missing from the trailers that pull the elderly veterans. But when I heard the applause and saw the flags waving, I knew that although these men are gone now, this is and always will be their town. As long as there is any semblance of freedom left in America, then these great men will own a piece of it. If freedom vanishes from our nation, no one will ever be able to blame this "Greatest Generation," which invested so many young lives, cut short, so that liberty could be extended into the hands of the future.

Watching only the trailer in front of me, I drove with as little movement as possible. I wanted to be a part of a moving memorial and not attract any attention away from the trailer. I wanted people to read the names and think about the price that was paid. It occurred to me this idea was similar to the way Bill Bennett lived his life, even as a Christian. He wanted to be a part of the plan but not attract attention away from what was really important. He lived his life to help point the way to Almighty God, who pursued us when we were hopelessly lost in our fallen state of sinfulness. Bill spent his entire life wanting to help others come to a place where they could stop and think about the price that was paid; paid by Christ Himself, on that cross so long ago. Bill not only gave a huge part of his life to preserve the physical freedom of a country, but he invested his entire life to help others find the eternal freedom of forgiveness and unity with Christ.

As I neared the end of the parade route, I couldn't help but see a young couple with three small children crouched on the curb to my right side. The children waved excitedly as I looked their way and I couldn't help but wave back. Their parents smiled as if I had given something to their children. Perhaps I had in some minuscule way, but the men whose names were on that trailer had given their children something much greater; something I hope they grow up to enjoy and cherish; something that will always make Memorial Day sacred.

Epilogue

Three years after Bill Bennett passed away, West Aurora High School was planning a Veteran's Day event to honor the family members of the students who had served in the United States military. During the event, to be held in the auditorium, the students would be given a chance to stand to represent their loved ones who served our country. Moses and Anne Cheng's daughter, Stephanie, was a junior at the time and her thoughts went to "Grandpa Bill," as was Bill's adopted name within the Cheng family. Stephanie knew of Bill's life-long commitment to the Marine Corps and asked her parents if they thought it would be okay if she stood to represent Bill at the ceremony. Of course, she was told that it sounded like a good idea. When the ceremony came and the United States Marine Corps was recognized, Stephanie stood to her feet in memory of Corporal William W. Bennett, U.S.M.C., Company D, 2nd Battalion, 18th Marine Regiment. Stephanie Cheng's thoughtfulness and respect for Bill was a touching reminder of Bill's remarkable warmth and openness toward others. Even very late in life, Bill had become a vital part of the Cheng family and his love for God and country had made an indelible imprint on their lives. Stephanie's story touched me as my first memory of Bill Bennett was of him standing to his feet to acknowledge his well-deserved association with the Marine Corps. On that day, now long ago, he was a stranger to me. Now I look back and can only thank God for allowing me to get to know Bill as a friend and to be able to say that without a doubt, he was the finest man I have ever known.

I think most people can be divided into two groups: those who believe in God and those who don't. I know there are a lot of extenuating circumstances attached to belief in God, but on a simple level, you have to find yourself on one side or the other. When I was a kid back in Aurora and I went to Vacation Bible School at Claim Street Baptist, I learned this Bible verse: Romans 8:28, "And we know that in all things God works for the good of those who love Him, who have been called according to His purpose." The essence of this statement is that God knows what is best for us and is always working behind the scenes to guide the life path of people who acknowledge Him and love Him.

One profound lesson that I have learned from closely examining Bill Bennett's life is that there were far too many amazing occurrences to be the sum total of random chance. I came to see the fingerprints of God on the details of Bill's life in the very same way that I see those fingerprints in the lives of Biblical characters. This is not as surprising as it might seem as God claims to be the "same yesterday, today and forever," so His handiwork would undoubtedly have some similarities throughout the ages. This would also apply to my life and yours, depending on our chosen disposition to God. Bill's life demonstrated the truth of God's promise in this verse.

The eighth chapter of Romans also contains some profound words that I find astounding in light of Bill's life experience:

If God is for us, who can be against us? Who shall separate us from the love of Christ? Shall trouble or hardship or persecution or famine or nakedness or danger or sword? For your sake we face death all day long: we are considered as sheep to be slaughtered. No, in all these things we are more than conquerors through Him who loved us. For I am convinced that neither death nor life, neither angels nor demons, neither the present nor the future, nor any powers, neither height nor depth, nor anything else in all creation, will be able to separate us from the love of God that is in Christ Jesus our Lord.

These words clearly describe God's commitment to Bill during his lifetime, and I know that Bill believed his path was ordered by God. Bill's life was not put together the way it was because Bill possessed super human skill or had superior intelligence; nor was it just a series of random coincidences. Bill's life was put together by the hand of God because Bill asked God to do so nearly every day of his life. Bill recognized his need for God and yielded his life's sovereignty back to his Creator. It is that simple. In the end, NOTHING could separate Bill from the love of God, and the love that Bill carried for others allowed God to touch their lives as well.

Knowing Bill, and his commitment to God, his family, his nation and his friends, made a powerful difference in my life. Bill's impact on lives around him spread outward like the ripples in a pond when you drop a stone into it. Whether you have been aware of it or not, each and every day that you live on this planet you have been building a legacy and impacting the world around you in some significant way. When you consider the hurt and destruction that will be left behind by so many who live only for themselves in comparison with the life that Bill Bennett lived, it should give you pause for reflection. Bill believed, with every fiber of his being, that one decision on his part, very early in life, set him on the course for wisely investing his entire life. That decision was the choice he made to accept the sacrifice that Jesus Christ, our Creator in human form, made for all of us on the cross. Bill knew that the blood Christ shed on the cross was specifically for him and he needed only to act in faith to accept it and receive it into his life. In return, God provided forgiveness and the Lord sent a part of Himself, His Holy Spirit, to fellowship with Bill and to guide him throughout his life.

During all the years of Bill's life he was never actually alone. Bill became acutely aware of the presence of the Holy Spirit just after his brush with death on Tarawa. Bill believed, as do I, that it was the voice of the Lord who whispered his name on Tarawa and spared his life. In doing so, God spared Bill's life and gave him the gift to live on when his friends were taken into eternity. Truitt Anderson and Bob Swigert had committed their lives to Christ before Tarawa and there is no doubt they were there to welcome Bill into heaven when he finally arrived. God kept his promise to Bill when He said, "Never will I leave you, never will I forsake you." [Hebrews 13:5]

Some men say that there is no God and that living your life to try and please an imaginary creator is a waste of time. I say they are wrong; dead wrong. Even if it were a verifiable fact (it is not) that there is no God, the cumulative good that men like Bill Bennett amassed during their lives has certainly made the world a better place. There is no arguing with that. To take a historical look back to America's "Greatest Generation" and not make note of their collective commitment to the Christ of the cross would be a massive oversight as well as a grievous inaccuracy. Many U.S. WW II combat veterans have noted that if there were any atheists or agnostics within their companies, they never knew about them. It seemed like they all believed in God to some extent; perhaps because they knew they may not be far from meeting Him at any particular time.

The true story of William Wesley Bennett, Sr., now belongs to the ages, along with those of so many great men and women of God. The true, long lasting value of Bill's story will now rest on the effect it will have on people who will go out into the world tomorrow and make decisions that will forever impact those around them. Bill's story is not his alone, but also the story of the Lord who walked unseen next to him every day of his life. It is a wondrous story of how God and man can not only reconcile through the cross of Calvary, but commune spiritually as friends to build an example for others who will follow ... once upon a lifetime.

Brent A. Peterson
Yorkville, Illinois
January, 2019

The Gospel According to Bill

If you are interested in knowing more about the life-changing relationship with God that Bill Bennett experienced and enjoyed during his lifetime, I encourage you to find a copy of The Holy Bible and begin by reading the Gospel of John. You will see how Jesus Christ came into the world to seek and save the lost human race, and how He paid the price for our freedom from sin and rebellion with His very own blood which was shed on the cross where He was brutally crucified by sinful men.

"Sin" is our rebellious nature to defy God's love for us and go our own way, to live our own way. Sin entered the human race way back at the beginning when Adam and Eve believed Satan's lie and decided that they knew more than the God who made them. Once sin entered the human realm, every sort of evil became common throughout the ages and is still just as rampant today, if not more so. God did not leave us to the ravages of sin and evil; our Creator Himself made the grand plan of redemption and came into the world in the form of the child, Jesus of Nazareth. He led a perfect, sinless life and performed miracles to attest to his true identity. He PROMISED that anyone who would seek Him would find Him and he promised to change lives in each case. He spoke of His "going away" and His "coming again." He was falsely accused, arrested and condemned in a rigged court. Sentenced to death, He was nailed to the cross between two condemned thieves.

After his death, he was buried in a borrowed tomb and ROSE AGAIN FROM THE DEAD on the third day, as he had promised His followers. Only one spiritual leader has ever conquered death to prove to us that He truly is who He said he was; our Creator. In His death, He who was without sin paid the full price for OUR sin and SET US FREE FROM SIN and DEATH; but action is still required on our part; We have to ACCEPT this great sacrifice, turn from our wickedness and seek a new life through Christ, who died for us. When we look to Him now and seek Him as He instructed us to do, He will hear us and take action on our behalf. Our sin and wickedness will be forgiven and we will be given a new life in place of our old; an eternal life that has no end. He will come and dwell WITHIN us through the miracle of His Holy Spirit, which is simply His unseen presence. This may all seem too wonderful to believe, but I will testify to the power of the Risen Christ as it transformed my life many years ago. At one moment I was filled with myself and pride, and the next I was a new creation capable of truly loving and forgiving for the first time. What God has done for you, and what He has provided for you, is due to His great love for you. He wants you to have a way out from your sin; which will ultimately result in your destruction, if left unchanged.

"There is a way that seems right to a man, but in the end it leads to death." [Proverbs 14:12] Left to our own way, we have some years to live on this Earth and then the certainty of death. The forgiveness and eternal life offered by Christ is the only way to union with God. This belief, in a nutshell, is what Bill believed and what brought him into a life-changing relationship with the Lord. The power of God's promise and the unity of God's Holy Spirit was the common bond that Bill and I shared. We knew that even though we were more than a generation apart in age, we carried the same signature and identity of those who have come face to face with the Risen Lord and Savior, Jesus Christ of Nazareth.

When all has been said and done by men, there is no one who can say it better than Jesus Himself in the Gospel of John, Chapter 14, verses 15-21:

If you love me, you will obey what I command. And I will ask the Father, and He will give you another Counselor to be with you forever—the Spirit of truth. The world cannot accept him, because it neither sees him nor knows him. But you know him, for he lives with you and will be in you. I will not leave you as orphans; I will come to you. Before long, the world will not see me anymore, but you will see me. Because I live, you also will live. On that day you will realize that I am in my Father, and you are in me, and I am in you. Whoever has my commands and obeys them, he is the one who loves me. He who loves me will be loved by my Father, and I too will love him and show myself to him.

Semper Fidelis, Bill. Semper Fi.

Once Upon a Lifetime: Research, Interviews, Bibliography and Sources
Compiled by Brent A. Peterson, August, 2014 through August, 2018.
All references from the Holy Bible are either King James Version or New International Version.

1. **A Guy Named Bill**
   Author's first-hand account

2. **True Pioneers**
   Archives of the Dutchess County Historical Society, Poughkeepsie, NY.
   Archives of the Ela Township Historical Society, Lake Zurich, IL
   Archives of the Floyd County Historical Society, Charles City, IA
   United States Census Records
   Ancestry.com

3. **A Change In Direction**
   Archives of the Floyd County Historical Society, Charles City, IA
   United States Census Records
   Aurora Historical Society, Aurora, IL
   Bennett Family Archives

4. **A New Bennett Family**
   Bennett Family Archives
   Bennett Family Photos
   United States Census records.
   Aurora Historical Society
   Aurora Beacon News Archives / Aurora Public Library
   Aurora City Directories, 1900-1919 / Aurora Public Library

5. **Arrival**
   Bennett Family Archives
   Bennett Family Photos
   United States Census records
   Aurora Historical Society
   Aurora Beacon News Archives / Aurora Public Library
   Aurora City Directories, 1900-1919 / Aurora Public Library

6. **The Early Years**
   Bennett Family Archives / Photos
   Aurora Beacon News Archives / Aurora Public Library
   Aurora City Directories / Aurora Public Library
   Aurora Historical Society Archives / Michael Fichtel
   Fourth Street Methodist Church / History Archives
   East Aurora High School / 1920-1924 Yearbooks / Aurora Public Library
   The Holy Bible / King James Version

7. **A New Kid In Town**
   Personal memories of William Wesley Bennett, Sr.
   Bennett Family Archives / Photos
   Stoner Family Archives / Photos
   Aurora Beacon News Archives / Aurora Public Library
   Aurora City Directories, 1927-1930 / Aurora Public Library
   Fourth Street Methodist Church / History Archives
   United States Census Records

8. **A Change of Address**
   Personal memories of William Wesley Bennett, Sr.
   Bennett Family Archives / Photos
   Author's tour of 454 Simms Street / Courtesy of the Cobb Family / 2016
   Aurora City Directory, 1925-1930 / Aurora Public Library
   United States Census Records
   Aurora Historical Society Archives
   Aurora Beacon News Archives / Aurora Public Library

9. **A New School**
   Aurora Historical Society Archives
   Aurora Beacon News Articles / Aurora Public Library
   Bennett Family Archives / Photos
   Personal interview of Ronald Olsen / 2016 / EAHS class of 1943 / C.M. Bardwell student
   Aurora Beacon News Archives / Aurora Public Library
   Chicago Tribune Archives

10. Close To Home
Bennett Family Archives / Photos
Aurora Beacon News Archives / Aurora Public Library

11. Becoming Bill
EAHS Yearbooks / various years.
Personal recollection of Fred C. Carter
Personal interview of Ronald Olsen / 2016
United States Census Records
Aurora City Directory / various years
Kane County (Illinois) Death Records
Aurora Beacon News Archives / Aurora Public Library

12. Champs!
Bennett Family Archives / Photos
Fourth Street Methodist Church History Archives / Weekly Bulletins
Aurora Beacon News Archives / Aurora Public Library

13. A Tale of Red and Black
Bennett Family Archives / Photos
East Aurora High School Speculum (yearbook) / various years.
West Aurora High School EOS (yearbook) / various years
Aurora Beacon News Archives / Aurora Public Library
Aurora City Directory / Aurora Public Library / various years.
Personal memories of William Wesley Bennett, Sr.
Personal memories of Fred C. Carter / EAHS class of 1934
Personal interview of Ronald Olsen / 2016 / EAHS class of 1943
Personal interview of Henry Cowherd / 2016 / EAHS class of 1945
Telephone interview of Jean Dix-Carson, 2017
Book: "Aurora's East-West Football Rivalry" by Steve Solarz: 2014 The History Press

14. The 1937 Tomcats
Bennett Family Archives / Photos
East Aurora High School Speculum (yearbook) / various years.
West Aurora High School EOS (yearbook) / various years
Aurora Beacon News Archives / Aurora Public Library
Aurora City Directory / Aurora Public Library / various years
Personal memories of William Wesley Bennett, Sr.
Personal memories of Fred C. Carter / EAHS class of 1934
Personal interview of Ronald Olsen / 2016 / EAHS class of 1943
Personal interview of Henry Cowherd / 2016 / EAHS class of 1945
Telephone interview of Jean Dix-Carson, 2017
Book: "Aurora's East-West Football Rivalry" by Steve Solarz: Copyright 2014 The History Press

15. From Denver, With Love
Bennett Family Archives / Photos
Personal letters of William Wesley Bennett, Sr.
Personal interview of Carole Casey-Boone, daughter of Mary Anne Swanson
East Aurora High School Speculum, 1937-1938
Aurora Beacon News Archives / Aurora Public Library
United States Census Records
Aurora City Directory, 1937 and 1938 / Aurora Public Library

16. The End Of An Era
Bennett Family Archives / Photos
Personal letters of William Wesley Bennett, Sr.
Personal interview of Carole Casey-Boone, daughter of Mary Anne Swanson
East Aurora High School Speculum, 1937-1938
Aurora Beacon News Archives / Aurora Public Library

United States Census Records

Aurora City Directory, 1937 and 1938 / Aurora Public Library

Personal memories of William Wesley Bennett, Sr.

Aurora Public Library / History Department Files

Aurora Historical Society Archives

17. Wedding Bells

Bennett Family Archives / Photos

Stoner Family Archives / Photos

Aurora Beacon News Archives / Aurora Public Library / Society Pages

United States Census Records

Aurora City Directory, 1938 and 1939 / Aurora Public Library

Aurora Public Library / History Department Files

Aurora Historical Society Archives

18. The Clippers

Bennett Family Archives / Photos

Aurora Beacon News Archives / Aurora Public Library / Society Pages

Personal Collection of Robert McCue

United States Census Records

Aurora City Directory, 1938 and 1939 / Aurora Public Library

Aurora Public Library / History Department Files

Aurora Historical Society Archives

Article: Fox Valley Sports Journal, November 3rd, 1983

Personal memories of William Wesley Bennett, Sr.

Chicago Tribune Archives

19. The Unexpected

Personal interview of Charles Manning, III / 2015 / 2016

Aurora Beacon News Archives / Aurora Public Library

Assistance of Rob Winder / Aurora Public Library

United States Census Records

Aurora City Directory, 1939 / Aurora Public Library

Aurora Historical Society Archives / Assisted by Michael Fichtel

Cedar Rapids Gazette Archives

State of Iowa / Senate Records

20. A Bitter Pill

Personal interview of Charles Manning, III / 2015 / 2016

Aurora Beacon News Archives / Aurora Public Library

Assistance of Rob Winder / Aurora Public Library

United States Census Records

Aurora City Directory, 1939-40 / Aurora Public Library

Aurora Historical Society Archives / Assisted by Michael Fichtel

Cedar Rapids Gazette Archives

Bennett Family Archives

21. Moving On

Personal Memories of William Wesley Bennett, Sr.

Article: Fox Valley Sports Journal, November 3rd, 1983

Aurora Beacon News Archives / Aurora Public Library

Aurora City Directory, 1939-40 / Aurora Public Library

North Central College Archives / Yearbooks, 1939 Curriculum

United States Census Records

Chicago Tribune Archives

Bennett Family Archives / letters

Stoner Family Archives

The Stoner Weekly News

Lewis University Archives

Michael Carpino, Aviator

22. Different Directions

Bennett Family Archives / Letters and Photos

Stoner Family Archives / Stoner Weekly News

Aurora Beacon News Archives / Aurora Public Library

United States Census Records

Chicago Tribune Archives

Aurora City Directory, 1939-40 / Aurora Public Library

United States Naval Records

Fourth Street Methodist Church History Archives / Assisted by Judy Bieritz

Richard and Debbie Cobb / Tour of 454 Simms Street

23. A New Flame

Bennett Family Archives / Letters and Photos

Personal Memories of William Wesley Bennett, Sr.

Telephone Interviews of Donald and Ronald Glossop

Telephone Interview of Carol June Glossop-Johnson

Aurora Beacon News Archives / Aurora Public Library

United States Census Records

Chicago Tribune Archives

Aurora City Directory, 1940-41 / Aurora Public Library

Aurora Historical Society Archives / Assisted by Michael Fichtel

Aurora Public Library / Industrial Records / Assisted by Rob Winder

United States Naval Records

Sandwich Historical Society / Joan Hardekopf and Vivian Wright

Personal Interview of Phyllis Cochran-Price, sister of Helen Cochran

Personal Interview of Susan Price-Johnson, niece of Helen Cochran

Sandwich High School Yearbooks, 1937-1940 / Sandwich Public Library

Telephone interview of Ada Scent-Hanson, 1940 Graduate of Sandwich High School

Fourth Street Methodist Church History Archives / Assisted by Judy Bieritz

24. Looking Ahead

Bennett Family Archives / Letters and Photos

Stoner Family Archives

Personal Memories of William Wesley Bennett, Sr.

Ripon College Yearbooks, 1940-41

Telephone Interviews of Donald and Ronald Glossop

Telephone Interview of Carol June Glossop

Aurora Beacon News Archives / Aurora Public Library

United States Census Records

Chicago Tribune Archives

Aurora City Directory, 1940-41 / Aurora Public Library

Aurora Historical Society Archives / Assisted by Michael Fichtel

Aurora Public Library / Industrial Records / Assisted by Rob Winder

United States Naval Records.

Sandwich Historical Society / Joan Hardekopf and Vivian Wright

Personal Interview of Phyllis Cochran, sister of Helen Cochran

Sandwich High School Yearbooks, 1937-1940 / Sandwich Public Library

Telephone interview of Ada Scent-Hanson, 1940 Graduate of Sandwich High School

Fourth Street Methodist Church History Archives / Assisted by Judy Bieritz

25. The Winds of War

Personal Memories of William Wesley Bennett, Sr.

Chicago Tribune Archives

Aurora Beacon News Archives / Aurora Public Library

Bennett Family Archives

Historic Radio Archives / Multiple Sources

26. Commitment

Personal Memories of William Wesley Bennett, Sr.

Chicago Tribune Archives

Aurora Beacon News Archives / Aurora Public Library

Bennett Family Archives

Historic Radio Archives / Multiple Sources

Richard and Debbie Cobb / Tour of 454 Simms Street

27. **The Wonder City**
    Personal Memories of William Wesley Bennett, Sr.
    Chicago Tribune Archives
    Aurora Beacon News Archives / Aurora Public Library
    Bennett Family Archives / Letters and Photos / Jessie's scrapbook
    Richard and Debbie Cobb / Tour of 454 Simms Street
    Telephone Interview of Jean A. Dix-Carson, daughter of Earl "Bud" Dix, Jr.
    Telephone Interviews of Donald and Ronald Glossop
    Telephone Interview of Carol June Glossop
    Sandwich Historical Society
    Personal Interview of Phyllis Cochran, sister of Helen Cochran
    Fourth Street Methodist Church History Archives / Assisted by Judy Bieritz
    U.S.M.C. Records

28. **The Corps**
    Personal Memories of William Wesley Bennett, Sr.
    Personal Letters of William Wesley Bennett, Sr.
    Chicago Tribune Archives
    Aurora Beacon News Archives / Aurora Public Library
    Bennett Family Archives / Letters and Photos / Jessie's scrapbook
    U.S.M.C. Records
    Personal Interviews of Emanuel E. "Manny" Bud / 2016
    "U.S.M.C. Uniforms & Equipment, 1941-1945" / Alberti-Pradier / Histoire & Collections, France / 2007

29. **Semper Fidelis**
    Personal Memories of William Wesley Bennett, Sr.
    Personal Letters of William Wesley Bennett, Sr.
    U.S.M.C. Records
    Personal Interviews of Emanuel E. "Manny" Bud / 2016
    M1903 range instruction courtesy of Michael and Donald Carpino
    Personal Interviews of Emanuel E. "Manny" Bud / 2016
    Basic Field Manual, Bayonet, M1905 / FM 23-25 / U. S. War Dept., 1940
    "U.S.M.C. Uniforms & Equipment, 1941-1945" / Alberti-Pradier / Histoire & Collections, France / 2007

30. **The 2nd Pioneers**
    Personal memories and letters of William Wesley Bennett, Sr.
    Personal interviews of Emanuel E. "Manny" Bud / 2016
    U.S.M.C. Records
    First United Methodist Church of San Diego / Bulletin
    Aurora Beacon News Archives / Aurora Public Library
    "Miss You" by Dinah Shore / 1942 RCA, Bluebird Records / 1929, Tobias Brothers
    United States Census Records
    "U.S.M.C. Uniforms & Equipment, 1941-1945" / Alberti-Pradier / Histoire & Collections, France / 2007

31. **Company A**
    Personal memories and letters of William Wesley Bennett, Sr.
    Personal interviews of Emanuel E. "Manny" Bud / 2016
    U.S.M.C. Records / Muster Rolls
    United States Census Records
    "Follow Me" / Richard W. Johnston / 1948, Random House
    "One Square Mile of Hell / John Wukovitz / NAL Caliber, 2006
    "Once A Marine, Always A Marine" / Mike Masters (Mike Matkovich) / 1988
    Telephone Interview of George P. Gabel, Jr. / 2016
    Emory Ashurst and Sharon Ashurst, 2018 interview and manuscript review

32. 746 Automatic Rifleman

Basic Field Manual, FM 23-15 / Browning Automatic Rifle, Caliber.30, M1918A2 With Bipod / U. S. War Dept. 1940

Personal memories and letters of William Wesley Bennett, Sr.

Personal interviews of Emanuel E. "Manny" Bud / 2016

U.S.M.C. Records / Muster Rolls

United States Census Records

"Follow Me" / Richard W. Johnston / 1948, Random House

Stoner Family Archives / Assisted by Carol Crawford and Suellen Stoner-Haynes.

"U.S.M.C. Uniforms & Equipment, 1941-1945" / Alberti-Pradier / Histoire & Collections, France / 2007

33. Shipping Out

Personal memories and letters of William Wesley Bennett, Sr.

Personal interviews of Emanuel E. "Manny" Bud / 2016

U.S.M.C. Records / Muster Rolls

United States Census Records

"Follow Me" / Richard W. Johnston / 1948, Random House

United States Naval Records

"U.S.M.C. Uniforms & Equipment, 1941-1945" / Alberti-Pradier / Histoire & Collections, France / 2007

"The Boat That Won The War" An Illustrated History of the Higgins LCVP" / Charles C. Roberts, Jr. / Seaforth / 2017

Author's Firsthand Experience with Higgins LCVP courtesy of Charles C. Roberts, Jr. / 2017

34. At Sea

"The Boat that Won the War" An Illustrated History of the Higgins LCVP / Charles C. Roberts, Jr. / Seaforth / 2017

Author's Firsthand Experience with Higgins LCVP courtesy of Charles C. Roberts, Jr. / 2017

"Once A Marine, Always A Marine" / Mike Masters (Mike Matkovich) / 1988

First Presbyterian Church of San Diego / Church Bulletin, Sunday, June 28th, 1942 / Bennett Family Archives

"This Above All" / Darryl F. Zanuck / 20th Century Fox / Released May 12th, 1942

35. Final Preparations

Personal Memories and Letters of William Wesley Bennett, Sr.

Personal Interviews of Emanuel E. "Manny" Bud / 2016

U.S.M.C. Records / Muster Rolls

United States Census Records

"Follow Me" / Richard W. Johnston / 1948, Random House

United States Naval Records

"U.S.M.C. Uniforms & Equipment, 1941-1945" / Alberti-Pradier / Histoire & Collections, France / 2007

"Once A Marine, Always A Marine" / Mike Masters (Mike Matkovich) / 1988

36. Into The Fray

Personal Memories and Letters of William Wesley Bennett, Sr.

Personal Interviews of Emanuel E. "Manny" Bud / 2016

U.S.M.C. Records / Muster Rolls

United States Census Records

"Follow Me" / Richard W. Johnston / 1948, Random House

United States Naval Records

"U.S.M.C. Uniforms & Equipment, 1941-1945" / Alberti-Pradier / Histoire & Collections, France / 2007

"Guadalcanal, Tarawa and Beyond" / William W. Rogal / McFarland & Company / 2010

Dan Nofziger / Lieutenant Harold A. Hayes, Jr. Family

37. Orphans

Personal Memories and Letters of William Wesley Bennett, Sr.

Personal Interviews of Emanuel E. "Manny" Bud / 2016

U.S.M.C. Records / Muster Rolls

"Once A Marine, Always A Marine" / Mike Masters (Mike Matkovich) / 1988

United States Census Records

"Follow Me" / Richard W. Johnston / 1948, Random House

United States Naval Records

"Guadalcanal, Tarawa And Beyond" / William W. Rogal / McFarland & Company / 2010

History Of United States Naval Operations In WW II / The Struggle for Guadalcanal / Samuel Elliot Morison / Little, Brown and Company / 1949

38. Stranded

Personal Memories and Letters of William Wesley Bennett, Sr.

Personal Interviews of Emanuel E. "Manny" Bud / 2016

U.S.M.C. Records / Muster Rolls

"Once A Marine, Always A Marine" / Mike Masters (Mike Matkovich) / 1988

United States Census Records

"Follow Me" / Richard W. Johnston / 1948, Random House

United States Naval Records

"Guadalcanal, Tarawa And Beyond" / William W. Rogal / McFarland & Company / 2010

"The Leathernecks Come Through" / Chaplain W. Wyeth Willard / Sixth Edition, 1985 / New England Classics

39. The Reunion

Personal Memories and Letters of William Wesley Bennett, Sr.

Personal Interviews of Emanuel E. "Manny" Bud / 2016

U.S.M.C. Records / Muster Rolls

"Once A Marine, Always A Marine" / Mike Masters (Mike Matkovich) / 1988

United States Census Records

"Follow Me" / Richard W. Johnston / 1948, Random House

United States Naval Records

"Guadalcanal, Tarawa And Beyond" / William W. Rogal / McFarland & Company / 2010

"We Buried Our Buddies & My Stories" / Charles Wysocki, Jr. / 2008 Trafford Publishing

Company D/2/18 photographs.

Swigert Family Photos

Dan Nofziger / Lieutenant Harold A. Hayes, Jr. Family

40. Letters From Home

Personal Memories and Letters of William Wesley Bennett, Sr.

Personal Interviews of Emanuel E. "Manny" Bud / 2016

U.S.M.C. Records / Muster Rolls

"Once A Marine, Always A Marine" / Mike Masters (Mike Matkovich) / 1988

United States Census Records

"Follow Me" / Richard W. Johnston / 1948, Random House

United States Naval Records

"Guadalcanal, Tarawa And Beyond" / William W. Rogal / McFarland & Company / 2010

"We Buried Our Buddies & My Stories" / Charles Wysocki, Jr. / 2008 Trafford Publishing

Company D/2/18 photographs.

Swigert Family Photos / Letters

41. Naval Nightmares

History of United States Naval Operations In WW II / The Struggle for Guadalcanal / Samuel Eliot Morison / Little, Brown and Company / 1949

Personal Memories and Letters of William Wesley Bennett, Sr.

Personal Interviews of Emanuel E. "Manny" Bud / 2016

U.S.M.C. Records / Muster Rolls

"Once A Marine, Always A Marine" / Mike Masters (Mike Matkovich) / 1988

United States Census Records

"Follow Me" / Richard W. Johnston / 1948, Random House

United States Naval Records

"Guadalcanal, Tarawa And Beyond" / William W. Rogal / McFarland & Company / 2010

"We Buried Our Buddies & My Stories" / Charles Wysocki, Jr. / 2008 Trafford Publishing

Company D/2/18 Platoon photographs

42. Relief

History of United States Naval Operations in WW II / The Struggle for Guadalcanal / Samuel Eliot Morison / Little, Brown and Company / 1949

Personal Memories and Letters of William Wesley Bennett, Sr.

Personal Interviews of Emanuel E. "Manny" Bud / 2016

U.S.M.C. Records / Muster Rolls

"Once A Marine, Always A Marine" / Mike Masters (Mike Matkovich) / 1988

United States Census Records

"Follow Me" / Richard W. Johnston / 1948, Random House

United States Naval Records

"Guadalcanal, Tarawa And Beyond" / William W. Rogal / McFarland & Company / 2010

"We Buried Our Buddies & My Stories" / Charles Wysocki, Jr. / 2008 Trafford Publishing

Company D/2/18 Platoon photographs

43. A Land Down Under

History of United States Naval Operations In WW II / The Struggle for Guadalcanal / Samuel Elliot -Morison / Little, Brown and Company / 1949

Personal Memories and Letters of William Wesley Bennett, Sr.

"Marine Pioneers, The Unsung Heroes of WW II" / Lieutenant Colonel Kerry Lane, Schiffer, 1997

Personal Interviews of Molly Burns (Anderson), nee Webby

Personal Interviews of Emanuel E. "Manny" Bud / 2016

U.S.M.C. Records / Muster Rolls

"Once A Marine, Always A Marine" / Mike Masters (Mike Matkovich) / 1988

"Follow Me" / Richard W. Johnston / 1948, Random House

United States Naval Records

"Guadalcanal, Tarawa And Beyond" / William W. Rogal / McFarland & Company / 2010

"We Buried Our Buddies & My Stories" / Charles Wysocki, Jr. / 2008 Trafford Publishing

Company D/2/18 photos of Charles Wysocki, Jr.

44. Company D

Personal Memories and Letters of William Wesley Bennett, Sr.

Personal Interviews of Emanuel E. "Manny" Bud / 2016

U.S.M.C. Records / Muster Rolls

United States Census Records

M1 Rifle Familiarization courtesy of Michael and Donald Carpino / Arlen Peterson

M1 Carbine Familiarization courtesy of Michael and Donald Carpino

M1 and M1 Carbine / Range Experience courtesy of Michael and Donald Carpino

"Once A Marine, Always A Marine" / Mike Masters (Mike Matkovich) / 1988

"Follow Me" / Richard W. Johnston / 1948, Random House

"Guadalcanal, Tarawa And Beyond" / William W. Rogal / McFarland & Company / 2010

"We Buried Our Buddies & My Stories" / Charles Wysocki, Jr. / 2008 Trafford Publishing

Company D/2/18 photos of Charles Wysocki, Jr. / Courtesy of John Ratomski

Dan Nofziger / Lieutenant Harold A. Hayes, Jr. Family

45. Liberty

Personal Memories and Letters of William Wesley Bennett, Sr.

Personal Interview of Molly Burns (Anderson) nee Webby, 2017

Proctor Family Photos

Personal Interview of Allison Mitchell / daughter of Lorna Proctor and Les Mitchell. 2016-17

Personal Interview of Greg Scott, son of Daphne Proctor-Scott, 2016

Personal Interview of Donald Scott, son of Daphne Proctor-Scott 2017

Scott Family Photos

Methodist Church of New Zealand Archives / Assisted by Jo Smith, 2016

Personal Interview of Alice Hunt, member of St. Paul's, 1943 / Palmerston North, N.Z. 2016

Internet assistance and N.Z. newspaper archive search assistance by Peter McQuarrie

Manawatu-Rangitikei Methodist Parish (formerly St. Paul's) / Palmerson North, N.Z. / Barbara Little

Emory B. Ashurst / Sharon Ashurst telephone interviews

46. The Stoner Weekly News

The Stoner Weekly News, 1942-1946 / Bennett Family Archives / Jessie Bennett

Personal Memories and Letters of William Wesley Bennett, Sr.

Additional Editions of The Stoner Weekly News courtesy of Carol Hard-Crawford

Personal Interviews of Carol Hard-Crawford and Dennis Hard, grandchildren of Sam and Margaret Stoner

Personal Interview of Suellen Stoner-Haynes, daughter of Dexter Stoner.

Personal Interview of William Stoner, son of Harley Stoner

Personal Interview of Tom Stoner, son of Harley Stoner

United States Census Records

Aurora City Directories / Aurora Public Library

47. 533 A New Specialty

Personal Memories and Letters of William Wesley Bennett, Sr.

U.S.M.C. Records / Muster Rolls

"We Buried Our Buddies & My Stories" / Charles Wysocki, Jr. / 2008 Trafford Publishing

Company D/2/18 photos of Charles Wysocki, Jr. / Courtesy of John Ratomski

"Once A Marine, Always A Marine" / Mike Masters (Mike Matkovich) / 1988

"Follow Me" / Richard W. Johnston / 1948, Random House

FM 21-105 Basic Field Manual / Engineer Soldier's Handbook / Chapter 6, Explosives and Demolitions

"The Leathernecks Come Through" / Chaplain W. Wyeth Willard / Sixth Edition, 1985 / New England Classics

48. Camp Life

Personal Memories and Letters of William Wesley Bennett, Sr.

U.S.M.C. Records / Muster Rolls

"We Buried Our Buddies & My Stories" / Charles Wysocki, Jr. / 2008 Trafford Publishing

Company D/2/18 photos of Charles Wysocki, Jr. / Courtesy of John Ratomski

"Once A Marine, Always A Marine" / Mike Masters (Mike Matkovich) / 1988

"Follow Me" / Richard W. Johnston / 1948, Random House

Article: "Paekakariki: Everything Went Wrong" / Frank Zalot, Jr. / 2009

49. Sentimental Ties

Personal Memories and Letters of William Wesley Bennett, Sr.

Sermon notes from Bill Bennett's notebook

Bennett Family Archives

Personal Letter of Mrs. Helen Taylor / Feb. 1943

Personal Interview of Alice Hunt, member of St. Paul's, 1943 / Palmerston North, N.Z. 2016

Manawatu-Rangitikei Methodist Parish (formerly St. Paul's) / Palmerson North, N.Z. / Barbara Little

Methodist Church of New Zealand Archives / Assisted by Jo Smith, 2016

Personal Interview of Allison Mitchell, daughter of Lorna Proctor and Les Mitchell. 2016-17

Holy Bible / King James Version

Personal Interview of Molly Burns (Anderson) nee Webby, 2017

Proctor Family Photos

Aurora Beacon News Archives / Aurora Public Library

50. Broken Hearts

Personal Memories and Letters of William Wesley Bennett, Sr.

Bennett Family Archives / Letters of George Garcia to Jessie Bennett

Personal Interviews of Emanuel E. "Manny" Bud / 2016

Swigert Family Archives / Letter from Manny Bud / Courtesy of Leo and Jackie Swigert / 2015-2016

U.S.M.C. Records / Muster Rolls

"We Buried Our Buddies & My Stories" / Charles Wysocki, Jr. / 2008 Trafford Publishing

Company D/2/18 photos of Charles Wysocki, Jr. / Courtesy of John Ratomski

"Once A Marine, Always A Marine" / Mike Masters (Mike Matkovich) / 1988

"Follow Me" / Richard W. Johnston / 1948, Random House

Personal Interview of Allison Mitchell, daughter of Lorna Proctor and Les Mitchell. 2016-17

Proctor Family Photos

"Bloody Tarawa" / Eric Hammel & John E. Lane / Zenith Press-MBI Pub. / 1998-2006

"Guadalcanal, Tarawa And Beyond" / William W. Rogal / McFarland & Company / 2010

51. A Combat Flier

The Stoner Weekly News

United States Naval Records

Personal Interview of Charlie Cartledge / Pilot of TBM-1C / 2016

Personal Interview of Captain Ken Glass / WW II Pilot of TBM-1C / 2016

52. The Sable and The Wolverine

The Stoner Weekly News

United States Naval Records

Article "Paddle Wheel Flattops of the Great Lakes" by Dave O'Malley / 2013 Vintage Wings of Canada

53. This Is It!

Personal Memories and Letters of William Wesley Bennett, Sr.

United States Naval Records

U.S.M.C. Records / Muster Rolls

54. Tarawa

Personal Memories and Letters of William Wesley Bennett, Sr.

Personal Interview of Molly Burns (Anderson) nee Webby, 2017 / Courtesy of Garry and Di Burns. Australia

U.S.M.C. Records / Muster Rolls

Births, Deaths and Marriages Office / Wellington, New Zealand / Assisted by Adam Bridge, 2017

Anderson Family Photos / Courtesy of Karen Welch, niece of PFC Truitt Alan Anderson

55. Getting Ready

Personal Memories and Letters of William Wesley Bennett, Sr.

"Tarawa: The Story of a Battle" Robert Sherrod / Admiral Nimitz Foundation, 1993 (original, 1944)

"Bloody Tarawa" / Eric Hammel & John E. Lane / Zenith Press-MBI Pub. / 1998-2006

"Guadalcanal, Tarawa And Beyond" / William W. Rogal / McFarland & Company / 2010

U.S.M.C. Records / Muster Rolls

United States Naval Records

"We Buried Our Buddies & My Stories" / Charles Wysocki, Jr. / 2008 Trafford Publishing

Company D/2/18 photos of Charles Wysocki, Jr. / Courtesy of John Ratomski

"Once A Marine, Always A Marine" / Mike Masters (Mike Matkovich) / 1988

"Follow Me" / Richard W. Johnston / 1948, Random House

"Utmost Savagery: The Three Days of Tarawa" / Colonel Joseph H. Alexander, U.S.M.C. (Ret.)

"One Square Mile of Hell" / John Wukovitz / NAL Caliber, 2006

Photo of Company OD/2/18 New Zealand One-pound Note Appears Courtesy of Dean Laubach

56. The Gauntlet

Personal Memories and Letters of William Wesley Bennett, Sr.

Bennett Family Archives / Personal Tarawa Battle Map of Bill Bennett

"Tarawa: The Story of a Battle" Robert Sherrod / Admiral Nimitz Foundation, 1993 (original, 1944)

"Bloody Tarawa" / Eric Hammel & John E. Lane / Zenith Press-MBI Pub. / 1998-2006

"Guadalcanal, Tarawa And Beyond" / William W. Rogal / McFarland & Company / 2010

U.S.M.C. Records / Muster Rolls

United States Naval Records

"We Buried Our Buddies & My Stories" / Charles Wysocki, Jr. / 2008 Trafford Publishing

Company D/2/18 photos of Charles Wysocki, Jr. / Courtesy of John Ratomski

"Once A Marine, Always A Marine" / Mike Masters (Mike Matkovich) / 1988

"Follow Me" / Richard W. Johnston / 1948, Random House

"Utmost Savagery: The Three Days of Tarawa" / Colonel Joseph H. Alexander, U.S.M.C. (Ret.)

"One Square Mile of Hell / John Wukovitz / NAL Caliber, 2006

Newspaper Article, Associated Press, 1943 / Ty Rupertus, embedded with Captain Farkas

57. The Whisper

Personal Memories and Letters of William Wesley Bennett, Sr.

Personal Interview of Brent Ellis, son of Fred Ellis

Bennett Family Archives / Personal Tarawa Battle Map of Bill Bennett

"Tarawa: The Story of a Battle" Robert Sherrod / Admiral Nimitz Foundation, 1993 (original, 1944)

"Bloody Tarawa" / Eric Hammel & John E. Lane / Zenith Press-MBI Pub. / 1998-2006

"Guadalcanal, Tarawa And Beyond" / William W. Rogal / McFarland & Company / 2010

U.S.M.C. Records / Muster Rolls

United States Naval Records

"We Buried Our Buddies & My Stories" / Charles Wysocki, Jr. / 2008 Trafford Publishing

Company D/2/18 photos of Charles Wysocki, Jr. / Courtesy of John Ratomski

"Once A Marine, Always A Marine" / Mike Masters (Mike Matkovich) / 1988

"Follow Me" / Richard W. Johnston / 1948, Random House

"Utmost Savagery: The Three Days of Tarawa" / Colonel Joseph H. Alexander, U.S.M.C. (Ret.)

"One Square Mile of Hell / John Wukovitz / NAL Caliber, 2006

58. Hell On Earth

Personal Memories and Letters of William Wesley Bennett, Sr.

Bennett Family Archives / Personal Tarawa Battle Map of Bill Bennett.

"Tarawa: The Story of a Battle" Robert Sherrod / Admiral Nimitz Foundation, 1993 (original, 1944)

"Bloody Tarawa" / Eric Hammel & John E. Lane / Zenith Press-MBI Pub. / 1998-2006

"Guadalcanal, Tarawa And Beyond" / William W. Rogal / McFarland & Company / 2010

U.S.M.C. Records / Muster Rolls United States Naval Records

"We Buried Our Buddies & My Stories" / Charles Wysocki, Jr. / 2008 Trafford Publishing

Company D/2/18 photos of Charles Wysocki, Jr. / Courtesy of John Ratomski

"Once A Marine, Always A Marine" / Mike Masters (Mike Matkovich) / 1988

"Follow Me" / Richard W. Johnston / 1948, Random House

"Utmost Savagery: The Three Days of Tarawa" / Colonel Joseph H. Alexander, U.S.M.C. (Ret.)

"One Square Mile of Hell / John Wukovitz / NAL Caliber, 2006

59. A Bitter Farewell

Personal Memories and Letters of William Wesley Bennett, Sr.

"A Brief History of the 6th Marines" / Lieutenant General William K. Jones, U.S.M.C. Retired, 1960, U.S.M.C. History Division

Personal Interview of Wendell Perkins / Company A, 1/6 U.S.M.C. Company Clerk / 2017

Tarawa's Gravediggers" / William L. Niven / 2015 Tate Publishing

"Tarawa: The Story of a Battle" Robert Sherrod / Admiral Nimitz Foundation, 1993 (original, 1944)

"Bloody Tarawa" / Eric Hammel & John E. Lane / Zenith Press-MBI Pub. / 1998-2006

"Guadalcanal, Tarawa And Beyond" / William W. Rogal / McFarland & Company / 2010

U.S.M.C. Records / Muster Rolls United States Naval Records

"We Buried Our Buddies & My Stories" / Charles Wysocki, Jr. / 2008 Trafford Publishing

Company D/2/18 photos of Charles Wysocki, Jr. / Courtesy of John Ratomski

"Once A Marine, Always A Marine" / Mike Masters (Mike Matkovich) / 1988

"Follow Me" / Richard W. Johnston / 1948, Random House

"Utmost Savagery: The Three Days of Tarawa" / Colonel Joseph H. Alexander, U.S.M.C. (Ret.)

"One Square Mile of Hell / John Wukovitz / NAL Caliber, 2006

60. Tarawa: The Aftermath

Personal Memories and Letters of William Wesley Bennett, Sr.

"Tarawa: The Story of a Battle" Robert Sherrod / Admiral Nimitz Foundation, 1993 (original, 1944)

"Bloody Tarawa" / Eric Hammel & John E. Lane / Zenith Press-MBI Pub. / 1998-2006

"Guadalcanal, Tarawa and Beyond" / William W. Rogal / McFarland & Company / 2010

U.S.M.C. Records / Muster Rolls United States Naval Records

"We Buried Our Buddies & My Stories" / Charles Wysocki, Jr. / 2008 Trafford Publishing

Company D/2/18 photos of Charles Wysocki, Jr. / Courtesy of John Ratomski

"Once A Marine, Always A Marine" / Mike Masters (Mike Matkovich) / 1988

"Follow Me" / Richard W. Johnston / 1948, Random House / U.S.M.C. 2nd Division History

"Utmost Savagery: The Three Days of Tarawa" / Colonel Joseph H. Alexander, U.S.M.C. (Ret.)

"One Square Mile of Hell" / John Wukovitz / NAL Caliber, 2006

61. Blue Hawaii

Personal Memories and Letters of William Wesley Bennett, Sr.

Bennett Family Archives

Personal letter to Bill Bennett from Mrs. Helen Taylor

Personal Interview of Molly Burns (widow of PFC Truitt Anderson) / 2017 / Courtesy of Garry and Di Burns / Australia

U.S.M.C. Records / Muster Rolls

United States Naval Records

"We Buried Our Buddies & My Stories" / Charles Wysocki, Jr. / 2008 Trafford Publishing

Company D/2/18 photos of Charles Wysocki, Jr. / Courtesy of John Ratomski

"Once A Marine, Always A Marine" / Mike Masters (Mike Matkovich) / 1988

"Follow Me" / Richard W. Johnston / 1948, Random House / U.S.M.C. 2nd Division History

Walker Family Photos

62. Disillusion

Personal Memories and Letters of William Wesley Bennett, Sr.

Bennett Family Archives / 2nd Division Rodeo Handbill

"Once A Marine, Always A Marine" / Mike Masters (Mike Matkovich) / 1988

"Follow Me" / Richard W. Johnston / 1948, Random House / U.S.M.C. 2nd Division History

63. The Meeting

Personal Memories and Letters of William Wesley Bennett, Sr.

U.S.M.C. Records / Muster Rolls

Aurora Beacon News Archives / Aurora Public Library

Aurora City Directories, 1935-1945 / Aurora Public Library

United States Census Records

East Aurora High School Yearbooks / 1935-1945 / Aurora Public Library

Bennett Family Archives / Beacon News Clippings of Jessie Bennett.

"With the Marines at Tarawa" / 1944 Documentary Film / U.S.M.C.

64. Replacements

Personal Memories and Letters of William Wesley Bennett, Sr.

"Once A Marine, Always A Marine" / Mike Masters (Mike Matkovich) / 1988

"Follow Me" / Richard W. Johnston / 1948, Random House / U.S.M.C. 2nd Division History

"Guadalcanal, Tarawa and Beyond" / William W. Rogal / McFarland & Company / 2010

"We Buried Our Buddies & My Stories" / Charles Wysocki, Jr. / 2008 Trafford Publishing

Company D/2/18 photos of Charles Wysocki, Jr. / Courtesy of John Ratomski

65. USS Nehenta Bay

United States Navy Records

The Stoner Weekly News

Personal Records of Onia Burton Stanley / Courtesy of the Stanley-Venema Family

Personal Interview of Peter Venema / Son-in-law of Onia Burton Stanley

66. Island X

Personal Memories and Letters of William Wesley Bennett, Sr.

U.S.M.C. Records / Muster Rolls

United States Navy Records / USS Nehenta Bay, CVE-74

The Stoner Weekly News

"Once A Marine, Always A Marine" / Mike Masters (Mike Matkovich) / 1988

"Follow Me" / Richard W. Johnston / 1948, Random House / U.S.M.C. 2nd Division History

Personal Records of Onia Burton Stanley / Courtesy of the Stanley-Venema Family

Personal Interview of Peter Venema, son-in-law of Onia Burton Stanley

"The Second Pearl Harbor" / Gene Eric Salecher / 2014 The University of Oklahoma Press

67. The Marianas

Personal Memories and Letters of William Wesley Bennett, Sr.

U.S.M.C. Records / Muster Rolls

Personal account of Setchan Akiyama (Vicky Vaughn) / 2004

"Saipan: Oral Histories of the Pacific War" / Bruce M. Petty / 2002 McFarland and Co., Inc.

"Once A Marine, Always A Marine" / Mike Masters (Mike Matkovich) / 1988

"Follow Me" / Richard W. Johnston / 1948, Random House / U.S.M.C. 2nd Division History

"Guadalcanal, Tarawa and Beyond" / William W. Rogal / McFarland & Company / 2010

"A Brief History of the 6th Marines" / Lieutenant General William K. Jones, U.S.M.C. Retired, 1960, U.S.M.C. History Division

"We Buried Our Buddies & My Stories" / Charles Wysocki, Jr. / 2008 Trafford Publishing

68. Counterattack

Personal Memories and Letters of William Wesley Bennett, Sr.

U.S.M.C. Records / Muster Rolls

"A Brief History of the 6th Marines" / Lieutenant General William K. Jones, U.S.M.C. Retired, 1960, U.S.M.C. History Division

"Guadalcanal, Tarawa and Beyond" / William W. Rogal / McFarland & Company / 2010

"We Buried Our Buddies & My Stories" / Charles Wysocki, Jr. / 2008 Trafford Publishing

"Follow Me" / Richard W. Johnston / 1948, Random House / U.S.M.C. 2nd Division History

69. Collateral Damage

Personal account of Setchan Akiyama (Vicky Vaughn) / 2004

"Saipan: Oral Histories of the Pacific War" / Bruce M. Petty / 2002 McFarland and Co., Inc.

Personal Memories and Letters of William Wesley Bennett, Sr.

U.S.M.C. Records / Muster Rolls

"Guadalcanal, Tarawa and Beyond" / William W. Rogal / McFarland & Company / 2010

70. The Long Haul

Personal Memories and Letters of William Wesley Bennett, Sr.

Personal letter from Johnnie C. Jones / Bennett Family Archives

"Saipan: Oral Histories of the Pacific War" / Bruce M. Petty / 2002 McFarland and Co., Inc.

U.S.M.C. Records / Muster Rolls

"A Brief History of the 6th Marines" / Lieutenant General William K. Jones, U.S.M.C. Retired, 1960, U.S.M.C. History Division

"Follow Me" / Richard W. Johnston / 1948, Random House / U.S.M.C. 2nd Division History

71. The Silver Star

"A Brief History of the 6th Marines" / Lieutenant General William K. Jones, U.S.M.C. Retired, 1960, U.S.M.C. History Division

U.S.M.C. Silver Star Citation for PFC Peter N. Andrews

U.S.M.C. Silver Star Citation of Corporal Channing B. Miller

Personal Interview of Wendell V. Perkins / Company A/1/6 Company Clerk

Personal Interview of Peter G. Andrews, nephew of PFC Peter N. Andrews, U.S.M.C.

72. The Combat Zone

Personal Memories and Letters of William Wesley Bennett, Sr.

U.S.M.C. Records / Muster Rolls

"A Brief History of the 6th Marines" / Lieutenant General William K. Jones, U.S.M.C. Retired, 1960, U.S.M.C. History Division

"Guadalcanal, Tarawa and Beyond" / William W. Rogal / McFarland & Company / 2010

Personal Interview of William Schell / nephew of Bill Bennett.

"Follow Me" / Richard W. Johnston / 1948, Random House / U.S.M.C. 2nd Division History

73. Banzai!

Personal Memories and Letters of William Wesley Bennett, Sr.

U.S.M.C. Records / Muster Rolls

"We Buried Our Buddies & My Stories" / Charles Wysocki, Jr. / 2008 Trafford Publishing

"A Brief History of the 6th Marines" / Lieutenant General William K. Jones, U.S.M.C. Retired, 1960, U.S.M.C. History Division

"Guadalcanal, Tarawa and Beyond" / William W. Rogal / McFarland & Company / 2010

"Follow Me" / Richard W. Johnston / 1948, Random House / U.S.M.C. 2nd Division History

74. Recuperation

Personal Memories and Letters of William Wesley Bennett, Sr.

U.S.M.C. Records / Muster Rolls

"We Buried Our Buddies & My Stories" / Charles Wysocki, Jr. / 2008 Trafford Publishing

"A Brief History of the 6th Marines" / Lieutenant General William K. Jones, U.S.M.C. Retired, 1960, U.S.M.C. History Division

"Guadalcanal, Tarawa and Beyond" / William W. Rogal / McFarland & Company / 2010

"Follow Me" / Richard W. Johnston / 1948, Random House / U.S.M.C. 2nd Division History

75. Tinian

Personal Memories and Letters of William Wesley Bennett, Sr.

U.S.M.C. Records / Muster Rolls

"We Buried Our Buddies & My Stories" / Charles Wysocki, Jr. / 2008 Trafford Publishing

"A Brief History of the 6th Marines" / Lieutenant General William K. Jones, U.S.M.C. Retired, 1960, U.S.M.C. History Division

"Guadalcanal, Tarawa and Beyond" / William W. Rogal / McFarland & Company / 2010

"Follow Me" / Richard W. Johnston / 1948, Random House / U.S.M.C. 2nd Division History

76. Bulls Eye!

Personal Memories and Letters of William Wesley Bennett, Sr.

U.S.M.C. Records / Muster Rolls

United States Naval Records / USS Nehenta Bay / LST-130 / LST-131

The Stoner Weekly News

Personal Interview of Carl Lee Davis, crew member, USS Nehenta Bay

Personal Interview of Armand Blackmore, crew member, USS Nehenta Bay

Personal Diary of Lieutenant Commander Onia Burton Stanley, U.S. Navy / Courtesy of the Stanley-Venema Family

"Follow Me" / Richard W. Johnston / 1948, Random House / U.S.M.C. 2nd Division History

Personal U.S.N. Flight Logbook of Lieutenant Robert F. Stoner courtesy of Chelsea Stoner-Bottari

77. The Unthinkable

Personal Memories and Letters of William Wesley Bennett, Sr.

Personal U.S.N. Flight Logbook of Lieutenant Robert F. Stoner courtesy of Chelsea Stoner-Bottari

U.S.M.C. Records / Muster Rolls

United States Naval Records / USS Nehenta Bay / LST-130 / LST-131

The Stoner Weekly News

Personal Interview of Carl Lee Davis / crew member, USS Nehenta Bay

Personal Interview of Armand Blackmore, crew member, USS Nehenta Bay

Personal Diary of Lieutenant Commander Onia Burton Stanley,

U.S. Navy / Courtesy of the Stanley-Venema Family

"Follow Me" / Richard W. Johnston / 1948, Random House / U.S.M.C. 2nd Division History

78. The Homecoming

Personal Memories and Letters of William Wesley Bennett, Sr.

The Stoner Weekly News

U.S.M.C. Records / Muster Rolls

Bennett Family Archives / Scrapbook of Jessie Bennett

Bennett Family Photos

United States Naval Records

79. Swamp Lejuene

Personal Memories and Letters of William Wesley Bennett, Sr.

Personal Letters of Sergeant George P. Gabel

U.S.M.C. Records / Muster Rolls

Personal Interviews of Emanuel E. "Manny" Bud / 2016

Bennett Family Archives / Photos

80. Home At Last

Personal Memories and Letters of William Wesley Bennett, Sr. / Herb Dale's letters

U.S.M.C. Records / Muster Rolls / Discharge

Bennett Family Archives / Glossop-Bennett Bank Records / Photos

Personal Interview of Ginny Schell, daughter of Jean(Bennett) and Linc Schell

Personal Interview of Carol June Glossop, daughter of Don and Helen Glossop

Personal Interview of Ronald Glossop, son of Don and Helen Glossop

Personal Interview of Donald Glossop, Jr., son of Don and Helen Glossop

81. A New Beginning

Personal Memories and Letters of William Wesley Bennett, Sr.

Bennett Family Archives / Church Bulletins, notes of Jessie Bennett

Personal Interview of Frances (Frannie) Ulferts-VanPelt, youngest sister of Edna May Ulferts

Personal Interview of Ginny Schell, daughter of Jean(Bennett) and Linc Schell

Personal interview with Jean Dix-Carson, daughter of Earl "Bud" Dix, Jr. / 2017

Personal Interview of Elmer "Bud" and Marlis Hutchinson, members of Fourth Street Methodist

Personal Interview of Kathy Bennett-Andrews and Sarah Bennett-Brauer

Personal Interview of William (Wes) Wesley Bennett, Jr.

City of Aurora Directories, 1944-1947 / Aurora Public Library

East Aurora High School Yearbooks, 1938-1945 / Aurora Public Library

United States Census Records

Aurora Beacon News Archives / Aurora Beacon News

United States Army Air Forces (U.S.A.A.F.) Records / Walter Truemper MOH citation

"Record of Aurora Illinois in WW II" / Judge J. W. Greenaway / 1952

82. Like No Other

Bennett Family Archives / Church Bulletins, notes of Jessie Bennett

Personal Interview of Frances (Frannie) Ulferts-VanPelt / youngest sister of Edna May Ulferts

Personal Interview of Elmer "Bud" and Marlis Hutchinson, members of Fourth Street Methodist

Personal Interview of Kathy Bennett-Andrews and Sarah Bennett-Brauer

Personal Interview of Ginny Schell, daughter of Jean(Bennett) and Linc Schell

Personal Interview of William (Wes) Wesley Bennett, Jr.

City of Aurora Directories, 1944-1947 / Aurora Public Library

East Aurora High School Yearbooks, 1938-1945 / Aurora Public Library

United States Census Records

Aurora Beacon News Archives / Aurora Beacon News

Stephens-Adamson History / Aurora Historical Society / Aurora Public Library / Aurora Beacon News

83. Challenges

Personal Interview of William (Wes) Wesley Bennett, Jr.

Personal Interview of Kathy Bennett-Andrews and Sarah Bennett-Brauer

Personal Interview of Frances (Frannie) Ulferts-VanPelt, youngest sister of Edna May Ulferts

Personal Interview of Ginny Schell, daughter of Jean(Bennett) and Linc Schell

Personal Interview of Peter G. Andrews, nephew of PFC Peter N. Andrews, U.S.M.C.

Personal Interview of Elmer "Bud" and Marlis Hutchinson, members of Fourth Street Methodist

United States Census Records

Aurora Beacon News Archives / Aurora Beacon News

84. Terry Allen

Personal Interview of Kathy Bennett-Andrews and Sarah Bennett-Brauer

Personal Interview of Frances (Frannie) Ulferts-VanPelt, youngest sister of Edna May Ulferts

Personal Interview of Ginny Schell, daughter of Jean(Bennett) and Linc Schell

Personal Interview of William (Wes) Wesley Bennett, Jr.

Personal Interview of Elmer "Bud" and Marlis Hutchinson, members of Fourth Street Methodist

85. The Good Life

Bennett Family Archives / Photos / Home Movies

Personal Interview of Kathy Bennett-Andrews and Sarah Bennett-Brauer

Personal Interview of Frances (Frannie) Ulferts-VanPelt, youngest sister of Edna May Ulferts-Bennett

Personal Interview of Ginny Schell, daughter of Jean(Bennett) and Linc Schell

Personal Interview of Bert Bennett, son of Al and Eunice Bennett

Personal Interview of Donna Bennett-Trinkle, daughter of Al and Eunice Bennett

United States Census Records

Aurora Beacon News Archives / Aurora Beacon News

Aurora City Directories, 1952-1960

Personal Interview of Brent Ellis, son of Fred Ellis

Personal Interview of Janet Simonson, daughter of Lieutenant Arthur K. Simonson

Personal Interview of William (Wes) Wesley Bennett, Jr., son of Bill and Edna Bennett

Personal Interview of Allison Mitchell, daughter of Lorna and Les Mitchell

Personal Interview of Peter G. Andrews, nephew of PFC Peter N. Andrews, U.S.M.C.

Personal Interview of William Schell, nephew of Bill Bennett

Personal Interview of Elmer "Bud" and Marlis Hutchinson, members of Fourth Street Methodist

86. Full Circle

Author's First-Hand Account

Personal Interview of Kathy Bennett-Andrews and Sarah Bennett-Brauer

Personal Interview of Elmer "Bud" and Marlis Hutchinson, members of Fourth Street Methodist

Bennett Family Archives / Photos

Newspaper Article and Photos by Wendy Derzewiec

United States Census Records

Aurora Beacon News Archives / Aurora Beacon News

87. **Getting To Know Bill Bennett**
    Author's First-Hand Account
    Bennett Family Archives / Photos

88. **To Japan**
    Author's First-Hand Account

89. **The Enemy Has A Face**
    Author's First-Hand Account

90. **Losing His Girl**
    Author's First-Hand Account
    Personal Interview of Kathy Bennett-Andrews and Sarah Bennett-Brauer
    Personal Interview of William (Wes) Wesley Bennett, Jr., son of Bill and Edna Bennett
    Bennett Family Archives / Photos
    Personal Interview of Moses Cheng

91. **Reliving Saipan**
    Author's First-Hand Account
    Personal Memories of Bill Bennett
    Personal Memories of Setchan Akiyama (Vicky Vaughn)

92. **Marine Corps Monument**
    Author's First-Hand Account

93. **An Historic Record**
    Author's First-Hand Account

94. **A Historic Flight**
    Bennett Family Archives / Photos
    Personal Interview of Kathy Bennett-Andrews
    Personal Interview of Peter G. Andrews
    Personal Interview of Herschel Luckinbill
    Honor Flight Chicago's Records

95. **The Arms of God**
    Bennett Family Archives / Photos
    Author's First-Hand Account
    Personal Interview of Kathy Bennett-Andrews and Sarah Bennett-Brauer
    Personal Interview of William (Wes) Wesley Bennett, Jr., son of Bill and Edna Bennett
    Personal Interview of Peter G. Andrews

96. **Memorial Day**
    Author's First-Hand Account

    Epilogue
    Author's Opinion
    Personal Interview of Moses Cheng

    The Gospel According to Bill.
    Author's Personal Interpretation of Bill Bennett's beliefs

About The Author

Brent A. Peterson first became familiar with William Wesley Bennett, Sr. in 1975 at the age of 12. From 1990 until 2011, Brent listened to Bill Bennett share first-hand accounts of his time with Company D, 2nd Battalion, 18th Marine Regiment. In 2014, Brent began a 4,000-hour project of researching the incredible, almost impossible to believe, stories of Bill Bennett's life. From recently declassified Navy documents to personal letters stored for over 75 years, Brent slowly rebuilt the remarkable details of this amazing man's life. A story of God's faithfulness to Bill and Bill's faithfulness to God emerged from the effort.

Brent lives in Illinois with his wife Belle, who contributed to this work in many ways. They have four grown children and a 17-year-old Jack Russell Terrier named Reilly.

Brent is a lifelong student of military history, specializing in World War II. He has worked from coast to coast within the United States and traveled extensively in Japan. He has earned AMA certificates in communication and negotiation, and arranged international business deals.

Brent has been involved in many facets of Christian ministry throughout his life and loves to encourage others to invest their lives in the things that have lasting value.

Brent is available on a limited basis for book-related events.

You can contact Brent in the following ways:

Once Upon A Lifetime, P.O. Box 445, Yorkville, IL 60560

info@bpetersonbooks.com

Facebook: bpetersonbooks

Website: bpetersonbooks.com